SIMULATION MODELING
AND ANALYSIS

SIMULATION MODELING AND ANALYSIS

Averill M. Law
Professor of Management Information Systems
University of Arizona

W. David Kelton
Professor of Administrative Sciences
Kent State University

McGraw-Hill Book Company

New York St. Louis San Francisco Auckland Bogotá Hamburg
Johannesburg London Madrid Mexico Montreal New Delhi
Panama Paris São Paulo Singapore Sydney Tokyo Toronto

This book was set in Times Roman by University Graphics, Inc.
The editors were Julienne V. Brown and Madelaine Eichberg;
the production supervisor was Joe Campanella.
The drawings were done by Fine Line Illustrations, Inc.
The cover was designed by Carla Bauer.
R. R. Donnelley & Sons Company was printer and binder.

SIMULATION MODELING AND ANALYSIS

67890 DODO 8987654

Library of Congress Cataloging in Publication Data
Law, Averill M.
 Simulation modeling and analysis.

 (McGraw-Hill series in industrial engineering and
management science)
 Includes bibliographical references and index.
 1. Digital computer simulation. I. Kelton,
W. David. II. Title. III. Series.
QA76.9.C65L38 001.4'34 81-5777
ISBN 0-07-036696-9   AACR2

To my wife, Steffi, and children, Heather and Adam, for their encouragement and understanding during the writing of this book.

AVERILL M. LAW

For Christie, who understood and helped more than I could tell her.

W. DAVID KELTON

CONTENTS

The goal of *Simulation Modeling and Analysis* is to give an up-to-date treatment of all the important aspects of a simulation study, including modeling, simulation languages, validation, and output data analysis. In addition, we have tried to present the material in a manner understandable to a person having only a basic familiarity with probability, statistics, and computer programming. The book does not sacrifice statistical correctness for expository convenience, but contains virtually no theorems or proofs. Technically difficult topics are placed in starred (*) sections or in an appendix to an appropriate chapter, and left for the advanced reader. (More difficult problems are also starred.) The book strives to motivate intuition about difficult topics and contains a large number of examples, figures, problems, and references for further study. There is also a solutions manual for instructors.

We feel that two of the book's major strengths are its treatment of modeling and of output data analysis. Chapters 1 and 2 show in complete detail how to build simulation models in FORTRAN of a simple queueing system, an inventory system, a time-shared computer model, a multiteller bank with jockeying, and a job-shop model. Chapter 8 contains what we believe is a complete and practical treatment of statistical analysis of simulation output data. Since lack of definitive output data analyses appears to have been a major shortcoming of most simulation studies, we feel that this chapter should enhance the practice of simulation.

We believe that *Simulation Modeling and Analysis* could serve as a textbook for the following types of courses:

1. A beginning course in simulation at the junior, senior, or first-year graduate level for engineering, business, or computer science students (Chaps. 1 through 4 and parts of Chaps. 5 through 8, 10, and 11).
2. A second, advanced course in simulation (most of Chaps. 7 through 12).
3. An introduction to simulation as part of a general course on operations research or management science (Chaps. 1 through 3).

The book should also be of interest to simulation practitioners. As a matter of fact, a large number of such practitioners from industry, government, and the military have used preliminary drafts of the manuscript while attending a seminar on simulation which has been given by the first author for the last four years.

There are a number of people and organizations that have contributed considerably to the writing of this book. Foremost among them are Dr. Thomas Varley and the Office of Naval Research, without whose research support during the past five years this book simply would not have been possible. We would also like to thank the Army Research Office for its research funding to the Mathematics Research Center at the University of Wisconsin. This support in 1980 allowed for the expeditious completion of the book. Most of the development of the simulation language SIM-LIB which is discussed in Chap. 2, and almost all of the research of the statistical methods in Chap. 5 was done by Stephen Vincent, a graduate student at Wisconsin. The organization and content of Chap. 7 benefitted greatly from our having in-depth discussions with Professor Bruce Schmeiser of Purdue University. In addition, conversations with the following people positively influenced our thinking on particular chapters of the book: William Biles (Penn State), Edward Dudewicz (Ohio State), James Henriksen (Wolverine Software), Stephen Lavenberg (IBM), Richard Nance (Virginia Tech), Alan Pritsker (Purdue), Edward Russell (CACI), Robert Sargent (Syracuse), Thomas Schriber (Michigan), Edward Silver (Waterloo), and Glenn Thomas (Kent State). Finally, we acknowledge the following graduate students at Wisconsin who read the entire manuscript and made many valuable suggestions: Steven Kimbrough, Lloyd Koenig, Insup Lee, and Muslim Yildiz.

Averill M. Law
W. David Kelton

BASIC SIMULATION MODELING

1.1 THE NATURE OF SIMULATION

This is a book about techniques for using computers to imitate, or *simulate,* the operations of various kinds of real-world facilities or processes. The facility or process of interest is usually called a *system,* and in order to study it scientifically we often have to make a set of assumptions about how it works. These assumptions, which usually take the form of mathematical or logical relationships, constitute a *model* which is used to try and gain some understanding of how the corresponding system behaves.

If the relationships which compose the model are simple enough, it may be possible to use mathematical methods (such as algebra, calculus, or probability theory) to obtain *exact* information on questions of interest; this is called an *analytic* solution. However, most real-world systems are too complex to allow realistic models to be evaluated analytically, and these models must be studied by means of simulation. In a *simulation* we use a computer to evaluate a model *numerically* over a time period of interest, and data are gathered to *estimate* the desired true characteristics of the model.

As an example of the use of simulation, consider a manufacturing firm that is contemplating building a large extension onto one of its plants but is not sure whether the potential gain in productivity would justify the construction cost. It certainly would not be cost-effective to build the extension and then remove it later if it does not work out. However, a careful simulation study could shed some light on the question by simulating the operation of the plant as it currently exists and as it *would* be *if* the plant were expanded.

Simulation is one of the most widely used techniques in operations research and management science, and by all indications its popularity is on the increase. There have been several impediments to its even wider acceptance and usefulness, however. First, models used to study large-scale systems tend to be very complex, and writing computer programs to execute them can be an arduous task indeed. This task has been eased in recent years by the development of several special-purpose computer languages that automatically provide many of the features needed to code a simulation model. A second problem with simulation of complex systems is that a large amount of computer time is often required. We anticipate, however, that this difficulty will become less severe as the cost of computing continues to fall. Finally, there appears to be an unfortunate impression that simulation is just an exercise in computer programming, albeit a complicated one. Consequently, many simulation "studies" have been composed of heuristic model building, coding, and a single run of the program to obtain "the answer." We fear that this attitude, which neglects the important issue of how a properly coded model should be used to draw inferences about the system of interest, has led to erroneous conclusions being drawn from many simulation studies. These questions of simulation *methodology,* which are largely independent of the programming language and computer hardware used, form an integral part of the latter chapters of this book.

In the remainder of this chapter (as well as in Chap. 2) we discuss systems and models in considerably more detail and then show how to write computer programs to simulate systems of varying degrees of complexity.

1.2 SYSTEMS, MODELS, AND SIMULATION

A *system* is defined to be a collection of entities, e.g., people or machines, which act and interact together toward the accomplishment of some logical end. (This definition was proposed by Schmidt and Taylor [14].†) In practice, what is meant by the system depends on the objectives of a particular study. The collection of entities which compose a system for one study might only be a subset of the overall system for another. For example, if one wants to study a bank to determine the number of tellers needed to provide adequate service for customers who only want to cash a check or make a savings deposit, the system can be defined to be that portion of the bank consisting of the tellers and the customers waiting in line or being served. If, on the other hand, the loan officer and the safety deposit boxes are to be included, the definition of the system must be expanded in an obvious way. We define the *state* of a system to be that collection of variables necessary to describe a system at a particular time, relative to the objectives of a study. In a study of a bank, examples of possible state variables are the number of busy tellers, the number of customers in the bank, and the time of arrival of each customer in the bank. We categorize systems to be of two types, discrete and continuous. A *discrete system* is one for which the state variables change only at a countable (or finite) number of points in time. A bank is an example of a discrete system since state variables, e.g., the number

---

†Numbers in brackets correspond to references at the end of the chapter.

of customers in the bank, change only when a customer arrives or when a customer finishes being served and departs. A *continuous system* is one for which the state variables change continuously with respect to time. An airplane moving through the air is an example of a continuous system since such state variables as position or velocity change continuously with respect to time. Few systems in practice are wholly discrete or continuous, but since one type of change predominates for most systems, it will usually be possible to classify a system as being either discrete or continuous.

Sometimes it is desired to study a system to understand the relationships between its various components or to predict its performance under a new operating policy. However, actual experimentation with the system may be infeasible, cost-ineffective, or disruptive of the present system's operation. This is particularly true when, as is often the case in practice, the system of interest does not yet exist. For example, suppose that it is desired to study (as a possible cost-saving measure) the effect of reducing the number of tellers in a bank. If the number of tellers in the bank were actually reduced temporarily, it might cause a significant increase in customers' delays and alienate them from doing future business with the bank. Because of the infeasibility of experimenting with many systems, a systems analyst often uses a model of a system to draw inferences about the operations of the actual system. We define a *model* to be a representation of a system developed for the purpose of studying that system. The model should be sufficiently detailed or "valid" to permit an analyst or decision maker to use it to make the same decisions about the system that would be made if it were feasible to experiment with the system itself.

In this book we restrict our attention to a particular type of *mathematical model* of a system which we call a *simulation model*. (Some models of systems are *physical* rather than mathematical, e.g., a scale model of an airplane tested in a wind tunnel.) Although we shall not explicitly define a simulation model in general, we distinguish between simulation models which are static or dynamic, deterministic or stochastic, and discrete or continuous. A *static* simulation model is a representation of a system at a particular time. Monte Carlo simulation models (Sec. 1.7.3) are typically of this type. A *dynamic* simulation model is a representation of a system as it evolves over time, e.g., a simulation model of a bank's activities over an 8-hour day. A simulation model is said to be *deterministic* if it contains no random variables. For a deterministic model, there is a unique set of model output data for a given set of inputs. On the other hand, a simulation model is *stochastic* if it contains one or more random variables. The output data for a stochastic model are themselves random and thus only estimates of the true characteristics of the model. A simulation model of a bank would normally treat the interarrival times and the service times of customers as random variables, each with their own probability distribution. Loosely speaking, we define *discrete* and *continuous* simulation models analogously to the way discrete and continuous systems were defined above. More precise definitions of discrete (event) simulation and continuous simulation are given in Secs. 1.3 and 1.7, respectively. It should be mentioned that a discrete model is not always used to model a discrete system and vice versa. The decision whether to use a discrete or continuous model for a particular system depends on the specific objectives of the study. For example, a model of traffic flow on a freeway would be discrete if the characteristics and movement of individual cars were important. Alternatively, if the cars can be treated in the "aggregate," the flow of traffic can be described by differential equations in a continuous model. The simulation models we consider in the remainder of this book, except for those in Sec. 1.7, will be discrete, dynamic, and stochastic and will henceforth be called *discrete-event simulation models*. (Since deterministic models are a special case of stochastic models, the restriction to stochastic models involves no loss of generality.)

1.3 DISCRETE-EVENT SIMULATION

Discrete-event simulation concerns the modeling of a system as it evolves over time by a representation in which the state variables change only at a countable number of points in time. These points in time are the ones at which an event occurs, where an *event* is defined to be an instantaneous occurrence which may change the state of a system. Although a discrete-event simulation could conceptually be done by hand calculations, the amount of data that must be stored and manipulated for most real-world systems dictates that discrete-event simulations be done on a digital computer.

> **Example 1.1** Consider a service facility with a single server, e.g., a one-operator barbershop or an information desk at an airport, for which we would like to estimate the average delay in queue (line) of arriving customers, where the delay in queue of a customer is the length of the time interval from the instant of his arrival at the facility to the instant he begins being served. For the objective of estimating the average delay of a customer, the state variables for a discrete-event simulation model of the facility would be the status of the server, i.e., either idle or busy, the number of customers waiting in queue to be served (if any), and the time of arrival of each person waiting in queue. The status of the server is needed to determine, upon a customer's arrival, whether the customer can be served immediately or must join the end of the queue. When the server completes serving a customer, the number of customers in the queue is used to determine whether the server will become idle or begin serving the first customer in the queue. The time of arrival of a customer is needed to compute his delay in queue, which is the time he begins being served (which will be known) minus his time of arrival. There are two types of events for this system, namely, the arrival of a customer and the completion of service for a customer, which results in the departure of the customer. An arrival is an event because it causes the (state variable) status to change from idle to busy or the (state variable) number of customers in the queue to increase by 1. Correspondingly, a departure is an event because it causes the status to change from busy to idle or the number of customers in the queue to decrease by 1. We show in detail how to build a discrete-event simulation model of this single-server queueing system in Sec. 1.4.

In the above example both types of events actually changed the state of the system, but in some discrete-event simulation models events are used for purposes which do not actually make such a change. For example, an event might be used to schedule the end of a simulation run at a particular time (see Sec. 1.4.5) or to schedule a decision about a system's operation at a particular time (see Sec. 1.5), which may not actually result in a change in the state of the system. This is why we originally said that an event *may* change the state of a system.

1.3.1 Time-Advance Mechanisms

Because of the dynamic nature of discrete-event simulation models, we need to keep track of the current value of simulated time as the simulation proceeds, and we also need a mechanism to advance simulated time from one value to another. We call the variable in a simulation model which gives the current value of simulated time the *simulation clock*. The unit of time for the simulation clock is never explicitly stated when a model is written in a general-purpose language like FORTRAN, and it is assumed to be in the same time units as the input parameters. Also, there is generally no relationship between simulated time and the time needed to run a simulation on the computer.

Historically, two principal approaches have been suggested for advancing the simulation clock, namely, *next-event time advance* and *fixed-increment time advance*. Since the first approach is used by all major simulation languages and by most people coding their model in a general-purpose language, and since the second is a special case of the first, we shall use the next-event time-advance approach for all discrete-event simulation models discussed in this book. A brief discussion of fixed-increment time advance is given in Appendix 1A (at the end of the chapter).

With the next-event time-advance approach, the simulation clock is initialized to zero and the times of occurrence of future events are determined. The simulation clock is then advanced to the time of occurrence of the *most imminent* (first) of these future events, at which point the state of the system is updated to account for the fact that an event has occurred, and our knowledge of the times of occurrence of future events is also updated. Then the simulation clock is advanced to the time of the (new) most imminent event, the state of the system is updated, and future event times are determined, etc. This process of advancing the simulation clock from one event time to another is continued until eventually some prespecified stopping condition is satisfied. Since all state changes occur only at event times for a discrete-event simulation model, periods of inactivity in a system are skipped over by jumping the clock from event time to event time. (Fixed-increment time advance does not skip over these inactive periods, which tends to eat up a lot of computer time; see Appendix 1A.) It should be noted that the successive jumps of the simulation clock are generally variable (or unequal) in size.

Example 1.2 We now illustrate in detail the next-event time-advance approach for the single-server queueing system of Example 1.1. We need the following notation:

t_i = time of arrival of ith customer ($t_0 = 0$)
$A_i = t_i - t_{i-1}$ = interarrival time between $(i - 1)$st and ith arrivals of customers
S_i = time server actually spends serving ith customer (exclusive of customer's delay in queue)
D_i = delay in queue of ith customer
$c_i = t_i + D_i + S_i$ = time ith customer completes service and departs
s_i = time of occurrence of ith event of any type (ith value simulation clock takes on, excluding value $s_0 = 0$)

Each of these defined quantities will generally be a random variable. Assume that the probability distributions of the interarrival times A_1, A_2, ... and the service times S_1, S_2, ... are known and are denoted by F_A and F_S, respectively. (In general, F_A and F_S would be determined by collecting data from the system of interest and then fitting distributions to these data using the techniques of Chap. 5.) At time $s_0 = 0$ the status of the server is idle, and the time of the first arrival, t_1, is determined by generating A_1 from F_A (techniques for generating random variables from a specified distribution are discussed in Chap. 7) and adding it to 0. The simulation clock is then advanced from s_0 to the time of the next (first) event, $s_1 = t_1$. (See Fig. 1.1, where the curved arrows rep-

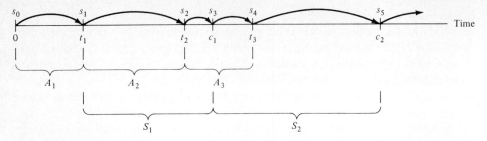

Figure 1.1 The next-event time-advance approach illustrated for the single-server queueing system.

resent the advancing of the simulation clock.) Since the customer arriving at time t_1 finds the server idle, he immediately enters service and has a delay in queue of $D_1 = 0$ and the status of the server is changed from idle to busy. The time, c_1, when the arriving customer will complete service is computed by generating S_1 from F_S and adding it to t_1. Finally, the time of the second arrival, t_2, is computed as $t_2 = t_1 + A_2$, where A_2 is generated from F_A. If $t_2 < c_1$, as depicted in Fig. 1.1, the simulation clock is advanced from s_1 to the time of the next event, $s_2 = t_2$. (If c_1 were less than t_2, the clock would be advanced from s_1 to c_1.) Since the customer arriving at time t_2 finds the server already busy, the number of customers in the queue is increased from 0 to 1 and the time of arrival of this customer is recorded; however, his service time S_2 is not generated at this time. Also, the time of the third arrival, t_3, is computed as $t_3 = t_2 + A_3$. If $c_1 < t_3$, as depicted in the figure, the simulation clock is advanced from s_2 to the time of the next event, $s_3 = c_1$, where the customer completing service departs, the customer in the queue (namely, the one who arrived at time t_2) begins service and his delay in queue and service completion time are computed as $D_2 = c_1 - t_2$ and $c_2 = c_1 + S_2$ (S_2 is now generated from F_S), and the number of customers in the queue is decreased from 1 to 0. If $t_3 < c_2$, the simulation clock is advanced from s_3 to the time of the next event, $s_4 = t_3$, etc. The simulation might eventually be terminated when, say, the number of customers whose delays have been observed reaches some specified value.

1.3.2 Components and Organization of a Discrete-Event Simulation Model

Although simulation has been applied to a great diversity of real-world systems, discrete-event simulation models all share a number of common components and there is a logical organization for these components which promotes the coding, debugging, and future changing of a simulation model's computer program. In particular, the following components will be found in most discrete-event simulation models using the next-event time-advance approach:

System state. The collection of state variables necessary to describe the system at a particular time

Simulation clock. A variable giving the current value of simulated time

Event list. A list containing the next time when each type of event will occur

Statistical counters. Variables used for storing statistical information about system performance

Initialization routine. A subroutine used to initialize the simulation model at time zero

Timing routine. A subroutine which determines the next event from the event list and then advances the simulation clock to the time when that event is to occur

Event routine. A subroutine which updates the system state when a particular type of event occurs (there is one event routine for each event type)

Report generator. A subroutine which computes estimates (from the statistical counters) of the desired measures of performance and prints a report when the simulation ends

Main program. A subprogram which calls the timing routine to determine the next event and then transfers control to the corresponding event routine to update the system state appropriately

The logical relationships (flow of control) between these components is shown in Fig. 1.2. The simulation begins at time zero with the main program's calling the initialization routine, where the simulation clock is set to zero, the system state and the statistical counters are initialized, and the event list is initialized. After control has been returned to the main program, it calls the timing routine to determine which type of event is most imminent. If an event of type i is the next to occur, the simulation clock is advanced to the time that event type i will occur and control is returned to the main program. Then the main program calls event routine i, where typically three types of activities occur: (1) updating the system state to account for the fact that an event of type i has occurred, (2) gathering information about system performance by updating the statistical counters, and (3) generating the times of occurrence of future events and adding this information to the event list. After all processing has been completed, either in event routine i or in the main program, a

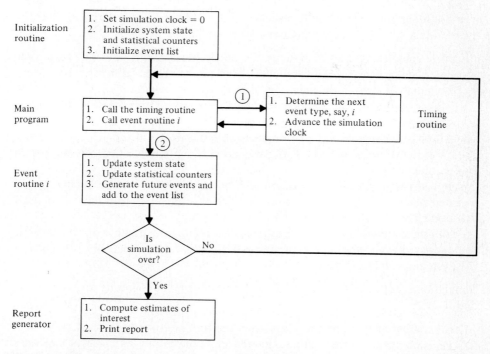

Figure 1.2 Flow of control for the next-event time-advance approach.

check is made to determine (relative to some stopping condition) whether the simulation should now be terminated. If it is time to terminate the simulation, the report generator is called from the main program to compute estimates (from the statistical counters) of the desired measures of performance and to print a report. If it is not time for termination, control is passed back to the main program and the main program–timing routine–main program–event routine–termination check cycle is continually repeated until the stopping condition is eventually satisfied.

Before concluding this section, a few additional words about the system state may be in order. As mentioned in Sec. 1.2, a system is a well-defined collection of *entities*. Entities are characterized by data values which are called *attributes,* and these attributes are part of the system state for a discrete-event simulation model. Furthermore, entities with some common property are often grouped together in *lists* (or *files* or *sets*). For each entity, there is a record in the list consisting of the entity's attributes, and the order in which the records are placed in the list depends on some specified rule. (See Chap. 2 for a discussion of efficient approaches for storing lists of records.) For the single-server queueing facility of Examples 1.1 and 1.2, the entities are the server and the customers in the facility. The server has the attribute "status," and the customers waiting in queue have the attribute "time of arrival." (The number of customers in the queue might also be considered an attribute of the server.) Furthermore, as we shall see in Sec. 1.4, these customers in queue will be grouped together in a list.

1.3.3 Advantages and Disadvantages of Simulation

The following are some possible reasons for the widespread popularity of discrete-event simulation (also see the discussion of models in Sec. 1.2):

1. Most complex, real-world systems with stochastic elements cannot be accurately described by a mathematical model which can be evaluated *analytically*. Thus, a simulation is often the only type of investigation possible.
2. Simulation allows one to estimate the performance of an existing system under some projected set of operating conditions.
3. Alternative proposed system designs (or alternative operating policies for a single system) can be compared via simulation to see which best meets a specified requirement.
4. In a simulation we can maintain much better control over experimental conditions than would generally be possible when experimenting with the system itself (see Chap. 11).
5. Simulation allows us to study a system with a long time frame, e.g., an economic system, in compressed time, or alternatively to study the detailed workings of a system in expanded time.

Simulation is not without its drawbacks. In particular, the following are some of its disadvantages:

1. Simulation models are often expensive and time-consuming to develop.
2. On each run a *stochastic* simulation model produces only *estimates* of a model's true characteristics for a particular set of input parameters. Thus, several inde-

pendent runs of the model will probably be required for each set of input parameters to be studied (see Chap. 8). For this reason, simulation models are generally not as good at optimization as they are at comparing a fixed number of specified alternative system designs. On the other hand, an analytic model, *if appropriate,* can often easily produce the *actual* true characteristics of that model for a variety of sets of input parameters. Thus, if a "valid" analytic model is available or can easily be developed, it will generally be preferable to a simulation model.

3. The large volume of numbers produced by a simulation study often creates a tendency to place greater confidence in a study's results than is justified. If a model is not a "valid" representation of a system under study, the simulation results, no matter how impressive they may appear, will provide little useful information about the actual system.

When deciding whether or not a simulation study is appropriate in a given situation, we can only advise that these advantages and drawbacks be kept in mind and that all other relevant facets of one's particular situation be brought to bear as well. Finally, it should be noted that in some studies both simulation and analytic models might be useful. In particular, simulation can be used to check the validity of assumptions needed in an analytic model. On the other hand, an analytic model can suggest reasonable alternatives to investigate in a simulation study.

1.4 SIMULATION OF A SINGLE-SERVER QUEUEING SYSTEM

This section shows in detail how to simulate a single-server queueing system such as a one-operator barbershop. Although this system seems very simple compared with those usually of interest in the real world, how it is simulated is actually quite representative of the operation of simulations of great complexity. Our discussion will essentially be in three parts. In Sec. 1.4.1 we describe the system of interest and state our objectives more precisely. We intuitively explain how to simulate this system in Sec. 1.4.2 by showing a "snapshot" of the simulated system just after each event occurs. Finally, in Secs. 1.4.3 to 1.4.5 we discuss a FORTRAN simulation model for this system.

1.4.1 Statement of the Problem

Consider a single-server queueing system (see Fig. 1.3) for which the interarrival times A_1, A_2, . . . are independent identically distributed (IID) random variables. ("Identically distributed" means that the interarrival times have a common probability distribution.) A customer who arrives and finds the server idle enters service immediately, and the service times S_1, S_2, . . . of the successive customers are I I D random variables independent of the interarrival times. A customer who arrives and finds the server busy joins the end of a single queue. On completing service for a customer, the server chooses a customer from the queue (if any) in a first-in, first-out (FIFO) manner. (For a discussion of other queue disciplines and queueing systems in general, see Appendix 1B.)

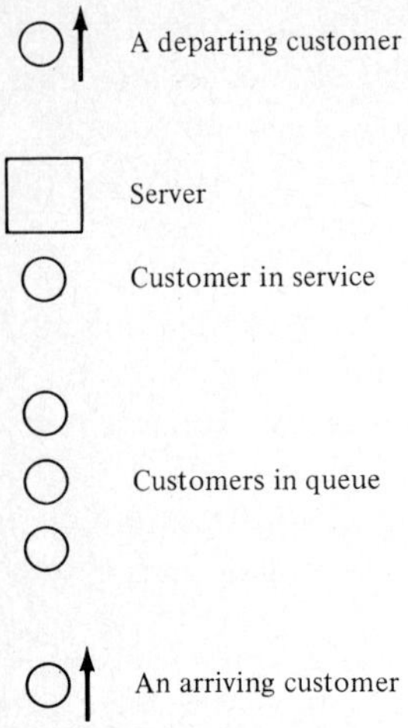

○↑ A departing customer

□ Server

○ Customer in service

○
○ Customers in queue
○

○↑ An arriving customer

Figure 1.3 A single-server queueing system.

We wish to simulate this system until n customers have completed their delays and to estimate the average delay of a customer, $d(n)$, and the time-average number of customers in queue, $Q(n)$. The measure of performance $d(n)$ is estimated by

$$\hat{d}(n) = \frac{\sum_{i=1}^{n} D_i}{n}$$

also called the *sample mean* of the D_i's and denoted by $\overline{D}(n)$. Throughout this book a hat (^) above a symbol denotes an estimator. The measure of performance $Q(n)$, on the other hand, is estimated by

$$\hat{Q}(n) = \frac{\int_0^T Q(t)\, dt}{T} = \frac{\sum_{i=1}^{m} R_i}{T}$$

where T = amount of time required for n customers to complete their delays (a random variable)

$Q(t)$ = number of customers in queue at time t $(0 \leq t \leq T)$

R_i = area of rectangle under $Q(t)$ between s_{i-1} and s_i (s_i is the time of the ith event of any type, and $s_0 = 0$)

m = number of events which occur in the interval $[0, T]$ (a random variable)

Recall from calculus that $\int_0^T Q(t)\, dt$ is the area under $Q(t)$ between 0 and T and thus $\hat{Q}(n)$ is the average value of the function $Q(t)$ over the interval $[0, T]$. The equality of $\int_0^T Q(t)\, dt$ and $\sum_{i=1}^{m} R_i$ is illustrated for the case $n = 3$ in Fig. 1.4.

The events for this system are the arrival of a customer and the departure of a customer (after a service completion); the state variables necessary to estimate $d(n)$ and $Q(n)$ are the status of the server, the number of customers in the queue, the time of arrival of each customer in the queue, and the time of the last (most recent) event.

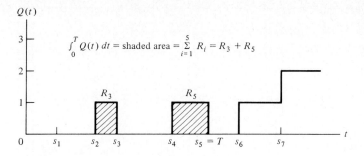

$Q(t)$

$$\int_0^T Q(t)\,dt = \text{shaded area} = \sum_{i=1}^5 R_i = R_3 + R_5$$

Figure 1.4 The equality of $\displaystyle\int_0^T Q(t)\,dt$ and $\displaystyle\sum_{i=1}^m R_i$ illustrated; arrivals occur at s_1, s_2, s_4, s_6, and s_7; departures occur at s_3 and s_5.

The time of the last event, which is defined to be s_{i-1} if $s_{i-1} \le t < s_i$ (t is the time), is needed to compute the area R_i at the time s_i of the ith event.

An estimator like $\hat{d}(n)$, which is the simple average of the D_i's, is called a *sample statistic*, while an estimator like $\hat{Q}(n)$, which is the average value of the function $Q(t)$ over the interval $[0, T]$, is called a *time-average statistic*. Both types of estimators are common in discrete-event simulation models.

1.4.2 Intuitive Explanation

We begin our explanation of how to simulate a single-server queueing system by showing how its simulation model would be represented inside the computer at time $s_0 = 0$ and at the times at which the successive events occur, s_1, s_2, ... For expository convenience, we assume that the interarrival and service times of customers are known and have the values

$$A_1 = 55,\ A_2 = 32,\ A_3 = 24,\ A_4 = 40,\ A_5 = 12,\ A_6 = 29, \ldots$$
$$S_1 = 43,\ S_2 = 36,\ S_3 = 34, \ldots$$

Thus, between 0 and the time when the first customer arrives there are 55 time units, between the arrivals of the first and second customers there are 32 time units, etc., and the service time of the first customer is 43 time units, etc. In an actual simulation (see Sec. 1.4.3) the A_i's and the S_i's would be generated from their corresponding probability distributions, as needed, during the course of the simulation.

Figure 1.5 gives a snapshot of the system itself and of a computer representation of the system at each of the times $s_0 = 0$, $s_1 = 55$, $s_2 = 87$, $s_3 = 98$, $s_4 = 111$, $s_5 = 134$, $s_6 = 151$, and $s_7 = 163$. Our discussion will focus on how the computer representation changes at each of these event times. At time 0, the main program calls the initialization routine to initialize the model. The computer representation after all initialization has been done is shown in the first section of the figure. Note that status, the number of customers in the queue, the time of the last event, the simulation clock, and all statistical counters are initially set to zero. (We use 0 to represent a server status of idle and 1 to represent a status of busy.) There is an array to store the times of arrivals of customers *in queue* which is initially empty.

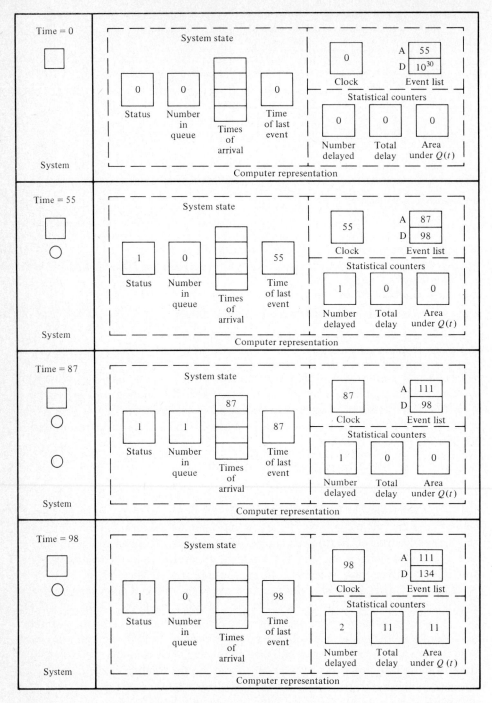

Figure 1.5 Snapshots of the system and of the computer representation of the system at TIME = 0 and each of the seven succeeding event times.

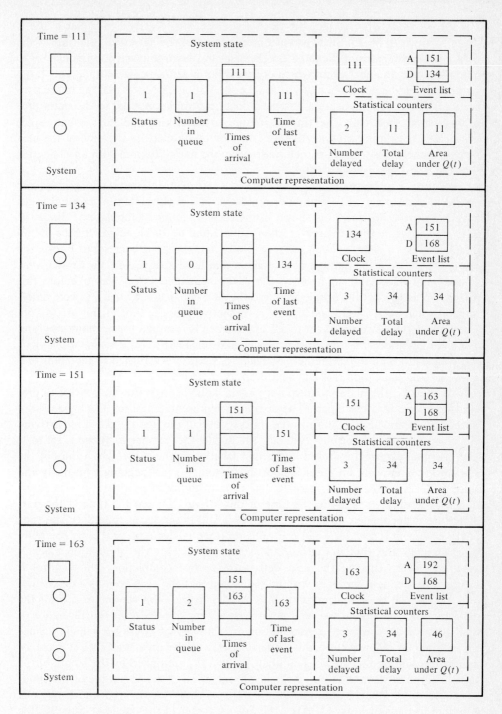

For the event list, observe that the time of the next (first) arrival (denoted by A) is set to 55 since $A_1 = 55$. Since no customer is currently being served, the time of the next customer departure (denoted by D) is set to the large positive number 10^{30} to guarantee that the next event which occurs is not a service completion. (This large number should be larger than any value the simulation clock will assume in the simulation.) After all initialization has been done, control is returned to the main program, which then calls the timing routine to determine the next event. Since $55 < 10^{30}$, the timing routine advances the simulation clock to the time of the next arrival, namely, 55. Control is then returned to the main program with an indication that the next event is an arrival.

At time 55, the main program calls the arrival event routine to process the arrival of a customer. (The computer representation of the system after all changes have been made at time 55 is shown in the second section of the figure.) Since the customer arrives to find the server idle (status equal to 0), he begins service immediately and has a delay in queue of zero. Note that status has been set to 1 since the server is now busy, the number of customers that have completed their delay is now 1, and total delay and area under $Q(t)$ are unchanged [$Q(t)$ was 0 before this arrival]. The times of the next arrival and the next departure, 87 and 98, were determined by adding $A_2 = 32$ and $S_1 = 43$, respectively, to the time of this arrival, 55. The time of the last event is set to 55, and control is returned to the main program. The main program calls the timing routine, and since $87 < 98$, the simulation clock is advanced to the time of the next arrival, 87. Control is returned to the main program with an indication that the next event is an arrival.

At time 87, the main program once again calls the arrival event routine to process the arrival of a customer. (The computer representation after all changes have been made at time 87 is shown in the third section of the figure.) Since the arriving customer finds the server busy, he joins the queue, the number in queue is set to 1, and his time of arrival is stored in the first location of the array. The values of the statistical counters are unchanged since the customer is just beginning his delay and since $Q(t)$ was 0 before this arrival. The time of the next arrival, 111, was determined by adding $A_3 = 24$ to the time of this arrival, 87, and the time of the next departure is unchanged. (The first customer is still in service at time 87.) The time of the last event is set to 87, and control is returned to the main program. The main program calls the timing routine, and since $98 < 111$, the simulation clock is advanced to the time of the next departure (service completion), 98. Control is returned to the main program with an indication that the next event is a departure.

At time 98, the main program calls the departure event routine to process the departure of a customer (the one who arrived at time 55). (See the fourth section of the figure for the computer representation after all changes have been made.) Since the number in queue before this departure was 1, the area under $Q(t)$ must be updated by adding this previous number in queue, 1, multiplied by the length of the time interval between the time of the last event, 87, and the new value of the simulation clock, 98 [that is 1 times $(98 - 87)$], to the previous area under $Q(t)$, 0, resulting in the new area, 11. Also, the first customer in the queue at time 98 (the one who arrived at time 87) enters service, reducing the number in queue from 1 to 0, increasing the number of customers delayed from 1 to 2, and increasing the total delay from 0 to 11 [11 = 0 + (98 − 87)]. [Note that it was necessary to update the area under $Q(t)$ before decrementing the number in queue.] The time of the next departure, 134, is computed by adding $S_2 = 36$ to the time the customer is beginning service, 98, and the time of the next arrival is unchanged. The time of the last event is set to 98, and control is returned to the main program. The main program calls the timing routine, and since $111 < 134$, the simulation clock is advanced to the time of the next arrival, 111. Control is returned to the main program with an indication that the next event is an arrival, etc.

The reader should carefully verify the correctness of the computer representations of the system after all changes have been made at the event times 111, 134, 151, and 163. In particular, note that time 163 is the first time when the total delay is not equal to the area under $Q(t)$ (why?). The simulation will be continued until the number of customers delayed is equal to n. At this point, the main program calls the report generator, and the average delay is estimated by dividing the total delay, $\sum_{i=1}^{n} D_i$, by the number delayed, n. Similarly, the time-average number in queue is estimated by dividing the area under $Q(t)$, $\int_{0}^{T} Q(t)\ dt$, by the final value of the simulation clock, T.

1.4.3 FORTRAN Program

At this point the reader should have an intuitive understanding of the nature of discrete-event simulation, but there is a big difference between an intuitive understanding and the ability to write efficient computer programs. Therefore, we now show how to write a FORTRAN program to simulate the single-server queueing system. Our reasons for choosing a general-purpose language like FORTRAN are twofold: (1) we have found that, despite the availability of several specialized simulation languages (see Chap. 3), many discrete-event simulation models are still written in FORTRAN, and (2) we feel that by learning to simulate in a language like FORTRAN (in which one has to pay attention to every detail) conceptual errors are less likely to occur if a switch is made later to a special-purpose simulation language which is, to some extent, a "black box."

To write a FORTRAN program, we need to make several additional assumptions about the single-server queueing system. In particular, we shall assume that interarrival times of customers to the system are IID exponential random variables with a mean of 1 minute and that service times of customers are IID exponential random variables with a mean of 0.5 minute. The exponential distribution, chosen because it is easy to generate from on a computer, is a continuous random variable with probability density function

$$f(x) = \frac{1}{\beta} e^{-x/\beta} \qquad \text{for } x \geq 0 \tag{1.1}$$

where the parameter $\beta > 0$ is also the mean (see Chap. 5 for further discussion of the exponential distribution). The queueing system we now have is commonly called the *M/M/1 queue,* as discussed in Appendix 1B. The stopping condition for the simulation is to run it until exactly $n = 1000$ customers have completed their delays.

We shall use the numbers 1 and 2 to refer to the two types of events for our model:

Event description	Event type
Arrival of a customer to the system	1
Departure of a customer from the system after completing service	2

Table 1.1 Subroutines, functions, and FORTRAN variables for the queueing model

Subprograms	Purpose
INIT	Initialization routine
TIMING	Timing routine
ARRIVE	Event routine which processes type 1 events
DEPART	Event routine which processes type 2 events
REPORT	Generates report (called when simulation ends)
EXPON(RMEAN)	Function which generates an exponential random variable with mean RMEAN

	Definition
Input parameters:	
MARRVT	Mean interarrival time
MSERVT	Mean service time
TOTCUS	Total number, *n*, of customers whose delays will be observed
Modeling variables:	
ANIQ	Area under number in queue function
DELAY	Delay in queue of a customer
NEVNTS	Number of event types for this model (used by timing routine; NEVNTS is 2 here)
NEXT	Event type (1 or 2) of next event to occur (determined by timing routine)
NIQ	Number of customers in queue
NUMCUS	Number of customers who have completed their delays
RMEAN	Mean of the exponential random variable to be generated
RMIN	Variable used by TIMING to determine time of occurrence of most imminent event
STATUS	Status of server (STATUS = 0 if server is idle and STATUS = 1 if server is busy)
TARRVL(I)	Time of arrival of Ith customer waiting in the queue (TARRVL has dimension 100)
TIME	Simulation clock
TLEVNT	Time of last event *which changed the number in queue*†
TNE(I)	Time of next occurrence of event type I (I = 1, 2), part of event list
TOTDEL	Total delay of all customers who have completed their delays
U	Random variable uniformly distributed between 0 and 1
Output variables:	
AVGDEL	Average delay in queue
AVGNIQ	Time-average number in queue

†This definition, which is different from the one given above, results in a more efficient program.

In addition to a main program, the program consists of the subroutines and functions shown in Table 1.1. The table also shows the FORTRAN variables the program uses (modeling variables include state variables, statistical counters, and variables that are used to facilitate the writing of the program).

The main program, whose FORTRAN listing is given in Fig. 1.6, essentially begins with the MODEL common block. The variables in MODEL are the ones we want to be global variables. (If a variable is in MODEL, its current value will be *global*, i.e., known in all subprograms which contain MODEL. A variable which is not in MODEL will be *local* to the subprogram in which it appears.) The two statements preceding the common declaration specify the mode (INTEGER or REAL) of each variable used in the main program. We have adopted the convention of declaring the mode of each variable explicitly, regardless of whether or not the first letter of the variable is consistent with its conventional FORTRAN mode. We also

```
C
C *** MAIN PROGRAM.
C
      INTEGER NEVNTS,NEXT,NIQ,NUMCUS,STATUS,TOTCUS
      REAL ANIQ,MARRVT,MSERVT,TARRVL(100),TIME,TLEVNT,TNE(2),TOTDEL
      COMMON /MODEL/ ANIQ,MARRVT,MSERVT,NEVNTS,NEXT,NIQ,NUMCUS,STATUS,
     1TARRVL,TIME,TLEVNT,TNE,TOTCUS,TOTDEL
C
C *** SPECIFY THE NUMBER OF EVENT TYPES FOR THE TIMING ROUTINE.
C
      NEVNTS=2
C
C *** READ INPUT PARAMETERS.
C
      READ 10,MARRVT,MSERVT
   10 FORMAT(2F10.0)
      READ 20,TOTCUS
   20 FORMAT(I10)
C
C *****************************************************************************
C
C *** INITIALIZE THE SIMULATION.
C
      CALL INIT
C
C *** DETERMINE THE NEXT EVENT.
C
   30 CALL TIMING
C
C *** CALL THE APPROPRIATE EVENT ROUTINE.
C
      GO TO (40,50),NEXT
   40 CALL ARRIVE
      GO TO 60
   50 CALL DEPART
C
C *** IF THE SIMULATION IS OVER, CALL THE REPORT GENERATOR AND END THE
C *** SIMULATION. IF NOT, CONTINUE THE SIMULATION.
C
   60 IF(NUMCUS.LT.TOTCUS) GO TO 30
      CALL REPORT
      STOP
      END
```

Figure 1.6 FORTRAN listing for the main program, queueing model.

specify the mode of each variable in MODEL, even if that variable is not used in the main program. The common declaration statement is followed by specifying the number of events for the model, reading the input parameters, and calling INIT to initialize the model at TIME = 0. The timing routine, TIMING, is then called to determine the event type, NEXT, of the next event to occur and to advance the simulation clock, TIME, to the time of occurrence of the next event. Then a "computed go to statement," based on NEXT, is used to pass control to the appropriate event routine. If NEXT = 1, event routine ARRIVE is called to process the arrival of a customer. If NEXT = 2, event routine DEPART is called to process the departure of a customer after completing service. After control is returned to the main program from ARRIVE or DEPART, a check is made to see whether the number of customers who have completed their delays, NUMCUS (which is incremented by 1 after each customer completes his delay), is still less than the number of customers whose delays we want to observe, TOTCUS. If so, TIMING is called to continue the simulation. If the specified number of delays has been observed, the report generator, REPORT, is called to compute and print estimates of the desired measures of performance and the simulation run is terminated.

A FORTRAN listing for subroutine INIT is given in Fig. 1.7. The program is quite straightforward, each statement in INIT corresponding to an element of the computer representation in the first section of Fig. 1.5. Note that the time of the first arrival, TNE(1), is determined by adding an exponential random variable with mean MARRVT, namely EXPON(MARRVT), to the simulation clock, TIME = 0. (We

```
      SUBROUTINE INIT
      INTEGER NEVNTS,NEXT,NIQ,NUMCUS,STATUS,TOTCUS
      REAL ANIQ,MARRVT,MSERVT,TARRVL(100),TIME,TLEVNT,TNE(2),TOTDEL
      COMMON /MODEL/ ANIQ,MARRVT,MSERVT,NEVNTS,NEXT,NIQ,NUMCUS,STATUS,
     1TARRVL,TIME,TLEVNT,TNE,TOTCUS,TOTDEL
C
C *** INITIALIZE THE SIMULATION CLOCK.
C
      TIME=0.
C
C *** INITIALIZE THE STATE VARIABLES.
C
      STATUS=0
      NIQ=0
      TLEVNT=0.
C
C *** INITIALIZE THE STATISTICAL COUNTERS.
C
      NUMCUS=0
      TOTDEL=0.
      ANIQ=0.
C
C *** INITIALIZE THE EVENT LIST. SINCE NO CUSTOMERS ARE PRESENT, THE
C *** TIME OF THE NEXT DEPARTURE (SERVICE COMPLETION) IS SET TO
C *** 'INFINITY.'
C
      TNE(1)=TIME+EXPON(MARRVT)
      TNE(2)=1.E+30
      RETURN
      END
```

Figure 1.7 FORTRAN listing for subroutine INIT, queueing model.

```
      SUBROUTINE TIMING
      INTEGER NEVNTS,NEXT,NIQ,NUMCUS,STATUS,TOTCUS
      REAL ANIQ,MARRVT,MSERVT,TARRVL(100),TIME,TLEVNT,TNE(2),TOTDEL
      REAL RMIN
      COMMON /MODEL/ ANIQ,MARRVT,MSERVT,NEVNTS,NEXT,NIQ,NUMCUS,STATUS,
     1TARRVL,TIME,TLEVNT,TNE,TOTCUS,TOTDEL
      RMIN=1.E+29
      NEXT=0
C
C *** DETERMINE THE EVENT TYPE OF THE NEXT EVENT TO OCCUR.
C
      DO 10 I=1,NEVNTS
      IF(TNE(I).GE.RMIN) GO TO 10
      RMIN=TNE(I)
      NEXT=I
   10 CONTINUE
C
C *** IF THE EVENT LIST IS EMPTY (I.E., NEXT=0), STOP THE SIMULATION.
C *** OTHERWISE, ADVANCE THE SIMULATION CLOCK.
C
      IF(NEXT.GT.0) GO TO 30
      PRINT 20
   20 FORMAT(1H1,5X,'EVENT LIST EMPTY')
      STOP
   30 TIME=TNE(NEXT)
      RETURN
      END
```

Figure 1.8 FORTRAN listing for subroutine TIMING, queueing model.

explicitly used TIME in this statement, although it has a value of 0, to show the general form of a statement to determine the time of a future event.) Since no customers are present at TIME = 0, the time of the next departure, TNE(2), is set to 1.E + 30 (FORTRAN notation for 10^{30}), which will guarantee that the first event will be an arrival.

A FORTRAN listing for subroutine TIMING is given in Fig. 1.8. The program compares TNE(1), TNE(2), ... , TNE(NEVNTS) and sets NEXT equal to the event type whose time of occurrence is the smallest. (Note that NEVNTS is set in the main program.) In case of ties, the lowest-numbered event type is chosen. Then the simulation clock is advanced to the time of occurrence of the chosen event type, namely TNE(NEXT). The program is made slightly more complicated by a check for the event list's being empty, which we define to mean that all events are scheduled to occur at TIME = 10^{30}. If this is ever the case (as indicated by NEXT = 0), the error message "event list empty" is printed and the simulation terminated.

A flowchart and FORTRAN listing for event subroutine (routine) ARRIVE are given in Figs. 1.9 and 1.10. The subroutine begins by scheduling the next arrival event at time TIME + EXPON(MARRVT). (Note that TIME is the time of arrival of the customer who is just now arriving.) Then a check is made to determine whether the server is idle, i.e., if STATUS = 0. If the server is idle, the delay of the arriving customer is set to 0, this delay is added to the counter TOTDEL, the number of customers delayed (that is, those who have completed their delays), NUMCUS, is incremented by 1, the server is made busy, and a departure event is scheduled for this customer at time TIME + EXPON(MSERVT). On the other hand, if the server is busy, the area under the number in queue function between the time of the

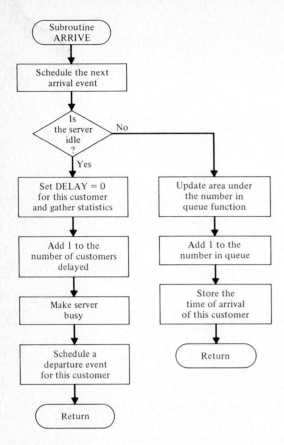

Figure 1.9 Flowchart for subroutine ARRIVE, queueing model.

last event, TLEVNT, and the present time, TIME, is added to the counter, ANIQ, and the time of the last event is set to the present time. Then the number of customers in the queue is incremented by 1 (the arriving customer joins the queue). If the (new) number in queue is less than or equal to 100 (the size of the array TARRVL), the time of arrival of the arriving customer is stored in the appropriate location in TARRVL. (In an actual simulation study, an adequate size for an array like TARRVL might be determined during a pilot run.) If there is no space in the array TARRVL to store the new time of arrival, the error message "overflow of the array TARRVL" is printed and the simulation terminated.

Event subroutine (routine) DEPART, whose flowchart and listing are given in Figs. 1.11 and 1.12, is called from the main program when a service completion (and subsequent departure) occurs. If the departing customer leaves no customer behind (as indicated by NIQ = 0), the server is made idle by setting STATUS = 0 and the time of the next departure, TNE(2), is set to 10^{30} since the next event must be an arrival. (If this latter statement is omitted, the program will get into an infinite loop.) If one or more customers are left behind by the departing customer, the area under the number in queue function is updated and the time of the last event is reset. Since the first customer in the queue will begin service, the number in queue is reduced by 1, the delay of this customer is computed as TIME − TARRVL(1) and

```
      SUBROUTINE ARRIVE
      INTEGER NEVNTS,NEXT,NIQ,NUMCUS,STATUS,TOTCUS
      REAL ANIQ,MARRVT,MSERVT,TARRVL(100),TIME,TLEVNT,TNE(2),TOTDEL
      REAL DELAY
      COMMON /MODEL/ ANIQ,MARRVT,MSERVT,NEVNTS,NEXT,NIQ,NUMCUS,STATUS,
     1TARRVL,TIME,TLEVNT,TNE,TOTCUS,TOTDEL
C
C *** SCHEDULE THE NEXT ARRIVAL.
C
      TNE(1)=TIME+EXPON(MARRVT)
C
C ********************************************************************
C
C *** IF THE SERVER IS IDLE, START SERVICE ON THE ARRIVING CUSTOMER.
C
      IF(STATUS.EQ.1) GO TO 10
C *** CUSTOMER HAS A DELAY OF ZERO. (THE FOLLOWING TWO STATEMENTS ARE
C *** FOR PROGRAM CLARITY AND DO NOT AFFECT THE RESULTS OF THE
C *** SIMULATION.)
C
      DELAY=0.
      TOTDEL=TOTDEL+DELAY
C
C *** ADD ONE TO THE NUMBER OF CUSTOMERS DELAYED.
C
      NUMCUS=NUMCUS+1
C
C *** MAKE SERVER BUSY.
C
      STATUS=1
C
C *** SCHEDULE A DEPARTURE (SERVICE COMPLETION).
C
      TNE(2)=TIME+EXPON(MSERVT)
      RETURN
C
C ********************************************************************
C
C *** SERVER IS BUSY. UPDATE THE AREA UNDER THE NUMBER IN QUEUE
C *** FUNCTION.
C
   10 ANIQ=ANIQ+NIQ*(TIME-TLEVNT)
      TLEVNT=TIME
C
C *** ADD ONE TO THE NUMBER OF CUSTOMERS IN THE QUEUE. IF AN OVERFLOW
C *** CONDITION EXISTS, STOP THE SIMULATION. OTHERWISE, STORE THE TIME
C *** OF ARRIVAL OF THE ARRIVING CUSTOMER IN THE ARRAY 'TARRVL.'
C
      NIQ=NIQ+1
      IF(NIQ.LE.100) GO TO 30
      PRINT 20
   20 FORMAT(1H1,5X,'OVERFLOW OF THE ARRAY TARRVL')
      STOP
   30 TARRVL(NIQ)=TIME
      RETURN
      END
```

Figure 1.10 FORTRAN listing for subroutine ARRIVE, queueing model.

added to the counter TOTDEL, the number delayed is increased by 1, and a departure event is scheduled for this customer. If there are still more customers in the queue, each time of arrival in the array TARRVL is moved up one location. This guarantees that the time of arrival of a customer entering service (after being delayed in queue) will always be stored in TARRVL(1).

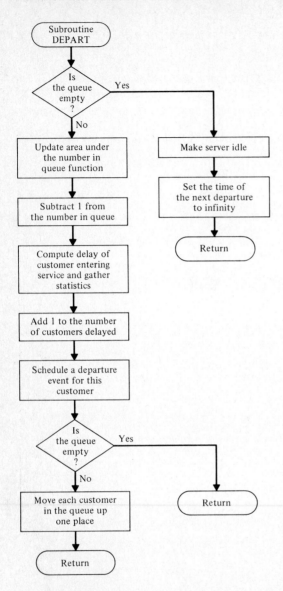

Figure 1.11 Flowchart for subroutine DEPART, queueing model.

The FORTRAN listing for subroutine REPORT is given in Fig. 1.13. The subroutine begins by printing the input parameters. This is always recommended to ensure that the input parameters were read into the computer correctly and to identify the input parameters corresponding to a particular set of output data. The average delay of a customer, AVGDEL, is computed as TOTDEL/NUMCUS and the average number of customers in queue, AVGNIQ, as ANIQ/TIME (here TIME is the time that customer number TOTCUS entered service), and then both quantities are printed. The print statement at the end of subroutine REPORT makes the simulation report page free of any extraneous printing.

```
      SUBROUTINE DEPART
      INTEGER NEVNTS,NEXT,NIQ,NUMCUS,STATUS,TOTCUS
      INTEGER I,I1
      REAL ANIQ,MARRVT,MSERVT,TARRVL(100),TIME,TLEVNT,TNE(2),TOTDEL
      REAL DELAY
      COMMON /MODEL/ ANIQ,MARRVT,MSERVT,NEVNTS,NEXT,NIQ,NUMCUS,STATUS,
     1TARRVL,TIME,TLEVNT,TNE,TOTCUS,TOTDEL
C
C *** IF THE QUEUE IS EMPTY, MAKE THE SERVER IDLE AND SET THE TIME OF
C *** THE NEXT DEPARTURE (SERVICE COMPLETION) TO 'INFINITY.'
C
      IF(NIQ.GT.0) GO TO 10
      STATUS=0
      TNE(2)=1.E+30
      RETURN
C
C ***********************************************************************
C
C *** QUEUE IS NOT EMPTY. UPDATE THE AREA UNDER THE NUMBER IN QUEUE
C *** FUNCTION.
C
   10 ANIQ=ANIQ+NIQ*(TIME-TLEVNT)
      TLEVNT=TIME
C
C *** SUBTRACT ONE FROM THE NUMBER OF CUSTOMERS IN THE QUEUE.
C
      NIQ=NIQ-1
C
C *** COMPUTE THE DELAY OF THE CUSTOMER WHO IS BEGINNING SERVICE.
C
      DELAY=TIME-TARRVL(1)
      TOTDEL=TOTDEL+DELAY
C
C *** ADD ONE TO THE NUMBER OF CUSTOMERS DELAYED.
C
      NUMCUS=NUMCUS+1
C
C *** SCHEDULE A DEPARTURE.
C
      TNE(2)=TIME+EXPON(MSERVT)
C
C *** IF THE QUEUE IS NOT EMPTY, MOVE EACH CUSTOMER IN THE QUEUE UP ONE
C *** PLACE.
C
      IF(NIQ.EQ.0) GO TO 30
      DO 20 I=1,NIQ
      I1=I+1
      TARRVL(I)=TARRVL(I1)
   20 CONTINUE
   30 RETURN
      END
```

Figure 1.12 FORTRAN listing for subroutine DEPART, queueing model.

The function EXPON, which generates an exponential random variable with mean RMEAN, is listed in Fig. 1.14. The program begins by obtaining a random variable U which is uniformly distributed on the interval 0 to 1 [such a random variable will henceforth be denoted by U(0, 1)]. The U(0, 1) random variable has the following probability density function:

$$f(x) = \begin{cases} 1 & \text{if } 0 \leq x \leq 1 \\ 0 & \text{otherwise} \end{cases}$$

```
      SUBROUTINE REPORT
      INTEGER NEVNTS,NEXT,NIQ,NUMCUS,STATUS,TOTCUS
      REAL ANIQ,MARRVT,MSERVT,TARRVL(100),TIME,TLEVNT,TNE(2),TOTDEL
      REAL AVGDEL,AVGNIQ
      COMMON /MODEL/ ANIQ,MARRVT,MSERVT,NEVNTS,NEXT,NIQ,NUMCUS,STATUS,
     1TARRVL,TIME,TLEVNT,TNE,TOTCUS,TOTDEL
C
C *** PRINT HEADING AND INPUT PARAMETERS.
C
      PRINT 10
   10 FORMAT(1H1,5X,'SINGLE-SERVER QUEUEING SYSTEM')
      PRINT 20,MARRVT
   20 FORMAT(1H0,5X,'MEAN INTERARRIVAL TIME',5X,F6.3,' MINUTES')
      PRINT 30,MSERVT
   30 FORMAT(1H0,5X,'MEAN SERVICE TIME',10X,F6.3,' MINUTES')
      PRINT 40,TOTCUS
   40 FORMAT(1H0,5X,'NUMBER OF CUSTOMERS',9X,I5)
C
C *** COMPUTE AND PRINT ESTIMATES OF THE DESIRED MEASURES OF PERFORMANCE.
C
      AVGDEL=TOTDEL/NUMCUS
      AVGNIQ=ANIQ/TIME
      PRINT 50
   50 FORMAT(//)
      PRINT 60,AVGDEL
   60 FORMAT(1H0,5X,'AVERAGE DELAY IN QUEUE',5X,F6.3,' MINUTES')
      PRINT 70,AVGNIQ
   70 FORMAT(1H0,5X,'AVERAGE NUMBER IN QUEUE',4X,F6.3)
      PRINT 80
   80 FORMAT(1H1)
      RETURN
      END
```

Figure 1.13 FORTRAN listing for subroutine REPORT, queueing model.

It is easy to show that the probability that a U(0, 1) random variable falls in any subinterval $[x, x + \Delta x]$ contained in the interval [0, 1] is (uniformly) Δx (see Chap. 5). This is why a U(0, 1) random variable is called "uniform." The U(0, 1) random variable is fundamental to simulation modeling because, as we shall see in Chap. 7, any random variable of interest can be generated by first generating one or more U(0, 1) random variables.

The U(0, 1) random variable U was generated on our particular computer by calling the library function RANUN(Z). Mechanisms for generating U(0, 1) random variables, such as RANUN, are called *random-number generators* and are dis-

```
      FUNCTION EXPON(RMEAN)
      REAL RMEAN,U
C
C *** GENERATE A U(0,1) RANDOM VARIABLE. THE FORM OF THIS STATEMENT
C *** DEPENDS ON THE COMPUTER USED.
C
      U=RANUN(Z)
C
C *** GENERATE AN EXPONENTIAL RANDOM VARIABLE WITH MEAN RMEAN.
C
      EXPON=-RMEAN*ALOG(U)
      RETURN
      END
```

Figure 1.14 FORTRAN listing for function EXPON, queueing model.

$F(x) = 1 - e^{-x/\beta}$

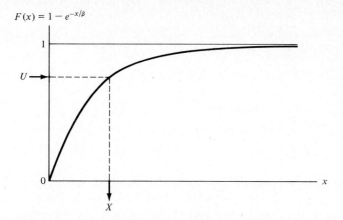

Figure 1.15 The inverse-transform approach for an exponential random variable.

cussed in Chap. 6. (Readers wishing to use EXPON should replace RANUN by the name of their random-number generator.)

To generate an exponential random variable with mean RMEAN, the natural logarithm (ln) of the U(0, 1) random variable U is taken and multiplied by the negative of the value of RMEAN, as seen in Fig. 1.14. We now try to provide some insight into why this is a correct method for generating an exponential random variable. If X is an exponential random variable with mean β, then for any $x \geq 0$ the probability that X is less than or equal to x is

$$P\{X \leq x\} = F(x) = \int_0^x f(t) \, dt = 1 - e^{-x/\beta}$$

where $f(t)$ is the density function given by Eq. (1.1) and $F(x)$ is the distribution function of X. If U is a U(0, 1) random variable, then for any $x \geq 0$,

$$P\{-\beta \ln U \leq x\} = P\{U \geq e^{-x/\beta}\} = 1 - e^{-x/\beta} = F(x)$$

so that the random variable $X = -\beta \ln U$ has an exponential distribution with mean β. Another way to derive a valid formula for X is to set $U = F(X)$ and solve for X (see Chap. 7); this procedure, illustrated in Fig. 1.15, is called the *inverse-transform* approach to generating random variables.

It should be mentioned that the FORTRAN program given above for the $M/M/1$ queue is certainly not the simplest one possible but was designed to illustrate how one might organize a program for a more complex simulation.

1.4.4 Simulation Output and Discussion

The simulation report is given in Fig. 1.16. Note that the average delay in queue was estimated to be 0.497 minute and the time-average number of customers in queue was estimated to be 0.500 (to three decimal places). (It is not a coincidence that these estimates are so close; see Appendix 1B.)

SINGLE-SERVER QUEUEING SYSTEM

MEAN INTERARRIVAL TIME	1.000 MINUTES
MEAN SERVICE TIME	.500 MINUTES
NUMBER OF CUSTOMERS	1000
AVERAGE DELAY IN QUEUE	.497 MINUTES
AVERAGE NUMBER IN QUEUE	.500

Figure 1.16 Simulation report for the queueing model.

In some simulation studies, we might want to estimate steady-state character-istics of the model (see Secs. 8.2 and 8.3), i.e., characteristics of a model after the simulation has been running a very long (an infinite) amount of time. For the simple $M/M/1$ queue we have been considering, it is possible to compute *analytically* the steady-state average delay in queue and the steady-state time-average number in queue, both of these measures of performance being 0.5 (see, for example, Gross and Harris [4, p. 58]). Thus, if we wanted to determine these steady-state measures, our estimates based on the stopping rule $n = 1000$ delays were actually quite close. However, we were lucky since $n = 1000$ was arbitrarily chosen! In practice, the choice of a stopping rule which will give good estimates of steady-state measures is quite difficult. To illustrate this point, suppose for the $M/M/1$ queue that the arrival rate of customers is increased by 80 percent from 1 per minute to 1.8 per minute (the mean interarrival time is now 0.556 minute), that the mean service time is unchanged, and that we wish to estimate the same steady-state measures from a run of length $n = 1000$ delays. We performed this simulation run and got estimates for the steady-state average delay and the steady-state average number in queue of 3.078 minutes and 5.501, respectively. Since the true values of these measures are 4.5 minutes and 8.1, it is clear that the stopping rule cannot be arbitrarily chosen. We discuss how to specify the run length for a steady-state simulation in Chap. 8.

The reader may have wondered why we did not estimate the average waiting time in system of a customer, $w(n)$, rather than the average delay in queue, $d(n)$, where the waiting time of a customer is defined as the time interval from the instant the customer arrives to the instant the customer completes service and departs. There were two reasons. First, for many queueing systems we believe that the customer's delay in queue while waiting for other customers to be served is the most troublesome part of the customer's wait in the system. Our second reason is one of statistical efficiency. The usual estimator of $w(n)$ would be

$$\hat{w}(n) = \frac{\sum_{i=1}^{n} W_i}{n} = \frac{\sum_{i=1}^{n} D_i}{n} + \frac{\sum_{i=1}^{n} S_i}{n} = \hat{d}(n) + \overline{S}(n) \qquad (1.2)$$

where $W_i = D_i + S_i$ is the waiting time in system of the ith customer. Since the service-time distribution would have to be known to perform a simulation in the first place, the expected or mean service time, $E(S)$, would also be known and an alternative estimator of $w(n)$ is

$$\tilde{w}(n) = \hat{d}(n) + E(S)$$

[Note that $\overline{S}(n)$ is an estimator of $E(S)$ in Eq. (1.2).] In almost all queueing simulations, $\tilde{w}(n)$ will be a more efficient (less variable) estimator of $w(n)$ than $\hat{w}(n)$ and is thus preferable (both estimators are unbiased). Therefore, if one wants an estimate of $w(n)$, estimate $d(n)$ by $\hat{d}(n)$ and add the known expected service time, $E(S)$. In general, the moral is to replace estimators by their expected values whenever possible (see the discussion of indirect estimators in Sec. 11.5).

1.4.5 Alternative Stopping Rules

In the above queueing example, the simulation was terminated when NUMCUS, the number of customers delayed, was equal to TOTCUS. In this case, the final value of TIME was a random variable. However, for many real-world queueing simulations, it is desired to stop the simulation after some fixed amount of time, say, 480 minutes (8 hours). However, since the A_i's and S_i's for our example are continuous random variables, the probability of the simulation's terminating after exactly 480 minutes is 0 (neglecting the finite accuracy of a computer). Therefore, to stop the simulation at a specified time, we introduce a dummy "end-simulation" event (call it an event of type 3) which is scheduled to occur at TIME = 480. When the time of occurrence of this event, TNE(3), is less than both TNE(1) and TNE(2), the report generator is called and the simulation is terminated. The number of customers delayed is now a random variable. These ideas can be implemented in the computer program by making changes in the main program, INIT, and REPORT, as shown in Figs. 1.17 to 1.19. In Fig. 1.17 note that NEVNTS is now 3, that the desired simulation run length, TEND, is now an input parameter and a member of the common block MODEL (TOTCUS has been removed), and that the statements after the "computed go to statement" have been changed. The only change to INIT (other than to the common block MODEL) is the addition of the statement TNE(3) = TEND, which schedules the end of the simulation. In Fig. 1.19, observe that a statement has been added to the beginning of REPORT to update the area under $Q(t)$ from the time of the last arrival or departure event to the time when the simulation actually ends, TEND. (Note that when REPORT is called, TIME is equal to TEND.) The reader should review carefully the changes that have been made to the three subprograms.

If the queueing system being considered had actually been a one-operator barbershop open from 9 A.M. to 5 P.M., stopping the simulation after exactly 8 hours might leave a customer with hair partially cut. In this case, it is desired to close the door of the barbershop after 8 hours but to continue to run the simulation until all customers present when the door closes (if any) have been served. The reader is asked in Prob. 1.1 to supply the program changes necessary to implement this stopping rule (see also Sec. 2.5).

```
C
C *** MAIN PROGRAM.
C
      INTEGER NEVNTS,NEXT,NIQ,NUMCUS,STATUS
      REAL ANIQ,MARRVT,MSERVT,TARRVL(100),TEND,TIME,TLEVNT,TNE(3),TOTDEL
      COMMON /MODEL/ ANIQ,MARRVT.MSERVT,NEVNTS,NEXT,NIQ,NUMCUS,STATUS,
     1TARRVL,TEND,TIME,TLEVNT,TNE,TOTDEL
C
C *** SPECIFY THE NUMBER OF EVENT TYPES FOR THE TIMING ROUTINE.
C
      NEVNTS=3
C
C *** READ INPUT PARAMETERS.
C
      READ 10,MARRVT,MSERVT
   10 FORMAT(2F10.0)
      READ 20,TEND
   20 FORMAT(F10.0)
C
C ************************************************************************
C
C *** INITIALIZE THE SIMULATION.
C
      CALL INIT
C
C *** DETERMINE THE NEXT EVENT.
C
   30 CALL TIMING
C
C *** CALL THE APPROPRIATE EVENT ROUTINE.
C
      GO TO (40,50,60),NEXT
   40 CALL ARRIVE
      GO TO 30
   50 CALL DEPART
      GO TO 30
C
C *** SINCE THE SIMULATION IS OVER. CALL THE REPORT GENERATOR AND END
C *** THE SIMULATION.
C
   60 CALL REPORT
      STOP
      END
```

Figure 1.17 FORTRAN listing for the main program, queueing model with fixed run length.

1.5 SIMULATION OF AN INVENTORY SYSTEM

We shall now see how simulation can be used to compare alternative ordering policies for an inventory system. Many of the elements of our model are representative of those found in actual inventory systems.

1.5.1 Statement of the Problem

Consider a company which sells a single product and would like to decide how many items to have in inventory for each of the next n months. The times between demands are IID exponential random variables with a mean of 0.1 month. The sizes of the

```
      SUBROUTINE INIT
      INTEGER NEVNTS,NEXT,NIQ,NUMCUS,STATUS
      REAL ANIQ,MARRVT,MSERVT,TARRVL(100),TEND,TIME,TLEVNT,TNE(3),TOTDEL
      COMMON /MODEL/ ANIQ,MARRVT,MSERVT,NEVNTS,NEXT,NIQ,NUMCUS,STATUS,
     1TARRVL,TEND,TIME,TLEVNT,TNE,TOTDEL
C
C *** INITIALIZE THE SIMULATION CLOCK.
C
      TIME=0.
C
C *** INITIALIZE THE STATE VARIABLES.
C
      STATUS=0
      NIQ=0
      TLEVNT=0.
C
C *** INITIALIZE THE STATISTICAL COUNTERS.
C
      NUMCUS=0
      TOTDEL=0.
      ANIQ=0.
C
C *** INITIALIZE THE EVENT LIST. SINCE NO CUSTOMERS ARE PRESENT, THE
C *** TIME OF THE NEXT DEPARTURE (SERVICE COMPLETION) IS SET TO
C *** 'INFINITY.'
C
      TNE(1)=TIME+EXPON(MARRVT)
      TNE(2)=1.E+30
      TNE(3)=TEND
      RETURN
      END
```

Figure 1.18 FORTRAN listing for subroutine INIT, queueing model with fixed run length.

demands, *D*, are IID random variables (independent of when the demands occur) with

$$D = \begin{cases} 1 & \text{w.p. } \frac{1}{6} \\ 2 & \text{w.p. } \frac{1}{3} \\ 3 & \text{w.p. } \frac{1}{3} \\ 4 & \text{w.p. } \frac{1}{6} \end{cases}$$

where w.p. is read "with probability."

At the beginning of each month, the company reviews the inventory level and decides how many items to order from its supplier. If the company orders Z items, it incurs a cost $K + iZ$, where $K = \$32$ is the *setup cost* and $i = \$3$ is the *incremental cost* per item. (If $Z = 0$, no cost is incurred.) When an order is placed, the time required for it to arrive (called the *delivery lag*) is a random variable which is uniformly distributed on the interval 0.5 to 1 month.

The company uses a stationary (s, S) policy to decide how much to order, i.e.,

$$Z = \begin{cases} S - I & \text{if } I < s \\ 0 & \text{if } I \geq s \end{cases}$$

where I is the inventory level at the beginning of the month (before ordering).

When a demand occurs, it is satisfied immediately if the inventory level is

```
      SUBROUTINE REPORT
      INTEGER NEVNTS,NEXT,NIQ,NUMCUS,STATUS
      REAL ANIQ,MARRVT,MSERVT,TARRVL(100),TEND,TIME,TLEVNT,TNE(3),TOTDEL
      REAL AVGDEL,AVGNIQ
      COMMON /MODEL/ ANIQ,MARRVT,MSERVT,NEVNTS,NEXT,NIQ,NUMCUS,STATUS,
     1TARRVL,TEND,TIME,TLEVNT,TNE,TOTDEL
C
C *** UPDATE THE AREA UNDER THE NUMBER IN QUEUE FUNCTION TO THE END OF
C *** THE SIMULATION.
C
      ANIQ=ANIQ+NIQ*(TIME-TLEVNT)
C
C *** PRINT HEADING AND INPUT PARAMETERS.
C
      PRINT 10
   10 FORMAT(1H1,5X,'SINGLE-SERVER QUEUEING SYSTEM')
      PRINT 20,MARRVT
   20 FORMAT(1H0,5X,'MEAN INTERARRIVAL TIME',5X,F6.3,' MINUTES')
      PRINT 30,MSERVT
   30 FORMAT(1H0,5X,'MEAN SERVICE TIME',10X,F6.3,' MINUTES')
      PRINT 40,TEND
   40 FORMAT(1H0,5X,'LENGTH OF THE SIMULATION',2X,F7.3,' MINUTES')
C
C *** COMPUTE AND PRINT ESTIMATES OF THE DESIRED MEASURES OF PERFORMANCE.
C
      AVGDEL=TOTDEL/NUMCUS
      AVGNIQ=ANIQ/TIME
      PRINT 50
   50 FORMAT(//)
      PRINT 60,AVGDEL
   60 FORMAT(1H0,5X,'AVERAGE DELAY IN QUEUE',5X,F6.3,' MINUTES')
      PRINT 70,AVGNIQ
   70 FORMAT(1H0,5X,'AVERAGE NUMBER IN QUEUE',4X,F6.3)
      PRINT 80
   80 FORMAT(1H1)
      RETURN
      END
```

Figure 1.19 FORTRAN listing for subroutine REPORT, queueing model with fixed run length.

greater than or equal to the demand size. If the demand size is greater than the inventory level, the excess of demand over supply is backlogged and satisfied by future deliveries. (In this case, the new inventory level is equal to the old inventory level minus the demand size, a negative integer.) When an order arrives, it is first used to eliminate as much of the backlog (if any) as possible and the remainder of the order (if any) is added to the inventory.

So far we have discussed only one type of cost incurred by the inventory system, namely, the ordering cost. However, most real-world inventory systems also have two additional types of costs, *holding* and *shortage costs,* which we discuss after introducing some additional notation. Let $I(t)$ be the inventory level at time t [$I(t)$ may be positive, zero, or negative], let $I^+(t) = \max \{I(t), 0\}$ be the number of items actually in the inventory at time t [$I^+(t) \geq 0$], and let $I^-(t) = \max \{-I(t), 0\}$ be the backlog at time t [$I^-(t) \geq 0$]. A possible realization of $I(t)$, $I^+(t)$, and $I^-(t)$ for $t \geq 0$ is shown in Fig. 1.20. The time points at which $I(t)$ decreases are the ones at which demands occur.

For our model, we shall assume that the company incurs an average holding cost for the n months of

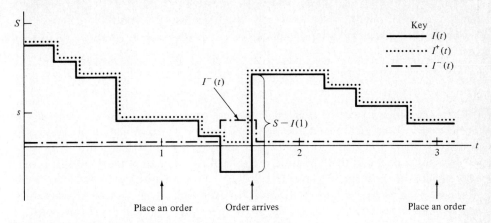

Figure 1.20 A realization of $I(t)$, $I^+(t)$, and $I^-(t)$ over time.

$$h \frac{\displaystyle\int_0^n I^+(t)\, dt}{n}$$

where h = \$1 per item per month and $\int_0^n I^+(t)\, dt/n$ is the time-average number of items actually in inventory. The holding cost includes such costs as warehouse rental, insurance, taxes, and maintenance. It also includes the opportunity cost of having capital tied up in inventory rather than invested elsewhere. [We have ignored in our formulation the fact that some holding costs are still incurred when $I^+(t) = 0$. However, since our goal is to *compare* ordering policies, ignoring this factor (which is independent of the policy used) will not affect our assessment of which policy is best.]

We shall also assume that the company incurs an average shortage cost for the n months of

$$\pi \frac{\displaystyle\int_0^n I^-(t)\, dt}{n}$$

where π = \$5 per item per month and $\int_0^n I^-(t)\, dt/n$ is the time-average number of items in backlog. The shortage cost includes the cost of extra record keeping when a backlog exists and also a cost due to the loss of customers' goodwill.

Assume that initially $I(0) = 60$ and that no order is outstanding. We simulate the inventory system for $n = 120$ months (10 years) and use the average total cost per month (which is the sum of the average ordering cost per month, the average holding cost per month, and the average shortage cost per month) to compare the following nine inventory ordering policies:

s	20	20	20	20	40	40	40	60	60
S	40	60	80	100	60	80	100	80	100

We do not address here the issue of how these particular policies were chosen for consideration; statistical techniques for making such a determination are discussed in Chap. 12.

It should be noted that the state variables for a simulation model of this inventory system are the inventory level $I(t)$, the amount of an outstanding order from the company to the supplier, and the time of the last event which changed the inventory level (which is needed to compute the areas under the $I^+(t)$ and $I^-(t)$ functions.

1.5.2 FORTRAN Program

Our model of the inventory system uses the following types of events:

Event description	Event type
Arrival of an order to the company from the supplier	1
Demand for the product from a customer	2
End of the simulation after n months	3
Inventory evaluation (and possible ordering) at the beginning of a month	4

We have chosen to make the end of the simulation event type 3 rather than 4, since at TIME = 120 both "end of the simulation" and "inventory evaluation" events will eventually be scheduled and we would like to execute the former event first at this time. (Since the simulation is over at TIME = 120, there is no sense in evaluating the inventory and possibly ordering.) The execution of event type 3 before 4 is guaranteed because the timing routine, TIMING, will give preference to the lowest-numbered event if two or more events are scheduled to occur at the same time (this is called a *time tie*). In general, a simulation model should be designed to process events in an appropriate order when time ties can occur.

Table 1.2 Subprograms and FORTRAN variables for the inventory model

Subprograms	Purpose
INIT	Initialization routine
TIMING	Timing routine
ORDARV	Event routine which processes type 1 events
DEMAND	Event routine which processes type 2 events
REPORT	Event routine which processes type 3 events (report generator)
EVALU8	Event routine which processes type 4 events
UPDATE	Subroutine to update areas under $I^+(t)$ and $I^-(t)$ functions when inventory level changes and when simulation ends (*not* an event routine)

Table 1.2 (*Continued*)

Subprograms	Purpose
EXPON(RMEAN)	Function which generates an exponential random variable with mean RMEAN
RANDI(Z)	Function which generates a random integer between 1 and NVALUE (a positive integer) in accordance with distribution function PROBD(I) (I = 1, 2, . . . , NVALUE), where Z is a dummy variable. [If X is the random integer, the probability that X takes on a value less than or equal to I is given by PROBD(I).] The values of NVALUE and PROBD(I) (I = 1, 2, . . . , NVALUE) are set in the main program and transmitted to RANDI by placing the following common block in the main program:
	COMMON /RANDOM/ NVALUE,PROBD(25)
	(This particular format for RANDI was chosen to make its use here consistent with Chap. 2)
UNIFRM(A,B)	Function which generates a continuous random variable uniformly distributed on the interval [A, B], where A and B are real-valued and A must be less than B

	Definition
Input parameters:	
BIGS	S, second number in the specification of (s, S) inventory policy
H	h, multiplier for average holding cost
INCRMC	i, incremental cost per item ordered
INITIL	Initial inventory level
MDEMDT	Mean interdemand time
NMNTHS	Length of the simulation in months
NPOLCY	Number of inventory policies being considered
NVALUE	Number of demand sizes
PI	π, multiplier for average shortage cost
PROBD(I)	Probability of a demand $\leq$ I
SETUPC	K, setup cost of placing an order
SMALLS	s, first number in specification of (s, S) inventory policy
Modeling variables:	
AMINUS	Area under $I^-(t)$ function
AMOUNT	Amount, Z, ordered by company from supplier
APLUS	Area under $I^+(t)$ function
DSIZE	Particular demand size
INVLEV	$I(t)$, inventory level
NEVNTS	Number of event types for model (i.e., 4)
NEXT	Event type (1, 2, 3, or 4) of next event to occur
TIME	Simulation clock
TLEVNT	Time of last event *which changed the inventory level*
TNE(I)	Time of occurrence of event type I (I = 1, 2, . . . , 4)
TORDC	Total ordering cost
TSLE	Time since last event
Output variables:	
ACOST	Average total cost per month
AHLDC	Average holding cost per month
AORDC	Average ordering cost per month
ASHRC	Average shortage cost per month

```
C
C *** MAIN PROGRAM.
C
      INTEGER AMOUNT,BIGS,INITIL,INVLEV,NEVNTS,NEXT,NMNTHS,SMALLS
      INTEGER I,NPOLCY
      REAL AMINUS,APLUS,H,INCRMC,MDEMDT,PI,SETUPC,TIME,TLEVNT,TNE(4),
     1TORDC
      COMMON /MODEL/ AMINUS,AMOUNT,APLUS,BIGS,H,INCRMC,INITIL,INVLEV,
     1MDEMDT,NEVNTS,NEXT,NMNTHS,PI,SETUPC,SMALLS,TIME,TLEVNT,TNE,TORDC
      COMMON /RANDOM/ NVALUE,PROBD(25)
C
C *** SPECIFY THE NUMBER OF EVENT TYPES FOR THE TIMING ROUTINE.
C
      NEVNTS=4
C
C *** READ INPUT PARAMETERS.
C
      READ 10,INITIL,NMNTHS,NPOLCY,NVALUE
   10 FORMAT(4I10)
      READ 20,MDEMDT,SETUPC,INCRMC,H,PI
   20 FORMAT(5F10.0)
      READ 30,(PROBD(I),I=1,NVALUE)
   30 FORMAT(8F10.0)
C
C ***********************************************************************
C
C *** PRINT REPORT HEADING.
C
      PRINT 40
   40 FORMAT(1H1,5X,'SINGLE-PRODUCT INVENTORY SYSTEM')
      PRINT 50,INITIL
   50 FORMAT(1H0,5X,'INITIAL INVENTORY LEVEL',21X,I3,' ITEMS')
      PRINT 60,NVALUE
   60 FORMAT(1H0,5X,'NUMBER OF DEMAND SIZES',22X,I3)
      PRINT 70,(PROBD(I),I=1,NVALUE)
   70 FORMAT(1H0,5X,'DISTRIBUTION FUNCTION OF DEMAND SIZES',5X,8(F5.3,3X
     1))
      PRINT 80,MDEMDT
   80 FORMAT(1H0,5X,'MEAN INTERDEMAND TIME',21X,F5.2,' MONTHS')
      PRINT 90,NMNTHS
   90 FORMAT(1H0,5X,'LENGTH OF THE SIMULATION',20X,I3,' MONTHS')
      PRINT 100,SETUPC,INCRMC,H,PI
  100 FORMAT(1H0,5X,'K = ',F5.1,3X,'I = ',F5.1,3X,'H = ',F5.1,3X,'PI = '
     1,F5.1)
      PRINT 110
  110 FORMAT(//)
      PRINT 120
  120 FORMAT(1H0,7X,'POLICY',6X,'AVERAGE COST',5X,'AVERAGE ORDERING COST
     1',5X,'AVERAGE HOLDING COST',5X,'AVERAGE SHORTAGE COST')
C
C ***********************************************************************
C
C *** RUN THE SIMULATION VARYING THE INVENTORY POLICY.
C
      DO 190 I=1,NPOLCY
C
C *** READ THE INVENTORY POLICY.
C
      READ 130,SMALLS,BIGS
  130 FORMAT(2I10)
C
C *** INITIALIZE THE SIMULATION.
C
      CALL INIT
C
C *** DETERMINE THE NEXT EVENT.
C
  140 CALL TIMING
C
C *** CALL THE APPROPRIATE EVENT ROUTINE.
C
      GO TO (150,160,180,170),NEXT
  150 CALL ORDARV
      GO TO 140
  160 CALL DEMAND
      GO TO 140
  170 CALL EVALU8
      GO TO 140
  180 CALL REPORT
  190 CONTINUE
      PRINT 200
  200 FORMAT(1H1)
      STOP
      END
```

Figure 1.21 FORTRAN listing for the main program, inventory model.

The computer program for this model consists of a main program and the sub-programs and FORTRAN variables listed in Table 1.2 (pages 32, 33).

The FORTRAN listing for the main program is given in Fig. 1.21. The program begins with the MODEL and RANDOM common blocks (the latter necessary since the function RANDI is being used), setting NEVNTS equal to 4, and reading the input parameters. Then, since subroutine REPORT will be called once for each inventory policy being considered, the heading for the report is printed in the main program (rather than in REPORT). Finally, for each of the desired simulation runs (each corresponding to a particular policy), the values of s and S for this run are read from a data card, the simulation is initialized by calling subroutine INIT, the event type of the next event to occur, NEXT, is determined by calling subroutine TIMING, and NEXT is used to pass control to the appropriate event routine. In particular, if NEXT = 3, REPORT is called and the simulation is ended for the policy under consideration. The reader should note the considerable similarity between the main programs for the inventory and queueing models.

Subroutine INIT, which is quite straightforward, is listed in Fig. 1.22. Observe that the first inventory evaluation is scheduled at TIME = 0 since, in general, the initial inventory level could be less than s. Subroutine TIMING, which (except for the common block MODEL) is identical to the one used for the queueing model, is listed in Fig. 1.23.

A flowchart and listing for event subroutine ORDARV are given in Figs. 1.24

```
      SUBROUTINE INIT
      INTEGER AMOUNT,BIGS,INITIL,INVLEV,NEVNTS,NEXT,NMNTHS,SMALLS
      REAL AMINUS,APLUS,H,INCRMC,MDEMDT,PI,SETUPC,TIME,TLEVNT,TNE(4),
     1TORDC
      COMMON /MODEL/ AMINUS,AMOUNT,APLUS,BIGS,H,INCRMC,INITIL,INVLEV,
     1MDEMDT,NEVNTS,NEXT,NMNTHS,PI,SETUPC,SMALLS,TIME,TLEVNT,TNE,TORDC
C
C *** INITIALIZE THE SIMULATION CLOCK.
C
      TIME=0.
C
C *** INITIALIZE THE STATE VARIABLES.
C
      INVLEV=INITIL
      TLEVNT=0.
C
C *** INITIALIZE THE STATISTICAL COUNTERS.
C
      TORDC=0.
      APLUS=0.
      AMINUS=0.
C
C *** INITIALIZE THE EVENT LIST. SINCE NO ORDER IS OUTSTANDING, THE TIME
C *** OF THE NEXT ORDER ARRIVAL IS SET TO 'INFINITY.'
C
      TNE(1)=1.E+30
      TNE(2)=EXPON(MDEMDT)
      TNE(3)=NMNTHS
      TNE(4)=0.
      RETURN
      END
```

Figure 1.22 FORTRAN listing for subroutine INIT, inventory model.

```
      SUBROUTINE TIMING
      INTEGER AMOUNT,BIGS,INITIL,INVLEV,NEVNTS,NEXT,NMNTHS,SMALLS
      REAL AMINUS,APLUS,H,INCRMC,MDEMDT,PI,SETUPC,TIME,TLEVNT,TNE(4),
     1TORDC
      REAL RMIN
      COMMON /MODEL/ AMINUS,AMOUNT,APLUS,BIGS,H,INCRMC,INITIL,INVLEV,
     1MDEMDT,NEVNTS,NEXT,NMNTHS,PI,SETUPC,SMALLS,TIME,TLEVNT,TNE,TORDC
      RMIN=1.E+29
      NEXT=0
C
C *** DETERMINE THE EVENT TYPE OF THE NEXT EVENT TO OCCUR.
C
      DO 10 I=1,NEVNTS
      IF(TNE(I).GE.RMIN) GO TO 10
      RMIN=TNE(I)
      NEXT=I
   10 CONTINUE
C
C *** IF THE EVENT LIST IS EMPTY (I.E., NEXT=0), STOP THE SIMULATION.
C *** OTHERWISE, ADVANCE THE SIMULATION CLOCK.
C
      IF(NEXT.GT.0) GO TO 30
      PRINT 20
   20 FORMAT(1H1,5X,'EVENT LIST EMPTY')
      STOP
   30 TIME=TNE(NEXT)
      RETURN
      END
```

Figure 1.23 FORTRAN listing for subroutine TIMING, inventory model.

and 1.25. The program first calls subroutine UPDATE to update the area under $I^+(t)$ and the area under $I^-(t)$ (see the description of UPDATE below for details) since the inventory level will change at the time of this event. Then the inventory level, INVLEV, is incremented by the amount previously ordered from the supplier, AMOUNT, and the time of the next order arrival, TNE(1), is set to 10^{30} since an order is no longer outstanding.

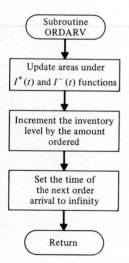

Figure 1.24 Flowchart for subroutine ORDARV, inventory model.

```
      SUBROUTINE ORDARV
      INTEGER AMOUNT,BIGS,INITIL,INVLEV,NEVNTS,NEXT,NMNTHS,SMALLS
      REAL AMINUS,APLUS,H,INCRMC,MDEMDT,PI,SETUPC,TIME,TLEVNT,TNE(4),
     1TORDC
      COMMON /MODEL/ AMINUS,AMOUNT,APLUS,BIGS,H,INCRMC,INITIL,INVLEV,
     1MDEMDT,NEVNTS,NEXT,NMNTHS,PI,SETUPC,SMALLS,TIME,TLEVNT,TNE,TORDC
C
C *** UPDATE 'APLUS' AND 'AMINUS.'
C
      CALL UPDATE
C
C *** INCREMENT THE INVENTORY LEVEL BY THE AMOUNT ORDERED.
C
      INVLEV=INVLEV+AMOUNT
C
C *** SINCE NO ORDER IS NOW OUTSTANDING, SET THE TIME OF THE NEXT ORDER
C *** ARRIVAL TO 'INFINITY.'
C
      TNE(1)=1.E+30
      RETURN
      END
```

Figure 1.25 FORTRAN listing for subroutine ORDARV, inventory model.

Event subroutine DEMAND, which is called when there is a demand for one or more items of the company's product, is flowcharted and listed in Figs. 1.26 and 1.27. Subroutine UPDATE is called to update the areas under $I^+(t)$ and $I^-(t)$ since the inventory level will change at the time of this demand event. The size of the demand which is to occur at the present time, DSIZE, is generated by the function RANDI and subtracted from the previous inventory level. Note that this could result in the inventory level's being negative, meaning that one or more items demanded cannot be supplied from available inventory and must be backlogged. The time of

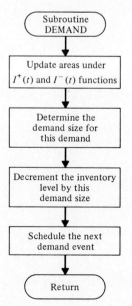

Figure 1.26 Flowchart for subroutine DEMAND, inventory model.

```
      SUBROUTINE DEMAND
      INTEGER AMOUNT,BIGS,INITIL,INVLEV,NEVNTS,NEXT,NMNTHS,SMALLS
      INTEGER DSIZE
      REAL AMINUS,APLUS,H,INCRMC,MDEMDT,PI,SETUPC,TIME,TLEVNT,TNE(4),
     1TORDC
      COMMON /MODEL/ AMINUS,AMOUNT,APLUS,BIGS,H,INCRMC,INITIL,INVLEV,
     1MDEMDT,NEVNTS,NEXT,NMNTHS,PI,SETUPC,SMALLS,TIME,TLEVNT,TNE,TORDC
C
C *** UPDATE 'APLUS' AND 'AMINUS.'
C
      CALL UPDATE
C
C *** GENERATE THE DEMAND SIZE.
C
      DSIZE=RANDI(Z)
C
C *** DECREMENT THE INVENTORY LEVEL BY THE DEMAND SIZE.
C
      INVLEV=INVLEV-DSIZE
C
C *** SCHEDULE THE NEXT DEMAND.
C
      TNE(2)=TIME+EXPON(MDEMDT)
      RETURN
      END
```

Figure 1.27 FORTRAN listing for subroutine DEMAND, inventory model.

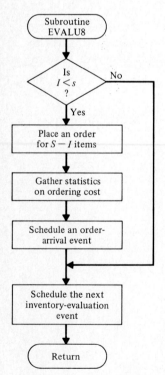

Figure 1.28 Flowchart for subroutine EVALU8, inventory model.

```
      SUBROUTINE EVALU8
      INTEGER AMOUNT,BIGS,INITIL,INVLEV,NEVNTS,NEXT,NMNTHS,SMALLS
      REAL AMINUS,APLUS,H,INCRMC,MDEMDT,PI,SETUPC,TIME,TLEVNT,TNE(4),
     1TORDC
      COMMON /MODEL/ AMINUS,AMOUNT,APLUS,BIGS,H,INCRMC,INITIL,INVLEV,
     1MDEMDT,NEVNTS,NEXT,NMNTHS,PI,SETUPC,SMALLS,TIME,TLEVNT,TNE,TORDC
C
C *** IF THE INVENTORY LEVEL IS LESS THAN 'SMALLS,' PLACE AN ORDER FOR
C *** 'BIGS'-'INVLEV' ITEMS.
C
      IF(INVLEV.GE.SMALLS) GO TO 10
      AMOUNT=BIGS-INVLEV
      TORDC=TORDC+SETUPC+(INCRMC*AMOUNT)
C
C *** SCHEDULE THE ARRIVAL OF THE ORDER.
C
      TNE(1)=TIME+UNIFRM(.5,1.)
C
C *** SCHEDULE THE NEXT INVENTORY EVALUATION.
C
   10 TNE(4)=TIME+1.
      RETURN
      END
```

Figure 1.29 FORTRAN listing for subroutine EVALU8, inventory model.

the next demand, TNE(2), is determined by adding an exponential random variable with mean MDEMDT to the present value of the simulation clock.

Event subroutine EVALU8, which is called at the beginning of each month to evaluate the inventory level and possibly to order, is flowcharted and listed in Figs. 1.28 and 1.29. If the inventory level INVLEV is less than the policy parameter SMALLS, an order is placed for AMOUNT = BIGS − INVLEV items, at a cost of SETUPC + (INCRMC*AMOUNT) and the time that the order will arrive, TNE(1), is determined by adding the delivery lag, which is uniformly distributed on

```
      SUBROUTINE REPORT
      INTEGER AMOUNT,BIGS,INITIL,INVLEV,NEVNTS,NEXT,NMNTHS,SMALLS
      REAL AMINUS,APLUS,H,INCRMC,MDEMDT,PI,SETUPC,TIME,TLEVNT,TNE(4),
     1TORDC
      REAL ACOST,AHLDC,AORDC,ASHRC
      COMMON /MODEL/ AMINUS,AMOUNT,APLUS,BIGS,H,INCRMC,INITIL,INVLEV,
     1MDEMDT,NEVNTS,NEXT,NMNTHS,PI,SETUPC,SMALLS,TIME,TLEVNT,TNE,TORDC
C
C *** UPDATE 'APLUS' AND 'AMINUS.'
C
      CALL UPDATE
C
C *** COMPUTE ESTIMATES OF THE DESIRED MEASURES OF PERFORMANCE.
C
      AORDC=TORDC/NMNTHS
      AHLDC=H*(APLUS/NMNTHS)
      ASHRC=PI*(AMINUS/NMNTHS)
      ACOST=AORDC+AHLDC+ASHRC
      PRINT 10,SMALLS,BIGS,ACOST,AORDC,AHLDC,ASHRC
   10 FORMAT(1H0,5X,'(',I3,',' I3,')',8X,F6.2,16X,F6.2,19X,F6.2,19X,F6.2
     1)
      RETURN
      END
```

Figure 1.30 FORTRAN listing for subroutine REPORT, inventory model.

the interval [0.5, 1.0] month, to TIME. Regardless of whether or not an order is placed, the time of the next evaluation, TNE(4), is set to TIME + 1. .

A listing for subroutine REPORT is given in Fig. 1.30. Subroutine UPDATE is first called to update the areas under the $I^+(t)$ and $I^-(t)$ functions from the time of the last event which changed the inventory level until the time when the simulation ends, TIME = MMNTHS. Then estimates of the desired measures of performance are computed in an obvious manner.

Subroutine UPDATE, which is *not* an event routine, is called at a particular time to update the areas under the $I^+(t)$ and $I^-(t)$ functions. The use of UPDATE, which is called from ORDARV, DEMAND, and REPORT, avoids having to write the same block of code three times. A flowchart and listing for UPDATE are given in Figs. 1.31 and 1.32. If the inventory level during the previous interval was negative, the area under $I^-(t)$ is updated and the area under $I^+(t)$ is unchanged. If the inventory level was zero, both areas remain unchanged. If the inventory level was positive, the area under $I^+(t)$ is updated and the area under $I^-(t)$ is unchanged.

The function EXPON used here is identical to the one listed in Fig. 1.14.

A listing for function RANDI is given in Fig. 1.33. The program is general in that it will generate an integer between 1 and NVALUE in accordance with distribution function PROBD(I), provided that NVALUE and PROBD(I) (I = 1, 2, ... , NVALUE) are specified. [In our particular case, NVALUE = 4 and PROBD(1) = $\frac{1}{6}$, PROBD(2) = $\frac{1}{2}$, PROBD(3) = $\frac{5}{6}$, and PROBD(4) = 1.] Let $p(1)$ = PROBD(1) and $p(I)$ = PROBD(I) − PROBD(I − 1) for I = 2, 3, ... , NVALUE. From the listing, it can be seen that the program will generate the integer 1 if the U(0, 1) random variable U falls in the interval [0, PROBD(1)), whose length is equal to $p(1)$, and will generate the integer 2 if U falls in the interval [PROBD(1), PROBD(2)), whose length is $p(2)$, etc. Since the probability that a U(0, 1) random variable falls in any subinterval of length Δx (contained in the interval [0, 1]) is

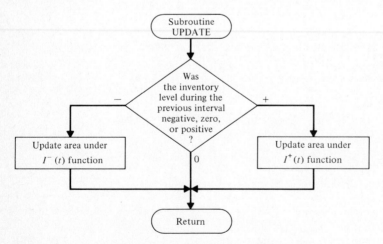

Figure 1.31 Flowchart for subroutine UPDATE, inventory model.

```
      SUBROUTINE UPDATE
      INTEGER AMOUNT,BIGS,INITIL,INVLEV,NEVNTS,NEXT,NMNTHS,SMALLS
      REAL AMINUS,APLUS,H,INCRMC,MDEMDT,PI,SETUPC,TIME,TLEVNT,TNE(4),
     1TORDC
      REAL TSLE
      COMMON /MODEL/ AMINUS,AMOUNT,APLUS,BIGS,H,INCRMC,INITIL,INVLEV,
     1MDEMDT,NEVNTS,NEXT,NMNTHS,PI,SETUPC,SMALLS,TIME,TLEVNT,TNE,TORDC
C
C *** COMPUTE THE TIME SINCE THE LAST EVENT WHICH CHANGED THE INVENTORY
C *** LEVEL.
C
      TSLE=TIME-TLEVNT
      TLEVNT=TIME
C
C *** DETERMINE WHETHER THE INVENTORY LEVEL DURING THE PREVIOUS INTERVAL
C *** WAS NEGATIVE, ZERO, OR POSITIVE.
C
      IF(INVLEV)10,20,30
C
C *** SINCE THE INVENTORY LEVEL DURING THE PREVIOUS INTERVAL WAS
C *** NEGATIVE, UPDATE 'AMINUS.'
C
   10 AMINUS=AMINUS+(-INVLEV*TSLE)
C
C *** THE INVENTORY LEVEL DURING THE PREVIOUS INTERVAL WAS ZERO.
C
   20 RETURN
C
C *** SINCE THE INVENTORY LEVEL DURING THE PREVIOUS INTERVAL WAS
C *** POSITIVE, UPDATE 'APLUS.'
C
   30 APLUS=APLUS+(INVLEV*TSLE)
      RETURN
      END
```

Figure 1.32 FORTRAN listing for subroutine UPDATE, inventory model.

```
      FUNCTION RANDI(Z)
      INTEGER I,N1
      REAL U
      COMMON /RANDOM/ NVALUE,PROBD(25)
C
C *** GENERATE A U(0,1) RANDOM VARIABLE. THE FORM OF THIS STATEMENT
C *** DEPENDS ON THE COMPUTER USED.
C
      U=RANUN(Z)
C
C *** GENERATE A RANDOM INTEGER BETWEEN 1 AND NVALUE IN ACCORDANCE WITH
C *** DISTRIBUTION FUNCTION 'PROBD.'
C
      N1=NVALUE-1
      DO 10 I=1,N1
      IF(U.GE.PROBD(I)) GO TO 10
      RANDI=I
      RETURN
   10 CONTINUE
      RANDI=NVALUE
      RETURN
      END
```

Figure 1.33 FORTRAN listing for function RANDI, inventory model.

```
      FUNCTION UNIFRM(A,B)
      REAL A,B,U
C
C *** GENERATE A U(O,1) RANDOM VARIABLE. THE FORM OF THIS STATEMENT
C *** DEPENDS ON THE COMPUTER USED.
C
      U=RANUN(Z)
C
C *** GENERATE A U(A,B) RANDOM VARIABLE.
C
      UNIFRM=A+(U*(B-A))
      RETURN
      END
```

Figure 1.34 FORTRAN listing for function UNIFRM, inventory model.

equal to Δx (see Chap. 5), we see that the program generates the integer 1 with probability $p(1) = \frac{1}{6}$, and generates the integer 2 with probability $p(2) = \frac{1}{3}$, etc.; this is the desired distribution for the random variable D, as given at the beginning of Sec. 1.5.1.

A listing for function UNIFRM is given in Fig. 1.34. Intuitively it is clear that the program generates a continuous random variable which is uniformly distributed on the interval [A, B]. For further justification, see Sec. 7.3.1.

1.5.3 Simulation Output and Discussion

The simulation report for the inventory model is given in Fig. 1.35. Based on the criterion of average total cost per month, it would *appear* that the (20, 80) policy is

```
SINGLE-PRODUCT INVENTORY SYSTEM

INITIAL INVENTORY LEVEL                 60 ITEMS

NUMBER OF DEMAND SIZES                   4

DISTRIBUTION FUNCTION OF DEMAND SIZES    .167    .500    .833    1.000

MEAN INTERDEMAND TIME                    .10 MONTHS

LENGTH OF THE SIMULATION                 120 MONTHS

K = 32.0   I =   3.0   H =   1.0   PI =   5.0
```

POLICY	AVERAGE COST	AVERAGE ORDERING COST	AVERAGE HOLDING COST	AVERAGE SHORTAGE COST
(20, 40)	123.92	98.80	8.91	16.21
(20, 60)	125.58	92.77	15.98	16.82
(20, 80)	118.24	82.95	27.04	8.25
(20,100)	126.13	82.07	35.96	8.10
(40, 60)	125.71	98.13	26.24	1.34
(40, 80)	123.58	86.72	35.98	.87
(40,100)	134.35	87.68	45.15	1.52
(60, 80)	145.69	101.20	44.29	.20
(60,100)	144.08	89.16	54.93	.00

Figure 1.35 Simulation report for the inventory model.

preferable. However, in the present context where the length of the simulation is fixed (the company wants a planning horizon of 10 years), what we *really* want to estimate for each policy is the *expected* average total cost per month for the first 120 months. The numbers in Fig. 1.35 are estimates of these expected values, each estimate based on a sample of size *one* (simulation run or replication). Since these estimates may have large variances, the ordering of these estimates may differ considerably from the ordering of the expected values, which is the desired information. In fact, if we rerun the nine simulations using different U(0, 1) random variables, the estimates obtained may differ greatly from those in Fig. 1.35. Furthermore, the ordering of the new estimates may also be different.

We conclude from the above discussion that when the simulation run length is fixed by the problem context, it will generally not be sufficient to make a single simulation run of each policy or system of interest. In Chap. 8 we address the issue of just how many runs are required to get a good estimate of a desired expected value. Chapters 9 and 12 consider related problems when we are concerned with several different expected values arising from alternative system designs.

1.6 STEPS IN A DISCRETE-EVENT SIMULATION STUDY

Figure 1.36 shows the steps that will compose a typical, sound simulation study and the relationships between them (see also Shannon [15, p. 23] and Gordon [3, p. 52]). The number beside the symbol representing each step refers to the more detailed discussion of that step below. Not all studies will necessarily contain all these steps and in the order stated; some studies may contain steps which are not depicted in the diagram. Furthermore, a simulation study is not a strictly sequential process. As one proceeds with a study and a better understanding of the system of interest is obtained, it is often necessary or desirable to go back to a previous step. For example, new insights about the system obtained during the study may necessitate reformulating the problem to be solved.

1. *Formulate problem and plan the study.* Every study must begin with a clear statement of the study's objectives; without such a statement there is little hope for success. The alternative system designs to be studied should be delineated (if possible), and criteria for evaluating the efficacy of these alternatives should be given. The overall study should be planned in terms of the number of people, the cost, and the time required for each aspect of the study.

2. *Collect data and define a model.* Data should be collected on the system of interest and used to estimate input parameters and to obtain probability distributions for the random variables used in the model (see Chap. 5). For example, in modeling a bank, one might collect interarrival times and service times and use these data to obtain theoretical interarrival-time and service-time distributions for use in the model. If possible, data on the performance of the system, e.g., delays in queue of customers in a bank, should be collected for validation purposes in step 6. The construction of a mathematical and logical model of a real-world system for a given

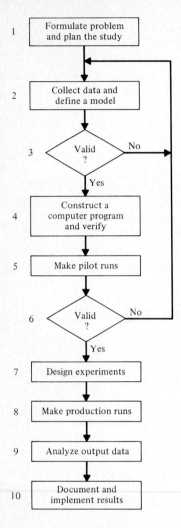

1 Formulate problem and plan the study

2 Collect data and define a model

3 Valid ?   No

   Yes

4 Construct a computer program and verify

5 Make pilot runs

6 Valid ?   No

   Yes

7 Design experiments

8 Make production runs

9 Analyze output data

10 Document and implement results

Figure 1.36 Steps in a simulation study.

objective is still much more an art than a science. Although there are few firm rules on how one should go about the modeling process, one point on which most authors agree is that it is always a good idea to start with a simple model which can later be made more sophisticated if necessary. A model should contain only enough detail to capture the essence of the system for the purposes for which the model is intended; it is not necessary to have a one-to-one correspondence between elements of the model and elements of the system. A model with excessive detail may be too expensive to program and to execute. A good discussion of the art of modeling can be found in [15].

3. *Valid?* Although we believe that validation (see Chap. 10) is something that should be done throughout the entire simulation study (rather than after the model has been built and only if there is time and money still remaining), there are several

points in the study where validation is particularly appropriate. One such point is during step 2. In building the model, it is imperative for the modelers to involve people in the study who are intimately familiar with the operations of the actual system. It is also advisable for the modelers to interact with the decision maker (or model's intended user) on a regular basis. This will increase the actual validity of the model, and the perceived validity of the model to the decision maker will be increased (see Chap. 10 for further discussion). In addition, the adequacy of the theoretical probability distributions fitted to the observed data should be tested using goodness-of-fit tests (see Sec. 5.5).

4. *Construct a computer program and verify.* The simulation modeler must decide whether to program the model in a general-purpose language like FORTRAN (Chaps. 1 and 2) or in a specially designed simulation language such as GASP, GPSS, or SIMSCRIPT (Chap. 3). A general-purpose language will probably already be known and available on the modeler's computer. It may also lead to a shorter execution time. On the other hand, by providing many of the features needed in programming a model, a simulation language may reduce the required programming time significantly. Chapter 7 discusses techniques for generating random variables on a computer with a specified probability distribution. This capability may be needed in programming a model, depending on the language used. Chapter 6 discusses the related topic of generating $U(0, 1)$ random variables (random numbers), which are the basis for generating all other types of random variables in Chap. 7. Techniques for verifying or debugging a computer program are discussed in Sec. 10.2.

5. *Make pilot runs.* Pilot runs of the verified model are made for validation purposes in step 6.

6. *Valid?* Pilot runs can be used to test the sensitivity of the model's output to small changes in an input parameter. If the output changes greatly, a better estimate of the input parameter must be obtained (see Sec. 10.4.2 for further discussion of this and other uses of sensitivity analysis). If a system similar to the one of interest currently exists, output data from pilot runs of a model of the existing system can be compared with output data from the actual existing system (collected in step 2). If the agreement is "good," the "validated" model is modified so that it represents the actual system of interest; we would hope that this modification is not too extensive. (See Secs. 10.4.3 and 10.6 for further discussion of this idea.)

7. *Design experiments.* It must be decided what system designs to simulate if, as is sometimes the case in practice, there are more alternatives than one can reasonably simulate. Often the complete decision cannot be made at this time. Instead, using output data from the production runs (from step 8) of certain selected system designs and techniques discussed in Chap. 12, the analyst can decide which additional systems to simulate. For each system design to be simulated, decisions have to be made on such issues as initial conditions for the simulation run(s), the length of the simulation run(s), and the number of independent simulation runs (replications) to make. These issues are discussed in Chap. 8. When designing and making the production runs, it is sometimes possible to use certain *variance-reduction techniques* to give results with greater statistical precision (the variances of the estimators are

decreased) at little or no additional cost. These techniques are discussed in Chap. 11. (A review of basic probability and statistics is given in Chap. 4.)

8. *Make production runs.* Production runs are made to provide performance data on the system designs of interest.

9. *Analyze output data.* Statistical techniques are used to analyze the output data from the production runs. Typical goals are to construct a confidence interval for a measure of performance for one particular system design (see Chap. 8) or to decide which simulated system is best relative to some specified measure of performance (see Chap. 9).

10. *Document and implement results.* Because simulation models are often used for more than one application, it is important to document the assumptions which went into the model as well as the computer program itself. Finally, a simulation study whose results are never implemented is most likely a failure. Thus, a study should never be considered complete until its results have been implemented.

1.7 OTHER TYPES OF SIMULATION

Although the emphasis in this book is on discrete-event simulation, several other types of simulation have considerable real-world importance. Our goal here is to explain these other types of simulation briefly and to contrast them with discrete-event simulation. In particular we shall discuss continuous, combined discrete-continuous, and Monte Carlo simulations.

1.7.1 Continuous Simulation

Continuous simulation concerns the modeling over time of a system by a representation in which the state variables change continuously with respect to time. Typically, continuous simulation models involve one or more differential equations which give relationships for the rates of change of the state variables with respect to time. If the differential equations are particularly simple, they can be solved analytically to give the values of the state variables for all values of time as a function of the values of the state variables at time zero. For most continuous models analytic solutions are not possible, however, and numerical analysis techniques, e.g., Runge-Kutta integration, are used to integrate the differential equations numerically, given *specific* values for the state variables at time zero.

A number of languages have been specifically designed for building continuous simulation models. For example, CSMP III is an equation-oriented language developed by IBM (see [7] and Speckhart and Green [16]). In addition, the discrete-event simulation languages GASP IV (see Pritsker [11]), SLAM (see Pritsker and Pegden [12]), and C-SIMSCRIPT (see Delfosse [2]) also have continuous modeling capabilities. These three languages have the added advantage of allowing both discrete and continuous components simultaneously in one model (see Sec. 1.7.2). Readers interested in applications of continuous simulation may wish to consult the journal *Simulation*.

Example 1.3 We now consider a continuous model of competition between two populations. Biological models of this type, which are called *predator-prey* (or *parasite-host*) *models,* have been considered by many authors, including Braun [1, p. 583] and Gordon [3, p. 103]. An environment consists of two populations, predators and prey, which interact with each other. The prey are passive, but the predators depend on the prey as their source of food. (For example, the predators might be sharks and the prey might be food fish; see [1].) Let $x(t)$ and $y(t)$ denote, respectively, the numbers of individuals in the prey and predator populations at time t. Suppose that there is an ample supply of food for the prey and, in the absence of predators, that the rate of growth is $rx(t)$ for some positive r. (We can think of r as the natural birth rate minus the natural death rate.) Because of the interaction between predators and prey, it is reasonable to assume that the death rate of the prey due to interaction is proportional to the product of the two population sizes, namely, $x(t)y(t)$. Therefore, the overall rate of change of the prey population, dx/dt, is given by

$$\frac{dx}{dt} = rx(t) - ax(t)y(t) \tag{1.3}$$

where a is a positive constant of proportionality. Since the predators depend on the prey for their very existence, the rate of change of the predators in the absence of prey is $-sy(t)$ for some positive s. Furthermore, the interaction between the two populations causes the predator population to increase at a rate which is also proportional to $x(t)y(t)$. Therefore, the overall rate of change of the predator population, dy/dt, is

$$\frac{dy}{dt} = -sy(t) + bx(t)y(t) \tag{1.4}$$

where b is a positive constant. Given initial conditions $x(0) > 0$ and $y(0) > 0$, the solution of the model given by Eqs. (1.3) and (1.4) has the interesting property that $x(t) > 0$ and $y(t) > 0$ for all $t \geq 0$ (see [1]). Thus, the prey population can never be completely extinguished by the predators. The solution $\{x(t), y(t)\}$ is also a periodic function of time. That is, there is a positive T such that $x(t + nT) = x(t)$ and $y(t + nT) = y(t)$ for all $n = 1, 2, \ldots$. This result is not unexpected. As the predator population increases, the prey population decreases. This causes a decrease in the rate of increase of the predators, which eventually results in a decrease in the number of predators. This in turn causes the number of prey to increase, etc.

Consider the particular values $r = 0.001$, $a = 2 \times 10^{-6}$, $s = 0.01$, $b = 10^{-6}$ and the initial population sizes $x(0) = 12,000$ and $y(0) = 600$. Figure 1.37 is a numerical solution of (1.3) and (1.4) resulting from the use of a computer package designed to solve systems of differential equations numerically (not explicitly a continuous simulation language).

1.7.2 Combined Discrete-Continuous Simulation

Since some real-world systems are neither completely discrete nor completely continuous, the need occasionally arises to construct a model with aspects of both discrete-event and continuous simulation. We call such a simulation a *combined discrete-continuous simulation.* Pritsker [11] and Pritsker and Pegden [12] describe the three fundamental types of interactions which can occur between discretely changing and continuously changing state variables:

1. A discrete event may cause a discrete change in the value of a continuous state variable.
2. A discrete event may cause the relationship governing a continuous state variable to change at a particular time.
3. A continuous state variable achieving a threshold value may cause a discrete event to occur or to be scheduled.

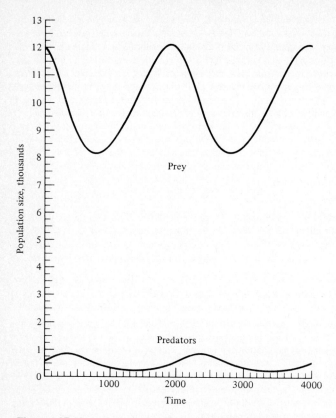

Figure 1.37 Numerical solution of a predator-prey model.

Combined discrete-continuous simulation models can be built in GASP IV [11], SLAM [12], and C-SIMSCRIPT [2], the first two languages being better documented and more readily accessible.

The example of a combined simulation below is a brief description of a model described in detail in [11, 12]. Combined models of a chemical reaction process and of a steel plant soaking pit furnace are given in [11] and [11, 12], respectively.

Example 1.4 Tankers carrying crude oil arrive at a single unloading dock, supplying a storage tank that in turn feeds a refinery through a pipeline. An unloading tanker delivers oil to the storage tank at a specified constant rate. (Tankers which arrive when the dock is busy form a queue.) The storage tank supplies oil to the refinery at a different specified rate. The dock is open from 6 A.M. to 12 P.M., and, because of safety considerations, unloading of a tanker ceases when the dock is closed.

The discrete events for this (simplified) model are the arrival of a tanker for unloading, the closing of the dock at 12 P.M., and the opening of the dock at 6 A.M. The levels of oil in the unloading tanker and in the storage tank are given by continuous state variables whose rates of change are given by differential equations (see [12] for details). The unloading of the tanker is considered to be complete when the level of oil in the tanker is less than 5 percent of its capacity, but unloading of a tanker must be temporarily stopped if the level of oil in the storage tank reaches its capacity.

Unloading can be resumed when the level of oil in the tank decreases to 80 percent of its capacity. If the level of oil in the tank ever falls below 5000 barrels, the refinery must be shut down temporarily. In order to avoid frequent start-ups and shutdowns of the refinery, the tank does not resume supplying oil to the refinery until the tank once again contains 50,000 barrels. Each of the five events concerning the levels of oil, e.g., the level of oil in the tanker falling below 5 percent of the tanker's capacity, is what Pritsker [11, p. 13] calls a *state event*. Unlike discrete events, state events are not scheduled but occur when a continuous state variable crosses a threshold.

1.7.3 Monte Carlo Simulation

We define *Monte Carlo simulation* to be a scheme employing random numbers, that is, U(0, 1) random variables, which is used for solving certain stochastic or deterministic problems where the passage of time plays no substantive role. Thus, Monte Carlo simulations are generally static rather than dynamic. The reader should note that although some authors define Monte Carlo simulation to be *any* simulation involving the use of random numbers, our definition is more restrictive. The name "Monte Carlo" simulation or method originated during World War II, when this approach was applied to problems related to the development of the atomic bomb. For a more detailed discussion of Monte Carlo simulation, see Hammersley and Handscomb [6] and Halton [5].

Example 1.5 Suppose we want to evaluate the integral $I = \int_a^b g(x)\, dx$, where $g(x)$ is a real-valued function which is not analytically integrable. (In practice, Monte Carlo simulation would probably not be used to evaluate a single integral since there are more efficient numerical analysis techniques for this purpose. It is more likely to be used on a multiple integral problem with an ill-behaved integrand.) To see how this *deterministic* problem can be approached by Monte Carlo simulation, let Y be the random variable $(b - a)g(X)$, where X is a continuous random variable uniformly distributed on the interval $[a, b]$ [such a random variable will henceforth be denoted by U(a, b)]. Then it can be shown that the expected value of Y is given by

$$E(Y) = E[(b - a)g(X)]$$

$$= (b - a)E[g(X)]$$

$$= (b - a)\int_a^b g(x)f_X(x)\, dx$$

$$= (b - a)\frac{\int_a^b g(x)\, dx}{b - a}$$

$$= I$$

where $f_X(x) = 1/(b - a)$ is the probability density function of a U(a, b) random variable (see Chap. 5). (For justification of the third equality, see, for example, Ross [13, p. 35].) Thus, the problem of evaluating the integral has been reduced to one of estimating the expected value $E(Y)$. In particular, we shall estimate $E(Y) = I$ by the sample mean

$$\bar{Y}(n) = \frac{\sum_{i=1}^{n} Y_i}{n} = (b - a)\frac{\sum_{i=1}^{n} g(X_i)}{n}$$

where $X_1, X_2, \ldots, X_n$ are IID U(a, b) random variables. [It is illustrative to think of $\bar{Y}(n)$ as an

Table 1.3 $\overline{Y}(n)$ **for various values of** n **resulting from applying Monte Carlo simulation to the evaluation of the integral**

$$\int_0^\pi \sin x \, dx = 2$$

n	10	20	40	80	160
$\overline{Y}(n)$	2.213	1.951	1.948	1.989	1.993

estimate of the area of the rectangle which has a base of length $b - a$ and height $\int_a^b g(x) \, dx / (b-a)$, which is the average value of $g(x)$ over the interval $[a, b]$.] Furthermore, it can be shown that $E[\overline{Y}(n)] = I$, that is, $\overline{Y}(n)$ is an unbiased estimator of I, and Var $[\overline{Y}(n)]$ = Var $(Y)/n$ (see Sec. 4.4). Since Var (Y) is a fixed number, it follows that $\overline{Y}(n)$ will be arbitrarily close to I for n sufficiently large.

To illustrate the above scheme numerically, suppose that we would like to evaluate the integral $\int_0^\pi \sin x \, dx$, which can be shown to have a value of 2. Table 1.3 shows the results of applying Monte Carlo simulation to the evaluation of this integral for various values of n.

Monte Carlo simulation is now widely used for solving certain problems in statistics which are not analytically tractable. For example, it has been applied to estimate the critical values or the power of a new hypothesis test. Determining the critical values for the Kolmogorov-Smirnov test for normality, discussed in Sec. 5.5.3 is such an application. The advanced reader might also enjoy perusing the technical journals *Communications in Statistics* (Part B, Simulation and Computation) and *Journal of Statistical Computation and Simulation,* both of which contain many examples of Monte Carlo simulation.

Finally, it should be mentioned that procedures discussed in Sec. 8.5 can be used to determine the sample size, n, required to obtain a specified precision in a Monte Carlo simulation study.

APPENDIX 1A FIXED-INCREMENT TIME ADVANCE

As mentioned in Sec. 1.3.1, the second principal approach for advancing the simulation clock in a discrete-event simulation model is called *fixed-increment time advance*. With this approach, the simulation clock is advanced in increments of exactly Δt time units for some appropriate choice of Δt. After each update of the clock, a check is made to determine whether any events should have occurred during the previous interval of length Δt. If one or more events were scheduled to have occurred during this interval, these events are considered to occur at the *end* of the interval and the system state (and statistical counters) are updated accordingly. The fixed-increment time-advance approach is illustrated in Fig. 1.38, where the curved arrows represent the advancing of the simulation clock and s_i ($i = 1, 2, \ldots$) is the

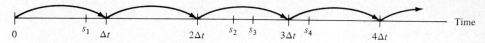

Figure 1.38 An illustration of fixed-increment time advance.

actual time of occurrence of the *i*th event of any type (*not* the *i*th value of the simulation clock). In the time interval $[0, \Delta t)$, an event occurs at time s_1 but is considered to occur at time Δt by the model. No events occur in the interval $[\Delta t, 2\Delta t)$, but the model checks to determine that this is the case. Events occur at the times s_2 and s_3 in the interval $[2\Delta t, 3\Delta t)$, but both events are considered to occur at time $3\Delta t$, etc. A set of rules must be built into the model to decide in what order to process events when two or more events are considered to occur at the same time by the model. Two disadvantages of fixed-increment time advance are the error introduced by processing events at the end of the interval in which they occur and the necessity of deciding which event to process first when events which are not simultaneous in reality are treated as such by the model. These problems can be made less severe by making Δt smaller, but this increases the amount of checking for event occurrences which must be done and results in an increase in execution time. Because of these considerations, fixed-increment time advance is generally not used for discrete-event simulation models when the times between successive events can vary greatly.

The primary use of this approach appears to be for systems where it can reasonably be assumed that all events *actually* occur at one of the times $n \Delta t$ ($n = 0, 1, 2, \dots$) for an appropriately chosen Δt. For example, data in economic systems are often available on a yearly basis, and it is natural in a simulation model to advance the simulation clock in increments of 1 year. (See Naylor [10] for a discussion of simulation of economic systems. See also Sec. 4.3 for the discussion of an inventory system which can be simulated, without loss of accuracy, by fixed-increment time advance.)

It should be noted that fixed-increment time advance can be realized when using the next-event time-advance approach by artificially scheduling "events" to occur every Δt time units.

APPENDIX 1B A PRIMER ON QUEUEING SYSTEMS

A *queueing system* is a system consisting of one or more servers which provide service of some kind to arriving customers. Customers who arrive to find all servers busy (generally) join one or more *queues* (or lines) in front of the servers, hence the name "queueing" system.

Historically, a large proportion of all discrete-event simulation studies have involved the modeling of a real-world queueing system, or at least some component

Table 1.4 Examples of real-world queueing systems

System	Servers	Customers
Bank	Tellers	Customers
Hospital	Doctors, nurses, beds	Patients
Computer system	Central processing unit, input-output devices	Jobs
Assembly line	Workers, machines	Items being manufactured
Airport	Runways, security check-in stations	Airplanes, travelers

of the system being simulated was a queueing system. Thus, we believe that it is important for the student of simulation to have at least a basic understanding of the components of a queueing system, standard notation for queueing systems, and measures of performance which are often used to indicate the quality of service being provided by a queueing system. Some examples of real-world queueing systems which have often been simulated are given in Table 1.4. For additional information on queueing systems, in general, see Gross and Harris [4] and Kleinrock [8, 9]. Reference 9 is particularly recommended for those interested in queueing models of computer systems.

1B.1 Components of a Queueing System

A queueing system is characterized by three components: arrival process, service mechanism, and queue discipline. Specifying the *arrival process* for a queueing system consists of describing how customers arrive to the system. Let A_i be the interarrival time between the arrivals of the $(i - 1)$st and ith customers (see Sec. 1.3). If $A_1, A_2, \ldots$ are assumed to be IID random variables, we shall denote the *mean* (or expected) *interarrival time* by $E(A)$ and call $\lambda = 1/E(A)$ the *arrival rate* of customers.

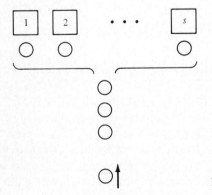

Figure 1.39 A *GI/G/s* queue.

The *service mechanism* for a queueing system is articulated by specifying the number of servers (denoted by s), whether each server has its own queue or there is one queue feeding all servers, and the probability distribution of customers' service times. Let S_i be the service time of the ith arriving customer. If $S_1, S_2, \ldots$ are IID random variables, we shall denote the *mean service time* of a customer by $E(S)$ and call $\omega = 1/E(S)$ the *service rate* of a server.

The *queue discipline* of a queueing system refers to the rule that a server uses to choose the next customer from the queue (if any) when the server completes the service of the current customer. Commonly used queue disciplines include:

FIFO. Customers are served in a first-in, first-out manner.
LIFO. Customers are served in a last-in, first-out manner (see Prob. 2.2).
Priority. Customers are served in order of their importance (see Prob. 2.8) or on the basis of their service requirements (see Probs. 1.7, 2.6, and 2.7).

1B.2 Notation for Queueing Systems

Certain queueing systems occur so often in practice that standard notations have been developed for them. In particular, consider the queueing system shown in Fig. 1.39, which has the following characteristics:

1. s servers in parallel and one FIFO queue feeding all servers.
2. $A_1, A_2, \ldots$ are IID random variables.
3. $S_1, S_2, \ldots$ are IID random variables.
4. The A_i's and S_i's are independent.

We call such a system a *GI/G/s* queue, where *GI* (general independent) refers to the distribution of the A_i's and *G* (general) refers to the distribution of the S_i's. If specific distributions are given for the A_i's and the S_i's (as is always the case for simulation), symbols denoting these distributions are used in place of *GI* and *G*. The symbol *M* is used for the exponential distribution because of the Markovian, i.e., memoryless, property of the exponential distribution (see Appendix 8A), the symbol E_k for a k-Erlang distribution (if X is a k-Erlang random variable, then $X = \sum_{i=1}^{k} Y_i$, where the Y_i's are IID exponential random variables), and *D* for deterministic (or constant) times. Thus, a single-server queueing system with exponential interarrival times and service times and a FIFO queue discipline is called an *M/M/1* queue.

For any *GI/G/s* queue, we shall call the quantity $\rho = \lambda/(s\omega)$ the *utilization factor* of the queueing system ($s\omega$ is the service rate of the system when all servers are busy). It is a measure of how heavily the resources of a queueing system are utilized.

1B.3 Measures of Performance for Queueing Systems

There are many possible measures of performance for queueing systems. We now describe four such measures which are usually used in the mathematical study of queueing systems. The reader should not infer from our choices that these measures are necessarily the most relevant or important in practice (see Secs. 8.2 and 8.3 for further discussion). As a matter of fact, for some real-world systems these measures may not even be well defined; i.e., they may not exist.

Let

$$D_i = \text{delay in queue of } i\text{th customer}$$
$$W_i = D_i + S_i = \text{waiting time in system of } i\text{th customer}$$
$$Q(t) = \text{number of customers in queue at time } t$$
$$L(t) = \text{number of customers in system at time } t \ [Q(t) \text{ plus number of customers being served at time } t]$$

Then the measures

$$d = \lim_{n \to \infty} \frac{\sum_{i=1}^{n} D_i}{n} \qquad \text{w.p. 1}$$

and

$$w = \lim_{n \to \infty} \frac{\sum_{i=1}^{n} W_i}{n} \qquad \text{w.p. 1}$$

(if they exist) are called the *steady-state average delay* and the *steady-state average waiting time*. Similarly, the measures

$$Q = \lim_{T \to \infty} \frac{\int_0^T Q(t) \, dt}{T} \qquad \text{w.p. 1}$$

and

$$L = \lim_{T \to \infty} \frac{\int_0^T L(t) \, dt}{T} \qquad \text{w.p. 1}$$

(if they exist) are called the *steady-state time-average number in queue* and the *steady-state time-average number in system*. Here and throughout this book, the qualifier "w.p. 1" (with probability 1) is given for mathematical correctness and has little practical significance. For example, suppose that $\sum_{i=1}^{n} D_i/n \to d$ as $n \to \infty$ (w.p. 1) for some queueing system. This means that if one performs a very large (an infinite) number of experiments, then in virtually every experiment $\sum_{i=1}^{n} D_i/n$ converges to the finite quantity d. Note that $\rho < 1$ is a necessary condition for d, w, Q, and L to exist for a $GI/G/s$ queue.

Among the most general and useful results for queueing systems are the *conservation equations*

$$Q = \lambda d \quad \text{and} \quad L = \lambda w$$

These equations hold for every queueing system for which d and w exist (see Stidham [17]). (Section 11.5 gives an application to simulation of these relationships.) Another equation of considerable practical value is given by

$$w = d + E(S)$$

(see Sec. 1.4.4 and also Sec. 11.5 for further discussion).

It should be mentioned that the measures of performance discussed above can be analytically computed for $M/M/s$ queues ($s \geq 1$), $M/G/1$ queues for any distribution G, and for certain other queueing systems. In general, the interarrival distribution, the service distribution, or both must be exponential (or a variant of exponential like k-Erlang) for analytic solutions to be possible (see [4] or [8, 9]).

PROBLEMS

1.1 For the single-server queueing facility of Sec. 1.4.3, suppose that the facility opens its doors at 9 A.M. and closes its doors at 5 P.M., but operates until all customers present (in service or in queue) at 5 P.M. have been served. Simulate the facility and estimate the average delay in queue of a customer, the time-average number of customers in queue, and the proportion of time the server is busy (the utilization of the server).

1.2 A service facility consists of two servers in series (tandem), each with its own FIFO queue (see Fig. 1.40). A customer completing service at server 1 proceeds to server 2, while a customer completing service at server 2 leaves the facility. Assume that the interarrival times of customers to server 1 are IID exponential random variables with mean 1 minute. Service times of customers at server 1 are IID exponential random variables with mean 0.7 minute, and at server 2 are IID exponential random variables with mean 0.9 minute. Run the simulation for exactly 1000 minutes and estimate for each server the average delay in queue of a customer and the time-average number of customers in queue.

1.3 For the inventory system of Sec. 1.5, suppose that if the inventory level I at the beginning of a month is less than zero, the company places an *express order* to its supplier. (If $0 \leq I < s$, the company still places a normal order.) An express order for Z items costs the company $48 + 4Z$ dollars, but the delivery lag is now uniformly distributed on the interval 0.25 to 0.50 month. Run the simulation for all nine policies and estimate the average total cost per month, the proporton of time that there is a backlog, that is, $I(t) < 0$, and the number of express orders.

1.4 Consider a service facility with s ($s \geq 1$) parallel servers. Assume that interarrival times of customers are IID exponential random variables with mean $E(A)$ and that service times of customers (regardless of the server) are IID exponential random variables with a mean of $E(S)$. If a customer arrives and finds one or more servers idle, the customer begins service immediately. Otherwise, the customer joins the tail of a *single* FIFO queue. (The queueing system we have described is known as the $M/M/s$ queue; see Appendix 1B.) Write a general program to simulate this system which will estimate the average delay in queue, the time-average number in queue, and the average utilization of the servers based on a stopping rule of n delays having been completed. The quantities s, $E(A)$, $E(S)$, and n should be input parameters. Run the model for $s = 5$, $E(A) = 1$, $E(S) = 4$, and $n = 1000$.

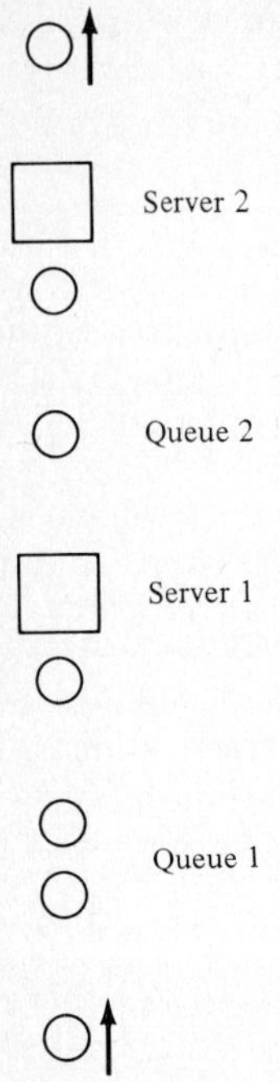

Figure 1.40 Two single-server queueing systems in series.

1.5 A manufacturing shop contains five machines, each subject to randomly occurring breakdowns. In particular, assume that a machine runs for an amount of time which is an exponential random variable with a mean of 8 hours before breaking down. There are s (s a fixed, positive integer) repairmen to fix broken machines, and it takes one repairman an exponential amount of time with a mean of 2 hours to complete the repair of one machine. If more than s machines are broken down at a given time, they form a FIFO "repair" queue and wait for the first available repairman. Further, a repairman works on a broken machine until it is fixed, regardless of what else is happening in the system. Assume that it costs the shop $50 for each hour that each machine is broken down and $10 an hour to employ each repairman. (The repairmen are paid their hourly wage whether they are actually working or not.) Simulate the shop for exactly 800 hours for each of the employment policies $s = 1, 2, \ldots, 5$, to determine which policy results in the smallest average cost per hour. Assume that at time zero all machines have just been "freshly" repaired.

1.6 For the facility of Prob. 1.1, suppose, in addition, that the server normally takes a 30-minute lunch break at the first time after 12 noon the facility is empty. If, however, the server has not gone to lunch by 1 P.M., the server will go after completing the customer in service at 1 P.M. (Assume in this case that all customers in the queue at 1 P.M. will wait until the server returns.) If a customer arrives while the server is at lunch, the customer *may* leave immediately without being served. (This is called *balking*.) Assume that whether such a customer leaves depends on the amount of time remaining before the server's return. (The server posts his time of return from lunch.) In particular, a customer who arrives during lunch will actually leave with the following probabilities:

Time remaining before server's return, minutes	Probability of customer's balking
[20, 30)	0.75
[10, 20)	0.50
[0, 10)	0.25

(The function RANDI, discussed in Sec. 1.5.2, can be used to determine whether a customer balks. For a simpler approach, see Sec. 7.4.1.) Run the simulation and estimate the same measures of performance as before. (Note that the server is not busy when at lunch and that the time-average number in queue is computed using data from the lunch break.) In addition, estimate the expected number of customers who balk.

1.7 For the single-server queueing facility of Sec. 1.4.3, suppose a customer's service time is known at the instant of arrival. On completing service to a customer, the server chooses from the queue (if any) the customer with the smallest service time. Run the simulation until 1000 customers have completed their delays and estimate the average delay in queue, the time-average number in queue, and the proportion of customers whose delay in queue is greater than 1 minute. (This priority queue discipline is called *shortest job first.*)

1.8 For the tandem queue of Prob. 1.2, suppose that with probability 0.2, a customer completing service at server 2 is *dissatisfied* with her overall service and must be completely served over again (at least once) by both servers. Define the delay in queue of a customer (in a particular queue) to be the total delay in that queue for all the customer's passes through the facility. Simulate the facility for each of the following cases (estimate the same measures as before):

 (*a*) Dissatisfied customers join the tail of queue 1.
 (*b*) Dissatisfied customers join the head of queue 1.

1.9 Consider a service facility consisting of two type A servers and one type B server. Assume that customers arrive at the facility with interarrival times that are IID exponential random variables with a mean of 1 minute. Upon arrival, a customer is determined to be either a type 1 customer or a type 2 customer, with respective probabilities of 0.75 and 0.25. A type 1 customer can be served by any server but will choose a type A server if one is available. Service times for type 1 customers are IID exponential random variables with a mean of 0.8 minute, regardless of the type of server. Type 1 customers who find all servers busy join a single FIFO queue *for type 1 customers.* A type 2 customer requires service from *both* a type A server *and* a type B server *simultaneously.* Service times for type 2 customers are uniformly distributed between 0.5 and 0.7 minute. Type 2 customers who arrive to find both type A servers busy *or* the type B server busy join a single FIFO queue *for type 2 customers.* Upon the completion of service of *any* customer, preference is given to a type 2 customer if one is present and if both a type A and the type B server are then idle. Otherwise, preference is given to a type 1 customer. Simulate the facility for exactly 1000 minutes and estimate the average delay in queue and the time-average number in queue for each type of customer. Also estimate the proportion of time that each server spends on each type of customer.

REFERENCES

1. Braun, M.: *Differential Equations and Their Applications,* Applied Mathematical Sciences, Vol. 15, Springer-Verlag, New York, 1975.
2. Delfosse, C. M.: *Continuous Simulation and Combined Simulation in SIMSCRIPT II.5,* CACI, Inc., Arlington, Va., 1976.
3. Gordon, G.: *System Simulation,* 2d ed., Prentice-Hall, Englewood Cliffs, N.J., 1978.
4. Gross, D., and C. M. Harris: *Fundamentals of Queueing Theory,* Wiley, New York, 1974.
5. Halton, J. H.: A Retrospective and Prospective Survey of the Monte Carlo Method, *SIAM Rev.,* **12:** 1–63 (1970).
6. Hammersley, J. M., and D. C. Handscomb: *Monte Carlo Methods,* Methuen, London, 1964.
7. IBM Corp.: CSMP III Program Reference Manual, Form SH 19-7001, White Plains, N.Y., 1972.
8. Kleinrock, L.: *Queueing Systems,* vol. I, *Theory,* Wiley, New York, 1975.
9. Kleinrock, L.: *Queueing Systems,* vol. II, *Computer Applications,* Wiley, New York, 1976.
10. Naylor, T. H.: *Computer Simulation Experiments with Models of Economic Systems,* Wiley, New York, 1971.
11. Pritsker, A. A. B.: *The GASP IV Simulation Language,* Wiley, New York, 1974.

12. Pritsker, A. A. B., and C. D. Pegden: *Introduction to Simulation and SLAM,* Systems Publishing, West Lafayette, Ind., 1979.
13. Ross, S. M.: *Introduction to Probability Models,* Academic, New York, 1972.
14. Schmidt, J. W., and R. E. Taylor: *Simulation and Analysis of Industrial Systems,* Irwin, Homewood, Ill., 1970.
15. Shannon, R. E.: *Systems Simulation: The Art and Science,* Prentice-Hall, Englewood Cliffs, N.J., 1975.
16. Speckhart, F. H., and W. L. Green: *A Guide to Using CSMP,* Prentice-Hall, Englewood Cliffs, N.J., 1976.
17. Stidham, S.: A Last Word on $L = \lambda W$, *Oper. Res.,* **22:** 417–421 (1974).

TWO

MODELING COMPLEX SYSTEMS

2.1 INTRODUCTION

The simulation models considered in Chap. 1 were really quite simple in that they contained either one or no lists of records other than the event list. Furthermore, the records in these lists consisted of a single attribute and were always processed in a FIFO manner. In the queueing example, there was a FIFO list containing the records of all customers waiting in queue, and each customer record consisted of the single attribute time of arrival. In the inventory example there were no lists other than the event list. However, many complex real-world simulations require large numbers of lists of records, each of which may contain many records, consisting in turn of possibly a large number of attributes. Furthermore, it is often necessary to process these lists in a manner other than FIFO. For example, in some models one must be able to remove that record in a list with the smallest value for a specified attribute (other than the time the record was placed in the list). If this large amount of information is not stored and manipulated efficiently, the model may require so much execution time and/or so many storage locations that the simulation study would not be feasible.

In the remainder of this section we discuss two approaches to storing lists of records in a computer, sequential and linked allocation, and then explain why the latter approach is preferable for complex simulations. In Sec. 2.2 we present a treatment of linked storage allocation sufficient for the development of a simple simulation language, called SIMLIB, in Sec. 2.3. This language, which can be completely mastered in just a few hours of study, provides considerable insight into the nature of the special-purpose simulation languages discussed in Chap. 3, which require much more time to learn. More importantly, SIMLIB provides a vehicle for explaining how to simulate considerably more complicated systems than those considered in

Chap. 1. In particular, SIMLIB is used to simulate a time-shared computer system, a multiteller bank with jockeying, and a job shop in Secs. 2.4, 2.5, and 2.6, respectively. These systems would require much more effort to simulate in brute-force FORTRAN; furthermore, we would not gain the insight into the basic nature of simulation modeling that is possible with SIMLIB. We conclude the chapter with a discussion in Sec. 2.7 of efficient event-list manipulation.

2.1.1 Approaches to Storing Lists in a Computer

There are two principal approaches to storing lists of records in a computer. In the *sequential-allocation* approach, used in Chap. 1, the records in a list are put into physically adjacent storage locations, one record after another. This was the approach taken with the list TARRVL in the queueing example of Chap. 1. In the *linked-allocation* approach, each record in a list contains its normal attributes and, in addition, one or more pointers (or links) which give the *logical* relationship of the record to other records in the list. Records in a list which follow each other logically may or may not be stored in physically adjacent storage locations. A detailed discussion of linked allocation is given in the next section.

The following are some advantages of using linked storage allocation for simulation modeling:

1. Linked allocation can reduce significantly the time required to process certain types of lists. For the queueing example of Chap. 1, every time a customer completed service (and left one or more customers behind) it was necessary to move each time of arrival in TARRVL up one storage location. This approach would be quite inefficient if TARRVL contained a large number of records. As we shall see in Example 2.1, the processing of TARRVL can be handled more efficiently using linked allocation.
2. For simulation models where the event list simultaneously contains a large number of event records, the use of linked allocation can reduce considerably the amount of time required to process the event list (see Example 2.2 and Sec. 2.7 for further discussion).
3. For some simulation models, the use of linked allocation can reduce the number of computer storage locations required (see the discussion at the end of Sec. 2.2).
4. Linked allocation provides a general framework which allows one to store and manipulate many lists simultaneously with ease, where records in different lists may be processed in different manners. This generality is one of the reasons for the use of the linked-allocation approach by all major simulation languages.

2.2 LINKED STORAGE ALLOCATION

In this section we present a discussion of linked storage allocation sufficient for the development of the simple simulation language SIMLIB, described in the next section. For a more complete and general discussion of list-processing principles, see, for example, Knuth [2, chap. 2].

Suppose that a list of records is to be stored in an array, that the rows of the array correspond to the records, and that the columns of the array correspond to the attributes (or data fields) which make up the records. For the queueing simulation of Chap. 1, customers waiting in the queue had the single attribute time of arrival. In general, customers might have additional attributes such as age, a priority number, their service time, etc.

A list of records is said to be a *doubly linked list* if each record has associated with it a predecessor link and a successor link. The *successor link* for a particular record gives the row in the array of the record which logically succeeds the specified record. If no record succeeds the specified record, the successor link is set to zero. The *predecessor link* for a particular record gives the row in the array of the record which logically precedes the specified record. If no record precedes the specified record, the predecessor link is set to zero. The row of the array which contains the first record in the list is identified by a *head pointer,* which is set to zero when the list contains no records. The row of the array which contains the last record in the list is identified by a *tail pointer,* which is also set to zero when the list is empty.

At any given time a list will probably occupy only a subset of the rows of the array in which it is physically stored. The "empty" rows of the array which are available for future use are linked together in a *list of available space.* The list of available space is usually processed in a LIFO (last-in, first-out) manner; this means that when a row is needed to store an additional record, it is taken from the head of the list of available space and when a row is no longer needed to store a record, it is returned to the head of the list of available space. Since all operations are done at the head of the list of available space, it requires neither a tail pointer nor predecessor links. (We call such a list a *singly linked list.*) At time zero in a simulation, all rows in the array are members of the list of available space, the successor link of row i is set to $i + 1$ (except for that of the last row, which is set to 0), all predecessor links are set to 0, and the head of the list of available space is set to 1. [The predecessor link for a particular row is set (to a positive integer) only when that row is occupied by a record.]

Example 2.1 For the queueing simulation of Chap. 1, consider the list containing the customers waiting in queue to be served. Each record in this list has the single attribute "time of arrival." Suppose that at TIME = 25 in the simulation there are three customers in queue, with times of arrival 10, 15, 25, and that these records are stored in rows 2, 3, and 1 of an array of dimension (5, 1). (To make the figures below manageable, we assume that there will never be more than five customers in queue at any time.) Rows 4 and 5 are members of the list of available space. The situation is depicted in Fig. 2.1. Note that the head pointer of the list is equal to 2, the successor link for the record in row 2 is equal to 3, the predecessor link for the record in row 3 is equal to 2, etc.

Suppose that the next event in the simulation (after TIME = 25) is the arrival of a customer at TIME = 40 and that we would like to add an appropriate record to the list, which is to be processed in a FIFO manner. Since the head pointer for the list of available space is equal to 4, the record for the arriving customer will be placed in row 4 of the array and the head pointer of the list of available space is now set to 5, which is the value of the successor link for row 4. Since the new record will be added to the tail of the list and the tail pointer for the list is now equal to 1, the successor link for the record in row 1 is set to 4, the predecessor link for the new record, i.e., the one in row 4, is set to 1, the successor link for the new record is set to 0, and the tail pointer for the list is set to 4. The state of both lists after these changes have been made is shown in Fig. 2.2.

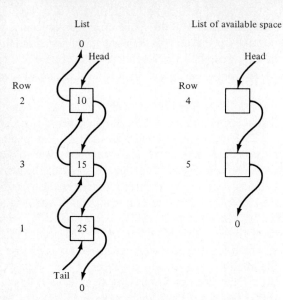

Figure 2.1 State of the lists for the queueing simulation at TIME = 25 in the simulation.

Suppose that the next event in the simulation (after TIME = 40) is the service completion at TIME = 50 of the customer who was being served (at least since TIME = 25) and that it is desired to remove the record of the customer at the head of the list so that this customer can begin service. Since the head pointer for the list is equal to 2 and the successor link for the record in row 2 is equal to 3, the time of arrival of the record in row 2 is used to compute the delay of the customer who will enter service (DELAY = 50 − 10), the head pointer for the list is set to 3, the

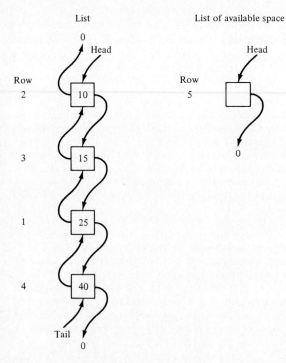

Figure 2.2 State of the lists for the queueing simulation at TIME = 40 in the simulation.

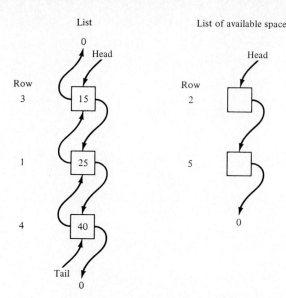

List

List of available space

0

Head

Head

Row
3

Row
2

15

1

25

5

4

40

0

Tail

0

Figure 2.3 State of the lists for
the queueing simulation at TIME
= 50 in the simulation.

Figure 2.3 State of the lists for the queueing simulation at TIME = 50 in the simulation.

predecessor link for the record in row 3 is set to 0, and row 2 (which is no longer needed) is placed at the head of the list of available space by setting the head pointer for the list of available space equal to 2 and the successor link for row 2 equal to 5 (the previous head of the list of available space). The state of both lists after these changes have been made is shown in Fig. 2.3.

Thus, removing a record from the head of the list always requires setting only four links or pointers. Contrast this with the brute-force approach of Chap. 1, which requires moving each record in the (sequential) list up by one location. If the list contained, say 100 records, this would be a much more time-consuming task than with the linked-list approach.

Example 2.2 For the inventory simulation of Chap. 1, the event list was stored in the array TNE, with each of the four event types having a dedicated location. If an event was not currently scheduled to occur, its entry in TNE was set to ∞ (represented as 10^{30} in the computer). However, for many complex simulations written in FORTRAN and for simulations which use the special-purpose simulation languages described in Chap. 3, the event list is stored as a linked list which is ranked in increasing order on event time. Now, events which have an event time of ∞ are not included in the event list. In particular, suppose that the event list for the inventory simulation is to be stored in an array of dimension (4, 2), column 1 being for the attribute event time and column 2 being for the attribute event type, that is, 1, 2, 3, or 4. Suppose that at TIME = 0 it is known that the first demad for the product (event type 2) will occur at TIME = 0.25, the first inventory evaluation (event type 4) will occur immediately at TIME = 0, the simulation will end (event type 3) at TIME = 120, and there is no outstanding order scheduled to arrive (event type 1). The state of the event list and the list of available space just after initialization at TIME = 0 is shown in Fig. 2.4. Note that event type 1 is not included in the event list and that event type 2 is in row 1 of the array physically since it was placed in the event list first.

To determine the next (first) event to occur at TIME = 0, the first record is removed from the event list, TIME is updated to the first attribute of this record, i.e., TIME is set to 0, the event type of the next event to occur, NEXT, is set to the second attribute of this record, i.e., NEXT is set to 4, and row 3 which contained this record is placed at the head of the list of available space. Since NEXT = 4, an inventory-evaluation event will occur next (at TIME = 0). Suppose that an order is placed at TIME = 0 and that it will arrive from the supplier at TIME = 0.6. To place this order-arrival event in the event list, first 0.6 and 1 are placed in columns 1 and 2, respectively, of row 3 (the head of the list of available space), and then this new record is added to the event list by logically proceeding down the event list (using the successor links) until the correct location

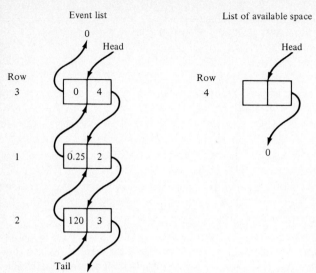

Figure 2.4 State of the lists for the inventory simulation just after initialization at TIME = 0.

is found. In particular, first attribute 1 of the new record, that is, 0.6, is compared with attribute 1 of the record in row 1, that is, 0.25. Since 0.6 is larger than 0.25, the new record should be farther down the event list. Next 0.6 is compared with attribute 1 of the record in row 2, that is, 120. (Note that the successor link of the record in row 1 is equal to 2.) Since 0.6 is less than 120, the new record is logically placed between the records in rows 1 and 2 by adjusting the successor

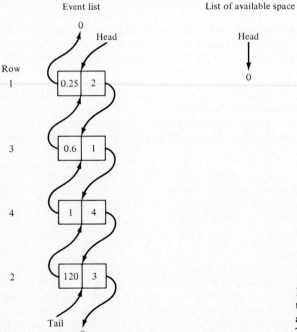

Figure 2.5 State of the lists for the inventory simulation after all processing has been done at TIME = 0.

and predecessor links for the three records. After this has been accomplished, another inventory-evaluation event is scheduled at TIME = 1 and placed in the event list in a manner similar to that for the order-arrival event. The state of both lists after all processing has been done at TIME = 0 is shown in Fig. 2.5.

In the above discussion, a single list was stored in an array where the empty rows were members of the list of available space, but there is no reason why many lists cannot be simultaneously stored logically in the same physical array. There is one list of available space, and the beginning and the end of each list are identified by head and tail pointers. This approach can result in a significant savings in storage space for some applications. For example, suppose a simulation requires 20 lists, each containing up to 100 records of 10 attributes each. Using the standard approach, 20 arrays each of dimension (100, 10) would be required for a total storage requirement of 20,000 locations. However, suppose that at any given time an average of only 25 percent of all available rows are actually being used. Then an alternative approach might be to store all 20 lists in one array of, say, dimension (1000, 10). This approach would require 10,000 locations for the array plus an additional 2040 locations for the links and pointers, for a grand total of 12,040 storage locations. Furthermore, at a particular point in a simulation, one or more lists may each be occupying more than their fair share of the available rows without causing an overflow condition.

The simple simulation language SIMLIB, developed in the next section, stores all lists (including the event list) in a single master array.

2.3 A SIMPLE SIMULATION LANGUAGE, SIMLIB

In this section we describe an easy-to-understand simulation language, SIMLIB, which is based on the concept of linked storage allocation presented in Sec. 2.2. The language makes it easy to file a record in a list (the record may be filed first in the list, last in the list, or so that the list is kept ranked in increasing or decreasing order on a specified attribute), to remove a record from a list (either the first record or the last record in the list may be removed), to process the event list, to compute sample statistics on a variable of interest (e.g., the average delay in queue in a queueing system), to compute time-average statistics on a variable of interest (e.g., the time-average number of items in inventory in an inventory system), and to generate the random variables used in the examples of Chap. 1. Although SIMLIB provides many of the important features found in special-purpose simulation languages (see Chap. 3), it is designed neither for absolute completeness nor computational efficiency. Our reasons for presenting it here are to provide some insight into the operation of simulation languages and, more important, a vehicle for understanding how to simulate systems considerably more complicated than those considered in Chap. 1.

The heart of SIMLIB is the real storage array MASTER, which has dimension (1000, 10). In this array one can store up to 1000 records, each with up to 10 attributes, in up to 25 different lists. However, list 25 is always reserved for the event list. Furthermore, attribute 1 for the event list is always the time that the event is to occur and attribute 2 is always the event type. The user has at his disposal the following variables which are contained in the common block SYSTEM:

LRANK(LIST)	The attribute of a record (the column of the array MASTER) on which list LIST is to be ranked, in either increasing or decreasing order, as desired (see the discussion below of subroutine FILE). If list LIST is to be a ranked list, then LRANK(LIST) is typically set in the main program. Otherwise, LRANK(LIST) does not need to be set. Note that LRANK(25) is automatically set to 1 by SIMLIB (attribute 1 for the event list is always the event time).
LSIZE(LIST)	The current number of records in list LIST, which is automatically updated by SIMLIB.
MAXATR	The maximum number of attributes for any record in a particular simulation model. If MAXATR is not set in the main program by the user, a default value of 10 is used by SIMLIB.
NEXT	The event type of the next event to occur. NEXT is determined by SIMLIB when the user calls the library subroutine TIMING (see below).
TIME	The simulation clock, which is updated by SIMLIB when the user calls the library subroutine TIMING.
TRNSFR	A real array of dimension 10 which is used for transferring records into and out of the array MASTER (see below for further discussion).

In addition to the array MASTER and the variables in the common block SYSTEM, the simulation language SIMLIB consists of 11 subroutines and functions, each designed to perform a commonly occurring simulation activity:

INITLK. This subroutine, which is called from the main program by the user at the beginning of a simulation, initializes the successor and predecessor links, initializes the head and tail pointers for each list, sets TIME = 0, and initializes the statistical subroutines SAMPST and TIMEST (see below). For a complete picture of the initialization done in INITLK, see the FORTRAN listings in Appendix 2A.

FILE(OPTION,LIST). This subroutine takes a record which has been placed in the TRNSFR array by the user and files it in list LIST (LIST = 1, 2, ... , 25) in accordance with option OPTION (OPTION = 1, 2, ... , 4). The following options are available to the user:

OPTION	Action
1	File record in TRNSFR array before first record in list LIST
2	File record in TRNSFR array after last record in list LIST
3	File record in TRNSFR array in list LIST so that list is kept ranked in increasing order on attribute LRANK(LIST) [if two records have same the value of atttribute LRANK(LIST), the rule is FIFO]
4	File record in TRNSFR array in list LIST so that list is kept ranked in decreasing order on attribute LRANK(LIST) [if two records have same the value of attribute LRANK(LIST), the rule is FIFO]

REMOVE(OPTION,LIST). This subroutine removes a record from list LIST (LIST = 1, 2, ..., 25) in accordance with option OPTION (OPTION = 1, 2) and places it in the TRNSFR array for the simulator's use. The following options are available to the user:

OPTION	Action
1	Remove first record from list LIST and place it in TRNSFR array
2	Remove last record from list LIST and place it in TRNSFR array

TIMING. This subroutine, which is called from the main program by the user, determines the event type, NEXT, of the next event to occur and updates the simulation clock, TIME. In determining the next event, TIMING uses subroutine REMOVE to remove from the event list the record corresponding to the most imminent event and places it in the TRNSFR array. Thus, attributes of the event record other than event time and event type (if any) are available for the simulator's use.

CANCEL(ETYPE). This subroutine cancels (removes) the first event in the event list with event type ETYPE (real-valued). The attributes of the canceled event are placed in the TRNSFR array.

SAMPST(VALUE,VARIBL). This subroutine computes the sample mean, the maximum, the minimum, and the number of observations in a set of observations on variable VARIBL (integer-valued). Each time a new value VALUE (real-valued) of variable VARIBL is computed during the course of a simulation, the statistical counters in SAMPST are updated by executing the statement CALL SAMPST(VALUE,VARIBL). This can be done for up to 20 different variables of interest. (For example, in the queueing simulation of Chap. 1, variable 1 might be the delay in queue of a customer and variable 2 the service time of a customer.) The statistical counters for SAMPST are initialized in subroutine INITLK, but additional initializations of all variables can be accomplished by executing the statement CALL SAMPST(0.,0). If the statement CALL SAMPST(0.,-VARIBL) is executed, the following summary statistics for variable VARIBL are computed and placed in the TRNSFR array for the simulator's use:

I	TRNSFR(I)
1	Sample mean of values of variable VARIBL observed
2	Number of values of variable VARIBL observed
3	Maximum value of variable VARIBL observed
4	Minimum value of variable VARIBL observed

TIMEST(VALUE,VARIBL). This subroutine computes the time average (mean), the maximum, and the minimum of a set of observations on variable VARIBL (integer-valued). Each time a new value VALUE (real-valued) of variable

VARIBL is computed during the course of a simulation, the statistical counters in TIMEST are updated by executing the statement CALL TIMEST(VALUE,VARIBL). This can be done for up to 20 variables of interest. [For example, in the inventory simulation of Chap. 1, variable 1 might be the actual number of items in inventory, $I^+(t)$, and variable 2 the size of the backlog, $I^-(t)$.] The statistical counters for TIMEST are initialized in subroutine INITLK under the assumption that each variable has an initial value of zero. To initialize variable VARIBL with a value VALUE (real-valued), the statement CALL TIMEST(VALUE,VARIBL) is executed just after subroutine INITLK is called from the main program. [To reinitialize all the statistical counters for TIMEST during the course of a simulation assuming an initial value of zero for each variable, the statement CALL TIMEST(0.,0) is executed. If variable VARIBL is to have an initial value VALUE at this point in the simulation, the statement CALL TIMEST(VALUE,VARIBL) must also be executed.] If the statement CALL TIMEST(0.,-VARIBL) is executed, the following summary statistics for variable VARIBL are computed and placed in the TRNSFR array for the simulator's use:

I	TRNSFR(I)
1	Time average (mean) of the values of variable VARIBL observed, *updated to time of this call*
2	Maximum value of variable VARIBL observed up to time of this call
3	Minimum value of variable VARIBL observed up to time of this call

FILEST(LIST). This subroutine computes the time-average number of records, the maximum number of records, and the minimum number of records in list (file) LIST (LIST = 1, 2, . . . , 25). (For the queueing simulation of Chap. 1, if list 1 contained the records of customers waiting in the queue, FILEST could be used to compute the time-average number of customers in queue.) By treating the number of records in list LIST as TIMEST variable 20 + LIST, SIMLIB *automatically* updates the statistical counters for FILEST each time a record is added to or deleted from list LIST. The statistical counters for FILEST are initialized in subroutine INITLK under the assumption that each list initially contains no records. To initialize the number of records in list LIST with a value VALUE (real-valued), the statement CALL TIMEST(VALUE,ILIST) is executed just after subroutine INITLK is called from the main program, where ILIST = 20 + LIST (integer-valued). [To reinitialize all the statistical counters for FILEST during the course of a simulation assuming that each list initially contains no records, the statement CALL TIMEST(0.,0) is executed. If the number of records in list LIST is to have an initial value VALUE at this point in the simulation, the statement CALL TIMEST(VALUE,ILIST) must also be executed. Note that the statement CALL TIMEST(0.,0) should never be executed more than once at a given time.] If the statement CALL FILEST(LIST) is executed, the following summary statistics for list LIST are computed and placed in the TRNSFR array for the simulator's use:

I	TRNSFR(I)
1	Time-average number of records in list LIST, *updated to time of this call*
2	Maximum number of records in list LIST up to time of this call
3	Minimum number of records in list LIST up to time of this call

EXPON(RMEAN). This function generates an exponential random variable with mean RMEAN.

RANDI(Z). This function generates a random integer between 1 and NVALUE (a positive integer) in accordance with the distribution function PROBD(I) (I = 1, 2, ... , NVALUE), where Z is a dummy variable. [If X is the random integer, the probability that X takes on a value less than or equal to I is given by PROBD(I).] The values of NVALUE and PROBD(I) (I = 1, 2, ... , NVALUE) are set in the main program and transmitted to RANDI by placing the following common block in the main program:

$$\text{COMMON /RANDOM/ NVALUE,PROBD(25)}$$

Note that NVALUE can have a maximum value of 25.

UNIFRM(A,B). This function generates a continuous random variable which is uniformly distributed on the interval [A, B], where A and B are real-valued and A must be less than B.

We now describe in somewhat more detail how the various components of SIMLIB are used to simulate a system of interest. First, the common block SYSTEM and a user-written common block MODEL are placed in appropriate subprograms. (MODEL contains the model-dependent global variables.) If the function RANDI is going to be used, the common block RANDOM is also placed in the main program. In the main program, the following activities take place, roughly in the order listed:

1. Read input parameters.
2. Call the library subroutine INITLK to initialize certain aspects of SIMLIB.
3. Set LRANK(LIST) if list LIST (LIST = 1, 2, ... , 24) is to be a ranked list and set MAXATR.
4. Call the library subroutine TIMEST to initialize a TIMEST variable or the number of records in a list to a value other than zero (optional).
5. Initialize the event list using the library subroutine FILE.
6. Call the library subroutine TIMING to determine the event type, NEXT, of the next event to occur.

7. Use a computed go to statement based on NEXT to call the appropriate event subroutine (user-written).
8. When the simulation has ended, call the user-written subroutine REPORT to print the desired results.

During the course of a simulation, the library subroutines FILE and REMOVE are used to keep lists of records in their proper order, and the library subroutines SAMPST and TIMEST are used to gather statistics on variables of interest. In REPORT, subroutines SAMPST, TIMEST, and FILEST are used to compute summary statistics of interest.

2.4 A TIME-SHARED COMPUTER MODEL

In this section we use the simulation language SIMLIB to simulate a model of a time-shared computer facility considered by Adiri and Avi-Itzhak [1].

2.4.1 Statement of the Problem

Consider a company with a time-shared computer system consisting of a single central processing unit (CPU) and n terminals, as shown in Fig. 2.6. The operator of each terminal "thinks" for an amount of time which is an exponential random variable with mean 25 seconds and then sends a message to the CPU with a service time which is an exponential random variable with mean 0.8 second. The arriving jobs join a single queue in front of the CPU but are served in a round-robin rather than FIFO manner. That is, the CPU allocates to each job a maximum service quantum of length $q = 0.1$ second. If the (remaining) service time of a job, s, is less than or equal to q, the CPU spends time s plus a fixed overhead $\tau = 0.015$ second processing the job and the job returns to its terminal. If s is greater than q, the CPU spends time q plus τ processing the job, the job joins the end of the queue, and its remaining service time is decremented by q seconds. This process is repeated until the job's service is eventually completed, at which point the job returns to its terminal.

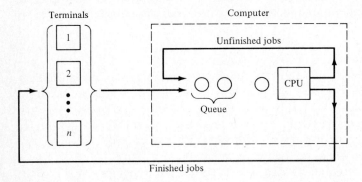

Figure 2.6 Time-shared computer model.

Define the response time of the ith job to finish service, R_i, to be the time elapsing between the instant the job leaves its terminal and the instant that it is finished being processed at the CPU. For each of the cases $n = 30, 35, \ldots, 70$, we use SIMLIB to simulate the computer system for 5000 job completions and estimate the average response time of the first 5000 jobs, the time-average number of jobs waiting in queue, and the utilization of the CPU (proportion of time the CPU is busy). Assume that all terminals are in the think state at time zero. The company would like to know how many terminals it can have on its system and still provide its users with an average response time of 30 seconds.

2.4.2 SIMLIB Program

The events for this simulation model are as follows:

Event description	Event type
Arrival of a job to the CPU from a terminal, at the end of a think time	1
End of a CPU run, when a job either completes its service requirement or has received the maximum processing quantum q	2
End of the simulation	3

Three lists of records are used for this model, one corresponding to the jobs in queue (list 1), one for the job being served by the CPU (list 2), and one for the event list (list 25). These lists have the following attributes:

List	Attribute 1	Attribute 2	Attribute 3	Attribute 4
1, queue	Time of arrival to queue	Terminal of origin	Number of full quantum-length CPU runs required	Remaining service time
2, CPU	Time of arrival to queue	Terminal of origin	Number of full quantum-length CPU runs required	Remaining service time
25, event list	Event time	Event type	Terminal number if event type = 1	

Note that list 2 will either be empty (if the CPU is idle) or contain only one record (if the CPU is busy). In addition to a main program (and the library subroutines and functions in SIMLIB), the program consists of the user-written subroutines and FORTRAN variables shown in Table 2.1. (Recall from Chap. 1 that modeling variables include state variables, statistical counters, and variables used to facilitate the writing of the program.)

The main program, whose FORTRAN listing is given in Fig. 2.7, begins with the MODEL (model-dependent global variables) and the SYSTEM common blocks,

Table 2.1 Subprograms and FORTRAN variables for computer model

Subprograms	Purpose
ARRIVE(ORIGIN)	Processes type 1 events where ORIGIN is the terminal of origin for a job
ENDRUN	Processes type 2 events
REPORT	Generates report (called when the simulation ends)
START	Removes a job from queue and places it in the CPU to start service (not an *event* subroutine)

	Definition
Input parameters:	
INCREM	Increment in number of terminals
MAXTER	Maximum number of terminals
MINTER	Minimum number of terminals
MSERVE	Mean service time
MTHINK	Mean think time
OVERHD	Overhead
QUANTM	Quantum
TOTJOB	Total number of jobs to be processed during the simulation
Modeling variables:	
INT	(Integer) number of full quantum-length CPU runs required for a job
JOBTIM	Total service time of a job
NTERML	Number of terminals for a particular simulation run
NUMJOB	Number of jobs processed
ORIGIN	Terminal of origin for a job
RESPTM	Response time of a job
RUNTIM	Amount of time required to process a job during a particular pass through the CPU
TERMNL	Terminal number
Output variables:	
ARESPT	Average response time
AVGNIQ	Average number in queue
UTILIZ	Utilization of the CPU

followed by the reading of the input parameters. Since the REPORT subroutine is called once for each desired simulation run, the report heading is printed in the main program. Then for each of the desired simulation runs (each run corresponding to a particular number of terminals) the simulation is initialized by calling INITLK, MAXATR is then set to 4 (the maximum number of attributes for any of the lists is 4), the event list is initialized with a job-arrival event for each terminal, TIMING is called to determine the event type of the next event to occur, NEXT, and NEXT is used to pass control to the appropriate event subroutine. Note that the argument of ARRIVE, TRNSFR(3), is set in TIMING when the event is removed from the event list. The print statement at the end of the main program again makes the simulation report page free of any extraneous printing.

A flowchart and FORTRAN listing for the ARRIVE event subroutine are given in Figs. 2.8 and 2.9. When a job arrives at the CPU, its total service requirement, JOBTIM, is generated. Taking the integral part of JOBTIM/QUANTM gives the number, INT, of required complete passes through the CPU for the job. The remain-

```
C
C *** MAIN PROGRAM.
C
      INTEGER INCREM,MAXTER,MINTER,NTERML,NUMJOB,TERMNL,TOTJOB
      REAL MSERVE,MTHINK,OVERHD,QUANTM
      COMMON /MODEL/ MSERVE,MTHINK,NTERML,NUMJOB,OVERHD,QUANTM,TOTJOB
      COMMON /SYSTEM/ LRANK(25),LSIZE(25),MAXATR,NEXT,TIME,TRNSFR(10)
C
C *** READ INPUT PARAMETERS.
C
      READ 10,MINTER,MAXTER,INCREM
   10 FORMAT(3I10)
      READ 20,TOTJOB
   20 FORMAT(I10)
      READ 30,MTHINK,MSERVE
   30 FORMAT(2F10.0)
      READ 40,QUANTM,OVERHD
   40 FORMAT(2F10.0)
C
C ***********************************************************************
C
C *** PRINT REPORT HEADING.
C
      PRINT 50
   50 FORMAT(1H1,5X,'TIME-SHARED COMPUTER MODEL')
      PRINT 60,MTHINK
   60 FORMAT(1H0,5X,'MEAN THINK TIME',7X,F6.3,' SECONDS')
      PRINT 70,MSERVE
   70 FORMAT(1H0,5X,'MEAN SERVICE TIME',5X,F6.3,' SECONDS')
      PRINT 80,QUANTM
   80 FORMAT(1H0,5X,'QUANTUM',15X,F6.3,' SECONDS')
      PRINT 90,OVERHD
   90 FORMAT(1H0,5X,'OVERHEAD',14X,F6.3,' SECONDS')
      PRINT 100,TOTJOB
  100 FORMAT(1H0,5X,'NUMBER OF JOBS PROCESSED',7X,I5)
      PRINT 110
  110 FORMAT(//)
      PRINT 120
  120 FORMAT(1H0,5X,'NUMBER OF TERMINALS',5X,'AVERAGE RESPONSE TIME',5X,
     1'AVERAGE NUMBER IN QUEUE',5X,'UTILIZATION OF CPU')
C
C ***********************************************************************
C
C *** RUN THE SIMULATION VARYING THE NUMBER OF TERMINALS.
C
      DO 180 NTERML=MINTER,MAXTER,INCREM
      NUMJOB=0
C
C *** INITIALIZE SUPPORT ROUTINES.
C
      CALL INITLK
      MAXATR=4
C
C *** SCHEDULE THE FIRST ARRIVAL TO THE CPU FROM EACH TERMINAL.
C
      DO 130 TERMNL=1,NTERML
      TRNSFR(1)=EXPON(MTHINK)
      TRNSFR(2)=1.
      TRNSFR(3)=TERMNL
      CALL FILE(3,25)
  130 CONTINUE
C
C *** DETERMINE THE NEXT EVENT.
C
  140 CALL TIMING
C
C *** CALL THE APPROPRIATE EVENT ROUTINE.
C
      GO TO (150,160,170),NEXT
  150 CALL ARRIVE(TRNSFR(3))
      GO TO 140
  160 CALL ENDRUN
      GO TO 140
  170 CALL REPORT
  180 CONTINUE
      PRINT 190
  190 FORMAT(1H1)
      STOP
      END
```

Figure 2.7 FORTRAN listing for the main program, computer model.

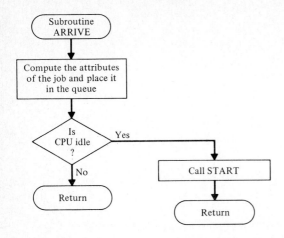

Figure 2.8 Flowchart for subroutine ARRIVE, computer model.

ing service time for the job is obtained by subtracting INT times QUANTM from JOBTIM. The record for the job, which contains four attributes, is then placed last (OPTION = 2 for the library subroutine FILE) in the queue, which is list 1. If the CPU (list 2) is idle, as indicated by LSIZE(2) = 0, service is started on the job by calling subroutine START.

START, which is not an *event* subroutine, is called at a particular time to start service on a job. The use of START, which is called from both ARRIVE and ENDRUN, avoids writing the same block of code twice. A flowchart and FORTRAN listing for START are given in Figs. 2.10 and 2.11. In START, the first job

```
      SUBROUTINE ARRIVE(ORIGIN)
      INTEGER INT,NTERML,NUMJOB,TOTJOB
      REAL JOBTIM,MSERVE,MTHINK,ORIGIN,OVERHD,QUANTM
      COMMON /MODEL/ MSERVE,MTHINK,NTERML,NUMJOB,OVERHD,QUANTM,TOTJOB
      COMMON /SYSTEM/ LRANK(25),LSIZE(25),MAXATR,NEXT,TIME,TRNSFR(10)
C
C *** PLACE THE JOB IN THE QUEUE.
C *** NOTE THAT THE FOLLOWING DATA ARE STORED FOR EACH JOB:
C ***      1. TIME OF ARRIVAL TO THE QUEUE.
C ***      2. THE TERMINAL OF ORIGIN.
C ***      3. THE NUMBER OF QUANTUM LENGTH CPU RUNS REQUIRED.
C ***      4. THE REMAINING AMOUNT OF SERVICE TIME REQUIRED.
C
      JOBTIM=EXPON(MSERVE)
      TRNSFR(1)=TIME
      TRNSFR(2)=ORIGIN
      INT=JOBTIM/QUANTM
      TRNSFR(3)=INT
      TRNSFR(4)=JOBTIM-(INT*QUANTM)
      CALL FILE(2,1)
C
C *** IF THE CPU IS IDLE, START A CPU RUN.
C
      IF(LSIZE(2).EQ.0) CALL START
      RETURN
      END
```

Figure 2.9 FORTRAN listing for subroutine ARRIVE, computer model.

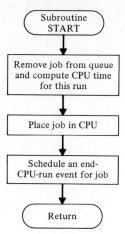

Figure 2.10 Flowchart for subroutine START, computer model.

```
      SUBROUTINE START
      INTEGER NTERML,NUMJOB,TOTJOB
      REAL MSERVE,MTHINK,OVERHD,QUANTM,RUNTIM
      COMMON /MODEL/ MSERVE,MTHINK,NTERML,NUMJOB,OVERHD,QUANTM,TOTJOB
      COMMON /SYSTEM/ LRANK(25),LSIZE(25),MAXATR,NEXT,TIME,TRNSFR(10)
C
C *** REMOVE JOB FROM QUEUE.
C
      CALL REMOVE(1,1)
C
C *** DETERMINE REQUIRED CPU TIME FOR THIS RUN.
C
      IF(TRNSFR(3).GT.0.5) GO TO 10
C
C *** LESS THAN A FULL QUANTUM IS NEEDED.
C
      RUNTIM=TRNSFR(4)+OVERHD
      TRNSFR(3)=-1.
      GO TO 20
C
C *** A FULL QUANTUM IS NEEDED.
C
   10 RUNTIM=QUANTM+OVERHD
      TRNSFR(3)=TRNSFR(3)-1.
C
C *** PLACE JOB IN CPU.
C
   20 CALL FILE(1,2)
C
C *** SCHEDULE THE END OF THE CPU RUN.
C
      TRNSFR(1)=TIME+RUNTIM
      TRNSFR(2)=2.
      CALL FILE(3,25)
      RETURN
      END
```

Figure 2.11 FORTRAN listing for subroutine START, computer model.

is removed from the queue (OPTION = 1 for REMOVE), and its remaining number of complete passes through the CPU is placed in TRNSFR(3). If one or more complete passes are required, as indicated by TRNSFR(3) > 0.5, a running time, RUNTIM, of QUANTM plus OVERHD is required for this pass. [Note that we check to see whether a job still needs at least a full quantum of CPU time by testing to see if TRNSFR(3) > 0.5 rather than, say, TRNSFR(3) ≥ 1.0, because of the possibility of floating-point roundoff error.] Otherwise, RUNTIM is equal to TRNSFR(4) (the remaining service time) plus OVERHD. In either case, 1 is subtracted from TRNSFR(3), and the job is placed in the CPU. [Note that if less than a full quantum of service time is required to complete the job currently being put in

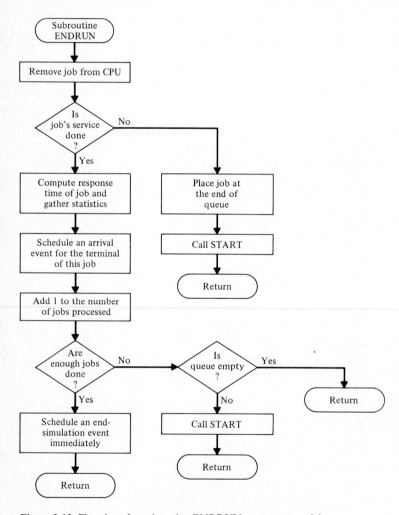

Figure 2.12 Flowchart for subroutine ENDRUN, computer model.

```
      SUBROUTINE ENDRUN
      INTEGER NTERML,NUMJOB,TOTJOB
      REAL MSERVE,MTHINK,ORIGIN,OVERHD,QUANTM,RESPTM
      COMMON /MODEL/ MSERVE,MTHINK,NTERML,NUMJOB,OVERHD,QUANTM,TOTJOB
      COMMON /SYSTEM/ LRANK(25),LSIZE(25),MAXATR,NEXT,TIME,TRNSFR(10)
C
C *** REMOVE JOB FROM THE CPU.
C
      CALL REMOVE(1,2)
C
C *** IF THIS JOB IS DONE, SCHEDULE ANOTHER ARRIVAL FOR THE SAME TERMINAL.
C
      IF(TRNSFR(3).GT.-0.5) GO TO 20
      RESPTM=TIME-TRNSFR(1)
      CALL SAMPST(RESPTM,1)
      ORIGIN=TRNSFR(2)
      TRNSFR(1)=TIME+EXPON(MTHINK)
      TRNSFR(2)=1.
      TRNSFR(3)=ORIGIN
      CALL FILE(3,25)
C
C *** INCREMENT THE NUMBER OF COMPLETED JOBS. IF ENOUGH JOBS ARE DONE,
C *** SCHEDULE THE END OF THE SIMULATION.
C
      NUMJOB=NUMJOB+1
      IF(NUMJOB.LT.TOTJOB) GO TO 10
      TRNSFR(1)=TIME
      TRNSFR(2)=3.
      CALL FILE(1,25)
      RETURN
C
C *** IF THE QUEUE IS NOT EMPTY, START ANOTHER JOB.
C
   10 IF(LSIZE(1).GT.0) CALL START
      RETURN
C
C *** SINCE THE JOB IS NOT FINISHED, PLACE IT AT THE END OF THE QUEUE.
C
   20 CALL FILE(2,1)
      CALL START
      RETURN
      END
```

Figure 2.13 FORTRAN listing for subroutine ENDRUN, computer model.

the CPU, TRNSFR(3) will be 0. after the CALL REMOVE(1, 1) statement. Thus the statement TRNSFR(3) = -1. is equivalent in this case to TRNSFR(3) = TRNSFR(3) - 1..] Finally, an end-CPU-run event (event type 2) is scheduled for the job.

Event subroutine ENDRUN is called from the main program when a job completes a pass through the CPU; it is flowcharted and listed in Figs. 2.12 and 2.13. The job is first removed from the CPU. If the job has finished being served, its response time, RESPTM, is computed, statistics are gathered by treating RESPTM as SAMPST variable 1, and another arrival event (event type 1) is scheduled for the terminal of this job. Then 1 is added to the number of jobs processed, and if enough jobs have been processed through completion, an end-simulation event is scheduled by placing a type 3 event record *first* in the event list and control is returned to the

```
      SUBROUTINE REPORT
      INTEGER NTERML,NUMJOB,TOTJOB
      REAL ARESPT,AVGNIQ,MSERVE,MTHINK,OVERHD,QUANTM,UTILIZ
      COMMON /MODEL/ MSERVE,MTHINK,NTERML,NUMJOB,OVERHD,QUANTM,TOTJOB
      COMMON /SYSTEM/ LRANK(25),LSIZE(25),MAXATR,NEXT,TIME,TRNSFR(10)
      CALL SAMPST(0.,-1)
      ARESPT=TRNSFR(1)
      CALL FILEST(1)
      AVGNIQ=TRNSFR(1)
      CALL FILEST(2)
      UTILIZ=TRNSFR(1)
      PRINT 10,NTERML,ARESPT,AVGNIQ,UTILIZ
   10 FORMAT(1H0,14X,I2,21X,F6.3,21X,F6.3,20X,F5.3)
      RETURN
      END
```

Figure 2.14 FORTRAN listing for subroutine REPORT, computer model.

main program. If the job is finished, not enough jobs have been processed through completion, and the queue is not empty [LSIZE(1) > 0], START is called.

If the job has not finished being served, it is placed last in the queue and START is called to start service on another job (possibly the one just removed from the CPU if all other jobs are at their terminals in the think state).

A FORTRAN listing for subroutine REPORT is given in Fig. 2.14. The average response time is computed and placed in TRNSFR(1) by calling SAMPST with VALUE = 0. and VARIBL = -1. (Recall that RESPTM is SAMPST variable 1.) The time-average number of jobs in queue (list 1) is then obtained by calling FILEST with LIST = 1, and the utilization of the CPU (the time-average number of jobs in the CPU) is obtained by calling FILEST with LIST = 2.

```
TIME-SHARED COMPUTER MODEL
MEAN THINK TIME        25.000 SECONDS
MEAN SERVICE TIME        .800 SECONDS
QUANTUM                  .100 SECONDS
OVERHEAD                 .015 SECONDS
NUMBER OF JOBS PROCESSED    5000
```

NUMBER OF TERMINALS	AVERAGE RESPONSE TIME	AVERAGE NUMBER IN QUEUE	UTILIZATION OF CPU
30	4.919	4.047	.917
35	7.610	7.131	.970
40	12.282	12.315	.997
45	16.252	16.780	.998
50	20.720	21.572	1.000
55	24.639	26.008	1.000
60	30.474	31.852	1.000
65	34.975	37.156	1.000
70	40.346	42.055	1.000

Figure 2.15 Simulation report for the computer model.

2.4.3 Simulation Output and Discussion

The simulation report is given in Fig. 2.15. Note that the CPU was busy continuously (to three decimal places) when there were 50 or more terminals. More importantly, observe that the company can have approximately 60 terminals on its computer system and still provide its users with an average response time of 30 seconds.

2.5 A MULTITELLER BANK WITH JOCKEYING

We now use SIMLIB to simulate a multiteller bank where customers are allowed to jockey (move) from queue to queue if it seems to be to their advantage. This model also illustrates how to deal with another common stopping rule for a simulation.

2.5.1 Statement of the Problem

A bank with five tellers opens its doors at 9 A.M. and closes its doors at 5 P.M., but operates until all customers in the bank by 5 P.M. have been served. Assume that the interarrival times of customers are IID exponential random variables with mean 1 minute and that the service times of customers are IID exponential random variables with mean 4.5 minutes.

Each teller has a separate queue. An arriving customer joins the shortest queue, the leftmost queue being joined in case of ties. Let n_i be the total number of customers (in service plus in queue) in front of teller i at a particular instant. If the completion of a customer's service at teller i causes $n_j > n_i + 1$ for some teller j, then the customer from the tail of queue j jockeys to the tail of queue i. (If there are two or more such tellers j, the customer corresponding to the closest, leftmost teller jockeys.) If teller i is idle, the customer from queue j begins service at teller i; see Fig. 2.16.

The bank's management is concerned with the quality of service currently provided to customers and is thinking of adding one or more new tellers. For each of the cases $n = 5$, 6, and 7 tellers, we use SIMLIB to simulate the bank and estimate the time-average total number of customers in queue, the average delay in queue, and the maximum delay in queue. In all cases we assume that no customers are present when the bank opens.

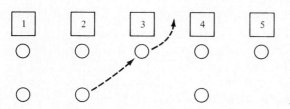

Figure 2.16 Customer being served by teller 3 completes service, causing the customer from the tail of queue 2 to jockey.

2.5.2 SIMLIB Program

The events for this model are as follows:

Event description	Event type
Arrival of a customer to the bank	1
Departure of a customer upon completion of his service	2
Bank closes its doors at 5 P.M.	3

This model requires $2n + 1$ lists of records, where n is the number of tellers for a particular simulation run. Lists 1 through n contain the records of the customers waiting in the respective queues. Lists $n + 1$ through $2n$ are used to indicate whether or not the tellers are busy. If list $n + i$ $(i = 1, 2, \ldots, n)$ contains one record, teller i is busy. If it contains no records, teller i is idle. Finally, list 25 is the event list. The attributes for all these lists are as follows:

List	Attribute 1	Attribute 2	Attribute 3
1 to n, queues	Time of arrival to queue		
$n + 1$ to $2n$, tellers	Irrelevant		
25, event list	Event time	Event type	Teller number if event type = 2

The program for this model consists of a main program and the user-written subroutines and FORTRAN variables shown in Table 2.2.

The FORTRAN listing for the bank model's main program is given in Fig. 2.17. The most interesting part of the main program is the treatment of the bank's closing. A close-doors event is scheduled for 60 times LENGTH minutes after the simulation begins. When this event actually occurs, the SIMLIB subroutine CANCEL is used to prevent the next customer from arriving since the doors are now closed. (Since an arrival is scheduled only by the previous arrival, this prevents any future arrivals.) If the event list is now empty, i.e., if LSIZE(25) = 0, all tellers must be idle and the simulation is ended by calling REPORT. If the event list is not empty, the simulation is allowed to continue until all customers in the bank have been served. If the event list is ever empty after a service completion occurs, it must be past 5 P.M. (otherwise there would be arrival and close-doors events in the event list) and the simulation is ended by calling REPORT.

A flowchart and listing for the ARRIVE event subroutine are given in Figs. 2.18 and 2.19. The subroutine begins by scheduling the next arrival event. Then a check is made to determine whether there is an available teller. This is accomplished by determining whether any of the lists which correspond to the tellers contain no records. If a teller is available, the delay of the arriving customer is set to 0, sample statistics for delays are updated, the available teller is made busy by placing a

Table 2.2 Subprograms and FORTRAN variables for bank model

Subprograms	Purpose
ARRIVE	Processes type 1 events
DEPART(RTEL)	Processes type 2 events, where RTEL (real-valued) is the number of the teller completing a service
JOCKEY(TELLER)	Jockeys a customer from one queue to another where TELLER (integer-valued) is the number of the teller completing a service (JOCKEY is called from DEPART and is not an *event* subroutine)
REPORT	Generates report and is called from the main program when the simulation ends (at *or after* 5 P.M.)

	Definition
Input parameters:	
LENGTH	Amount of time (hours) bank's doors are open
MARRVT	Mean interarrival time
MAXTEL	Maximum number of tellers
MINTEL	Minimum number of tellers
MSERVT	Mean service time
Modeling variables:	
CHOICE	Number of queue an arriving customer will join
DELAY	Delay in queue of a customer
DIFF	Absolute value of the difference between TELLER and the number of the queue from which a customer will jockey
INDEX	Number of list corresponding to teller TELLER
INDEXS	Number of list corresponding to teller SERVER
K	Absolute value of TELLER $-$ SERVER
NUMS	Number of customers in front of teller SERVER
NUMT	Number of customers in front of teller TELLER, plus 1
NUMTEL	Number of tellers for a particular simulation run
ORIGIN	Number of queue from which a customer will jockey
RTEL	Number of teller completing service
SERVER	Number of queue being considered for jockeying
SHORT	Number of customers in the shortest queue upon a customer's arrival
TELLER	Number of a particular teller or corresponding queue
Output variables:	
AVGDEL	Average delay in queue
AVGNIQ	Average total number of customers in queue
MAXDEL	Maximum delay in queue

dummy record in the teller's corresponding list, and a departure event is scheduled for the customer. If all tellers are busy, a record containing the time of arrival of the arriving customer is placed at the tail of the list corresponding to the shortest queue.

Event subroutine DEPART, with the flowchart and listing given in Figs. 2.20 and 2.21, is called from the main program when a customer completes service. If no customers are waiting in the queue of the teller who has just completed the service, this teller becomes idle (by removing the dummy record from the corresponding list) and subroutine JOCKEY is called to determine whether a customer from another

```
C
C *** MAIN PROGRAM.
C
      INTEGER MAXTEL,MINTEL,NUMTEL
      REAL LENGTH,MARRVT,MSERVT
      COMMON /MODEL/ MARRVT,MSERVT,NUMTEL
      COMMON /SYSTEM/ LRANK(25),LSIZE(25),MAXATR,NEXT,TIME,TRNSFR(10)
C
C *** READ INPUT PARAMETERS.
C
      READ 10,MINTEL,MAXTEL
   10 FORMAT(2I10)
      READ 20,MARRVT,MSERVT
   20 FORMAT(2F10.0)
      READ 30,LENGTH
   30 FORMAT(F10.0)
C
C *****************************************************************
C
C *** PRINT REPORT HEADING.
C
      PRINT 40
   40 FORMAT(1H1,5X,'BANK WITH EACH TELLER HAVING ITS OWN QUEUE AND JOCK
     1EYING')
      PRINT 50,MARRVT
   50 FORMAT(1H0,5X,'MEAN INTERARRIVAL TIME',5X,F6.3,' MINUTES')
      PRINT 60,MSERVT
   60 FORMAT(1H0,5X,'MEAN SERVICE TIME',10X,F6.3,' MINUTES')
      PRINT 70,LENGTH
   70 FORMAT(1H0,5X,'BANK CLOSES AFTER',10X,F6.3,' HOURS')
      PRINT 80
   80 FORMAT(//)
      PRINT 90
   90 FORMAT(1H0,5X,'NUMBER OF TELLERS',5X,'AVERAGE NUMBER IN QUEUE',5X,
     1'AVERAGE DELAY IN QUEUE',5X,'MAXIMUM DELAY IN QUEUE')
C
C *****************************************************************
C
C *** RUN THE SIMULATION VARYING THE NUMBER OF TELLERS.
C
      DO 150 NUMTEL=MINTEL,MAXTEL
C
C *** INITIALIZE SUPPORT ROUTINES.
C
      CALL INITLK
      MAXATR=3
C *** SCHEDULE THE FIRST ARRIVAL.
C
      TRNSFR(1)=EXPON(MARRVT)
      TRNSFR(2)=1.
      CALL FILE(3,25)
C
C *** SCHEDULE THE BANK CLOSING.
C
      TRNSFR(1)=60.*LENGTH
      TRNSFR(2)=3.
      CALL FILE(3,25)
C
C *** DETERMINE THE NEXT EVENT.
C
  100 CALL TIMING
C
C *** CALL THE APPROPRIATE EVENT ROUTINE.
C
      GO TO (110,120,130),NEXT
  110 CALL ARRIVE
      GO TO 100
  120 CALL DEPART(TRNSFR(3))
      GO TO 140
  130 CALL CANCEL(1.)
C
C *** IF THE BANK IS CLOSED AND NO CUSTOMERS ARE PRESENT, END THE
C *** SIMULATION.
C
  140 IF(LSIZE(25).GT.0) GO TO 100
      CALL REPORT
  150 CONTINUE
      PRINT 160
  160 FORMAT(1H1)
      STOP
      END
```

Figure 2.17 FORTRAN listing for the main program, bank model.

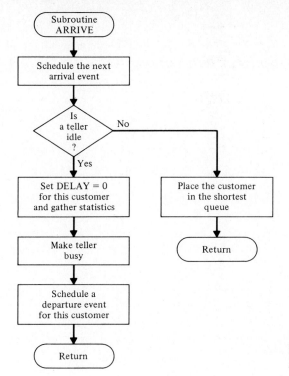

Figure 2.18 Flowchart for subroutine ARRIVE, bank model.

queue can jockey. If the queue of the completing teller is not empty, the first customer in the queue is removed, his delay is computed, delay statistics are updated,
a departure event is scheduled for him, and subroutine JOCKEY is called.

Subroutine JOCKEY is called with an argument of TELLER to see whether a
customer can jockey to the queue corresponding to teller TELLER from another
(longer) queue. Its flowchart and listing are given in Figs. 2.22 and 2.23. The number
of the queue from which a customer will jockey is determined, using the rule given
in Sec. 2.5.1, and placed in the variable ORIGIN. (If there is no customer to jockey,
as indicated by ORIGIN = 0, control is returned to the main program.) Then the
customer from the tail of queue ORIGIN is removed. If teller TELLER is idle, the
delay of the jockeying customer is computed, teller TELLER is made busy, and
service is begun on the customer. If the teller is busy, the jockeying customer is
placed at the tail of queue TELLER.

A listing for the report generator, subroutine REPORT, is given in Fig. 2.24.
The time-average number of customers in queue TELLER is computed by calling
library subroutine FILEST with an argument of TELLER. By summing these averages over all tellers, the time-average total number of customers in queue, AVGNIQ,
is obtained. The average and maximum customer delay are computed and placed in
TRNSFR(1) and TRNSFR(3), respectively, by appropriately calling SAMPST.

```
      SUBROUTINE ARRIVE
      INTEGER CHOICE,INDEX,NUMTEL,SHORT,TELLER
      REAL DELAY,MARRVT,MSERVT
      COMMON /MODEL/ MARRVT,MSERVT,NUMTEL
      COMMON /SYSTEM/ LRANK(25),LSIZE(25),MAXATR,NEXT,TIME,TRNSFR(10)
C
C *** SCHEDULE THE NEXT ARRIVAL.
C
      TRNSFR(1)=TIME+EXPON(MARRVT)
      TRNSFR(2)=1.
      CALL FILE(3,25)
C
C ***********************************************************************
C
C *** IF A TELLER IS IDLE, START SERVICE ON THE ARRIVING CUSTOMER.
C
      DO 10 TELLER=1,NUMTEL
      INDEX=NUMTEL+TELLER
      IF(LSIZE(INDEX).EQ.0) GO TO 20
   10 CONTINUE
      GO TO 30
C
C *** CUSTOMER HAS A DELAY OF ZERO.
C
   20 DELAY=0.
      CALL SAMPST(DELAY,1)
C
C *** MAKE TELLER BUSY (ATTRIBUTES ARE IRRELEVANT).
C
      CALL FILE(1,INDEX)
C
C *** SCHEDULE A SERVICE COMPLETION.
C
      TRNSFR(1)=TIME+EXPON(MSERVT)
      TRNSFR(2)=2.
      TRNSFR(3)=TELLER
      CALL FILE(3,25)
      RETURN
C
C ***********************************************************************
C
C *** ALL TELLERS ARE BUSY, FIND THE SHORTEST QUEUE.
C
   30 SHORT=1000000
      DO 40 TELLER=1,NUMTEL
      IF(LSIZE(TELLER).GE.SHORT) GO TO 40
      SHORT=LSIZE(TELLER)
      CHOICE=TELLER
   40 CONTINUE
C
C *** PLACE THE CUSTOMER IN THE SHORTEST QUEUE.
C
      TRNSFR(1)=TIME
      CALL FILE(2,CHOICE)
      RETURN
      END
```

Figure 2.19 FORTRAN listing for subroutine ARRIVE, bank model.

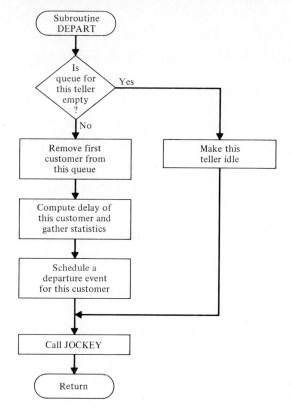

Figure 2.20 Flowchart for subroutine DEPART, bank model.

2.5.3 Simulation Output and Discussion

The results from simulating the bank with $n = 5$, 6, and 7 tellers are given in Fig. 2.25. It appears that it would be desirable for the bank to add a sixth teller since this would reduce the average delay from 3.69 to 0.85 minute. The addition of a seventh teller might be questionable, depending on the cost of hiring a teller.

2.6 A JOB-SHOP MODEL

In this section, we use SIMLIB to simulate a model of a manufacturing facility. This example, the most complex one we have considered, illustrates how simulation can be used to identify bottlenecks in a production process.

2.6.1 Statement of the Problem

A manufacturing shop consists of five groups of machines, and at present groups 1, 2, ..., 5 consist of 3, 2, 4, 3, and 1 identical machines, respectively (see Fig. 2.26).

```
      SUBROUTINE DEPART(RTEL)
      INTEGER INDEX,NUMTEL,TELLER
      REAL DELAY,MARRVT,MSERVT,RTEL
      COMMON /MODEL/ MARRVT,MSERVT,NUMTEL
      COMMON /SYSTEM/ LRANK(25),LSIZE(25),MAXATR,NEXT,TIME,TRNSFR(10)
      TELLER=RTEL
C
C *** IF THE QUEUE IS EMPTY, MAKE THE TELLER IDLE.
C
      IF(LSIZE(TELLER).GT.0) GO TO 10
      INDEX=NUMTEL+TELLER
      CALL REMOVE(1,INDEX)
      GO TO 20
C
C ***********************************************************************
C
C *** SINCE THE QUEUE IS NOT EMPTY, START SERVICE ON A CUSTOMER.
C
   10 CALL REMOVE(1,TELLER)
      DELAY=TIME-TRNSFR(1)
      CALL SAMPST(DELAY,1)
      TRNSFR(1)=TIME+EXPON(MSERVT)
      TRNSFR(2)=2.
      TRNSFR(3)=TELLER
      CALL FILE(3,25)
C
C ***********************************************************************
C
C *** LET ANOTHER CUSTOMER JOCKEY IF POSSIBLE.
C
   20 CALL JOCKEY(TELLER)
      RETURN
      END
```

Figure 2.21 FORTRAN listing for subroutine DEPART, bank model.

(In effect, the shop is a network of five multiserver queues.) Assume that jobs arrive at the shop with interarrival times that are IID exponential random variables with mean 0.25 hour. There are three types of jobs, and jobs are of types 1, 2, 3 with respective probabilities 0.3, 0.5, and 0.2. Job types 1, 2, 3 require 4, 3, 5 tasks to be done, respectively, and each task must be done at a specified machine group and in a prescribed order. The routings for the different job types are as follows:

Job type	Machine groups in routing
1	3, 1, 2, 5
2	4, 1, 3
3	2, 5, 1, 4, 3

Thus, type 2 jobs first have a task done at group 4, then have a task done at group 1, and finally have a task done at group 3.

If a job arrives at a particular machine group and finds all machines in that group already busy, the job joins a single FIFO queue at that machine group. The time to perform a task at a particular machine is an independent 2-Erlang random variable whose mean depends on the job type and the group to which the machine belongs. (If X is a 2-Erlang random variable with mean m, then $X = Y_1 + Y_2$,

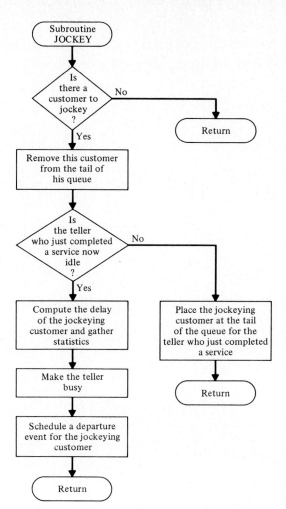

Figure 2.22 Flowchart for subroutine JOCKEY, bank model.

where Y_1 and Y_2 are independent exponential random variables with mean $m/2$. Alternatively, X is known as a gamma random variable with shape parameter 2 and scale parameter $m/2$. See Chap. 5 for further details.) We chose the 2-Erlang distribution to represent service times because experience has shown that if one collects data on the time to perform some task in the real world, the histogram of these data will often have a shape similar to that of the density function for a 2-Erlang distribution. The mean service time for each job type and each task are as follows:

Job type	Mean service times for successive tasks, hours
1	0.50, 0.60, 0.85, 0.50
2	1.10, 0.80, 0.75
3	1.20, 0.25, 0.70, 0.90, 1.00

```
      SUBROUTINE JOCKEY(TELLER)
      INTEGER DIFF,INDEX,INDEXS,K,NUMS,NUMT,NUMTEL,ORIGIN,SERVER,TELLER
      REAL DELAY,MARRVT,MSERVT
      COMMON /MODEL/ MARRVT,MSERVT,NUMTEL
      COMMON /SYSTEM/ LRANK(25),LSIZE(25),MAXATR,NEXT,TIME,TRNSFR(10)
C
C *** FIND THE ORIGIN OF THE CUSTOMER WHO WILL JOCKEY TO QUEUE 'TELLER,'
C *** IF THERE IS SUCH A CUSTOMER.
C
      ORIGIN=0
      DIFF=1000
      INDEX=NUMTEL+TELLER
      NUMT=LSIZE(TELLER)+LSIZE(INDEX)+1
      DO 10 SERVER=1,NUMTEL
      IF(SERVER.EQ.TELLER) GO TO 10
      INDEXS=NUMTEL+SERVER
      NUMS=LSIZE(SERVER)+LSIZE(INDEXS)
      K=IABS(TELLER-SERVER)
      IF((NUMS.LE.NUMT).OR.(K.GE.DIFF)) GO TO 10
      DIFF=K
      ORIGIN=SERVER
   10 CONTINUE
C
C *** IF NO CUSTOMER WAS FOUND, RETURN.
C
      IF(ORIGIN.EQ.0) RETURN
C
C *** SINCE A CUSTOMER WAS FOUND, REMOVE HIM FROM HIS ORIGINAL QUEUE.
C
      CALL REMOVE(2,ORIGIN)
C
C *** IF THE TELLER OF THE NEW QUEUE IS BUSY, PLACE THE CUSTOMER IN THE
C *** QUEUE.
C
      IF(LSIZE(INDEX).EQ.0) GO TO 20
      CALL FILE(2,TELLER)
      RETURN
C
C *** SINCE THE TELLER IS IDLE, START SERVICE ON THE JOCKEYING CUSTOMER.
C
   20 DELAY=TIME-TRNSFR(1)
      CALL SAMPST(DELAY,1)
      CALL FILE(1,INDEX)
      TRNSFR(1)=TIME+EXPON(MSERVT)
      TRNSFR(2)=2.
      TRNSFR(3)=TELLER
      CALL FILE(3,25)
      RETURN
      END
```

Figure 2.23 FORTRAN listing for subroutine JOCKEY, bank model.

```
      SUBROUTINE REPORT
      INTEGER NUMTEL,TELLER
      REAL AVGDEL,AVGNIQ,MARRVT,MAXDEL,MSERVT
      COMMON /MODEL/ MARRVT,MSERVT,NUMTEL
      COMMON /SYSTEM/ LRANK(25),LSIZE(25),MAXATR,NEXT,TIME,TRNSFR(10)
      AVGNIQ=0.
      DO 10 TELLER=1,NUMTEL
      CALL FILEST(TELLER)
      AVGNIQ=AVGNIQ+TRNSFR(1)
   10 CONTINUE
      CALL SAMPST(0.,-1)
      AVGDEL=TRNSFR(1)
      MAXDEL=TRNSFR(3)
      PRINT 20,NUMTEL,AVGNIQ,AVGDEL,MAXDEL
   20 FORMAT(1H0,13X,I1,21X,F6.3,22X,F6.3,21X,F6.3)
      RETURN
      END
```

Figure 2.24 FORTRAN listing for subroutine REPORT, bank model.

```
BANK WITH EACH TELLER HAVING ITS OWN QUEUE AND JOCKEYING
MEAN INTERARRIVAL TIME      1.000 MINUTES
MEAN SERVICE TIME           4.500 MINUTES
BANK CLOSES AFTER           8.000 HOURS


NUMBER OF TELLERS    AVERAGE NUMBER IN QUEUE    AVERAGE DELAY IN QUEUE    MAXIMUM DELAY IN QUEUE
       5                    3.851                     3.691                    24.467
       6                     .895                      .854                    13.310
       7                     .334                      .318                    10.229
```

Figure 2.25 Simulation report for the bank model.

Thus, a type 2 job requires a mean service time of 1.10 hours at machine group 4 (the group where its first task will be done).

Assuming no loss of continuity between successive days' operations of the shop, we simulate the shop for 365 eight-hour days and estimate the average total delay in queue (exclusive of service times) for each job type and the overall average job total delay. We use the true probabilities 0.3, 0.5, 0.2 in computing the latter quantity. In addition, we estimate the average number in queue, the average utilization

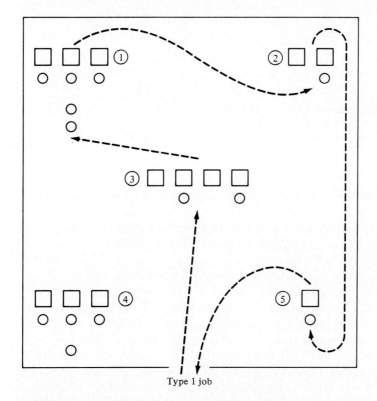

Figure 2.26 Manufacturing shop with five machine groups, showing the route of type 1 jobs.

(using the library subroutine TIMEST), and the average delay in queue for each machine group.

Suppose all machines cost approximately the same amount and the shop has enough money to purchase one new machine with an eye toward improving the shop's efficiency. We use the results of the above simulation to decide what additional simulation runs should be made. (Each of these runs will involve 14 total machines, which is 1 more than the original number.) From these additional runs, we use the overall average job total delay to decide what type of machine the shop should purchase.

2.6.2 SIMLIB Program

The events for this model are quite straightforward and are as follows:

Event description	Event type
Arrival of a job to the shop	1
Departure of a job from a particular machine group	2
End of the simulation	3

The required lists for this model and their attributes are:

List	Attribute 1	Attribute 2	Attribute 3	Attribute 4
1 to 5, queues	Time of arrival to machine group	Job type	Task number	
25, event list	Event time	Event type	Job type	Task number

(By "task number" we mean the number of the current task for a particular job. For example, task number 2 for job type 3 refers to the task which is to be done at machine group 5.) The program for this model consists of a main program and the user-written subprograms and FORTRAN variables shown in Table 2.3.

The FORTRAN listing for the main program is given in Fig. 2.27. Note that the main program contains the labeled common block RANDOM since the library function RANDI is used to generate the job type of an arriving job.

Subroutine ARRIVE, flowcharted and listed in Figs. 2.28 and 2.29, begins with a check to determine whether this is a new arrival to the shop (NEW = 1) or if this arrival has been routed from another machine group (NEW = 2). If NEW = 1, the job type of the arrival, JOBTYP, is generated by calling RANDI and TASK is set to 1. In addition, the next (new) arrival event is scheduled. If NEW = 2, then JOBTYP and TASK were set in subroutine DEPART and are members of the com-

Table 2.3 Subprograms and FORTRAN variables for job-shop model

Subprograms	Purpose
ARRIVE(NEW)	Processes arrival of a job where NEW = 1 if this is a new job arriving to the shop (type 1 event) and NEW = 2 if the job has been routed after completing service at another machine group
DEPART	Processes type 2 events
REPORT	Generates report, called when the simulation ends (type 3 event)
ERLANG(K,RMEAN)	Generates a K-Erlang random variable (K = positive integer) with mean RMEAN (real-valued)

	Definition
Input parameters:	
LENGTH	Length of the simulation, 8-hour days
MARRVT	Mean interarrival time of jobs, hours
MSERVT(I,J)	Mean service time of task J for job type I, hours
NGROUP	Number of machine groups
NMACHS(I)	Number of machines in machine group I
NTASKS(I)	Number of tasks for job type I
NTYPES	Number of job types
PROBD(I)	Probability of a job type $\leq$ I
ROUTE(I,J)	Number of the machine group corresponding to task J for job type I
Modeling variables:	
DELAY	Delay of a job at a particular machine group
GROUP	Machine group of a particular job
INDEX	Number of SAMPST variable corresponding to delays for a particular job type
JOBTQ	Job type of a job leaving *queue* and entering service at a particular machine group
JOBTYP	Job type of a job
NBUSY(I)	Number of busy machines in machine group I
NEW	See discussion of event subroutine ARRIVE above
RNBUSY	Number of busy machines at a particular machine group (real-valued)
SUM	Distribution function of a particular job type's occurring (used in subroutine REPORT)
TASK	Current task number of a job [1 $\leq$ TASK $\leq$ NTASKS(I) for job type I]
TASKQ	Current task number of a job leaving *queue* and entering service at a particular machine group
Output variables:	
AJDEL(I)	Average total delay in queue for job type I
AMDEL(I)	Average delay in queue at machine group I
AUTIL(I)	Average utilization of the machines in machine group I
AVGNIQ(I)	Average number in queue at machine group I
OAJDEL	Overall average job delay in queue

```
C
C *** MAIN PROGRAM.
C
      INTEGER I,J,JOBTYP,NBUSY(8),NGROUP,NMACHS(8),NTASKS(8),NTSKS
      INTEGER NTYPES,ROUTE(8,8),TASK
      REAL LENGTH,MARRVT,MSERVT(8,8)
      COMMON /MODEL/ JOBTYP,LENGTH,MARRVT,MSERVT,NBUSY,NGROUP,NMACHS,
     1NTASKS,NTYPES,ROUTE,TASK
      COMMON /RANDOM/ NVALUE,PROBD(25)
      COMMON /SYSTEM/ LRANK(25),LSIZE(25),MAXATR,NEXT,TIME,TRNSFR(10)
C
C *** READ INPUT PARAMETERS.
C
      READ 10,NGROUP
   10 FORMAT(I10)
      READ 20,(NMACHS(I),I=1,NGROUP)
   20 FORMAT(8I10)
      READ 10,NTYPES
      READ 20,(NTASKS(I),I=1,NTYPES)
      DO 40 I=1,NTYPES
      NTSKS=NTASKS(I)
      READ 20,(ROUTE(I,J),J=1,NTSKS)
      READ 30,(MSERVT(I,J),J=1,NTSKS)
   30 FORMAT(8F10.0)
   40 CONTINUE
      READ 50,MARRVT
   50 FORMAT(F10.0)
      READ 30,(PROBD(I),I=1,NTYPES)
      READ 50,LENGTH
C
C *** SPECIFY NVALUE FOR LIBRARY FUNCTION RANDI.
C
      NVALUE=NTYPES
C
C *********************************************************************
C
      DO 60 I=1,NGROUP
      NBUSY(I)=0
   60 CONTINUE
C
C *** INITIALIZE SUPPORT ROUTINES.
C
      CALL INITLK
      MAXATR=4
C
C *** SCHEDULE THE ARRIVAL OF THE FIRST JOB.
C
      TRNSFR(1)=EXPON(MARRVT)
      TRNSFR(2)=1.
      CALL FILE(3,25)
C
C *** SCHEDULE THE END OF THE SIMULATION.
C
      TRNSFR(1)=8.*LENGTH
      TRNSFR(2)=3.
      CALL FILE(3,25)
C
C *** DETERMINE THE NEXT EVENT.
C
   70 CALL TIMING
C
C *** CALL THE APPROPRIATE EVENT ROUTINE.
C
      GO TO (80,90,100),NEXT
   80 CALL ARRIVE(1)
      GO TO 70
   90 CALL DEPART
      GO TO 70
  100 CALL REPORT
      PRINT 110
  110 FORMAT(1H1)
      STOP
      END
```

Figure 2.27 FORTRAN listing for the main program, job-shop model.

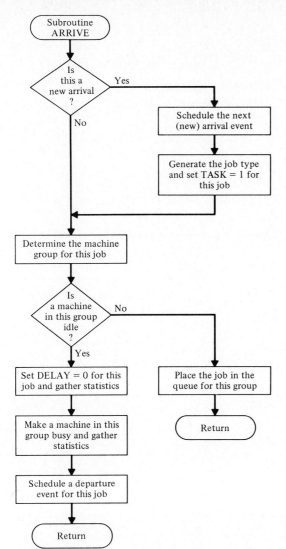

Figure 2.28 Flowchart for subroutine ARRIVE, job-shop model.

mon block MODEL. In either case, JOBTYP and TASK are used to determine the machine group of the arriving job, GROUP, and then the job is processed as in previous queueing examples. Observe that two types of statistics are computed for the delay of a job, DELAY. By calling SAMPST with arguments of DELAY and GROUP, statistics on the delays of all jobs at a particular machine group are obtained. On the other hand, calling SAMPST with arguments of DELAY and INDEX = NGROUP + JOBTYP produces statistics on the delays for jobs with job type JOBTYP. (See the discussion of REPORT for further comment.) Time-average statistics on the number of busy machines at machine group GROUP are obtained by calling TIMEST with arguments of RNBUSY = NBUSY(GROUP) and GROUP. (Recall that the first argument for TIMEST must be real-valued.)

```
      SUBROUTINE ARRIVE(NEW)
      INTEGER GROUP,INDEX,JOBTYP,NBUSY(8),NEW,NGROUP,NMACHS(8),NTASKS(8)
      INTEGER NTYPES,ROUTE(8,8),TASK
      REAL DELAY,LENGTH,MARRVT,MSERVT(8,8),RNBUSY
      COMMON /MODEL/ JOBTYP,LENGTH,MARRVT,MSERVT,NBUSY,NGROUP,NMACHS,
     1NTASKS,NTYPES,ROUTE,TASK
      COMMON /SYSTEM/ LRANK(25),LSIZE(25),MAXATR,NEXT,TIME,TRNSFR(10)
C
C *** IF THIS IS A NEW ARRIVAL TO THE SHOP, GENERATE THE TIME OF THE
C *** NEXT ARRIVAL AND DETERMINE THE JOB TYPE AND TASK NUMBER OF THE
C *** ARRIVING JOB.
C
      IF(NEW.GT.1) GO TO 10
      TRNSFR(1)=TIME+EXPON(MARRVT)
      TRNSFR(2)=1.
      CALL FILE(3,25)
      JOBTYP=RANDI(Z)
      TASK=1
   10 GROUP=ROUTE(JOBTYP,TASK)
C
C ******************************************************************************
C
C *** IF A MACHINE IN THIS GROUP IS IDLE, START SERVICE ON THE ARRIVING
C *** JOB.
C
      IF(NBUSY(GROUP).EQ.NMACHS(GROUP)) GO TO 20
C
C *** THE JOB HAS A DELAY OF ZERO.
C
      DELAY=0.
      CALL SAMPST(DELAY,GROUP)
      INDEX=NGROUP+JOBTYP
      CALL SAMPST(DELAY,INDEX)
      NBUSY(GROUP)=NBUSY(GROUP)+1
      RNBUSY=NBUSY(GROUP)
      CALL TIMEST(RNBUSY,GROUP)
C
C *** SCHEDULE A SERVICE COMPLETION.
C
      TRNSFR(1)=TIME+ERLANG(2,MSERVT(JOBTYP,TASK))
      TRNSFR(2)=2.
      TRNSFR(3)=JOBTYP
      TRNSFR(4)=TASK
      CALL FILE(3,25)
      RETURN
C
C ******************************************************************************
C
C *** SINCE ALL MACHINES IN THIS GROUP ARE BUSY, PLACE THE ARRIVING JOB
C *** IN THE APPROPRIATE QUEUE. NOTE THAT THE FOLLOWING DATA ARE STORED
C *** FOR EACH JOB:
C ***     1. TIME OF ARRIVAL TO THIS MACHINE GROUP.
C ***     2. JOB TYPE.
C ***     3. CURRENT TASK NUMBER.
C
   20 TRNSFR(1)=TIME
      TRNSFR(2)=JOBTYP
      TRNSFR(3)=TASK
      CALL FILE(2,GROUP)
      RETURN
      END
```

Figure 2.29 FORTRAN listing for subroutine ARRIVE, job-shop model.

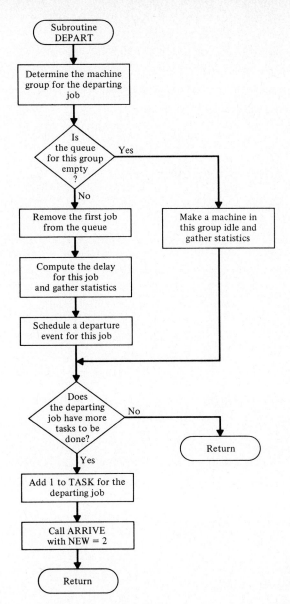

Figure 2.30 Flowchart for subroutine DEPART, job-shop model.

A flowchart and listing for subroutine DEPART are given in Figs. 2.30 and 2.31. The job type, JOBTYP, and task number, TASK, of the departing job are obtained from the departure event record which was placed in the TRNSFR array by TIMING, and then processing proceeds in a straightforward manner. The subroutine concludes with a check to determine whether the departing job has one or more machine groups yet to visit. If so, TASK is incremented by 1 and the job is routed to its next machine group by calling ARRIVE with NEW = 2.

```
      SUBROUTINE DEPART
      INTEGER GROUP,INDEX,JOBTQ,JOBTYP,NBUSY(8),NGROUP,NMACHS(8)
      INTEGER NTASKS(8),NTYPES,ROUTE(8,3),TASK,TASKQ
      REAL DELAY,LENGTH,MARRVT,MSERVT(8,8),RNBUSY
      COMMON /MODEL/ JOBTYP,LENGTH,MARRVT,MSERVT,NBUSY,NGROUP,NMACHS,
     1NTASKS,NTYPES,ROUTE,TASK
      COMMON /SYSTEM/ LRANK(25),LSIZE(25),MAXATR,NEXT,TIME,TRNSFR(10)
C
C *** DETERMINE THE MACHINE GROUP OF THE DEPARTING JOB.
C
      JOBTYP=TRNSFR(3)
      TASK=TRNSFR(4)
      GROUP=ROUTE(JOBTYP,TASK)
C
C *** IF THE QUEUE FOR THIS MACHINE GROUP IS EMPTY, MAKE A MACHINE IN
C *** THIS GROUP IDLE.
C
      IF(LSIZE(GROUP).GT.0) GO TO 10
      NBUSY(GROUP)=NBUSY(GROUP)-1
      RNBUSY=NBUSY(GROUP)
      CALL TIMEST(RNBUSY,GROUP)
      GO TO 20
C
C *********************************************************************
C
C *** SINCE THE QUEUE FOR THIS MACHINE GROUP IS NOT EMPTY, START SERVICE
C *** ON A JOB.
C
   10 CALL REMOVE(1,GROUP)
      DELAY=TIME-TRNSFR(1)
      CALL SAMPST(DELAY,GROUP)
      JOBTQ=TRNSFR(2)
      TASKQ=TRNSFR(3)
      INDEX=NGROUP+JOBTQ
      CALL SAMPST(DELAY,INDEX)
      TRNSFR(1)=TIME+ERLANG(2,MSERVT(JOBTQ,TASKQ))
      TRNSFR(2)=2.
      TRNSFR(3)=JOBTQ
      TRNSFR(4)=TASKQ
      CALL FILE(3,25)
C
C *********************************************************************
C
C *** IF THE DEPARTING JOB HAS ONE OR MORE TASKS YET TO BE DONE, SEND
C *** THE JOB TO THE NEXT MACHINE GROUP ON ITS ROUTE.
C
   20 IF(TASK.EQ.NTASKS(JOBTYP)) RETURN
      TASK=TASK+1
      CALL ARRIVE(2)
      RETURN
      END
```

Figure 2.31 FORTRAN listing for subroutine DEPART, job-shop model.

The FORTRAN listing for the report generator REPORT is given in Fig. 2.32. In order to compute the average total delay for job type I, SAMPST is called with argument of 0. and $-INDEX = -(NGROUP + I)$ and the desired quantity is then given by TRNSFR(1) times NTASKS(I) since SAMPST was called NTASKS(I) times for each job (exclusive of the calls for the machine groups) rather than once.

The program for function ERLANG is straightforward and is listed in Fig. 2.33.

```
      SUBROUTINE REPORT
      INTEGER I,INDEX,J,JOBTYP,NBUSY(8),NGROUP,NMACHS(8),NTASKS(8),NTSKS
      INTEGER NTYPES,ROUTE(8,8),TASK
      REAL AJDEL(8),AMDEL(8),AUTIL(8),AVGNIQ(8),LENGTH,MARRVT
      REAL MSERVT(8,8),OAJDEL,SUM
      COMMON /MODEL/ JOBTYP,LENGTH,MARRVT,MSERVT,NBUSY,NGROUP,NMACHS,
     1NTASKS,NTYPES,ROUTE,TASK
      COMMON /RANDOM/ NVALUE,PROBD(25)
      COMMON /SYSTEM/ LRANK(25),LSIZE(25),MAXATR,NEXT,TIME,TRNSFR(10)
      PRINT 10
   10 FORMAT(1H1,5X,'JOB SHOP MODEL - INPUT DATA')
      PRINT 20
   20 FORMAT(//)
      PRINT 30,NGROUP
   30 FORMAT(1H0,5X,'NUMBER OF MACHINE GROUPS',15X,I5)
      PRINT 40,(NMACHS(I),I=1,NGROUP)
   40 FORMAT(1H0,5X,'NUMBER OF MACHINES IN EACH GROUP',7X,8I5)
      PRINT 50,NTYPES
   50 FORMAT(1H0,5X,'NUMBER OF JOB TYPES',20X,I5)
      PRINT 60,(NTASKS(I),I=1,NTYPES)
   60 FORMAT(1H0,5X,'NUMBER OF TASKS FOR EACH JOB TYPE',6X,8I5)
      PRINT 70,(PROBD(I),I=1,NTYPES)
   70 FORMAT(1H0,5X,'DISTRIBUTION FUNCTION OF JOB TYPES',5X,8(F5.3,3X))
      PRINT 80,MARRVT
   80 FORMAT(1H0,5X,'MEAN INTERARRIVAL TIME OF JOBS',9X,F5.2,' HOURS')
      PRINT 90,LENGTH
   90 FORMAT(1H0,5X,'LENGTH OF THE SIMULATION',15X,F5.1,' EIGHT HOUR DAY
     1S')
      PRINT 20
      PRINT 100
  100 FORMAT(1H0,5X,'ROUTING FOR EACH JOB TYPE:')
      PRINT 20
      PRINT 110
  110 FORMAT(1H0,5X,'JOB TYPE',5X,'MACHINE GROUPS')
      DO 130 I=1,NTYPES
      NTSKS=NTASKS(I)
      PRINT 120,I,(ROUTE(I,J),J=1,NTSKS)
  120 FORMAT(1H0,9X,I1,8X,8I5)
  130 CONTINUE
      PRINT 20
      PRINT 140
  140 FORMAT(1H0,5X,'MEAN SERVICE TIME FOR EACH JOB TYPE AND EACH TASK:'
     1)
      PRINT 20
      PRINT 150
  150 FORMAT(1H0,5X,'JOB TYPE',5X,'MEAN SERVICE TIMES(IN HOURS) FOR SUCC
     1ESSIVE TASKS')
      DO 170 I=1,NTYPES
      NTSKS=NTASKS(I)
      PRINT 160,I,(MSERVT(I,J),J=1,NTSKS)
  160 FORMAT(1H0,9X,I1,8X,8(F5.2,3X))
  170 CONTINUE
C
C *** COMPUTE THE AVERAGE TOTAL DELAY IN QUEUE FOR EACH JOB TYPE AND THE
C *** OVERALL AVERAGE CUSTOMER DELAY.
C
      OAJDEL=0.
      SUM=0.
      DO 180 I=1,NTYPES
      INDEX=NGROUP+I
      CALL SAMPST(0.,-INDEX)
      AJDEL(I)=TRNSFR(1)*NTASKS(I)
      OAJDEL=OAJDEL+(PROBD(I)-SUM)*AJDEL(I)
      SUM=PROBD(I)
  180 CONTINUE
```

Figure 2.32 FORTRAN listing for subroutine REPORT, job-shop model.

```
C
C *** COMPUTE THE AVERAGE NUMBER IN QUEUE, THE AVERAGE UTILIZATION, AND
C *** THE AVERAGE DELAY IN QUEUE FOR EACH MACHINE GROUP.
C
      DO 190 I=1,NGROUP
      CALL SAMPST(0.,-I)
      AMDEL(I)=TRNSFR(1)
      CALL FILEST(I)
      AVGNIQ(I)=TRNSFR(1)
      CALL TIMEST(0.,-I)
      AUTIL(I)=TRNSFR(1)/NMACHS(I)
  190 CONTINUE
      PRINT 200
  200 FORMAT(1H1,5X,'JOB SHOP MODEL - JOB TYPE REPORT')
      PRINT 20
      PRINT 210
  210 FORMAT(1H0,5X,'JOB TYPE',5X,'AVERAGE TOTAL DELAY IN QUEUE')
      DO 230 I=1,NTYPES
      PRINT 220,I,AJDEL(I)
  220 FORMAT(1H0,9X,I1,19X,F6.3)
  230 CONTINUE
      PRINT 20
      PRINT 240,OAJDEL
  240 FORMAT(1H0,5X,'OVERALL AVERAGE JOB TOTAL DELAY',5X,F6.3)
      PRINT 250
  250 FORMAT(1H1,5X,'JOB SHOP MODEL - MACHINE GROUP REPORT')
      PRINT 20
      PRINT 260
  260 FORMAT(1H0,5X,'MACHINE GROUP',5X,'AVERAGE NUMBER IN QUEUE',5X,'AVE
     1RAGE UTILIZATION',5X,'AVERAGE DELAY IN QUEUE')
      DO 280 I=1,NGROUP
      PRINT 270,I,AVGNIQ(I),AUTIL(I),AMDEL(I)
  270 FORMAT(1H0,11X,I1,19X,F6.3,21X,F5.3,20X,F6.3)
  280 CONTINUE
      RETURN
      END
```

Figure 2.32 (*continued*)

```
      FUNCTION ERLANG(K,RMEAN)
      INTEGER I,K
      REAL MEXP,RMEAN,SUM
C
C *** THIS FUNCTION GENERATES A K - ERLANG RANDOM VARIABLE.
C
      MEXP=RMEAN/K
      SUM=0.
      DO 10 I=1,K
      SUM=SUM+EXPON(MEXP)
   10 CONTINUE
      ERLANG=SUM
      RETURN
      END
```

Figure 2.33 FORTRAN listing for function ERLANG, job-shop model.

2.6.3 Simulation Output and Discussion

Figures 2.34 to 2.36 give the output resulting from running the simulation model with the job shop's current configuration of machines. From the machine-group report, it appears that machine groups 2, 4, and 1 may be bottlenecks for the job shop. We thus made three additional runs to see which type of new machine will have the greatest impact on the shop's efficiency. (For the first of these runs, the number of machines in group 2 was increased by 1, while the numbers of machines

```
JOB SHOP MODEL - INPUT DATA


NUMBER OF MACHINE GROUPS                5

NUMBER OF MACHINES IN EACH GROUP        3    2    4    3    1

NUMBER OF JOB TYPES                     3

NUMBER OF TASKS FOR EACH JOB TYPE       4    3    5

DISTRIBUTION FUNCTION OF JOB TYPES     .300     .800    1.000

MEAN INTERARRIVAL TIME OF JOBS         .25 HOURS

LENGTH OF THE SIMULATION            365.0 EIGHT HOUR DAYS



ROUTING FOR EACH JOB TYPE:


JOB TYPE      MACHINE GROUPS
   1              3    1    2    5
   2              4    1    3
   3              2    5    1    4    3



MEAN SERVICE TIME FOR EACH JOB TYPE AND EACH TASK:


JOB TYPE      MEAN SERVICE TIMES(IN HOURS) FOR SUCCESSIVE TASKS
   1            .50     .60     .85     .50
   2           1.10     .80     .75
   3           1.20     .25     .70     .90     1.00
```

Figure 2.34 Listing of the input data for the job-shop model.

```
JOB SHOP MODEL - JOB TYPE REPORT


JOB TYPE        AVERAGE TOTAL DELAY IN QUEUE
   1                       13.293

   2                        8.066

   3                       17.879
```

Figure 2.35 Job-type report for the job-shop model.

```
OVERALL AVERAGE JOB TOTAL DELAY       11.597
```

in the other groups was held constant.) The estimated overall average job total delays from these runs and the original run are summarized in Table 2.4. From these results it appears that a machine should be added to group 2 (see Prob. 9.3).

2.7 EFFICIENT EVENT-LIST MANIPULATION

In SIMLIB the event list is stored as a linked list which is ranked in increasing order on event time. To determine the next event which is to occur in a simulation, subroutine REMOVE is called (with OPTION = 1) by the timing routine TIMING to remove the first event record in the event list. To add a new event record to the event list, subroutine FILE is called with OPTION = 3. The proper location for the new record in the event list is determined by beginning at the head of the list and then searching through the list by means of the successor links.

A number of other algorithms could have been used for adding new records to the event list (see McCormack [3] and McCormack and Sargent [4] for a comprehensive survey). For example, one could start at the tail of the event list and then search through the list using the predecessor links. This approach is used by GASP IV and GPSS V (see Chap. 3 for discussion of these languages). Alternatively, one could add an additional pointer to indicate the middle record in the event list. This pointer is used to determine whether the new event record should be in the front or

```
JOB SHOP MODEL - MACHINE GROUP REPORT


MACHINE GROUP    AVERAGE NUMBER IN QUEUE    AVERAGE UTILIZATION    AVERAGE DELAY IN QUEUE
     1                  11.192                     .950                    2.814

     2                  17.999                     .958                    9.161

     3                    .725                     .721                     .182

     4                  14.084                     .966                    5.041

     5                   1.926                     .796                     .980
```

Figure 2.36 Machine-group report for the job-shop model.

Table 2.4 Estimated overall average job total delays for current and proposed machine configurations

Number of machines in groups	Overall average job total delays, hours
3, 2, 4, 3, 1 (current configuration)	11.597
3, 3, 4, 3, 1 (add 1 to group 2)	7.983
3, 2, 4, 4, 1 (add 1 to group 4)	8.459
4, 2, 4, 3, 1 (add 1 to group 1)	9.174

back half of the event list. If the new record should be in the front half, this half is scanned by beginning at the head of that half. Conversely, if the new record should be in the back half, this half is scanned by beginning at the tail of that half.

Results in [3, 4] indicate that for some simulation models the choice of the event-list-insertion algorithm can have a significant impact on model execution time. If one wants to use SIMLIB on a real-world simulation model where the event list can contain a large number of events, we recommend writing a new subroutine (see Prob. 2.13) which uses the middle-pointer algorithm for new-event insertion. This recommendation is based on empirical results in [3, 4] for the three algorithms discussed as well as for other algorithms which are more difficult to implement.

APPENDIX 2A FORTRAN LISTINGS FOR SIMLIB

FORTRAN listings for the subroutines and functions which compose the simulation language SIMLIB are given on the following pages. Subroutines INITLK, FILE, REMOVE, and CANCEL contain the common block LLISTS which consists of the following variables:

HEAD(LIST)	Head pointer for list LIST (LIST = 1, 2, . . . , 25)
LINKPR(I)	Predecessor link for row I of array MASTER (I = 1, 2, . . . , 1000)
LINKSR(I)	Successor link for row I of array MASTER (I = 1, 2, . . . , 1000)
MASTER(I,J)	Value (real) of the entry in Ith row and Jth column of array MASTER (I = 1, 2, . . . , 1000 and J = 1, 2, . . . , 10)
NAR	Next available row in array MASTER, i.e., head of list of available space
TAIL(LIST)	Tail pointer for list LIST (LIST = 1, 2, . . . , 25)

Note that in the functions EXPON, RANDI, and UNIFRM, we call the function RANUN(Z), which is our random-number generator. These three statements would have to be modified to change RANUN to the name of the user's random-number generator.

```
      SUBROUTINE INITLK
      INTEGER HEAD(25),LINKPR(1000),LINKSR(1000),LIST,NAR,ROW,TAIL(25)
      REAL MASTER(1000,10)
      COMMON /LLISTS/ HEAD,LINKPR,LINKSR,MASTER,NAR,TAIL
      COMMON /SYSTEM/ LRANK(25),LSIZE(25),MAXATR,NEXT,TIME,TRNSFR(10)
C
C *** INITIALIZE LINKS.
C
      DO 10 ROW=1,1000
      LINKPR(ROW)=0
      LINKSR(ROW)=ROW+1
   10 CONTINUE
      LINKSR(1000)=0
C
C *** INITIALIZE LIST ATTRIBUTES.
C
      DO 20 LIST=1,25
      HEAD(LIST)=0
      TAIL(LIST)=0
      LSIZE(LIST)=0
      LRANK(LIST)=0
   20 CONTINUE
C
C *** INITIALIZE SYSTEM ATTRIBUTES.
C
      TIME=0.
      NAR=1
      LRANK(25)=1
      MAXATR=10
C
C *** INITIALIZE STATISTICAL ROUTINES.
C
      CALL SAMPST(0.,0)
      CALL TIMEST(0.,0)
      RETURN
      END
```

```
      SUBROUTINE FILE(OPTION,LIST)
      INTEGER AHEAD,BEHIND,HEAD(25),IHEAD,ITAIL,ITEM,LINKPR(1000),
     1LINKSR(1000),LIST,NAR,OPTION,ROW,TAIL(25)
      REAL MASTER(1000,10),SIZE
      COMMON /LLISTS/ HEAD,LINKPR,LINKSR,MASTER,NAR,TAIL
      COMMON /SYSTEM/ LRANK(25),LSIZE(25),MAXATR,NEXT,TIME,TRNSFR(10)
C
C *** IF THE MASTER STORAGE ARRAY IS FULL, STOP THE SIMULATION.
C
      IF(NAR.GT.0) GO TO 20
      PRINT 10, TIME
   10 FORMAT(1H1,5X,'MASTER STORAGE ARRAY OVERFLOW AT TIME ',E10.3)
      STOP
C
C *** IF THE LIST VALUE IS IMPROPER, STOP THE SIMULATION.
C
   20 IF((LIST.GE.1).AND.(LIST.LE.25)) GO TO 40
      PRINT 30, LIST,TIME
   30 FORMAT(1H1,I10,' IS AN IMPROPER VALUE FOR FILE LIST AT TIME ',
     1E10.3)
      STOP
```

```
C
C *** INCREMENT THE LIST SIZE.
C
   40 LSIZE(LIST)=LSIZE(LIST)+1
C
C *** IF THE OPTION VALUE IS IMPROPER, STOP THE SIMULATION.
C
      IF((OPTION.GE.1).AND.(OPTION.LE.4)) GO TO 60
      PRINT 50, OPTION,TIME
   50 FORMAT(1H1,I10,' IS AN IMPROPER VALUE FOR FILE OPTION AT TIME ',
     1E10.3)
      STOP
C
C *** FILE ACCORDING TO THE DESIRED OPTION.
C
   60 GO TO (300,200,100,100), OPTION
C
C ***************************************************************************
C
C *** THE LIST IS RANKED. DETERMINE THE ITEM ON WHICH THE LIST IS TO
C *** BE RANKED.
C
  100 ITEM=LRANK(LIST)
C
C *** IF AN INVALID ITEM HAS BEEN SPECIFIED, STOP THE SIMULATION.
C
      IF((ITEM.GE.1).AND.(ITEM.LE.MAXATR)) GO TO 120
      PRINT 110, ITEM,LIST
  110 FORMAT(1H1,I10,' IS AN IMPROPER VALUE FOR THE RANK OF LIST ',I2)
      STOP
C
C *** IF THIS IS NOT THE FIRST RECORD IN THIS LIST, CONTINUE.
C
  120 IF(LSIZE(LIST).EQ.1) GO TO 400
C
C *** SEARCH THE LIST FOR THE PROPER LOCATION.
C
      ROW=HEAD(LIST)
  130 IF(OPTION.EQ.4) GO TO 140
C
C *** RANK THE LIST IN INCREASING ORDER.
C
      IF(TRNSFR(ITEM).GE.MASTER(ROW,ITEM)) GO TO 160
C
C *** THE CORRECT LOCATION HAS BEEN FOUND.
C
      GO TO 150
C
C *** RANK THE LIST IN DECREASING ORDER.
C
  140 IF(TRNSFR(ITEM).LE.MASTER(ROW,ITEM)) GO TO 160
C
C *** THE CORRECT LOCATION HAS BEEN FOUND.
C
C *** INSERT BEFORE THE LAST RECORD EXAMINED.
C
  150 IF(ROW.EQ.HEAD(LIST)) GO TO 300
C
C *** INSERT IN THE PROPER LOCATION BETWEEN THE PRECEDING AND
C *** SUCCEEDING RECORDS (BEHIND AND AHEAD).
C
      AHEAD=LINKSR(BEHIND)
      ROW=NAR
      NAR=LINKSR(ROW)
      IF(NAR.GT.0) LINKPR(NAR)=0
      LINKPR(ROW)=BEHIND
      LINKSR(BEHIND)=ROW
      LINKPR(AHEAD)=ROW
      LINKSR(ROW)=AHEAD
```

```
C
C *** GO TO TRANSFER THE DATA.
C
      GO TO 500
C
C *** CONTINUE SEARCHING, CONSIDER THE NEXT ROW.
C
  160 BEHIND=ROW
      ROW=LINKSR(BEHIND)
C
C *** IF THE LAST ROW CONSIDERED WAS NOT THE TAIL OF THE LIST,
C *** CONTINUE.
C
      IF(TAIL(LIST).NE.BEHIND) GO TO 130
C
C ***********************************************************************
C
C *** INSERT AFTER THE LAST RECORD IN THE LIST.
C
  200 IF(LSIZE(LIST).EQ.1) GO TO 400
      ROW=NAR
      NAR=LINKSR(ROW)
      IF(NAR.GT.0) LINKPR(NAR)=0
      ITAIL=TAIL(LIST)
      LINKPR(ROW)=ITAIL
      LINKSR(ITAIL)=ROW
      LINKSR(ROW)=0
      TAIL(LIST)=ROW
C
C *** GO TO TRANSFER THE DATA.
C
      GO TO 500
C
C ***********************************************************************
C
C *** INSERT BEFORE THE FIRST RECORD IN THE LIST.
C
  300 IF(LSIZE(LIST).EQ.1) GO TO 400
      ROW=NAR
      NAR=LINKSR(ROW)
      IF(NAR.GT.0) LINKPR(NAR)=0
      IHEAD=HEAD(LIST)
      LINKPR(IHEAD)=ROW
      LINKSR(ROW)=IHEAD
      LINKPR(ROW)=0
      HEAD(LIST)=ROW
C
C *** GO TO TRANSFER THE DATA.
C
      GO TO 500
C
C ***********************************************************************
C
C *** INSERT THE FIRST RECORD IN THE LIST.
C
  400 ROW=NAR
      NAR=LINKSR(ROW)
      IF(NAR.GT.0) LINKPR(NAR)=0
      LINKSR(ROW)=0
      HEAD(LIST)=ROW
      TAIL(LIST)=ROW
```

```
C
C    ***************************************************************************
C
C    *** TRANSFER THE DATA.
C
  500 DO 510 ITEM=1,MAXATR
      MASTER(ROW,ITEM)=TRNSFR(ITEM)
  510 CONTINUE
C
C    *** UPDATE THE AREA UNDER THE NUMBER IN LIST CURVE.
C
      SIZE=LSIZE(LIST)
      CALL TIMEST(SIZE,20+LIST)
      RETURN
      END


      SUBROUTINE REMOVE(OPTION,LIST)
      INTEGER HEAD(25),IHEAD,ITAIL,ITEM,LINKPR(1000),LINKSR(1000),LIST,
     1NAR,OPTION,ROW,TAIL(25)
      REAL MASTER(1000,10),SIZE
      COMMON /LLISTS/ HEAD,LINKPR,LINKSR,MASTER,NAR,TAIL
      COMMON /SYSTEM/ LRANK(25),LSIZE(25),MAXATR,NEXT,TIME,TRNSFR(10)
C
C    *** IF THE LIST VALUE IS IMPROPER, STOP THE SIMULATION.
C
      IF((LIST.GE.1).AND.(LIST.LE.25)) GO TO 20
      PRINT 10, LIST,TIME
   10 FORMAT(1H1,I10,' IS AN IMPROPER VALUE FOR REMOVE LIST AT TIME ',
     1E10.3)
      STOP
C
C    *** IF THE LIST IS EMPTY, STOP THE SIMULATION.
C
   20 IF(LSIZE(LIST).GT.0) GO TO 40
      PRINT 30, LIST,TIME
   30 FORMAT(1H1,5X,'UNDERFLOW OF LIST ',I2,' AT TIME ',E10.3)
      STOP
C
C    *** DECREMENT THE LIST SIZE.
C
   40 LSIZE(LIST)=LSIZE(LIST)-1
C
C    *** IF THE OPTION VALUE IS IMPROPER, STOP THE SIMULATION.
C
      IF((OPTION.EQ.1).OR.(OPTION.EQ.2)) GO TO 60
      PRINT 50, OPTION,TIME
   50 FORMAT(1H1,I10,' IS AN IMPROPER VALUE FOR REMOVE OPTION AT TIME ',
     1E10.3)
      STOP
C
C    *** IF THERE IS MORE THAN ONE RECORD IN THE LIST, CONTINUE.
C
   60 IF(LSIZE(LIST).EQ.0) GO TO 300
C
C    *** REMOVE ACCORDING TO THE DESIRED OPTION.
C
      GO TO (100,200), OPTION
C
C    ***************************************************************************
C
C    *** REMOVE THE FIRST RECORD IN THE LIST.
C
```

```
  100 ROW=HEAD(LIST)
      IHEAD=LINKSR(ROW)
      LINKPR(IHEAD)=0
      HEAD(LIST)=IHEAD
C
C *** GO TO TRANSFER THE DATA.
C
      GO TO 400
C
C ************************************************************************
C
C *** REMOVE THE LAST RECORD IN THE LIST.
C
  200 ROW=TAIL(LIST)
      ITAIL=LINKPR(ROW)
      LINKSR(ITAIL)=0
      TAIL(LIST)=ITAIL
C
C *** GO TO TRANSFER THE DATA.
C
      GO TO 400
C
C ************************************************************************
C
C *** REMOVE THE ONLY RECORD IN THE LIST.
C
  300 ROW=HEAD(LIST)
      HEAD(LIST)=0
      TAIL(LIST)=0
C
C ************************************************************************
C
C *** TRANSFER THE DATA.
C
  400 LINKSR(ROW)=NAR
      LINKPR(ROW)=0
      NAR=ROW
      DO 410 ITEM=1,MAXATR
      TRNSFR(ITEM)=MASTER(ROW,ITEM)
  410 CONTINUE
C
C *** UPDATE THE AREA UNDER THE NUMBER IN LIST CURVE.
C
      SIZE=LSIZE(LIST)
      CALL TIMEST(SIZE,20+LIST)
      RETURN
      END




      SUBROUTINE TIMING
      COMMON /SYSTEM/ LRANK(25),LSIZE(25),MAXATR,NEXT,TIME,TRNSFR(10)
C
C *** REMOVE THE FIRST EVENT FROM THE EVENT LIST.
C
      CALL REMOVE(1,25)
C
C *** CHECK FOR A TIME REVERSAL.
C
      IF(TRNSFR(1).GE.TIME) GO TO 20
      PRINT 10,TRNSFR(2),TRNSFR(1),TIME
   10 FORMAT(1H1,5X,'ATTEMPT TO SCHEDULE AN EVENT OF TYPE ',F3.0,
     1' AT TIME ',E10.3,' WHEN THE CLOCK IS ',E10.3)
      STOP
C
C *** ADVANCE THE SIMULATION CLOCK.
```

```
C
   20 TIME=TRNSFR(1)
      NEXT=TRNSFR(2)
      RETURN
      END


      SUBROUTINE CANCEL(ETYPE)
      INTEGER AHEAD,BEHIND,HEAD(25),ITEM,LINKPR(1000),LINKSR(1000),NAR,
     1ROW,TAIL(25)
      REAL ETYPE,HIGH,LOW,MASTER(1000,10),SIZE,VALUE
      COMMON /LLISTS/ HEAD,LINKPR,LINKSR,MASTER,NAR,TAIL
      COMMON /SYSTEM/ LRANK(25),LSIZE(25),MAXATR,NEXT,TIME,TRNSFR(10)
C
C *** SEARCH THE EVENT LIST.
C
      IF(LSIZE(25).EQ.0) RETURN
      ROW=HEAD(25)
      LOW=ETYPE-0.1
      HIGH=ETYPE+0.1
   10 VALUE=MASTER(ROW,2)
      IF((LOW.LT.VALUE).AND.(HIGH.GT.VALUE)) GO TO 20
C
C *** GO TO THE NEXT EVENT.
C
      IF(ROW.EQ.TAIL(25)) RETURN
      ROW=LINKSR(ROW)
      GO TO 10
C
C ***********************************************************************
C
C *** CANCEL THIS EVENT.
C
   20 IF(ROW.NE.HEAD(25)) GO TO 30
C
C *** REMOVE THE FIRST EVENT IN THE EVENT LIST.
C
      CALL REMOVE(1,25)
      RETURN
   30 IF(ROW.NE.TAIL(25)) GO TO 40
C
C *** REMOVE THE LAST EVENT IN THE EVENT LIST.
C
      CALL REMOVE(2,25)
      RETURN
C
C *** REMOVE THIS EVENT WHICH IS SOMEWHERE IN THE MIDDLE OF THE EVENT
C *** LIST.
C
   40 AHEAD=LINKSR(ROW)
      BEHIND=LINKPR(ROW)
      LINKSR(BEHIND)=AHEAD
      LINKPR(AHEAD)=BEHIND
      LINKSR(ROW)=NAR
      LINKPR(ROW)=0
      NAR=ROW
      LSIZE(25)=LSIZE(25)-1
C
C *** PLACE THE ATTRIBUTES OF THE CANCELED EVENT IN THE TRNSFR ARRAY.
C
      DO 50 ITEM=1,MAXATR
      TRNSFR(ITEM)=MASTER(ROW,ITEM)
   50 CONTINUE
C
C *** UPDATE THE AREA UNDER THE NUMBER IN LIST CURVE.
C
      SIZE=LSIZE(25)
      CALL TIMEST(SIZE,45)
      RETURN
      END
```

```
      SUBROUTINE SAMPST(VALUE,VARIBL)
      INTEGER IVAR,NOBS(20),VARIBL
      REAL MAX(20),MIN(20),SUM(20),VALUE
      COMMON /SYSTEM/ LRANK(25),LSIZE(25),MAXATR,NEXT,TIME,TRNSFR(10)
C
C *** IF THE VARIABLE VALUE IS IMPROPER, STOP THE SIMULATION.
C
      IF((VARIBL.GE.-20).AND.(VARIBL.LE.20)) GO TO 20
      PRINT 10, VARIBL,TIME
   10 FORMAT(1H1,I10,' IS AN IMPROPER VALUE FOR A SAMPST VARIABLE ',
     1'AT TIME ',E10.3)
      STOP
C
C *** EXECUTE THE DESIRED OPTION.
C
   20 IF(VARIBL) 300,100,200
C
C ********************************************************************
C
C *** INITIALIZE THE ROUTINE.
C
  100 DO 110 IVAR=1,20
      SUM(IVAR)=0.
      MAX(IVAR)=-1.E+30
      MIN(IVAR)=1.E+30
      NOBS(IVAR)=0
  110 CONTINUE
      RETURN
C
C ********************************************************************
C
C *** COLLECT DATA.
C
  200 SUM(VARIBL)=SUM(VARIBL)+VALUE
      IF(VALUE.GT.MAX(VARIBL)) MAX(VARIBL)=VALUE
      IF(VALUE.LT.MIN(VARIBL)) MIN(VARIBL)=VALUE
      NOBS(VARIBL)=NOBS(VARIBL)+1
      RETURN
C
C ********************************************************************
C
C *** REPORT THE RESULTS.
C
  300 IVAR=-VARIBL
      TRNSFR(1)=0.
      TRNSFR(2)=NOBS(IVAR)
      TRNSFR(3)=MAX(IVAR)
      TRNSFR(4)=MIN(IVAR)
      IF(NOBS(IVAR).EQ.0) RETURN
      TRNSFR(1)=SUM(IVAR)/TRNSFR(2)
      RETURN
      END




      SUBROUTINE TIMEST(VALUE,VARIBL)
      INTEGER IVAR,VARIBL
      REAL AREA(45),MAX(45),MIN(45),PREVAL(45),TLVC(45),VALUE,TRESET
      COMMON /SYSTEM/ LRANK(25),LSIZE(25),MAXATR,NEXT,TIME,TRNSFR(10)
C
C *** IF THE VARIABLE VALUE IS IMPROPER, STOP THE SIMULATION.
C
      IF((VARIBL.GE.-45).AND.(VARIBL.LE.45)) GO TO 20
      PRINT 10, VARIBL,TIME
```

```
   10 FORMAT(1H1,I10,' IS AN IMPROPER VALUE FOR A TIMEST VARIABLE ',
     1'AT TIME ',E10.3)
      STOP
C
C *** EXECUTE THE DESIRED OPTION.
C
   20 IF(VARIBL) 300,100,200
C
C ***************************************************************************
C
C
C *** INITIALIZE THE ROUTINE.
C
  100 DO 110 IVAR=1,45
      AREA(IVAR)=0.
      MAX(IVAR)=-1.E+30
      MIN(IVAR)=1.E+30
      PREVAL(IVAR)=0.
      TLVC(IVAR)=TIME
  110 CONTINUE
      TRESET=TIME
      RETURN
C
C ***************************************************************************
C
C *** COLLECT DATA.
C
  200 AREA(VARIBL)=AREA(VARIBL)+(TIME-TLVC(VARIBL))*PREVAL(VARIBL)
      IF(VALUE.GT.MAX(VARIBL)) MAX(VARIBL)=VALUE
      IF(VALUE.LT.MIN(VARIBL)) MIN(VARIBL)=VALUE
      PREVAL(VARIBL)=VALUE
      TLVC(VARIBL)=TIME
      RETURN
C
C ***************************************************************************
C
C *** REPORT THE RESULTS.
C
  300 IVAR=-VARIBL
      AREA(IVAR)=AREA(IVAR)+(TIME-TLVC(IVAR))*PREVAL(IVAR)
      TLVC(IVAR)=TIME
      TRNSFR(1)=AREA(IVAR)/(TIME-TRESET)
      TRNSFR(2)=MAX(IVAR)
      TRNSFR(3)=MIN(IVAR)
      RETURN
      END



      SUBROUTINE FILEST(LIST)
      INTEGER ILIST,LIST
      COMMON /SYSTEM/ LRANK(25),LSIZE(25),MAXATR,NEXT,TIME,TRNSFR(10)
C
C *** COMPUTE SUMMARY STATISTICS FOR THE LIST.
C
      ILIST=-(20+LIST)
      CALL TIMEST(0.,ILIST)
      RETURN
      END



      FUNCTION EXPON(RMEAN)
      REAL RMEAN,U
C
C *** GENERATE A U(0,1) RANDOM VARIABLE. THE FORM OF THIS STATEMENT
C *** DEPENDS UPON THE COMPUTER USED.
C
```

```
      U=RANUN(Z)
C
C *** GENERATE AN EXPONENTIAL RANDOM VARIABLE WITH MEAN RMEAN.
C
      EXPON=-RMEAN*ALOG(U)
      RETURN
      END



      FUNCTION RANDI(Z)
      INTEGER I,N1
      REAL U
      COMMON /RANDOM/ NVALUE,PROBD(25)
C
C *** GENERATE A U(0,1) RANDOM VARIABLE. THE FORM OF THIS STATEMENT
C *** DEPENDS UPON THE COMPUTER USED.
C
      U=RANUN(Z)
C
C *** GENERATE A RANDOM INTEGER BETWEEN 1 AND NVALUE IN ACCORDANCE WITH
C *** DISTRIBUTION FUNCTION 'PROBD.'
C
      N1=NVALUE-1
      DO 10 I=1,N1
      IF(U.GE.PROBD(I)) GO TO 10
      RANDI=I
      RETURN
   10 CONTINUE
      RANDI=NVALUE
      RETURN
      END



      FUNCTION UNIFRM(A,B)
      REAL A,B,U
C
C *** GENERATE A U(0,1) RANDOM VARIABLE. THE FORM OF THIS STATEMENT
C *** DEPENDS UPON THE COMPUTER USED.
C
      U=RANUN(Z)
C
C *** GENERATE A U(A,B) RANDOM VARIABLE.
C
      UNIFRM=A+(U*(B-A))
      RETURN
      END
```

PROBLEMS

The following problems are to be done using the simulation language SIMLIB.

2.1 For the inventory example of Chap. 1, suppose that the delivery lag is uniformly distributed between 1 and 3 months. Thus, it is possible for there to be between 0 and 3 outstanding orders at a particular time. As a result, the company bases its ordering decision at the beginning of each month on the sum of the (net) inventory level [denoted by $I(t)$ in Chap. 1] and the inventory on order, which can be positive, zero, or negative. For each of the nine inventory policies, run the model for 120 months and estimate the average total cost per month and the proportion of time there is a backlog. Note that holding and shortage costs are still based on the net inventory level.

2.2 For the inventory system of Prob. 2.1, suppose that the inventory is perishable and has a shelf life which is uniformly distributed between 1.5 and 2.5 months. That is, if an item has a shelf life of l

months, l months after it is placed in the inventory it spoils and is of no value to the company. (Note that different items in an order from the supplier will have different shelf lives.) The company discovers that an item is spoiled only upon its examination before a sale. If an item is determined to be spoiled, it is discarded and the next item in the inventory is examined. Run the model assuming that the items in the inventory are processed (a) LIFO and (b) FIFO.

2.3 For the time-shared computer model considered in Sec. 2.4, suppose that instead of processing jobs in the queue in a round-robin manner the CPU chooses the job from the queue which has made the fewest number of previous passes through the CPU. In case of ties, the rule is FIFO. (This is equivalent to using time of arrival to the queue to break ties.) Run the model with $n = 60$ terminals for 1000 job completions.

2.4 Ships arrive at a harbor with interarrival times that are IID exponential random variables with a mean of 1.25 days. The harbor contains a dock which has two berths and two cranes for unloading the ships; ships which arrive when both berths are occupied join a FIFO queue. The time for one crane to unload a ship is uniformly distributed between 0.5 and 1.5 days. If only one ship is in the harbor, both cranes unload the ship and the unloading time is cut in half. When two ships are in the harbor, one crane works on each ship. If both cranes are unloading one ship when a second ship arrives, one of the cranes immediately begins serving the second ship and the remaining service time of the first ship is doubled. Assuming that no ships are in the harbor at time zero, run the simulation for 90 days and estimate the minimum, maximum, and average time that ships are in the harbor. Also estimate the utilization of each berth and the utilization of the cranes. (This problem is a paraphrasing of an example in Russell [6, p. 134].)

2.5 For the original configuration of the job shop considered in Sec. 2.6, run the model for 100 eight-hour days but use only the data from the last 90 days to estimate the quantities of interest. In effect, the state of the system at TIME = 10 days is the initial condition for the simulation. The idea of warming up the model before beginning data collection is a common simulation practice, explained in Chap. 8.

2.6 Jobs arrive at a computer facility with a single CPU with interarrival times that are IID exponential random variables with a mean of 1 minute. Each job specifies upon its arrival the maximum amount of processing time it requires, and the maximum times for successive jobs are IID exponential random variables with a mean of 1.1 minutes. However, if m is the specified maximum processing time for a particular job, the actual processing time is uniformly distributed between $0.55m$ and $1.05m$. The CPU will never process a job for more time than its specified maximum; a job whose required processing time exceeds its specified maximum leaves the facility without completing service. Simulate the computer facility until 1000 jobs have left the CPU if (a) jobs in the queue are processed in a FIFO manner and (b) jobs in the queue are ranked in increasing order of their specified maximum processing time. Estimate, for each case, the average delay in queue of jobs, the proportion of jobs which are delayed in queue more than 5 minutes, and the maximum number of jobs ever in queue.

2.7 In a quarry, trucks deliver ore from three shovels to a single, primary crusher. Trucks are assigned to specific shovels, so that a truck will always return to its assigned shovel after dumping a load at the crusher. Two different truck sizes are in use, 20 and 50 tons. The size of the truck affects its loading time at the shovel, travel time to the crusher, dumping time at the crusher, and return trip time from the crusher back to the appropriate shovel, as follows:

Truck size, tons	Time, minutes			
	Load	Travel	Dump	Return
20	Exponentially distributed with mean 5	Constant 2.5	Exponentially distributed with mean 2	Constant 1.5
50	Exponentially distributed with mean 10	Constant 3	Exponentially distributed with mean 4	Constant 2

To each shovel is assigned two 20-ton trucks and one 50-ton truck. The shovel queues are all FIFO, and the crusher queue is ranked in decreasing order of truck size, the rule being FIFO in case of ties. Assume that at time 0 all trucks are at their respective shovels with the 50-ton trucks just beginning to be loaded. Run the simulation model for 8 hours and estimate the time-average number in queue for each shovel and for the crusher. Also estimate the utilizations of all four pieces of equipment. (This problem is taken from Pritsker and Pegden [5, p. 184].)

2.8 A computer facility with a single CPU opens its doors at 7 A.M. and closes its doors at 12 A.M., but operates until all jobs present at 12 have been served. Assume that jobs arrive at the facility with inter-arrival times that are IID exponential random variables with mean 1.91 minutes. Jobs request either express (class 4), normal (class 3), deferred (class 2), or convenience (class 1) service and the classes occur with respective probabilities 0.05, 0.50, 0.30, and 0.15. When the CPU is idle, it will process the highest-class (priority) job present, the rule being FIFO within a class. The times required for the CPU to process class 4, 3, 2, and 1 jobs are 3-Erlang random variables (see Sec. 2.6) with respective means 0.25, 1.00, 1.50, and 3.00 minutes. Simulate the computer facility for each of the following cases:

(*a*) A job being processed by the CPU is not preempted.

(*b*) If a job of class i is being processed and a job of class j ($j > i$) arrives, the arriving job preempts the job being processed. The preempted job joins the queue and takes the highest priority in its class, and only its remaining service time needs to be completed at some future time.

Estimate for each class the time-average number of jobs in queue and the average delay in queue. Also estimate the proportion of time that the CPU is busy and the proportion of CPU busy time the CPU spends on each class. Note that it is convenient to have one list for each class's queue and also an input parameter PREMPT which is set to 0 for case (*a*) and set to 1 for case (*b*).

2.9 A port in Africa is used to load tankers with crude oil for overwater shipment, and the port has facilities for loading as many as three tankers simultaneously. The tankers, which arrive at the port every 11 ± 7 hours, are of three different types. (All times given as a range in this problem are uniformly distributed over the range.) The relative frequency of the various types and their loading-time requirements are as follows:

Type	Relative frequency	Loading time, hours
1	0.25	18 ± 2
2	0.25	24 ± 3
3	0.50	36 ± 4

There is one tug at the port. Tankers of all types require the services of a tug to move from the harbor into a berth and later to move out of a berth into the harbor. When the tug is available, any berthing or deberthing activity takes approximately 1 hour. It takes the tug 0.25 hour to travel from the harbor to the berths, or vice versa, when it is not pulling a tanker. When the tug finishes a berthing activity, it will deberth the first tanker in the deberthing queue if this queue is not empty. If the deberthing queue is empty but the harbor queue is not, the tug will travel to the harbor and begin berthing the first tanker in the harbor queue. When the tug finishes a deberthing activity, it will berth the first tanker in the harbor queue if this queue is not empty and a berth is available. Otherwise, the tug will travel to the berths, and if the deberthing queue is not empty, will begin deberthing the first tanker in the queue. If the deberthing queue is empty, the tug will remain idle at the berths.

The situation is complicated because the area experiences frequent storms which last 4 ± 2 hours. The time between the end of one storm and the onset of the next is an exponential random variable with mean 48 hours. The tug will not start a new activity when a storm is in progress but will always finish an existing activity. If the tug is traveling from the berths to the harbor without a tanker when a storm begins, it will turn around and head for the berths.

Run the simulation model for a 1-year period (8760 hours) and estimate:

(*a*) The proportion of time the tug is idle, is traveling without a tanker, and is engaged in either a berthing or deberthing activity

(*b*) The proportion of time each berth is unoccupied, is occupied but not loading, and is loading (*c*) The time-average number of tankers in the deberthing queue and in the harbor queue

(*d*) The average in-port residence time of each type of tanker

A shipper considering bidding on a contract to transport oil from the port to the United Kingdom has determined that five tankers of a particular type would have to be committed to this task to meet contract specifications. These tankers would require 21 ± 3 hours to load oil at the port. After loading and deberthing, they would travel to the United Kingdom, offload the oil, return to the port for reloading, etc. The round-trip travel time, including offloading, is estimated to be 240 ± 24 hours. Rerun the simulation and estimate, in addition, the average in-port residence time of the proposed additional tankers. Assume that at time 0 the five additional tankers are in the harbor queue. (This problem is an embellishment of one in Schriber [7, p. 329].)

2.10 Write a FORTRAN function, called FIND, to find the row in the array MASTER which contains the first record with a value VALUE (a real-valued representation of an integer, for example, 5.) for attribute ITEM (ITEM = 1, 2, . . . , MAXATR) in list LIST (LIST = 1, 2, . . . , 25). To determine the desired row, a statement of the form ROW = FIND(ITEM,VALUE,LIST) is executed. In addition, copy the record which has been found into the TRNSFR array. If no record is found, set FIND equal to -1.

2.11 Write a FORTRAN subroutine, called DELETE, to delete the record from list LIST (LIST = 1, 2, . . . , 25) which is in row ROW (ROW = 1, 2, . . . , 1000) of the array MASTER. To delete the desired record, a statement of the form CALL DELETE(ROW,LIST) is executed. If there is an error condition, print out an error message and stop the simulation. Also, update the statistics for list LIST by calling TIMEST (see the listing of REMOVE in Appendix 2A).

2.12 For the bank model considered in Sec. 2.5, suppose that after a customer has waited in queue a certain amount of time, the customer *may* leave without being served. (This is called *reneging*.) Assume that the amount of time a customer will wait in queue before considering leaving without service is uniformly distributed between 5 and 10 minutes; if this amount of time actually elapses while the customer is in queue, the customer will actually leave with the following probabilities:

Position in queue when time elapses	1	2	3	≥ 4
Probability of customer's actually leaving	0	0.25	0.50	1

Using routines FIND and DELETE from Probs. 2.10 and 2.11, run the simulation model with five tellers and estimate (in addition to what was estimated before) the proportion of customers who leave without being served and the average delay in queue of these customers.

2.13 Write a FORTRAN subroutine, called INSERT, to insert a new event record into the event list using the middle-pointer algorithm discussed in Sec. 2.7. If two event records have the same event time, give preference to the event record with the smallest event type.

REFERENCES

1. Adiri, I., and B. Avi-Itzhak: A Time-Sharing Queue with a Finite Number of Customers, *J. Ass. Comput. Mach.,* **16:** 315–323 (1969).
2. Knuth, D. E.: *The Art of Computer Programming,* vol. 1, Addison-Wesley, Reading, Mass., 1975.
3. McCormack, W. M.: Analysis of Future Event Set Algorithms for Discrete Event Simulation, *Va. Polytech. Inst. State Univ. Comput. Sci. Depart. Tech. Rep.* CS80002-R, Blacksburg, Va., 1980.
4. McCormack, W. M., and R. G. Sargent: Comparison of Future Event Set Algorithms for Simulations of Closed Queueing Systems, chap. 5 in N. R. Adam and A. Dogramaci (eds.), *Current Issues in Computer Simulation,* Academic, New York, 1979.
5. Pritsker, A. A. B., and C. D. Pegden: *Introduction to Simulation and SLAM,* Systems Publishing, West Lafayette, Ind., 1979.
6. Russell, E. C.: *Simulation and SIMSCRIPT II.5,* CACI, Inc., Los Angeles, 1976.
7. Schriber, T. J.: *Simulation Using GPSS,* Wiley, New York, 1974.

THREE

SIMULATION LANGUAGES

3.1 INTRODUCTION

In studying the simulation examples in Chaps. 1 and 2, the reader probably noticed several features needed in programming most discrete-event simulation models. They include the following:

1. Generating random numbers, that is U(0, 1) random variables
2. Generating random variables from a specified distribution
3. Advancing simulated time
4. Determining the next event from the event list and passing control to the appropriate block of code
5. Adding records to, or deleting records from, a list
6. Collecting and analyzing data
7. Reporting the results
8. Detecting error conditions

As a matter of fact, it is the commonality of these and other features to most simulation programs that led to the development of special-purpose simulation languages. Furthermore, we believe that the improvement, standardization, and greater availability of these languages has been one of the major factors in the increased popularity of simulation in recent years.

We discuss in Sec. 3.2 the relative merits of using a simulation language rather than a general-purpose language like FORTRAN for programming simulation models. Most simulation languages in use today use one of two different modeling approaches or orientations. These two orientations, called the *event-scheduling* and the *process-interaction approaches,* are discussed in Sec. 3.3. In Secs. 3.4 to 3.6 we present a brief description of GASP IV, SIMSCRIPT II.5, and GPSS, probably the most widely used simulation languages in the United States. A simulation model of the $M/M/1$ queue is also given in each language. In Sec. 3.4 we also discuss a new language, SLAM, which is likely to be the successor to GASP IV. We do not, however, discuss SIMULA (see Birtwistle et al. [1] and Franta [6]). Although considered by many to be one of the better simulation languages, SIMULA has not received much attention in the United States because of its ALGOL base. (It has gained greater acceptance in Europe.) Finally, in Sec. 3.7 we give a set of criteria to be considered when trying to decide which simulation language to purchase or lease for an organization's use or which simulation language to use on a particular project.

3.2 COMPARISON OF SIMULATION LANGUAGES WITH GENERAL-PURPOSE LANGUAGES

One of the most important decisions a modeler or analyst must make in performing a simulation study is the choice of a language. An inappropriate choice may in itself kill a simulation project if it cannot be completed in time. The following are some advantages of programming a simulation model in a simulation language rather than a general-purpose language, e.g., FORTRAN, PL/1, and BASIC:

1. Simulation languages automatically provide most (if not all) of the features needed in programming a simulation model (see Sec. 3.1), resulting in a decrease in programming time which can often be significant.
2. They provide a natural framework for simulation modeling. Their basic building blocks are more closely akin to simulation than those in a language like FORTRAN.
3. Simulation models are generally easier to change when written in a simulation language.
4. Most simulation languages provide dynamic storage allocation during execution. This is not the case with FORTRAN.
5. They provide better error detection because many potential types of errors have been identified and are checked for automatically. Since fewer lines of code have to be written, the chance of making an error will probably be smaller. (Conversely, errors in a new version of a simulation language itself may be difficult for a user to find.)

On the other hand, many simulation models are still written in a general-purpose language. Some advantages of such a choice are as follows:

1. Most modelers already know a general-purpose language, but this is often not the case with a simulation language.
2. FORTRAN or BASIC are available on virtually every computer, but a particular simulation language may not be accessible on the computer that the analyst wants to use.

3. An *efficiently* written FORTRAN program may require less execution time than the corresponding program written in a simulation language. This is because a simulation language is designed to model a wide variety of systems with one set of building blocks, whereas a FORTRAN program can be tailored to the particular application.
4. General-purpose languages allow greater programming flexibility than certain simulation languages. For example, complicated numerical calculations are not easy in GPSS; see Sec. 3.6 for further discussion.

Although there are clearly advantages to using both types of languages, we believe, in general, that a modeler would be prudent to give serious consideration to the use of a simulation language. If such a decision has indeed been made, the criteria discussed in Sec. 3.7 may be helpful in deciding which particular simulation language to use.

3.3 APPROACHES TO DISCRETE-EVENT SIMULATION MODELING

Almost all simulation languages use one of two basic approaches to discrete-event simulation modeling; these approaches are also used by modelers using a general-purpose language. In the *event-scheduling approach,* used in the programs in Chaps. 1 and 2, a system is modeled by identifying its characteristic events and then writing a set of event routines which give a detailed description of the state changes taking place at the time of each event. The simulation evolves over time by executing the events in increasing order of their time of occurrence. Here a basic property of an event routine is that no simulated time passes during its execution. The event-scheduling approach is used by GASP IV and it is one of the approaches employed by SIMSCRIPT II.5 and SLAM.

We define a *process* to be a time-ordered sequence of events, separated by lapses of time, which describes the entire experience of a "customer as it flows through a system." In the *process-interaction approach,* a system is modeled by writing a process routine which delineates everything that happens to a customer as it moves through its corresponding process. Unlike the event-scheduling approach, the total history of a customer is described by a single (process) routine which also explicitly contains the passage of simulated time. The name "process-interaction approach" is derived from the fact that at a given time, a system may contain many (customer) processes interacting with each other while competing for a set of system resources.

To illustrate the nature of the process-interaction approach more succinctly, Fig. 3.1 gives a flowchart for a prototype customer-process routine in the case of a single-server queueing system. (This process routine describes the entire experience of a customer as it progresses through the system.) Unlike an event routine, this process routine has multiple entry points at blocks 1, 5, and 9. Entry into this routine at block 1 corresponds to the arrival event for a customer process that is the most imminent event in the event list. At block 1 an arrival event record is placed in the event list for the *next* customer process to arrive. (This next process will arrive at a

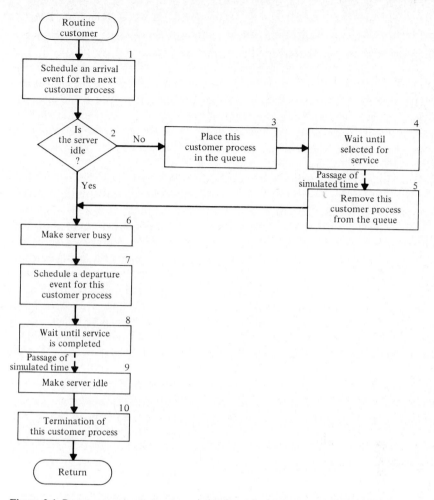

Figure 3.1 Prototype customer-process routine for a single-server queueing system.

time equal to the time the *current* customer process arrives plus an interarrival time.) To determine whether the currently arriving customer process can begin service, a check is made (at block 2) to see whether the server is idle. If the server is busy, this customer process is placed at the end of the queue (block 3) and made to wait (at block 4) until selected for service at some undetermined time in the future. (This is called a *conditional wait*.) Control is then returned to the "timing routine" to determine what customer process's event is the most imminent *now*. (If we think of a flowchart like the one in Fig. 3.1 as existing for each customer process in the system, control will next be passed to the appropriate entry point for the flowchart corresponding to the most imminent event.) When this customer process (the one made to wait at block 4) is activated at some point in the future (when another customer process completes service and makes the server idle), it is removed from the queue *at block 5* and begins service immediately, thereby making the server busy (block 6). A customer process which arrives to find the server idle also begins service immediately (at block 6); in either case, we are now at block 7. At block 7, the departure time for the customer process beginning service is determined, and a corresponding event record is placed in the event list. This customer process is then made to wait (at block 8) until its service has been completed. (This is an *unconditional wait* since its activation time is known.) Control is returned to the timing routine to determine what customer process will be processed next. When the customer process made to wait at block 8 is activated at the end of its service, it makes the server idle *at block 9* (allowing the first customer process in the queue to become active immediately), and then this customer process is removed from the system at block 10.

The process-interaction approach has several advantages over the event-scheduling approach. First, for many types of systems it provides a more natural framework for modeling because the entire experience of a customer as it flows through a system is described in a single process routine. Furthermore, when this approach is implemented in a simulation language, the language provides powerful *macrostatements,* which automatically translate certain situations commonly occurring in a simulation model, e.g., customers arriving to a queueing system, into the corresponding event logic. As a result, a model written using this approach may require significantly fewer lines of code than the corresponding model using the event-scheduling approach. On the other hand, a simulation language using the process-interaction approach exclusively may offer less programming flexibility because it restricts the user to a standard set of macrostatements, which often are oriented toward queueing models.

The process-interaction approach is used by GPSS and is allowed in SIMSCRIPT II.5 and SLAM. Additional references on the process-interaction approach are Fishman [4, p. 40; 5, chap. 4], Franta [6], and Pritsker and Pegden [15, p. 68].

3.4 GASP IV AND RELATED LANGUAGES

GASP IV (see Pritsker [12]) is an event-oriented simulation language consisting of more than 30 FORTRAN subroutines and functions, each of which performs a required simulation activity. (A historical perspective of GASP developments is given by Pritsker [14].) GASP IV is very similar to, but more complete and sophisticated than, the simulation language SIMLIB, presented in Chap. 2. Because GASP IV is written in FORTRAN, it is very easy to learn and is usable on almost any computer with a FORTRAN compiler. (It requires approximately 20,000 words of storage.) GASP IV and SLAM (see Sec. 3.4.2) are the two languages with the best documented and most accessible capabilities of performing continuous and combined discrete-continuous simulations in addition to discrete-event simulation. Because it is an extension of FORTRAN, GASP IV might be considered less elegant and less powerful than some languages specifically designed for simulation, but because it can be obtained at low cost, it has been a very economical choice for many organizations. The GASP IV language is distributed by Pritsker and Associates, Inc. (West Lafayette, Indiana), who also offer a seminar on the language.

A GASP IV discrete-event simulation model views a system as consisting of *entities,* their associated *attributes,* and *files* which contain entities with common characteristics. (Files were called lists in SIMLIB.) As in SIMLIB, all files are stored in one master array (called NSET in GASP IV). The language provides the user with an executive routine called GASP, which automatically performs such activities as determining the next event from the event list and advancing the simulation clock. On the other hand, the user must write a main program, an initialization subroutine INTLC (optional), a subroutine EVNTS, the usual event routines, and a report subroutine OTPUT (optional). In the main program, the total amount of storage required for the simulation is specified by dimensioning NSET, the user-defined variables that are to remain constant over all simulation runs are initialized, and the statement CALL GASP is executed to begin the simulation. Subroutine INTLC is used to initialize user-defined variables at the start of each simulation run. Subroutine EVNTS, which is called by subroutine GASP with the event type of the next event which will occur (denoted by NEXT in Fig. 3.4), uses a computed go to statement to pass control to the appropriate user-written event routine. GASP IV automatically provides the user with a standard output report at the end of the simulation. In the simulation of the $M/M/1$ queue, discussed below, this standard report is sufficient to provide estimates of both desired measures of performance. If the user wants additional output data, they can be obtained by writing a subroutine called OTPUT, which is automatically called by subroutine GASP when the simulation terminates.

3.4.1 Simulation of the $M/M/1$ Queue

We now present a GASP IV program for the $M/M/1$ queue simulated in Sec. 1.4.3 using FORTRAN. Recall that the stopping rule was the completion of 1000 delays and that the desired measures of performance were the average delay in queue and the time-average number of customers in queue. The user-defined variables here

```
C
C *** MAIN PROGRAM.
C
      INTEGER TOTCUS
      REAL MARRVT,MSERVT
      DIMENSION NSET(500)
      COMMON QSET(500)
      COMMON /GCOM1/ ATRIB(30),JEVNT,MFE(100),MLE(100),MSTOP,NCRDR,
     1NNAPT,NNATR(100),NNFIL,NNQ(100),NPRNT,PPARM(50,4),TNOW,TTBEG,
     2TTCLR,TTFIN,TTRIB(30),TTSET,MMATR,MMFA(5)
      COMMON /MODEL/ MARRVT,MSERVT,TOTCUS
      EQUIVALENCE (NSET(1),QSET(1))
C
C *** SET THE DEVICE NUMBERS FOR THE CARD READER AND PRINTER.
C
      NCRDR=5
      NPRNT=6
      CALL GASP
      WRITE(NPRNT,10)
   10 FORMAT(1H1)
      STOP
      END
```

Figure 3.2 Listing of the GASP IV main program, queueing model.

```
      SUBROUTINE INTLC
      INTEGER TOTCUS
      REAL MARRVT,MSERVT
      COMMON /GCOM1/ ATRIB(30),JEVNT,MFE(100),MLE(100),MSTOP,NCRDR,
     1NNAPT,NNATR(100),NNFIL,NNQ(100),NPRNT,PPARM(50,4),TNOW,TTBEG,
     2TTCLR,TTFIN,TTRIB(30),TTSET,MMATR,MMFA(5)
      COMMON /MODEL/ MARRVT,MSERVT,TOTCUS
C
C *** READ INPUT PARAMETERS.
C
      READ(NCRDR,10) MARRVT,MSERVT
   10 FORMAT(2F10.0)
      READ(NCRDR,20) TOTCUS
   20 FORMAT(I10)
C
C *** SCHEDULE THE FIRST ARRIVAL.
C
      ATRIB(1)=EXPON(MARRVT,1)
      ATRIB(2)=1.
      CALL FILEM(1)
      RETURN
      END
```

Figure 3.3 Listing of GASP IV subroutine INTLC, queueing model.

have exactly the same meaning as in the FORTRAN program. (We shall not explain every detail of the GASP IV program, such as the required GASP IV input data cards. The interested reader should consult [12].)

The listing for the GASP IV main program is given in Fig. 3.2. Note that the storage array NSET has been dimensioned to 500, which is more storage than actually necessary. The common block GCOM1, which must be included in every discrete-event program, contains GASP IV-defined global variables.

Subroutine INTLC is listed in Fig. 3.3. After reading in the input parameters, the subroutine determines the time of the first arrival and places an arrival event record in the event list (file 1). The first and second attributes of an event record are

```
      SUBROUTINE EVNTS(NEXT)
      INTEGER NEXT,NUMCUS,TOTCUS
      REAL MARRVT,MSERVT
      COMMON /GCOM1/ ATRIB(30),JEVNT,MFE(100),MLE(100),MSTOP,NCRDR,
     1NNAPT,NNATR(100),NNFIL,NNQ(100),NPRNT,PPARM(50,4),TNOW,TTBEG,
     2TTCLR,TTFIN,TTRIB(30),TTSET,MMATR,MMFA(5)
      COMMON /GCOM6/ EENQ(100),IINN(100),KKRNK(100),MMAXQ(100),
     1QQTIM(100),SSOBV(25,5),SSTPV(25,6),VVNQ(100)
      COMMON /MODEL/ MARRVT,MSERVT,TOTCUS
C
C *** CALL THE APPROPRIATE EVENT ROUTINE.
C
      GO TO (10,20),NEXT
   10 CALL ARRIVE
      GO TO 30
   20 CALL DEPART
C
C *** IF ENOUGH CUSTOMERS HAVE COMPLETED THEIR DELAYS, END THE
C *** SIMULATION.
C
   30 NUMCUS=SSOBV(1,3)
      IF(NUMCUS.GE.TOTCUS) MSTOP=-1
      RETURN
      END
```

Figure 3.4 Listing of GASP IV subroutine EVNTS, queueing model.

the time of occurrence of the event and the event type (1 for an arrival, 2 for a departure), and the records in the event list are always ranked in increasing order on attribute 1. The attributes of the arrival event record are put into the array ATRIB (ATRIB is analogous to the array TRNSFR in SIMLIB), and then the event record is placed in the event list by calling the GASP IV subroutine FILEM (which corresponds to subroutine FILE in SIMLIB) with an argument of 1 for the event list. Note that the time of the first arrival is determined by using the GASP IV exponential function, EXPON, with the first argument equal to the desired mean interarrival time, MARRVT, and the second argument equal to the number of the random-number stream to be used. (GASP IV has six random-number streams.)

A listing for subroutine EVNTS, which is quite straightforward, is given in Fig. 3.4. In statement number 30, SSOBV(1, 3) is a GASP IV-defined statistical counter containing the number of customers who have completed their delays. On the following line, note that MSTOP (a GASP IV variable) is set to -1 when the desired

```
      SUBROUTINE ARRIVE
      INTEGER TOTCUS
      REAL MARRVT,MSERVT
      COMMON /GCOM1/ ATRIB(30),JEVNT,MFE(100),MLE(100),MSTOP,NCRDR,
     1NNAPT,NNATR(100),NNFIL,NNQ(100),NPRNT,PPARM(50,4),TNOW,TTBEG,
     2TTCLR,TTFIN,TTRIB(30),TTSET,MMATR,MMFA(5)
      COMMON /MODEL/ MARRVT,MSERVT,TOTCUS
C
C *** SCHEDULE THE NEXT ARRIVAL.
C
      ATRIB(1)=TNOW+EXPON(MARRVT,1)
      ATRIB(2)=1.
      CALL FILEM(1)
C
C ******************************************************************
C
C *** IF THE SERVER IS IDLE, START SERVICE ON THE ARRIVING CUSTOMER.
C
      IF(NNQ(3).EQ.1) GO TO 10
C
C *** CUSTOMER HAS A DELAY OF ZERO.
C
      CALL COLCT(0.,1)
C
C *** MAKE SERVER BUSY.
C
      CALL FILEM(3)
C
C *** SCHEDULE A DEPARTURE.
C
      ATRIB(1)=TNOW+EXPON(MSERVT,2)
      ATRIB(2)=2.
      CALL FILEM(1)
      RETURN
C
C ******************************************************************
C
C *** SERVER IS BUSY. PLACE ARRIVING CUSTOMER IN THE QUEUE.
C
   10 ATRIB(1)=TNOW
      CALL FILEM(2)
      RETURN
      END
```

Figure 3.5 Listing of GASP IV subroutine ARRIVE, queueing model.

```
      SUBROUTINE DEPART
      INTEGER TOTCUS
      REAL DELAY,MARRVT,MSERVT
      COMMON /GCOM1/ ATRIB(30),JEVNT,MFE(100),MLE(100),MSTOP,NCRDR,
     1NNAPT,NNATR(100),NNFIL,NNQ(100),NPRNT,PPARM(50,4),TNOW,TTBEG,
     2TTCLR,TTFIN,TTRIB(30),TTSET,MMATR,MMFA(5)
      COMMON /MODEL/ MARRVT,MSERVT,TOTCUS
C
C *** IF THE QUEUE IS EMPTY, MAKE THE SERVER IDLE.
C
      IF(NNQ(2).GT.0) GO TO 10
      CALL RMOVE(MFE(3),3)
      RETURN
C
C ***********************************************************************
C
C *** QUEUE IS NOT EMPTY. REMOVE THE FIRST CUSTOMER FROM THE QUEUE.
C
   10 CALL RMOVE(MFE(2),2)
C
C *** COMPUTE THE DELAY OF THE CUSTOMER WHO IS BEGINNING SERVICE.
C
      DELAY=TNOW-ATRIB(1)
      CALL COLCT(DELAY,1)
C
C *** SCHEDULE A DEPARTURE.
C
      ATRIB(1)=TNOW+EXPON(MSERVT,2)
      ATRIB(2)=2.
      CALL FILEM(1)
      RETURN
      END
```

Figure 3.6 Listing of GASP IV subroutine DEPART, queueing model.

stopping rule has been satisfied. When control is passed from subroutine EVNTS back to subroutine GASP, a check is made to see whether MSTOP is equal to -1. If so, the simulation is terminated and the standard output report is printed. (Subroutine OTPUT, if used, would also be executed at this time.)

Subroutine ARRIVE, the arrival event routine, is listed in Fig. 3.5. The first thing done in this subroutine is to schedule the arrival of the next customer. (TNOW is the GASP IV simulation clock.) Then a check is made to determine whether the arriving customer finds the server idle. We use file 3 to correspond to the server. If file 3 contains no records, the server is idle, and if it contains one record (the attributes of this record are irrelevant), the server is busy. [NNQ(3) is the number of records in file 3.] If the server is indeed idle, the arriving customer has a delay of 0, which is recorded by calling the GASP IV subroutine COLCT. (The use and arguments of COLCT are similar to those of subroutine SAMPST in SIMLIB.) Then the server is made busy, and a departure event is scheduled for the arriving customer using random-number stream 2. If the arriving customer finds the server busy, a record containing the time of arrival of this customer is placed in file 2 (the queue).

A listing for subroutine DEPART is given in Fig. 3.6. In this subroutine, the statement CALL RMOVE(MFE(I),I) will remove the first record from file I and place its attributes in the array ATRIB. (RMOVE corresponds to subroutine REMOVE in SIMLIB.) The rest of the subroutine should be self-explanatory.

The GASP IV standard output report (with the exception of a listing of the GASP IV input data) is given in Fig. 3.7. Note that the estimates of average delay

```
                          **GASP SUMMARY REPORT**

                      SIMULATION PROJECT NUMBER   1  BY  LAW

                      DATE  6/ 20/ 1980      RUN NUMBER    1 OF    1

                      CURRENT TIME =    .9474+03


PARAMETER SET      1 =     .0000         .0000        .1000+21       .0000


                         **STATISTICS FOR VARIABLES BASED ON OBSERVATION**
               MEAN        STD DEV      SD OF MEAN        CV        MINIMUM       MAXIMUM    OBS
DELAYINQ     .5593+00      .8761+00      .2771-01     .1566+01      .0000        .4690+01   1000


                      **GASP FILE STORAGE AREA DUMP AT TIME    .9474+03**

                   MAXIMUM NUMBER OF WORDS USED IN FILE STORAGE AREA =    40
                          EQUIVALENT TO  10 ENTRIES OF MAXIMUM SIZE.


                              PRINTOUT OF FILE NUMBER   1
                                TNOW =    .9474+03
                                QQTIM=    .9474+03

                              TIME PERIOD FOR STATISTICS   .9474+03
                              AVERAGE NUMBER IN FILE       1.5420
                              STANDARD DEVIATION            .4982
                              MAXIMUM NUMBER IN FILE        2

                                   FILE CONTENTS
ENTRY   1   =     .9477+03      .1000+01
ENTRY   2   =     .9432+03      .2000+01


                              PRINTOUT OF FILE NUMBER   2
                                TNOW =    .9474+03
                                QQTIM=    .9474+03

                              TIME PERIOD FOR STATISTICS   .9474+03
                              AVERAGE NUMBER IN FILE        .5904
                              STANDARD DEVIATION           1.1492
                              MAXIMUM NUMBER IN FILE        7

                                 THE FILE IS EMPTY


                              PRINTOUT OF FILE NUMBER   3
                                TNOW =    .9474+03
                                QQTIM=    .9460+03

                              TIME PERIOD FOR STATISTICS   .9474+03
                              AVERAGE NUMBER IN FILE        .5420
                              STANDARD DEVIATION            .4982
                              MAXIMUM NUMBER IN FILE        1

                                   FILE CONTENTS
ENTRY   1   =     .9460+03
```

Figure 3.7 GASP IV standard output report, queueing model.

and average number in queue are 0.5593 (see "mean" under "statistics for variables based on observation") and 0.5904 (see "average number in file" for file number 2), respectively. The statistics on delay were computed by subroutine COLCT. (The output statistics on various standard deviations may not be statistically meaningful because of autocorrelation in the output data; see Sec. 4.4.)

3.4.2 SLAM

SLAM (*S*imulation *L*anguage for *A*lternative *M*odeling) is an event-oriented or a process-oriented simulation language developed by Pegden and Pritsker (see [15]). The event orientation in SLAM is similar to that in GASP IV. In the process orientation in SLAM, a modeler combines a set of standard symbols, called *nodes* and *branches,* into an interconnected *network* structure which represents the system of interest pictorially. [This network representation is based on similar concepts in Q-GERT (see Pritsker [13]).] Thus, one can think of a network as a pictorial representation of the "process through which customers in the system flow." After the network model of the system has been developed, it is translated into an equivalent set of SLAM program statements for execution on the computer.

The real appeal of SLAM appears to be the diversity of modeling approaches it affords. The analyst can build discrete-event models using either the event or the process orientation (or both), continuous models employing differential or difference equations, and combined models using all these elements. Because SLAM retains the positive features of GASP IV and also offers increased modeling flexibility and power, it seems likely that SLAM will eventually replace GASP IV.

SLAM is distributed by Pritsker and Associates, which also offers a seminar on its use.

3.5 SIMSCRIPT II.5

SIMSCRIPT II.5 is an event-oriented or process-oriented simulation language considered by many to be the most powerful simulation language available today. After having been developed by the Rand Corporation in the early 1960s, SIMSCRIPT evolved through a number of versions; the latest and most comprehensive version, SIMSCRIPT II.5, is a proprietary product of CACI, Inc. (Los Angeles, Calif.). SIMSCRIPT II.5 is available for major computers manufactured by IBM, UNIVAC, CDC, Honeywell, DEC, and also on many time-sharing networks. References for SIMSCRIPT II.5 include the *SIMSCRIPT II.5 Reference Handbook* [2], Kiviat, Villaneuva, and Markowitz [10], and Russell [17]. A seminar on SIMSCRIPT II.5 is given by CACI monthly.

Because of the power and diversity of the statements available in SIMSCRIPT, general programming tasks can be done more efficiently than in FORTRAN. Furthermore, its English-like and free-form syntax makes SIMSCRIPT programs easy to read and almost self-documenting. SIMSCRIPT II.5 is the only major simulation language with a package for performing statistical analyses of simulation output data (see Law [11]). Continuous and combined discrete-continuous simulations can be performed in SIMSCRIPT II.5 by means of an extension to the language called C-SIMSCRIPT (see Delfosse [3]). One drawback of SIMSCRIPT II.5 at present is that it does not have a textbook comparable to those available for the other simulation languages. This difficulty should be remedied in the near future, since a textbook is in preparation by CACI (see Russell [18]). Another possible drawback of SIMSCRIPT II.5 compared with the other simulation languages, except possibly GPSS/H, is its high purchase or lease cost. As a result, it tends to be used by organizations having a large amount of simulation activity, or on large and expensive simulation projects where the programming power of SIMSCRIPT II.5 is the overriding consideration.

We now shall give a brief survey of how one builds a simulation model in SIMSCRIPT using the event-scheduling approach (see Sec. 3.5.2 for a discussion of the process-interaction approach). A SIMSCRIPT II.5 model views a system as consisting of *entities, attributes,* and *sets.* Entities are of two types, permanent and temporary. *Permanent entities* correspond to objects in a system, e.g., servers in a queueing system, whose number remains fairly constant during the simulation. Conversely, *temporary entities* represent objects in a system, e.g., customers arriving to a queueing system, whose number may vary considerably during the simulation. Attributes are data values which characterize either type of entity, and sets are collections of entities with a common property. (Sets were called files in GASP IV.) To construct a discrete-event simulation model in SIMSCRIPT II.5, the modeler must write a preamble, a main program, and the usual event routines. The *preamble,* which does not contain any executable statements, is used to give a static description of the entire model, including the required events, entities, and sets. Global variables are also defined in the preamble. The main program is used to initialize the event list, to initialize state variables, and to read input parameters. The statement START SIMULATION, which calls the SIMSCRIPT II.5 timing routine, is also executed there to start the actual running of the simulation.

3.5.1 Simulation of the $M/M/1$ Queue

This section shows how to simulate the $M/M/1$ queue considered in Chap. 1 using the event orientation of SIMSCRIPT II.5. (The line numbers in Figs. 3.8 to 3.12 and 3.14 are for expository purposes and are not part of the actual program.) The preamble is given in Fig. 3.8. The events required for the model are declared in line 2. Here, REPORT is an event which will be scheduled to occur when the simulation ends and used to print the output report. Lines 4 and 5 define a generic temporary entity, CUSTOMER, which has the single attribute TIME.OF.ARRIVAL and may belong to the set QUEUE. (Note that variable names can be up to 80 characters long and contain embedded periods.) The set QUEUE will contain the records of all customers waiting in the queue. In line 6, the system as a whole is defined to have

```
 1    PREAMBLE
 2         EVENT NOTICES INCLUDE ARRIVE,DEPART,AND REPORT
 3
 4         TEMPORARY ENTITIES
 5              EVERY CUSTOMER HAS A TIME.OF.ARRIVAL AND MAY BELONG TO THE QUEUE
 6              THE SYSTEM HAS A STATUS AND OWNS THE QUEUE
 7
 8         DEFINE IDLE TO MEAN 0
 9         DEFINE BUSY TO MEAN 1
10         DEFINE DELAY,MARRVT,AND MSERVT AS VARIABLES
11         DEFINE NUMCUS,STATUS,AND TOTCUS AS INTEGER VARIABLES
12         DEFINE MINUTES TO MEAN UNITS
13
14         SUBSTITUTE THESE 4 LINES FOR CHECK.FOR.TERMINATION
15              ADD 1 TO NUMCUS
16              IF NUMCUS=TOTCUS
17                   SCHEDULE A REPORT NOW
18              ALWAYS
19
20         TALLY AVGDEL AS THE AVERAGE OF DELAY
21         ACCUMULATE AVGNIQ AS THE AVERAGE OF N.QUEUE
22    END
```

Figure 3.8 Listing of the SIMSCRIPT II.5 preamble, queueing model.

an attribute STATUS, i.e., idle or busy, and to be the owner of the set QUEUE. (For this example, the system can be thought of as the server.) Every set in SIM-SCRIPT II.5 must have an owner since it uses linked storage allocation. In line 8, the program is told to substitute 0 for every occurrence of the word IDLE. A similar substitution is defined in line 9. The three quantities in line 10 are defined to be global real variables. (In SIMSCRIPT II.5, all variables are by default real, regardless of the letter they begin with.) The quantities in line 11 are correspondingly defined to be global integer variables. In line 12, minutes is defined to be the basic unit of time for all internal program calculations; the default is days. In line 14, the program is told to substitute the statements in lines 15 to 18 for every occurrence of the expression CHECK.FOR.TERMINATION. The TALLY statement in line 20 says to compute the average delay of the customers and store it in the variable AVGDEL; its purpose is similar to that of subroutine COLCT in GASP IV. The ACCUMULATE statement in line 21 computes the time-average number of records (customers) in the set QUEUE and stores it in AVGNIQ.

The main program, which is quite short for this example, is listed in Fig. 3.9. In line 2, a free-form read statement is used to read in the three input parameters. The SCHEDULE statement in line 3 places an ARRIVE event in the event list at a time equal to the present value of simulated time (0) plus an exponential interarrival time with mean MARRVT, using random-number stream 1. (There are 10 such streams in SIMSCRIPT.) Note the ease of event scheduling in SIMSCRIPT compared with GASP IV and SIMLIB. Finally, the statement in line 4 calls the timing routine, as discussed above.

Event routine ARRIVE is listed in Fig. 3.10. The SCHEDULE statement in line 2 schedules the arrival of the next customer to the system just as in the main program. A check is then made in line 4 to see whether the server is busy when the current customer arrives. If the server is busy, storage is allocated for the arriving customer's record by the CREATE statement in line 5, the time of arrival of this customer is set to the current value of the simulation clock, TIME.V, in line 6, and the customer's record is filed last in the set QUEUE in line 7. If the arriving customer finds the server idle (line 10), the delay of this customer is set to 0 in line 11, the server is made busy in line 12, and a DEPART event is scheduled for this customer using random-number stream 2 in line 13. When the statement CHECK.FOR.TERMINATION is executed in line 14 (see the preamble), 1 is added to the number of customers previously delayed, NUMCUS (which was automatically initialized to 0), and then a check is made to see whether NUMCUS is equal to the number of customers whose delays we want to observe, TOTCUS. If so, a REPORT event is scheduled to occur immediately (NOW) upon return to the timing routine. Otherwise, control is simply returned to the timing routine.

```
1    MAIN
2         READ MARRVT,MSERVT,AND TOTCUS
3         SCHEDULE AN ARRIVE IN EXPONENTIAL.F(MARRVT,1) MINUTES
4         START SIMULATION
5    END
```

Figure 3.9 Listing of the SIMSCRIPT II.5 main program, queueing model.

```
 1      EVENT ARRIVE
 2          SCHEDULE AN ARRIVE IN EXPONENTIAL.F(MARRVT,1) MINUTES
 3
 4          IF STATUS=BUSY
 5              CREATE A CUSTOMER
 6              LET TIME.OF.ARRIVAL(CUSTOMER)=TIME.V
 7              FILE THE CUSTOMER IN THE QUEUE
 8              RETURN
 9
10          ELSE
11              LET DELAY=0.
12              LET STATUS=BUSY
13              SCHEDULE A DEPART IN EXPONENTIAL.F(MSERVT,2) MINUTES
14              CHECK.FOR.TERMINATION
15              RETURN
16      END
```

Figure 3.10 Listing of the SIMSCRIPT II.5 event routine ARRIVE, queueing model.

A listing for event routine DEPART is given in Fig. 3.11. If the queue is empty just before a customer departs (line 2), the server is made idle in line 3 and control is returned to the timing routine. If one or more customers are left behind (line 6), the first customer is removed from the queue in line 7, its delay is computed in line 8, the storage space for this customer's record is returned by the DESTROY statement in line 9 to the pool of available space, and a DEPART event is scheduled for the customer entering service in line 10. A check for termination is performed in line 11 exactly as in event routine ARRIVE.

Event routine REPORT, which is called when the desired number of delays has been observed, is listed in Fig. 3.12. The print statement in line 2 states that literally 7 lines of output are to be printed as specified by the following 7 lines and that these lines are to include the variables MARRVT, MSERVT, and TOTCUS. The format **.*** in line 5 corresponds to the first of these variables, etc. After three blank lines are printed by the statement in line 10, estimates of the desired measures of performance, AVGDEL and AVGNIQ, are printed by line 11. Note that no calculations were necessary to compute these quantities after they were defined in the preamble. Lines 15 to 17 make the output report free of any extraneous printing. The simulation terminates upon encountering the STOP statement in line 18.

The desired output report, as printed by event routine REPORT, is displayed in Fig. 3.13.

```
 1      EVENT DEPART
 2          IF QUEUE IS EMPTY
 3              LET STATUS=IDLE
 4              RETURN
 5
 6          ELSE
 7              REMOVE THE FIRST CUSTOMER FROM THE QUEUE
 8              LET DELAY=TIME.V-TIME.OF.ARRIVAL(CUSTOMER)
 9              DESTROY CUSTOMER
10              SCHEDULE A DEPART IN EXPONENTIAL.F(MSERVT,2) MINUTES
11              CHECK.FOR.TERMINATION
12              RETURN
13      END
```

Figure 3.11 Listing of the SIMSCRIPT II.5 event routine DEPART, queueing model.

```
 1      EVENT REPORT
 2          PRINT 7 LINES WITH MARRVT,MSERVT,AND TOTCUS THUS
 3      SINGLE-SERVER QUEUEING SYSTEM
 4
 5      MEAN INTERARRIVAL TIME        **.*** MINUTES
 6
 7      MEAN SERVICE TIME             **.*** MINUTES
 8
 9      NUMBER OF CUSTOMERS             *****
10          SKIP 3 LINES
11          PRINT 3 LINES WITH AVGDEL AND AVGNIQ THUS
12      AVERAGE DELAY IN QUEUE        **.*** MINUTES
13
14      AVERAGE NUMBER IN QUEUE       **.***
15          START NEW PAGE
16          PRINT 1 LINE THUS
17
18          STOP
19      END
```

Figure 3.12 Listing of the SIMSCRIPT II.5 event routine REPORT, queueing model.

3.5.2 The Process-Interaction Approach in SIMSCRIPT II.5

For most of SIMSCRIPT's history it was an event-oriented simulation language, as described above, but in 1975 CACI added two new concepts, *processes* and *resources,* to SIMSCRIPT II.5 (see Russell [16, 18]), thereby allowing a modeler to use either the event orientation, the process orientation, or both simultaneously. (Processes were defined in Sec. 3.3, and resources may be thought of as the objects requested by the process objects.) In order to give the reader a brief idea of the process orientation in SIMSCRIPT, Fig. 3.14 gives the customer-process routine corresponding to a (process) SIMSCRIPT II.5 simulation model of the $M/M/1$ queue. This process routine, which describes the entire experience of a customer as it flows through the queueing system, takes the place of event routines ARRIVE and DEPART in the model of Sec. 3.5.1. (Note that small changes must also be made to the preamble and the main program and that event routine REPORT is replaced by an almost identical process routine by the same name; we omit explicit listings of these minor changes. Furthermore, the new model will use two types of processes, CUSTOMER and REPORT, and one type of resource, SERVER.) The ACTI-VATE statement in line 3 of the process routine schedules the arrival of the *next* customer process to the system. The time of arrival of the currently arriving customer process is recorded in line 5, and then this process *requests* the use of the server

```
SINGLE-SERVER QUEUEING SYSTEM

MEAN INTERARRIVAL TIME      1.000 MINUTES

MEAN SERVICE TIME           0.500 MINUTES

NUMBER OF CUSTOMERS         1000


AVERAGE DELAY IN QUEUE      0.431 MINUTES

AVERAGE NUMBER IN QUEUE     0.431
```

Figure 3.13 SIMSCRIPT II.5 output report, queueing model.

```
 1    PROCESS CUSTOMER
 2           DEFINE TIME.OF.ARRIVAL AS A VARIABLE
 3           ACTIVATE A CUSTOMER IN EXPONENTIAL.F(MARRVT,1) MINUTES
 4
 5           LET TIME.OF.ARRIVAL=TIME.V
 6           REQUEST 1 SERVER
 7           LET DELAY=TIME.V-TIME.OF.ARRIVAL
 8           CHECK.FOR.TERMINATION
 9           WORK EXPONENTIAL.F(MSERVT,2) MINUTES
10           RELINQUISH 1 SERVER
11    END
```

Figure 3.14 Listing of the SIMSCRIPT II.5 process routine CUSTOMER, queueing model.

resource in line 6. If the server is already busy serving another customer process, the arriving process joins the queue and waits to be served at some point in the future. (In this case the REQUEST statement automatically provides for the passage of simulated time.) If the server is idle, the delay in queue of the arriving customer process is computed (line 7) and a check for termination of the simulation run is made (line 8). (If the server was busy when the customer process arrived, lines 7 and 8 are executed *after* the customer process has completed its delay in queue.) The server then *works* on the service request of the customer process in line 9. After service has been completed, the customer process *relinquishes* the server in line 10 and is then removed from the system. The reader may find it instructive to compare the SIMSCRIPT II.5 process routine CUSTOMER to the flowchart in Fig. 3.1.

In summary, the process routine requires 10 lines of code whereas the corresponding event routines ARRIVE and DEPART required a total of 26 lines. The programming power of the process orientation is apparent.

3.6 GPSS

GPSS (*General-Purpose Simulation System*) is a process-oriented simulation language particularly well suited for queueing systems. Originally developed by the IBM Corporation in the early 1960s, it has evolved through several versions, the latest two IBM versions being called GPSS/360 and GPSS V. (All other IBM versions are obsolete, and GPSS V is a superset of GPSS/360.) Historically, GPSS has been the most popular simulation language, probably due to the queueing nature of many simulations and to IBM's strong influence on the computer industry. GPSS 360/V is available on IBM 360 and 370 computers; versions developed by other companies are available for most major computers and on time-sharing networks. (These versions are not completely compatible with GPSS 360/V.) The most exciting new implementation is GPSS/H (see [9]), developed by James O. Henriksen, of Wolverine Software, Falls Church, Virginia. GPSS/H is a compiler language, compared with the interpretive approach taken by GPSS 360/V. Due to this and other improvements, GPSS/H programs are reported to run, on the average, 5 times faster than corresponding GPSS 360/V programs. A good introduction to GPSS, in general, can be found in Gordon [8]. A more detailed description, including numerous examples, is given by Schriber [20] (see also Gordon [7]). A seminar on GPSS is given every summer at the University of Michigan by Professor Thomas J. Schriber.

The principal appeal of GPSS is the ease and speed with which simulation models can be built. Since many simulation projects operate against tight time deadlines, this programming power can be a very important consideration. However, like the other simulation languages, GPSS has drawbacks of its own. In GPSS the simulation clock is integer-valued, and the simulator must implicitly choose a basic unit of time in which to represent all activity times. For the GPSS program of the $M/M/1$ queue given in Sec. 3.6.1, we choose the basic unit of time as 1 second and represent, for example, a mean interarrival time of 1 minute as 60 basic units. (Thus, a generated interarrival time can take on only the integer values 0, 1, 2, . . . seconds.) GPSS 360/V has no exact automatic mechanism for generating random variables from the standard probability distributions, e.g., exponential or normal. Instead, the user must approximate the inverse of the distribution function of the desired random variable by a sequence of straight-line segments. GPSS offers less programming flexibility than GASP IV (which is an extension of FORTRAN) or SIMSCRIPT II.5 (which contains statements comparable in power to those in ALGOL, FORTRAN, or PL/1). The analyst who wants to do complicated numerical calculations or obtain a special output report when using GPSS will have to write a subroutine in, say, FORTRAN and interface it with his program by means of the GPSS HELP statement. (A HELP statement could also be used to generate a random variable without resorting to the above approximation.) Finally, the GPSS 360/V random-number generator has certain shortcomings. For example, all eight random-number streams are identical by default; see Schriber [20, p. 172] for a discussion of how to make these streams different (but not necessarily independent). It should be noted, however, that certain other versions of GPSS use other random-number generators.

The GPSS language consists of more than 40 standard statements, each of which has a corresponding pictorial representation (called a *block*) that is intended to be suggestive of the operation performed by the statement. Building a GPSS model can be thought of as combining a set of the standard blocks into a block diagram which represents the path taken by a typical customer as it progresses through the system of interest. After the block-diagram model has been constructed, it is translated into the corresponding set of GPSS statements for execution on the computer. However, the block diagram itself is often useful in explaining the nature of the model to a manager, who may not be familiar with any programming language. Customers or temporary entities which require service of some kind from the system of interest are called *transactions* in GPSS. The servers or permanent entities which provide the service required by the transactions are called *facilities* or *storages,* corresponding to a single server or a group of servers, respectively.

3.6.1 Simulation of the $M/M/1$ Queue

A block diagram and a statement listing for a GPSS/360 program of the $M/M/1$ queue are given in Figs. 3.15 and 3.16, respectively. In Fig. 3.16 note the relatively

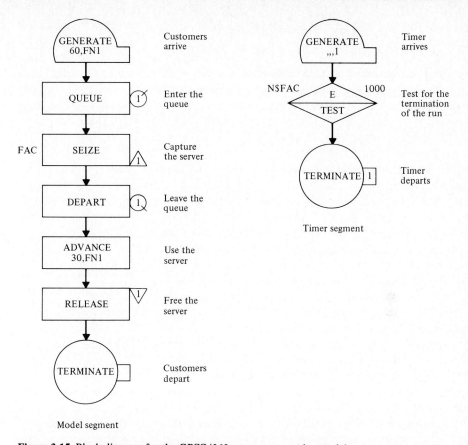

Model segment

Figure 3.15 Block diagram for the GPSS/360 program, queueing model.

small number of statements required by the GPSS program compared with the number required by the corresponding GASP IV and SIMSCRIPT II.5 programs. (Statements with an asterisk (*) in column 1 are comments. Also, in lines 15 to 31 the words after column 30 are comments. Line numbers are not part of the program.) We describe each of the statements in the program briefly. The SIMULATE statement (line 4 of the program) is a control statement necessary for execution of the program. Lines 8 to 11 define a function, denoted by FN1 in the remainder of the program, used to generate a random variable that is *approximately* exponentially distributed with a mean of 1 second; see, for example, Schriber [20, p. 163] for details. (Recall from above that 1 second is the basic unit of time.) The next part of the program, model segment 1, describes the flow of customers through the system. The GENERATE statement (line 15) creates transactions representing customers with interarrival times that are approximately exponentially distributed with a mean of 60 seconds (or 1 minute). (FN1 is used to generate exponential random variables with a mean of 1 which are multiplied by 60 to give exponential random variables

```
 1    *
 2    *         SIMULATION OF THE M/M/1 QUEUE
 3    *
 4              SIMULATE
 5    *
 6    *         DEFINE FUNCTION NUMBER 1
 7    *
 8    1    FUNCTION   RN1,C24
 9    0,0/.1,.104/.2,.222/.3,.355/.4,.509/.5,.69/.6,.915/.7,1.2/.75,1.38
10    .8,1.6/.84,1.83/.88,2.12/.9,2.3/.92,2.52/.94,2.81/.95,2.99/.96,3.2
11    .97,3.5/.98,3.9/.99,4.6/.995,5.3/.998,6.2/.999,7/.9998,8
12    *
13    *         MODEL SEGMENT 1
14    *
15              GENERATE   60,FN1        CUSTOMERS ARRIVE
16              QUEUE      1             ENTER THE QUEUE
17    FAC       SEIZE      1             CAPTURE THE SERVER
18              DEPART     1             LEAVE THE QUEUE
19              ADVANCE    30,FN1        USE THE SERVER
20              RELEASE    1             FREE THE SERVER
21              TERMINATE                CUSTOMERS DEPART
22    *
23    *         MODEL SEGMENT 2
24    *
25              GENERATE   ,,,1          TIMER ARRIVES
26              TEST E     N$FAC,1000    TEST FOR TERMINATION OF THE RUN
27              TERMINATE  1             TIMER DEPARTS
28    *
29    *         CONTROL CARDS
30    *
31              START      1             MAKE 1 SIMULATION RUN
32              END
```

Figure 3.16 Listing of the GPSS/360 program, queueing model.

with a mean of 60.) The QUEUE statement (line 16) and the DEPART statement (line 18) correspond to a customer's entering and leaving the queue, respectively; the use of these statements results in estimates of the average delay and the time-average number in queue being computed automatically and then printed in the standard output report. The SEIZE statement (line 17) and the RELEASE statement (line 20), which define a facility, correspond to a transaction's seizing the server when it becomes idle and releasing the server after the transaction's service has been completed. The actual service time of a transaction, which in this case will be approximately exponentially distributed with a mean of 30 seconds, is experienced at the ADVANCE statement (line 19). The transaction is destroyed (removed from the system) at the TERMINATE statement (line 21).

Model segment 2 is used to terminate the simulation after 1000 customers have completed their delays. The GENERATE statement (line 25) causes a *single* timer transaction to arrive at time 1. The timer transaction is prevented from proceeding by the TEST statement (line 26) until the number of normal transactions, N$FAC, which have entered the SEIZE statement labeled FAC (line 17) is equal to 1000. When the number of normal transactions which have completed their delays reaches the desired number, the timer transaction continues to the TERMINATE statement (line 27), where it is destroyed and reduces a termination counter by 1. Since the termination counter was initially set to 1 by the START statement (line 31), the

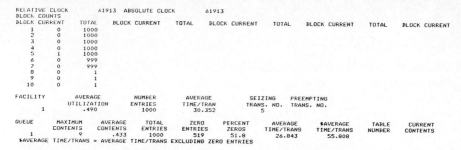

Figure 3.17 GPSS/360 standard output report, queueing model.

timer transaction's decrementing the counter reduces the counter value to 0 and results in the termination of the simulation.

The GPSS/360 standard output report is shown in Fig. 3.17. Note that the estimates of average delay and the average number in queue are 26.843 seconds and 0.433 (see "average time/trans" and "average contents" for queue 1), respectively.

3.7 CRITERIA FOR SELECTING A SIMULATION LANGUAGE

We assume in this section that a decision has been made to use a simulation language rather than a general-purpose language, and we present criteria which may be useful in selecting such a language. As suggested by Shannon [21, p. 107], there are two levels at which a decision with regard to a simulation language may be made. At the first level an organization must decide what language or languages to purchase or lease for its general use. One should not necessarily feel that a single language must be chosen, since for a given application, one language could be more appropriate than another. At the second level, an analyst must decide what language to use for a particular simulation study.

The following are some of the criteria that should be considered in selecting a simulation language for an organization (see [21] and also Sargent [19]):

1. Availability of the language for the company's computer system
2. Cost of installing and maintaining the language
3. Number of simulation studies likely to be done
4. Types of systems that will be simulated
5. Quality of the language's documentation (textbooks and user's manuals)
6. Ease of learning the language
7. Computer storage requirements of the language
8. Computer time efficiency of the language
9. Flexibility and power of the language

When an analyst must pick a simulation language for a particular application, many of the above criteria are still relevant. In addition, however, the following factors are important:

1. Availability of languages, either in-house or on a time-sharing network
2. Nature of the problem to be solved
3. Languages known by the analyst
4. Amount of time available for the simulation study and the programming effort required by the language
5. Portability of a model written in the language (often important to governmental and military organizations)
6. Language's ability to communicate the nature of a model to a person other than the programmer, e.g., the model's user or a manager

In order to provide the reader with some additional guidance in choosing a simulation language, Table 3.1 presents a comparison of GASP IV, SIMSCRIPT II.5, and GPSS (either GPSS 360/V or GPSS/H) relative to 14 selected criteria. Our list of criteria is *not exhaustive*. In particular, we have chosen not to include computer time efficiency, since we believe that this depends heavily on the computer used, programmer skill, and the application. A number of the criteria evaluated are application-dependent, and our comparison is aimed at indicating how the languages would fare relative to these criteria in general. Furthermore, evaluation of a language is really somewhat subjective, depending on such factors as programming skill, educational background, and personal bias.

Two criteria evaluated in the table deserve additional discussion. First, our cost evaluations are *relative* rather than absolute; thus, whether or not a language is actually expensive in an absolute sense depends on the size of the organization involved and the nature of the simulation study. To give some indication of actual language costs, it might be mentioned that GPSS V, which was evaluated as having a medium cost, can be leased from IBM for approximately $1000 a year. The other criterion we would like to discuss is the availability of an output-data analysis package. All the simulation languages provide a mechanism for obtaining *estimates* of desired measures of performance from a single simulation run, but since these estimates are random variables which may have large variances, in a particular run these estimates could differ greatly from the corresponding true answers. Furthermore, the usual estimates of these variances provided by simulation languages are often highly biased (see Sec. 4.4). Recently, an output-data analysis package has been made available as an extension of SIMSCRIPT II.5 (see [11]) which addresses issues related to the accuracy of simulation output. However, analysts (after reading Chap. 8) could develop a similar package of their own for use with some other simulation language.

We have not included an evaluation of SLAM in Table 3.1 (see Prob. 3.4) because not enough time has elapsed since its introduction to allow for a thorough evaluation of its capabilities. We do feel, however, that SLAM provides a considerable improvement over GASP IV with regard to many of the criteria discussed, e.g., programming power and natural framework for simulation modeling, and is likely to be a popular simulation language during the next several years.

Table 3.1 Comparison of the simulation languages GASP IV, SIMSCRIPT II.5, and GPSS

	Language		
Criterion	GASP IV	SIMSCRIPT II.5	GPSS
Types of systems oriented toward	General	General	Queueing[a]
Relative cost (purchase or lease)	Low	High	GPSS V, medium; GPSS/H, high
Event-scheduling approach	Yes	Yes	No
Process-interaction approach	No	Yes	Yes
Combined discrete-continuous simulation	Yes	Yes[b]	No
Mechanism for generating random variables easily	Yes	Yes	No[c]
Output-data analysis package	Limited	Yes[b]	Limited
Natural framework for simulation modeling	Fair	Good	Very good[d]
Ease of learning[e] (discrete aspects of the language)	Very good	Fair	Good
Availability for different computers and portability of programs	Excellent	Good	Fair
Documentation (textbooks and user's manuals)	Very good	Fair[f]	Very good
Language flexibility	Excellent	Excellent	Fair
Language programming power	Fair	Excellent	Excellent[g]
Communication ability[h]	Fair	Very good	Excellent

[a]Our definition of a queueing system is quite general, including such systems as computer systems, assembly lines, transportation systems, etc.

[b]Available as a free extension of the language.

[c]This capability should be available in GPSS/H by 1981 (personal communication with James O. Henriksen).

[d]GPSS's capability with regard to this criterion for *queueing systems* is very good; for other types of systems its capability is somewhat less.

[e]This attribute assumes a knowledge of FORTRAN and a desire to obtain a *thorough* understanding of the language. For nonprogrammers, GPSS would rate higher.

[f]This evaluation should improve considerably when Russell [18] becomes available.

[g]GPSS's capability with regard to this criterion for *queueing systems* is excellent; for other types of systems its capability is somewhat less.

[h]This evaluation is based on the block diagrams of GPSS and the self-documenting syntax of SIMSCRIPT II.5.

PROBLEMS

The following problems are to be done with the assistance of the references for this chapter.

3.1 Build a simulation model of the service facility consisting of two servers in series discussed in Prob. 1.2 using each of the languages GASP IV, SIMSCRIPT II.5, and GPSS.

3.2 Build a simulation model of the service facility consisting of s parallel servers and a single FIFO queue discussed in Prob. 1.4 using each of the languages GASP IV, SIMSCRIPT II.5, and GPSS.

3.3 Build a simulation model of the job shop presented in Sec. 2.6 using each of the languages GASP IV, SIMSCRIPT II.5, and GPSS.

3.4 Learn enough about the simulation language SLAM from reading [15] to be able to add a corresponding column to Table 3.1.

3.5 Using the criteria presented in Sec. 3.7 and any others that seem appropriate, determine which language or languages might be the most appropriate for your company or university.

REFERENCES

1. Birtwistle, G. M., O. J. Dahl, B. Myhrhaug, and K. Nygaard: *SIMULA Begin,* Auerbach, Philadelphia, 1973.
2. CACI, Inc.: *SIMSCRIPT II.5 Reference Handbook,* Los Angeles, 1976.
3. Delfosse, C. M.: *Continuous Simulation and Combined Simulation in SIMSCRIPT II.5,* CACI, Inc., Arlington, Va., 1976.
4. Fishman, G. S.: *Concepts and Methods in Discrete Event Digital Simulation,* Wiley, New York, 1973.
5. Fishman, G. S.: *Principles of Discrete Event Simulation,* Wiley, New York, 1978.
6. Franta, W. R.: *The Process View of Simulation,* Elsevier North-Holland, New York, 1977.
7. Gordon, G.: *The Application of GPSS V to Discrete System Simulation,* Prentice-Hall, Englewood Cliffs, N.J., 1975.
8. Gordon, G.: *System Simulation,* 2d ed., Prentice-Hall, Englewood Cliffs, N.J., 1978.
9. Henriksen, J. O.: *The GPSS/H User's Manual,* Wolverine Software, Falls Church, Va., 1979.
10. Kiviat, P. J., R. Villaneuva, and H. M. Markowitz: *SIMSCRIPT II.5 Programming Language,* E. C. Russell (ed.), CACI, Inc., Los Angeles, 1973.
11. Law, A. M.: *Statistical Analysis of Simulation Output Data with SIMSCRIPT II.5,* CACI, Inc., Los Angeles, 1979.
12. Pritsker, A. A. B.: *The GASP IV Simulation Language,* Wiley, New York, 1974.
13. Pritsker, A. A. B.: *Modeling and Analysis Using Q-GERT Networks,* 2d ed., Halsted, New York, 1979.
14. Pritsker, A. A. B.: GASP, in J. Belzer, A. G. Holzman, and A. Kent (eds.), *Encyclopedia of Computer Science and Technology,* vol. 8, Dekker, New York, 1977.
15. Pritsker, A. A. B., and C. D. Pegden: *Introduction to Simulation and SLAM,* Systems Publishing, West Lafayette, Ind., 1979.
16. Russell, E. C.: *Simulating with Processes and Resources in SIMSCRIPT II.5,* CACI, Inc., Los Angeles, 1976.
17. Russell, E. C.: *Simulation and SIMSCRIPT II.5,* CACI, Inc., Los Angeles, 1976.
18. Russell, E. C.: *Building Simulation Models with SIMSCRIPT II.5,* CACI, Inc., Los Angeles, 1981.
19. Sargent, R. G.: An Introduction to the Selection and Use of Simulation Languages, *Syracuse Univ. Dept. Ind. Eng. Oper. Res. Tech. Rep.* 79-1. Syracuse, N.Y., 1979.
20. Schriber, T. J.: *Simulation Using GPSS,* Wiley, New York, 1974.
21. Shannon, R. E.: *Systems Simulation: The Art and Science,* Prentice-Hall, Englewood Cliffs, N.J., 1975.

FOUR

REVIEW OF BASIC PROBABILITY AND
STATISTICS

4.1 INTRODUCTION

The completion of a successful simulation study involves much more than constructing a flowchart of the system under study, translating the flowchart into a computer
language, and then making one or a few replications of each proposed system design.
The use of probability and statistics is such an integral part of a simulation study
that every simulation modeling team should include at least one person thoroughly
trained in such techniques. In particular, probability and statistics are needed for
choosing the input probability distributions (Chap. 5), generating the random variables corresponding to these distributions (Chaps. 6 and 7), validation of the simulation model (Chap. 10), statistical analysis of the simulation output data (Chaps.
8 and 9), and designing the simulation experiments (Chaps. 11 and 12).

In this chapter we establish a statistical notation used throughout the book and
review some basic probability and statistics particularly relevant to simulation. We
also point out the potential dangers of applying classical statistical techniques based
on independent observations to simulation output data, which are rarely independent.

4.2 RANDOM VARIABLES AND THEIR PROPERTIES

We assume that the reader has a basic understanding of what is meant by a random
variable, and we denote random variables by capital letters such as X, Y, Z and the
values that random variables take on by small letters such as x, y, z. A random
variable X is said to be *discrete* if it can take on at most a countable number of
values, say, x_1, x_2, ... (Thus, a random variable which takes on a finite number of

values $x_1, x_2, \ldots, x_n$ is discrete.) The probability that the discrete random variable X takes on the value x_i is given by

$$P\{X = x_i\} = p(x_i) \qquad \text{for} \qquad i = 1, 2, \ldots$$

and
$$\sum_{i=1}^{\infty} p(x_i) = 1$$

All probability statements about X can (at least in principle) be computed from $p(x)$, which is called the *probability mass function* for the discrete random variable X. If $I = [a, b]$, where a and b are any real numbers such that $a \leq b$, then

$$P\{X \in I\} = \sum_{\{i: a \leq x_i \leq b\}} p(x_i)$$

(the symbol $\in$ means "contained in" and the colon is read "such that"). If $I = (-\infty, x]$ for any real number x, then

$$P\{X \in I\} = P\{X \leq x\} = \sum_{\{i: x_i \leq x\}} p(x_i) = F(x)$$

where $F(x)$ is called the *distribution function* of X.

Example 4.1 For the inventory example of Chap. 1, the size of the demand for the product is a discrete random variable X which takes on the values 1, 2, 3, 4 with respective probabilities $\frac{1}{6}, \frac{1}{3}$, $\frac{1}{3}, \frac{1}{6}$. The probability mass function and the distribution function for X are given in Figs. 4.1 and 4.2.

A random variable X is said to be *continuous* if there exists a nonnegative function $f(x)$ such that for any set of real numbers B

$$P\{X \in B\} = \int_B f(x)\, dx \qquad \text{and} \qquad \int_{-\infty}^{\infty} f(x)\, dx = 1$$

(If X is a nonnegative random variable, as is often the case, the second range of integration is from 0 to ∞.) All probability statements about X can (in principle) be computed from $f(x)$, which is called the *probability density function* for the contin-

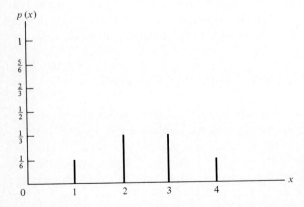

Figure 4.1 $p(x)$ for the demand-size random variable X.

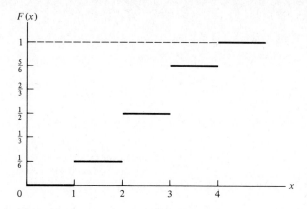

Figure 4.2 $F(x)$ for the demand-size random variable X.

uous random variable X. The distribution function of X is given by

$$F(x) = P\{X \le x\} = \int_{-\infty}^{x} f(y)\, dy \qquad \text{for all } -\infty < x < \infty$$

Furthermore, if $I = [a, b]$ for any real numbers a and b such that $a < b$, then

$$P\{X \in I\} = \int_{a}^{b} f(y)\, dy = F(b) - F(a)$$

Example 4.2 In Chap. 1 the exponential random variable was used for the interarrival times and for the service times in the queueing example and for the interdemand times in the inventory example. The probability density function and the distribution function for an exponential random variable with parameter β are given in Figs. 4.3 and 4.4.

So far in this chapter we have considered only one random variable at a time, but in a simulation study one must usually deal with many random variables simultaneously. For example, in the queueing model of Chap. 1 we were interested in the (input) service-time random variables $S_1, S_2, \ldots, S_n$ and the (output) delay random variables $D_1, D_2, \ldots, D_n$. In general, let $X_1, X_2, \ldots, X_n$ be random variables of interest, and let

$$F_{X_1, X_2, \ldots, X_n}(x_1, x_2, \ldots, x_n) = P\{X_1 \le x_1, X_2 \le x_2, \ldots, X_n \le x_n\}$$

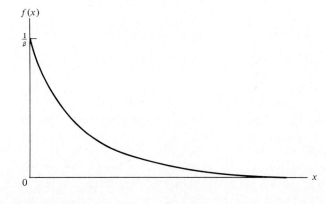

Figure 4.3 $f(x)$ for an exponential random variable with parameter β.

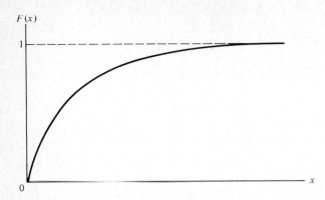

$F(x)$

1

0

x

Figure 4.4 $F(x)$ for an exponential random variable with parameter β.

be the *joint distribution function* of $X_1, X_2, \ldots, X_n$ for the values $x_1, x_2, \ldots, x_n$. Here and below, we use subscripts on distribution, density, and mass functions to indicate explicitly which random variables we are dealing with. We say that the random variables $X_1, X_2, \ldots, X_n$ are *mutually independent* if

$$F_{X_1,X_2,\ldots,X_n}(x_1, x_2, \ldots, x_n) = \prod_{i=1}^{n} F_{X_i}(x_i) \qquad \text{for all } x_1, x_2, \ldots, x_n \qquad (4.1)$$

where the symbol Π means "product" and $F_{X_i}(x_i)$ is the (marginal) distribution function of X_i evaluated at x_i. (Intuitively, $n = 2$ random variables are independent if knowing the value that one random variable takes on tells us nothing about the distribution of the other random variable.) For jointly continuous random variables definition (4.1) is equivalent to

$$f_{X_1,X_2,\ldots,X_n}(x_1, x_2, \ldots, x_n) = \prod_{i=1}^{n} f_{X_i}(x_i) \qquad \text{for all } x_1, x_2, \ldots, x_n$$

where $f_{X_1,X_2,\ldots,X_n}(x_1, x_2, \ldots, x_n)$ is the *joint probability density function* of $X_1, X_2, \ldots, X_n$ and $f_{X_i}(x_i)$, the density function of X_i, can be computed from

$$f_{X_i}(x_i) = \int_{-\infty}^{\infty} \int_{-\infty}^{\infty} \cdots \int_{-\infty}^{\infty} f_{X_1,X_2,\ldots,X_n}(x_1, x_2, \ldots, x_n) \, dx_1 \, dx_2 \ldots dx_{i-1} \, dx_{i+1} \ldots dx_n$$

Similarly, for jointly discrete random variables (4.1) is equivalent to

$$p_{X_1,X_2,\ldots,X_n}(x_1, x_2, \ldots, x_n) = \prod_{i=1}^{n} p_{X_i}(x_i) \qquad \text{for all } x_1, x_2, \ldots, x_n$$

where $p_{X_1,X_2,\ldots,X_n}(x_1, x_2, \ldots, x_n)$ is the *joint probability mass function* of $X_1, X_2, \ldots, X_n$ and $p_{X_i}(x_i)$, the mass function of X_i, can be computed by appropriately summing $p_{X_1,X_2,\ldots,X_n}(x_1, x_2, \ldots, x_n)$. If the random variables $X_1, X_2, \ldots, X_n$ are not independent, we say that they are *dependent*.

We now discuss some characteristics of the single random variable X_i and also some measures of the dependence which may exist between two random variables X_i

and X_j. The *mean* or *expected value* of the random variable X_i ($i = 1, 2, \ldots, n$) will be denoted by μ_i or $E(X_i)$ and is defined by

$$\mu_i = \begin{cases} \displaystyle\sum_{j=1}^{\infty} x_j p_{X_i}(x_j) & \text{if } X_i \text{ is discrete} \\ \displaystyle\int_{-\infty}^{\infty} x f_{X_i}(x) \, dx & \text{if } X_i \text{ is continuous} \end{cases}$$

The mean is a measure of the central tendency of a random variable. The *variance* of the random variable X_i ($i = 1, 2, \ldots, n$) will be denoted by σ_i^2, $\sigma^2(X_i)$, or Var (X_i) and is defined by

$$\sigma_i^2 = E[(X_i - \mu_i)^2] = E(X_i^2) - \mu_i^2$$

where $E(X_i^2)$, the second moment of X_i, is just the expectation of the random variable X_i^2. The variance, which is always nonnegative, is a measure of the dispersion of a random variable about its mean. The *covariance* between the random variables X_i and X_j ($i = 1, 2, \ldots, n; j = 1, 2, \ldots, n$), which is a measure of their (linear) dependence, will be denoted by C_{ij} or Cov (X_i, X_j) and is defined by

$$C_{ij} = E[(X_i - \mu_i)(X_j - \mu_j)] = E(X_i X_j) - \mu_i \mu_j \qquad (4.2)$$

Note that covariances are symmetric, that is, $C_{ij} = C_{ji}$, and that if $i = j$, then $C_{ij} = C_{ii} = \sigma_i^2$.

If $C_{ij} = 0$, the random variables X_i and X_j are said to be *uncorrelated*. It is easy to show that if X_i and X_j are independent random variables, then $C_{ij} = 0$ (see Prob. 4.3). In general, though, the converse is not true (see Prob. 4.4). However, suppose that X_i has a normal distribution with mean μ_i and variance σ_i^2 for $i = 1, 2, \ldots, n$. That is, suppose that the marginal density of X_i is

$$f_{X_i}(x) = \frac{1}{\sqrt{2\pi\sigma_i^2}} \exp\left[-\frac{(x - \mu_i)^2}{2\sigma_i^2} \right] \qquad \text{for } -\infty < x < \infty$$

Then it can be shown that $C_{ij} = 0$ implies that X_i and X_j are independent (see Prob. 4.5). This fact will be used in Chap. 8 when we discuss the method of batch means for steady-state simulations.

We now give two definitions which will shed some light on the significance of the covariance C_{ij}. If $C_{ij} > 0$, then X_i and X_j are said to be *positively correlated*. In this case, $X_i > \mu_i$ and $X_j > \mu_j$ tend to occur together, and $X_i < \mu_i$ and $X_j < \mu_j$ also tend to occur together [see Eq. (4.2)]. Thus, for positively correlated random variables, if one is large, the other is likely to be large also. If $C_{ij} < 0$, then X_i and X_j are said to be *negatively correlated*. In this case, $X_i > \mu_i$ and $X_j < \mu_j$ tend to occur together, and $X_i < \mu_i$ and $X_j > \mu_j$ also tend to occur together. Thus, for negatively correlated random variables, if one is large, the other is likely to be small. We give examples of positively and negatively correlated random variables in the next section.

If $X_1, X_2, \ldots, X_n$ are simulation output data (for example, X_i might be the delay D_i for the queueing example of Chap. 1), we shall often need to know not only the mean μ_i and the variance σ_i^2 for $i = 1, 2, \ldots, n$, but also a measure of the dependence between X_i and X_j for $i \neq j$. However, the difficulty with using C_{ij} as a measure of the dependence between X_i and X_j is that it is not dimensionless, which makes its interpretation troublesome. As a result, we use the *correlation* ρ_{ij}, defined by

$$\rho_{ij} = \frac{C_{ij}}{\sqrt{\sigma_i^2 \sigma_j^2}} \qquad \begin{array}{l} i = 1, 2, \ldots, n \\ j = 1, 2, \ldots, n \end{array} \qquad (4.3)$$

as our primary measure of the dependence between X_i and X_j. [We shall also denote the correlation between X_i and X_j by Cor (X_i, X_j).] Since the denominator in (4.3) is positive, it is clear that ρ_{ij} has the same sign as C_{ij}. Furthermore, it can be shown that $-1 \leq \rho_{ij} \leq 1$ for all i and j (see Prob. 4.6). If ρ_{ij} is close to $+1$, then X_i and X_j are highly positively correlated. On the other hand, if ρ_{ij} is close to -1, then X_i and X_j are highly negatively correlated.

4.3 SIMULATION OUTPUT DATA AND STOCHASTIC PROCESSES

Since most simulation models use random variables as input, the simulation output data are themselves random and care must be taken in drawing conclusions about the model's true characteristics, e.g., the (expected) average delay in the queueing example of Chap. 1. In this and the next three sections we lay the groundwork for a careful treatment of output data analysis in Chap. 8.

A *stochastic process* is a collection of random variables $\{X_t, t \in T\}$ all defined on a common sample (probability) space (see, for example, Ross [5, p. 2]). For our purposes t will always have the connotation of time and T, which is called the *index set*, determines the number of random variables in the collection. The set of all possible values that X_t can take on for any value of t is called the *state space* of the stochastic process. If T is a countable set (usually the positive integers), $\{X_t, t \in T\}$ is called a *discrete-time* stochastic process. If T is an uncountable subset of the set of real numbers (usually the nonnegative real numbers), $\{X_t, t \in T\}$ is called a *continuous-time* stochastic process.

Example 4.3 Consider a single-server queueing system, e.g., the $M/M/1$ queue, with IID interarrival times $A_1, A_2, \ldots$ (see Chap. 1 for the exact definition), IID service times $S_1, S_2, \ldots$, and customers served in a FIFO manner. Relative to the experiment of generating the random variables $A_1, A_2, \ldots$ and $S_1, S_2, \ldots$, one can define the discrete-time stochastic process of delays in queue $\{D_i, i \geq 1\}$ as follows (see Prob. 4.7):

$$D_1 = 0$$

$$D_{i+1} = \max \{D_i + S_i - A_{i+1}, 0\} \qquad \text{for } i = 1, 2, \ldots$$

Here, the index set is the positive integers $\{1, 2, \ldots\}$, and the state space is the set of nonnegative real numbers.

Example 4.4 For the queueing system of Example 4.3, let $Q(t)$ be the number of customers in queue at time t. Then relative to the experiment of generating the random variables $A_1, A_2, \ldots$ and $S_1, S_2, \ldots$, one can define the continuous-time stochastic process $\{Q(t), t \geq 0\}$ as follows (see Prob. 4.8):

$$Q(t) = \sum_{i=1}^{\infty} Y_i(t) \qquad \text{for } t \geq 0$$

$$Y_i(t) = \begin{cases} 1 & \text{if } t_i \leq t < t_i + D_i \\ 0 & \text{otherwise} \end{cases} \quad \text{for } t \geq 0$$

and t_i, the time of arrival of the ith customer, is given by

$$t_i = \sum_{j=1}^{i} A_j \quad \text{for } i = 1, 2, \dots$$

The index set for this stochastic process is the set of nonnegative real numbers, and the state space is the set of nonnegative integers $\{0, 1, 2, \dots\}$.

Sometimes, in order to be able to draw inferences about an underlying stochastic process from a set of simulation output data, one must make assumptions about the stochastic process which may not be strictly true in practice. (Without such assumptions, however, statistical analysis of the output data may not be possible.) An example of this is to assume that a stochastic process is covariance stationary, a property which we now define. A discrete-time stochastic process $\{X_i, i \geq 1\}$ is said to be *covariance stationary* if

$$\mu_i = \mu \qquad \begin{array}{l} \text{for } i = 1, 2, \dots \\ \text{and } -\infty < \mu < \infty \end{array}$$

$$\sigma_i^2 = \sigma^2 \qquad \begin{array}{l} \text{for } i = 1, 2, \dots \\ \text{and } \sigma^2 < \infty \end{array}$$

and $\quad C_{i,i+j} = \text{Cov}\,(X_i, X_{i+j})$ is independent of $i \qquad$ for $j = 1, 2, \dots$

Thus, for a covariance stationary process the mean and variance are stationary over time (the common mean and variance are denoted by μ and σ^2, respectively) and the covariance between two observations X_i and X_{i+j} depends only on the separation j and not on the actual time values i and $i + j$. (It is also possible to define a covariance stationary continuous-time stochastic process $\{X_t, t \geq 0\}$.)

For a covariance stationary process, we denote the covariance and correlation between X_i and X_{i+j} by C_j and ρ_j, respectively, where

$$\rho_j = \frac{C_{i,i+j}}{\sqrt{\sigma_i^2 \sigma_{i+j}^2}} = \frac{C_j}{\sigma^2} = \frac{C_j}{C_0} \qquad \text{for } j = 0, 1, 2, \dots$$

Example 4.5 Consider the output process $\{D_i, i \geq 1\}$ for a covariance stationary (see Appendix 4A for a discussion of this technical detail) $M/M/1$ queue with $\rho = \lambda/\omega < 1$ (recall that λ is the arrival rate and ω is the service rate). From results in Daley [3], one can compute ρ_j, which we plot in Fig. 4.5 for $\rho = 0.5$ and 0.9. (Do not confuse ρ_j and ρ.) Note that the correlations ρ_j are positive and monotonically decrease to zero as j increases. In particular, $\rho_1 = 0.99$ for $\rho = 0.9$ and $\rho_1 = 0.78$ for $\rho = 0.5$. Furthermore, the convergence of ρ_j to zero is considerably slower for $\rho = 0.9$; in fact, ρ_{50} is (amazingly) 0.69. (In general, our experience indicates that output processes for queueing systems are positively correlated.)

Example 4.6 Consider an (s, S) inventory system with zero delivery lag and backlogging. (For this inventory system, which is a simpler version of the one considered in Chap. 1, it is possible to compute the desired correlations analytically.) Let I_i, J_i, and Q_i denote, respectively, the amount of inventory on hand before ordering, the amount of inventory on hand after ordering, and the demand, each in month i. Assume that Q_i has a Poisson distribution (see Sec. 5.2.3 for further discussion) with a mean of 25, that is,

$$p(x) = P\{Q_i = x\} = \frac{e^{-25}(25)^x}{x!} \qquad \text{for } x = 0, 1, 2, \dots$$

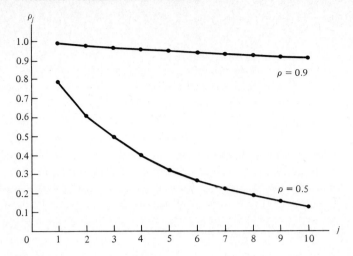

Figure 4.5 Correlation function ρ_j of the process $\{D_i, i \geq 1\}$ for the $M/M/1$ queue.

If $I_i < s$, we order $S - I_i$ items ($J_i = S$) and incur an ordering cost $K + i(S - I_i)$, where $K = 32$ and $i = 3$. If $I_i \geq s$, no order is placed ($J_i = I_i$) and no ordering cost is incurred. After J_i has been determined, the demand Q_i occurs. If $J_i - Q_i \geq 0$, a holding cost $h(J_i - Q_i)$ is incurred, where $h = 1$. If $J_i - Q_i < 0$, a shortage cost $\pi(Q_i - J_i)$ is incurred, where $\pi = 5$. In either case, $I_{i+1} = J_i - Q_i$. Let C_i be the total cost in month i and assume that $s = 17$, $S = 57$, and $I_1 = S$. From results in Wagner [6, p. A19], one can compute ρ_j for the output process $\{C_i, i \geq 1\}$, which we plot in Fig. 4.6. (See Appendix 4A for discussion of a technical detail.) Note that ρ_j can be positive or negative and that the convergence to zero is not monotone, as in Example 4.5.

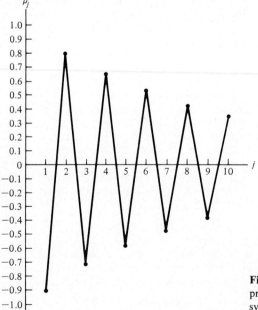

Figure 4.6 Correlation function ρ_j of the process $\{C_i, i \geq 1\}$ for an (s, S) inventory system.

4.4 ESTIMATION OF MEANS, VARIANCES, AND CORRELATIONS

Suppose that $X_1, X_2, \ldots, X_n$ are IID random variables (observations) with finite population mean μ and finite population variance σ^2 and that our primary objective is to estimate μ; the estimation of σ^2 is of secondary interest. Then the *sample mean*

$$\overline{X}(n) = \frac{\sum\limits_{i=1}^{n} X_i}{n}$$

is an unbiased (point) estimator of μ; that is, $E[\overline{X}(n)] = \mu$ (see Prob. 4.9). [Intuitively, $\overline{X}(n)$ an unbiased estimator of μ means that if we perform a very large number of independent experiments each resulting in an $\overline{X}(n)$, the average of the $\overline{X}(n)$'s will be μ.] Similarly, the *sample variance*

$$s^2(n) = \frac{\sum\limits_{i=1}^{n} [X_i - \overline{X}(n)]^2}{n - 1}$$

is an unbiased estimate of σ^2 since $E[s^2(n)] = \sigma^2$ (see Prob. 4.9).

The difficulty with using $\overline{X}(n)$ as an estimator of μ without any additional information is that we have no way of assessing how close $\overline{X}(n)$ is to μ. Because $\overline{X}(n)$ has a variance $\sigma^2[\overline{X}(n)]$, on one experiment $\overline{X}(n)$ may be close to μ while on another $\overline{X}(n)$ may differ from μ by a large amount. (Recall that $\sigma^2[\overline{X}(n)]$ denotes the variance of $\overline{X}(n)$.) The usual way to assess the accuracy of $\overline{X}(n)$ as an estimator of μ is to construct a confidence interval for μ, which we discuss in the next section. However, the first step in constructing a confidence interval is to estimate $\sigma^2[\overline{X}(n)]$. Since

$$\sigma^2[\overline{X}(n)] = \sigma^2 \left(\frac{1}{n} \sum_{i=1}^{n} X_i \right) = \left(\frac{1}{n} \right)^2 \sigma^2 \left(\sum_{i=1}^{n} X_i \right)$$

$$= \frac{1}{n^2} \sum_{i=1}^{n} \sigma^2(X_i) \qquad \text{(because the } X_i\text{'s are independent)}$$

$$= \frac{1}{n^2} n\sigma^2 = \frac{\sigma^2}{n} \tag{4.4}$$

it is clear that, in general, the bigger the sample size n the closer $\overline{X}(n)$ should be to μ. Furthermore, an unbiased estimator of $\sigma^2[\overline{X}(n)]$ is obtained by replacing σ^2 in (4.4) by $s^2(n)$, resulting in

$$\hat{\sigma}^2[\overline{X}(n)] = \frac{s^2(n)}{n} = \frac{\sum\limits_{i=1}^{n} [X_i - \overline{X}(n)]^2}{n(n - 1)}$$

Observe that the expression for $\hat{\sigma}^2[\overline{X}(n)]$ has both an n and an $n - 1$ in the denominator when it is rewritten in terms of the X_i's and $\overline{X}(n)$.

Finally, note that if the X_i's are independent, they are uncorrelated, and thus $\rho_j = 0$ for $j = 1, 2, \ldots, n - 1$.

It has been our experience that simulation output data are always correlated. (If there are simulations with independent output data, we have never seen one.) Thus, the above discussion about IID observations is not *directly* applicable to analyzing simulation output data. In order to understand the dangers of treating simulation output data as if they were independent, we shall use the covariance stationary model discussed in the last section. In particular, assume that the random variables $X_1, X_2, \ldots, X_n$ are from a covariance stationary stochastic process. Then it is still true that the sample mean $\overline{X}(n)$ is an unbiased estimator of μ; however, the sample variance $s^2(n)$ is no longer an unbiased estimator of σ^2. In fact, it can be shown (see Anderson [1, p. 448]) that

$$E[s^2(n)] = \sigma^2 \cdot \left[1 - 2 \sum_{j=1}^{n-1} \frac{(1 - j/n)\rho_j}{n - 1} \right] \tag{4.5}$$

Thus, if $\rho_j > 0$ (positive correlation), as is very often the case in practice, $s^2(n)$ will have a negative bias: $E[s^2(n)] < \sigma^2$. This is significant since all three of the major simulation languages (see Chap. 3) use $s^2(n)$ to estimate the variance of a set of simulation output data, which will generally lead to serious errors in analysis.

Let us now consider the problem of estimating the variance of the sample mean $\sigma^2[\overline{X}(n)]$ (which will be used to construct a confidence interval for μ in the next section) when $X_1, X_2, \ldots, X_n$ are from a covariance stationary process. It can be shown (see Prob. 4.10) that

$$\sigma^2[\overline{X}(n)] = \sigma^2 \cdot \frac{\left[1 + 2 \sum_{j=1}^{n-1} (1 - j/n)\, \rho_j \right]}{n} \tag{4.6}$$

Thus, if one estimates $\sigma^2[\overline{X}(n)]$ from $s^2(n)/n$ (the expression correct in the IID case), which has often been done historically, there are two sources of error: the bias in $s^2(n)$ as an estimator of σ^2 and the neglect of the correlation terms in (4.6). As a matter of fact, if we combine (4.5) and (4.6), we get

$$E\left[\frac{s^2(n)}{n} \right] = \frac{[n/a(n)] - 1}{n - 1} \sigma^2[\overline{X}(n)] \tag{4.7}$$

where $a(n)$ denotes the quantity in square brackets in (4.6).

Example 4.7 Suppose that we have the data $D_1, D_2, \ldots, D_{10}$ from the process of delays $\{D_i, i \geq 1\}$ for a covariance stationary $M/M/1$ queue with $\rho = 0.9$. Then substituting the true correlations ρ_j ($j = 1, 2, \ldots, 9$) into (4.5) and (4.7), we get

$$E[s^2(10)] = 0.0328\sigma^2$$

and

$$E\left[\frac{s^2(10)}{10} \right] = 0.0034\sigma^2[\overline{D}(10)]$$

where

$$\sigma^2 = \sigma^2(D_i) \qquad \overline{D}(10) = \frac{\sum_{i=1}^{10} D_i}{10} \qquad \text{and} \qquad s^2(10) = \frac{\sum_{i=1}^{10} [D_i - \overline{D}(10)]^2}{9}$$

Thus, on the average $s^2(10)/10$ will be a gross underestimate of $\sigma^2[\overline{D}(10)]$, and we are likely to be over optimistic about the closeness of $\overline{D}(10)$ to $\mu = E(D_i)$.

Sometimes one is interested in estimating the ρ_j's from data $X_1, X_2, \ldots, X_n$. (For example, estimates of the ρ_j's might be substituted into (4.6) to obtain a better estimate of $\sigma^2[\overline{X}(n)]$.) If this is the case, ρ_j (for $j = 1, 2, \ldots, n - 1$) can be estimated as follows:

$$\hat{\rho}_j = \frac{\hat{C}_j}{s^2(n)} \qquad \hat{C}_j = \frac{\sum_{i=1}^{n-j} [X_i - \overline{X}(n)][X_{i+j} - \overline{X}(n)]}{n - j} \tag{4.8}$$

(Other estimates of ρ_j are also used. For example, one could replace the $n - j$ in the denominator of $\hat{C}_j$ by n.) The difficulty with the estimate $\hat{\rho}_j$ (or any other estimate of ρ_j) is that it is biased, it has a large variance unless n is very large, and it is correlated with other correlation estimates; that is, $\text{Cov}(\hat{\rho}_j, \hat{\rho}_k) \neq 0$. (In particular, $\hat{\rho}_{n-1}$ will be a poor estimate of ρ_{n-1} since it is based on the single product $[X_1 - \overline{X}(n)][X_n - \overline{X}(n)]$.) Thus, in general, accurate estimates of the ρ_j's will be difficult to obtain unless n is very large and j is small relative to n.

Example 4.8 Suppose we have the data $D_1, D_2, \ldots, D_{100}$ considered in Example 4.7. In Fig. 4.7 we plot $\hat{\rho}_j$ [as computed from (4.8)] and ρ_j for $j = 1, 2, \ldots, 10$. Note the poor quality of the correlation estimates.

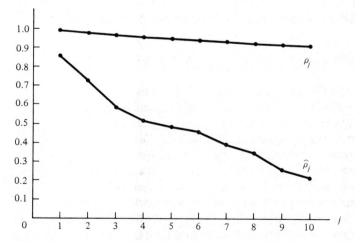

Figure 4.7 ρ_j and $\hat{\rho}_j$ of the process $\{D_i, i \geq 1\}$ for the $M/M/1$ queue with $\rho = 0.9$.

We have seen that simulation output data are correlated, and thus that formulas from classical statistics based on IID observations cannot be used directly for estimating variances. However, we shall see in Chap. 8 that it will often be possible to group simulation output data into new "observations" to which the formulas based on IID observations can be applied. Thus, the formulas in this and the next two sections based on IID observations are indirectly applicable to analyzing simulation output data.

4.5 CONFIDENCE INTERVALS AND HYPOTHESIS TESTS FOR THE MEAN

Let $X_1, X_2, \ldots, X_n$ be IID random variables with finite mean μ and finite variance σ^2. (Also assume that $\sigma^2 > 0$, so that the X_i's are not degenerate random variables.) In this section we discuss how to construct a confidence interval for μ and also the complementary problem of testing the hypothesis that $\mu = \mu_0$.

We begin with a statement of the most important result in probability theory, the classical central limit theorem. Let $Z^{(n)}$ be the random variable $[\overline{X}(n) - \mu] / \sqrt{\sigma^2/n}$, and let $F_Z^{(n)}(z)$ be the distribution function of $Z^{(n)}$ for a sample size of n; that is, $F_Z^{(n)}(z) = P\{Z^{(n)} \leq z\}$. Then the central limit theorem is as follows (see Chung [2, p. 169] for a proof).

> **Theorem 4.1** $F_Z^{(n)}(z) \to \Phi(z)$ as $n \to \infty$, where $\Phi(z)$, the distribution function of a normal random variable with $\mu = 0$ and $\sigma^2 = 1$ (henceforth, called a *standard normal random variable*), is given by
>
> $$\Phi(z) = \frac{1}{\sqrt{2\pi}} \int_{-\infty}^{z} e^{-(1/2)y^2}\, dy \qquad \text{for } -\infty < z < \infty$$

Furthermore, the theorem remains true if we replace σ^2 by $s^2(n)$ in the expression for $Z^{(n)}$. With this change the theorem says that if n is "sufficiently large," the distribution function of $t^{(n)} = [\overline{X}(n) - \mu] / \sqrt{s^2(n)/n}$ is closely approximated by that of a standard normal random variable. It follows for large n that

$$P\left\{ -z_{1-\alpha/2} \leq \frac{\overline{X}(n) - \mu}{\sqrt{s^2(n)/n}} \leq z_{1-\alpha/2} \right\}$$

$$= P\left\{ \overline{X}(n) - z_{1-\alpha/2} \sqrt{\frac{s^2(n)}{n}} \leq \mu \leq \overline{X}(n) + z_{1-\alpha/2} \sqrt{\frac{s^2(n)}{n}} \right\}$$

$$\approx 1 - \alpha \qquad (4.9)$$

where the symbol $\approx$ means "approximately equal" and $z_{1-\alpha/2}$ (for $0 < \alpha < 1$) is the upper $1 - \alpha/2$ critical point for a standard normal distribution (see Fig. 4.8 and the last line of Table T.1 of the Appendix at the end of the book). Therefore, if n is sufficiently large, an approximate $100(1 - \alpha)$ percent confidence interval for μ is

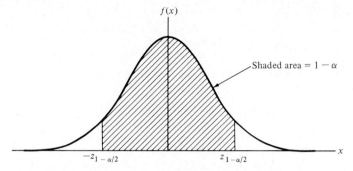

Figure 4.8 Density function for a standard normal distribution.

given by

$$\bar{X}(n) \pm z_{1-\alpha/2} \sqrt{\frac{s^2(n)}{n}} \tag{4.10}$$

For a given set of data $X_1, X_2, \ldots, X_n$, the lower confidence-interval endpoint $l(n, \alpha)$ = $\bar{X}(n) - z_{1-\alpha/2}\sqrt{s^2(n)/n}$ and the upper confidence-interval endpoint $u(n, \alpha)$ = $\bar{X}(n) + z_{1-\alpha/2}\sqrt{s^2(n)/n}$ are just numbers and the confidence interval $[l(n, \alpha), u(n, \alpha)]$ either contains μ or does not contain μ. Thus, there is nothing probabilistic about the single confidence interval $[l(n, \alpha), u(n, \alpha)]$. The correct interpretation to give to the confidence interval (4.10) is as follows [see (4.9)]: if one constructs a very large number of $100(1 - \alpha)$ percent confidence intervals each based on n observations, where n is sufficiently large, the proportion of these confidence intervals which contain (cover) μ should be $1 - \alpha$. We call this proportion the *coverage* for the confidence interval.

The difficulty in using (4.10) to construct a confidence interval for μ is in knowing what "n sufficiently large" means. It turns out that the more nonnormal the distribution of the X_i's, the larger the value of n needed for the distribution of $t^{(n)}$ to be closely approximated by $\Phi(z)$. (See Chap. 8 for further discussion.) If n is chosen too small, the actual coverage of a desired $100(1 - \alpha)$ percent confidence interval will generally be less than $1 - \alpha$. This is why the confidence interval given by (4.10) is stated to be only approximate.

In light of the above discussion, we now develop an alternative confidence-interval expression. If the X_i's are *normal* random variables, the random variable $t^{(n)} = [\bar{X}(n) - \mu]/\sqrt{s^2(n)/n}$ has a t distribution with $n - 1$ degrees of freedom (df) (see, for example, Hogg and Craig [4, p. 195]) and an *exact* (for any $n \geq 2$) $100(1 - \alpha)$ percent confidence interval for μ is given by

$$\bar{X}(n) \pm t_{n-1,1-\alpha/2} \sqrt{\frac{s^2(n)}{n}} \tag{4.11}$$

where $t_{n-1,1-\alpha/2}$ is the upper $1 - \alpha/2$ critical point for the t distribution with

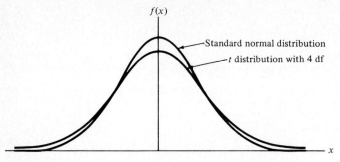

Figure 4.9 Density functions for the t distribution with 4 df and for a standard normal distribution.

$n - 1$ df. These critical points are given in Table T.1. Plots of the density functions for the t distribution with 4 df and for the standard normal distribution are given in Fig. 4.9. Note that the t distribution is less peaked and has longer tails than the normal distribution.

In practice, the distribution of the X_i's will rarely be normal, and the confidence interval given by (4.11) will also be approximate in terms of coverage. Since $t_{n-1,1-\alpha/2} > z_{1-\alpha/2}$, the confidence interval given by (4.11) will be larger than the one given by (4.10) and will generally have coverage closer to the desired level $1 - \alpha$. For this reason, we recommend using (4.11) to construct a confidence interval for μ. Note that $t_{n-1,1-\alpha/2} \to z_{1-\alpha/2}$ as $n \to \infty$; in particular, $t_{40,0.95}$ differs from $z_{0.95}$ by less than 3 percent. However, in most of our applications of (4.11) in Chaps. 8 and 9, n will be small enough for the difference between (4.10) and (4.11) to be appreciable.

Example 4.9 Suppose that the 10 observations 0.202, 0.498, 0.680, 0.888, -0.048, 0.486, 0.583, 0.553, -0.497, and 0.089 are from a normal distribution with unknown mean μ and that our objective is to construct a 90 percent confidence interval for μ. From these data we get

$$\overline{X}(10) = 0.343 \quad \text{and} \quad s^2(10) = 0.167$$

which results in the following confidence interval for μ:

$$\overline{X}(10) \pm t_{9,0.95} \sqrt{\frac{s^2(10)}{10}} = 0.343 \pm 1.833 \sqrt{\frac{0.167}{10}} = 0.343 \pm 0.237$$

Note that (4.11) was used to construct the confidence interval and that $t_{9,0.95}$ was taken from Table T.1. Therefore, subject to the interpretation stated above, we claim with 90 percent confidence that μ is in the interval [0.106, 0.580].

Assume that $X_1, X_2, \ldots, X_n$ are normally distributed (or are approximately so) and that we would like to test the null hypothesis H_0 that $\mu = \mu_0$, where μ_0 is a fixed, hypothesized value for μ. Intuitively, we would expect that if $|\overline{X}(n) - \mu_0|$ is large [recall that $\overline{X}(n)$ is the point estimator for μ], H_0 is not likely to be true. However, in order to develop a test with known statistical properties, we need a statistic (a function of the X_i's) whose distribution is known when H_0 is true. It follows from the above discussion that if H_0 is true, the statistic $t^{(n)} = [\overline{X}(n) - \mu_0]/\sqrt{s^2(n)/n}$ will have a t distribution with $n - 1$ df. Therefore, consistent with our intuitive discussion above, the form of our hypothesis test for $\mu = \mu_0$ is

$$\text{If } |t^{(n)}| \begin{cases} > t_{n-1,1-\alpha/2} & \text{reject } H_0 \\ \leq t_{n-1,1-\alpha/2} & \text{accept } H_0 \end{cases} \tag{4.12}$$

The portion of the real line which corresponds to rejection of H_0, namely, $\{x : |x| > t_{n-1,1-\alpha/2}\}$, is called the *critical region* for the test, and the probability that the statistic $t^{(n)}$ falls in the critical region given that H_0 is true, which is clearly equal to α, is called the *level* of the test. Typically, an experimenter will choose the level α equal to 0.05 or 0.1.

When one performs a hypothesis test, two types of errors can be made. If one rejects H_0 when in fact it is true, this is called a Type I error. The probability of a Type I error is equal to the level α and is thus under the experimenter's control. Therefore, if $\alpha = 0.05$ and we reject H_0, we can be 95 percent sure that we made the correct decision. If one accepts H_0 when it is false, i.e., when an alternative hypothesis H_1 is true, this is called a Type II error. For a fixed level α and sample size n, the probability of a Type II error, which we denote by δ, depends on the form of H_1 and may be unknown. We call $1 - \delta$ the *power* of a test, and it is equal to the probability of rejecting H_0 when it is false. If α and H_1 are fixed, the power of a test can be increased only by increasing n. Since the power of a test may be low and unknown to us, we shall henceforth say that we "fail to reject H_0" (instead of "accept H_0") when the statistic $t^{(n)}$ does not lie in the critical region. (When H_0 is not rejected, we generally do not know with any certainty whether H_0 is true or whether H_0 is false, since our test might not be powerful enough to detect any difference between H_0 and H_1.)

Example 4.10 For the data of Example 4.9, suppose we would like to test the null hypothesis H_0 that $\mu = 0$. Since

$$t^{(10)} = \frac{\overline{X}(10) - 0}{\sqrt{s^2(10)/10}} = \frac{0.343}{\sqrt{0.167/10}} = 2.654 > 1.833 = t_{9,0.95}$$

we reject H_0.

It should be mentioned that there is an intimate relationship between the confidence interval given by (4.11) and the hypothesis test given by (4.12). In particular, rejection of the null hypothesis H_0 that $\mu = \mu_0$ is equivalent to μ_0 not being contained in the confidence interval.

4.6 THE STRONG LAW OF LARGE NUMBERS

The second most important result in probability theory (after the central limit theorem) is arguably the strong law of large numbers. Let $X_1, X_2, \ldots, X_n$ be IID random variables with finite mean μ. Then the strong law of large numbers is as follows (see Chung [2, p. 126] for a proof).

Table 4.1 $\overline{X}(n)$ **for various values of** n **when the** X_i's **are normal random variables with** $\mu = 1$ **and** $\sigma^2 = 0.01$

n	$\overline{X}(n)$	n	$\overline{X}(n)$	n	$\overline{X}(n)$	n	$\overline{X}(n)$
1	0.880	11	0.974	21	0.975	31	0.998
2	0.938	12	0.950	22	0.977	32	0.996
3	0.960	13	0.950	23	0.975	33	1.001
4	0.973	14	0.959	24	0.983	34	1.003
5	0.959	15	0.952	25	0.982	35	1.003
6	0.962	16	0.957	26	0.987	36	1.001
7	0.947	17	0.963	27	0.987	37	0.997
8	0.952	18	0.969	28	0.992	38	0.998
9	0.958	19	0.971	29	0.997	39	0.997
10	0.954	20	0.973	30	0.997	40	0.999

Theorem 4.2 $\overline{X}(n) \to \mu$ w.p. 1 (with probability one) as $n \to \infty$.

The theorem says, in effect, that if one performs an infinite number of experiments each resulting in an $\overline{X}(n)$ and n is sufficiently large, then $\overline{X}(n)$ will be arbitrarily close to μ for almost all of the experiments.

Example 4.11 Suppose that X_1, X_2, ... are IID normal random variables with $\mu = 1$ and $\sigma^2 = 0.01$. Table 4.1 gives the values of $\overline{X}(n)$ for various n which resulted from sampling from this distribution. Note that $\overline{X}(n)$ differs from μ by less than 1 percent for $n \geq 28$.

APPENDIX 4A COMMENTS ON COVARIANCE STATIONARY PROCESSES

Consider the process $\{D_i, i \geq 1\}$ for the $M/M/1$ queue when no customers are present at time 0. Clearly, $D_1 = 0$, but $P\{D_i > 0\} > 0$ for $i = 2, 3, \ldots$. Therefore, $E(D_1) = 0$ and $E(D_i) > 0$ for $i = 2, 3, \ldots$, which implies that $\{D_i, i \geq 1\}$ is *not* covariance stationary. However, if $\rho < 1$, it can be shown for all $x \geq 0$ that

$$P\{D_i \leq x\} \to (1 - \rho) + \rho(1 - e^{-(\omega - \lambda)x}) \qquad \text{as } i \to \infty \qquad (4.13)$$

It follows from (4.13) and the equation for D_{i+1} in Example 4.3 that if we delete the first k observations from $D_1, D_2, \ldots$ and k is sufficiently large, then the process D_{k+1}, D_{k+2}, ... will be (approximately) covariance stationary. Therefore, when we say "consider the process $\{D_i, i \geq 1\}$ for the covariance stationary $M/M/1$ queue," we mean that we let the $M/M/1$ queue "warm up" for some amount of time before observing the first delay.

Consider the process $\{C_i, i \geq 1\}$ for the inventory system of Example 4.6 when $I_1 = S$. Since $P\{I_i = S\} \neq 1$ for $i = 2, 3, \ldots$, it follows that $\{C_i, i \geq 1\}$ is not covariance stationary. However, it can be shown that $P\{C_i \leq x\}$ converges to a limiting distribution function as $i \rightarrow \infty$ (see Wagner [6, p. A48]). Furthermore, the correlations plotted in Fig. 4.6 are for an inventory system warmed up for some amount of time before the first cost is observed.

PROBLEMS

4.1 Suppose that X and Y are jointly discrete random variables with

$$p_{X,Y}(x, y) = \begin{cases} \dfrac{2}{n(n+1)} & \text{for } x = 1, 2, \ldots, n \text{ and } y = 1, 2, \ldots, x \\ 0 & \text{otherwise} \end{cases}$$

Compute $p_X(x)$ and $p_Y(y)$ and then determine whether X and Y are independent.

4.2 Suppose that X and Y are jointly continuous random variables with

$$f_{X,Y}(x, y) = \begin{cases} y - x & \text{for } 0 < x < 1 \text{ and } 1 < y < 2 \\ 0 & \text{elsewhere} \end{cases}$$

Compute $E(X)$, $E(Y)$, $\sigma^2(X)$, $\sigma^2(Y)$, Cov (X, Y), and Cor (X, Y).

4.3 If X and Y are jointly continuous random variables with joint probability density function $f_{X,Y}(x, y)$ and X and Y are independent, show that Cov $(X, Y) = 0$. Therefore, X and Y independent implies that $E(XY) = E(X)E(Y)$.

4.4 Suppose that X is a discrete random variable with $p_X(x) = \frac{1}{4}$ for $x = -2, -1, 1, 2$. Let Y also be a discrete random variable such that $Y = X^2$. Clearly, X and Y are not independent. However, show that Cov $(X, Y) = 0$. Therefore, uncorrelated random variables are not necessarily independent.

4.5 Suppose that X_1 and X_2 are jointly normally distributed random variables with joint probability density function

$$f_{X_1,X_2}(x_1, x_2) = \frac{1}{2\pi \sqrt{\sigma_1^2 \sigma_2^2 (1 - \rho_{12}^2)}} e^{-q/2} \qquad \begin{array}{l} \text{for } -\infty < x_1 < \infty \\ \text{and } -\infty < x_2 < \infty \end{array}$$

where

$$q = \frac{1}{1 - \rho_{12}^2} \left[\frac{(x_1 - \mu_1)^2}{\sigma_1^2} - 2\rho_{12} \frac{(x_1 - \mu_1)(x_2 - \mu_2)}{\sqrt{\sigma_1^2 \sigma_2^2}} + \frac{(x_2 - \mu_2)^2}{\sigma_2^2} \right]$$

If $\rho_{12} = 0$, show that X_1 and X_2 are independent.

4.6 If X_1 and X_2 are random variables, then $E(X_1^2)E(X_2^2) \geq [E(X_1 X_2)]^2$ by Schwarz's inequality. Use this fact to show that $-1 \leq \rho_{12} \leq 1$.

4.7 Justify the equation for D_{i+1} in Example 4.3.

4.8 Justify the equations for $Q(t)$ in Example 4.4.

4.9 Using the fact that $E\left(\sum_{i=1}^{n} a_i X_i\right) = \sum_{i=1}^{n} a_i E(X_i)$ for any random variables $X_1, X_2, \ldots, X_n$ and any numbers $a_1, a_2, \ldots, a_n$, show that if $X_1, X_2, \ldots, X_n$ are IID random variables with mean μ and variance σ^2, then $E[\overline{X}(n)] = \mu$ and $E[s^2(n)] = \sigma^2$.

4.10 Show that Eq. (4.6) is correct.

4.11 For any random variables X_1, X_2 and any numbers a_1, a_2 show that Var $(a_1 X_1 + a_2 X_2) = a_1^2$ Var $(X_1) + 2a_1 a_2$ Cov $(X_1, X_2) + a_2^2$ Var (X_2).

4.12 Using the equation for D_{i+1} in Example 4.3, write a FORTRAN program requiring approximately 15 lines of code to simulate the $M/M/1$ queue with a mean interarrival time of 1 and a mean service time of 0.5. Run the program until 1000 D_i's have been observed and compute $\overline{D}(1000)$. The program should not require a simulation clock, an event list, or a timing routine.

REFERENCES

1. Anderson, T. W.: *The Statistical Analysis of Time Series,* Wiley, New York, 1971.
2. Chung, K. L.: *A Course in Probability Theory,* 2d ed., Academic, New York, 1974.
3. Daley, D. J.: The Serial Correlation Coefficients of Waiting Times in a Stationary Single Server Queue, *J. Austrl. Math. Soc.,* **8**: 683–699 (1968).
4. Hogg, R. V., and A. T. Craig: *Introduction to Mathematical Statistics,* 3d ed., Macmillan, New York, 1970.
5. Ross, S. M.: *Introduction to Probability Models,* 2d ed., Academic, New York, 1980.
6. Wagner, H. M.: *Principles of Operations Research,* Prentice-Hall, Englewood Cliffs, N.J., 1969.

SELECTING INPUT PROBABILITY DISTRIBUTIONS

5.1 INTRODUCTION

In order to carry out a simulation of a system having inputs (such as interarrival times or demand sizes) which are random variables we have to specify the probability distributions of these inputs. For example, in the simulation of the single-server queueing system in Sec. 1.4.3, the interarrival times were taken to be IID exponential random variables with a mean of 1 minute; the demand sizes in the inventory simulation of Sec. 1.5 were specified to be 1, 2, 3, or 4 items with respective probabilities $\frac{1}{6}$, $\frac{1}{3}$, $\frac{1}{3}$, and $\frac{1}{6}$. Then, *given* that the input random variables to a model follow a particular distribution, the simulation proceeds by *generating* values of these input random variables from the appropriate distribution; Chaps. 6 and 7 discuss methods of generating random variables from a given distribution. Our concern in this chapter is with *how* the analyst might go about specifying these input probability distributions.

Usually, we would expect to be able to collect data on the input random variables of interest; most of this chapter is concerned with how these data are then used to specify input distributions. For example, we could observe the arrivals of customers at an existing queueing facility of interest and record the times when arrivals occur. Assuming, then, that data on an input random variable of interest are available, they can be used in one of two general approaches to specify a distribution:

1. Standard techniques of statistical inference are used to "fit" a *theoretical* distribution form, e.g., exponential, normal, or Poisson, to the data and to perform hypothesis tests to determine how good the fit is. When an acceptably good fit is obtained for some distribution form with certain values for its parameters, this

distribution is then used to generate the corresponding random variables during the simulation.

2. The values of the data themselves are used directly to define an *empirical* distribution without relying on any of the common theoretical distribution forms. In the simulation, we then sample directly from this empirical distribution.

Approach 2, discussed in Sec. 5.2.4, does have its uses, e.g., a situation in which we simply cannot find a theoretical distribution form that fits the data adequately. We feel, however, that approach 1 should be used (or at least attempted) whenever possible, for three reasons: (1) The data which are collected are themselves random, so that an empirical distribution obtained from one set of observations on, say, an arrival process of customers might differ greatly from that obtained from another set of observations on the same process taken at a different time. By fitting a theoretical distribution form to the data, we are trying to infer from the data something about the nature of the *underlying* distribution; distributions specified in this way should be less sensitive to the vagaries of random fluctuation in the particular observations we happen to have obtained. (2) If empirical distributions are defined in the usual way (see Sec. 5.2.4), their use in the simulation implies that no random variables will be generated which fall outside the range of the observed data (see Sec. 7.3.10). This is unfortunate since many measures of performance for simulated systems depend heavily on the probability of an "extreme" event's occurring, e.g., generation of a very large service-time random variable. With a fitted theoretical distribution, on the other hand, random variables outside the range of the observed data can be generated. (3) There might be a compelling physical reason in some situations for using a certain theoretical distribution form as a model for a particular input random variable. Even when we are fortunate enough to have this kind of information, it is a good idea to use observed data to provide empirical support for the use of this particular distribution form.

Throughout this chapter, we are tacitly assuming that our data are independent observations taken from a single underlying distribution. If this is not the case (for example, when correlation is present in the data), then most of the techniques discussed here are not directly applicable.

The remainder of the chapter discusses various topics related to selecting input distributions. Section 5.2 treats generally how theoretical distributions are parameterized, provides a compendium of relevant facts on most of the commonly used continuous and discrete distributions, and discusses how empirical distributions can be specified. Sections 5.3 to 5.5 discuss the three basic steps in specifying a theoretical distribution on the basis of observed data. Section 5.6 suggests possible methods of specifying input distributions when we are not able to obtain any actual data. Section 5.7 discusses several useful probabilistic models for events (such as customer arrivals) that occur randomly through time. Finally, Appendix 5A discusses a technical consideration of considerable use in modifying the forms of some standard theoretical distributions so that they can be made to fit certain kinds of data more closely.

In this chapter, we are really in the province of statistics, and the particular topics we have chosen to present are only some of a much larger group of statistical questions and techniques of potential interest in simulation. For example, the question of whether or not it is valid to "pool" observations from different sources might come up when we seek to estimate parameters of a distribution (see, for example, Breiman [6, chap. 9]). For questions of this sort the analyst should seek out advice in the statistics literature or from an applied statistician.

5.2 USEFUL PROBABILITY DISTRIBUTIONS

The purpose of this section is to discuss a variety of distributions which have been found useful in simulation modeling and to provide a unified listing of relevant properties of these distributions. Section 5.2.1 provides a short discussion of common methods by which distributions are defined, or parameterized. Then, Secs. 5.2.2 and 5.2.3 contain compilations of properties of several continuous and discrete distributions. Finally, Sec. 5.2.4 suggests how the data themselves can be used directly to define a distribution.

5.2.1 Parameterization of Distributions

For a given family of distributions, e.g., normal or gamma, there are usually several alternative ways to define, or *parameterize,* the probability density or probability mass function. Most parameters used to define a distribution can be classified, on the basis of their physical or geometric interpretation, as being one of three basic types: location, scale, or shape parameters.

A *location parameter* γ specifies an abscissa (x-axis) location point of a distribution's range of values; usually γ is the midpoint or lower endpoint of the range. (Location parameters are also called *shift parameters.*) As γ changes, the associated distribution merely shifts left or right without otherwise changing. A *scale parameter* β determines the scale (or unit) of measurement of the values in the range of the distribution. When γ is fixed at 0, a change in β compresses or expands the associated distribution without altering its basic form. A *shape parameter* α determines, distinctly from location and scale, the basic form or shape of a distribution within the general family of distributions of interest. A change in α generally alters a distribution's properties more fundamentally than changes in location or scale. Some distributions do not have a shape parameter, e.g., exponential and normal, while others may have several (the beta distribution has two).

Two random variables X and Y (from the same family of distributions) are said to *differ only in location* if there is a real number γ such that $\gamma + X$ and Y have the same distribution. Similarly, we say that X and Y *differ only in scale* if βX has the same distribution as Y for some positive real number β. Finally, X and Y *differ only in location and scale* if we can find γ and β such that $\gamma + \beta X$ and Y are identically distributed. However, if the distributions of X and Y have different shape parameters, they are more fundamentally distinct in that no amount of rescaling and relocating can make them the same.

5.2.2 Continuous Distributions

Table 5.1 gives information relevant to simulation modeling applications for eight continuous distributions. Possible applications are given first to indicate *some* (certainly not all) uses of the distribution (see Hahn and Shapiro [17] for other applications). Then the density function and distribution function (if it exists in simple closed form) are listed. Next is a short description of the parameters, including their possible values. The range indicates the interval where the associated random variable can take on values. Also listed are the mean (expectation), variance, and mode, i.e., the value at which the density function is maximized. The MLE refers to the maximum-likelihood estimator(s) of the parameter(s), treated later in Sec. 5.4. General comments include relationships of the distribution under study to other distributions. Graphs are given of the density functions for each distribution. The notation following the name of each distribution is our abbreviation for that distribution, which includes the parameters. The symbol $\sim$ is read "is distributed as."

Table 5.1 Continuous distributions

Uniform	$U(a, b)$
Possible applications	Used as a "first" model for a quantity that is felt to be randomly varying between a and b but about which little else is known. The $U(0, 1)$ distribution is essential in generating random variables from all other distributions (see Chaps. 6 and 7)
Density (see Fig. 5.1)	$$f(x) = \begin{cases} \dfrac{1}{b - a} & \text{if } a \leq x \leq b \\ 0 & \text{otherwise} \end{cases}$$
Distribution	$$F(x) = \begin{cases} 0 & \text{if } x < a \\ \dfrac{x - a}{b - a} & \text{if } a \leq x \leq b \\ 1 & \text{if } b < x \end{cases}$$
Parameters	a and b real numbers with $a < b$; a is a location parameter, $b - a$ is a scale parameter
Range	$[a, b]$
Mean	$\dfrac{a + b}{2}$
Variance	$\dfrac{(b - a)^2}{12}$
Mode	Does not uniquely exist
MLE	$\hat{a} = \min\limits_{1 \leq i \leq n} X_i, \ \hat{b} = \max\limits_{1 \leq i \leq n} X_i$
Comments	1. The $U(0, 1)$ distribution is a special case of the beta distribution (when $\alpha_1 = \alpha_2 = 1$) 2. If $X \sim U(0, 1)$ and $[x, x + \Delta x]$ is a subinterval of $[0, 1]$ with $\Delta x \geq 0$, $$P\{X \in [x, x + \Delta x]\} = \int_{x}^{x+\Delta x} 1\, dx = (x + \Delta x) - x = \Delta x$$

Table 5.1 (*Continued*)

Exponential	expo(β)

Possible applications	Times between independent events, e.g., arrivals at a service facility, that occur at a constant rate; lifetimes of devices with constant hazard rate
Density (see Fig. 5.2)	$$f(x) = \begin{cases} \left(\dfrac{1}{\beta}\right) e^{-x/\beta} & \text{if } x \geq 0 \\ 0 & \text{otherwise} \end{cases}$$
Distribution	$$F(x) = \begin{cases} 1 - e^{-x/\beta} & \text{if } x \geq 0 \\ 0 & \text{otherwise} \end{cases}$$
Parameter	Scale parameter $\beta > 0$
Range	$[0, \infty)$
Mean	β
Variance	β^2
Mode	0
MLE	$\hat{\beta} = \bar{X}(n)$
Comments	1. The expo(β) distribution is a special case of both the gamma and Weibull distributions (for shape parameter $\alpha = 1$ and scale parameter β in both cases)
	2. If $X_1, X_2, \ldots, X_m$ are independent expo(β) random variables, then $X_1 + X_2 + \cdots + X_m \sim$ gamma(m, β), also called the m-Erlang distribution
	3. The exponential distribution is the only continuous distribution with the memoryless property (see Appendix 8A)

Gamma	gamma(α, β)

Possible applications	Time to complete some task, e.g., customer service or machine repair
Density (see Fig. 5.3)	$$f(x) = \begin{cases} \dfrac{\beta^{-\alpha} x^{\alpha-1} e^{-x/\beta}}{\Gamma(\alpha)} & \text{if } x > 0 \\ 0 & \text{otherwise} \end{cases}$$
	where $\Gamma(\alpha)$ is the *gamma function*, defined by $\Gamma(z) = \displaystyle\int_0^\infty t^{z-1} e^{-t}\, dt$ for any real number $z > 0$. Some properties of the gamma function: $\Gamma(z + 1) = z\Gamma(z)$ for any $z > 0$, $\Gamma(k + 1) = k!$ for any nonnegative integer k, $\Gamma(k + \frac{1}{2}) = \sqrt{\pi} \cdot 1 \cdot 3 \cdot 5 \cdots (2k - 1)/2^k$ for any positive integer k, $\Gamma(1/2) = \sqrt{\pi}$
Distribution	If α is not an integer, there is no closed form. If α is a positive integer, then
	$$F(x) = \begin{cases} 1 - e^{-x/\beta} \displaystyle\sum_{j=0}^{\alpha-1} \dfrac{(x/\beta)^j}{j!} & \text{if } x > 0 \\ 0 & \text{otherwise} \end{cases}$$
Parameters	Shape parameter $\alpha > 0$, scale parameter $\beta > 0$
Range	$[0, \infty)$
Mean	$\alpha\beta$
Variance	$\alpha\beta^2$
Mode	$\beta(\alpha - 1)$ if $\alpha \geq 1$, 0 if $\alpha < 1$

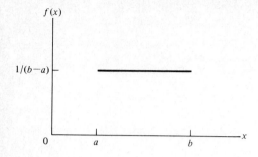

Figure 5.1 U(a, b) density function.

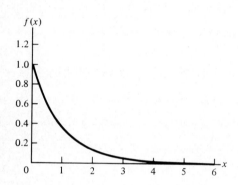

Figure 5.2 expo(1) density function.

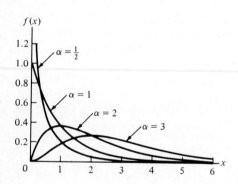

Figure 5.3 gamma(α, 1) density functions.

Table 5.1 (*Continued*)

Gamma	gamma(α, β)

MLE	The following two equations must be satisfied:

$$\ln \hat{\beta} + \Psi(\hat{\alpha}) = \frac{\sum_{i=1}^{n} \ln X_i}{n}, \qquad \hat{\alpha}\hat{\beta} = \bar{X}(n)$$

which could be solved numerically. [$\Psi(\hat{\alpha}) = \Gamma'(\hat{\alpha})/\Gamma(\hat{\alpha})$ and is called the *digamma function;* Γ' denotes the derivative of Γ.] Alternatively, approximations to $\hat{\alpha}$ and $\hat{\beta}$ can be obtained by letting $T = \left[\ln \bar{X}(n) - \sum_{i=1}^{n} \ln X_i/n \right]^{-1}$, using Table 5.11 (see Appendix 5B) to obtain $\hat{\alpha}$ as a function of T, and letting $\hat{\beta} = \bar{X}(n)/\hat{\alpha}$. (See Choi and Wette [9] for the derivation of this procedure and of Table 5.11)

Comments	1. The expo(β) and gamma(1, β) distributions are the same

2. For a positive integer m, the gamma(m, β) distribution is called the m-Erlang(β) distribution
3. The chi-square distribution with k df is the same as the gamma($k/2$, 2) distribution
4. If $X_1, X_2, \ldots, X_m$ are independent random variables with $X_i \sim$ gamma(α_i, β), then $X_1 + X_2 + \cdots + X_m \sim$ gamma($\alpha_1 + \alpha_2 + \cdots + \alpha_m$, β)
5. If X_1 and X_2 are independent random variables with $X_i \sim$ gamma(α_i, β), then $X_1/(X_1 + X_2) \sim$ beta(α_1, α_2)
6.

$$\lim_{x \to 0} f(x) = \begin{cases} \infty & \text{if } \alpha < 1 \\ \dfrac{1}{\beta} & \text{if } \alpha = 1 \\ 0 & \text{if } \alpha > 1 \end{cases}$$

Weibull	Weibull(α, β)

Possible applications	Widely used in reliability models for lifetimes of devices; time to complete some task (density takes on shapes similar to gamma densities)
Density (see Fig. 5.4)	$f(x) = \begin{cases} \alpha\beta^{-\alpha}x^{\alpha-1}e^{-(x/\beta)^{\alpha}} & \text{if } x > 0 \\ 0 & \text{otherwise} \end{cases}$
Distribution	$F(x) = \begin{cases} 1 - e^{-(x/\beta)^{\alpha}} & \text{if } x > 0 \\ 0 & \text{otherwise} \end{cases}$
Parameters	Shape parameter $\alpha > 0$, scale parameter $\beta > 0$
Range	$[0, \infty)$
Mean	$\dfrac{\beta}{\alpha}\Gamma\left(\dfrac{1}{\alpha}\right)$
Variance	$\dfrac{\beta^2}{\alpha}\left\{ 2\Gamma\left(\dfrac{2}{\alpha}\right) - \dfrac{1}{\alpha}\left[\Gamma\left(\dfrac{1}{\alpha}\right)\right]^2 \right\}$
Mode	$\begin{cases} \beta\left(\dfrac{\alpha-1}{\alpha}\right)^{1/\alpha} & \text{if } \alpha \geq 1 \\ 0 & \text{if } \alpha < 1 \end{cases}$

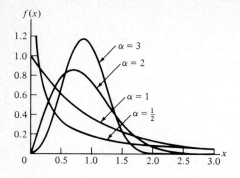

Figure 5.4 Weibull(α, 1) density functions.

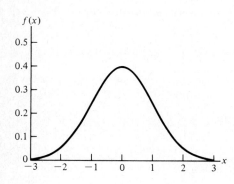

Figure 5.5 N(0, 1) density function.

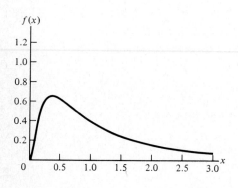

Figure 5.6 LN(0, 1) density function.

Table 5.1 (*Continued*)

Weibull	Weibull(α, β)

MLE	The following two equations must be satisfied:

$$\frac{\sum_{i=1}^{n} X_i^{\hat{\alpha}} \ln X_i}{\sum_{i=1}^{n} X_i^{\hat{\alpha}}} - \frac{1}{\hat{\alpha}} = \frac{\sum_{i=1}^{n} \ln X_i}{n}, \qquad \hat{\beta} = \left(\frac{\sum_{i=1}^{n} X_i^{\hat{\alpha}}}{n} \right)^{1/\hat{\alpha}}$$

The first can be solved for $\hat{\alpha}$ numerically by Newton's method, and the second equation then gives $\hat{\beta}$ directly. The general recursive step for the Newton iterations is

$$\hat{\alpha}_{k+1} = \hat{\alpha}_k + \frac{A + 1/\hat{\alpha}_k - C_k/B_k}{1/\hat{\alpha}_k^2 + (B_k H_k - C_k^2)/B_k^2}$$

where

$$A = \frac{\sum_{i=1}^{n} \ln X_i}{n}, \qquad B_k = \sum_{i=1}^{n} X_i^{\hat{\alpha}_k}, \qquad C_k = \sum_{i=1}^{n} X_i^{\hat{\alpha}_k} \ln X_i,$$

and

$$H_k = \sum_{i=1}^{n} X_i^{\hat{\alpha}_k} (\ln X_i)^2$$

(See Thoman, Bain, and Antle [43] for these formulas, as well as for confidence intervals on the true α and β.) As a starting point for the iterations, the estimate

$$\hat{\alpha}_0 = \left\{ \frac{6 \left[\sum_{i=1}^{n} (\ln X_i)^2 - \left(\sum_{i=1}^{n} \ln X_i \right)^2 / n \right]}{\pi^2 \quad n - 1} \right\}^{-1/2}$$

which is Menon's [28] estimator of α, was suggested in [43]. With this choice of $\hat{\alpha}_0$, it was reported in [43] that an average of only 3.5 Newton iterations were needed to achieve four-place accuracy

Comments	1. The expo(β) and Weibull(1, β) distributions are the same
	2. $X \sim$ Weibull(α, β) if and only if $X^{\alpha} \sim$ expo(β^{α})
	3. The (natural) logarithm of a Weibull random variable has a distribution known as the *extreme-value* or *Gumbel distribution* [see [17], Mann [26], and part (*b*) of Prob. 7.1]
	4. As $\alpha \to \infty$, the Weibull distribution becomes degenerate at β. Thus, Weibull densities for large α have a sharp peak at the mode
	5.

$$\lim_{x \to 0} f(x) = \begin{cases} \infty & \text{if } \alpha < 1 \\ \dfrac{1}{\beta} & \text{if } \alpha = 1 \\ 0 & \text{if } \alpha > 1 \end{cases}$$

Normal	N(μ, σ^2)

Possible applications	Represents quantities, e.g., measurement errors, that are sums of a large number of other quantities (by virtue of central limit theorems)

Density (see Fig. 5.5)	$f(x) = \dfrac{1}{\sqrt{2\pi\sigma^2}} e^{-(x-\mu)^2/2\sigma^2}$ for all real numbers x

Table 5.1 (*Continued*)

Normal	$N(\mu, \sigma^2)$

Distribution	No closed form
Parameters	Location parameter $\mu \in (-\infty, \infty)$, scale parameter $\sigma > 0$
Range	$(-\infty, \infty)$
Mean	μ
Variance	σ^2
Mode	μ
MLE	$\hat{\mu} = \bar{X}(n), \qquad \hat{\sigma} = \left[\dfrac{n-1}{n} s^2(n) \right]^{1/2}$

Comments

1. If two normal random variables are uncorrelated, they are also independent For distributions other than normal, this implication is not true in general
2. Suppose that the joint distribution of $X_1, X_2, \ldots, X_m$ is multivariate normal, and let $\mu_i = E(X_i)$ and $C_{ij} = \text{Cov}(X_i, X_j)$. Then for any real numbers a, $b_1, b_2, \ldots, b_m$, the random variable $a + b_1 X_1 + b_2 X_2 + \cdots + b_m X_m$ has a normal distribution with mean $\mu = a + \sum\limits_{i=1}^{m} b_i \mu_i$ and variance

$$\sigma^2 = \sum_{i=1}^{m} \sum_{j=1}^{m} b_i b_j C_{ij}$$

Note that we need *not* assume independence of the X_i's. If the X_i's *are* independent, then

$$\sigma^2 = \sum_{i=1}^{m} b_i^2 \text{ Var}(X_i)$$

3. The $N(0, 1)$ distribution is often called the *standard* or *unit normal distribution*
4. If $X_1, X_2, \ldots, X_k$ are independent standard normal random variables, then $X_1^2 + X_2^2 + \cdots + X_k^2$ has a chi-square distribution with k df, which is also the gamma($k/2$, 2) distribution
5. If $X \sim N(\mu, \sigma^2)$, then e^X has the *lognormal distribution* with parameters μ and σ, denoted $LN(\mu, \sigma^2)$
6. If $X \sim N(0, 1)$, if Y has a chi-square distribution with k df, and if X and Y are independent, then $X/\sqrt{Y/k}$ has a t distribution with k df (sometimes called *Student's t distribution*)
7. As $\sigma \to 0$, the normal distribution becomes degenerate at μ

Lognormal	$LN(\mu, \sigma^2)$

Possible applications	Represents quantities, e.g., measurement errors, that are the products of a large number of other quantities; time to accomplish some task [density takes on shapes similar to gamma(α, β) densities for $\alpha > 1$]
Density (see Fig. 5.6)	$f(x) = \begin{cases} \dfrac{1}{x\sqrt{2\pi\sigma^2}} \exp \dfrac{-(\ln x - \mu)^2}{2\sigma^2} & \text{if } x > 0 \\ 0 & \text{otherwise} \end{cases}$
Distribution	No closed form
Parameters	Shape parameter $\sigma > 0$, scale parameter $\mu \in (-\infty, \infty)$
Range	$[0, \infty)$
Mean	$e^{\mu + \sigma^2/2}$

Table 5.1 (*Continued*)

Lognormal	$LN(\mu, \sigma^2)$

Variance	$e^{2\mu + \sigma^2}(e^{\sigma^2} - 1)$
Mode	$e^{\mu - \sigma^2}$

MLE

$$\hat{\mu} = \frac{\displaystyle\sum_{i=1}^{n} \ln X_i}{n}, \qquad \hat{\sigma} = \left[\frac{\displaystyle\sum_{i=1}^{n} (\ln X_i - \hat{\mu})^2}{n}\right]^{1/2}$$

Comments

1. $X \sim LN(\mu, \sigma^2)$ if and only if $\ln X \sim N(\mu, \sigma^2)$. Thus, if one has data $X_1, X_2, \ldots, X_n$ which are thought to be lognormal, the logarithms of the data points, $\ln X_1, \ln X_2, \ldots, \ln X_n$, can be treated as normally distributed data for purposes of hypothesizing a distribution, parameter estimation, and goodness-of-fit testing
2. As $\sigma \to 0$, the lognormal distribution becomes degenerate at e^μ. Thus, lognormal densities for small σ have a sharp peak at the mode
3. $\lim_{x \to 0} f(x) = 0$, regardless of the parameters

Beta	$beta(\alpha_1, \alpha_2)$

Possible applications

Used as a rough model in the absence of data (see Sec. 5.6); distribution of a random proportion, such as the proportion of defective items in a shipment; time to complete a task, e.g., in a PERT network

Density (see Fig. 5.7)

$$f(x) = \begin{cases} \dfrac{x^{\alpha_1 - 1}(1 - x)^{\alpha_2 - 1}}{B(\alpha_1, \alpha_2)} & \text{if } 0 < x < 1 \\[2mm] 0 & \text{otherwise} \end{cases}$$

where $B(\alpha_1, \alpha_2)$ is the *beta function* defined by

$$B(z_1, z_2) = \int_0^1 t^{z_1 - 1}(1 - t)^{z_2 - 1}\, dt$$

for any real numbers $z_1 > 0$ and $z_2 > 0$. Some properties of the beta function:

$$B(z_1, z_2) = B(z_2, z_1), \qquad B(z_1, z_2) = \frac{\Gamma(z_1)\Gamma(z_2)}{\Gamma(z_1 + z_2)}$$

Distribution

No closed form, in general. If either α_1 or α_2 is a positive integer, a binomial expansion can be used to obtain $F(x)$, which will be a polynomial in x, and the powers of x will be, in general, positive real numbers ranging from 0 through $\alpha_1 + \alpha_2 - 1$

Parameters — Shape parameters $\alpha_1 > 0$ and $\alpha_2 > 0$

Range — $[0, 1]$

Mean

$$\frac{\alpha_1}{\alpha_1 + \alpha_2}$$

Variance

$$\frac{\alpha_1 \alpha_2}{(\alpha_1 + \alpha_2)^2 (\alpha_1 + \alpha_2 + 1)}$$

Mode

$$\begin{cases} \dfrac{\alpha_1 - 1}{\alpha_1 + \alpha_2 - 2} & \text{if } \alpha_1 > 1, \alpha_2 > 1 \\[2mm] 0 \text{ and } 1 & \text{if } \alpha_1 < 1, \alpha_2 < 1 \\[2mm] 0 & \text{if } \alpha_1 < 1, \alpha_2 \geq 1 \qquad \text{if } \alpha_1 = 1, \alpha_2 > 1 \\[2mm] 1 & \text{if } \alpha_1 \geq 1, \alpha_2 < 1 \qquad \text{if } \alpha_1 > 1, \alpha_2 = 1 \\[2mm] \text{does not uniquely exist} & \text{if } \alpha_1 = \alpha_2 = 1 \end{cases}$$

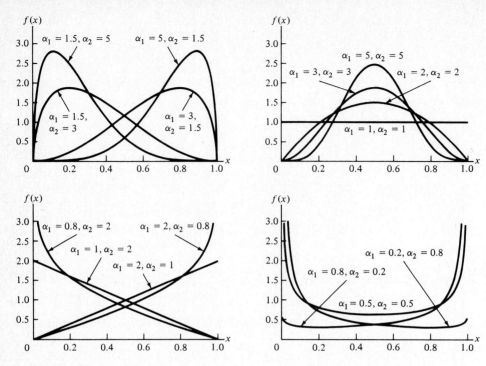

Figure 5.7 beta(α_1, α_2) density functions.

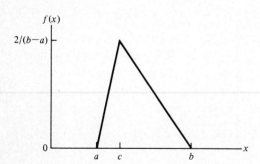

Figure 5.8 triang(a, b, c) density functions.

Table 5.1 (*Continued*)

Beta	beta(α_1, α_2)

MLE

The following two equations must be satisfied:

$$\Psi(\hat{\alpha}_1) - \Psi(\hat{\alpha}_1 + \hat{\alpha}_2) = \ln G_1, \qquad \Psi(\hat{\alpha}_2) - \Psi(\hat{\alpha}_1 + \hat{\alpha}_2) = \ln G_2$$

where Ψ is the digamma function, $G_1 = \left(\prod_{i=1}^{n} X_i \right)^{1/n}$, and $G_2 =$

$\left[\prod_{i=1}^{n} (1 - X_i) \right]^{1/n}$ (see Gnanadesikan, Pinkham, and Hughes [15]); note that $G_1 + G_2 \leq 1$. These equations could be solved numerically (see Beckman and Tietjen [3]), or approximations to $\hat{\alpha}_1$ and $\hat{\alpha}_2$ can be obtained from Table 5.12 (see Appendix 5B), which was computed for particular (G_1, G_2) pairs by modifications of the methods in [3]

Comments

1. The U(0, 1) and beta(1, 1) distributions are the same
2. If X_1 and X_2 are independent random variables with $X_i \sim$ gamma(α_i, β), then $X_1/(X_1 + X_2) \sim$ beta(α_1, α_2)
3. A beta random variable X on [0, 1] can be rescaled and shifted to obtain a beta random variable on [a, b] of the same shape by the transformation $a + (b - a)X$
4. $X \sim$ beta(α_1, α_2) if and only if $1 - X \sim$ beta(α_2, α_1)
5. The beta(1, 2) density is a left triangle, and the beta(2, 1) density is a right triangle
6.

$$\lim_{x \to 0} f(x) = \begin{cases} \infty & \text{if } \alpha_1 < 1 \\ \alpha_2 & \text{if } \alpha_1 = 1 \\ 0 & \text{if } \alpha_1 > 1 \end{cases}, \qquad \lim_{x \to 1} f(x) = \begin{cases} \infty & \text{if } \alpha_2 < 1 \\ \alpha_1 & \text{if } \alpha_2 = 1 \\ 0 & \text{if } \alpha_2 > 1 \end{cases}$$

7. The density is symmetric about $x = \frac{1}{2}$ if and only if $\alpha_1 = \alpha_2$. Also, the mean and the mode are equal if and only if $\alpha_1 = \alpha_2$

Triangular	triang(a, b, c)

Possible applications

Used as a rough model in the absence of data (see Sec. 5.6)

Density (see Fig. 5.8)

$$f(x) = \begin{cases} \dfrac{2(x - a)}{(b - a)(c - a)} & \text{if } a \leq x \leq c \\ \dfrac{2(b - x)}{(b - a)(b - c)} & \text{if } c < x \leq b \\ 0 & \text{otherwise} \end{cases}$$

Distribution

$$F(x) = \begin{cases} 0 & \text{if } x < a \\ \dfrac{(x - a)^2}{(b - a)(c - a)} & \text{if } a \leq x \leq c \\ 1 - \dfrac{(b - x)^2}{(b - a)(b - c)} & \text{if } c < x \leq b \\ 1 & \text{if } b < x \end{cases}$$

Parameters

a, b, and c real numbers with $a < c < b$. a is a location parameter, $b - a$ is a scale parameter, c is a shape parameter

Range

[a, b]

Mean

$\dfrac{a + b + c}{3}$

Table 5.1 (*Continued*)

Triangular	triang(a, b, c)
Variance	$\dfrac{a^2 + b^2 + c^2 - ab - ac - bc}{18}$
Mode	c
MLE	Our use of the triangular distribution, as described in Sec. 5.6, is as a rough model when there are no data. Thus, MLEs are not relevant
Comment	The limiting cases as $c \to b$ and $c \to a$ are called the *right triangular* and *left triangular distributions*, respectively, and are discussed in Prob. 7.7. For $a = 0$ and $b = 1$, both the left and right triangular distributions are special cases of the beta distribution

5.2.3 Discrete Distributions

The descriptions of the six discrete distributions in Table 5.2 follow the same pattern as for the continuous distributions in Table 5.1.

Table 5.2 Discrete distributions

Bernoulli	Bernoulli(p)
Possible applications	Indicator of the outcome of an event with two possible outcomes; used to generate other discrete random variables, e.g., binomial, geometric, and negative binomial
Mass (see Fig. 5.9)	$p(x) = \begin{cases} 1 - p & \text{if } x = 0 \\ p & \text{if } x = 1 \\ 0 & \text{otherwise} \end{cases}$
Distribution	$F(x) = \begin{cases} 0 & \text{if } x < 0 \\ 1 - p & \text{if } 0 \leq x < 1 \\ 1 & \text{if } 1 \leq x \end{cases}$
Parameter	$p \in (0, 1)$
Range	$\{0, 1\}$
Mean	p
Variance	$p \cdot (1 - p)$
Mode	$\begin{cases} 0 & \text{if } p < \frac{1}{2} \\ 0 \text{ and } 1 & \text{if } p = \frac{1}{2} \\ 1 & \text{if } p > \frac{1}{2} \end{cases}$
MLE	$\hat{p} = \overline{X}(n)$
Comments	1. A Bernoulli(p) random variable X can be thought of as the outcome of an experiment that either "fails" or "succeeds." If the probability of success is p, and we let $X = 0$ if the experiment fails and $X = 1$ if it succeeds, then $X \sim$ Bernoulli(p). Such an experiment, often called a *Bernoulli trial*, provides a convenient way of relating several other discrete distributions to the Bernoulli distribution 2. If t is a positive integer and X_1, X_2, . . .,X_t are independent Bernoulli(p) random variables, $X_1 + X_2 + \cdots + X_t$ has the binomial distribution with

Table 5.2 (*Continued*)

Bernoulli	Bernoulli(p)

parameters t and p. Thus, a binomial random variable can be thought of as the number of successes in a fixed number of independent Bernoulli trials

3. Suppose we begin making independent replications of a Bernoulli trial with probability p of success on each trial. Then the number of failures *before* observing the first success has a geometric distribution with parameter p. For a positive integer s, the number of failures before observing the sth success has a negative binomial distribution with parameters s and p

4. The Bernoulli(p) distribution is a special case of the binomial distribution (with $t = 1$ and the same value for p)

Discrete uniform	DU(i, j)

Possible applications	Indicator of the outcome of an event with several possible outcomes, each of which is equally likely; used as a "first" model for a quantity that is varying among the integers i through j but about which little else is known

Mass (see Fig. 5.10)

$$p(x) = \begin{cases} \dfrac{1}{j - i + 1} & \text{if } x \in \{i, i+1, \ldots, j\} \\ 0 & \text{otherwise} \end{cases}$$

Distribution

$$F(x) = \begin{cases} 0 & \text{if } x < i \\ \dfrac{\lfloor x \rfloor - i + 1}{j - i + 1} & \text{if } i \leq x \leq j \\ 1 & \text{if } j < x \end{cases}$$

where $\lfloor x \rfloor$ denotes the largest integer $\leq x$

Parameters i and j integers with $i \leq j$; i is a location parameter

Range $\{i, i + 1, \ldots, j\}$

Mean $\dfrac{i + j}{2}$

Variance $\dfrac{(j - i + 1)^2 - 1}{12}$

Mode   Does not uniquely exist

MLE $\hat{i} = \min_{1 \leq k \leq n} X_k, \qquad \hat{j} = \max_{1 \leq k \leq n} X_k$

Comment   The DU(0, 1) and Bernoulli($\frac{1}{2}$) distributions are the same

---

Binomial	bin(t, p)

Possible applications	Number of successes in t independent Bernoulli trials with probability p of success on each trial; number of "defective" items in a batch of size t; number of items in a batch (for example, a group of people) of random size; number of items demanded from an inventory

Mass (see Fig. 5.11)

$$p(x) = \begin{cases} \dbinom{t}{x} p^x (1 - p)^{t-x} & \text{if } x \in \{0, 1, \ldots, t\} \\ 0 & \text{otherwise} \end{cases}$$

where $\dbinom{t}{x}$ is the *binomial coefficient*, defined by

$$\binom{t}{x} = \frac{t!}{x!(t - x)!}$$

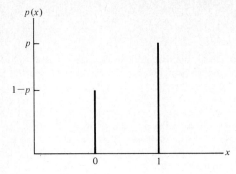

Figure 5.9 Bernoulli(p) mass function ($p > 0.5$ here).

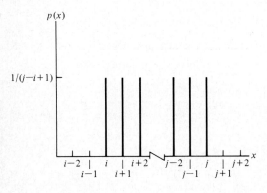

Figure 5.10 DU(i, j) mass function.

Table 5.2 (*Continued*)

Binomial	bin(t, p)

Distribution	$$F(x) = \begin{cases} 0 & \text{if } x < 0 \\ \sum_{i=0}^{\lfloor x \rfloor} \binom{t}{i} p^i(1-p)^{t-i} & \text{if } 0 \le x \le t \\ 1 & \text{if } t < x \end{cases}$$
Parameters	t a positive integer, $p \in (0, 1)$
Range	$\{0, 1, \ldots, t\}$
Mean	tp
Variance	$tp \cdot (1 - p)$
Mode	$\begin{cases} p \cdot (t+1) - 1 \text{ and } p \cdot (t+1) & \text{if } p \cdot (t+1) \text{ is an integer} \\ \lfloor p \cdot (t+1) \rfloor & \text{otherwise} \end{cases}$
MLE	If t is known, then $\hat{p} = \overline{X}(n)/t$. If both t and p are unknown, finding $\hat{t}$ and $\hat{p}$ is considerably more difficult; the following approach could be taken. Let $M = \max_{1 \le i \le n} X_i$, and for $k = 0, 1, \ldots, M$, let f_k be the number of X_i's $\ge k$. Then it can be shown that $\hat{t}$ and $\hat{p}$ are the values for t and p which maximize the function $$g(t, p) = \sum_{k=1}^{M} f_k \ln(t - k + 1) + nt \ln(1 - p) + n\overline{X}(n) \ln \frac{p}{1-p}$$ subject to the constraints that $t \in \{M, M+1, \ldots\}$ and $0 < p < 1$. It is easy to see that for a fixed value of t, say t_0, the value of p which maximizes $g(t_0, p)$ is $\overline{X}(n)/t_0$, so $\hat{t}$ and $\hat{p}$ are the values of t and $\overline{X}(n)/t$ which lead to the largest value of $g[t, \overline{X}(n)/t]$ for $t \in \{M, M+1, \ldots\}$. Since this would involve infinitely many evaluations of g, a practical operational procedure might be to evaluate $g[M, \overline{X}(n)/M]$, $g[M+1, \overline{X}(n)/(M+1)]$, $g[M+2, \overline{X}(n)/(M+2)]$, etc., until it appears that further increases in t will only decrease g. $\hat{t}$ and $\hat{p}$ are then chosen to be the values of t and $\overline{X}(n)/t$ which led to the largest observed value of $g[t, \overline{X}(n)/t]$. Strictly speaking, however, this procedure does not absolutely guarantee that the true MLEs will be obtained
Comments	1. If $Y_1, Y_2, \ldots, Y_t$ are independent Bernoulli(p) random variables, then $Y_1 + Y_2 + \cdots + Y_t \sim$ bin(t, p) 2. If $X_1, X_2, \ldots, X_m$ are independent random variables and $X_i \sim$ bin(t_i, p), then $X_1 + X_2 + \cdots + X_m \sim$ bin($t_1 + t_2 + \cdots + t_m, p$) 3. The bin($t, p$) distribution is symmetric if and only if $p = \frac{1}{2}$ 4. $X \sim$ bin(t, p) if and only if $t - X \sim$ bin($t, 1 - p$) 5. The bin($1, p$) and Bernoulli(p) distributions are the same

Geometric	geom(p)

Possible applications	Number of failures before the first success in a sequence of independent Bernoulli trials with probability p of success on each trial; number of items inspected before encountering the first defective item; number of items in a batch of random size; number of items demanded from an inventory
Mass (see Fig. 5.12)	$$p(x) = \begin{cases} p \cdot (1 - p)^x & \text{if } x \in \{0, 1, \ldots\} \\ 0 & \text{otherwise} \end{cases}$$
Distribution	$$F(x) = \begin{cases} 1 - (1 - p)^{\lfloor x \rfloor + 1} & \text{if } x \ge 0 \\ 0 & \text{otherwise} \end{cases}$$

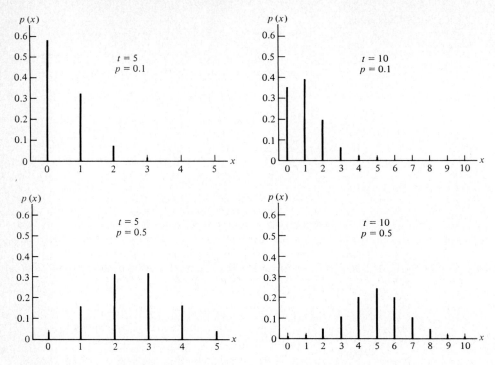

Figure 5.11 bin(t, p) mass functions.

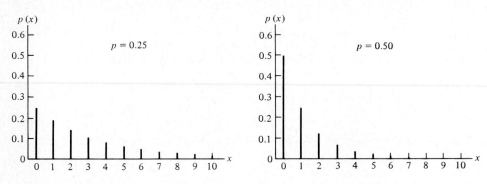

Figure 5.12 geom(p) mass functions.

Table 5.2 (*Continued*)

Geometric	geom(p)

Parameter	$p \in (0, 1)$
Range	$\{0, 1, \ldots\}$
Mean	$\dfrac{1 - p}{p}$
Variance	$\dfrac{1 - p}{p^2}$
Mode	
MLE	$\hat{p} = \dfrac{1}{\overline{X}(n) + 1}$
Comments	1. If $Y_1, Y_2, \ldots$ is a sequence of independent Bernoulli(p) random variables and $X = \min\{i : Y_i = 1\} - 1$, then $X \sim$ geom(p).
	2. If $X_1, X_2, \ldots, X_s$ are independent geom(p) random variables, then $X_1 + X_2 + \cdots + X_s$ has a negative binomial distribution with parameters s and p
	3. The geometric distribution is the discrete analogue of the exponential distribution, in the sense that it is the only discrete distribution with the memoryless property (see Appendix 8A)
	4. The geom(p) distribution is a special case of the negative binomial distribution (with $s = 1$ and the same value for p)

Negative binomial	negbin(s, p)

Possible applications	Number of failures before the sth success in a sequence of independent Bernoulli trials with probability p of success on each trial; number of good items inspected before encountering the sth defective item; number of items in a batch of random size; number of items demanded from an inventory
Mass (see Fig. 5.13)	$p(x) = \begin{cases} \dbinom{s + x - 1}{x} p^s (1 - p)^x & \text{if } x \in \{0, 1, \ldots\} \\ 0 & \text{otherwise} \end{cases}$
Distribution	$F(x) = \begin{cases} \displaystyle\sum_{i=0}^{\lfloor x \rfloor} \dbinom{s + i - 1}{i} p^s (1 - p)^i & \text{if } x \geq 0 \\ 0 & \text{otherwise} \end{cases}$
Parameters	s a positive integer, $p \in (0, 1)$
Range	$\{0, 1, \ldots\}$
Mean	$\dfrac{s(1 - p)}{p}$
Variance	$\dfrac{s(1 - p)}{p^2}$
Mode	Let $y = [s(1 - p) - 1]/p$; then
	$\text{Mode} = \begin{cases} y \text{ and } y + 1 & \text{if } y \text{ is an integer} \\ \lfloor y \rfloor + 1 & \text{otherwise} \end{cases}$
MLE	If s is known, then $\hat{p} = s/[\overline{X}(n) + s]$. If both s and p are unknown, finding $\hat{s}$ and $\hat{p}$ is more difficult and resembles the problem of finding MLEs for both binomial parameters. Let $M = \max_{1 \leq i \leq n} X_i$, and for $k = 0, 1, \ldots, M$, let f_k be the number of X_i's $\geq k$. Then we can show that $\hat{s}$ and $\hat{p}$ are the values for s and

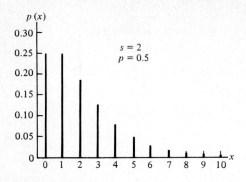

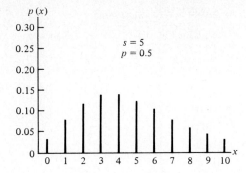

Figure 5.13 negbin(s, p) mass functions.

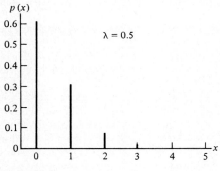

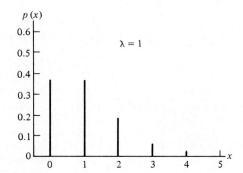

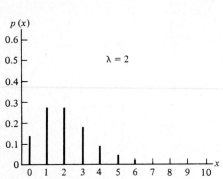

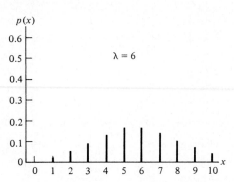

Figure 5.14 Poisson(λ) mass functions.

Table 5.2 (*Continued*)

Negative binomial	negbin(s, p)

p that maximize the function

$$h(s, p) = \sum_{k=1}^{M} f_k \ln(s + k - 1) + ns \ln p + n\bar{X}(n) \ln(1 - p)$$

subject to the constraints that $s \in \{1, 2, \ldots\}$ and $0 < p < 1$. For a fixed value of s, say s_0, the value of p that maximizes $h(s_0, p)$ is $s_0/[\bar{X}(n) + s_0]$, so that we could examine $h(1, 1/[\bar{X}(n) + 1])$, $h(2, 2/[\bar{X}(n) + 2])$, etc., until it appears that further increases in s will only decrease h. $\hat{s}$ and $\hat{p}$ are then chosen to be the values of s and $s/[\bar{X}(n) + s]$ which led to the biggest observed value of $h(s, s/[\bar{X}(n) + s])$. Again, this operational procedure is not absolutely guaranteed to yield the true MLEs

Comments

1. If $Y_1, Y_2, \ldots, Y_s$ are independent geom(p) random variables, then $Y_1 + Y_2 + \cdots + Y_s \sim$ negbin(s, p)
2. If $Y_1, Y_2, \ldots$ is a sequence of independent Bernoulli(p) random variables and $X = \min \{i: \sum_{j=1}^{i} Y_j = s\} - s$, then $X \sim$ negbin(s, p)
3. If $X_1, X_2, \ldots, X_m$ are independent random variables and $X_i \sim$ negbin(s_i, p), then $X_1 + X_2 + \cdots + X_m \sim$ negbin($s_1 + s_2 + \cdots + s_m, p$)
4. The negbin($1, p$) and geom(p) distributions are the same

Poisson	Poisson(λ)
Possible applications	Number of events that occur in an interval of time when the events occur independently of each other (see Sec. 5.7); number of items in a batch of random size; number of items demanded from an inventory

Mass (see Fig. 5.14)

$$p(x) = \begin{cases} \dfrac{e^{-\lambda}\lambda^x}{x!} & \text{if } x \in \{0, 1, \ldots\} \\ 0 & \text{otherwise} \end{cases}$$

Distribution

$$F(x) = \begin{cases} 0 & \text{if } x < 0 \\ e^{-\lambda} \sum_{i=0}^{\lfloor x \rfloor} \dfrac{\lambda^i}{i!} & \text{if } 0 \leq x \end{cases}$$

Parameter	$\lambda > 0$
Range	$\{0, 1, \ldots\}$
Mean	λ
Variance	λ
Mode	$\begin{cases} \lambda - 1 \text{ and } \lambda & \text{if } \lambda \text{ is an integer} \\ \lfloor \lambda \rfloor & \text{otherwise} \end{cases}$
MLE	$\hat{\lambda} = \bar{X}(n)$

Comments

1. Let $Y_1, Y_2, \ldots$ be a sequence of nonnegative IID random variables, and let $X = \max \{i: \sum_{j=1}^{i} Y_j \leq 1\}$. Then the distribution of the Y_i's is expo($1/\lambda$) if and only if $X \sim$ Poisson(λ). Also, if $X' = \max \{i: \sum_{j=1}^{i} Y_j \leq \lambda\}$, then the Y_i's are expo(1) if and only if $X' \sim$ Poisson(λ) (see also Sec. 5.7)
2. If $X_1, X_2, \ldots, X_m$ are independent random variables and $X_i \sim$ Poisson(λ_i), then $X_1 + X_2 + \cdots + X_m \sim$ Poisson($\lambda_1 + \lambda_2 + \cdots + \lambda_m$)

5.2.4 Empirical Distributions

In some situations we might want to use the observed data themselves to specify directly (in some sense) a distribution, called an *empirical distribution,* from which samples are drawn during the simulation, rather than fitting a theoretical distribution to the data. For example, it could happen that we simply cannot find a theoretical distribution which fits the data adequately (see Secs. 5.3 to 5.5). This section explores ways of specifying empirical distributions.

For continuous random variables the type of empirical distribution that can be defined depends on whether we have the actual values of the individual original observations $X_1, X_2, \ldots, X_n$ rather than only the *number* of X_i's which fall into each of several specified intervals. (The latter case is called *grouped data* or *data in the form of a histogram.*) If the original data are available, we can define a continuous, piecewise linear distribution function F by first sorting the X_i's into increasing order. Let $X_{(i)}$ denote the ith smallest of the X_j's, so that $X_{(1)} \le X_{(2)} \le \cdots \le X_{(n)}$. Then F is given by

$$
F(x) = \begin{cases}
0 & \text{if } x < X_{(1)} \\
\dfrac{i-1}{n-1} + \dfrac{x - X_{(i)}}{(n-1)(X_{(i+1)} - X_{(i)})} & \text{if } X_{(i)} \le x < X_{(i+1)} \\
& \quad \text{for } i = 1, 2, \ldots, n-1 \\
1 & \text{if } X_{(n)} \le x
\end{cases}
$$

Figure 5.15 gives an illustration for $n = 6$. Note that $F(x)$ rises most rapidly over those ranges of x in which the X_i's are most densely distributed, as desired. Also, for each i, $F(X_{(i)}) = (i-1)/(n-1)$, which is approximately (for large n) the proportion of the X_j's that are less than $X_{(i)}$; this is also the way we would like a *continuous* distribution function to behave. However, one clear disadvantage of specifying this particular empirical distribution is that random variables generated from it during a simulation run can never be less than $X_{(1)}$ or more than $X_{(n)}$ (see Sec. 7.3.10).

If, on the other hand, the data are grouped, a different approach must be taken since we do not know the values of the individual X_i's. Suppose that the n X_i's are grouped into k adjacent intervals $[a_0, a_1), [a_1, a_2), \ldots, [a_{k-1}, a_k)$ so that the jth interval contains n_j observations, where $n_1 + n_2 + \cdots + n_k = n$. (Often the a_j's will be equally spaced, but we need not make this assumption.) A reasonable piece-

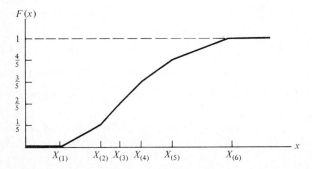

Figure 5.15 Continuous, piecewise linear empirical distribution function from original data.

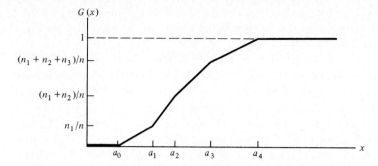

Figure 5.16 Continuous, piecewise linear empirical distribution function from grouped data.

wise linear empirical distribution function G could be specified by first letting $G(a_0) = 0$ and $G(a_j) = (n_1 + n_2 + \cdots + n_j)/n$ for $j = 1, 2, \ldots, k$. Then interpolating linearly between the a_j's, we define

$$
G(x) = \begin{cases}
0 & \text{if } x < a_0 \\[2mm]
G(a_{j-1}) + \dfrac{x - a_{j-1}}{a_j - a_{j-1}}[G(a_j) - G(a_{j-1})] & \begin{aligned}&\text{if } a_{j-1} \leq x < a_j \\ &\text{for } j = 1, 2, \ldots, k\end{aligned} \\[2mm]
1 & \text{if } a_k \leq x
\end{cases}
$$

Figure 5.16 illustrates this specification of an empirical distribution function for $k = 4$. In this case, $G(a_j)$ is the proportion of the X_i's that are less than a_j, and $G(x)$ rises most rapidly over ranges of x where the observations are most dense. The random variables generated from this distribution, however, will still be bounded both below (by a_0) and above (by a_k); see Sec. 7.3.10.

We emphasize that the above two paragraphs give only two possible ways in which empirical distributions can be specified for continuous random variables. Depending on the situation, other methods could be devised which would eliminate the boundedness, such as putting an "exponential tail" on one or both sides.

For discrete data, it is quite simple to define an empirical distribution, provided that the original data values $X_1, X_2, \ldots, X_n$ are available. For each possible value x an empirical mass function $p(x)$ can be defined to be the proportion of the X_i's that are equal to x. For grouped discrete data we could define a mass function such that the *sum* of the $p(x)$'s over all possible values of x in an interval is equal to the proportion of the X_i's in that interval. How the individual $p(x)$'s are allocated for the possible values of x within an interval is essentially arbitrary.

5.3 HYPOTHESIZING A FAMILY OF DISTRIBUTIONS

The first step in selecting a particular input distribution is to decide what general *family*, e.g., exponential, gamma, normal, or Poisson, of distributions appears to be appropriate, without worrying (yet) about the particular parameter values for the family. This section describes some general methods that can be used to *hypothesize* (some might call it guess) a family of distributions that can be used to generate a particular random variable in a simulation.

In some situations, use can be made of *prior knowledge* about a certain random variable's role in a system to select a modeling distribution or at least to rule out some distributions; this is done on theoretical bases and does not require any data at all. For example, if we feel sure that customers arrive at a service facility one at a time, at a constant rate, and so that the numbers of customers arriving in disjoint time intervals are independent, there are theoretical reasons (see Sec. 5.7.1) for postulating that the interarrival times are IID exponential random variables. Recall also that several discrete distributions, e.g., binomial, geometric, and negative binomial, were developed from a physical model. Often the range of a distribution rules it out as a modeling distribution. Service times, for example, should not be generated directly from a normal distribution (at least in theory), since a random variable from *any* normal distribution can be negative. The proportion of defective items in a large batch should not be assumed to have a gamma distribution, since proportions must be between 0 and 1, whereas gamma random variables have no upper bound. Prior information should be used whenever available, but supporting the postulated distribution with data is also recommended.

In practice, we seldom have enough of this kind of theoretical prior information to select a single distribution, and the task of hypothesizing a distribution form from observed data is much less structured. In the remainder of this section, we discuss various *heuristics*, or guidelines, that can be used to help one select an appropriate distribution form. Since these heuristics tend to take different forms for continuous and discrete data, and since we usually have enough prior knowledge to know whether a continuous or discrete distribution is appropriate, we consider these two cases separately.

5.3.1 Continuous Distributions

We describe three different kinds of heuristics applicable to selecting an appropriate continuous distribution form: *point statistics, histograms,* and *probability plots.*

Point statistics. Some continuous distributions are characterized by values of functions of their *true* parameters. One such function that has been used is the *coefficient of variation* of a distribution, $\delta = \sqrt{\text{Var}(X)}/E(X)$, where Var (X) and $E(X)$ are the variance and mean, respectively, of the distribution. Table 5.3 gives δ and, where possible, the range of values for δ as a function of the parameters of a distribution. For the gamma and Weibull distributions, we see that δ is greater than, equal to, or less than 1 according as the shape parameter α is less than, equal to, or greater than 1, respectively. In particular, $\delta = 1$ for the exponential distribution, regardless of β. For the uniform, normal, lognormal, beta, and triangular distributions, δ is not particularly useful. [In fact, for distributions such as the U$(-c, c)$ (for $c > 0$) or N$(0, \sigma^2)$, δ is not even well defined since the mean is zero.]

Since δ depends on the true (unknown) parameters of a distribution, it must be

Table 5.3 Coefficients of variation for continuous distributions

Distribution	δ	Range of δ
$U(a, b)$	$\dfrac{b - a}{\sqrt{3}(a + b)}$	$(-\infty, \infty]\dagger$
$\text{expo}(\beta)$	1	$\{1\}$
$\text{gamma}(\alpha, \beta)$	$\alpha^{-1/2}$	$\begin{cases} > 1 & \text{if } \alpha < 1 \\ = 1 & \text{if } \alpha = 1 \\ < 1 & \text{if } \alpha > 1 \end{cases}$
$\text{Weibull}(\alpha, \beta)$	$\left\{ \dfrac{\Gamma((2/\alpha) + 1)}{[\Gamma((1/\alpha) + 1)]^2} - 1 \right\}^{1/2}$	$\begin{cases} > 1 & \text{if } \alpha < 1 \\ = 1 & \text{if } \alpha = 1 \\ < 1 & \text{if } \alpha > 1 \end{cases}$
$N(\mu, \sigma^2)$	$\dfrac{\sigma}{\mu}$	$(-\infty, \infty]\dagger$
$LN(\mu, \sigma^2)$	$(e^{\sigma^2} - 1)^{1/2}$	$(0, \infty)$
$\text{beta}(\alpha_1, \alpha_2)$	$\left[\dfrac{\alpha_1}{\alpha_2}(\alpha_1 + \alpha_2 + 1) \right]^{-1/2}$	$(0, \infty)$
$\text{triang}(a, b, c)$	$\dfrac{(a^2 + b^2 + c^2 - ab - ac - bc)^{1/2}}{\sqrt{2}(a + b + c)}$	$(-\infty, \infty]\dagger$

$\dagger$Except 0.

estimated from data. Let $X_1, X_2, \ldots, X_n$ be n IID observations which we have collected on the random variable of interest, and let

$$\overline{X}(n) = \frac{\sum\limits_{i=1}^{n} X_i}{n} \quad \text{and} \quad s^2(n) = \frac{\sum\limits_{i=1}^{n} [X_i - \overline{X}(n)]^2}{n - 1}$$

be the usual sample mean and variance. [Recall from Chap. 4 that $\overline{X}(n)$ and $s^2(n)$ are unbiased estimators of the *true* mean and variance, respectively, of the distribution of the X_i's.] Then a natural (but not necessarily unbiased) estimate of δ is

$$\hat{\delta}(n) = \frac{\sqrt{s^2(n)}}{\overline{X}(n)}$$

Thus, if we are considering the exponential distribution as a modeling distribution, we would look for a value of $\hat{\delta}(n)$ near 1. Similarly, $\hat{\delta}(n) > 1$ might suggest gamma or Weibull with $\alpha < 1$, and $\hat{\delta}(n) < 1$ would suggest gamma or Weibull with $\alpha > 1$.

Estimating δ by $\hat{\delta}(n)$ in this way is certainly a very quick and easy thing to do and can sometimes be of assistance, but there are several clear drawbacks. As we saw in Table 5.3, δ does not uniquely determine a distribution form. Other functions of a distribution's parameters might therefore be considered, e.g., the coefficients of skewness and kurtosis (see, for example, Kendall and Stuart [20]), that discriminate better between alternative distributions. All such measures, however, have to be estimated from the data, and these estimates (being random variables themselves) usually are not very reliable. For example, it could well be that the true (unknown) distribution of the X_i's is exponential, yet due to sampling fluctuation we could get a value of $\hat{\delta}(n)$ that is far from 1. In the absence of a more reliable and formal statistical evaluation (such as a hypothesis test), the simple computation of a point statistic is a very rough guide, at best.

Histograms. A histogram is essentially a graphical estimate of the plot of the density function corresponding to the distribution of our data $X_1, X_2, \ldots, X_n$. Density functions, as shown in Figs. 5.1 to 5.7, tend to have recognizable shapes in many cases. Therefore, a graphical estimate of a density should provide a good clue to the distributions that might be tried as a model for the data.

To make a histogram, we break up the range of values covered by the data into k disjoint adjacent intervals $[b_0, b_1), [b_1, b_2), \ldots, [b_{k-1}, b_k)$. All the intervals should be the same width, say $\Delta b = b_j - b_{j-1}$, which might necessitate throwing out a few extremely large or small X_i's to avoid getting an unwieldly looking histogram plot. (Discarded data should be noted on the histogram plot itself in some way.) For $j = 1, 2, \ldots, k$, let q_j be the proportion of the X_i's that are in the jth interval $[b_{j-1}, b_j)$. Finally, we define the function

$$h(x) = \begin{cases} 0 & \text{if } x < b_0 \\ q_j & \text{if } b_{j-1} \le x < b_j \quad \text{for } j = 1, 2, \ldots, k \\ 0 & \text{if } b_k \le x \end{cases}$$

which we plot as a function of x. (See Example 5.1 below for an example of a histogram.) The plot of h, which is piecewise constant, is then compared with plots of densities of various distributions on the basis of shape alone (location and scale differences are ignored) to see what distributions have densities that resemble the histogram h.

To see why the shape of h should resemble the true density f of the data, let X be a random variable with density f, so that X is distributed as the X_i's. Then for any fixed j ($j = 1, 2, \ldots, k$),

$$P\{b_{j-1} \le X \le b_j\} = \int_{b_{j-1}}^{b_j} f(x) \, dx = \Delta b \, f(y)$$

for some particular number $y \in (b_{j-1}, b_j)$. (The first equation is by the definition of a continuous random variable, and the second follows from the mean-value theorem of calculus.) On the other hand, the probability that X falls in the jth interval is approximated by q_j, which is the value of $h(y)$. Therefore,

$$h(y) = q_j \approx \Delta b \, f(y)$$

so that $h(y)$ is roughly proportional to $f(y)$; that is, h and f have roughly the same shape. (Actually, an *estimate* of f is obtained by dividing the function h by the constant Δb.)

Histograms are simple to construct, are applicable to any distribution, and provide an easily interpreted visual synopsis of the data. Furthermore, it is relatively easy to "eyeball" a graph in reference to possible density functions. There are, however, some difficulties. Most vexing is the absence of any kind of guide in choosing the intervals and their width. About the only thing we can say is that the analyst might try several different values of Δb and choose the one which yields the "best" or "smoothest" looking histogram. This is clearly a matter of great subjectivity and represents the major problem in using histograms (see Example 5.1 below). Another disadvantage of historgrams is the loss of information incurred in grouping the data.

As we have noted, a histogram is an estimate (except for rescaling) of the density function. There are many other ways in which the density function can be estimated from data, some of these quite sophisticated. We refer the interested reader to the survey papers of Tarter and Kronmal [42] and Wegman [44].

Probability plots. As we just saw, a histogram can be thought of as an estimate of the shape of a density function. Probability plots can be thought of as a graphical comparison of an estimate of the distribution function of our data $X_1, X_2, \ldots, X_n$ with the distribution function of one of the standard distributions being considered as a model for the data. There are many different kinds (and uses) of probability plots, only one of which we describe here; see Barnett [1], Hahn and Shapiro [17], and Wilk and Gnanadesikan [47] for more complete treatments.

As in Sec. 5.2.4, let $X_{(i)}$ be the ith smallest of the X_j's, sometimes called the *ith order statistic* of the n X_j's. Recall that the distribution function F of a random variable X is defined so that for any x, $F(x) = P\{X \leq x\}$. If X has the same distribution as the X_j data, a reasonable approximation to $F(x)$ is thus the proportion of the X_j's that are less than or equal to x. In particular, we might want to define an empirical distribution function $\tilde{F}_n(x)$ so that $\tilde{F}_n(X_{(i)}) = i/n$, since this *is* the proportion of the X_j's that are less than or equal to $X_{(i)}$. For purposes of probability plotting, however, it turns out to be somewhat inconvenient to have $\tilde{F}_n(X_{(n)}) = 1$, that is, to have an empirical distribution function that is equal to 1 for a finite value of x. We therefore make a small adjustment and define

$$\tilde{F}_n(X_{(i)}) = \frac{i - 0.5}{n}$$

for $i = 1, 2, \ldots, n$. [Clearly, for moderately large n, this adjustment is quite small. Other adjustments have been suggested, such as $i/(n + 1)$.] A straightforward procedure would then be to plot the n points $(X_{(1)}, 0.5/n)$, $(X_{(2)}, 1.5/n)$, $\ldots$, $(X_{(n)}, (n - 0.5)/n)$, compare this result with plots of the distribution functions of several of the distributions being considered as a model for the data, and look for similarities. However, distribution functions generally do not have as characteristic an appearance as densities. In fact, many distribution functions have some sort of an "S" shape, and eyeballing for differences or similarities in shapes between S-shaped curves is somewhat perplexing.

Most of us, however, *can* recognize whether or not a set of plotted points appears to lie more or less along a *straight* line, and probability plotting techniques reduce the problem of comparing distribution functions to one of looking for a straight line. The particular technique we propose is based on a comparison of *quantiles* of distributions. For $0 < q < 1$, the q quantile of a distribution F is a number x_q that satisfies $F(x_q) = q$. (Quantiles were called *critical points* in Chap. 4.) Thus, if F^{-1} denotes the inverse of the distribution function F, a formula for the q quantile of F is $x_q = F^{-1}(q)$. (F^{-1} will exist if F is continuous and strictly increasing.) If F and G are two distribution functions, it is clear that $F = G$ if and only if each of the quantiles of F is the same as the corresponding quantile of G. Thus, if x_q and y_q are the q quantiles of F and G, respectively, a plot of the points (x_q, y_q) for various values of q will produce points along a straight line having slope 1 (a 45° line) and passing through the origin, since $x_q = y_q$ for all q. Furthermore, if the random variables corresponding to F and G differ only in location and scale (see Sec. 5.2.1), then for some real numbers γ and β ($\beta > 0$) we have $G(x) = F[(x - \gamma)/\beta]$ for all x. In this case, it is easy to see that for all q, $y_q = \gamma + \beta x_q$, so that a plot of the points (x_q, y_q) produces a *straight* line of points which has a slope not necessarily 1 and which need not pass through the origin. Thus, distributions having the same shape (but which may differ in location and scale) have quantiles which are linearly related. A plot of pairs of quantiles such as (x_q, y_q) is called a *probability plot*. (This particular version is often called a *Q-Q plot*.)

Probability plots provide a way of assessing whether the empirical distribution function $\tilde{F}_n$, defined at the $X_{(i)}$ points, has the same shape as a distribution function from one of the theoretical families. Suppose that we are considering a *particular* distribution form, e.g., exponential or gamma, and that if this distribution has any shape parameters, they have already been estimated from the data. (We return to this point concerning shape parameters later.) Location and scale parameters, however, need not be uniquely specified; it is usually convenient to take the location parameter to be 0 and the scale parameter to be 1, although any values will do. (The scale parameter must be positive.) Let the resulting distribution function be denoted by F, which represents a trial hypothesized distribution *shape*, with unspecified location and scale. We want to compare $\tilde{F}_n$ with F, and we can do so by a (Q-Q) probability plot of the quantile pairs for $q = (i - 0.5)/n$ for $i = 1, 2, \ldots, n$, as follows. By definition, the $(i - 0.5)/n$ quantile of $\tilde{F}_n$ is precisely $X_{(i)}$. The $(i - 0.5)/n$ quantile of F is simply $F^{-1}[(i - 0.5)/n]$. Thus, we plot the points

$$\left(X_{(i)}, F^{-1}\left(\frac{i - 0.5}{n} \right) \right)$$

for $i = 1, 2, \ldots, n$, and if the resulting points appear to lie along a straight line (*any* straight line, regardless of slope or intercept), we have informal confirmation that, except for adjustments in location and scale, F is a good distribution function for our data.

Several specific issues regarding probability plots need to be addressed.

Uniform and exponential distributions. The above procedure really has no problems, since a simple formula for $F^{-1}[(i - 0.5)/n]$ can easily be found. For the uniform distribution F would be taken to be the U(0, 1) distribution function, and for the exponential distribution we would use the expo(1) distribution function.

Gamma and beta distributions. We suggest first estimating the shape parameters by their maximum-likelihood estimators (see Sec. 5.4) and setting $\beta = 1$ in the gamma distribution. No formula can be found for F^{-1} in either of these cases, so that $F^{-1}[(i - 0.5)/n]$ must be computed by numerical methods. For the gamma distribution, Best and Roberts [4] provide an algorithm (and FORTRAN program) for inverting the chi-square distribution function for the general case of degrees of freedom which need not be an integer. Thus, since the chi-square distribution with $2\alpha > 0$ df is the same as the gamma(α, 2) distribution, their method is applicable to any gamma distribution. (We would be taking the scale parameter β to be 2 instead of 1 if we used this relationship between the gamma and chi-square distributions directly to invert F; again, the choice of any $\beta > 0$ is arbitrary for probability plotting.) For numerical inversion of the beta distribution function, see Cran, Martin, and Thomas [12].

Normal distribution. Inversion of F must also be done numerically; see Beasley and Springer [2]. If the plot is done by hand, however, special normal probability paper is commercially available which automatically scales one of the axes to an F^{-1} scale and leaves the other axis as a standard linear scale. Thus, we would simply plot the pairs $(X_{(i)}, (i - 0.5)/n)$ with the $X_{(i)}$'s on the linear axis and the values of $(i - 0.5)/n$ on the normal probability (or F^{-1}) axis.

Lognormal distribution. Replace the data values by their natural logarithms and treat these logarithms as being normally distributed; that is, if X'_i for $i = 1, 2, \ldots, n$ are the raw data points which we think may have a lognormal distribution, simply let $X_i = \ln X'_i$ and treat the X_i's as data points from a normal distribution.

Weibull distribution. It is possible to avoid estimation of the shape parameter α. The Weibull distribution function is easy to invert analytically, and a probability plot is based on the assumption that

$$X_{(i)} \approx \beta \left(-\ln \frac{n - i + 0.5}{n} \right)^{1/\alpha}$$

which would seem to imply that the shape parameter α would have to be estimated. However, in this case a logarithmic transformation yields

$$\ln X_{(i)} \approx \ln \beta + \left(\frac{1}{\alpha} \right) \ln \left(-\ln \frac{n - i + 0.5}{n} \right)$$

so that we can plot the pairs

$$\left(\ln X_{(i)}, \ln \left(-\ln \frac{n - i + 0.5}{n} \right) \right)$$

and look for linearity in the points. Thus in this particular case, we need not estimate the shape parameter.

Probability plots have the advantage of being widely applicable, easy to interpret (we simply look for a straight line of points as opposed to systematic deviations from linearity), and not requiring the troublesome interval specification (and loss of information due to grouping) necessary for construction of histograms. Disadvantages of probability plotting include the need to specify beforehand which distribution form is of interest (not necessary in using histograms), possibly having to estimate shape parameters before making a plot, and difficulty in inverting some distribution functions.

Example 5.1 A simulation model was developed for a drive-up banking facility, and data were collected on the arrival pattern of cars. Over a fixed 90-minute period, 220 cars arrived, and we noted the interarrival time X_i (in minutes) between cars i and $i + 1$, for $i = 1, 2, \ldots, 219$. Table 5.4 lists these $n = 219$ interarrival times after they have been sorted into increasing order. The first step in fitting a distribution to these data (for use in sampling interarrival times in a simulation run of the facility) is to hypothesize a distribution form. We carried out the three kinds of heuristics discussed in this section. Since $\overline{X}(219) = 0.399$ and $s^2(219) = 0.144$, an estimate of the coefficient of variation is $\hat{\delta}(219) = \sqrt{0.144/0.399} = 0.951$. Since this is quite close to 1, the exponential distribution is suggested. Next we made three different histograms of the data using $b_0 = 0$ in each case and $\Delta b = 0.050, 0.075,$ and 0.100, as shown in Fig. 5.17. The "smoothest" looking

Table 5.4 $n = 219$ interarrival times (minutes) sorted into increasing order

0.01	0.06	0.12	0.23	0.38	0.53	0.88
0.01	0.07	0.12	0.23	0.38	0.53	0.88
0.01	0.07	0.12	0.24	0.38	0.54	0.90
0.01	0.07	0.13	0.25	0.39	0.54	0.93
0.01	0.07	0.13	0.25	0.40	0.55	0.93
0.01	0.07	0.14	0.25	0.40	0.55	0.95
0.01	0.07	0.14	0.25	0.41	0.56	0.97
0.01	0.07	0.14	0.25	0.41	0.57	1.03
0.02	0.07	0.14	0.26	0.43	0.57	1.05
0.02	0.07	0.15	0.26	0.43	0.60	1.05
0.03	0.07	0.15	0.26	0.43	0.61	1.06
0.03	0.08	0.15	0.26	0.44	0.61	1.09
0.03	0.08	0.15	0.26	0.45	0.63	1.10
0.04	0.08	0.15	0.27	0.45	0.63	1.11
0.04	0.08	0.15	0.28	0.46	0.64	1.12
0.04	0.09	0.17	0.28	0.47	0.65	1.17
0.04	0.09	0.18	0.29	0.47	0.65	1.18
0.04	0.10	0.19	0.29	0.47	0.65	1.24
0.04	0.10	0.19	0.30	0.48	0.69	1.24
0.05	0.10	0.19	0.31	0.49	0.69	1.28
0.05	0.10	0.20	0.31	0.49	0.70	1.33
0.05	0.10	0.21	0.32	0.49	0.72	1.38
0.05	0.10	0.21	0.35	0.49	0.72	1.44
0.05	0.10	0.21	0.35	0.50	0.72	1.51
0.05	0.10	0.21	0.35	0.50	0.74	1.72
0.05	0.10	0.21	0.36	0.50	0.75	1.83
0.05	0.11	0.22	0.36	0.51	0.76	1.96
0.05	0.11	0.22	0.36	0.51	0.77	
0.05	0.11	0.22	0.37	0.51	0.79	
0.06	0.11	0.23	0.37	0.52	0.84	
0.06	0.11	0.23	0.38	0.52	0.86	
0.06	0.12	0.23	0.38	0.53	0.87	

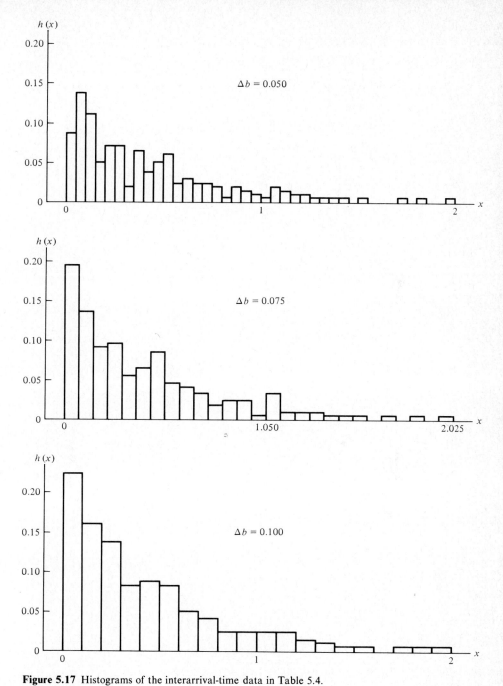

Figure 5.17 Histograms of the interarrival-time data in Table 5.4.

$F^{-1}[(i-0.5)/n]$

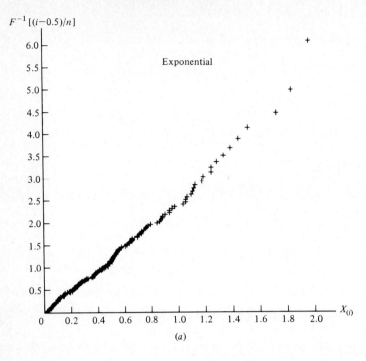

(a)

$\Phi^{-1}[(i-0.5)/n]$

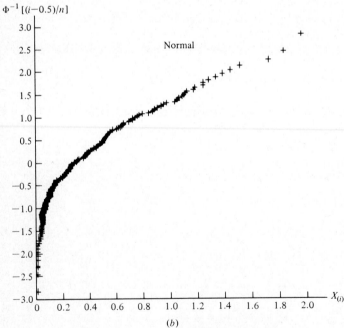

(b)

Figure 5.18 Probability plots of the interarrival-time data in Table 5.4: (a) exponential; (b) normal.

histogram appears to be for $\Delta b = 0.100$, and its shape resembles that of an exponential density. At this point, since the exponential distribution appears to be a good candidate, we made a probability plot using this distribution. To find a formula for F^{-1}, we solve the equation $y = F(x)$ for x; in the exponential case we get $x = F^{-1}(y) = -\beta \ln (1 - y)$. Since β is a scale parameter, we can set it arbitrarily to 1, so that a probability plot consists of plotting the pairs

$$\left(X_{(i)}, -\ln \frac{n - i + 0.5}{n} \right)$$

for $i = 1, 2, \ldots, n$. These pairs, as shown in the first plot of Fig. 5.18, indeed appear to form a line that is quite straight, further supporting the exponential distribution. To give the reader an idea of what a probability plot might look like when an inappropriate distribution is hypothesized, we made a probability plot for the normal distribution, i.e., we plotted the pairs

$$\left(X_{(i)}, \Phi^{-1} \left(\frac{i - 0.5}{n} \right) \right)$$

where Φ is the distribution function of the N(0, 1) distribution. (We computed Φ^{-1} by a numerical method.) The resulting normal probability plot in Fig. 5.18 displays obvious nonlinearity at the lower end. (See Hahn and Shapiro [17, pp. 264–282] for several examples of how probability plots appear when using both the "right" and "wrong" distributions.)

5.3.2 Discrete Distributions

Heuristics helpful in hypothesizing discrete distributions are similar to those for continuous distributions, with some exceptions. In particular, Q-Q probability plotting in the discrete case is not generally possible since discrete distribution functions are not continuous, so that $F^{-1}(y)$ may not be well defined. (Other kinds of probability plots can be done for discrete distributions with the aid of special graph paper that depends on the distribution; see, for example, Blank [5, pp. 439–441].) The discrete versions of histograms, called *line graphs,* however, are more appealing than histograms for continuous distributions since the problems of interval specification and data grouping do not exist.

Point statistics. For discrete distributions, the ratio $\tau = \text{Var }(X)/E(X)$ can be useful in discriminating between possibilities. Table 5.5 gives τ and its range of values for the discrete distributions given in Sec. 5.2.3.

Table 5.5 Formulas and ranges of τ for discrete distributions

Distribution	τ	Range of τ
Bernoulli(p)	$1 - p$	$(0, 1)$
DU(i, j)	$\dfrac{(j - i + 1)^2 - 1}{6(i + j)}$	$(-\infty, \infty]$
bin(t, p)	$1 - p$	$(0, 1)$
geom(p)	$\dfrac{1}{p}$	$(1, \infty)$
negbin(s, p)	$\dfrac{1}{p}$	$(1, \infty)$
Poisson(λ)	1	$\{1\}$

Table 5.6 $n = 87$ demand sizes sorted into increasing order

1	3	4	4	5	6	6	6	7	8	8	9	11
1	3	4	5	5	6	6	6	7	8	8	9	12
2	3	4	5	5	6	6	6	7	8	9	9	12
2	3	4	5	5	6	6	7	7	8	9	9	
2	3	4	5	5	6	6	7	7	8	9	9	
2	4	4	5	5	6	6	7	7	8	9	10	
3	4	4	5	6	6	6	7	8	8	9	11	

Like point statistics in the continuous case, τ must be estimated from the data $X_1, X_2, \ldots, X_n$; an estimator analogous to $\hat{\delta}(n)$ is $\hat{\tau}(n) = s^2(n)/\overline{X}(n)$. From Table 5.5, $\hat{\tau}(n) < 1$ might suggest a binomial distribution, $\hat{\tau}(n)$ near 1 suggests Poisson, and $\hat{\tau}(n) > 1$ would be characteristic of negative binomial or geometric (a special case of negative binomial). As in the continuous case, however, caution must be used in interpreting $\hat{\tau}(n)$ since it is a random variable. (Coefficients of skewness and kurtosis can also be defined in the discrete case.)

Line graphs. The mass function of discrete data can be estimated in an entirely natural way. For each possible value x_j which can be assumed by the data, let h_j be the proportion of the X_i's that are equal to x_j. Vertical lines of height h_j are plotted versus x_j, and this is compared with plots of the theoretical mass functions of various discrete distributions (such as those in Sec. 5.2.3) to look for similarities in shape.

The justification for line graphs stems from the fact that h_j (which is a random variable) is an unbiased estimator of $p(x_j)$, where $p(x)$ is the true (unknown) mass function of the data (see Prob. 5.1). Line graphs are quite similar to histograms in their construction, interpretation, and use but are more appealing since we need not make any arbitrary subjective decisions about interval width and placement.

Example 5.2 Table 5.6 lists $n = 87$ observations on the number of items demanded in a day from an inventory, sorted into increasing order. Since $\overline{X}(87) = 6.115$ and $s^2(87) = 5.777$, we estimate τ by $\hat{\tau}(87) = 5.777/6.115 = 0.945$. Since this is only a little less than 1, the first distribution that comes to mind is the Poisson. (Another possibility might be the binomial with a very small value of p.) A line graph of the data (Fig. 5.19) appears to be consistent with the possible shapes of a Poisson mass function.

5.4 ESTIMATION OF PARAMETERS

After a family of distributions has been hypothesized, we must somehow specify the value(s) of its parameter(s) in order to determine completely the distribution from which we shall sample during the simulation. Our IID data $X_1, X_2, \ldots, X_n$ were used to help us hypothesize a distribution family, and these same data can also be used to specify a distribution's parameter(s). When data are used in this way directly to specify a numerical value for an unknown parameter, we say that we are *estimating* that parameter from the data.

An *estimator* is a numerical function of the data. There are many different ways to specify the form of an estimator for a particular parameter of a given distribution, and many alternative ways exist to evaluate the quality of an estimator. We shall consider explicitly only one type, *maximum-likelihood estimators* (MLEs), for three reasons: (1) MLEs have several desirable properties often not enjoyed by alternative methods of estimation, e.g., least-squares estimators, unbiased estimators, and the method of moments; (2) the use of MLEs turns out to be important in justifying the chi-square goodness-of-fit test (see Sec. 5.5.2); and (3) the central idea of maximum-likelihood estimation has a strong intuitive appeal.

The basis for MLEs is most easily understood in the discrete case. Suppose that we have hypothesized a discrete distribution for our data which has one unknown parameter θ. Let $p_\theta(x)$ denote the probability mass function for this distribution, so that the parameter θ is part of the notation. *Given that we have already observed* the IID data $X_1, X_2, \ldots, X_n$, we define the *likelihood function* $L(\theta)$ as follows:

$$L(\theta) = p_\theta(X_1)p_\theta(X_2) \cdots p_\theta(X_n)$$

$L(\theta)$, which is just the joint probability mass function since the data are independent (see Sec. 4.2), gives the probability (likelihood) of obtaining our observed data if θ is the value of the unknown parameter. Then, the MLE of the unknown value of θ, which we denote by $\hat{\theta}$, is defined to be the value of θ which maximizes $L(\theta)$; that is, $L(\hat{\theta}) \geq L(\theta)$ for all possible values of θ. Thus, $\hat{\theta}$ "best explains" the data we have collected. In the continuous case, MLEs do not have quite as simple an intuitive explanation, since the probability that a continuous random variable *equals* any fixed number is always 0 (see Breiman [6, pp. 67–68] for an intuitive justification of MLEs in the continuous case). Nevertheless, MLEs for continuous distributions are defined analogously to the discrete case. If $f_\theta(x)$ denotes the hypothesized density function (again we assume that there is only one unknown parameter θ), the likelihood function is given by

$$L(\theta) = f_\theta(X_1)f_\theta(X_2) \cdots f_\theta(X_n)$$

The MLE $\hat{\theta}$ of θ is defined to be the value of θ that maximizes $L(\theta)$ over all permissible values of θ. The following two examples show how to compute MLEs for the distributions hypothesized earlier in Examples 5.1 and 5.2.

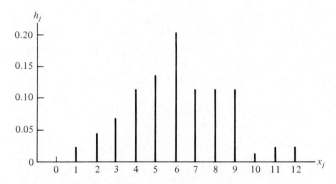

Figure 5.19 Line graph of the demand-size data in Table 5.6.

Example 5.3 For the exponential distribution, $\theta = \beta$ $(\beta > 0)$ and $f_\beta(x) = (1/\beta)e^{-x/\beta}$ for $x \geq 0$. The likelihood function is

$$L(\beta) = \left(\frac{1}{\beta} e^{-X_1/\beta}\right)\left(\frac{1}{\beta} e^{-X_2/\beta}\right) \cdots \left(\frac{1}{\beta} e^{-X_n/\beta}\right)$$

$$= \beta^{-n} \exp\left(-\frac{1}{\beta}\sum_{i=1}^{n} X_i\right)$$

and we seek the value of β which maximizes $L(\beta)$ over all $\beta > 0$. This task is more easily accomplished if, instead of working directly with $L(\beta)$, we work with its logarithm. Thus, we define the *log likelihood function* as

$$l(\beta) = \ln L(\beta) = -n \ln \beta - \frac{1}{\beta}\sum_{i=1}^{n} X_i$$

Since the logarithm function is strictly increasing, maximizing $L(\beta)$ is equivalent to maximizing $l(\beta)$, which is much easier; that is, $\hat{\beta}$ maximizes $L(\beta)$ if and only if $\hat{\beta}$ maximizes $l(\beta)$. Standard differential calculus can be used to maximize $l(\beta)$ by setting its derivative to zero and solving for β. That is,

$$\frac{dl}{d\beta} = \frac{-n}{\beta} + \frac{1}{\beta^2}\sum_{i=1}^{n} X_i$$

which equals zero if and only if $\beta = \sum_{i=1}^{n} X_i/n = \bar{X}(n)$. To make sure that $\beta = \bar{X}(n)$ is a maximizer of $l(\beta)$ (as opposed to a minimizer or an inflection point), a sufficient (but not necessary) condition is that $d^2l/d\beta^2$, evaluated at $\beta = \bar{X}(n)$, be negative. But

$$\frac{d^2l}{d\beta^2} = \frac{n}{\beta^2} - \frac{2}{\beta^3}\sum_{i=1}^{n} X_i$$

which is easily seen to be negative when $\beta = \bar{X}(n)$ since the X_i's are positive. Thus, the MLE of β is $\hat{\beta} = \bar{X}(n)$. Notice that the MLE is quite natural here since β is the mean of the hypothesized distribution and the MLE is the *sample* mean. For the data of Example 5.1, $\hat{\beta} = \bar{X}(219) = 0.399$.

Example 5.4 The discrete data of Example 5.2 were hypothesized to have come from a Poisson distribution. Here, $\theta = \lambda$ $(\lambda > 0)$ and $p_\lambda(x) = e^{-\lambda}\lambda^x/x!$ for $x = 0, 1, 2, \ldots$. The likelihood function is

$$L(\lambda) = \frac{e^{-n\lambda}\,\lambda^{n\bar{X}(n)}}{\prod_{i=1}^{n} X_i!}$$

which is once again amenable to the logarithmic transformation to obtain

$$l(\lambda) = \ln L(\lambda) = -n\lambda + \left(\sum_{i=1}^{n} X_i\right)\ln \lambda - \ln\left(\prod_{i=1}^{n} X_i!\right)$$

Differentiating $l(\lambda)$, we get

$$\frac{dl}{d\lambda} = -n + \frac{1}{\lambda}\sum_{i=1}^{n} X_i$$

which equals zero if and only if $\lambda = \bar{X}(n)$. To make sure that $\lambda = \bar{X}(n)$ is a maximizer, note that

$$\frac{d^2l}{d\lambda^2} = -\frac{1}{\lambda^2}\sum_{i=1}^{n} X_i < 0$$

for any $\lambda > 0$. Thus, the MLE of λ is $\hat{\lambda} = \bar{X}(n)$. For the demand-size data of Example 5.2, $\hat{\lambda} = \bar{X}(87) = 6.115$.

The above two examples illustrate two important practical tools for deriving MLEs, namely, the use of the log likelihood function and setting a derivative equal to zero to find the MLE. While these tools are often useful in finding MLEs, the reader should be cautioned against assuming that finding a MLE is always a simple matter of setting a derivative to zero and solving easily for $\hat{\theta}$. For some distributions, neither the log likelihood function nor differentiation is useful; probably the best-known example is the uniform distribution (see Prob. 5.2). For other distributions, both tools are useful, but solving $dl/d\theta = 0$ cannot be accomplished by simple algebra and numerical methods must be used; the gamma, Weibull, and beta distributions are (multiparameter) examples of this general situation. We refer the reader to [6, pp. 65–84] for examples of techniques used to find MLEs for a variety of distributions.

We have said that MLEs have several desirable statistical properties, some of which are as follows (see [6, pp. 85–88] and Kendall and Stuart [21, chap. 18]):

1. For most of the common distributions, the MLE is unique; that is, $L(\hat{\beta})$ is *strictly* greater than $L(\beta)$ for any other value of β.
2. Although MLEs need not be unbiased, in general, the asymptotic distribution (as $n \to \infty$) of $\hat{\theta}$ has mean equal to θ (see property 4 below).
3. MLEs are *invariant;* i.e., if $\phi = h(\theta)$ for some function h, then the MLE of ϕ is $h(\hat{\theta})$. (Unbiasedness is not invariant.) For example, the variance of an expo(β) random variable is β^2, so that the MLE of this variance is $[\bar{X}(n)]^2$.
4. MLEs are asymptotically normally distributed; i.e., $\sqrt{n}(\hat{\theta} - \theta) \xrightarrow{\mathcal{D}} N(0, v(\theta))$, where $v(\theta) = -1/E(d^2l/d\theta^2)$ (the expectation is with respect to X_i, assuming that X_i has the hypothesized distribution) and $\xrightarrow{\mathcal{D}}$ denotes convergence in distribution. Furthermore, if $\tilde{\theta}$ is any other estimator such that $\sqrt{n}(\tilde{\theta} - \theta) \xrightarrow{\mathcal{D}} N(0, \sigma^2)$, then $v(\theta) \leq \sigma^2$. (Thus, MLEs are called *best asymptotically normal*.)
5. MLEs are *strongly consistent;* that is, $\lim_{n \to \infty} \hat{\theta} = \theta$ (w.p. 1).

The proofs of these and other properties sometimes require additional mild "regularity" assumptions; see [21].

Property 4 is of special interest, since it allows us to establish an approximate confidence interval for θ. If we define $v(\theta)$ as in property 4 above, it can be shown that

$$\frac{\hat{\theta} - \theta}{\sqrt{v(\hat{\theta})/n}} \xrightarrow{\mathcal{D}} N(0, 1)$$

as $n \to \infty$. Thus, for large n an approximate $100(1 - \alpha)$ percent confidence interval for θ is

$$\hat{\theta} \pm z_{1-\alpha/2} \sqrt{\frac{v(\hat{\theta})}{n}} \tag{5.1}$$

This suggests a way of checking how sensitive a simulation output measure of performance is to a particular input parameter. The simulation could be run for θ set at, say, the left endpoint, the center ($\hat{\theta}$), and the right endpoint of the confidence interval in (5.1). If the measure of performance appeared to be insensitive to values of θ in this range, we could feel confident that we have an adequate estimate of θ for our purposes. On the other hand, if the simulation seemed to be sensitive to θ, we might seek a better estimate of θ; this would usually entail collecting more data.

So far, we have explicitly treated only distributions with a single unknown parameter. If a distribution has several parameters, we can define MLEs of these parameters in a natural way. For instance, the gamma distribution has two parameters (α and β), and the likelihood function is defined to be

$$L(\alpha, \beta) = \frac{\beta^{-n\alpha} \left(\prod_{i=1}^{n} X_i \right)^{\alpha-1} \exp\left(-\frac{1}{\beta} \sum_{i=1}^{n} X_i \right)}{[\Gamma(\alpha)]^n}$$

The MLEs $\hat{\alpha}$ and $\hat{\beta}$ of the unknown values of α and β are defined to be the values of α and β which (jointly) maximize $L(\alpha, \beta)$. [Finding $\hat{\alpha}$ and $\hat{\beta}$ usually proceeds by letting $l(\alpha, \beta) = \ln L(\alpha, \beta)$ and trying to solve the equations $\partial l/\partial \alpha = 0$ and $\partial l/\partial \beta = 0$ simultaneously for α and β.] Analogues of the properties of MLEs listed above also hold in this multiparameter case. Unfortunately, the process of finding MLEs when there are several parameters is usually quite difficult. (The normal case is a notable exception.)

For each of the distributions in Secs. 5.2.2 (except for the triangular distribution) and 5.2.3, we listed either formulas for the MLEs or a method for obtaining them numerically. For the gamma MLEs, Table 5.11 can be used with standard linear interpolation. For the beta MLEs, Table 5.12 can be used; one could either simply pick ($\hat{\alpha}_1, \hat{\alpha}_2$) corresponding to the closest table values of G_1 and G_2 or devise a scheme for two-dimensional interpolation.

5.5 GOODNESS-OF-FIT TESTS

After we have hypothesized a distribution form for our data and have estimated its parameters, we must examine whether the *fitted* distribution is in agreement with our observed data $X_1, X_2, \ldots, X_n$. The question we are really asking is this: Is it plausible to have obtained our observed data by sampling from the fitted distribution? If $\hat{F}$ is the distribution function of the fitted distribution, this question can be addressed by a hypothesis test (see Sec. 4.5) with a null hypothesis

H_0: The X_i's are IID random variables with distribution function $\hat{F}$

This is called a *goodness-of-fit test* since it tests how well the fitted distribution "fits" the observed data. In this section we discuss a variety of goodness-of-fit tests.

We feel compelled to comment on the formal structure and properties of these hypothesis tests before going on. In reality, H_0 will probably *never* be *literally* true; i.e., we can probably never obtain the *exact* distribution of the X_i's. Thus, failure to reject H_0 should *not* be interpreted as "accepting" H_0 as being true. Instead, goodness-of-fit hypothesis tests should be regarded as a way of trying systematically to detect fairly gross disagreement between the data and the fitted distribution. Furthermore, many of these kinds of tests are not very powerful; i.e., they are not very sensitive to subtle disagreements between the data and the fitted distribution. (This is generally true of the chi-square and Kolmogorov-Smirnov tests, presented below.) The literature on goodness-of-fit tests is quite extensive, and Sec. 5.5.5 gives references to some recent tests which have been designed chiefly to obtain higher power.

5.5.1 Informal Visual Assessment

As a rough initial guide to how well a fitted distribution agrees with the data, we can visually compare its density with a histogram of the data in the continuous case or its mass function with the line graph of the data in the discrete case. These are only very informal heuristic procedures and are not tests in the strict statistical sense.

For continuous data, recall from Sec. 5.3.1 that the histogram function $h(x)$ can be viewed as an estimate of $\Delta b\, f(x)$, where Δb is the histogram interval width and $f(x)$ is the true density function of the data. If $\hat{f}(x)$ is the density of the fitted distribution, we would plot the function $g(x) = \Delta b\, \hat{f}(x)$ on the same set of axes with the histogram and look for similarity between $h(x)$ and $g(x)$. Another visual method for continuous data is to compute the *expected* proportion of observations, r_j, that would fall in the jth histogram interval if the fitted distribution were in fact the true one. If the r_j's agree well with the corresponding q_j's (the histogram levels), a good fit is indicated; the values of the r_j's can also be displayed on the histogram plot.

Example 5.5 For the interarrival time data of Example 5.1, we hypothesized an exponential distribution and obtained the MLE $\hat{\beta} = 0.399$ in Example 5.3. Thus, the density of the fitted distribution is

$$\hat{f}(x) = \begin{cases} 2.506 e^{-x/0.399} & \text{if } x \geq 0 \\ 0 & \text{otherwise} \end{cases}$$

For the histogram in Fig. 5.17 with $\Delta b = 0.1$, we superimpose $\Delta b\, \hat{f}(x)$ over this histogram in Fig. 5.20, and the agreement with the histogram appears satisfactory. The expected proportion of observations, r_j, in the histogram interval $[b_{j-1}, b_j)$ is given by

$$r_j = \int_{b_{j-1}}^{b_j} \hat{f}(x)\, dx = e^{-b_{j-1}/0.399} - e^{-b_j/0.399} = 0.285 e^{-0.251j}$$

since $b_j = (\Delta b)\, j = 0.1j$ for $j = 0, 1, \ldots, k$, in this case. The values of r_j are plotted in Fig. 5.20 as horizontal dashed lines over their corresponding intervals, and the agreement with the histogram levels appears reasonable.

For discrete data, a simple visual assessment of goodness of fit can be made by superimposing the mass function $\hat{p}(x)$ of the fitted distribution over the line graph of the data. If the two seem to be in agreement, we have visual confirmation of a good fit.

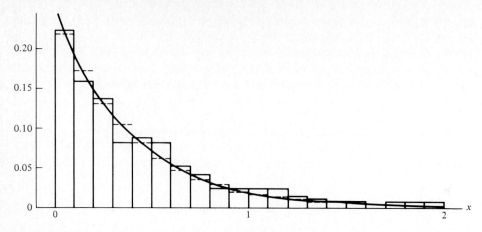

Figure 5.20 Informal visual assessment of the fitted exponential density function, interarrival-time data.

Example 5.6 The demand-size data of Example 5.2 were hypothesized to have come from a Poisson distribution, and the MLE of the Poisson parameter λ was found in Example 5.4 to be $\hat{\lambda} = 6.115$. Thus, the mass function of the fitted distribution is

$$\hat{p}(x) = \begin{cases} \dfrac{e^{-6.115}(6.115)^x}{x!} & \text{if } x \in \{0, 1, \dots\} \\ 0 & \text{otherwise} \end{cases}$$

In Fig. 5.21 we plot $\hat{p}(x)$ (with crosses) on top of the line graph of the data from Fig. 5.19, and the agreement appears reasonably good.

5.5.2 Chi-Square Tests

The oldest goodness-of-fit hypothesis test is the *chi-square test,* which dates back at least to 1900 with the paper of K. Pearson [31]. As we shall see, a chi-square test

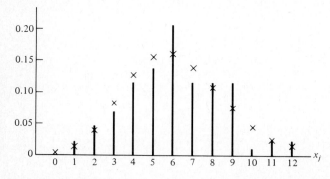

Figure 5.21 Informal visual assessment of the fitted Poisson mass function, demand-size data.

may be thought of as a more formal comparison of a histogram or line graph with the fitted density or mass function.

To compute the chi-square test statistic in either the continuous or discrete case, we must first divide the entire range of the fitted distribution into k adjacent intervals $[a_0, a_1)$, $[a_1, a_2)$, $\ldots$, $[a_{k-1}, a_k)$, where it could be that $a_0 = -\infty$, in which case the first interval is $(-\infty, a_1)$, or $a_k = +\infty$, or both. Then we tally

$$N_j = \text{number of } X_i\text{'s in the } j\text{th interval } [a_{j-1}, a_j)$$

for $j = 1, 2, \ldots, k$. (Note that $\sum_{j=1}^{k} N_j = n$.) Next, we compute the expected *proportion* p_j of the X_i's that would fall in the jth interval if we were sampling from the fitted distribution. In the continuous case,

$$p_j = \int_{a_{j-1}}^{a_j} \hat{f}(x)\, dx$$

where $\hat{f}$ is the density of the fitted distribution. For discrete data,

$$p_j = \sum_{\{i:a_{j-1} \le x_i < a_j\}} \hat{p}(x_i)$$

where $\hat{p}$ is the mass function of the fitted distribution. Finally, the test statistic is

$$\chi^2 = \sum_{j=1}^{k} \frac{(N_j - np_j)^2}{np_j}$$

Since np_j is the expected number of the n X_i's that would fall in the jth interval if H_0 were true, we would expect χ^2 to be small if the fit is good. Therefore, we reject H_0 if χ^2 is too large. The precise form of the test depends on whether or not we have estimated any of the parameters of the fitted distribution from our data.

First, suppose that all parameters of the fitted distribution are known; i.e., we specified the fitted distribution without making use of the data in any way. [This all-parameters-known case might appear to be of little practical use, but there are at least two applications for it in simulation: (1) in the Poisson process test (Sec. 5.5.4) we test to see whether times of arrivals can be regarded as being IID U(0, T) random variables, where T is a constant independent of the data, and (2) in empirical testing of random-number generators (Sec. 6.4.1) we test for a U(0, 1) distribution.] Then if H_0 is true, χ^2 converges in distribution (as $n \to \infty$) to a chi-square distribution with $k - 1$ df. Thus, for large n, a test with *approximate* level α is obtained by rejecting H_0 if $\chi^2 > \chi^2_{k-1,1-\alpha}$, where $\chi^2_{k-1,1-\alpha}$ is the upper $1 - \alpha$ critical point for a chi-square distribution with $k - 1$ df. (Values for $\chi^2_{k-1,1-\alpha}$ can be found in Table T.2 at the end of the book.) Note that the chi-square test is only *valid*, i.e., is of level α, asymptotically as $n \to \infty$.

Second, suppose that in order to specify the fitted distribution we had to estimate m parameters ($m \ge 1$) from the data. When *MLEs are used*, Chernoff and Lehmann [8] showed that if H_0 is true, then as $n \to \infty$ the distribution function of χ^2 converges to a distribution function that lies *between* the distribution functions of

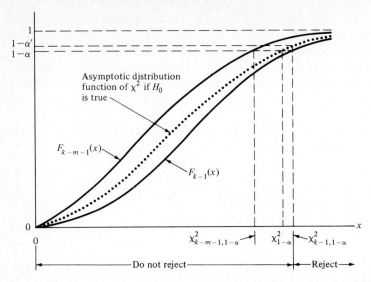

Figure 5.22 The chi-square test when m parameters are estimated by their MLEs.

chi-square distributions with $k - 1$ and $k - m - 1$ df. (See Fig. 5.22, where F_{k-1} and F_{k-m-1} represent the distribution functions of chi-square distributions with $k - 1$ and $k - m - 1$ df, respectively, and the dotted distribution function is the one to which the distribution function of χ^2 converges as $n \to \infty$.) If we let $\chi^2_{1-\alpha}$ be the upper $1 - \alpha$ critical point of the asymptotic distribution of χ^2, then $\chi^2_{k-m-1,1-\alpha} \leq \chi^2_{1-\alpha} \leq \chi^2_{k-1,1-\alpha}$, as shown in Fig. 5.22; unfortunately, the value of $\chi^2_{1-\alpha}$ will not be known in general. It is clear that we should reject H_0 if $\chi^2 > \chi^2_{k-1,1-\alpha}$ and we should not reject H_0 if $\chi^2 < \chi^2_{k-m-1,1-\alpha}$; an ambiguous situation occurs when $\chi^2_{k-m-1,1-\alpha} \leq \chi^2 \leq \chi^2_{k-1,1-\alpha}$. It is often recommended that we reject H_0 only if $\chi^2 > \chi^2_{k-1,1-\alpha}$, since this is *conservative;* i.e., the actual probability α' of committing a Type I error [rejecting H_0 when it is true (see Sec. 4.5)] is at *least* as small as the *stated* probability α (see Fig. 5.22). This choice, however, will entail loss of power (probability of rejecting a false H_0) of the test. Usually, m will be no more than 2, and if k is fairly large, the difference between $\chi^2_{k-m-1,1-\alpha}$ and $\chi^2_{k-1,1-\alpha}$ will not be too great.) Thus, we reject H_0 if (and only if) $\chi^2 > \chi^2_{k-1,1-\alpha}$, as in the all-parameters-known case. The rejection region for χ^2 is indicated in Fig. 5.22.

The most troublesome aspect of carrying out a chi-square test is choosing the intervals. This is a difficult problem, and no definitive prescription can be given that is guaranteed to produce good results (validity and high power) for all hypothesized distributions and all sample sizes. There are, however, a few generally accepted guidelines which should be followed if possible. First, it is recommended that the intervals be chosen so that $p_1 = p_2 = \cdots = p_k$ or at least so that the p_j's are nearly equal. In the discrete case, it will generally not be possible to make the p_j's exactly equal (see Example 5.8 below); in the continuous case it might be inconvenient to do so for some distributions since the distribution function of the fitted distribution must be inverted (see Example 5.7 below). One reason for recommending that the p_j's be equal is that it makes the test *unbiased*; i.e., it is more likely that we shall reject H_0 when it is false than when it is true (see [21, pp. 446–453]; we certainly would not want to use a test that is biased). Second, a common recommendation is that the intervals be chosen so that the values of np_j are not too small; a widely used rule of thumb is that we want $np_j \geq 5$ for all (or nearly all) j. The reason for this recommendation is that the agreement between the *true* distribution of χ^2 (for fixed, finite n) and its *asymptotic* (as $n \rightarrow \infty$) chi-square distribution (used to obtain the critical value for a test) is better if the values of np_j are not too small. This contributes to the validity of the test.

Thus, we see from the previous paragraph that there are good reasons for choosing the intervals so that the p_j's are approximately equal to each other and so that $np_j \geq 5$ for all but one or two (at most) values of j. However, these recommendations do not provide a complete answer to the problem of interval choice; in particular, we have not said much about how to decide on the *number* of intervals k. The choice of k mainly affects the power of the test, and choosing the optimal k (the one which results in highest power) can be very dependent on the alternative distribution form; it has been suggested that k be no larger than 30 or 40 (roughly) regardless of how large n may be. Unfortunately, there is simply no good answer to this question in general, and this is the major drawback of the chi-square test. In some situations, entirely different conclusions can be reached from the *same* data set depending on how the intervals are specified. The chi-square test nevertheless remains in wide use since it can be applied to any hypothesized distribution; as we shall see in Sec. 5.5.3, other goodness-of-fit tests do not enjoy such a wide range of applicability.

Example 5.7 We now use a chi-square test to compare the $n = 219$ interarrival times of Table 5.4 with the fitted exponential distribution having distribution function $\hat{F}(x) = 1 - e^{-x/0.399}$ for $x \geq 0$. If we form, say, $k = 20$ intervals with $p_j = 1/k = 0.05$ for $j = 1, 2, \ldots, 20$, then $np_j = (219)(0.05) = 10.950$, so that this satisfies the guidelines that the intervals be chosen with equal p_j's and $np_j \geq 5$. In this case, it is easy to find the a_j's since $\hat{F}$ can be inverted. That is, we set $a_0 = 0$ and $a_{20} = \infty$, and for $j = 1, 2, \ldots, 19$ we want a_j to satisfy $\hat{F}(a_j) = j/20$; this is equivalent to setting $a_j = -0.399 \ln (1 - j/20)$ for $j = 1, 2, \ldots, 19$ since $a_j = \hat{F}^{-1}(j/20)$. (For continuous distributions such as the normal, gamma, and beta, the inverse of the distribution function does not have a simple closed form. $\hat{F}^{-1}$ in these cases, however, can be evaluated by numerical methods; consult the references given in Sec. 5.3.1.) The computations for the test are given in Table 5.7, and the value of the test statistic is $\chi^2 = 22.188$. Referring to Table T.2, we see that $\chi^2_{19,0.90} = 27.204$, which is not exceeded by χ^2, so that we would not reject H_0 at the $\alpha = 0.10$ level. (Note that we would also not reject H_0 for certain larger values of α such as 0.25.) Thus, this test gives us no reason to conclude that our data are poorly fitted by the expo(0.399) distribution.

Example 5.8 As an illustration of the use of the chi-square test in the discrete case, we test how well the fitted Poisson(6.115) distribution (see Example 5.4) agrees with the demand-size data of Table 5.6. As is usually the case for discrete distributions, we cannot make the p_j's exactly equal, but by grouping together adjacent points on which the mass function $\hat{p}$ is defined (here, the nonnegative integers), we can define intervals which make the p_j's roughly the same. One way to do this is to note that the mode of the fitted distribution is $\lfloor 6.115 \rfloor = 6$; thus, $\hat{p}(6) = 0.160$ is the largest value of the mass function. Then, we can (by trial and error) group adjacent nonnegative integers together into sets such that the sum of their masses (under H_0) is near 0.160. Finally, intervals are chosen to encompass the desired groups of integers. (There certainly are other ways

Table 5.7 A chi-square goodness-of-fit test for the interarrival-time data

j	Interval	N_j	np_j	$\dfrac{(N_j - np_j)^2}{np_j}$
1	[0, 0.020)	8	10.950	0.795
2	[0.020, 0.042)	11	10.950	0.000
3	[0.042, 0.065)	14	10.950	0.850
4	[0.065, 0.089)	14	10.950	0.850
5	[0.089, 0.115)	16	10.950	2.329
6	[0.115, 0.142)	10	10.950	0.082
7	[0.142, 0.172)	7	10.950	1.425
8	[0.172, 0.204)	5	10.950	3.233
9	[0.204, 0.239)	13	10.950	0.384
10	[0.239, 0.277)	12	10.950	0.101
11	[0.277, 0.319)	7	10.950	1.425
12	[0.319, 0.366)	7	10.950	1.425
13	[0.366, 0.419)	12	10.950	0.101
14	[0.419, 0.480)	10	10.950	0.082
15	[0.480, 0.553)	20	10.950	7.480
16	[0.553, 0.642)	9	10.950	0.347
17	[0.642, 0.757)	11	10.950	0.000
18	[0.757, 0.919)	9	10.950	0.347
19	[0.919, 1.195)	14	10.950	0.850
20	[1.195, ∞)	10	10.950	0.082
				$\chi^2 = 22.188$

of choosing the intervals in the discrete case, but they all involve grouping the x_i's together in some way.) Deciding on the intervals in this way, we chose $k = 7$, with the intervals being defined to group the nonnegative integers together as follows:

$$\{0, 1, 2, 3\}, \{4\}, \{5\}, \{6\}, \{7\}, \{8, 9\}, \text{ and } \{10, 11, \dots\}$$

The calculations are shown in Table 5.8 (note that the intervals are simply contrived to get the desired groupings of the nonnegative integers), and we get $\chi^2 = 4.310$. Since $\chi^2 < \chi^2_{6,0.90} = 10.645$, we would not reject H_0 at the $\alpha = 0.10$ level. Thus, this test gives us no reason to believe that the demand-size data are not fitted well by a Poisson(6.115) distribution.

Table 5.8 A chi-square goodness-of-fit test for the demand-size data

j	Interval	N_j	np_j	$\dfrac{(N_j - np_j)^2}{np_j}$
1	[−0.5, 3.5)	12	12.267	0.006
2	[3.5, 4.5)	10	11.223	0.133
3	[4.5, 5.5)	12	13.659	0.201
4	[5.5, 6.5)	18	13.920	1.196
5	[6.5, 7.5)	10	12.180	0.390
6	[7.5, 9.5)	20	15.660	1.203
7	[9.5, ∞)	5	8.091	1.181
				$\chi^2 = 4.310$

5.5.3 Kolmogorov-Smirnov Tests

As we just saw, chi-square tests can be thought of as a more formal comparison of a histogram of the data with the density or mass function of the fitted distribution. We also identified a real difficulty in using a chi-square test in the continuous case, namely, that of deciding how to specify the intervals. *Kolmogorov-Smirnov* (K-S) *tests* for goodness of fit, on the other hand, compare an empirical *distribution* function with the *distribution* function $\hat{F}$ of the hypothesized distribution. As we shall see, K-S tests do not require us to group our data in any way, so that no information is lost; this also eliminates the troublesome problem of interval specification. Another advantage of K-S tests is that they are valid (exactly) for any sample size n, whereas chi-square tests are generally valid only in an asymptotic sense.

Nevertheless, K-S tests do have some drawbacks, at least at present. Most seriously, their range of applicability is much more limited than that for chi-square tests. First, the hypothesized distribution must be continuous; i.e., K-S tests are not valid for discrete data. [K-S tests can formally be applied in the discrete case, where they are conservative in the sense of yielding a smaller probability of a Type I error than that specified (see Noether [29]); this generally results in low power. Pettitt and Stephens [32] discuss a modified K-S test for discrete and grouped data.] However, grouping discrete data for a chi-square test is not as troublesome as in the continuous case. Second, the *original* form of the K-S test is valid only if *all* the parameters of the hypothesized distribution are *known;* i.e., the parameters cannot have been estimated from the data. In recent years, however, the K-S test has been extended to allow for estimation of the parameters in the cases of normal, exponential, and Weibull distributions. Although the K-S test in its original (all-parameters-known) form has often been applied directly for any distribution with estimated parameters, it is not really valid in this case; the effect of this misapplication is not well understood (see [6, p. 213]).

To define the K-S statistic, we must first define an empirical distribution function. As we have already seen in this chapter, there are several different reasonable ways to do this. For the K-S test, we define an empirical distribution function $F_n(x)$ from our data $X_1, X_2, \ldots, X_n$ as

$$F_n(x) = \frac{\text{number of } X_i\text{'s} \leq x}{n}$$

for all real numbers x. Thus, $F_n(x)$ is a (right-continuous) step function such that $F_n(X_{(i)}) = i/n$ for each $i = 1, 2, \ldots, n$. If $\hat{F}(x)$ is the fitted distribution function, a natural assessment of goodness of fit is some kind of measure of the closeness between the functions F_n and $\hat{F}$. The K-S test statistic D_n is simply the *largest* (vertical) distance between $F_n(x)$ and $\hat{F}(x)$ for all values of x and is defined formally by

$$D_n = \sup_{x} \{|F_n(x) - \hat{F}(x)|\}$$

["sup" is used instead of the simpler and more familiar "max" since, depending on the situation, there might not be a value of x such that $D_n = |F_n(x) - \hat{F}(x)|$. However, it is always true that no number strictly smaller than D_n can be greater

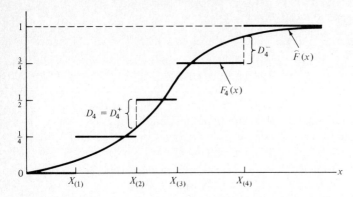

Figure 5.23 Geometric meaning of the K-S test statistic D_n for $n = 4$.

than or equal to $|F_n(x) - \hat{F}(x)|$ for every x.] D_n can be computed by calculating

$$D_n^+ = \max_{1 \le i \le n} \left\{ \frac{i}{n} - \hat{F}(X_{(i)}) \right\}, \qquad D_n^- = \max_{1 \le i \le n} \left\{ \hat{F}(X_{(i)}) - \frac{i-1}{n} \right\}$$

and finally letting

$$D_n = \max \{D_n^+, D_n^-\}$$

An example is given in Fig. 5.23 for $n = 4$, where $D_n = D_n^+$. [*Beware!* Incorrect computational formulas are often given for D_n. In particular, one sometimes sees

$$D_n' = \max_{1 \le i \le n} \left\{ \left| \frac{i}{n} - \hat{F}(X_{(i)}) \right| \right\}$$

as a "formula" for D_n. For the situation of Fig. 5.23, it *is* true that $D_n' = D_n$. Consider, however, Fig. 5.24, where $D_n' = \hat{F}(X_{(2)}) - \frac{2}{4}$ but the correct value for D_n is $\hat{F}(X_{(2)}) - \frac{1}{4}$, which occurs *just before* $x = X_{(2)}$. Clearly, $D_n' \ne D_n$ in this case.] Direct

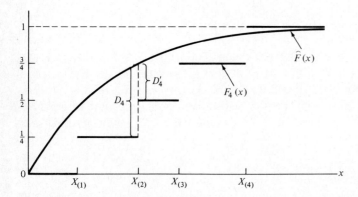

Figure 5.24 An example where the K-S test statistic D_n is not equal to D_n'.

computation of D_n^+ and D_n^- requires sorting the data to obtain the $X_{(i)}$'s. For moderate values of n (up to several hundred) sorting can be done quickly by simple methods. If n is large, however, even sophisticated sorting methods become expensive (computing time is proportional to $n \ln n$). Gonzalez, Sahni, and Franta [16] provide an algorithm for computing D_n^+ and D_n^- without sorting; their algorithm's computation time is proportional to n.

Clearly, a large value of D_n indicates a poor fit, so that the form of the test is to reject the null hypothesis H_0 if D_n exceeds some constant $d_{n,1-\alpha}$, where α is the specified level of the test. The numerical value of the critical point $d_{n,1-\alpha}$ depends on how the hypothesized distribution was specified, and we must distinguish several cases.

Case 1. If *all parameters of $\hat{F}$ are known,* i.e., none of the parameters of $\hat{F}$ is estimated in any way from the data, the distribution of D_n does not depend on $\hat{F}$, assuming (of course) that $\hat{F}$ is continuous. This rather remarkable fact means that a single table of values for $d_{n,1-\alpha}$ will suffice for all continuous distribution forms; these tables are widely available (see, for example, Owen [30].) Stephens [39] devised an accurate approximative scheme which eliminates the need for all but a tiny table; instead of testing for $D_n > d_{n,1-\alpha}$, we reject H_0 if

$$\left(\sqrt{n} + 0.12 + \frac{0.11}{\sqrt{n}} \right) D_n > c_{1-\alpha}$$

where values for $c_{1-\alpha}$ (which do not depend on n) are given in the all-parameters-known line of Table 5.9. This all-parameters-known case is the original form of the K-S test.

Case 2. Suppose the hypothesized distribution is $N(\mu, \sigma^2)$ with both μ and σ^2 unknown. We can estimate μ and σ^2 by $\overline{X}(n)$ and $s^2(n)$, respectively, and define the distribution function $\hat{F}$ to be that of the $N(\overline{X}(n), s^2(n))$ distribution; i.e., let $\hat{F}(x) = \Phi\{[x - \overline{X}(n)]/\sqrt{s^2(n)}\}$, where Φ is the distribution function of the standard normal distribution. Using this $\hat{F}$ (which *has* estimated parameters), D_n is computed in the same way, but different critical points must be used. Lilliefors [23] estimated (via Monte Carlo simulation) the critical points of D_n as a function of

Table 5.9 Critical values $c_{1-\alpha}$, $c'_{1-\alpha}$, and $c''_{1-\alpha}$ for adjusted K-S test statistics

Case	Adjusted test statistic	1 − α				
		0.850	0.900	0.950	0.975	0.990
All parameters known	$\left(\sqrt{n} + 0.12 + \frac{0.11}{\sqrt{n}} \right) D_n$	1.138	1.224	1.358	1.480	1.628
$N(\overline{X}(n), s^2(n))$	$\left(\sqrt{n} - 0.01 + \frac{0.85}{\sqrt{n}} \right) D_n$	0.775	0.819	0.895	0.955	1.035
$\text{expo}(\overline{X}(n))$	$\left(D_n - \frac{0.2}{n} \right)\left(\sqrt{n} + 0.26 + \frac{0.5}{\sqrt{n}} \right)$	0.926	0.990	1.094	1.190	1.308

n (and $1 - \alpha$). Stephens [39] performed further Monte Carlo simulations and provided an accurate approximation which obviates the need for large tables; namely, we reject H_0 if

$$\left(\sqrt{n} - 0.01 + \frac{0.85}{\sqrt{n}} \right) D_n > c'_{1-\alpha}$$

where values for $c'_{1-\alpha}$ are given in the $N(\overline{X}(n), s^2(n))$ line of Table 5.9. (This case includes a K-S test for the lognormal distribution if the X_i's are the *logarithms* of the basic data points we have hypothesized to have a lognormal distribution; see Sec. 5.2.2.)

Case 3. Suppose the hypothesized distribution is expo(β) with β unknown. β is estimated by its MLE $\overline{X}(n)$, and we define $\hat{F}$ to be the expo($\overline{X}(n)$) distribution function; that is, $\hat{F}(x) = 1 - e^{-x/\overline{X}(n)}$ for $x \geq 0$. In this case, critical values for D_n were originally estimated by Lilliefors [24] in a Monte Carlo study, and exact tables were later obtained by Durbin [13] (see also Margolin and Maurer [27]). Stephens' [39] approximation in this case is to reject H_0 if

$$\left(D_n - \frac{0.2}{n} \right) \left(\sqrt{n} + 0.26 + \frac{0.5}{\sqrt{n}} \right) > c''_{1-\alpha}$$

where $c''_{1-\alpha}$ can be found in the expo($\overline{X}(n)$) line of Table 5.9.

Case 4. Suppose the hypothesized distribution is Weibull with both shape parameter α and scale parameter β unknown; we estimate these parameters by their respective MLEs $\hat{\alpha}$ and $\hat{\beta}$. (See the discussion of the Weibull MLEs in Sec. 5.2.2.) $\hat{F}$ is taken to be the Weibull($\hat{\alpha}, \hat{\beta}$) distribution function, $\hat{F}(x) = 1 - \exp[-(x/\hat{\beta})^{\hat{\alpha}}]$ for $x \geq 0$, and D_n is computed in the usual fashion. Critical values $d_{n,1-\alpha}$ for D_n were estimated by Littell, McClave, and Offen [25] and are given in Table 5.10. Unfortunately, the values of $d_{n,1-\alpha}$ run only through $n = 40$. (For an alternative K-S test

Table 5.10 Critical values $d_{n,1-\alpha}$ for the K-S test for the Weibull distribution†

n	$1 - \alpha$				
	0.80	0.85	0.90	0.95	0.99
10	0.218	0.228	0.240	0.260	0.300
15	0.181	0.190	0.201	0.217	0.251
20	0.158	0.165	0.175	0.191	0.220
25	0.142	0.149	0.157	0.170	0.195
30	0.130	0.136	0.144	0.156	0.179
35	0.121	0.126	0.134	0.146	0.173
40	0.113	0.118	0.125	0.136	0.158

†Reprinted from [25, p. 262], by courtesy of Marcel Dekker, Inc.

for the Weibull distribution based on its relationship with the extreme value distribution, see Chandra, Singpurwalla, and Stephens [7].)

> **Example 5.9** In Example 5.7 we used a chi-square test to check the goodness of fit of the fitted expo(0.399) distribution for the interarrival-time data of Table 5.4. We can also apply a K-S test with $\hat{F}(x) = 1 - e^{-x/0.399}$ for $x \geq 0$, by using case 3 above. Using the formulas for D_{219}^{+} and D_{219}^{-}, we found that $D_{219} = 0.047$, so that the adjusted test statistic is
>
> $$\left(D_{219} - \frac{0.2}{219} \right) \left(\sqrt{219} + 0.26 + \frac{0.5}{\sqrt{219}} \right) = 0.696$$
>
> Since 0.696 is less than $0.990 = c''_{0.90}$ (from the last line of Table 5.9), we do not reject H_0 at the $\alpha = 0.10$ level.

5.5.4 Poisson Process Test

Suppose that we observe a Poisson process (see Sec. 5.7.1 below) for a *fixed* interval of time $[0, T]$, where T is a constant that is decided upon before we start our observation. Let n be the number of events we observe in the interval $[0, T]$, and let t_i be the time of the ith event for $i = 1, 2, \ldots, n$. [Thus, $0 \leq t_1 \leq t_2 \leq \cdots \leq t_n \leq T$. If $t_n < T$, then no events occurred in the interval $(t_n, T]$.] Then the joint distribution of $t_1, t_2, \ldots, t_n$ is related to the U$(0, T)$ distribution in the following way. Assume that $Y_1, Y_2, \ldots, Y_n$ (the same n as above) are IID random variables with the U$(0, T)$ distribution, and let $Y_{(1)}, Y_{(2)}, \ldots, Y_{(n)}$ be their corresponding order statistics (see Sec. 5.3.1). Then a property of the Poisson process is that $t_1, t_2, \ldots, t_n$ have the same joint distribution as $Y_{(1)}, Y_{(2)}, \ldots, Y_{(n)}$. (See Ross [34, pp. 17–18] for a proof.)

One way of interpreting this property is that if someone simply showed us the *values* of $t_1, t_2, \ldots, t_n$ without telling us that t_i was obtained as the time of the ith event in some sequence of events, it would appear (in a statistical sense) that these n numbers had been obtained by taking a sample of n IID random variables from the U$(0, T)$ distribution and then sorting them into increasing order. Alternatively, one could think of this property as saying that if we consider $t_1, t_2, \ldots, t_n$ as unordered random variables, they are IID with the U$(0, T)$ distribution. This is why we sometimes see a Poisson process described as one in which events occur "at random," since the instants at which events occur are uniformly distributed over time.

In any case, this property provides us with a different way of testing the null hypothesis that an observed sequence of events was generated by a Poisson process. (We have already seen one way this hypothesis can be tested, namely, testing whether the interevent times appear to be IID exponential random variables; see Sec. 5.7.1 and Examples 5.7 and 5.9.) We simply test whether the event times $t_1, t_2, \ldots, t_n$ appear to be IID U$(0, T)$ random variables using any applicable testing procedure.

> **Example 5.10** The interarrival-time data of Table 5.4 were collected over a fixed 90-minute period, and $n = 220$ arrivals were recorded during this interval. (It was decided beforehand to start observing the process at exactly 5 P.M., rather than at the first time after 5:00 when an arrival happened to take place. Also, data collection terminated promptly at 6:30 P.M., regardless of any arrivals that occurred later. It is important for the validity of this test that the data collection be

designed in this way, i.e., independent of the actual event times.) The times of arrivals were $t_1 = 1.53$, $t_2 = 1.98, \ldots, t_{220} = 88.91$ (in minutes after 5 P.M.). To test whether these numbers can be regarded as being independent with the U(0, 90) distribution, we used the *all-parameters-known* cases of the chi-square and K-S tests. [The density and distribution function of the fitted distribution are, respectively, $\hat{f}(x) = 1/90$ and $\hat{F}(x) = x/90$, for $0 \le x \le 90$. Note also that our "data" points are already sorted, conveniently.] We carried out a chi-square test with the $k = 17$ equal-sized intervals [0, 5.294), [5.294, 10.588), $\ldots$, [84.706, 90], so that $np_j = 220/17 = 12.941$ for $j = 1, 2, \ldots, 17$. The resulting value of χ^2 was 13.827, and since $\chi^2_{16,0.90} = 23.542$, we cannot reject the null hypothesis that the arrivals occurred in accordance with a Poisson process. The K-S test resulted in $D_{220} = 0.045$, and the value of the adjusted test statistic from the all-parameters-known line of Table 5.9 is thus 0.673. Since this is well below $c_{0.90} = 1.224$, once again we cannot reject the null hypothesis.

5.5.5 Other Tests

In addition to the chi-square and K-S goodness-of-fit tests discussed in Secs. 5.5.2 and 5.5.3, there are several other kinds of tests that can be used for the same purpose. Two of them, the Anderson-Darling and Cramér-von Mises tests, can be applied in the same four cases to which the K-S test is applicable (see Sec. 5.5.3); they also appear to be preferable to K-S tests in that they are usually more powerful. We refer the interested reader to Stephens [39, 40] and Littell, McClave, and Offen [25].

There are also a number of goodness-of-fit tests designed for a specific distribution form in the null hypothesis. A partial listing of references for these follows:

Uniform—Quesenberry and Miller [33]
Exponential—Stephens [41], Gail and Gastwirth [14]
Weibull—Stephens [40] (Recall that X has a Weibull distribution if and only if
ln X has an extreme value distribution.)
Normal—Shapiro and Wilk [36, 37], Shapiro, Wilk, and Chen [38], Shapiro and
Francia [35], Weisberg [45], and Weisberg and Bingham [46]

As we mentioned at the beginning of this section, there is an extremely large literature on the subject of goodness-of-fit tests. We suggest that the reader who wants to keep up with the frequent developments in this field scan the current contents of such journals as *Technometrics, Journal of the American Statistical Association, Biometrika, Journal of the Royal Statistical Society* (Series B), *The Annals of Statistics, Communications in Statistics* (Series B), and *Journal of Statistical Computation and Simulation.*

5.6 SELECTING A DISTRIBUTION IN THE ABSENCE OF DATA

In some simulation studies, it may not be possible to collect data on a random quantity of interest, so the techniques discussed in Secs. 5.3 to 5.5 are not applicable to the problem of selecting a corresponding probability distribution. For example, if the system being studied does not currently exist in some form, collecting data from the system is obviously not possible. In this section, we discuss two heuristic procedures for choosing a distribution in the absence of data, which we have found are used by many simulation practitioners.

Let us assume that the random quantity of interest is a continuous random variable X. It will also be useful to think of this random variable as being the time to perform some task, e.g., the time required to construct part of a new ship, or as being the duration of an activity, e.g., the time to failure of a new computer component. The first step in using either heuristic approach is to identify an interval $[a, b]$ (a and b real numbers such that $a < b$) in which it is felt that X will lie with probability close to 1; that is, $P\{X < a \text{ or } X > b\} \approx 0$. In order to obtain *subjective* estimates of a and b, "experts" are asked for their most optimistic and pessimistic estimates, respectively, of the time to perform the task. Once an interval $[a, b]$ has been subjectively identified, the next step is to place a probability density function on $[a, b]$ which is thought to be representative of X.

In the triangular approach, the experts are also asked for their subjective estimate of the most likely time to perform the task. This most likely value m is the mode of the distribution of X. Given a, b, and m, the random variable X is then considered to have a triangular distribution (see Sec. 5.2.2) on the interval $[a, b]$ with mode m. A graph of a triangular density function is given in Fig. 5.8 ($c = m$ there). Furthermore, an algorithm for generating a triangular random variable is given in Sec. 7.3.9.

A second approach to placing a density function on $[a, b]$ is to assume that the random variable X has a beta distribution (see Sec. 5.2.2) on this interval with shape parameters α_1 and α_2. This approach offers more modeling flexibility because of the variety of shapes the beta density function can assume (see Fig. 5.7). On the other hand, it is not clear how to choose the parameters α_1 and α_2 so as to specify the distribution completely. We can suggest two possible ideas. If one is willing to assume that X is equally likely to take on any value between a and b, choose $\alpha_1 = \alpha_2 = 1$, which results in the U(a, b) distribution (see Fig. 5.7). (This model might be used if very little is known about the random variable X other than its range $[a, b]$.) An alternative idea, which we feel is generally more realistic, is to assume that the density function of X is skewed to the right. (Our experience with real-world data indicates that density functions corresponding to the time to perform some task often have this shape.) This density shape corresponds to $\alpha_2 > \alpha_1 > 1$ in the beta distribution (see Fig. 5.7). Furthermore, such a beta distribution has a mean μ and a mode m, given by

$$\mu = a + \frac{\alpha_1(b - a)}{\alpha_1 + \alpha_2} \qquad \text{and} \qquad m = a + \frac{(\alpha_1 - 1)(b - a)}{\alpha_1 + \alpha_2 - 2}$$

Given subjective estimates of μ and m, these equations can be solved to obtain the following estimates of α_1 and α_2:

$$\tilde{\alpha}_1 = \frac{(\mu - a)(2m - a - b)}{(m - \mu)(b - a)} \qquad \text{and} \qquad \tilde{\alpha}_2 = \frac{(b - \mu)\tilde{\alpha}_1}{\mu - a}$$

(Note that μ must be greater than m for the density to be skewed to the right; if $\mu < m$, it will be skewed to the left.) A beta random variable X defined on the interval $[a, b]$ and with shape parameters $\tilde{\alpha}_1$ and $\tilde{\alpha}_2$ can be generated using algorithms discussed in Sec. 7.3.8.

5.7 MODELS OF ARRIVAL PROCESSES

In many simulations we need to generate a sequence of random points in time, $0 = t_0 \leq t_1 \leq t_2 \leq \cdots$, such that the ith event of some kind occurs at time t_i ($i = 1, 2, \ldots$) and the distribution of the event times $\{t_i\}$ follows some specified form. Let $N(t) = \max\{i{:}t_i \leq t\}$ be the number of events to occur at or before time t for $t \geq 0$. We call the stochastic process $\{N(t), t \geq 0\}$ an *arrival process* since, for our purposes, the events of interest are usually arrivals of customers to a service facility of some kind. In what follows, we call $A_i = t_i - t_{i-1}$ ($i = 1, 2, \ldots$) the *interarrival time* between the $(i - 1)$st and the ith customers.

In Sec. 5.7.1 we discuss the Poisson process, which is an arrival process for which the A_i's are IID exponential random variables. The Poisson process is the most commonly used model for the arrival process of customers to a queueing system. Section 5.7.2 discusses the nonstationary Poisson process, which is often used as a model of the arrival process to a system when the arrival rate varies with time. Finally, in Sec. 5.7.3, we describe an approach to modeling arrival processes where each event is the arrival of a "batch" of customers.

A general reference for this section is Çinlar [10, chap. 4].

5.7.1 Poisson Process

In this section we define a Poisson process, state some of its important properties, and in the course of doing so explain why the interarrival times for many real-world systems closely resemble IID exponential random variables. The stochastic process $\{N(t), t \geq 0\}$ is said to be a *Poisson process* if:

1. Customers arrive one at a time.
2. $N(t + s) - N(t)$ (the number of arrivals in the interval $(t, t + s]$) is independent of $\{N(u), 0 \leq u \leq t\}$.
3. The distribution of $N(t + s) - N(t)$ is independent of t for all $t, s \geq 0$.

Properties 1 and 2 are characteristic of many actual arrival processes. Property 1 would not hold if customers arrived in batches; see Sec. 5.7.3. Property 2 says that the number of arrivals in the interval $(t, t + s]$ is independent of the number of arrivals in the interval $[0, t]$ and also of the times at which these arrivals occur. This property could be violated if, for example, a large number of arrivals in $[0, t]$ caused some customers arriving in $(t, t + s]$ to balk, i.e., go away immediately without being served, because they find the system highly congested. Property 3, on the other hand, will not be satisfied by most real-life arrival processes since it implies that the arrival rate of customers does not depend on the time of day, etc. If, however, the time period of interest for the system is relatively short, say, a 1- or 2-hour period of peak demand, we have found that for many systems (but certainly not all) the arrival rate is reasonably constant over this interval and the Poisson process is a good model (for the process during this interval). (See Theorem 5.2 below and then Example 5.1.)

The following theorem, proved in [10, pp. 74–76], explains where the Poisson process gets its name.

> **Theorem 5.1** If $\{N(t), t \geq 0\}$ is a Poisson process, then the number of arrivals in any interval of length s is a Poisson random variable with parameter λs (λ a positive real number). That is,
>
> $$P\{N(t + s) - N(t) = k\} = \frac{e^{-\lambda s}(\lambda s)^k}{k!} \qquad \text{for } k = 0, 1, 2, \ldots$$
>
> $$\text{and } t, s \geq 0$$

Therefore, $E[N(s)] = \lambda s$ (see Sec. 5.2.3) and, in particular, $E[N(1)] = \lambda$. Thus, λ is the expected number of arrivals in any interval of length 1. We also call λ the *arrival rate* of the process.

We now see that the interarrival times for a Poisson process are IID exponential random variables; see [10, pp. 79–80].

> **Theorem 5.2** If $\{N(t), t \geq 0\}$ is a Poisson process with rate λ, then its corresponding interarrival times $A_1, A_2, \ldots$ are IID exponential random variables with parameter $1/\lambda$.

This result together with our above discussion explains why we have found that interarrival times during a restricted time period are often approximately IID exponential random variables. For example, recall that the interarrival times of cars for the drive-up bank of Example 5.1 were found to be approximately exponential during a 90-minute period.

The converse of Theorem 5.2 is also true. Namely, if the interarrival times A_1, $A_2, \ldots$ for an arrival process $\{N(t), t \geq 0\}$ are IID exponential random variables with parameter $1/\lambda$, then $\{N(t), t \geq 0\}$ is a Poisson process with rate λ ([10, p. 80]).

5.7.2 Nonstationary Poisson Process

Let $\lambda(t)$ be the arrival rate of customers to some system at time t. [See below for some insight into the meaning of $\lambda(t)$.] If customers arrive at the system in accordance with a Poisson process with rate λ, then $\lambda(t) = \lambda$ for all $t \geq 0$. However, for many real-world systems, $\lambda(t)$ is a function of t. For example, the arrival rate of customers to a fast-food restaurant will be larger during the noon rush hour than in the middle of the afternoon. Also, traffic on a freeway will be heavier during the morning and evening rush hours. If the arrival rate $\lambda(t)$ does in fact change as a function of time, then the interarrival times $A_1, A_2, \ldots$ are *not* identically distributed; thus, it is not appropriate to fit a single probability distribution to the A_i's using the techniques discussed in Secs. 5.3 to 5.5. In this section, we discuss a commonly used model for arrival processes with time-varying arrival rates.

The stochastic process $\{N(t),\ t \geq 0\}$ is said to be a *nonstationary Poisson process* if:

1. Customers arrive one at a time.
2. $N(t + s) - N(t)$ is independent of $\{N(u),\ 0 \leq u \leq t\}$.

Thus, for a nonstationary Poisson process, customers still must arrive one at a time, and the numbers of arrivals in disjoint intervals are independent, but now the arrival rate $\lambda(t)$ is allowed to be a function of time. If, however, $\lambda(t) = \lambda$ (a constant) for all $t \geq 0$, then $\{N(t),\ t \geq 0\}$ is a (stationary) Poisson process.

Let $a(t) = E[N(t)]$ for all $t \geq 0$. If $a(t)$ is differentiable for a particular value of t, we formally define $\lambda(t)$ as

$$\lambda(t) = \frac{d}{dt}\,a(t)$$

Intuitively, $\lambda(t)$ will be large in intervals for which the expected number of arrivals is large. We call $a(t)$ and $\lambda(t)$ the *expectation function* and the *rate function*, respectively, for the nonstationary Poisson process.

The following theorem shows that the number of arrivals in the interval $(t,\ t + s]$ for a nonstationary Poisson process is a Poisson random variable whose parameter depends on *both* t and s.

Theorem 5.3 If $\{N(t),\ t \geq 0\}$ is a nonstationary Poisson process with continuous expectation function $a(t)$, then

$$P\{N(t + s) - N(t) = k\} = \frac{e^{-b(t,s)}[b(t,\ s)]^k}{k!} \qquad \begin{array}{l} \text{for } k = 0, 1, 2, \ldots \\ \text{and } t, s \geq 0 \end{array}$$

where $b(t, s) = a(t + s) - a(t) = \displaystyle\int_{t}^{t+s} \lambda(y)\,dy$, the last equality holding if $da(t)/dt$ is bounded on $[t,\ t + s]$ and if $da(t)/dt$ exists and is continuous for all but finitely many points in $[t,\ t + s]$.

We have not yet addressed the question of how to estimate $\lambda(t)$ [or $a(t)$] from a set of observations on an arrival process of interest. The following example gives a heuristic but practical approach (for a discussion of alternative approaches, see, for example, Lewis and Shedler [22]).

Example 5.11 A simulation model was developed for a xerographic copy shop, and data were collected on the times of arrivals of customers between 11 A.M. and 1 P.M. for 8 different days. From observing the characteristics of the arriving customers, it was felt that properties 1 and 2 for the nonstationary Poisson process were applicable and, in addition, that $\lambda(t)$ varied over the 2-hour interval. To obtain an estimate of $\lambda(t)$, the 2-hour interval was divided into the following 12 subintervals:

$$[11:00, 11:10), [11:10, 11:20), \ldots, [12:40, 12:50), [12:50, 1:00]$$

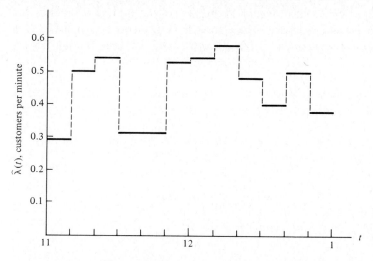

Figure 5.25 Plot of the estimated rate function $\hat{\lambda}(t)$ in customers per minute for the arrival process to a copy shop between 11 A.M. and 1 P.M.

For each day, the number of arrivals in each of these subintervals was determined. Then for each subinterval, the average number of arrivals in that subinterval over the 8 days was computed. These 12 averages are estimates of the expected number of arrivals in the corresponding subintervals. Finally, for each subinterval, the average number of arrivals in that subinterval was divided by the subinterval length, 10 minutes, to obtain an estimate of the arrival rate for that subinterval. The estimated arrival rate $\hat{\lambda}(t)$ (in customers per minute) is plotted in Fig. 5.25. Note that the estimated arrival rate varies by a factor of 2 from the subinterval [11:00, 11:10) to the subinterval [12:10, 12:20).

One might legitimately ask how we decided on these subintervals of 10 minutes. Actually, we computed estimates of $\lambda(t)$ in the above manner for subintervals of length 5, 10, and 15 minutes. The estimate of $\lambda(t)$ based on subintervals of length 5 minutes was rejected because it was felt that the corresponding plot of $\hat{\lambda}(t)$ was too ragged; i.e., a subinterval length of 5 minutes was too small. On the other hand, the estimate of $\lambda(t)$ based on subintervals of length 15 minutes was not chosen because the corresponding plot of $\hat{\lambda}(t)$ seemed too "smooth," meaning that information on the true nature of $\lambda(t)$ was being lost. In general, the problem of choosing a subinterval length here is similar to that of choosing the interval widths for a histogram (see Sec. 5.3.1).

5.7.3 Batch Arrivals

For some real-world systems, customers arrive in *batches,* or groups, so that property 1 of the Poisson process and of the nonstationary Poisson process is violated. For example, people arriving at a sporting event or at a cafeteria often come in batches. We now consider how one might model such an arrival process.

Let $N(t)$ now be the number of *batches* of customers which have arrived by time t. By applying the techniques discussed previously in this chapter to the times of arrivals of the successive batches, we can develop a model for the process $\{N(t), t \geq 0\}$. For example, if the interarrival times of batches appear to be approximately IID exponential random variables, $\{N(t), t \geq 0\}$ can be modeled as a Poisson process. Next, we fit a discrete distribution to the sizes of the successive batches; the batch sizes will be positive integers. Thus, for the original arrival process, it is assumed that batches of customers arrive in accordance with the arrival process $\{N(t), t \geq 0\}$ and that the number of customers in each batch is a random variable with the fitted discrete distribution.

The above informal discussion can be made more precise. If $X(t)$ is the total number of customers to arrive by time t, and if B_i is the number of customers in the ith batch, then $X(t)$ is given by

$$X(t) = \sum_{i=1}^{N(t)} B_i \qquad \text{for } t \geq 0$$

If the B_i's are assumed to be IID random variables which are also independent of $\{N(t), t \geq 0\}$, and if $\{N(t), t \geq 0\}$ is a Poisson process, then the stochastic process $\{X(t), t \geq 0\}$ is said to be a *compound Poisson process*.

APPENDIX 5A SHIFTED AND TRUNCATED DISTRIBUTIONS

Several of the continuous distributions of Sec. 5.2.2, including the exponential, gamma, Weibull, and lognormal distributions, had range $[0, \infty)$. Thus, if X has any of these distributions, it can take on arbitrarily small positive values. However, it is frequently the case in practice that if X represents the time to accomplish some task (such as a customer service), it is simply impossible for X to be less than some fixed positive number. For example, in a bank it is probably not possible to serve anyone in less than, say, 30 seconds; this will be reflected in the service-time data we might collect on the bank's operation. Thus, in reality $P\{X < 30 \text{ seconds}\} = 0$; however, for a fitted gamma or Weibull distribution, for instance, there is a *positive* probability of generating a random variable X which is less than 30 seconds. Thus, it would appear that some modification of these distribution forms would provide a more realistic model and might result in a better fit. There are at least two possible approaches to making such a modification.

The first approach involves *shifting* the distribution some distance to the right. What this really amounts to is generalizing the density function of the distribution in question to include a location parameter (see Sec. 5.2.1). For example, the gamma distribution shifted to the right by an amount $\gamma > 0$ has density

$$f(x) = \begin{cases} \dfrac{\beta^{-\alpha}(x - \gamma)^{\alpha-1}e^{-(x-\gamma)/\beta}}{\Gamma(\alpha)} & \text{if } x > \gamma \\ 0 & \text{otherwise} \end{cases}$$

which has the same shape and scale as the gamma(α, β) distribution but is shifted γ units to the right. (This is often called the *three-parameter gamma distribution*.) Shifted exponential, Weibull, and lognormal distributions are defined similarly, by replacing x by $x - \gamma$ in the density functions (including the domains of definition).

With these shifted distributions, we then have to estimate γ as well as the other parameters. This can be done formally by finding the MLE for γ in addition to the MLEs for the original parameters. For the shifted exponential, $\hat{\gamma}$ and $\hat{\beta}$ are relatively easy to find (see Prob. 5.6). However, finding MLEs for the three-parameter gamma, Weibull, and lognormal distributions is quite difficult and must be done by numerical methods (see Harter and Moore [19], Harter [18, pp. 96–110], Zanakis [48], and Cohen and Whitten [11]). Generating random variables from shifted distributions is very easy (given the ability to generate from the original unshifted distribution); see Prob. 7.15.

The second approach involves *truncating* the distribution in some way. If f is, say, the (unshifted) gamma(α, β) density, let $a(\gamma) = \int_{\gamma}^{\infty} f(x)\, dx$, which is less than 1 if $\gamma > 0$. Then define

$$f^*(x) = \begin{cases} f(x)/a(\gamma) & \text{if } x > \gamma \\ 0 & \text{otherwise} \end{cases}$$

so that f^* is a proper density which jumps from 0 to $f(\gamma)/a(\gamma)$ at $x = \gamma$. Depending on the data (and, for example, how the histogram appears), a truncated distribution may provide a better fit than a shifted distribution. Estimating γ here is also troublesome. Techniques for generating random variables from distributions truncated in this way are discussed in Sec. 7.2.1 and in Prob. 7.3.

Example 5.12 Figure 5.26 is a histogram of $n = 200$ observations on the service times (in seconds) of customers in a bank. Note that no service times were observed to be less than 20 seconds (the minimum of the actual observations was 35 seconds). A lognormal distribution (unshifted) was

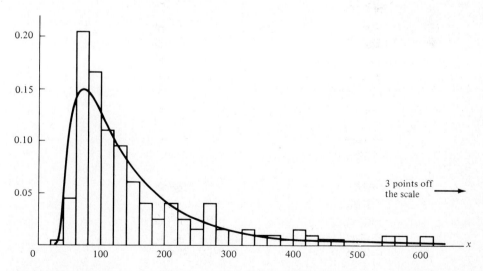

Figure 5.26 Histogram of service times and a (rescaled) plot of the density function of the fitted shifted lognormal distribution.

fitted to these data (using MLEs), but an extremely poor fit was indicated by a chi-square test; examination of the individual $(N_j - np_j)^2/np_j$ terms revealed that the fit was the worst in the regions near $x = 0$. Thus, it was decided to postulate a shifted lognormal distribution with $\gamma = 31$. (This value of γ was arrived at by simple inspection of the data; it is *not* a MLE.) Assuming $\gamma = 31$, MLEs of μ and σ in the lognormal density were obtained by subtracting 31 from each X_i and viewing the resulting data as having an unshifted lognormal distribution. From the formulas in Sec. 5.2.2, the MLEs $\hat{\mu} = 4.489$ and $\hat{\sigma} = 0.887$ were obtained from the data $X_1 - 31$, $X_2 - 31, \ldots, X_{200} - 31$. Thus, the fitted density is

$$\hat{f}(x) = \begin{cases} \dfrac{1}{(x - 31)\sqrt{2\pi\hat{\sigma}^2}} \exp \dfrac{-[\ln(x - 31) - \hat{\mu}]^2}{2\hat{\sigma}^2} & \text{if } x > 31 \\ 0 & \text{otherwise} \end{cases}$$

The function $\Delta b\, \hat{f}(x)$ is plotted over the histogram (for which $\Delta b = 20$) in Fig. 5.26. The fit appears reasonable, and a chi-square test did not indicate a poor fit.

Specifying γ as in the preceding example (simple inspection or guessing) certainly cannot be defended on formal statistical grounds, although it might be a reasonable operational procedure. For more rigorous statistical methods of estimating shift parameters, see the references cited earlier in this section and Prob. 5.6.

APPENDIX 5B TABLES OF MLEs FOR THE GAMMA AND BETA DISTRIBUTIONS

Table 5.11 $\hat{\alpha}$ as a function of T, gamma distribution

T	$\hat{\alpha}$	T	$\hat{\alpha}$	T	$\hat{\alpha}$	T	$\hat{\alpha}$
0.01	0.010	1.40	0.827	5.00	2.655	13.00	6.662
0.02	0.019	1.50	0.879	5.20	2.755	13.50	6.912
0.03	0.027	1.60	0.931	5.40	2.856	14.00	7.163
0.04	0.036	1.70	0.983	5.60	2.956	14.50	7.413
0.05	0.044	1.80	1.035	5.80	3.057	15.00	7.663
0.06	0.052	1.90	1.086	6.00	3.157	15.50	7.913
0.07	0.060	2.00	1.138	6.20	3.257	16.00	8.163
0.08	0.068	2.10	1.189	6.40	3.357	16.50	8.413
0.09	0.076	2.20	1.240	6.60	3.458	17.00	8.663
0.10	0.083	2.30	1.291	6.80	3.558	17.50	8.913
0.11	0.090	2.40	1.342	7.00	3.658	18.00	9.163
0.12	0.098	2.50	1.393	7.20	3.759	18.50	9.414
0.13	0.105	2.60	1.444	7.40	3.859	19.00	9.664
0.14	0.112	2.70	1.495	7.60	3.959	19.50	9.914
0.15	0.119	2.80	1.546	7.80	4.059	20.00	10.164
0.16	0.126	2.90	1.596	8.00	4.159	20.50	10.414
0.17	0.133	3.00	1.647	8.20	4.260	21.00	10.664
0.18	0.140	3.10	1.698	8.40	4.360	21.50	10.914
0.19	0.147	3.20	1.748	8.60	4.460	22.00	11.164
0.20	0.153	3.30	1.799	8.80	4.560	22.50	11.414
0.30	0.218	3.40	1.849	9.00	4.660	23.00	11.664

Table 5.11 (*Continued*)

T	$\hat{\alpha}$	T	$\hat{\alpha}$	T	$\hat{\alpha}$	T	$\hat{\alpha}$
0.40	0.279	3.50	1.900	9.20	4.760	23.50	11.914
0.50	0.338	3.60	1.950	9.40	4.860	24.00	12.164
0.60	0.396	3.70	2.001	9.60	4.961	24.50	12.414
0.70	0.452	3.80	2.051	9.80	5.061	25.00	12.664
0.80	0.507	3.90	2.101	10.00	5.161	30.00	15.165
0.90	0.562	4.00	2.152	10.50	5.411	35.00	17.665
1.00	0.616	4.20	2.253	11.00	5.661	40.00	20.165
1.10	0.669	4.40	2.353	11.50	5.912	45.00	22.665
1.20	0.722	4.60	2.454	12.00	6.162	50.00	25.166
1.30	0.775	4.80	2.554	12.50	6.412		

Table 5.12 $\hat{\alpha}_1$ and $\hat{\alpha}_2$ as functions of G_1 and G_2, beta distribution

If $G_1 \leq G_2$, use the first line of labels; if $G_2 \leq G_1$, use the second line of labels

G_1 G_2	G_2 G_1	$\hat{\alpha}_1$ $\hat{\alpha}_2$	$\hat{\alpha}_2$ $\hat{\alpha}_1$	G_1 G_2	G_2 G_1	$\hat{\alpha}_1$ $\hat{\alpha}_2$	$\hat{\alpha}_2$ $\hat{\alpha}_1$
0.01	0.01	0.112	0.112	0.15	0.35	0.405	0.563
0.01	0.05	0.126	0.157	0.15	0.40	0.432	0.653
0.01	0.10	0.135	0.192	0.15	0.45	0.464	0.762
0.01	0.15	0.141	0.223	0.15	0.50	0.502	0.903
0.01	0.20	0.147	0.254	0.15	0.55	0.550	1.090
0.01	0.25	0.152	0.285	0.15	0.60	0.612	1.353
0.01	0.30	0.157	0.318	0.15	0.65	0.701	1.752
0.01	0.35	0.163	0.354	0.15	0.70	0.842	2.429
0.01	0.40	0.168	0.395	0.15	0.75	1.111	3.810
0.01	0.45	0.173	0.441	0.15	0.80	1.884	8.026
0.01	0.50	0.179	0.495	0.15	0.84	7.908	42.014
0.01	0.55	0.185	0.559	0.20	0.20	0.395	0.395
0.01	0.60	0.192	0.639	0.20	0.25	0.424	0.461
0.01	0.65	0.200	0.741	0.20	0.30	0.456	0.537
0.01	0.70	0.210	0.877	0.20	0.35	0.491	0.626
0.01	0.75	0.221	1.072	0.20	0.40	0.531	0.735
0.01	0.80	0.237	1.376	0.20	0.45	0.579	0.873
0.01	0.85	0.259	1.920	0.20	0.50	0.640	1.057
0.01	0.90	0.299	3.162	0.20	0.55	0.720	1.314
0.01	0.95	0.407	8.232	0.20	0.60	0.834	1.701
0.01	0.98	0.850	42.126	0.20	0.65	1.016	2.352
0.05	0.05	0.180	0.180	0.20	0.70	1.367	3.669
0.05	0.10	0.195	0.223	0.20	0.75	2.388	7.654
0.05	0.15	0.207	0.263	0.20	0.79	10.407	39.649
0.05	0.20	0.217	0.302	0.25	0.25	0.500	0.500
0.05	0.25	0.228	0.343	0.25	0.30	0.543	0.588
0.05	0.30	0.238	0.387	0.25	0.35	0.592	0.695
0.05	0.35	0.248	0.437	0.25	0.40	0.651	0.830
0.05	0.40	0.259	0.494	0.25	0.45	0.724	1.007
0.05	0.45	0.271	0.560	0.25	0.50	0.822	1.254
0.05	0.50	0.284	0.640	0.25	0.55	0.962	1.624
0.05	0.55	0.299	0.739	0.25	0.60	1.186	2.243
0.05	0.60	0.317	0.867	0.25	0.65	1.620	3.486

Table 5.12 (*Continued*)

G_1 G_2	G_2 G_1	$\hat{\alpha}_1$ $\hat{\alpha}_2$	$\hat{\alpha}_2$ $\hat{\alpha}_1$	G_1 G_2	G_2 G_1	$\hat{\alpha}_1$ $\hat{\alpha}_2$	$\hat{\alpha}_2$ $\hat{\alpha}_1$
0.05	0.65	0.338	1.037	0.25	0.70	2.889	7.230
0.05	0.70	0.366	1.280	0.25	0.74	12.905	37.229
0.05	0.75	0.403	1.655	0.30	0.30	0.647	0.647
0.05	0.80	0.461	2.305	0.30	0.35	0.717	0.777
0.05	0.85	0.566	3.682	0.30	0.40	0.804	0.947
0.05	0.90	0.849	8.130	0.30	0.45	0.920	1.182
0.05	0.94	2.898	45.901	0.30	0.50	1.086	1.532
0.10	0.10	0.245	0.245	0.30	0.55	1.352	2.115
0.10	0.15	0.262	0.291	0.30	0.60	1.869	3.280
0.10	0.20	0.278	0.337	0.30	0.65	3.387	6.779
0.10	0.25	0.294	0.386	0.30	0.69	15.402	34.780
0.10	0.30	0.310	0.441	0.35	0.35	0.879	0.879
0.10	0.35	0.327	0.503	0.35	0.40	1.013	1.101
0.10	0.40	0.345	0.576	0.35	0.45	1.205	1.430
0.10	0.45	0.365	0.663	0.35	0.50	1.514	1.975
0.10	0.50	0.389	0.770	0.35	0.55	2.115	3.060
0.10	0.55	0.417	0.909	0.35	0.60	3.883	6.313
0.10	0.60	0.451	1.093	0.35	0.64	17.897	32.315
0.10	0.65	0.497	1.356	0.40	0.40	1.320	1.320
0.10	0.70	0.560	1.756	0.40	0.45	1.673	1.827
0.10	0.75	0.660	2.443	0.40	0.50	2.358	2.832
0.10	0.80	0.846	3.864	0.40	0.55	4.376	5.837
0.10	0.85	1.374	8.277	0.40	0.59	20.391	29.841
0.10	0.89	5.406	44.239	0.45	0.45	2.597	2.597
0.15	0.15	0.314	0.314	0.45	0.50	4.867	5.354
0.15	0.20	0.335	0.367	0.45	0.54	22.882	27.359
0.15	0.25	0.357	0.424	0.49	0.49	12.620	12.620
0.15	0.30	0.380	0.489	0.49	0.50	24.873	25.371

PROBLEMS

5.1 For discrete distributions, prove that the line graph (Sec. 5.3.2) is an unbiased estimate of the (unknown) mass function; i.e., show that $E(h_j) = p(x_j)$ for all j. *Hint:* For j fixed, define

$$Y_i = \begin{cases} 1 & \text{if } X_i = x_j \\ 0 & \text{otherwise} \end{cases} \quad \text{for } i = 1, 2, \ldots, n$$

5.2 For each of the following distributions, derive formulas for the MLEs of the indicated parameters. Assume that we have IID data $X_1, X_2, \ldots, X_n$ from the distribution in question.

  (a) U(0, b), MLE for b
  (b) U(a, 0), MLE for a
  (c) U(a, b), joint MLEs for a and b
  (d) N(μ, σ^2), joint MLEs for μ and σ
  (e) LN(μ, σ^2), joint MLEs for μ and σ
  (f) Bernoulli(p), MLE for p
  (g) DU(i, j), joint MLEs for i and j
  (h) bin(t, p), MLE for p assuming that t is known
  (i) geom(p), MLE for p
  (j) negbin(s, p), MLE for p assuming that s is known
  (k) U($\theta - 0.5$, $\theta + 0.5$), MLE for θ

Table 5.13 Service-time data

0.02	4.04	0.37	4.85	8.22	3.14	2.19
1.39	4.85	2.66	2.39	1.04	1.95	1.65
5.02	4.75	0.99	4.06	3.27	2.13	1.52
3.04	16.44	2.83	5.03	2.66	2.54	3.67
3.45	6.71	4.45	11.51	2.14	1.58	5.49
1.85	1.92	3.78	2.57	7.23	3.19	0.71
0.83	2.28	7.66	1.99	3.43	6.88	3.46
4.39	2.50	6.03	10.29	3.07	7.12	3.26
4.39	3.34	3.41	4.73	7.98	0.94	8.52
7.78	3.79	1.16	5.00	0.86	7.02	4.95
2.66	6.03	4.21	4.19	5.08	3.29	3.57
3.37	2.80	2.82	1.03	5.16	3.35	
5.83	5.97	4.56	4.05	5.79	2.34	
0.72	2.10	7.15	6.64	1.36	10.79	
0.89	2.82	5.08	2.12	0.51	3.23	
3.43	3.47	2.07	2.93	4.46	2.08	
4.33	3.09	0.84	5.12	6.36	1.15	

5.3 Assume that the data in Table 5.13 are independent observations on service times (in minutes) at a single-server queueing system. Use all appropriate techniques from Secs. 5.3 to 5.5 to hypothesize a distribution form, estimate its parameter(s) (using MLE estimation), and perform goodness-of-fit test(s).

5.4 Suppose the data in Table 5.14 are independent observations on deviations from the desired diameter of ball bearings produced by a new high-speed machine. Use all appropriate techniques from Secs.

Table 5.14 Data on errors in the diameter of ball bearings

2.31	0.94	1.55	1.10	1.68	−0.16	0.48
1.49	1.20	1.48	0.85	3.21	1.71	4.01
2.10	0.26	1.97	1.09	2.72	1.18	0.28
0.30	1.40	0.59	1.99	2.14	1.59	1.50
0.48	2.12	1.15	2.54	0.70	1.63	1.47
1.71	1.41	0.95	1.55	1.28	0.44	−1.72
0.19	2.73	0.45	0.49	1.23	2.44	−1.62
−0.00	1.33	−0.51	1.62	0.06	2.20	1.87
0.66	0.26	2.36	2.40	1.00	2.30	1.74
−1.27	3.11	1.03	0.59	1.37	1.30	0.78
1.01	0.99	0.24	2.18	2.24	0.22	1.01
−0.54	0.24	2.66	1.14	1.06	1.09	1.63
1.70	1.35	1.00	1.21	1.75	3.27	1.62
2.58	0.60	0.19	1.43	2.21	0.49	0.46
0.56	1.17	2.28	2.02	1.71	1.08	2.08
0.38	1.12	0.01	1.82	1.96	0.77	1.70
0.77	2.79	0.31	1.11	1.69	1.23	2.05
2.29	0.17	−0.12	2.69	1.78	2.26	0.02
1.55	0.44	0.89	1.51	−0.67	1.06	−0.05
0.27	0.78	0.60	1.06	2.29	1.13	1.85
1.62	1.50	0.21	2.04	1.26	1.98	1.50
0.94	0.17	1.90	1.64	1.12	0.89	0.49

Table 5.15 Demand-size data

2	7	1	3	6	1	3
2	0	1	5	11	5	3
2	8	1	7	4	8	4
4	0	2	20	0	2	5
1	6	12	7	0	5	11
8	6	2	0	4	2	4
8	10	6	6	5	2	6
3	6	5	0	1	3	1
0	2	1	8	5	6	1
0	1	9	4	1	4	2
2	1	1	2	1	4	

5.3 to 5.5 to hypothesize a distribution form, estimate its parameter(s) (using MLE estimation), and perform goodness-of-fit test(s).

5.5 Assume that the number of items demanded per day from an inventory on different days are IID random variables and that the data in Table 5.15 are those demand sizes on 76 different days. Use all appropriate techniques from Secs. 5.3 to 5.5 to hypothesize a distribution form, estimate its parameter(s) (using MLE estimation), and perform goodness-of-fit test(s).

5.6 Consider the shifted (two-parameter) exponential distribution, which has density function

$$f(x) = \begin{cases} \dfrac{1}{\beta} e^{-(x-\gamma)/\beta} & \text{if } x \geq \gamma \\ 0 & \text{otherwise} \end{cases}$$

for $\beta > 0$ and any real number γ. Given a sample $X_1, X_2, \ldots, X_n$ of IID random variables from this distribution, find formulas for the joint MLEs $\hat{\gamma}$ and $\hat{\beta}$. *Hint:* Remember that γ cannot exceed any X_i.

5.7 Let $LN(\gamma, \mu, \sigma^2)$ denote the shifted (three-parameter) lognormal distribution, which has density

$$f(x) = \begin{cases} \dfrac{1}{(x-\gamma)\sqrt{2\pi\sigma^2}} \exp\dfrac{-[\ln(x-\gamma)-\mu]^2}{2\sigma^2} & \text{if } x > \gamma \\ 0 & \text{otherwise} \end{cases}$$

for $\sigma > 0$ and any real numbers γ and μ. [Thus $LN(0, \mu, \sigma^2)$ is the original $LN(\mu, \sigma^2)$ distribution.]

(*a*) Verify that $X \sim LN(\gamma, \mu, \sigma^2)$ if and only if $X - \gamma \sim LN(\mu, \sigma^2)$.

(*b*) Show that for a fixed, known value of γ, the MLEs of μ and σ in the $LN(\gamma, \mu, \sigma^2)$ distribution are

$$\hat{\mu} = \frac{\sum_{i=1}^{n} \ln(X_i - \gamma)}{n} \quad \text{and} \quad \hat{\sigma} = \left\{\frac{\sum_{i=1}^{n} [\ln(X_i - \gamma) - \hat{\mu}]^2}{n}\right\}^{1/2}$$

i.e., we simply shift the data by an amount $-\gamma$ and then treat them as being (unshifted) lognormal data.

REFERENCES

1. Barnett, V.: Probability Plotting Methods and Order Statistics, *Appl. Statist.*, **24**: 95–108 (1975).
2. Beasley, J. D., and S. G. Springer: The Percentage Points of the Normal Distribution, *Appl. Statist.*, **26**: 118–121 (1977).

3. Beckman, R. J., and G. L. Tietjen: Maximum Likelihood Estimation for the Beta Distribution, *J. Statist. Comput. Simul.,* **7:** 253–258 (1978).

4. Best, D. J., and D. E. Roberts: The Percentage Points of the χ^2 Distribution, *Appl. Statist.,* **24:** 385–388 (1975).

5. Blank, L.: *Statistical Procedures for Engineering, Management, and Science,* McGraw-Hill, New York, 1980.

6. Breiman, L.: *Statistics: With a View Toward Applications,* Houghton-Mifflin, Boston, 1973.

7. Chandra, M., N. D. Singpurwalla, and M. A. Stephens: Kolmogorov Statistics for Tests of Fit for the Extreme Value and Weibull Distributions, George Washington University, Department of Operations Research, Washington, 1980.

8. Chernoff, H., and E. L. Lehmann: The Use of Maximum Likelihood Estimates in χ^2 Tests for Goodness of Fit, *Ann. Math. Statist.,* **25:** 579–586 (1954).

9. Choi, S. C., and R. Wette: Maximum Likelihood Estimation of the Parameters of the Gamma Distribution and their Bias, *Technometrics,* **11:** 683–690 (1969).

10. Çinlar, E.: *Introduction to Stochastic Processes,* Prentice-Hall, Englewood Cliffs, N.J., 1975.

11. Cohen, A. C., and B. J. Whitten: Estimation in the Three-Parameter Lognormal Distribution, *J. Am. Statist. Ass.,* **75:** 399–404 (1980).

12. Cran, G. W., K. J. Martin, and G. E. Thomas: A Remark on Algorithms AS63: The Incomplete Beta Integral, AS64: Inverse of the Incomplete Beta Function Ratio, *Appl. Statist.,* **26:** 111–114 (1977).

13. Durbin, J.: Kolmogorov-Smirnov Tests When Parameters Are Estimated with Applications to Tests of Exponentiality and Tests on Spacings, *Biometrika,* **62:** 5–22 (1975).

14. Gail, M. H., and J. L. Gastwirth: A Scale-Free Goodness-of-Fit Test for the Exponential Distribution Based on the Gini Statistic, *J. R. Statist. Soc.,* **B40:** 350–357 (1978).

15. Gnanadesikan, R., R. S. Pinkham, and L. P. Hughes: Maximum Likelihood Estimation of the Parameters of the Beta Distribution from Smallest Order Statistics, *Technometrics,* **9:** 607–620 (1967).

16. Gonzalez, T., S. Sahni, and W. R. Franta: An Efficient Algorithm for the Kolmogorov-Smirnov and Lilliefors Tests, *ACM Trans. Math. Software,* **3:** 60–64 (1977).

17. Hahn, G. J., and S. S. Shapiro: *Statistical Models in Engineering,* Wiley, New York, 1967.

18. Harter, H. L.: *Order Statistics and Their Use in Testing and Estimation,* Government Printing Office, Washington, 1970.

19. Harter, H. L., and A. H. Moore: Maximum-Likelihood Estimation of the Parameters of Gamma and Weibull Populations from Complete and from Censored Samples, *Technometrics,* **7:** 639–643 (1965).

20. Kendall, M. G., and A. Stuart: *The Advanced Theory of Statistics,* 3d ed., vol. 1, Hafner, New York, 1969.

21. Kendall, M. G., and A. Stuart: *The Advanced Theory of Statistics,* 3d ed., vol. 2, Hafner, New York, 1973.

22. Lewis, P. A. W., and G. S. Shedler: Statistical Analysis of Non-Stationary Series of Events in a Data Base System, *IBM J. Res. Dev.,* **20:** 465–482 (1976).

23. Lilliefors, H. W.: On the Kolmogorov-Smirnov Test for Normality with Mean and Variance Unknown, *J. Am. Statist. Ass.,* **62:** 399–402 (1967).

24. Lilliefors, H. W.: On the Kolmogorov-Smirnov Test for the Exponential Distribution with Mean Unknown, *J. Am. Statist. Ass.,* **64:** 387–389 (1969).

25. Littell, R. C., J. T. McClave, and W. W. Offen: Goodness-of-Fit Tests for the Two Parameter Weibull Distribution, *Commun. Statist.,* **B8:** 257–269 (1979).

26. Mann, N. R.: Point and Interval Estimation Procedures for the Two-Parameter Weibull and Extreme-Value Distributions, *Technometrics,* **10:** 231–256 (1968).

27. Margolin, B. H., and W. Maurer: Tests of the Kolmogorov-Smirnov Type for Exponential Data with Unknown Scale, and Related Problems, *Biometrika,* **63:** 149–160 (1976).

28. Menon, M. V.: Estimation of the Shape and Scale Parameters of the Weibull Distribution, *Technometrics,* **5:** 175–182 (1963).

29. Noether, G. E.: *Elements of Nonparametric Statistics,* Wiley, New York, 1967.

30. Owen, D. B.: *Handbook of Statistical Tables,* Addison-Wesley, Reading, Mass., 1962.

31. Pearson, K.: On a Criterion That a Given System of Deviations from the Probable in the Case of a Correlated System of Variables Is Such That It Can Be Reasonably Supposed to Have Arisen in Random Sampling, *Phil. Mag.*, (5)**50:** 157–175 (1900).
32. Pettitt, A. N., and M. A. Stephens: The Kolmogorov-Smirnov Goodness-of-Fit Statistic with Discrete and Grouped Data, *Technometrics,* **19:** 205–210 (1977).
33. Quesenberry, C. P., and F. L. Miller, Jr.: Power Studies of Some Tests for Uniformity, *J. Statist. Comput. Simul.,* **5:** 169–191 (1977).
34. Ross, S. M.: *Applied Probability Models with Optimization Applications,* Holden-Day, San Francisco, 1970.
35. Shapiro, S. S., and R. S. Francia: An Approximate Analysis of Variance Test for Normality, *J. Am. Statist. Ass.,* **67:** 215–216 (1972).
36. Shapiro, S. S., and M. B. Wilk: An Analysis of Variance Test for Normality (Complete Samples), *Biometrika,* **52:** 591–611 (1965).
37. Shapiro, S. S., and M. B. Wilk: Approximations for the Null Distribution of the *W* Statistic, *Technometrics,* **10:** 861–866 (1968).
38. Shapiro, S. S., M. B. Wilk, and H. J. Chen: A Comparative Study of Various Tests for Normality, *J. Am. Statist. Ass.,* **63:** 1343–1372 (1968).
39. Stephens, M. A.: EDF Statistics for Goodness of Fit and Some Comparisons, *J. Am. Statist. Ass.,* **69:** 730–737 (1974).
40. Stephens, M. A.: Goodness of Fit for the Extreme Value Distribution, *Biometrika,* **64:** 583–588 (1977).
41. Stephens, M. A.: Goodness of Fit Tests with Special Reference to Tests for Exponentiality, *Stanford Univ. Dept. Statist. Tech. Rep. 22,* Stanford, Calif., 1978.
42. Tarter, M. E., and R. A. Kronmal: An Introduction to the Implementation and Theory of Nonparametric Density Estimation, *Am. Statist.,* **30:** 105–112 (1976).
43. Thoman, D. R., L. J. Bain, and C. E. Antle: Inferences on the Parameters of the Weibull Distribution, *Technometrics,* **11:** 445–460 (1969).
44. Wegman, E. J.: Nonparametric Probability Density Estimation: I. A Summary of Available Methods, *Technometrics,* **14:** 533–546 (1972).
45. Weisberg, S.: An Empirical Comparison of the Percentage Points of *W* and *W'*, *Biometrika,* **61:** 644–646 (1974).
46. Weisberg, S., and C. Bingham: An Approximate Analysis of Variance Test for Non-Normality Suitable for Machine Calculation, *Technometrics,* **17:** 133–134 (1975).
47. Wilk, M. B., and R. Gnanadesikan: Probability Plotting Methods for the Analysis of Data, *Biometrika,* **55:** 1–17 (1968).
48. Zanakis, S. H.: Extended Pattern Search with Transformations for the Three-Parameter Weibull MLE Problem, *Manag. Sci.,* **25:** 1149–1161 (1979).

SIX

RANDOM-NUMBER GENERATORS

6.1 INTRODUCTION

A simulation of any system or process in which there are inherently random components requires a method of generating or obtaining numbers that are *random,* in some sense. For example, the queueing and inventory models of Chaps. 1 and 2 required interarrival times, service times, demand sizes, etc., that were "drawn" from some specified distribution, such as an exponential or Erlang distribution. In this and the next chapter, we discuss how the desired random variables can be conveniently and efficiently generated for use in executing simulation models. Strictly speaking, one should not talk about "generating random variables," since a random variable is defined (in mathematical probability theory) to be a *function* satisfying certain conditions. Thus, when we talk about "generating a random variable," we really mean that we are generating a possible *numerical value* that the random variable *can take on*, in accordance with the appropriate probability distribution.

This entire chapter is devoted to methods of generating random numbers from the uniform distribution on the interval $[0, 1]$; this distribution was denoted by $U(0, 1)$ in Chap. 5. Although this is the simplest continuous distribution of all, it is extremely important that we be able to obtain such independent $U(0, 1)$ random variables. This prominent role of the $U(0, 1)$ distribution stems from the fact that random variables from all other distributions (normal, gamma, binomial, etc.) and realizations of various random processes, e.g., a nonstationary Poisson process, can be obtained by transforming IID $U(0, 1)$ random variables in a way determined by the desired distribution or process. This chapter discusses ways to obtain $U(0, 1)$

random variables, and the following chapter treats methods of transforming them to obtain random quantities from other distributions and processes.

The methodology of generating random numbers has a long and interesting history; see Hull and Dobell [10] for an entertaining account. The earliest methods were essentially carried out by hand, using such methods as casting lots, throwing dice, dealing out cards, or drawing numbered balls from a "well-stirred urn." Many lotteries are still operated in this way, as is well known by American males who were of draft age in the late 1960s and early 1970s. In the early twentieth century, statisticians joined gamblers in their interest in random numbers, and mechanized devices were built to generate random numbers more quickly; in the late 1930s, Kendall and Babington-Smith [14] used a rapidly spinning disk to prepare a table of 100,000 random digits. Some time later, electric circuits based on randomly pulsating vacuum tubes were designed that delivered random digits at rates of up to 50 per second. One such random-number machine, the Electronic Random Number Indicator Equipment (ERNIE) was used by the British General Post Office to pick the winners in the Premium Savings Bond lottery (see Thomson [30]). Another electronic device was used by the Rand Corporation [27] to generate a table of a million random digits. Many other schemes have been contrived, such as picking numbers "randomly" out of phone books or census reports, or using the digits in an expansion of π to 100,000 decimal places.

As computers (and simulation) became more widely used, increasing attention was paid to methods of random-number generation compatible with the way computers work. One possibility would be to hook up an electronic random-number machine, such as ERNIE, directly to the computer. This has several disadvantages, chiefly that we could not reproduce a previously generated random-number stream exactly. (The desirability of being able to do this is discussed later in this section.) Another alternative would be to read in a table, such as the Rand Corporation table, but this would entail either large memory requirements or a lot of time for relatively slow input operations. (Also, it is not at all uncommon for a modern large-scale simulation to use far more than a million random *numbers,* each of which would require several individual random *digits.*) Therefore, research in the 1940s and 1950s turned to *numerical* or *arithmetic* ways to generate "random" numbers. Usually, the random numbers are generated in a sequence, each new number's being determined by one or several of its predecessors according to a fixed mathematical formula. The first such arithmetic generator, proposed by von Neumann and Metropolis in the 1940s, is the famous *midsquare method,* an example of which follows.

Example 6.1 Start with a four-digit positive integer Z_0 and square it to obtain an integer with up to eight digits; if necessary, append zeros to the left to make it exactly eight digits. Take the *middle four* digits of this eight-digit number as the next four-digit number, Z_1. Place a decimal point at the left of Z_1 to obtain the first "U(0, 1) random number," U_1. Then let Z_2 be the middle four digits of Z_1^2 and let U_2 be Z_2 with a decimal point at the left, and so on. Table 6.1 lists the first few Z_i's and U_i's for $Z_0 = 7182$ (the first four digits to the right of the decimal point in the number e).

Intuitively the midsquare method seems to provide a good scrambling of one number to obtain the next, and so we might think that such a haphazard rule would

Table 6.1 The midsquare method

i	Z_i	U_i	Z_i^2
0	7182	—	51,581,124
1	5811	0.5811	33,767,721
2	7677	0.7677	58,936,329
3	9363	0.9363	87,665,769
4	6657	0.6657	44,315,649
5	3156	0.3156	09,960,336

provide a fairly good way of generating random numbers. In fact, it does not work very well at all. One serious problem (among others) is that it has a strong tendency to degenerate fairly rapidly to zero, where it will stay forever. (Continue Table 6.1 for just a few more steps, or try Z_0 = 1009, the first four digits from the Rand Corporation tables.) This illustrates the danger in assuming that a good random-number generator will always be obtained by doing something strange and nefarious to one number to obtain the next.

A more fundamental objection to the midsquare method is that it is not "random" at all, in the sense of being unpredictable. Indeed, if we know one number, the next is completely determined since the rule to obtain it is fixed; actually, when Z_0 is specified, the *whole sequence* of Z_i's and U_i's is determined. This objection applies to all arithmetic generators (the only kind we consider in the rest of this chapter), and arguing about it usually leads one quickly into mystical discussions about the true nature of truly random numbers. (Sometimes arithmetic generators are called *pseudo random,* an awkward term which we avoid, even though it is probably more accurate.) We agree, however, with most writers that arithmetic generators, if designed carefully, can produce numbers which *appear* to be independent draws from the U(0, 1) distribution, in that they pass a series of statistical tests (see Sec. 6.4). This is a useful definition of "random numbers," to which we subscribe.

A "good" arithmetic random-number generator should possess several properties. Above all, the numbers produced should appear to be distributed uniformly on [0, 1] and should not exhibit any correlation with each other. From a practical standpoint, we would naturally like the generator to be fast and avoid the need for a lot of storage. Finally, we want to be able to reproduce a given stream of random numbers exactly, for at least two reasons. First, this can sometimes make debugging or verification of the computer program easier. More importantly, we might want to reuse the same random numbers in different simulation runs in order to increase the precision of the simulation output; Chap. 11 discusses this in detail. Most of the commonly used generators are quite fast, require very little storage, and can easily reproduce a given stream of random numbers. Unfortunately, not all random-number generators satisfy the uniformity and independence criteria, and these statistical properties are absolutely necessary if one hopes to obtain correct simulation results.

In Sec. 6.2 we discuss the most popular kind of generator, and Sec. 6.3 mentions some alternative methods. Sec. 6.4 discusses how one can test a given random-number generator for the desired statistical properties. (On a first reading, we suggest that only Secs. 6.2, 6.4.1, and 6.4.3 be studied in detail.) The subject of random-number generators is a complicated one and involves such disparate disciplines as abstract algebra and number theory on the one hand, and systems programming and computer hardware engineering on the other. Its importance, however, should be clear since random-number generators are at the very heart of a simulation.

6.2 LINEAR CONGRUENTIAL GENERATORS

The great majority of random-number generators in use today are *linear congruential generators* (LCGs), introduced by Lehmer [18] in 1951. A sequence of integers $Z_1, Z_2, \ldots$ is defined by the recursive formula

$$Z_i = (aZ_{i-1} + c)(\text{mod } m) \tag{6.1}$$

where m (the *modulus*), a (the *multiplier*), c (the *increment*), and Z_0 (the *seed* or *starting value*) are nonnegative integers. Thus, (6.1) says that to obtain Z_i, divide $aZ_{i-1} + c$ by m and let Z_i be the *remainder* of this division. Therefore, $0 \le Z_i \le m - 1$, and to obtain the desired random numbers U_i (for $i = 1, 2, \ldots$) on $[0, 1]$, we let $U_i = Z_i/m$; we shall concentrate our attention for the most part on the Z_i's. In addition to nonnegativity, the integers m, a, c, and Z_0 should satisfy $0 < m$, $a < m$, $c < m$, and $Z_0 < m$.

Immediately, two objections could be raised against LCGs. The first objection is one common to all (pseudo) random-number generators, namely, that the Z_i's defined by (6.1) are not really random at all. In fact, one can show by induction that for $i = 1, 2, \ldots$,

$$Z_i = \left[a^i Z_0 + \frac{c(a^i - 1)}{a - 1} \right] (\text{mod } m)$$

so that *every* Z_i is completely determined by m, a, c, and Z_0. However, by a careful choice of these four parameters we try to induce behavior in the Z_i's which makes the corresponding U_i's *appear* to be IID U(0, 1) random variables when subjected to a variety of tests (see Sec. 6.4). The second objection to LCGs might be that the U_i's can take on only the rational values $0, 1/m, 2/m, \ldots, (m - 1)/m$; thus the "probability" of getting an actual value of U_i between, say, $0.1/m$ and $0.9/m$ is 0 whereas it *should* be $0.8/m > 0$. As we shall see, the modulus m is usually chosen to be very large, say 10^9 or more, so that the points in $[0, 1]$ where the U_i's can fall are very dense; for $m \ge 10^9$, there are at least a billion possible values for U_i, equally spaced. This should provide an approximation to the true U(0, 1) distribution sufficient for most purposes.

Example 6.2 Consider the LCG defined by $m = 16$, $a = 5$, $c = 3$, and $Z_0 = 7$. Table 6.2 gives Z_i and U_i (to three decimal places) for $i = 1, 2, \ldots, 19$. Note that $Z_{17} = Z_1 = 6$, $Z_{18} = Z_2 = 1$, and so on. That is, from $i = 17$ through 32, we shall obtain *exactly* the same values of Z_i (and hence U_i) that we did from $i = 1$ through 16, and in *exactly* the same order. (We do not seriously suggest that anyone use this generator since m is so small; it only illustrates the arithmetic of LCGs.)

The "looping" behavior of the LCG in Example 6.2 is inevitable. By the definition in (6.1), whenever Z_i takes on a value it has had previously, exactly the same sequence of values is generated, and this cycle repeats itself endlessly. The length of a cycle is called the *period* of a generator, which we denote by p. For LCGs, Z_i depends *only* on the previous integer Z_{i-1}, and since $0 \leq Z_i \leq m - 1$, it is clear that $p \leq m$; if $p = m$, the LCG is said to have *full period*. (The LCG in Example 6.2 has full period.)

Since large-scale simulation projects can use hundreds of thousands of random numbers, it is manifestly desirable to have LCGs with long periods. Furthermore, it is comforting to have full-period LCGs, since we are assured that every integer between 0 and $m - 1$ will occur exactly once in each cycle, which should contribute to the uniformity of the U_i's. (Even full-period LCGs, however, can exhibit nonuniform behavior in segments within a cycle. For example, if we generate only $m/2$ consecutive Z_i's, they may leave large "gaps" in the sequence $0, 1, \ldots, m - 1$ of possible values.) Thus, it is useful to know how to choose m, a, and c so that the corresponding LCG will have full period. The following theorem, proved by Hull and Dobell [10], gives such a characterization.

Theorem 6.1 The LCG defined in (6.1) has full period if and only if the following three conditions hold:
(*a*) The only positive integer that (exactly) divides both m and c is 1.
(*b*) If q is a prime number (divisible only by itself and 1) that divides m, then q divides $a - 1$.
(*c*) If 4 divides m, then 4 divides $a - 1$.

[Condition (*a*) in Theorem 6.1 is often stated as "c is relatively prime to m."]
Obtaining a full (or at least a long) period is just one desirable property in finding good LCGs; as indicated in Sec. 6.1, we also want good statistical properties (such as independence), computational and storage efficiency, and reproducibility. (The last property is no problem with LCGs, since we can save the seed Z_0. Also, *we can easily resume generating the Z_i's at any point by saving the last Z_i; this is the usual way to obtain independent random-number streams.*) In the remainder of this section we consider the choice of parameters for obtaining good LCGs and identify some notably poor LCGs which are probably still in frequent use. Because of condition (*a*) in Theorem 6.1, LCGs tend to behave differently for $c > 0$ (called *mixed* LCGs) than for $c = 0$ (called *multiplicative* LCGs).

Table 6.2 The LCG $Z_i = (5Z_{i-1} + 3)(\text{mod } 16)$ with $Z_0 = 7$

i	Z_i	U_i	i	Z_i	U_i	i	Z_i	U_i	i	Z_i	U_i
0	7	—	5	10	0.625	10	9	0.563	15	4	0.250
1	6	0.375	6	5	0.313	11	0	0.000	16	7	0.438
2	1	0.063	7	12	0.750	12	3	0.188	17	6	0.375
3	8	0.500	8	15	0.938	13	2	0.125	18	1	0.063
4	11	0.688	9	14	0.875	14	13	0.813	19	8	0.500

6.2.1 Mixed Generators

For $c > 0$, condition (a) of Theorem 6.1 is possible, so we might be able to obtain full period, $p = m$. We first discuss the choice of m.

For a large period and high density of the U_i's on $[0, 1]$ we want m to be large. Furthermore, dividing by m to obtain the remainder in (6.1) is a relatively slow arithmetic operation, and it would be desirable to avoid having to do this division explicitly. A choice of m which is good in all these respects is $m = 2^b$, where b is the number of bits (*bi*nary dig*its*) in a word on the computer being used that are available for actual data storage. (For example, IBM 360 and 370 computers have 32-bit words, the leftmost bit being a sign bit; thus $b = 31$. For UNIVAC 1100 series computers, the word length is 36 bits, the leftmost of which is a sign bit, so $b = 35$.) If b is reasonably large, say $b \geq 31$, then m *is* quite large; for example, $m \geq 2^{31} > 2.1$ billion. Furthermore, choosing $m = 2^b$ *does* allow us to avoid explicit division by m on most computers by taking advantage of *integer overflow*. The largest integer that can be represented is $2^b - 1$, and any attempt to store a larger integer W (with, say, $h > b$ binary digits) will result in loss of the left (most significant) $h - b$ binary digits of this oversized integer. What remains in the retained b bits is precisely $W \pmod{2^b}$. The following example illustrates modulo division by overflow for $m = 2^b$.

> **Example 6.3** Suppose that the LCG of Example 6.2 is implemented on a mythical computer with $b = 4$ bits per word available for data storage; $m = 16 = 2^b$, conveniently. How can overflow be used to obtain $Z_7 = 12$ from $Z_6 = 5$? Now $5Z_6 + 3 = 28$, which in binary representation is 11100. Since our 4-bit computer can store only four binary digits, the leftmost digit of the binary number 11100 is dropped, leaving the binary number 1100, which *is* the binary representation of $12 = Z_7$.

We caution the reader to check out exactly how integer overflow is handled; e.g., the sign bit might be turned on in the operation, necessitating an adjustment which depends on the computer's architecture, the format for representing integers, and the language being used.

Thus, $m = 2^b$ would appear to be a good choice for the modulus. With this choice, Theorem 6.1 says that we shall obtain full period if c is odd and $a - 1$ is divisible by 4; with such a full-period generator, Z_0 can be any integer between 0 and $m - 1$ without affecting the generator's period. We next consider the choice of the multiplier a.

Early work on LCGs emphasized efficiency in effecting the multiplication of Z_{i-1} by a, which led to multipliers of the form

$$a = 2^l + 1 \tag{6.2}$$

for some positive integer l. Then

$$aZ_{i-1} = 2^l Z_{i-1} + Z_{i-1}$$

so that aZ_{i-1} can be obtained by "shifting" Z_{i-1} l bits to the left and adding Z_{i-1}. Thus, the explicit multiplication can be replaced by the shift-and-add operations.

However, more recent work has indicated that multipliers of the form (6.2) should be avoided for at least two reasons: (1) the explicit multiplication of Z_{i-1} by a can actually be *faster* than the shift-and-add operations on modern computers (see Knuth [15, p. 22]) and (2) (most important) choosing a as in (6.2) has produced generators with poor statistical properties (see Sec. 6.4).

How, then, should one choose a and c when $m = 2^b$ to obtain a "good" mixed LCG? Tentatively, we might address this question by suggesting that consideration be given to not using a mixed LCG; the simpler and better understood multiplicative LCGs (treated in Sec. 6.2.2) have generally performed as well as mixed LCGs and are in wider use. Nevertheless, we can identify two mixed LCGs that have been suggested as providing adequate performance. The first, for $b = 35$, was examined by Coveyou and MacPherson [4]:

$$Z_i = (5^{15}Z_{i-1} + 1)(\text{mod } 2^{35})$$

(Our empirical experiments in Chaps. 8 to 12 used this generator.) The second mixed LCG is for $b = 31$ and was suggested by Kobayashi [16, p. 240], based on recommendations by Knuth [15, pp. 155–156]:

$$Z_i = (314{,}159{,}269\,Z_{i-1} + 453{,}806{,}245)(\text{mod } 2^{31})$$

6.2.2 Multiplicative Generators

Multiplicative LCGs are advantageous in that the addition of c is not needed, but they cannot have full period since condition (a) of Theorem 6.1 cannot be satisfied (because, for example, m is positive and divides both m and $c = 0$). As we shall see, however, it is possible to obtain period $p = m - 1$ if m and a are chosen carefully. Multiplicative LCGs came before mixed LCGs historically and have been studied more intensively. The majority of the LCGs in use today *are* multiplicative, since the improvement in performance hoped for in the more recent mixed LCGs has not been demonstrated conclusively; many researchers on random-number generators have thus chosen to stick with the original multiplicative LCGs.

As with mixed generators, it is still computationally efficient to choose $m = 2^b$ and thus avoid an explicit division. However, it can be shown (see, for example, [15, pp. 18–19]) that $p \leq 2^{b-2}$, that is, only *one-fourth* of the integers 0 through $m - 1$ can be obtained as values for the Z_i's. (In fact, $p = 2^{b-2}$ if Z_0 is odd and a is of the form $8k + 3$ or $8k + 5$ for some $k = 0, 1, \ldots$.) Furthermore, we generally shall not know *where* these $m/4$ integers will fall; i.e., there might be unacceptably large gaps in the Z_i's obtained. Additionally, if we choose a to be of the form $a = 2^l + j$ (so that the multiplication of Z_{i-1} by a is replaced by a shift and j adds), poor statistical properties can be induced. Unfortunately, the generator RANDU in IBM's old Scientific Subroutine Package is of this form ($m = 2^{31}$, $a = 2^{16} + 3$, $c = 0$) and has been shown to have very undesirable statistical properties; use of RANDU should therefore be avoided. (IBM has replaced RANDU by the multiplicative generator defined by $m = 2^{31} - 1$ and $a = 7^5$ and called it GGL in its Subroutine Library—Mathematics; this is a much better generator, and we shall have more to say about it later.) Greenberger [8] showed that another generator of this form (with $m = 2^{35}$ and $a = 2^{18} + 3$) also exhibits poor statistical behavior. Even if one does not choose $a = 2^l + j$, using $m = 2^b$ in multiplicative LCGs is probably not a good idea, if only because of the shorter period of $m/4$ and the resulting possibility of gaps.

Because of these difficulties associated with choosing $m = 2^b$ in multiplicative LCGs, attention was paid to finding other ways of specifying m. Such a method, which has proved to be quite successful, was reported by Hutchinson [11], who attributed the idea to D. H. Lehmer. Instead of letting $m = 2^b$, it was proposed that m be the largest prime number which is less than 2^b. Now for m prime, it can be shown that the period $p = m - 1$ if a is a *primitive element modulo m*; that is, the smallest integer l for which $a^l - 1$ is divisible by m is $l = m - 1$; see [15, p. 19]. With m and a chosen in this way, we obtain each integer $1, 2, \ldots, m - 1$ exactly once in each cycle, so that Z_0 can be any integer from 1 through $m - 1$ and a period of $m - 1$ will still result. These are called *prime modulus multiplicative LCGs* (PMMLCGs).

Two questions immediately arise concerning PMMLCGs: (1) How does one obtain a primitive element modulo m? Although Knuth [15, p. 19] gives some characterizations, the task is quite complicated from a computational standpoint. We shall, in essence, finesse this point by referring the reader to the end of this section, where we explicitly give some "tried and true" PMMLCGs. (2) Since we are not choosing 2^b as the modulus, we can no longer use the overflow mechanism directly to effect the division modulo m. A technique for avoiding explicit division in this case, which also uses overflow, was given by Payne, Rabung, and Bogyo [26] and has been called *simulated division*. (See also Fishman [5, 6], Kobayashi [16, pp. 237–238], and Schrage [28].) For PMMLCGs, m is of the form $2^b - q$ for some positive integer q. To obtain $Z_i = (aZ_{i-1})(\bmod\ 2^b - q)$ from Z_{i-1}, let $Z_i' = (aZ_{i-1})(\bmod\ 2^b)$, which can be obtained without division by taking advantage of overflow. If k is the greatest integer which is less than or equal to $aZ_{i-1}/2^b$, then

$$Z_i = \begin{cases} Z_i' + kq & \text{if } Z_i' + kq < 2^b - q \\ Z_i' + kq - (2^b - q) & \text{if } Z_i' + kq \geq 2^b - q \end{cases}$$

(Schrage's "portable" FORTRAN generators, which we list below, use simulated division.)

We close this section by giving examples of specific PMMLCGs which have performed well. For $b = 35$ (UNIVAC 1100 series), the largest prime less than 2^{35} is $m = 2^{35} - 31 = 34,359,738,337$, and Hutchinson [11] tested the generator with $a = 5^5 = 3125$ (which is a primitive element modulo $2^{35} - 31$). He reported that this generator performed well statistically and also gave an assembly-language code for it.

For $b = 31$ (IBM 360 and 370) it was somewhat more difficult to find good PMMLCGs. The largest prime less than 2^{31} is, very agreeably, $m = 2^{31} - 1 = 2,147,483,647$, and two well-known (and widely used) choices for a are $a_1 = 7^5 = $

16,807 (Lewis, Goodman, and Miller [19]), and $a_2 = 630,360,016$ (see [26]), both of which are primitive elements modulo $2^{31} - 1$. (a_1 is used in the LLRANDOM package [17], IBM's GGL [12], IMSL's GGUBS [13], and Schrage's portable FORTRAN functions given below. a_2 is used in SIMSCRIPT II.5.) An assembly-language program (with explicit hardware division rather than simulated division) using a_1 is listed in [19]. Schrage [28] gave very portable FORTRAN functions (*with* simulated division) using a_1, which we list in Figs. 6.1 and 6.2. Both functions are called with IX set to the initial seed and return in IX the next integer Z_i, and the function name contains the next U_i; it is important that all parentheses be included. The function RAND in Fig. 6.1 can be used on machines with words of at least 32 bits (including the sign bit), assuming only that all integers from $-2^{31} + 1$ through $2^{31} - 1$ are properly computed and stored. The function DRAND in

```
FUNCTION RAND(IX)
INTEGER A,P,IX,B15,B16,XHI,XALO,LEFTLO,FHI,K
DATA A/16807/,B15/32768/,B16/65536/,P/2147483647/
XHI=IX/B16
XALO=(IX-XHI*B16)*A
LEFTLO=XALO/B16
FHI=XHI*A+LEFTLO
K=FHI/B15
IX=(((XALO-LEFTLO*B16)-P)+(FHI-K*B15)*B16)+K
IF(IX.LT.0)IX=IX+P
RAND=FLOAT(IX)*4.656612875E-10
RETURN
END
```

Figure 6.1 FORTRAN function RAND for PMMLCG $Z_i = (7^5 Z_{i-1}) \pmod{2^{31} - 1}$ for 32-bit (or larger) words.†

```
DOUBLE PRECISION FUNCTION DRAND(IX)
DOUBLE PRECISION A,P,IX,B15,B16,XHI,XALO,LEFTLO,FHI,K
DATA A/16807.D0/,B15/32768.D0/,B16/65536.D0/,P/2147483647.D0/
XHI=IX/B16
XHI=XHI-DMOD(XHI,1.D0)
XALO=(IX-XHI*B16)*A
LEFTLO=XALO/B16
LEFTLO=LEFTLO-DMOD(LEFTLO,1.D0)
FHI=XHI*A+LEFTLO
K=FHI/B15
K=K-DMOD(K,1.D0)
IX=(((XALO-LEFTLO*B16)-P)+(FHI-K*B15)*B16)+K
IF(IX.LT.0.D0)IX=IX+P
DRAND=IX*4.656612875D-10
RETURN
END
```

Figure 6.2 FORTRAN function DRAND for PMMLCG $Z_i = (7^5 Z_{i-1}) \pmod{2^{31} - 1}$ for 16-bit (or larger) words.†

Fig. 6.2 can be used on machines with words as short as 16 bits (such as many minicomputers) by doing all calculations in double precision; to use DRAND, both DRAND and IX must be declared DOUBLE PRECISION in the calling program. (Naturally, RAND is much faster than DRAND. As a check to see whether your function is correct, set $Z_0 = 1$. Then Z_{1000} should be 522,329,230 for both RAND and DRAND.) For $m = 2^{31} - 1$, Hoaglin [9] and Fishman and Moore [7] identified some values for a other than a_1 and a_2 exhibiting statistical properties that were somewhat better (namely, 397,204,094 and 764,261,123, with the former slightly preferable). However, their values for a cannot be substituted for $a_1 = 7^5$ in the programs in Figs. 6.1 and 6.2 since they are considerably larger and could cause numerical difficulties. In the absence of anything better, we would feel comfortable in recommending the use of the PMMLCG with $m = 2^{31} - 1$ and $a = 7^5$, with the aid of Schrage's FORTRAN functions RAND (if possible) or DRAND (if necessary due to short word length), as given in Figs. 6.1 and 6.2.

6.3 OTHER KINDS OF GENERATORS

Although LCGs are by far the most widely used and best understood kind of random-number generator, there are many alternative types. (We have already seen one alternative in Sec. 6.1, the midsquare method, which is not recommended.) Most of these other generators have been developed in an attempt to obtain longer periods and better statistical properties. Often, however, a simple LCG with carefully chosen parameters can perform nearly as well as (sometimes better than) these more complicated alternatives. Our treatment in this section is not meant to be an exhaustive compendium of all kinds of generators but only to indicate some of the main alternatives to LCGs.

6.3.1 More General Congruences

LCGs can be thought of as a special case of generators defined by

$$Z_i = g(Z_{i-1}, Z_{i-2}, \ldots)(\text{mod } m) \tag{6.3}$$

where g is a fixed deterministic function of previous Z_j's. As with LCGs, the Z_i's defined by (6.3) lie between 0 and $m - 1$, and the U(0, 1) random numbers are given by $U_i = Z_i/m$. [For LCGs, the function g is, of course, $g(Z_{i-1}, Z_{i-2}, \ldots) = aZ_{i-1} + c$.] Here we simply mention a few of these kinds of generators and refer the reader to Knuth [15, pp. 25–28] for a more detailed discussion.

The most obvious generalization of LCGs would be to let $g(Z_{i-1}, Z_{i-2}, \ldots) = a'Z_{i-1}^2 + aZ_{i-1} + c$, which produces a *quadratic* congruential generator. A special case of this quadratic congruence that has received some attention is when $a' = a = 1$, $c = 0$, and m is a power of 2; although this particular generator turns out to be a close relative of the midsquare method (see Sec. 6.1), it has better statistical properties. Since Z_i still depends only on Z_{i-1} (and not on earlier Z_j's), and since $0 \leq Z_i < m - 1$, the period of quadratic congruential generators is at most m, as for LCGs.

A different generalization of LCGs is to maintain linearity but to use earlier Z_j's; this gives rise to generators defined by

$$g(Z_{i-1}, Z_{i-2}, \ldots) = a_1 Z_{i-1} + a_2 Z_{i-2} + \cdots + a_q Z_{i-q} \qquad (6.4)$$

where $a_1, a_2, \ldots, a_q$ are constants. Huge periods (as high as $m^q - 1$) then become possible if the parameters are chosen properly. Most attention to generators with g of the form (6.4) used in (6.3) has focused on g's defined as $Z_{i-1} + Z_{i-q}$, which includes the old Fibonacci generator

$$Z_i = (Z_{i-1} + Z_{i-2})(\bmod\ m)$$

(The Fibonacci generator tends to have a period in excess of m but is not acceptable from a statistical standpoint.)

6.3.2 Composite Generators

Several researchers have developed methods which take two *separate* generators (usually two different LCGs) and combine them in some way to generate the final random numbers. It is hoped that this composite generator will exhibit better statistical behavior than either of the simple generators composing it. The price paid, of course, is that the cost of obtaining each U_i is more than that of using one of the simple generators alone. We shall discuss two different kinds of composite generators.

The best known of the composite generators uses the second LCG to *shuffle* the output from the first LCG; it was developed by MacLaren and Marsaglia [21] and extended by Marsaglia and Bray [24]. Initially, a vector $\mathbf{V} = (V_1, V_2, \ldots, V_k)$ is filled (sequentially) with the first k U_i's from the first LCG ($k = 128$ was originally suggested). Then the second LCG is used to generate a random integer I distributed uniformly on the integers $1, 2, \ldots, k$ (see Sec. 7.4.2), and V_I is returned as the first $U(0, 1)$ random number; the first LCG then replaces this Ith location in $\mathbf{V}$ with its next U_i, and the second LCG randomly chooses the next returned random number from this updated $\mathbf{V}$, etc. Shuffling has a natural intuitive appeal, especially since we would expect it to break up any autocorrelation and greatly extend the period. Indeed, MacLaren and Marsaglia were able to obtain a shuffling generator with very good statistical behavior even though the two individual LCGs used were quite poor. In a recent evaluation of shuffling, Nance and Overstreet [25] confirm that shuffling one bad LCG by another bad LCG can result in a good composite generator, e.g., by extending the period when used on computers with short word lengths, but that little is accomplished by shuffling a good LCG; in addition, they found that a vector of length $k = 2$ works as well as much larger vectors.

An altogether different way of combining two LCGs was developed and tested by Westlake [33]. Let $Z_i^{(1)}$ and $Z_i^{(2)}$ be the values of Z_i produced by the first and second LCGs, respectively. First, the bits of $Z_i^{(1)}$ are used to "rotate circularly" the bits of $Z_i^{(2)}$, resulting in another integer $Z_i^{(3)}$ between 0 and $m - 1$ (see [33] for details). Next, the corresponding bits of $Z_i^{(1)}$ and $Z_i^{(3)}$ are added modulo 2 (equivalent to the "exclusive or" instruction discussed in the next section) to obtain $Z_i^{(4)}$, and the returned random number is then $U_i = Z_i^{(4)}/m$. Westlake tested this arithmetic composition using two rather poor multiplicative LCGs and noted good statistical performance; we are not aware of any studies examining whether Westlake's method appreciably improves good LCGs.

6.3.3 Tausworthe Generators

Several very interesting and promising kinds of generators have been developed on the basis of a paper by Tausworthe [29]. These generators, which are related to cryptographic methods, operate directly with bits to form random numbers.

Define a sequence $b_1, b_2, \ldots$ of binary digits by the recurrence

$$b_i = (c_1 b_{i-1} + c_2 b_{i-2} + \cdots + c_q b_{i-q})(\mathrm{mod}\ 2) \tag{6.5}$$

where $c_1, c_2, \ldots, c_q$ are constants which are either 0 or 1. Note the similarity of the recurrence for b_i with (6.4); the maximum period here is $2^q - 1$. In essentially all applications of Tausworthe generators, only two of the c_j coefficients are nonzero, in which case (6.5) becomes

$$b_i = (b_{i-r} + b_{i-q})(\mathrm{mod}\ 2) \tag{6.6}$$

for integers r and q satisfying $0 < r < q$. Execution of (6.6) is expedited by noting that addition modulo 2 is equivalent to the *exclusive or* instruction on bits; that is, (6.6) can be expressed as

$$b_i = \begin{cases} 0 & \text{if } b_{i-r} = b_{i-q} \\ 1 & \text{if } b_{i-r} \neq b_{i-q} \end{cases}$$

To initialize the $\{b_i\}$ sequence, the first q b_i's must be specified somehow; this is akin to specifying the seed Z_0 for LCGs.

Example 6.4 Let $r = 3$ and $q = 5$ in (6.6), and let $b_1 = b_2 = \cdots = b_5 = 1$. (This example is given by Lewis and Payne [20].) Thus, for $i \geq 6$, b_i is the "exclusive or" of b_{i-3} with b_{i-5}. The first 42 b_i's are then

111110001101110101000010010110011111000110

Note that the period (of the bits) is $31 = 2^q - 1$.

With this sequence $\{b_i\}$ so defined, the question arises: How should it be transformed into U(0, 1) random numbers? One natural possibility is to string together l consecutive b_i's to form an l-bit binary integer between 0 and $2^l - 1$, which is then divided by 2^l. (In Example 6.4, choosing $l = 4$ results in the sequence of random numbers 15/16, 8/16, 13/16, 13/16, 4/16, 2/16, 5/16, 9/16, 15/16, 1/16, ...) However, l would have to be no more than the word size of the computer. There is disagreement over how well this works, so another possibility would be to use l consecutive bits for the first integer, then *skip* some number of the following b_i's, then use the next *l* bits for the second integer, etc. A much more sophisticated bit-selection algorithm was given in [20] and further studied by Bright and Enison [2]. The important question of how *r* and *q* are specified was also treated by Tausworthe [29], Tootill, Robinson, and Adams [31], and Tootill, Robinson, and Eagle [32]. These papers also discuss various tests of several particular Tausworthe generators.

Tausworthe generators offer a number of advantages over LCGs. They are essentially independent of the computer used and its word size, and one can readily obtain periods of unthinkable length (such as $2^{521} - 1 > 10^{156}$, or more) even on 16-bit minicomputers. Furthermore, they have appealing theoretical properties (see [29, 32]). However, it is safe to say that LCGs are much better understood and that empirical evidence on certain Tausworthe generators is not conclusive (see, for example, [31]). We agree with Fishman [6] that more work on Tausworthe generators would be welcomed. Finally, we note that a Tausworthe generator is used in GPSS/H (see Chap. 3).

6.4 TESTING RANDOM-NUMBER GENERATORS

As we have seen in Secs. 6.1 to 6.3, all random-number generators currently used in computer simulation are actually completely deterministic. Thus, we can only hope that the U_i's generated *appear* as if they *were* IID U(0, 1) random variables. In this section we discuss several tests to which a random-number generator can be subjected to ascertain how well the generated U_i's do (or can) resemble values of true IID U(0, 1) random variables.

Most computer installations have a "canned" random-number generator as part of the available software. Before such a generator is actually used in a simulation, we strongly recommend that one identify exactly what kind of generator it is and what its numerical parameters are. Unless a generator is one of the "good" ones identified (and tested) somewhere in the literature (or is one of the specific LCGs recommended in Sec. 6.2), the responsible simulator should subject it (at least) to the empirical tests discussed below.

There are two quite different kinds of tests, which we discuss separately in Secs. 6.4.1 and 6.4.2. *Empirical* tests are the usual kinds of statistical tests and are based on the actual U_i's produced by a generator. *Theoretical* tests are not tests in the statistical sense but use the numerical parameters of a generator to assess it in a global manner without actually generating any U_i's at all.

6.4.1 Empirical Tests

Perhaps the most direct way to test a generator is to *use* it to generate some U_i's, which are then examined statistically to see how closely they resemble IID U(0, 1) random variables. We discuss three such empirical tests; several others are treated in [15, 6].

The first test is designed to check whether the U_i's appear to be uniformly distributed between 0 and 1, and it is a special case of a test we have seen before (in Chap. 5), the chi-square test with all parameters known. We divide $[0, 1]$ into k subintervals of equal length and generate $U_1, U_2, \ldots, U_n$. (As a general rule, k should be at least 100 here, and n/k should be at least 5.) For $j = 1, 2, \ldots, k$, let f_j be the number of the U_i's that are in the jth subinterval, and let

$$\chi^2 = \frac{k}{n} \sum_{j=1}^{k} \left(f_j - \frac{n}{k} \right)^2$$

Then for large n, χ^2 will approximately have a chi-square distribution with $k - 1$ df under the null hypothesis that the U_i's are IID $U(0, 1)$ random variables. Thus, we reject this hypothesis at level α if $\chi^2 > \chi^2_{k-1,1-\alpha}$, where $\chi^2_{k-1,1-\alpha}$ is the upper $1 - \alpha$ critical point of the chi-square distribution with $k - 1$ df. [For the large values of k likely to be encountered here, we can use the approximation

$$\chi^2_{k-1,1-\alpha} \approx (k - 1) \left\{ 1 - \frac{2}{9(k-1)} + z_{1-\alpha} \left[\frac{2}{9(k-1)} \right]^{1/2} \right\}^3$$

where $z_{1-\alpha}$ is the upper $1 - \alpha$ critical point of the N(0, 1) distribution.]

Example 6.5 We applied the chi-square test of uniformity to the PMMLCG $Z_i = (7^5 Z_{i-1})(\text{mod } 2^{31} - 1)$ with $Z_0 = 12{,}345{,}678$ and used the FORTRAN function RAND in Fig. 6.1. We took $k = 2^{12} = 4096$ (so that the most significant 12 bits of the U_i's are being examined) and let $n = 2^{16} = 65{,}536$. (These values for Z_0, k, and n were used in [19] for testing this generator.) We obtained $\chi^2 = 4001.625$ and using the above approximation for the critical point, $\chi^2_{4095,0.90} \approx 4211.402$, so that we fail to reject the null hypothesis at the 0.10 level. Therefore, *these particular* 65,536 U_i's produced by this generator do not behave in a way which is significantly different (at the 0.10 level, at least) from what would be expected from truly IID $U(0, 1)$ random variables, so far as this chi-square test can ascertain.

Our second empirical test, the *serial test,* is really just a generalization of the chi-square test to higher dimensions. If the U_i's were really IID $U(0, 1)$ random variables, the nonoverlapping d-tuples

$$\mathbf{U}_1 = (U_1, U_2, \ldots, U_d)$$

$$\mathbf{U}_2 = (U_{d+1}, U_{d+2}, \ldots, U_{2d})$$

should be IID random *vectors* distributed uniformly on the d-dimensional unit hypercube $[0, 1]^d$. Divide $[0, 1]$ into k subintervals of equal size and generate $\mathbf{U}_1$, $\mathbf{U}_2, \ldots, \mathbf{U}_n$ (requiring nd U_i's). Let $f_{j_1 j_2 \cdots j_d}$ be the number of $\mathbf{U}_i$'s having first component in subinterval j_1 and second component in subinterval j_2, etc. (It is easier to tally the $f_{j_1 j_2 \cdots j_d}$'s than might be expected; see Prob. 6.7.) If we let

$$\chi^2(d) = \frac{k^d}{n} \sum_{j_1=1}^{k} \sum_{j_2=1}^{k} \cdots \sum_{j_d=1}^{k} \left(f_{j_1 j_2 \cdots j_d} - \frac{n}{k^d} \right)^2$$

then $\chi^2(d)$ will approximately have a chi-square distribution with $k^d - 1$ df. (Again, it is advisable to have $n/k^d \geq 5$.) The test for d-dimensional uniformity is carried out exactly as for the one-dimensional chi-square test above.

Example 6.6 For $d = 2$, we tested the null hypothesis that the pairs (U_1, U_2), (U_3, U_4), ... , (U_{2n-1}, U_{2n}) are IID random vectors distributed uniformly over the unit square. Again we used the function RAND in Fig. 6.1 and generated $n = 65,536$ pairs of U_i's, with an initial seed 137,751,267. (This was the final Z_i obtained in Example 6.5, so that we simply continued the Z_i stream from where it left off earlier.) We took $k = 64$, so that the degrees of freedom were again $4095 = k^2 - 1$. The value of $\chi^2(2)$ was 3981.75, which indicates acceptable uniformity in two dimensions. For $d = 3$, we continued through the same random-number stream and again took $n = 65,536$ (thus requiring 196,608 additional U_i's) but let $k = 16$ this time, so that the degrees of freedom were $k^3 - 1 = 4095$, again. $\chi^2(3)$ was 3994.375, which indicates acceptable uniformity in three dimensions.

Why should we care about this kind of uniformity in *higher* dimensions? If the individual U_i's are correlated, the distribution of the d-vectors $\mathbf{U}_i$ will deviate from d-dimensional uniformity; thus, the serial test provides an indirect check on the assumption that the individual U_i's are independent. For example, if adjacent U_i's tend to be positively correlated, the pairs (U_i, U_{i+1}) will tend to cluster around the southwest-northeast diagonal in the unit square and $\chi^2(2)$ should pick this up. Finally, it should be apparent that the serial test for $d > 3$ would be quite costly because of the large storage requirements needed to tally the k^d values of $f_{j_1 j_2 \cdots j_d}$. (Choosing $k = 16$ in Example 6.6 when $d = 3$ is probably not a sufficiently fine division of $[0, 1]$.)

The final empirical test we consider, the *runs* (or *runs-up*) *test,* is a more direct test of the independence assumption. (In fact, it is a test of independence only; i.e., we are not testing for uniformity in particular.) We examine the U_i sequence (or, equivalently the Z_i sequence) for unbroken subsequences of maximal length within which the U_i's monotonically increase; such a subsequence is called a *run up*. For example, consider the following sequence $U_1, U_2, \ldots, U_{10}$:

$$0.855, \ 0.108, \ 0.226, \ 0.032, \ 0.132, \ 0.055, \ 0.545, \ 0.642, \ 0.870, \ 0.104$$

(These were generated by RAND with $Z_0 = 853,506,241$.) The sequence starts with a run up of length 1 (0.855), followed by a run up of length 2 (0.108, 0.226), then another run up of length 2 (0.032, 0.132), then a run up of length 4 (0.055, 0.545, 0.642, 0.870), and finally another run up of length 1 (0.104). From a sequence of n U_i's, we count the number of runs up of length 1, 2, 3, 4, 5, and ≥ 6 and define

$$r_i = \begin{cases} \text{number of runs up of length } i & \text{for } i = 1, 2, \ldots, 5 \\ \text{number of runs up of length} \geq 6 & \text{for } i = 6 \end{cases}$$

(See Prob. 6.8 for an algorithm to tally the r_i's. For the 10 U_i's above, $r_1 = 2$, $r_2 = 2$, $r_3 = 0$, $r_4 = 1$, $r_5 = 0$, and $r_6 = 0$.) The test statistic is then

$$R = \frac{1}{n} \sum_{i=1}^{6} \sum_{j=1}^{6} a_{ij}(r_i - nb_i)(r_j - nb_j)$$

where a_{ij} is the (i, j)th element of the matrix

$$\begin{bmatrix} 4{,}529.4 & 9{,}044.9 & 13{,}568 & 18{,}091 & 22{,}615 & 27{,}892 \\ 9{,}044.9 & 18{,}097 & 27{,}139 & 36{,}187 & 45{,}234 & 55{,}789 \\ 13{,}568 & 27{,}139 & 40{,}721 & 54{,}281 & 67{,}852 & 83{,}685 \\ 18{,}091 & 36{,}187 & 54{,}281 & 72{,}414 & 90{,}470 & 111{,}580 \\ 22{,}615 & 45{,}234 & 67{,}852 & 90{,}470 & 113{,}262 & 139{,}476 \\ 27{,}892 & 55{,}789 & 83{,}685 & 111{,}580 & 139{,}476 & 172{,}860 \end{bmatrix}$$

and the b_i's are given by

$$(b_1, b_2, \ldots, b_6) = (\tfrac{1}{6}, \tfrac{5}{24}, \tfrac{11}{120}, \tfrac{19}{720}, \tfrac{29}{5040}, \tfrac{1}{840})\dagger$$

(See [15] for the derivation of these constants. The a_{ij}'s given above are accurate to five significant digits.) For large n (Knuth recommends $n \geq 4000$), R will approximately have a chi-square distribution with 6 df, under the null hypothesis that the U_i's are IID random variables.

> **Example 6.7** We subjected the generator in RAND to the runs-up test with $n = 65{,}536$ and $Z_0 = 146{,}067{,}020$ (the seed at the end of generation for Example 6.6). We obtained
>
> $$(r_1, r_2, \ldots, r_6) = (10{,}864, 13{,}695, 5884, 1778, 401, 84)$$
>
> which led to $R = 8.206$. Since $\chi^2_{6,0.90} = 10.6$, we do not reject (at the 0.10 level) the null hypothesis that the U_i's are IID.

The runs-up test can be reversed in the obvious manner to obtain a runs-down test; the a_{ij} and b_i constants are the same. There are several other kinds of runs tests, such as counting runs up or down in the same sequence, or simply counting the number of runs without regard to their length; we refer the reader to Conover [3] or Fishman [6], for example. Since runs tests look solely for independence (and not specifically for uniformity), it would probably be a good idea to apply a runs test *before* performing the chi-square or serial tests, since the last two tests implicitly assume independence. Knuth feels that the runs test is more powerful than the chi-square and serial tests, in the sense that many generators have passed the chi-square and serial tests but fail the runs tests; his explanation is that LCGs with small multipliers and increments tend to generate longer runs than would be expected for truly IID U_i's.

As mentioned above, these are just three of many possible empirical tests. For example, the Kolmogorov-Smirnov test discussed in Chap. 5 (for the case with all parameters known) could be applied instead of the chi-square test for one-dimensional uniformity. In general, we feel that as many empirical tests as are practicable should be performed. One potential disadvantage of empirical tests is that they are only *local*; i.e., only that segment of a cycle (for LCGs, for example) which was actually used to generate the U_i's for the test is examined, so we cannot say anything about how the generator might perform in other segments of the cycle. On the other

---

†Knuth, *The Art of Computer Programming,* vol. 2, 1969, Addison-Wesley Publishing Company, Inc., chap. 3, page 60. Reprinted with permission.

hand, this local nature of empirical tests can be advantageous, since it might allow us to examine the actual random numbers that will be used later in a simulation. (Often we can calculate ahead of time how many random numbers will be used in a simulation, or at least get a conservative estimate, by analyzing the model's operation and the techniques used for generating the necessary random variables.) Then this entire random-number stream can be tested empirically, one would hope without excessive cost. (The CPU time required on our computer to generate all the 458,752 random numbers and perform all of the tests in Examples 6.5 to 6.7 was 22 seconds; the total job charge was 58 cents.) A more global empirical test could be performed by replicating an entire test several times and statistically comparing the test statistics against the distribution under the null hypothesis; Fishman [6] suggests this approach. For example, the runs-up test of Example 6.7 could be done, say, 100 times using 100 separate random-number streams from the same generator, each of length 65,536. This would result in 100 independent values for R, which could then be compared with the chi-square distribution with 6 df using, for example, the K-S test with all parameters known. Fishman's approach could be used to identify "bad" segments within a cycle of a LCG; this was done for the generator $Z_i = (630,360,016 Z_{i-1})(\text{mod } 2^{31} - 1)$ used in SIMSCRIPT II.5, and a bad segment was indeed discovered and eliminated (see [5, p. 183]).

*6.4.2 Theoretical Tests†

We now briefly discuss two theoretical tests for LCGs. Since these tests are quite sophisticated and mathematically complex, we shall describe them only qualitatively; for detailed accounts, see [6, 15]. As mentioned earlier, theoretical tests do not require us to generate any U_i's at all but are a priori; i.e., they indicate how well a LCG *can* perform by looking at the constants m, a, and c. Theoretical tests also differ from empirical tests in that they are *global;* i.e., a LCG's behavior over its *entire* cycle is examined. As we indicated in Sec. 6.4.1, it is debatable whether local or global tests are preferable; global tests have a natural appeal but do not generally indicate how well a specific segment of a cycle will behave.

Both theoretical tests are based on the rather upsetting observation by Marsaglia [22] that "random numbers fall mainly in the planes." That is, if $U_1, U_2, \ldots$ is a sequence of random numbers generated by a LCG, the d-tuples $(U_1, U_2, \ldots, U_d)$, $(U_2, U_3, \ldots, U_{d+1})$, $\ldots$ will all fall in a relatively small number of $(d-1)$-dimensional parallel hyperplanes passing through the d-dimensional unit hypercube $[0, 1]^d$. For example, if $d = 2$, the pairs (U_1, U_2), (U_2, U_3), $\ldots$ will be arranged in a "crystalline" or "lattice" fashion along several different families of parallel lines going through the unit square. (The lines within a family are parallel to each other, but lines from different families are not parallel.) Such regularity in the U_i's is certainly not very "random," and our two theoretical tests try to quantify the effect of this regularity.

---

†The meaning of starred sections is explained in the Preface.

Both the *spectral test* (developed originally by Coveyou and MacPherson [4]) and the *lattice test* (proposed independently by Beyer, Roof, and Williamson [1] and by Marsaglia [23]) are aimed at identifying how densely the d-tuples of U_i's *can* fill up $[0, 1]^d$ by looking at the particular crystalline pattern of d-tuples generated by the LCG of interest. If one or both of these tests indicates that there are large gaps in $[0, 1]^d$ which cannot contain any d-tuples, we have evidence that the LCG being tested will exhibit poor behavior, at least in d dimensions. Usually the spectral and lattice tests are applied separately for each dimension from 2 to as high as 10. As exemplified in [4] and by Hoaglin [9], a given LCG might pass these tests nicely in some dimensions but fail them miserably in others. Thus, one should interpret the results of these theoretical tests in the light of the proposed use of an LCG.

It seems that the information obtained from both of these theoretical tests might tend to be similar. In applying both tests to some 50 LCGs, Hoaglin [9] found that this was often the case, although it would be safe to say that there is not complete agreement on the relative merits of the spectral and lattice tests.

6.4.3 Some General Observations on Testing

The number, variety, and range of complexity of tests for random-number generators is truly bewildering. To make matters worse, there has been (and probably always will be) considerable controversy over which tests are best, whether theoretical tests are really more definitive than empirical tests, and so on. Indeed, no amount of testing can ever absolutely convince everyone that some particular generator is absolutely "the best." One piece of advice that is often offered, however, is that a random-number generator should be tested in a way consistent with its intended use. This would entail, for example, examining the behavior of pairs of U_i's (perhaps with the serial test) if random numbers are naturally used in pairs in the simulation itself. In a broader sense, this advice would imply that one should be more careful in choosing and testing a random-number generator if the simulation in which it will be used is very costly, requires high-precision results, or is a particularly critical component of a larger study.

PROBLEMS

6.1 For the LCG of Example 6.2, find Z_{500} using only pencil and paper.

6.2 For the following multiplicative LCGs, compute Z_i for enough values of $i \geq 1$ to cover an entire cycle:

(*a*) $Z_i = (11 Z_{i-1})(\text{mod } 16)$, $Z_0 = 1$
(*b*) $Z_i = (11 Z_{i-1})(\text{mod } 16)$, $Z_0 = 2$
(*c*) $Z_i = (2 Z_{i-1})(\text{mod } 13)$, $Z_0 = 1$
(*d*) $Z_i = (3 Z_{i-1})(\text{mod } 13)$, $Z_0 = 1$

Note that (*a*) and (*b*) have m of the form 2^b; (*c*) is a PMMLCG, for which $a = 2$ is a primitive element modulo $m = 13$.

6.3 Without actually computing any Z_i's, determine which of the following mixed LCGs have full period:

    (a) $Z_i = (13Z_{i-1} + 13)(\bmod\ 16)$
    (b) $Z_i = (12Z_{i-1} + 13)(\bmod\ 16)$
    (c) $Z_i = (13Z_{i-1} + 12)(\bmod\ 16)$
    (d) $Z_i = (Z_{i-1} + 12)(\bmod\ 13)$

6.4 For the four mixed LCGs in Prob. 6.3, compute Z_i for enough values of $i \geq 1$ to cover an entire cycle; let $Z_0 = 1$ in each case. Comment on the results.

6.5 Implement the PMMLCG $Z_i = (7^5 Z_{i-1})(\bmod\ 2^{31} - 1)$ on your computer using the FORTRAN function RAND in Fig. 6.1 (if your word size is at least 32 bits) or DRAND in Fig. 6.2 (if your word size is less than 32 bits but at least 16 bits). Check your program by setting $Z_0 = 1$, that is, set IX to 1 before the first call, and printing out Z_{1000} (the returned value of IX after the 1000th call), which should be 522,329,230.

6.6 Use the multiplicative LCG in part (a) of Prob. 6.2 to shuffle the output from the mixed LCG in part (d) of Prob. 6.3, using a vector **V** of length 2. Let the seed for both LCGs be 1 and list the first 100 values of **V**, I, and V_I. Identify the period and comment generally on the results.

6.7 For the chi-square test of uniformity, verify the following algorithm for computing $f_1, f_2, \ldots, f_k$ from the generated numbers $U_1, U_2, \ldots, U_n$:

  1. Set $f_j = 0$ for $j = 1, 2, \ldots, k$ and let $i = 0$.
  2. Replace i by $i + 1$. If $i > n$, stop. Otherwise, proceed to step 3.
  3. Generate U_i, let $J = \lceil kU_i \rceil$, add 1 to f_J, and return to step 2.

(For a real number z, $\lceil z \rceil$ denotes the smallest integer that is greater than or equal to z.) Generalize this algorithm to compute the k^d values of $f_{j_1 j_2 \cdots j_d}$ for the d-dimensional serial test for $d = 2$ and $d = 3$.

6.8 Show that the following algorithm correctly computes $r_1, r_2, \ldots, r_6$ for the runs-up test from the generated numbers $U_1, U_2, \ldots, U_n$:

  1. Set $r_j = 0$ for $j = 1, 2, \ldots, 6$ and let $i = 1$.
  2. Generate U_1, set $A = U_1$, and let $J = 1$.
  3. Replace i by $i + 1$. If $i > n$, go to step 9. Otherwise, proceed to step 4.
  4. Generate U_i and set $B = U_i$.
  5. If $A < B$, go to step 8. Otherwise, proceed to step 6.
  6. If $J > 6$, set $J = 6$.
  7. Add 1 to r_J, reset J to 1, replace A by B, and return to step 3.
  8. Add 1 to J, replace A by B, and return to step 3.
  9. If $J > 6$, set $J = 6$.
 10. Add 1 to r_J, and stop.

6.9 Subject the canned random-number generator on your computer to the chi-square test, two- and three-dimensional serial tests, and the runs-up test. Use the same values for n, k, and α that were used in Examples 6.5 to 6.7. (If your generator does not pass these tests, we suggest that you exercise caution in using it until you can obtain more information on it, either from the literature or from your own further testing.)

6.10 A general approach to testing a random-number generator empirically is to use it to simulate a *simple* stochastic model and obtain estimates of *known* parameters; a standard statistical test is then used to compare the estimate(s) against the known parameter(s). For example, we know that in throwing two fair dice independently, the sum of the two scores will be 2, 3, $\ldots$, 12 with respective probabilities $\frac{1}{36}, \frac{1}{18}, \frac{1}{12}, \frac{1}{9}, \frac{5}{36}, \frac{1}{6}, \frac{5}{36}, \frac{1}{9}, \frac{1}{12}, \frac{1}{18}$, and $\frac{1}{36}$. Simulate 1000 independent throws of a pair of independent fair dice and compare the observed proportion of 1s, 2s, $\ldots$, 12s with the known probabilities, using an appropriate test from Chap. 5. Use the canned generator on your computer or the generators in Fig. 6.1 or 6.2.

6.11 For the LCGs of Example 6.2 and part (d) of Prob. 6.3, plot the pairs $(U_1, U_2), (U_2, U_3), \ldots$ and observe the lattice structures obtained. Note that both LCGs have full period.

REFERENCES

1. Beyer, W. A., R. B. Roof, and D. Williamson: The Lattice Structure of Multiplicative Congruential Pseudo-Random Vectors, *Math. Comput.*, **25:** 345–363 (1971).
2. Bright, H. S., and R. L. Enison: Quasi-Random Number Sequences from a Long-Period TLP Generator with Remarks on Application to Cryptography, *Comp. Surveys*, **11:** 357–370 (1979).
3. Conover, W. J.: *Practical Nonparametric Statistics*, Wiley, New York, 1971.
4. Coveyou, R. R., and R. D. MacPherson: Fourier Analysis of Uniform Random Number Generators, *J. Ass. Comput. Mach.*, **14:** 100–119 (1967).
5. Fishman, G. S.: *Concepts and Methods in Discrete Event Digital Simulation*, Wiley, New York, 1973.
6. Fishman, G. S.: *Principles of Discrete Event Simulation*, Wiley, New York, 1978.
7. Fishman, G. S., and L. R. Moore: A Statistical Evaluation of Multiplicative Congruential Generators with Modulus $2^{31} - 1$, *Univ. N.C. Curric. Oper. Res. Systems Anal. Tech. Rep.* 78-11, Chapel Hill, N.C., 1978.
8. Greenberger, M.: Method in Randomness, *Commun. Ass. Comput. Mach.*, **8:** 177–179 (1965).
9. Hoaglin, D. C.: Theoretical Properties of Congruential Random-Number Generators: An Empirical View, *Harvard Univ. Dept. Statist. Mem.* NS-340, 1976.
10. Hull, T. E., and A. R. Dobell: Random Number Generators, *SIAM Rev.*, **4:** 230–254 (1962).
11. Hutchinson, D. W.: A New Uniform Pseudorandom Number Generator, *Commun. Ass. Comput. Mach.*, **9:** 432–433 (1966).
12. IBM Corporation: Subroutine GGL, pp. 79–82 in *IBM Subroutine Library—Mathematics, User's Guide*, White Plains, N.Y., 1974.
13. International Mathematical and Statistical Libraries, Inc.: *IMSL Library Reference Manual*, vol. 2, IMSL, Inc., Houston, Tex., 1979.
14. Kendall, M. G., and B. Babington-Smith: Randomness and Random Sampling Numbers, *J. R. Statist. Soc.*, **101A:** 147–166 (1938).
15. Knuth, D. E.: *The Art of Computer Programming*, vol. 2, Addison-Wesley, Reading, Mass., 1969.
16. Kobayashi, H.: *Modeling and Analysis: An Introduction to System Performance Evaluation Methodology*, Addison-Wesley, Reading, Mass., 1978.
17. Learmonth, G. P., and P. A. W. Lewis: Naval Postgraduate School Random Number Generator Package LLRANDOM, Naval Postgraduate School, Monterey, Calif., 1973.
18. Lehmer, D. H.: Mathematical Methods in Large-Scale Computing Units, *Ann. Comput. Lab.* [*Harvard Univ.*], **26:** 141–146 (1951).
19. Lewis, P. A. W., A. S. Goodman, and J. M. Miller: A Pseudo-Random Number Generator for the System/360, *IBM Syst. J.*, **8:** 136–146 (1969).
20. Lewis, T. G., and W. H. Payne: Generalized Feedback Shift Register Pseudorandom Number Algorithm, *J. Ass. Comput. Mach.*, **20:** 456–468 (1973).
21. MacLaren, M. D., and G. Marsaglia: Uniform Random Number Generators, *J. Ass. Comput. Mach.*, **12:** 83–89 (1965).
22. Marsaglia, G.: Random Numbers Fall Mainly in the Planes, *Natl. Acad. Sci. Proc.*, **61:** 25–28 (1968).
23. Marsaglia, G: The Structure of Linear Congruential Sequences, pp. 249–285 in S. K. Zaremba (ed.), *Applications of Number Theory to Numerical Analysis*, Academic, New York, 1972.
24. Marsaglia, G., and T. A. Bray: One-Line Random Number Generators and Their Use in Combinations, *Commun. Ass. Comput. Mach.*, **11:** 757–759 (1968).
25. Nance, R. E., and C. Overstreet, Jr.: Some Experimental Observations on the Behavior of Composite Random Number Generators, *Oper. Res.*, **26:** 915–935 (1978).
26. Payne, W. H., J. R. Rabung, and T. P. Bogyo: Coding the Lehmer Pseudorandom Number Generator, *Commun. Ass. Comput. Mach.*, **12:** 85–86 (1969).
27. Rand Corporation: *A Million Random Digits with 100,000 Normal Deviates*, Free Press, Glencoe, Ill., 1955.

28. Schrage, L.: A More Portable Fortran Random Number Generator, *ACM Trans. Math. Software,* **5:** 132–138 (1979).

29. Tausworthe, R. C.: Random Numbers Generated by Linear Recurrence Modulo Two, *Math. Comput.,* **19:** 201–209 (1965).

30. Thomson, W. E.: ERNIE–A Mathematical and Statistical Analysis, *J. R. Statist. Soc.,* **122A:** 301–324 (1959).

31. Tootill, J. P. R., W. D. Robinson, and A. G. Adams: The Runs Up-and-Down Performance of Tausworthe Pseudo-Random Number Generators, *J. Ass. Comput. Mach.,* **18:** 381–399 (1971).

32. Tootill, J. P. R., W. D. Robinson, and D. J. Eagle: An Asymptotically Random Tausworthe Sequence, *J. Ass. Comput. Mach.,* **20:** 469–481 (1973).

33. Westlake, W. J.: A Uniform Random Number Generator Based on the Combination of Two Congruential Generators, *J. Ass. Comput. Mach.,* **14:** 337–340 (1967).

SEVEN

GENERATING RANDOM VARIABLES

7.1 INTRODUCTION

A simulation having any random aspects at all must involve sampling, or *generating* random variables from one or more distributions. These distributions often are specified as a result of fitting some appropriate distributional form, e.g., exponential, gamma, or Poisson, to observed data, as discussed in Chap. 5. In this chapter we assume that a distribution has already been specified somehow (including the values of the parameters), and we address the issue of how we can generate random variables with this distribution in order to run the simulation model. For example, the queueing-type models discussed in Chaps. 1 and 2 required generation of interarrival and service times in order to drive the simulation through time, and the inventory model of Chap. 1 needed randomly generated demand sizes at the times when a demand occurred.

As we shall see in this chapter, the basic ingredient needed for *every* method of generating random variables from *any* distribution or random process is a source of IID U(0, 1) random variables. For this reason, it is very important that a statistically reliable U(0, 1) random-number generator be available. Most computer installations and simulation languages have a convenient random-number generator, but some of them (especially the older ones) do not perform adequately (see Chap. 6). Without an acceptable random-number generator it is impossible to generate random variables correctly from any distribution. In the remainder of this chapter, we therefore assume that a good source of random numbers is available.

There are usually several alternative algorithms that can be used for generating random variables from a given distribution, and a number of factors should be considered when choosing which algorithm to use in a particular simulation study.

Unfortunately, these different factors often are in conflict with each other, so that the simulator's judgment of which algorithm to use must involve a number of trade-offs. All we can do here is raise some of the pertinent issues.

The first issue is that of *exactness*. We feel that, if possible, one should use an algorithm which results in random variables with exactly the desired distribution, within the unavoidable external limitations of machine accuracy and exactness of the U(0, 1) random-number generator. For most of the commonly used distributions, efficient and exact algorithms are now available, obviating the need to consider any older, approximate methods. (Many of these approximations, e.g., the well-known technique of obtaining a "normal" random variable as 6 less than the average of 12 U(0, 1) random variables, are based on the central limit theorem.) On the other hand, the practitioner may argue that a specified distribution is really only an approximation to reality anyway, so that an approximate generation method should suffice; since this depends on the situation and is often difficult to quantify, we still would prefer to use an exact method.

Given that we have a choice, then, of alternative exact algorithms, we would like to use one which is *efficient,* in terms of both storage space and execution time. Some algorithms require *storage* of a large number of constants or of large tables, which could prove troublesome. As for execution time, there are really two factors. Obviously, we hope that we can accomplish the generation of each random variable in a small amount of time; this is called the *marginal execution time.* Second, some algorithms have to do some initial computing to specify constants or tables that depend on the particular distribution and parameters; the time required to do this is called the *setup time.* In most simulations, we shall be generating a large number of random variables from a given distribution, so that marginal execution time is likely to be more important than setup time. If the parameters of a distribution change often or randomly during the course of the simulation, however, setup time could become an important consideration.

A somewhat subjective issue in choosing an algorithm is its overall *complexity,* including conceptual as well as implementational factors. One must ask whether the potential gain in efficiency which might be experienced by using a more complicated algorithm is worth the extra effort to understand and implement it. This issue should be considered relative to the purpose in implementing a method for random-variable generation; a more efficient but more complex algorithm might be appropriate for use as permanent software but not for a "one-time" simulation model.

Finally, there are a few issues of a more technical nature. Some algorithms rely on a source of random variables from distributions other than U(0, 1), which is undesirable, other things being equal. Another technical issue is that a given algorithm may be efficient for some parameter values but costly for others. We would like to have algorithms that are efficient for all parameter values (this is sometimes called *robustness* of the algorithm). One last technical point is relevant if we want to use certain kinds of variance-reduction techniques in order to obtain better (less variable) estimates (see Chap. 11 and also Chaps. 9 and 12). Two commonly used variance-reduction techniques (common random numbers and antithetic variates) require synchronization of the basic U(0, 1) input random variables used in the simulation of the system(s) under study, and this synchronization is more easily accomplished for certain types of random-variable generation algorithms. In particular, the general inverse-transform approach can be very helpful in facilitating the desired synchronization and variance reduction; Sec. 7.2.1 treats this point more precisely.

There is a fairly large literature on the subject of generating random variables, and we have organized our treatment as follows. In Sec. 7.2 we survey the most important general approaches used for generating random variables, including examples and discussions of the relative merits of the various approaches. Sections 7.3 and 7.4 then discuss algorithms for generating random variables from particular continuous and discrete distributions that have been useful in simulation. Finally, Secs. 7.5 and 7.6 discuss two more specialized topics, generating correlated random variables and generating realizations of both stationary and nonstationary arrival processes.

On a first reading, we suggest that only Sec. 7.2 be studied in detail. The remainder of the chapter can be viewed as a reference to be consulted for particular problems in generating random variables.

7.2 GENERAL APPROACHES TO GENERATING RANDOM VARIABLES

There are many techniques for generating random variables, and the particular algorithm used must, of course, depend on the distribution from which we wish to generate; however, nearly all these techniques can be classified according to their theoretical basis. In this section we discuss these general approaches.

7.2.1 Inverse Transform

Suppose that we wish to generate a random variable X which is continuous (see Sec. 4.2) and has distribution function F which is continuous and strictly increasing when $0 < F(x) < 1$. [This means that if $x_1 < x_2$ and $0 < F(x_1) \leq F(x_2) < 1$, then in fact $F(x_1) < F(x_2)$.] Let F^{-1} denote the inverse of the function F. Then an algorithm for generating a random variable X having distribution function F is as follows (recall that $\sim$ is read "is distributed as"):

1. Generate $U \sim U(0, 1)$.
2. Set $X = F^{-1}(U)$ and return.

Note that $F^{-1}(U)$ will always be defined, since $0 \leq U \leq 1$ and the range of F is [0, 1]. Figure 7.1 illustrates the algorithm graphically.

To show that the value X returned by the above algorithm, called the general *inverse-transform method,* has the desired distribution F, we must show that for any real number x, $P\{X \leq x\} = F(x)$. Since F is invertible, we have

$$P\{X \leq x\} = P\{F^{-1}(U) \leq x\} = P\{U \leq F(x)\} = F(x)$$

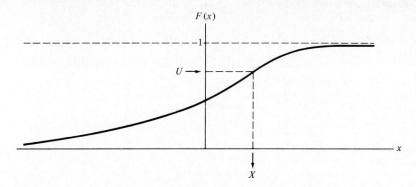

Figure 7.1 Inverse-transform method for continuous random variables.

where the last equality follows since $U \sim U(0, 1)$ and $0 \le F(x) \le 1$. (See the discussion of the uniform distribution in Sec. 5.2.2.)

Example 7.1 Let X have the exponential distribution with parameter β (see Sec. 5.2.2). The distribution function is

$$F(x) = \begin{cases} 1 - e^{-x/\beta} & \text{if } x \ge 0 \\ 0 & \text{otherwise} \end{cases}$$

so to find F^{-1}, we set $u = F(x)$ and solve for x to obtain

$$F^{-1}(u) = -\beta \ln (1 - u)$$

Thus, to generate the desired random variable we first generate a $U \sim U(0, 1)$ and then let $X = -\beta \ln U$. [It is possible in this case to use U instead of $1 - U$, since $1 - U$ and U have the same $U(0, 1)$ distribution. This saves a subtraction.]

The inverse-transform method can also be used when X is discrete. Here the distribution function is

$$F(x) = P\{X \le x\} = \sum_{\{i: x_i \le x\}} p(x_i)$$

where $p(x_i)$ is the probability mass function

$$p(x_i) = P\{X = x_i\}$$

(We assume that X can take on only the values $x_1, x_2, \ldots$ and that $x_1 < x_2 < \cdots$.) Then the algorithm is as follows:

1. Generate a $U \sim U(0, 1)$.
2. Determine the smallest positive integer I such that $U \le F(x_I)$, set $X = x_I$, and return.

Figure 7.2 illustrates the method, where we generate $X = x_4$ in this case. Although this algorithm might not seem related to the inverse-transform method for continuous random variables, the similarity between Figs. 7.1 and 7.2 is apparent.

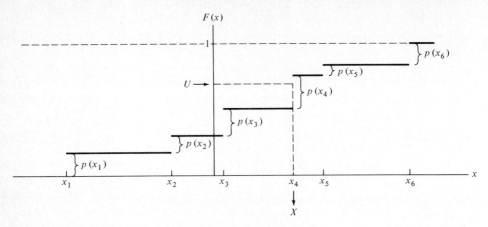

Figure 7.2 Inverse-transform method for discrete random variables.

To verify that the discrete inverse-transform method is valid, we need to show that $P\{X = x_i\} = p(x_i)$ for all i. For $i = 1$, we get $X = x_1$ if and only if $U \leq F(x_1)$ $= p(x_1)$, since we have arranged the x_i's in increasing order. Since $U \sim U(0, 1)$, $P\{X = x_1\} = p(x_1)$, as desired. For $i \geq 2$, the algorithm sets $X = x_i$ if and only if $F(x_{i-1}) < U \leq F(x_i)$, since the i chosen by the algorithm is the smallest positive integer such that $U \leq F(x_i)$. Further, since $U \sim U(0, 1)$ and $0 \leq F(x_{i-1}) < F(x_i)$ ≤ 1,

$$P\{X = x_i\} = P\{F(x_{i-1}) < U \leq F(x_i)\} = F(x_i) - F(x_{i-1}) = p(x_i)$$

Example 7.2 Recall the inventory example of Sec. 1.5, where the demand-size random variable X is discrete, taking on the values 1, 2, 3, 4 with respective probabilities $\frac{1}{6}, \frac{1}{3}, \frac{1}{3}, \frac{1}{6}$; the distribution function F is given in Fig. 4.2. To generate an X, first generate $U \sim U(0, 1)$ and set X to either 1, 2, 3, or 4, depending on the subinterval in [0, 1] in which U falls. If $U \leq \frac{1}{6}$, then let $X = 1$; if $\frac{1}{6} < U \leq \frac{1}{2}$, let $X = 2$; if $\frac{1}{2} < U \leq \frac{5}{6}$, let $X = 3$; finally, if $\frac{5}{6} < U$, let $X = 4$.

Although both Fig. 7.2 and Example 7.2 deal with discrete random variables taking on only finitely many values, the discrete inverse-transform method can also be used directly as stated to generate random variables with an infinite range, e.g., the Poisson, geometric, or negative binomial.

The discrete inverse-transform method, when written as in Example 7.2, is really quite intuitive. We split the unit interval into contiguous subintervals of width $p(x_1)$, $p(x_2)$, ... and assign X according to whichever of these subintervals contains the generated U. For example, U will fall in the second subinterval with probability $p(x_2)$, in which case we let $X = x_2$. The efficiency of the algorithm will depend on how we look for the subinterval which contains a given U. The simplest approach would be to start at the left and move up; first check whether $U \leq p(x_1)$, in which case we set $X = x_1$ and return. If $U > p(x_1)$, check whether $U \leq p(x_1) + p(x_2)$, in which case we set $X = x_2$ and return, etc. The number of comparisons needed to determine a value for X is thus dependent on U and the $p(x_i)$'s. If, for example, the first several $p(x_i)$'s are very small, the probability is high that we will have to do a large number of comparisons before the algorithm terminates. This suggests that we might be well advised to perform this search in a more sophisticated manner, using appropriate sorting and searching techniques from the computer science literature (see, for example, Knuth [25]). One simple improvement would be first to check whether U lies in the widest subinterval, since this would be the single most likely case. If not, we would check the second widest subinterval, etc. This method would be particularly useful when some $p(x_i)$ values are considerably greater than others and there are many x_i's; see Prob. 7.2 for more on this idea.

Let us now consider some general advantages and disadvantages of the inverse-transform method in both the continuous and discrete cases. One possible impediment to use of the method in the continuous case is having to be able to evaluate $F^{-1}(u)$. Since we might not be able to write a formula for F^{-1} in closed form for the desired distribution, e.g., the normal and gamma distributions, simple use of the method, as in Example 7.1, might not be possible. However, even if F^{-1} does not have a simple closed-form expression, we might be able to use numerical methods, e.g., a power-series expansion, to evaluate F^{-1}. (See, for example, the discussion in Sec. 7.3 of the generation of normal and gamma random variables.) In that these numerical methods can yield accuracy matching that inherent in machine roundoff error, they are exact for all practical purposes. A second possible disadvantage is that for a given distribution the inverse-transform method may not be the fastest way to generate the corresponding random variable; in Secs. 7.3 and 7.4 we discuss the efficiency of alternative algorithms for each distribution considered.

Despite these possible drawbacks, there are a number of important advantages in using the inverse-transform method. The first follows from the fact that we always need exactly one U(0, 1) random variable to produce one value of the desired X. [Other methods to be discussed later may involve several U(0, 1) random variables to obtain a single value of X, or the number of such U(0, 1) random variables might itself be random, as in the acceptance-rejection method.] This observation is important if the analyst wants to use certain variance-reduction techniques (see Chap. 11) which call for some sort of synchronization of the input random numbers between different simulation runs; two important examples of such variance-reduction techniques which require this are common random numbers and antithetic variates. If the inverse-transform technique is used, the synchronization is made easier, since one U yields one X, and could eliminate the need for storage of many generated values of X.

The second advantage concerns ease of generating from a truncated distribution. In the continuous case, suppose that we have a density f with corresponding distribution function F. For $a < b$ (with the possibility that $a = -\infty$ or $b = +\infty$) we define the *truncated density*

$$f^*(x) = \begin{cases} \dfrac{f(x)}{F(b) - F(a)} & \text{if } a \leq x \leq b \\ 0 & \text{otherwise} \end{cases}$$

which has corresponding *truncated distribution function*

$$F^*(x) = \begin{cases} 0 & \text{if } x < a \\ \dfrac{F(x) - F(a)}{F(b) - F(a)} & \text{if } a \leq x \leq b \\ 1 & \text{if } b < x \end{cases}$$

(The discrete case is analogous.) Then an algorithm for generating an X having distribution function F^* is as follows:

1. Generate $U \sim U(0, 1)$.
2. Let $V = F(a) + [F(b) - F(a)] U$.
3. Set $X = F^{-1}(V)$ and return.

We leave it as an exercise (Prob. 7.3) to show that the X defined by this algorithm indeed has distribution function F^*. Note that the inverse-transform idea is really used twice: first in step 2 to distribute V uniformly between $F(a)$ and $F(b)$ and then in step 3 to obtain X. (See Prob. 7.3 for another way to generate X and Prob. 7.4 for a different type of truncation which results in a distribution function which is *not* the same as F^*.)

Finally, the inverse-transform method can be quite useful for generating order statistics. Suppose that $Y_1, Y_2, \ldots, Y_n$ are IID with common distribution function F and that for $i = 1, 2, \ldots, n$, $Y_{(i)}$ denotes the ith smallest of the Y_j's. Recall from Chap. 5 that $Y_{(i)}$ is called the ith order statistic from a sample of size n. [Order statistics have been useful in simulation when one is concerned with the reliability, or *lifetime*, of some system having components subject to failure. If Y_j is the lifetime of the jth component, then $Y_{(1)}$ is the lifetime of a system consisting of n such components connected in series and $Y_{(n)}$ is the lifetime of the system if the components are connected in parallel.] One direct way of generating $X = Y_{(i)}$ is first to generate n IID values $Y_1, Y_2, \ldots, Y_n$ with distribution function F, then sort them into increasing order, and finally set X to the ith value of the Y_j's after sorting. This method, however, requires generating n separate values with distribution function F and then sorting them, which can be very slow if n is large. As an alternative, we can use the following algorithm to generate $X = Y_{(i)}$:

1. Generate $V \sim \text{beta}(i, n - i + 1)$.
2. Set $X = F^{-1}(V)$ and return.

The validity of this algorithm is established in Prob. 7.5. Note that step 1 requires generating from a beta distribution, which we discuss below in Sec. 7.3.8. No sorting is required, and we need to evaluate F^{-1} only once; this is particularly advantageous if n is large or the evaluation of F^{-1} is slow. Two important special cases concern generating either the minimum or maximum of the n Y_j's, where step 1 becomes particularly simple. For the minimum, $i = 1$, and V in step 1 can be defined by $V = 1 - U^{1/n}$, where $U \sim U(0, 1)$. For the maximum, $i = n$, and we can set

$V = U^{1/n}$ in step 1. (See Prob. 7.5 for verification of these methods for these two special cases.) For more on generating order statistics, see Ramberg and Tadikamalla [36], Schmeiser [39, 40], and Schucany [46].

7.2.2 Composition

The *composition* technique applies when the distribution function F from which we wish to sample can be expressed as a convex combination of other distribution functions $F_1, F_2, \ldots$. We would hope to be able to sample from the F_j's more easily than from the original F.

Specifically, we assume that for all x, $F(x)$ can be written as

$$F(x) = \sum_{j=1}^{\infty} p_j F_j(x)$$

where $p_j \geq 0$, $\sum_{j=1}^{\infty} p_j = 1$, and each F_j is a distribution function. (Although we have written this combination as an infinite sum, there may be a k such that $p_k > 0$ but $p_j = 0$ for $j > k$, in which case the sum is actually finite.) Equivalently, if X has density f which can be written as

$$f(x) = \sum_{j=1}^{\infty} p_j f_j(x)$$

where the f_j's are other densities, the method of composition still applies; the discrete case is analogous. The general composition algorithm, then, is as follows:

1. Generate a positive random integer J such that

$$P\{J = j\} = p_j \text{ for } j = 1, 2, \ldots$$

2. Given that $J = j$, generate X with distribution function F_j and return.

Step 1 can be thought of as choosing the distribution function F_j with probability p_j and could be accomplished, for example, by the discrete inverse-transform method. Given that $J = j$, the generating of X in step 2 should be done, of course, independently of J. By conditioning on the value of J generated in step 1, we can easily see that the X returned by the algorithm will have distribution function F:

$$P\{X \leq x\} = \sum_{j=1}^{\infty} P\{X \leq x \mid J = j\} P\{J = j\} = \sum_{j=1}^{\infty} F_j(x) p_j = F(x)$$

Sometimes we can give a geometric interpretation to the composition method. For X a continuous random variable with density f, for example, we might be able to divide the area under f into regions of areas $p_1, p_2, \ldots$, corresponding to the decomposition of f into its convex-combination representation. Then we can think of step 1 as choosing a region and step 2 as generating from the distribution corresponding to the chosen region. The following two examples allow this kind of geometric interpretation.

Example 7.3 The *double exponential* (or *Laplace*) distribution has density $f(x) = 0.5e^{-|x|}$ for all real x; this density is plotted in Fig. 7.3. From the plot we see that except for the normalizing factor 0.5, $f(x)$ is two exponential densities placed back to back; this suggests the use of composition. Indeed, we can express the density as

$$f(x) = 0.5e^x I_{(-\infty,0)}(x) + 0.5e^{-x} I_{[0,\infty)}(x)$$

where I_A denotes the *indicator function* of the set A, defined by

$$I_A(x) = \begin{cases} 1 & \text{if } x \in A \\ 0 & \text{otherwise} \end{cases}$$

Thus, $f(x)$ is a convex combination of $f_1(x) = e^x I_{(-\infty,0)}(x)$ and $f_2(x) = e^{-x} I_{[0,\infty)}(x)$, both of which are densities, and $p_1 = p_2 = 0.5$. Therefore, we can generate an X with density f by composition. First generate U_1 and U_2 as IID U(0, 1). If $U_1 \leq 0.5$, let $X = -\ln U_2$ and return. On the other hand, if $U_1 > 0.5$, let $X = \ln U_2$ and return. Note that we are essentially generating an exponential random variable with parameter 1 and then changing its sign with probability 0.5. Alternatively, we are generating from the left half of the density in Fig. 7.3 with probability equal to the corresponding area (0.5) and from the right half with probability 0.5.

Note that in Example 7.3, step 2 of the general composition algorithm was accomplished by means of the inverse-transform method for exponential random variables; this illustrates how different general approaches for generating random variables might be combined to obtain the final desired random variable. Also, we see that *two* U(0, 1) random variables are required to generate a single X in this example; in general, we shall need *at least two* U(0, 1) random variables to use the composition method. (The reader may find it interesting to compare Example 7.3 with the inverse-transform method for generating a double exponential random variable; see Prob. 7.6.)

In Example 7.3 we obtained the representation for f by dividing the area below the density with a vertical line, namely, the ordinate axis. In the following example, we make a horizontal division instead.

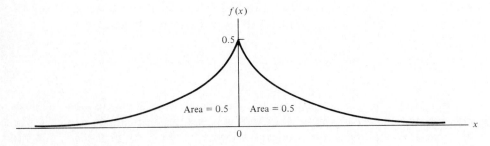

Figure 7.3 Double exponential density.

Example 7.4 For $0 < a < 1$, the *right trapezoidal* distribution has density

$$f(x) = \begin{cases} a + 2(1 - a)x & \text{if } 0 \le x \le 1 \\ 0 & \text{otherwise} \end{cases}$$

(see Fig. 7.4). As suggested by the dashed lines, we can think of dividing the area under f into a rectangle having area a and a right triangle with area $1 - a$. Now $f(x)$ can be decomposed as

$$f(x) = aI_{[0,1]}(x) + (1 - a)2xI_{[0,1]}(x)$$

so that $f_1(x) = I_{[0,1]}(x)$, which is simply the U(0, 1) density, and $f_2(x) = 2xI_{[0,1]}(x)$ is a right triangular density. Clearly, $p_1 = a$ and $p_2 = 1 - a$. The composition method thus calls for generating $U_1 \sim$ U(0, 1) and checking whether $U_1 \le a$. If so, generate an independent $U_2 \sim$ U(0, 1), set $X = U_2$, and return. If $U_1 > a$, however, we must generate from the right triangular distribution. This can be accomplished either by generating $U_2 \sim$ U(0, 1) and setting $X = \sqrt{U_2}$, or by generating U_2 and U_3 distributed as IID U(0, 1) and letting $X = \max\{U_2, U_3\}$ (see Prob. 7.7). Since the time to take a square root is probably greater than that required to generate an extra U(0, 1) random variable *and* perform a comparison, the latter method would appear to be a faster way of generating an X with density f_2.

Again, the reader is encouraged to develop the inverse-transform method of generating a random variable from the right trapezoidal distribution in Example 7.4. Note that especially if a is large, the composition method will be faster than the inverse transform, since the latter *always* requires that a square root be taken, while it is quite likely (with probability a) that the former will simply return with $X = U_2 \sim$ U(0, 1). This increase in speed must be played off by the analyst against the possible disadvantage of having to generate two or three U(0, 1) random variables to obtain one value of X. Trapezoidal distributions like that in Example 7.4 play an important role in the efficient method developed by Schmeiser and Lal [44] for generating gamma random variables and for beta generation in Schmeiser and Babu [42].

7.2.3 Convolution

For several important distributions, the desired random variable X can be expressed as a sum of other random variables which are IID and can be generated more readily

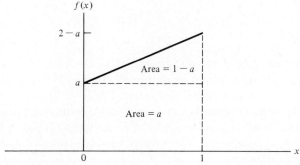

Figure 7.4 Right trapezoidal density.

than direct generation of X. We assume that there are IID random variables Y_1, Y_2, ..., Y_m (for fixed m) such that $Y_1 + Y_2 + \cdots + Y_m$ has the same distribution as X; hence we write

$$X = Y_1 + Y_2 + \cdots + Y_m$$

The name of this method, *convolution,* comes from terminology in stochastic processes, where the distribution of X is called the *m-fold convolution* of the distribution of a Y_j. The reader should take care not to confuse this situation with the method of composition. Here we assume that the *random variable X* can be represented as a sum of other *random variables,* whereas the assumption behind the method of composition is that the *distribution function* of X is a (weighted) sum of other *distribution functions;* the two situations are fundamentally different.

The algorithm for generating the desired random variable X is quite intuitive (let F be the distribution function of X and G be the distribution function of a Y_j):

1. Generate Y_1, Y_2, ..., Y_m IID each with distribution function G.
2. Set $X = Y_1 + Y_2 + \cdots + Y_m$ and return.

To demonstrate the validity of this algorithm, recall that we assumed that X and $Y_1 + Y_2 + \cdots + Y_m$ have the same distribution function, namely, F. Thus,

$$P\{X \le x\} = P\{Y_1 + Y_2 + \cdots + Y_m \le x\} = F(x)$$

Example 7.5 The m-Erlang random variable X with mean β can be defined as being the sum of m IID exponential random variables with common parameter β/m. Thus, to generate X, we can first generate Y_1, Y_2, ..., Y_m as IID exponential with parameter β/m (see Example 7.1), then set $X = Y_1 + Y_2 + \cdots + Y_m$ and return. (See Sec. 7.3.3 for an improvement in efficiency of this algorithm.)

The convolution method, when it can be used, is very simple, provided that we can generate the required Y_j's easily. However, depending on the particular parameters of the distribution of X, it may not be the most efficient way. For example, to generate the m-Erlang random variable by the convolution method (as in Example 7.5) when m is large could be very slow. In this case it would be better to recall that the m-Erlang distribution is a special case of the gamma distribution (see Sec. 5.2.2) and use a general method for generating gamma random variables (see Sec. 7.3.4).

7.2.4 Acceptance-Rejection

The three general approaches for generating random variables discussed so far (inverse transform, composition, and convolution) might be called *direct* in the sense that they deal directly with the distribution or random variable desired. The *acceptance-rejection method,* which we now consider, is less direct in its approach and can be useful when the direct methods fail or are inefficient. Our discussion is for the continuous case, where we want to generate X having distribution function F and density f; the discrete case is exactly analogous and is treated in Prob. 7.9. The underlying idea dates back at least to 1951 and is evidently due to von Neumann [49].

The acceptance-rejection method requires us to specify a function t which *majorizes* the density f; that is, $t(x) \geq f(x)$ for all x. Now t will not, in general, be a density since

$$c = \int_{-\infty}^{\infty} t(x) \, dx \geq \int_{-\infty}^{\infty} f(x) \, dx = 1$$

but the function $r(x) = t(x)/c$ clearly *is* a density. (We assume that t is such that $c < \infty$.) We must be able to generate (easily and quickly, we hope) a random variable Y having density r. The general algorithm follows:

1. Generate Y having density r.
2. Generate $U \sim U(0, 1)$, independent of Y.
3. If $U \leq f(Y)/t(Y)$, set $X = Y$ and return. Otherwise, go back to step 1 and try again.

The algorithm continues looping back to step 1 until finally we generate a (Y, U) pair in steps 1 and 2 for which $U \leq f(Y)/t(Y)$, when we "accept" the value Y for X. Since demonstrating the validity of this algorithm is more complicated than for the three previous methods, we refer the reader to Appendix 7A for a proof.

Example 7.6 The beta(4, 3) distribution (on the unit interval) has density

$$f(x) = \begin{cases} 60x^3(1 - x)^2 & \text{if } 0 \leq x \leq 1 \\ 0 & \text{otherwise} \end{cases}$$

[Since the distribution function $F(x)$ is a sixth-degree polynomial, the inverse-transform method is not simple, involving numerical methods to find polynomial roots.] By standard methods of differential calculus, i.e., setting $df/dx = 0$, we see that the maximum value of $f(x)$ occurs at $x = 0.6$, where $f(0.6) = 2.0736$ (exactly). Thus, if we define

$$t(x) = \begin{cases} 2.0736 & \text{if } 0 \leq x \leq 1 \\ 0 & \text{otherwise} \end{cases}$$

then t majorizes f. Next, $c = \int_0^1 2.0736 \, dx = 2.0736$, so that the density $r(x)$ is just the $U(0, 1)$ density. The functions f, t, and r are shown in Fig. 7.5. The algorithm first generates Y and U as IID $U(0, 1)$ random variables in steps 1 and 2; then in step 3 we check whether

$$U \leq 60Y^3(1 - Y)^2/2.0736$$

If so, we set $X = Y$ and return; otherwise, we reject Y and go back to step 1.

Note that in the preceding example, X is bounded on an interval (the unit interval in this case), and so we were able to choose t to be a constant over this interval, which in turn led to r's being a uniform density. The acceptance-rejection method is often stated *only* for such bounded random variables X and *only* for this uniform choice of r; our treatment is more general.

Although this technique generates a value of X with the desired distribution regardless of the choice of the majorizing function t, this choice will play a major

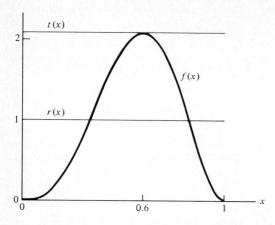

Figure 7.5 Acceptance-rejection method for the beta(4, 3) distribution.

role in the efficiency of the acceptance-rejection method in two ways. First, since step 1 requires generating Y with density $t(x)/c$, we want to choose t so that this can be accomplished rapidly. (The uniform t chosen in Example 7.6 certainly satisfies this wish.) Second, we hope that the probability of rejection in step 3 can be made small, since we have to start all over if this rejection occurs. In Appendix 7A we show that on any given iteration through the algorithm the probability of rejection in step 3 is $1 - 1/c$; we therefore would like to choose t so that c is small. Thus, we want to find a t which fits closely above f, bringing c closer down to 1, its lower bound. (From this standpoint, then, we see that the uniform choice of t in Example 7.6 might not be so wise after all, since it does not fit down on top of f very snugly. Since $c = 2.0736$, the probability of rejection is approximately 0.5177, which is higher than we would like.)

Since these two goals, ease of generation from $t(x)/c$ and a small value of c, may well conflict with each other, the choice of t is by no means obvious and deserves care. Recent research has been aimed at identifying good choices of t for a given distribution. (See, for example, Ahrens and Dieter [1, 2], Atkinson [4], Atkinson and Whittaker [7], Schmeiser [41], Schmeiser and Babu [42], Schmeiser and Lal [44], Schmeiser and Shalaby [45], and Tadikamalla [48].) One popular method of finding a suitable t is *first* to specify $r(x)$ to be some common density, e.g., a normal or double exponential, then find the smallest c such that $t(x) = c \cdot r(x) \geqslant f(x)$ for all x.

7.2.5 Special Properties

Although most methods for generating random variables can be classified into one of the four approaches discussed so far in Sec. 7.2, some techniques simply rely on some *special property* of the desired distribution function F or the random variable X. Frequently, the special property will take the form of representing X in terms of other random variables which are more easily generated; in this sense the method of convolution is a "special" special property. Since there is no general form for these techniques, we shall give examples of the kinds of things which can be done.

Example 7.7 If $Y \sim N(0, 1)$ (the standard normal distribution), then Y^2 has a chi-square distribution with 1 df. [We write $X \sim \chi^2(k)$ to mean that X has a chi-square distribution with k df.] Thus, to generate $X \sim \chi^2(1)$, generate $Y \sim N(0, 1)$ (see Sec. 7.3.6), set $X = Y^2$, and return.

Example 7.8 If $Z_1, Z_2, \ldots, Z_k$ are IID $\chi^2(1)$ random variables then $X = Z_1 + \cdots + Z_k \sim \chi^2(k)$. Thus, to generate $X \sim \chi^2(k)$, first generate $Y_1, Y_2, \ldots, Y_k$ as IID $N(0, 1)$ random variables, then let $X = Y_1^2 + Y_2^2 + \cdots + Y_k^2$ (see Example 7.7), and return. Since for large k this may be quite slow, we might want to exploit the fact that the $\chi^2(k)$ distribution is a gamma distribution with shape parameter $\alpha = k/2$ and scale parameter $\beta = 2$. Then X can be obtained directly from the gamma generation methods discussed in Sec. 7.3.4.

Example 7.9 If $Y \sim N(0, 1)$, $Z \sim \chi^2(k)$, and Y and Z are independent, then $X = Y/\sqrt{Z/k}$ is said to have *Student's t distribution* with k df, which we denote $X \sim t(k)$. Thus, to generate $X \sim t(k)$, we generate $Y \sim N(0, 1)$ and $Z \sim \chi^2(k)$ independently of Y (see Example 7.8), set $X = Y/\sqrt{Z/k}$, and return.

Example 7.10 If $Z_1 \sim \chi^2(k_1)$, $Z_2 \sim \chi^2(k_2)$, and Z_1 and Z_2 are independent, then

$$X = (Z_1/k_1)/(Z_2/k_2)$$

is said to have an *F distribution* with (k_1, k_2) df, denoted $X \sim F(k_1, k_2)$. We thus generate $Z_1 \sim \chi^2(k_1)$ and $Z_2 \sim \chi^2(k_2)$ independently, set $X = (Z_1/k_1)/(Z_2/k_2)$, and return.

Although Examples 7.7 to 7.10 all have to do with normal-theory random variables, these kinds of observations can be used to generate random variables which may not have anything to do with the normal distribution. (For example, see the discussion of the beta distribution in Sec. 7.3.8.)

7.3 GENERATING CONTINUOUS RANDOM VARIABLES

In this section we discuss particular algorithms for generating random variables from several commonly occurring continuous distributions; Sec. 7.4 contains a similar treatment for discrete random variables. Although there may be a number of different algorithms for generating from a given distribution, we explicitly present only one technique in each case and provide references for other algorithms which may be better in some sense, e.g., in terms of speed at the expense of increased setup cost and greater complexity. In deciding which algorithm to present, we have tried to choose those which are simple to describe and implement and reasonably efficient as well. We also prefer exact (up to machine accuracy) to approximate methods. If speed is of critical importance, however, we urge the reader to pursue the various references given for the desired distribution. For definitions of density functions, mass functions, and distribution functions, see Sec. 5.2.

7.3.1 Uniform

The distribution function of a $U(a, b)$ random variable is easily inverted by solving $u = F(x)$ for x to obtain, for $0 \leq u \leq 1$,

$$x = F^{-1}(u) = a + (b - a)u$$

Thus, we can use the inverse-transform method to generate X:

1. Generate $U \sim U(0, 1)$.
2. Set $X = a + (b - a)U$ and return.

If many X values are to be generated, the constant $b - a$ should, of course, be computed beforehand and stored for use in the algorithm.

7.3.2 Exponential

The exponential random variable with parameter $\beta > 0$ was considered in Example 7.1, where we derived the following inverse-transform algorithm:

1. Generate $U \sim U(0, 1)$.
2. Set $X = -\beta \ln U$ and return.

This is certainly a simple technique and has all the advantages of the inverse-transform method discussed in Sec. 7.2.1. It is also reasonably fast, most of the computing time's being taken up in evaluation of the logarithm (72 percent of the total time in the experiments of Ahrens and Dieter [1]). In fact, this method was the fastest of the four algorithms considered in [1] if the programming is done in FORTRAN. If one is willing to program in assembly language, however, there are other methods (von Neumann [49], Marsaglia [30], and MacLaren, Marsaglia, and Bray [29]) which avoid the logarithm and are faster, although considerably more complex and involving various amounts of preliminary setup. We refer the interested reader to [1] and to Fishman [20] for further discussion.

7.3.3 *m*-Erlang

As discussed in Example 7.5, if X is an m-Erlang random variable with mean β, we can write $X = Y_1 + Y_2 + \cdots + Y_m$, where the Y_i's are IID exponential random variables, each with parameter β/m. This led to the convolution algorithm described in Example 7.5. Its efficiency can be improved, however, as follows. If we use the inverse-transform method of Sec. 7.3.2 to generate the exponential Y_i's [$Y_i = (-\beta/m) \ln U_i$, where $U_1, U_2, \ldots, U_m$ are IID $U(0, 1)$ random variables], then

$$X = \sum_{i=1}^{m} Y_i = \sum_{i=1}^{m} \frac{-\beta}{m} \ln U_i = \frac{-\beta}{m} \ln \left(\prod_{i=1}^{m} U_i \right)$$

so that we need to compute only one logarithm (rather than m logarithms). Then the statement of the algorithm is as follows:

1. Generate $U_1, U_2, \ldots, U_m$ as IID $U(0, 1)$.
2. Set $X = \frac{-\beta}{m} \ln \left(\prod_{i=1}^{m} U_i \right)$ and return.

(Again, one should compute β/m beforehand and store it for repeated use.) This algorithm is really a combination of the composition and inverse-transform methods.

Since we must generate m U(0, 1) random variables and perform m multiplications, the execution time of the algorithm is approximately proportional to m. Therefore, one might look for an alternative method when m is large. Fortunately, the m-Erlang distribution is a special case of the gamma distribution (with shape parameter α equal to the integer m), so that we can use one of the methods for generating gamma random variables here as well (see Sec. 7.3.4 for discussion of gamma generation). The precise threshold for m beyond which one should switch to general gamma generation will depend on the method used for generating a gamma random variable as well as on languages, compilers, and hardware; preliminary experimentation in one's particular situation might prove worthwhile. (For the gamma generator stated in Sec. 7.3.4 for the case $\alpha > 1$, timing experiments in Cheng [13] indicate that using his general gamma generator becomes faster than the above m-Erlang algorithm for $m \geq 10$, approximately.)

7.3.4 Gamma

General gamma random variables are more complicated to generate than the three types of random variables considered so far in this section, since the distribution function has no simple closed form for which we could try to find an inverse. First note that given $X \sim$ gamma(α, 1), we can obtain, for any $\beta > 0$, a gamma(α, β) random variable X' by letting $X' = \beta X$, so that it is sufficient to restrict attention to generating from the gamma(α, 1) distribution. Furthermore, recall that the gamma(1, 1) distribution is just the exponential distribution with parameter 1, so that we need only consider $0 < \alpha < 1$ and $\alpha > 1$. Since the available algorithms for generating gamma random variables are for the most part valid for only one of these ranges of α, we shall discuss them separately.

We first consider the case $0 < \alpha < 1$. [Note that if $\alpha = 0.5$, we have a rescaled $\chi^2(1)$ distribution and X can be easily generated using Example 7.7; the algorithm stated below is nevertheless valid for $\alpha = 0.5$.] Atkinson and Pearce [6] tested three alternative algorithms for this case, and we present one of them, due to Ahrens and Dieter [2]. (The algorithm of Forsythe [21] was usually the fastest in the comparisons in [6], but is considerably more complicated; if speed is of critical importance, we refer the reader to [6].) This algorithm, denoted GS in [2], is an acceptance-rejection technique, with majorizing function

$$t(x) = \begin{cases} 0 & \text{if } x \leq 0 \\ \dfrac{x^{\alpha-1}}{\Gamma(\alpha)} & \text{if } 0 < x \leq 1 \\ \dfrac{e^{-x}}{\Gamma(\alpha)} & \text{if } 1 < x \end{cases}$$

Thus, $c = \displaystyle\int_0^\infty t(x)\, dx = b/[\alpha\Gamma(\alpha)]$, where $b = (e + \alpha)/e > 1$, which yields the density $r(x) = t(x)/c$ as

$$
r(x) = \begin{cases}
0 & \text{if } x \le 0 \\[2mm]
\dfrac{\alpha x^{\alpha-1}}{b} & \text{if } 0 < x \le 1 \\[3mm]
\dfrac{\alpha e^{-x}}{b} & \text{if } 1 < x
\end{cases}
$$

Generating a random variable Y with density $r(x)$ can be done by the inverse-transform method; the distribution function corresponding to r is

$$
R(x) = \int_0^x r(y)\, dy = \begin{cases}
\dfrac{x^\alpha}{b} & \text{if } 0 \le x \le 1 \\[3mm]
1 - \dfrac{\alpha e^{-x}}{b} & \text{if } 1 < x
\end{cases}
$$

which can be inverted to obtain

$$
R^{-1}(u) = \begin{cases}
(bu)^{1/\alpha} & \text{if } u \le \dfrac{1}{b} \\[3mm]
-\ln\dfrac{b(1-u)}{\alpha} & \text{otherwise}
\end{cases}
$$

Thus to generate Y with density r, we first generate $U_1 \sim U(0, 1)$. If $U_1 \le 1/b$, we set $Y = (bU_1)^{1/\alpha}$. (Note that in this case, $Y \le 1$.) Otherwise, if $U_1 > 1/b$, set $Y = -\ln[b(1 - U_1)/\alpha]$, which will be greater than 1. Noting that

$$
\frac{f(Y)}{t(Y)} = \begin{cases}
e^{-Y} & \text{if } 0 \le Y \le 1 \\
Y^{\alpha-1} & \text{if } 1 < Y
\end{cases}
$$

we obtain the final algorithm [$b = (e + \alpha)/e$ must be computed beforehand]:

1. Generate $U_1 \sim U(0, 1)$, and let $P = bU_1$. If $P > 1$, go to step 3. Otherwise, proceed to step 2.
2. Let $Y = P^{1/\alpha}$, and generate $U_2 \sim U(0, 1)$. If $U_2 \le e^{-Y}$, set $X = Y$ and return. Otherwise, go back to step 1.
3. Let $Y = -\ln[(b - P)/\alpha]$ and generate $U_2 \sim U(0, 1)$. If $U_2 \le Y^{\alpha-1}$, set $X = Y$ and return. Otherwise, go back to step 1.

We now consider the case $\alpha > 1$, where there are several good algorithms currently available. In view of recent timing experiments by Schmeiser and Lal [44] and Cheng and Feast [15], we will present a modified acceptance-rejection method due to Cheng [13], who calls this the GB algorithm. This algorithm has a "capped" execution time; i.e., its execution time is bounded as $\alpha \to \infty$ and in fact appears to become faster as α grows. (The modification of the general acceptance-rejection method consists of adding a faster pretest for acceptance.) To obtain a majorizing function $t(x)$, first let $\lambda = (2\alpha - 1)^{1/2}$, $\mu = \alpha^\lambda$, and $c = 4\alpha^\alpha e^{-\alpha}/[\lambda\Gamma(\alpha)]$. Then define $t(x) = c \cdot r(x)$, where

$$
r(x) = \begin{cases} \dfrac{\lambda\mu x^{\lambda-1}}{(\mu + x^\lambda)^2} & \text{if } x > 0 \\[2ex] 0 & \text{otherwise} \end{cases}
$$

The distribution function corresponding to the density $r(x)$ is

$$
R(x) = \begin{cases} \dfrac{x^\lambda}{\mu + x^\lambda} & \text{if } x \geq 0 \\[2ex] 0 & \text{otherwise} \end{cases}
$$

which is easily inverted to obtain

$$
R^{-1}(u) = \left(\frac{\mu u}{1 - u} \right)^{1/\lambda} \qquad \text{for } 0 < u < 1
$$

To verify that $t(x)$ indeed majorizes $f(x)$, see [13]. Note that this is an example of obtaining a majorizing function by first specifying a known distribution [here, $R(x)$ is known as the *log logistic distribution*] and then rescaling the density $r(x)$ to majorize $f(x)$. Thus, we use the inverse-transform method to generate Y with density r. After adding an advantageous pretest for acceptance and streamlining for computational efficiency, Cheng [13] recommends the following algorithm [the prespecified constants are $a = (2\alpha - 1)^{-1/2}$, $b = \alpha - \ln 4$, $q = \alpha + 1/a$, $\theta = 4.5$, and $d = 1 + \ln \theta$]:

1. Generate U_1 and U_2 as IID $U(0, 1)$.
2. Let $V = a \ln [U_1/(1 - U_1)]$, $Y = \alpha e^V$, $Z = U_1^2 U_2$, and $W = b + qV - Y$.
3. If $W + d - \theta Z \geq 0$, set $X = Y$ and return. Otherwise, proceed to step 4.
4. If $W \geq \ln Z$, set $X = Y$ and return. Otherwise, go back to step 1.

Step 3 is the added pretest, which (if passed) avoids computing the logarithm in the regular acceptance-rejection test in step 4. (If step 3 were removed, the algorithm would still be valid and would be equivalent to the usual acceptance-rejection method.)

As mentioned above, there are several other good algorithms which could be used when $\alpha > 1$. Schmeiser and Lal [44] present another rejection method with $t(x)$ piecewise linear in the "body" of $f(x)$ and exponential in the tails; their algorithm was roughly twice as fast as the one we chose to present above, for α ranging from 1.0001 through 1000. However, the algorithm in [44] is considerably more complicated and requires more time to set up the necessary constants for a given value of α. This is a typical kind of trade-off which the analyst must consider in choosing from alternative algorithms for generating random variables.

Finally, we consider direct use of the inverse-transform method to generate gamma random variables. Since neither the gamma distribution function nor its inverse has a simple closed form, we must resort to numerical methods. Best and Roberts [10] give a numerical procedure for inverting the distribution function of a χ^2 random variable with degrees of freedom that need not be an integer, so is applicable for gamma(α, 1) generation for any $\alpha > 0$. [If $Y \sim \chi^2(\nu)$, where $\nu > 0$ need not be an integer, then $Y \sim$ gamma($\nu/2$, 2). If we want $X \sim$ gamma (α, 1), first generate $Y \sim \chi^2(2\alpha)$, then set $X = Y/2$.] A FORTRAN subroutine for the procedure is also provided in [10].

7.3.5 Weibull

The Weibull distribution function is easily inverted to obtain

$$F^{-1}(u) = \beta[-\ln (1 - u)]^{1/\alpha}$$

which leads to the following inverse-transform algorithm:

1. Generate $U \sim$ U(0, 1).
2. Set $X = \beta(-\ln U)^{1/\alpha}$ and return.

Again we are exploiting the fact that U and $1 - U$ have the same U(0, 1) distribution. [This algorithm can also be justified by recalling that if Y has an exponential distribution with parameter β^α, then $Y^{1/\alpha} \sim$ Weibull(α, β); see Sec. 5.2.2.]

7.3.6 Normal

First note that given $X \sim$ N(0, 1), we can obtain $X' \sim$ N(μ, σ^2) by setting $X' = \mu + \sigma X$, so that we can restrict our attention to generating standard normal random variables. Efficient generation of normal random variables is important since the normal density has often been used to provide majorizing functions for acceptance-rejection generation of random variables from other distributions, e.g., Ahrens and Dieter's [2] gamma and beta generators; normal random variables can also be transformed directly into random variables from other distributions, e.g., the lognormal. Also, statisticians seeking to estimate empirically, in a Monte Carlo study (simulation), the null distribution of a test statistic for normality will need an efficient source of normal random variables. (See, for example, Filliben [18], Lilliefors [28], or Shapiro and Wilk [47].)

One of the early methods for generating N(0, 1) random variables, due to Box and Muller [11], is evidently still in wide use despite the current availability of much faster algorithms. It does have the advantage, however, of maintaining a one-to-one correspondence between the U(0, 1) random variables and the N(0, 1) random variables produced; it may thus prove useful for maintaining synchronization in the use of common random numbers as a variance-reduction technique. The method simply says to generate U_1 and U_2 as IID U(0, 1) random variables, then set $X_1 = (-2 \ln U_1)^{1/2} \cos 2\pi U_2$ and $X_2 = (-2 \ln U_1)^{1/2} \sin 2\pi U_2$. Then X_1 and X_2 are IID N(0, 1) random variables. Since we obtain the desired random variables in pairs, we could, on odd-numbered calls to the subprogram, actually compute X_1 and X_2 as just described and return only X_1, saving X_2 for immediate return on the next (even-numbered) call. Thus, this method uses *two* U(0, 1) random variables to produce *two* N(0, 1) random variables.

An improvement to the Box and Muller method, which eliminates the trigonometric calculations and was described in Marsaglia and Bray [31], has become known as the *polar method*. It relies on a special property of the normal distribution and was found by Atkinson and Pearce [6] to be between 9 and 31 percent faster in FORTRAN programming than the Box and Muller method, depending on the machine used. (Ahrens and Dieter [1] experienced a 27 percent reduction in time.) The polar method, which also generates N(0, 1) random variables in pairs, is as follows:

1. Generate U_1 and U_2 as IID U(0, 1), let $V_i = 2U_i - 1$ for $i = 1, 2$, and let $W = V_1^2 + V_2^2$.
2. If $W > 1$, go back to step 1. Otherwise, let $Y = [(-2 \ln W)/W]^{1/2}$, $X_1 = V_1 Y$, and $X_2 = V_2 Y$. Then X_1 and X_2 are IID N(0, 1) random variables.

Since a "rejection" of U_1 and U_2 can occur in step 2 (with probability $1 - \pi/4$, by Prob. 7.12), the polar method will require a random number of U(0, 1) random variables to generate each pair of N(0, 1) random variables. More recently, a very fast algorithm for generating N(0, 1) random variables was developed by Kinderman and Ramage [24] which is more complicated but required 30 percent less time than the polar method in their FORTRAN experiments.

For direct use of the inverse-transform method in normal generation, one must use a numerical method, since neither the normal distribution function nor its inverse has a simple closed-form expression. Such a method, complete with a FORTRAN subroutine for implementation, is given in Beasley and Springer [9].

7.3.7 Lognormal

A special property of the lognormal distribution, namely, that if $Y \sim \text{N}(\mu, \sigma^2)$ then $e^Y \sim \text{LN}(\mu, \sigma^2)$, is used to obtain the following algorithm:

1. Generate $Y \sim \text{N}(\mu, \sigma^2)$.
2. Set $X = e^Y$ and return.

To accomplish step 1, any method discussed in Sec. 7.3.6 for normal generation can be used.

Note that μ and σ^2 are *not* the mean and variance of the LN(μ, σ^2) distribution. In fact, if $X \sim \text{LN}(\mu, \sigma^2)$ and we let $\mu_l = E(X)$ and $\sigma_l^2 = \text{Var}(X)$, then $\mu_l = e^{\mu + \sigma^2/2}$ and $\sigma_l^2 = e^{2\mu + \sigma^2}(e^{\sigma^2} - 1)$. Thus, if we want to generate a lognormal random variable with *given mean* μ_l and *variance* σ_l^2, we should solve for μ and σ^2 in terms of μ_l and σ_l^2 first, *before* generating the desired random variables. The formulas are easily obtained as $\mu = \ln [\mu_l^2/(\sigma_l^2 + \mu_l^2)^{1/2}]$ and $\sigma^2 = \ln [(\sigma_l^2 + \mu_l^2)/\mu_l^2]$.

7.3.8 Beta

First note that we can obtain $X' \sim \text{beta}(\alpha_1, \alpha_2)$ on the interval $[a, b]$ for $a < b$ by setting $X' = a + (b - a)X$, where $X \sim \text{beta}(\alpha_1, \alpha_2)$ on the interval $[0, 1]$, so that it is sufficient to consider only the latter case, which we henceforth refer to as *the* beta(α_1, α_2) distribution.

Some properties of the beta(α_1, α_2) distribution for certain (α_1, α_2) combinations facilitate generation of beta random variables. First, if $X \sim \text{beta}(\alpha_1, \alpha_2)$, then $1 - X \sim \text{beta}(\alpha_2, \alpha_1)$, so that we can readily generate a beta(α_2, α_1) random variable if we can obtain a beta(α_1, α_2) random variable easily. One such situation occurs when either α_1 or α_2 is equal to 1. If $\alpha_2 = 1$, for example, then for $0 \le x \le 1$ we have $f(x) = \alpha_1 x^{\alpha_1 - 1}$; so the distribution function is $F(x) = x^{\alpha_1}$, and we can easily generate $X \sim \text{beta}(\alpha_1, 1)$ by the inverse-transform method, i.e., by setting $X = U^{1/\alpha_1}$, for $U \sim \text{U}(0, 1)$. Finally, the beta $(1, 1)$ distribution is simply U$(0, 1)$.

A general method for generating a beta(α_1, α_2) random variable for any $\alpha_1 > 0$ and $\alpha_2 > 0$ is a result of the fact that if $Y_1 \sim \text{gamma}(\alpha_1, 1)$, $Y_2 \sim \text{gamma}(\alpha_2, 1)$, and Y_1 and Y_2 are independent, then $Y_1/(Y_1 + Y_2) \sim \text{beta}(\alpha_1, \alpha_2)$. This leads to the following algorithm:

1. Generate $Y_1 \sim \text{gamma}(\alpha_1, 1)$ and $Y_2 \sim \text{gamma}(\alpha_2, 1)$ independent of Y_1.
2. Set $X = Y_1/(Y_1 + Y_2)$ and return.

Generating the two gamma random variables Y_1 and Y_2 can be done by any appropriate algorithm for gamma generation (see Sec. 7.3.4), so that we must take care to check whether α_1 and α_2 are less than or greater than 1.

This method is quite convenient, in that it is essentially done provided that we have gamma$(\alpha, 1)$ generators for all $\alpha > 0$; its efficiency will, of course, depend on the speed of the chosen gamma generators. There are, however, considerably faster (and more complicated, as usual) algorithms for generating from the beta distribution directly. For $\alpha_1 > 1$ and $\alpha_2 > 1$, Schmeiser and Babu [42] present a very fast acceptance-rejection method, where the majorizing function is piecewise linear over the center of $f(x)$ and exponential over the tails; a fast acceptance pretest is specified by a piecewise linear function $b(x)$ that minorizes $f(x)$. If $\alpha_1 < 1$ or $\alpha_2 < 1$ (or both), algorithms for generating beta(α_1, α_2) random variables directly are given by Atkinson and Whittaker [7, 8], Cheng [14], and Jöhnk [22]. Cheng's [14] method BA is quite simple and is valid as well for any $\alpha_1 > 0, \alpha_2 > 0$ combination; the same is true for Jöhnk's [22] algorithm.

The inverse-transform method for generating beta(α_1, α_2) random variables must rely on numerical methods to evaluate $F^{-1}(U)$, as was the case for the gamma and normal distributions. One such method is given (with a FORTRAN program) by Cran, Martin, and Thomas [17].

7.3.9 Triangular

First notice that, if we have $X \sim \text{triang}(0, 1, (c - a)/(b - a))$, then $X' = a + (b - a)X \sim \text{triang}(a, b, c)$, so we can restrict attention to $\text{triang}(0, 1, c)$ random variables, where $0 < c < 1$. (For the limiting cases $c = 0$ or $c = 1$, giving rise to a left or right triangle, see Prob. 7.7.) The distribution function is easily inverted to obtain, for $0 \leq u \leq 1$,

$$F^{-1}(u) = \begin{cases} (cu)^{1/2} & \text{if } 0 \leq u \leq c \\ 1 - [(1 - c)(1 - u)]^{1/2} & \text{if } c < u \leq 1 \end{cases}$$

Therefore, we can state the following inverse-transform algorithm for generating $X \sim \text{triang}(0, 1, c)$:

1. Generate $U \sim \text{U}(0, 1)$.
2. If $U \leq c$, set $X = (cU)^{1/2}$ and return. Otherwise, set $X = 1 - [(1 - c)(1 - U)]^{1/2}$ and return.

(Note that if $U > c$ in step 2, we *cannot* replace the $1 - U$ in the formula for X by U. Why?) For an alternative method of generating a triangular random variable (by composition), see Prob. 7.13.

7.3.10 Empirical Distributions

In this section we give algorithms for generating random variables from the continuous empirical distribution functions F and G, defined in Sec. 5.2.4. Recall that there were two cases: when the original individual observations are available, and when we only have grouped data. In both cases, the inverse-transform approach can be used.

First suppose we have the original individual observations, which we use to define the empirical distribution function $F(x)$ given in Sec. 5.2.4 (see also Fig. 5.15). Although an inverse-transform algorithm might at first appear to involve some kind of a search, the fact that the "corners" of F occur precisely at the levels $0, 1/(n - 1), 2/(n - 1), \ldots, (n - 2)/(n - 1), 1$ allows us to avoid an explicit search. We leave it to the reader to verify that the following algorithm *is* the inverse-transform method (recall that $\lfloor z \rfloor$ denotes the greatest integer that is less than or equal to the real number z):

1. Generate $U \sim \text{U}(0, 1)$, let $P = (n - 1)U$, and let $I = \lfloor P \rfloor + 1$.
2. Set $X = X_{(I)} + (P - I + 1)(X_{(I+1)} - X_I)$ and return.

Note that the $X_{(i)}$'s must be stored and that storing a separate array containing the values of $X_{(I+1)} - X_{(I)}$ would eliminate a subtraction in step 2. Also, the values of X generated will always be between $X_{(1)}$ and $X_{(n)}$; this limitation is a possible disadvantage of specifying an empirical distribution in this way. The lack of a search makes the marginal execution time of this algorithm essentially independent of n, although large n entails more storage and setup time for the sorting of the X_i's.

Now suppose that our data are grouped; that is, we have k adjacent intervals $[a_0, a_1), [a_1, a_2), \ldots, [a_{k-1}, a_k]$, and the jth interval contains n_j observations, with $n_1 + n_2 + \cdots + n_k = n$. In this case, we defined an empirical distribution function $G(x)$ in Sec. 5.2.4 (see also Fig. 5.16), and the following inverse-transform algorithm generates a random variable with this distribution:

1. Generate $U \sim U(0, 1)$.
2. Find the nonnegative integer J ($0 \leq J \leq k - 1$) such that $G(a_J) \leq U < G(a_{J+1})$, set $X = a_J + [U - G(a_J)](a_{J+1} - a_J)/[G(a_{J+1}) - G(a_J)]$, and return.

Note that the value of J found in step 2 satisfies $G(a_J) < G(a_{J+1})$, so that no X can be generated in an interval for which $n_j = 0$. (Also, it is clear that $a_0 \leq X \leq a_k$.) The determination of J in step 2 could be done by a straightforward left-to-right search or by a search starting with the value of j for which $G(a_{j+1}) - G(a_j)$ is largest, then next largest, etc. As an alternative which avoids the search entirely (at the expense of extra storage) we could initially define a vector $(m_1, m_2, \ldots, m_n)$ by setting the first n_1 m_i's to 0, the next n_2 m_i's to 1, etc., with the last n_k m_i's being set to $k - 1$. (If some n_j is 0, no m_i's are set to $j - 1$. For example, if $k \geq 3$ and $n_1 > 0$, $n_2 = 0$, and $n_3 > 0$, the first n_1 m_i's are set to 0 and the *next* n_3 m_i's are set to 2.) Then the value of J in step 2 can be determined by setting $L = \lfloor nU \rfloor + 1$ and letting $J = m_L$. Whether or not this is worthwhile depends on the particular characteristics of the data and on the importance of any computational speed that might be gained relative to the extra storage and programming effort. Finally, Chen and Asau [12] give another method for determining J in step 2, based on preliminary calculations which reduce the range of search for a given U; it requires only 10 extra memory locations. (Their treatment is for a discrete empirical distribution function but can also be applied to the present case.)

7.4 GENERATING DISCRETE RANDOM VARIABLES

This section discusses particular algorithms for generating random variables from various discrete distributions which might be useful for modeling in a simulation study. As in Sec. 7.3, we usually present for each distribution one algorithm which is fairly simple to implement and reasonably efficient. References will be made to alternative algorithms which might be faster, usually at the expense of a higher degree of complexity.

The discrete inverse-transform method, as described in Sec. 7.2.1, can be used for any discrete distribution, whether the range of possible values is finite or (countably) infinite. Many of the algorithms presented in this section *are* the discrete inverse-transform method, although in some cases this fact is very well disguised due to the particular way the required search is performed, which often takes advantage of the special form of the probability mass function. As was the case for continuous random variables, however, the inverse-transform method may not be the most efficient way to generate a random variable from a given distribution.

One other general approach should be mentioned here, which can be used for generating *any* discrete random variable having a *finite* range of values. This is the *alias method,* developed by Walker [50] and refined by Kronmal and Peterson [26]; it is very general and efficient. The method does require some initial setup calculations and extra storage, but not very much. We discuss the alias method in more detail in Sec. 7.4.3, but the reader should keep in mind that it is applicable to *any* discrete distribution with a finite range (such as the binomial). For an infinite range, the alias method can be used indirectly in conjunction with the general composition approach (see Sec. 7.2.2); this is also discussed in Sec. 7.4.3.

A final comment concerns the apparent loss of generality in considering below only distributions which have range $S_n = \{0, 1, 2, \ldots, n\}$ or $S = \{0, 1, 2, \ldots\}$, which may appear to be more restrictive than our original definition of a discrete random variable having general range $T_n = \{x_1, x_2, \ldots, x_n\}$ or $T = \{x_1, x_2, \ldots\}$. However, no generality is actually lost. If we really want a random variable X with mass function $p(x_i)$ and general range T_n (or T), we can first generate a random variable I with range S_{n-1} (or S) such that $P\{I = i - 1\} = p(x_i)$ for $i = 1, 2, \ldots, n$ (or $i = 1, 2, \ldots$). Then the random variable $X = x_{I+1}$ is returned and has the desired distribution. (Given I, x_{I+1} could be determined from a stored table of the x_i's, or from a formula which computes x_i as a function of i.)

7.4.1 Bernoulli

The following algorithm is quite intuitive and is equivalent to the inverse-transform method (the roles of U and $1 - U$ are reversed):

1. Generate $U \sim U(0, 1)$.
2. If $U \leq p$, set $X = 1$ and return. Otherwise, set $X = 0$ and return.

7.4.2 Discrete Uniform

Again, the straightforward intuitive algorithm given below is (exactly) the inverse-transform method:

1. Generate $U \sim U(0, 1)$.
2. Set $X = i + \lfloor (j - i + 1)U \rfloor$ and return.

Note that no search is required. The constant $j - i + 1$ should, of course, be computed ahead of time and stored.

7.4.3 Arbitrary Discrete Distribution

Consider the very general situation where we have *any* probability mass function $p(0)$, $p(1)$, $p(2)$, ... on the nonnegative integers S, and we want to generate a discrete random variable X with the corresponding distribution. The $p(i)$'s could have been specified theoretically by some distributional form or empirically from a data set directly. The case of finite range S_n is included here by setting $p(i) = 0$ for all $i \geq n + 1$. (Note that this formulation includes *every* special discrete distribution form.)

The direct inverse-transform method, for either the finite- or infinite-range case, is as follows (define the empty sum to be 0):

1. Generate $U \sim U(0, 1)$.
2. Find the nonnegative integer I satisfying

$$\sum_{j=0}^{I-1} p(j) \leq U < \sum_{j=0}^{I} p(j)$$

Set $X = I$ and return.

Note that this algorithm will never return a value $X = i$ for which $p(i) = 0$, since the strict inequality between the two summations in step 2 would fail. Step 2 does require a search, which may be time-consuming. As an alternative we could initially sort the $p(i)$'s into decreasing order so that the search would be most likely to terminate after a smaller number of comparisons; see Prob. 7.2 for an example.

Due to the generality of the present situation, we depart from our usual practice of giving only one algorithm and present two other methods which are useful when the desired random variable has *finite* range S_n. The first of these methods assumes that each $p(i)$ is exactly equal to a q-place decimal; for exposition we take the case $q = 2$, so that $p(i)$ is of the form $0.01 k_i$ for some integer $k_i \in \{0, 1, \dots, 100\}$ ($i = 0, 1, \dots, n$), and $\sum_{i=0}^{n} k_i = 100$. We initialize a vector $(m_1, m_2, \dots, m_{100})$ by setting the first k_0 m_j's to 0, the next k_1 m_j's to 1, etc., and the last k_n m_j's to n. (If $k_i = 0$ for some i, no m_j's are set to i.) Then an algorithm for generating the desired random variable X is as follows:

1. Generate $J \sim DU(1, 100)$.
2. Set $X = m_J$ and return.

(See Sec. 7.4.2 to accomplish step 1.) Note that this method requires 10^q extra storage locations and an array reference in step 2; it is, however, the inverse-transform method provided that J is generated by the algorithm in Sec. 7.4.2. If three or four decimal places are needed to specify the $p(i)$'s exactly, the value 100 in step 1 would be replaced by 1000 or 10,000, respectively, and the storage requirements would also grow by one or two orders of magnitude. Even if the $p(i)$'s are not *exactly* q-place decimals for some small value of q, the simulator might be able to obtain sufficient accuracy by rounding the $p(i)$'s to the nearest hundredth or thousandth; this is an attractive alternative especially when the $p(i)$'s are proportions obtained directly from data, and may not be accurate beyond two or three decimal places anyway. When rounding the $p(i)$'s, however, it is important to remember that they must sum exactly to 1.

The second attractive technique to use when X has range S_n is the alias method mentioned above. The method requires that we initially calculate two arrays of length $n + 1$ each, from the given $p(i)$'s. The first array contains the *cutoff* values $F_i \in [0, 1]$ for $i = 0, 1, \ldots, n$, and the second array gives the *aliases* $L_i \in S_n$ for $i = 0, 1, \ldots, n$; an explicit algorithm for computing the cutoff values and aliases from the $p(i)$'s is given in Kronmal and Peterson [26]. Then the alias method is as follows:

1. Generate $I \sim DU(0, n)$ and $U \sim U(0, 1)$ independent of I.
2. If $U \leq F_I$, set $X = I$ and return. Otherwise, set $X = L_I$ and return.

Thus, step 2 involves a kind of "rejection," but upon rejecting I we need *not* start over but only return I's alias, L_I, rather than I itself. The cutoff values are seen to be the probabilities with which we return I rather than its alias. There is only one comparison needed to generate each X, and we need exactly two $U(0, 1)$ random variables for each X if I is generated as in Sec. 7.4.2. (See [26] for a way to accomplish step 1 with only *one* $U(0, 1)$ random variable.) The setup algorithm is not complicated and involves $2(n + 1)$ extra storage locations. (A method is mentioned in [26] to reduce this to $n + 1$ extra locations if n is large or storage capacity is very limited.) We feel that the alias method is an attractive possibility, especially when we need a large number of random variables, so that the setup is justified.

Although the alias method is limited to discrete random variables with a finite range, it can be used indirectly for discrete distributions with an infinite range, such as the geometric, negative binomial, or Poisson, by combining it with the general composition method. For example, if X can be any nonnegative integer, we can examine the $p(i)$'s to find an n such that $q = \sum_{i=0}^{n} p(i)$ is close to 1, so that the probability is high that $X \in S_n$. Then, noting that for any i we can write

$$p(i) = q \left[\frac{p(i)}{q} I_{S_n}(i) \right] + (1 - q) \left\{ \frac{p(i)}{1-q} [1 - I_{S_n}(i)] \right\}$$

we obtain the following general algorithm:

1. Generate $U \sim U(0, 1)$. If $U \leq q$, go to step 2. Otherwise, go to step 3.
2. Use the alias method to generate X on S_n with probability mass function $p(i)/q$ for $i = 0, 1, \ldots, n$ and return.
3. Use any other method to generate X on $\{n+1, n+2, \ldots\}$ with probability mass function $p(i)/(1-q)$ for $i = n + 1, n + 2, \ldots$ and return.

In step 3, we could use the inverse-transform method, for example. Since n was chosen to make q close to 1, we would expect to avoid step 3 most of the time.

7.4.4 Binomial

To generate a bin(t, p) random variable, recall from Sec. 5.2.3 that the sum of t IID Bernoulli(p) random variables has the bin(t, p) distribution. This relation leads to the following convolution algorithm:

1. Generate Y_1, Y_2, ..., Y_t as IID Bernoulli(p) random variables.
2. Set $X = Y_1 + Y_2 + \cdots + Y_t$ and return.

Since the execution time of this algorithm is proportional to t, we might want to look for an alternative if t is large. One possibility would be the direct inverse-transform method with an efficient search. Another alternative is direct application of the alias method (see Sec. 7.4.3), since the range of X is finite. Finally, algorithms specific to the binomial distribution that are efficient for large t are discussed by Ahrens and Dieter [2].

7.4.5 Geometric

The following algorithm is equivalent to the inverse-transform method if we replace U by $1 - U$ in step 2 (see Prob. 7.14):

1. Generate $U \sim U(0, 1)$.
2. Set $X = \lfloor \ln U / \ln (1 - p) \rfloor$ and return.

The constant $\ln (1 - p)$ should, of course, be computed beforehand. If p is near 0, $\ln (1 - p)$ will also be near zero, so that double-precision arithmetic should be considered to avoid excessive roundoff error in the division in step 2. For p near 1, $\ln (1 - p)$ will be a large negative number, which also could cause numerical difficulties; fortunately, for large p it is more efficient to use an altogether different algorithm based on the relationship between geometric and Bernoulli random variables described in Sec. 5.2.3 (see Prob. 7.14).

7.4.6 Negative Binomial

The relation between the negbin(s, p) and geom(p) distributions in Sec. 5.2.3 leads to the following convolution algorithm:

1. Generate Y_1, Y_2, ..., Y_s as IID geom(p) random variables.
2. Set $X = Y_1 + Y_2 + \cdots + Y_s$ and return.

This is a simple method, but its execution time is proportional to s. For large s, consideration might be given to an alternative method discussed by Fishman [20], which makes use of a special relationship between the negative binomial, gamma, and Poisson distributions; its efficiency depends on the ability to generate rapidly from the gamma and Poisson distributions. Other alternatives are discussed in [2].

7.4.7 Poisson

Our algorithm for generating Poisson(λ) random variables is based essentially on the relationship between the Poisson(λ) and expo($1/\lambda$) distributions stated in Sec. 5.2.3. The algorithm is as follows:

1. Let $a = e^{-\lambda}$, $b = 1$, and $i = 0$.
2. Generate $U_{i+1} \sim U(0, 1)$ and replace b by bU_{i+1}. If $b < a$, set $X = i$ and return. Otherwise, go to step 3.
3. Replace i by $i + 1$ and go back to step 2.

The algorithm is justified by noting that $X = i$ if and only if

$$\sum_{j=1}^{i} Y_j \leq 1 < \sum_{j=1}^{i+1} Y_j$$

where $Y_j = (-1/\lambda) \ln U_j \sim \text{expo}(1/\lambda)$ and the Y_j's are independent. That is, $X = \max \{i: \sum_{j=1}^{i} Y_j \leq 1\}$, so that $X \sim \text{Poisson}(\lambda)$ by the first comment in the description of the Poisson distribution in Table 5.2.

Unfortunately, this algorithm becomes slow as λ increases, since a large λ means that $a = e^{-\lambda}$ is smaller, requiring more executions of step 2 to bring the cumulative product of the U_{i+1}'s down under a. [In fact, since X is 1 less than the number of U_{i+1}'s required, the expected number of executions of step 2 is $E(X) + 1 = \lambda + 1$, so that execution time grows with λ in an essentially linear fashion.] One alternative would be to use the alias method in concert with the composition approach (since the range of X is infinite), as described in Sec. 7.4.3. Another possibility would be the inverse-transform method with an efficient search. Recently, Atkinson [5] examined several such search procedures and reported that an indexed search similar to the method of Chen and Asau [12], discussed earlier in Sec. 7.3.10, performed well. (This search procedure, called PQM by Atkinson, requires a small amount of initialization and extra storage but is still quite simple to implement.)

*7.5 GENERATING CORRELATED RANDOM VARIABLES

So far in this chapter we have really only considered generation of a single random variable at a time from various *univariate distributions*. Applying one of these algorithms repeatedly with independent sets of U(0, 1) random variables produces a sequence of IID random variables from the desired distribution. In some simulation models, however, we may want to generate a random *vector* $\mathbf{X} = (X_1, X_2, \ldots, X_k)^T$ from a specified *joint* (or *multivariate*) *distribution*, where the individual components of the vector might not be independent. (A^T denotes the transpose of a vector or matrix A.) Even if we cannot specify the exact, full joint distributions of X_1, X_2,

..., X_m, we might want to generate them so that the individual X_i's have specified univariate distributions (called the *marginal distributions* of the X_i's) and so that the correlations, ρ_{ij}, between X_i and X_j are specified by the modeler. In this section we give examples of methods for generating such correlated random variables in some specific cases. There are several other problems related to generating correlated random variables which we do not explicitly discuss, e.g., simulating autoregressive processes and generating from a multivariate exponential distribution; we refer the reader to Fishman [19, 20], Mitchell and Paulson [33], and Marshall and Olkin [32].

It is not difficult to think of models where correlated random variables would be appropriate. For example, consider a maintenance shop which can be modeled as a tandem queue with two service stations. At the first station, incoming items are inspected, and any defects are marked for repair at the second station. Since a badly damaged item would require more time for *both* inspection *and* repair, we would expect the two service times for a given item to be positively correlated. Mitchell, Paulson, and Beswick [34] found that ignoring this correlation in modeling a system can lead to serious inaccuracies in the results of a simulation, which underscores the need to be able to generate correlated random variables.

7.5.1 Using Conditional Distributions

Suppose that we have a specified joint distribution function $F_{X_1,X_2,\ldots,X_n}(x_1, x_2, \ldots, x_n)$ from which we would like to generate a random vector $\mathbf{X} = (X_1, X_2, \ldots, X_n)^T$. Also assume that for $k = 2, 3, \ldots, n$ we can obtain the *conditional distribution* of X_k given that $X_i = x_i$ for $i = 1, 2, \ldots, k - 1$; denote this conditional distribution function by $F_k(x_k \mid x_1, x_2, \ldots, x_{k-1})$. (See any probability text, such as Mood, Graybill, and Boes [35] for a discussion of conditional distributions.) In addition, let $F_{X_i}(x_i)$ be the marginal distribution function of X_i for $i = 1, 2, \ldots, n$. Then a general algorithm for generating a random vector $\mathbf{X}$ with joint distribution function $F_{X_1,X_2,\ldots,X_n}$ is as follows:

1. Generate X_1 with distribution function F_{X_1}.
2. Generate X_2 with distribution function $F_2(\cdot \mid X_1)$.
3. Generate X_3 with distribution function $F_3(\cdot \mid X_1, X_2)$.

  . . . .

n. Generate X_n with distribution function $F_n(\cdot \mid X_1, X_2, \ldots, X_{n-1})$.

$n + 1$. Let $\mathbf{X} = (X_1, X_2, \ldots, X_n)^T$ and return.

Note that in steps 2 through n the conditional distributions used are those with the previously generated X_i's; for example, if x_1 is the value generated for X_1 in step 1, the conditional distribution function used in step 2 is $F_2(\cdot \mid x_1)$, etc. The proof of the validity of this algorithm relies on the definition of conditional distributions and is left to the reader.

As general as this approach may be, its practical usefulness is probably quite limited. Not only is specification of the entire joint distribution required, but also derivation of many marginal and conditional distributions must be carried out. Such a level of detail is probably rarely obtainable in a complicated simulation.

7.5.2 Multivariate Normal and Multivariate Lognormal

The n-dimensional multivariate normal distribution with mean $\mu = (\mu_1, \mu_2, \ldots, \mu_n)^T$ and covariance matrix Σ, where the (i, j)th entry is σ_{ij}, has joint density function

$$f(\mathbf{x}) = (2\pi)^{-n/2}|\Sigma|^{-1/2} \exp\left[\frac{-(\mathbf{x} - \mu)^T\Sigma^{-1}(\mathbf{x} - \mu)}{2}\right]$$

where $\mathbf{x} = (x_1, x_2, \ldots, x_n)^T$ is any point in n-dimensional real space and $|\Sigma|$ is the determinant of Σ. We denote this joint distribution as $N_n(\mu, \Sigma)$ and note that if $\mathbf{X} = (X_1, X_2, \ldots, X_n)^T \sim N_n(\mu, \Sigma)$, then $E(X_i) = \mu_i$ and $\text{Cov}(X_i, X_j) = \sigma_{ij} = \sigma_{ji}$; that is, Σ is symmetric and is positive definite.

Although the conditional distribution method of Sec. 7.5.1 can be applied, a simpler method due to Scheuer and Stoller [38] is available, which uses a special property of the multivariate normal distribution. Since Σ is symmetric and positive definite, we can factor it uniquely as $\Sigma = CC^T$, where the $n \times n$ matrix C is lower triangular. (See [19, p. 217] for an algorithm to compute C.) If c_{ij} is the (i, j)th element of C, an algorithm for generating the desired multivariate normal vector $\mathbf{X}$ is as follows:

1. Generate $Z_1, Z_2, \ldots, Z_n$ as IID $N(0, 1)$ random variables.

2. For $i = 1, 2, \ldots, n$, let $X_i = \mu_i + \sum_{j=1}^{i} c_{ij}Z_j$ and return.

To accomplish the univariate normal generation in step 1, see Sec. 7.3.6. In matrix notation, if we let $\mathbf{Z} = (Z_1, Z_2, \ldots, Z_n)^T$, the algorithm is just $\mathbf{X} = \mu + C\mathbf{Z}$; note the similarity with the transformation $X' = \mu + \sigma X$ for generating $X' \sim N(\mu, \sigma^2)$ given $X \sim N(0, 1)$.

For a discussion of generating a random vector from a multivariate lognormal distribution, see Johnson and Ramberg [23].

7.5.3 Correlated Gamma Random Variables

We now come to a case where we cannot write the entire joint distribution but only specify the marginal distributions (gamma) and the correlations between the component random variables of the $\mathbf{X}$ vector. (Indeed, there is not even agreement about what the "multivariate gamma" distribution should be. Unlike the multivariate normal case, specification of the marginal distributions and the correlation matrix does *not* completely determine the joint distribution here.)

The problem, then, is as follows. For a given set of shape parameters $\alpha_1, \alpha_2,$

..., α_m, scale parameters $\beta_1, \beta_2, \ldots, \beta_m$, and correlations ρ_{ij} ($i = 1, 2, \ldots, n; j = 1, 2, \ldots, n$) we want to generate a random vector $\mathbf{X} = (X_1, X_2, \ldots, X_n)^T$ so that $X_i \sim \text{gamma}(\alpha_i, \beta_i)$ and Cor $(X_i, X_j) = \rho_{ij}$. An immediate difficulty is that not all ρ_{ij} values between -1 and $+1$ are theoretically consistent with a given set of α_i's; that is, a given set of α_i's places a limitation on the possible ρ_{ij}'s (see Schmeiser and Lal [43]). The next difficulty is that, even for a set of α_i's and ρ_{ij}'s that *are* theoretically possible, there might not be an algorithm currently available that will do the job. For this reason, we must be content at present with generating correlated gamma random variables in some restricted cases.

One situation in which there *is* a simple algorithm is the bivariate case, $n = 2$. A further restriction is that $\rho = \rho_{12} \geq 0$, that is, positive correlation, and yet another restriction is that $\rho \leq [\min \{\alpha_1, \alpha_2\}]/(\alpha_1\alpha_2)^{1/2}$. Nevertheless, this does include many useful situations, especially when α_1 and α_2 are close together. (If $\alpha_1 = \alpha_2$, the upper bound on ρ is removed.) Notice that any two positively correlated exponential random variables are included by setting $\alpha_1 = \alpha_2 = 1$. The algorithm, using a general technique developed by Arnold [3], relies on a special property of gamma distributions:

1. Generate $Y_1 \sim \text{gamma}(\alpha_1 - \rho(\alpha_1\alpha_2)^{1/2}, 1)$.
2. Generate $Y_2 \sim \text{gamma}(\alpha_2 - \rho(\alpha_1\alpha_2)^{1/2}, 1)$, independent of Y_1.
3. Generate $Y_3 \sim \text{gamma}(\rho(\alpha_1\alpha_2)^{1/2}, 1)$, independent of Y_1 and Y_2.
4. Set $X_1 = \beta_1(Y_1 + Y_3)$, $X_2 = \beta_2(Y_2 + Y_3)$, and return.

This technique is known as *trivariate reduction,* since the three random variables Y_1, Y_2, and Y_3 are "reduced" to the two final random variables X_1 and X_2. Note that the algorithm does not control the joint distribution of X_1 and X_2; this point is addressed in [43].

Correlated gamma random variables can also be generated in some less restrictive cases. Schmeiser and Lal [43] give algorithms for generating bivariate gamma random vectors with any theoretically possible correlation, either positive or negative. Ronning [37] treats the general multivariate case ($n \geq 2$) but again restricts consideration to certain positive correlations.

7.6 GENERATING ARRIVAL PROCESSES

In this section, we show how to generate the times of arrivals $t_1, t_2, \ldots$ for the arrival processes discussed in Sec. 5.7.

7.6.1 Poisson Process

The (stationary) Poisson process with rate $\lambda > 0$, discussed in Sec. 5.7.1, has the property that the interarrival times $A_i = t_i - t_{i-1}$ ($i = 1, 2, \ldots$) are IID exponential random variables with common parameter $1/\lambda$. Thus, we can generate the t_i's recursively, as follows (assume that t_{i-1} has been determined and we want to generate the next arrival time, t_i):

1. Generate $U \sim U(0, 1)$ independent of any previous random variables.
2. Set $t_i = t_{i-1} - (1/\lambda) \ln U$ and return.

The recursion starts by computing t_1 (recall that $t_0 = 0$).

This algorithm can be easily modified to generate any arrival process where the interarrival times are IID random variables, whether or not they are exponential. Step 2 would just add an independently generated interarrival time to t_{i-1} in order to get t_i; the form of step 2 as given above is simply a special case for exponential interarrival times.

7.6.2 Nonstationary Poisson Process

We now discuss how to generate arrival times which follow a nonstationary Poisson process (see Sec. 5.7.2).

It is tempting to modify the algorithm of Sec. 7.6.1 to generate t_i given t_{i-1} by substituting $\lambda(t_{i-1})$ in step 2 for λ. However, this would be incorrect, as can be seen from Fig. 7.6. (This figure might represent traffic arrival rates at an intersection over a 24-hour day.) If $t_{i-1} = 5$, for example, this erroneous "algorithm" would tend to generate a large interarrival time before t_i, since $\lambda(5)$ is low compared with $\lambda(s)$ for s between 6 and 9. Thus, we would miss this upcoming rise in the arrival rate and would not generate the high traffic density associated with the morning rush; indeed, if t_i turned out to be 11, we would miss the morning rush altogether.

Care must be taken, then, to generate a nonstationary Poisson process in a valid way. A general and simple method recently proposed by Lewis and Shedler [27],

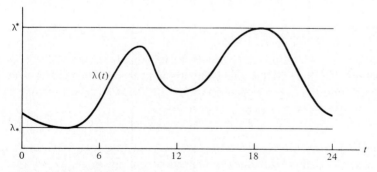

Figure 7.6 Nonstationary Poisson process.

known as *thinning*, can be used. We present a special case of the thinning algorithm which works when $\lambda^* = \max_s \{\lambda(s)\}$ is finite. Briefly, we generate a stationary Poisson process with constant rate λ^* and arrival times $\{t_i^*\}$ (using, for example, the algorithm of Sec. 7.6.1), then "thin out" the t_i^*'s by throwing away (rejecting) each t_i^* as an arrival, with probability $1 - \lambda(t_i^*)/\lambda^*$. Thus, we are more likely to accept t_i^* as an arrival if $\lambda(t_i^*)$ is high, yielding the desired property that arrivals will occur more frequently in intervals for which $\lambda(s)$ is high. An equivalent algorithm, in a more convenient recursive form, is as follows (again we assume that t_{i-1} has been validly generated and we want to generate the next arrival time t_i):

1. Set $t = t_{i-1}$.
2. Generate U_1 and U_2 as IID U(0, 1) independent of any previous random variables.
3. Replace t by $t - (1/\lambda^*) \ln U_1$.
4. If $U_2 \leq \lambda(t)/\lambda^*$, set $t_i = t$ and return. Otherwise, go back to step 2.

(Once again the algorithm is started by computing t_1.) If the evaluation of $\lambda(t)$ is slow [which might be the case if, for example, $\lambda(t)$ is a complicated function involving exponential and trigonometric calculations], computation time might be saved in step 4 by adding an acceptance pretest; i.e., the current value for t is accepted as the next arrival time if $U_2 \leq \lambda_*/\lambda^*$, where $\lambda_* = \min_s \{\lambda(s)\}$. This would be useful especially when $\lambda(s)$ is fairly flat.

Although the thinning algorithm is simple, it might be inefficient in some cases. For example, if $\lambda(s)$ is relatively low except for a few high and narrow peaks, λ^* will be a lot larger than $\lambda(s)$ most of the time, resulting in thinning out most of the t_i^*'s. In such cases, other methods might be used, such as a more general thinning algorithm (see [27]) or the method described by Çinlar [16], which involves inverting the expectation function $a(s) = \int_0^s \lambda(y)\, dy$. For a discussion of the relative merits of these and other alternatives, see [27].

7.6.3 Batch Arrivals

Consider an arrival process where the ith batch of customers arrives at time t_i and the number of customers in this batch is a discrete random variable B_i. Assume that the B_i's are IID and, in addition, are independent of the t_i's. Then a general recursive algorithm for generating this arrival process is as follows:

1. Generate the next arrival time t_i.
2. Generate the discrete random variable B_i independently of any previous B_j's and also independently of $t_1, t_2, \ldots, t_i$.
3. Return with the information that B_i customers are arriving at time t_i.

Note that the arrival times $\{t_i\}$ are arbitrary; in particular, they could be from a nonstationary Poisson process.

*APPENDIX 7A VALIDITY OF THE ACCEPTANCE-REJECTION METHOD

We show here that the acceptance-rejection method for continuous random variables (Sec. 7.2.4) is valid by checking that for any x, $P\{X \le x\} = \displaystyle\int_{-\infty}^{x} f(y)\ dy$.

Let A denote the event that acceptance occurs in step 3 of the algorithm. Now X is defined only on the event (or set) A, which is a *subset* of the entire space on which Y and U (of steps 1 and 2) are defined. Thus, *unconditional* probability statements about X alone are really *conditional* probability statements (conditioned on A) about Y and U. Since, given that A occurs we have $X = Y$, we can write

$$P\{X \le x\} = P\{Y \le x \,|\, A\} \tag{7.1}$$

We shall evaluate the right side of (7.1).

By the definition of conditional probability,

$$P\{Y \le x \,|\, A\} = \frac{P\{A,\, Y \le x\}}{P\{A\}} \tag{7.2}$$

We shall solve explicitly for the two probabilities on the right side of (7.2). To do this, it will be convenient first to note that for any y,

$$P\{A \,|\, Y = y\} = P\left\{U \le \frac{f(y)}{t(y)}\right\} = \frac{f(y)}{t(y)} \tag{7.3}$$

where the first equality follows since U is independent of Y and the second equality since $U \sim U(0, 1)$ and $f(y) \le t(y)$.

We now use (7.3) to show that

$$P\{A,\, Y \le x\} = \int_{-\infty}^{x} P\{A,\, Y \le x \,|\, Y = y\} r(y)\ dy$$

$$= \int_{-\infty}^{x} P\{A \,|\, Y = y\} \frac{t(y)}{c}\ dy$$

$$= \frac{1}{c} \int_{-\infty}^{x} f(y)\,dy \tag{7.4}$$

Next, we note that $P\{A\} = \displaystyle\int_{-\infty}^{\infty} P\{A \,|\, Y = y\} r(y)\ dy = 1/c$ [by (7.3) and the fact that f is a density, so integrates to 1]. This, together with (7.4), (7.2), and (7.1), yields the desired result.

PROBLEMS

7.1 Give algorithms for generating random variables with the following densities:

(a) Cauchy

$$f(x) = \left\{ \pi\beta \left[1 + \left(\frac{x - \alpha}{\beta} \right)^2 \right] \right\}^{-1} \quad \text{where } -\infty < \alpha < \infty, \beta > 0, -\infty < x < \infty$$

(b) Gumbel or extreme value

$$f(x) = \frac{1}{\beta} \exp\left[-e^{-(x-\alpha)/\beta} - (x - \alpha)/\beta \right] \quad \text{where } -\infty < \alpha < \infty, \beta > 0, -\infty < x < \infty$$

(c) Logistic

$$f(x) = \frac{(1/\beta)e^{-(x-\alpha)/\beta}}{(1 + e^{-(x-\alpha)/\beta})^2} \quad \text{where } -\infty < \alpha < \infty, \beta > 0, -\infty < x < \infty$$

(d) Pareto

$$f(x) = \frac{\theta a^\theta}{x^{\theta+1}} \quad \text{where } a > 0, \theta > 0, x > a$$

For $\alpha = 0$ and $\beta = 1$ in each of (a), (b), and (c), use your algorithms to generate IID random variables $X_1, X_2, \ldots, X_{5000}$ and print out $\overline{X}(n) = \sum_{i=1}^{n} X_i/n$ for $n = 50, 100, 150, \ldots, 5000$ to verify empirically the strong law of large numbers (Sec. 4.6), i.e., that $\overline{X}(n)$ converges to $E(X_i)$ (if it exists); do the same for (d) with $a = 1$ and $\theta = 2$.

7.2 Let X be discrete with probability mass function $p(1) = 0.05$, $p(2) = 0.05$, $p(3) = 0.1$, $p(4) = 0.1$, $p(5) = 0.6$, and $p(6) = 0.1$, and for $i = 1, 2, \ldots, 6$, let $q(i) = p(1) + p(2) + \cdots + p(i)$. Convince yourself that the following algorithm is explicitly the discrete inverse-transform method with a simple left-to-right search:

   1. Generate $U \sim U(0, 1)$ and set $i = 1$.
   2. If $U \leq q(i)$, set $X = i$ and return. Otherwise, go to step 3.
   3. Replace i by $i + 1$ and go back to step 2.

Let N be the number of times step 2 is executed (so N is also the number of comparisons). Show that N has the same distribution as X, so that $E(N) = E(X) = 4.45$. This algorithm can be represented as in Fig. 7.7, where the circled numbers are the values to which X is set if U falls in the interval directly below them and the search is left to right.

Alternatively, we could first sort the $p(i)$'s into decreasing order and form a coding vector $i'(i)$, as follows. Let $q'(1) = 0.6$, $q'(2) = 0.7$, $q'(3) = 0.8$, $q'(4) = 0.9$, $q'(5) = 0.95$, and $q'(6) = 1$; also let $i'(1) = 5$, $i'(2) = 3$, $i'(3) = 4$, $i'(4) = 6$, $i'(5) = 1$, and $i'(6) = 2$. Show that the following algorithm is valid:

   1'. Generate $U \sim U(0, 1)$ and set $i = 1$.
   2'. If $U \leq q'(i)$, set $X = i'(i)$ and return. Otherwise, go to step 3'.
   3'. Replace i by $i + 1$ and go back to step 2'.

If N' is the number of comparisons for this second algorithm, show that $E(N') = 2.05$, which is less than half of $E(N)$. This saving in marginal execution time will depend on the particular distribution and must be weighed against the extra setup time and storage for the coding vector $i'(i)$. This second algorithm can be represented as in Fig. 7.8.

Figure 7.7 Representation of the first algorithm in Prob. 7.2.

Figure 7.8 Representation of the second algorithm in Prob. 7.2.

7.3 Recall the truncated distribution function F^* and the algorithm for generating from it, as given in Sec. 7.2.1.

(*a*) Show that the algorithm stated in Sec. 7.2.1 is valid when F is continuous and strictly

3. Replace i by $i + 1$ and go back to step 2.

1. Generate $U \sim U(0, 1)$.
2. If $F(a) \leq U \leq F(b)$, set $X = F^{-1}(U)$ and return. Otherwise, go back to step 1.

Which algorithm do you think is "better"? In what sense? Under what conditions?

7.4 A truncation of a distribution function F can be defined differently from the F^* of Sec. 7.2.1. Again for $a < b$, define the distribution function

$$\tilde{F}(x) = \begin{cases} 0 & \text{if } x < a \\ F(x) & \text{if } a \leq x < b \\ 1 & \text{if } b \leq x \end{cases}$$

Find a method for generating from the distribution function $\tilde{F}$, assuming that we already have a method for generating from F. Demonstrate the validity of your algorithm.

7.5 Show that the algorithm in Sec. 7.2.1 for generating the ith order statistic is valid when F is strictly increasing. [*Hint:* Use the fact that if $U_1, U_2, \ldots, U_n$ are IID U(0, 1), then $U_{(i)} \sim \text{beta}(i, n - i + 1)$.] Verify directly that for $i = 1$ and $i = n$ it is valid to let $V = 1 - U^{1/n}$ and $V = U^{1/n}$, respectively.

7.6 Derive the inverse-transform algorithm for the double exponential distribution of Example 7.3 and compare it with the composition algorithm as given in the example. Which would you prefer?

7.7 For $a < b$, the *right triangular distribution* has density function

$$f_R(x) = \begin{cases} \dfrac{2(x - a)}{(b - a)^2} & \text{if } a \leq x \leq b \\ 0 & \text{otherwise} \end{cases}$$

and the *left triangular distribution* has density function

$$f_L(x) = \begin{cases} \dfrac{2(b - x)}{(b - a)^2} & \text{if } a \leq x \leq b \\ 0 & \text{otherwise} \end{cases}$$

These distributions are denoted by RT(a, b) and LT(a, b), respectively.

(*a*) Show that if $X \sim$ RT(0, 1), then $X' = a + (b - a)X \sim$ RT(a, b); verify the same relation between LT(0, 1) and LT(a, b). Thus it is sufficient to generate from RT(0, 1) and LT(0, 1).

(*b*) Show that if $X \sim$ RT(0, 1), then $1 - X \sim$ LT(0, 1). Thus it is enough to restrict further our attention to generating from RT(0, 1).

(*c*) Derive the inverse-transform algorithm for generating from RT(0, 1). Despite the result in (*b*), also derive the inverse-transform algorithm for generating directly from LT(0, 1).

(*d*) As an alternative to the inverse-transform method, show that if U_1 and U_2 are IID U(0, 1) random variables, then max $\{U_1, U_2\} \sim$ RT(0, 1). Do you think that this is better than the inverse-transform method? In what sense? (See Example 7.4.)

7.8 In each of the following cases, give an algorithm which uses exactly *one* U(0, 1) random variable for generating a random variable with the same distribution as X.

(*a*) $X = $ min $\{U_1, U_2\}$, where U_1 and U_2 are IID U(0, 1).

(b) $X = \max \{U_1, U_2\}$, where U_1 and U_2 are IID U(0, 1).

(c) $X = \min \{Y_1, Y_2\}$, where Y_1 and Y_2 are IID exponential with common parameter β.

Compare (a) and (b) with Prob. 7.7. Compare your one-U algorithms in (a) to (c) with the direct ones of actually generating the U_i's or Y_i's and then taking the minimum or maximum.

*7.9 The general acceptance-rejection method of Sec. 7.2.4 has the following discrete analogue. Let X be discrete with probability mass function $p(x_i)$ for $i = 0, \pm 1, \pm 2, \ldots$, let the majorizing function be

$t(x_i) \geq p(x_i)$ for all i, let $c = \sum_{i=-\infty}^{\infty} t(x_i)$, and let $r(x_i) = t(x_i)/c$ for $i = 0, \pm 1, \pm 2, \ldots$.

1'. Generate Y having probability mass function r.

2'. Generate $U \sim$ U(0, 1), independent of Y.

3'. If $U \leq p(Y)/t(Y)$, set $X = Y$ and return. Otherwise, return to step 1' and try again.

Show that this algorithm is valid by following steps similar to those in Appendix 7A. What considerations are important in choosing the function $t(x_i)$?

7.10 For the general acceptance-rejection method (either continuous, as in Sec. 7.2.4, or discrete, as in Prob. 7.9) find the distribution of the number of (Y, U) pairs that are rejected before acceptance occurs. What is the expected number of rejections?

7.11 Give inverse-transform, composition, and acceptance-rejection algorithms for generating from each of the following densities. Discuss which algorithm is preferable for each density. (First plot the densities.)

(a)

$$f(x) = \begin{cases} \dfrac{3x^2}{2} & \text{if } -1 \leq x \leq 1 \\ 0 & \text{otherwise} \end{cases}$$

(b) For $0 < a < \frac{1}{2}$,

$$f(x) = \begin{cases} 0 & \text{if } x \leq 0 \\ \dfrac{x}{a(1-a)} & \text{if } 0 \leq x \leq a \\ \dfrac{1}{1-a} & \text{if } a \leq x \leq 1-a \\ \dfrac{1-x}{a(1-a)} & \text{if } 1-a \leq x \leq 1 \\ 0 & \text{if } 1 \leq x \end{cases}$$

7.12 Recall the polar method of Sec. 7.3.6 for generating N(0, 1) random variables. Show that the probability of "acceptance" of W in step 2 is $\pi/4$ and find the distribution of the number of "rejections" of W before "acceptance" finally occurs. What is the expected value of the number of executions of step 1?

7.13 Give a composition algorithm for generating from the triang(0, 1, c) distribution ($0 < c < 1$) of Sec. 7.3.9. Compare it with the inverse-transform algorithm in Sec. 7.3.9. (*Hint*: See Prob. 7.7.)

7.14 (a) Demonstrate the validity of the algorithm given in Sec. 7.4.5 for generating from the geom(p) distribution. (*Hint*: For a real number z and an integer i, $\lfloor z \rfloor = i$ if and only if $i \leq z < i + 1$.) Also verify (with $1 - U$ in place of U) that this *is* the inverse-transform algorithm.

(b) Show that the following algorithm is also valid for generating $X \sim$ geom(p):

1. Let $i = 0$.

2. Generate $U \sim$ U(0,1) independent of any previously generated U(0,1) random variables.

3. If $U \leq p$, set $X = i$ and return. Otherwise, replace i by $i+1$ and go back to step 2.

Note that if p is large (close to 1), this algorithm is an attractive alternative to the one given in Sec. 7.4.5, since no logarithms are required and early termination is likely.

7.15 Recall the shifted exponential, gamma, Weibull, and lognormal distributions discussed in Appendix 5A. Assuming the ability to generate random variables from the original (unshifted) versions of these distributions, give a general algorithm for generating random variables from the shifted versions. (Assume that the shift parameter γ is specified.)

REFERENCES

1. Ahrens, J. H., and U. Dieter: Computer Methods for Sampling from the Exponential and Normal Distributions, *Commun. Ass. Comput. Mach.,* **15**: 873–882 (1972).
2. Ahrens, J. H., and U. Dieter: Computer Methods for Sampling from Gamma, Beta, Poisson and Binomial Distributions, *Computing,* **12**: 223–246 (1974).
3. Arnold, B. C.: A Note on Multivariate Distributions with Specified Marginals, *J. Am. Statist. Ass.,* **62**: 1460–1461 (1967).
4. Atkinson, A. C.: A Family of Switching Algorithms for the Computer Generation of Beta Random Variables, *Biometrika,* **66**: 141–145 (1979).
5. Atkinson, A. C.: The Computer Generation of Poisson Random Variables, *Appl. Statist.,* **28**: 29–35 (1979).
6. Atkinson, A. C., and M. C. Pearce: The Computer Generation of Beta, Gamma and Normal Random Variables, *J. R. Statist. Soc.,* **A139**: 431–448 (1976).
7. Atkinson, A. C., and J. Whittaker: A Switching Algorithm for the Generation of Beta Random Variables with at Least One Parameter less than 1, *J. R. Statist. Soc.,* **A139**: 462–467 (1976).
8. Atkinson, A. C., and J. Whittaker: The Generation of Beta Random Variables with One Parameter Greater Than and One Parameter Less Than 1, *Appl. Statist.,* **28**: 90–93 (1979).
9. Beasley, J. D., and S. G. Springer: The Percentage Points of the Normal Distribution, *Appl. Statist.,* **26**: 118–121 (1977).
10. Best, D. J., and D. E. Roberts: The Percentage Points of the χ^2 Distribution, *Appl. Statist.,* **24**: 385–388 (1975).
11. Box, G. E. P., and M. E. Muller: A Note on the Generation of Random Normal Deviates, *Ann. Math. Statist.,* **29**: 610–611 (1958).
12. Chen, H., and Y. Asau: On Generating Random Variates from an Empirical Distribution, *AIIE Trans.,* **6**: 163–166 (1974).
13. Cheng, R. C. H.: The Generation of Gamma Variables with Non-integral Shape Parameter, *Appl. Statist.,* **26**: 71–75 (1977).
14. Cheng, R. C. H.: Generating Beta Variates with Nonintegral Shape Parameters, *Commun. Ass. Comput. Mach.,* **21**: 317–322 (1978).
15. Cheng, R. C. H., and G. M. Feast: Some Simple Gamma Variate Generators, *Appl. Statist.,* **28**: 290–295 (1979).
16. Çinlar, E.: *Introduction to Stochastic Processes,* Prentice-Hall, Englewood Cliffs, N.J., 1975.
17. Cran, G. W., K. J. Martin, and G. E. Thomas: A Remark on Algorithms AS63: The Incomplete Beta Integral, AS64: Inverse of the Incomplete Beta Function Ratio, *Appl. Statist.,* **26**: 111–114 (1977).
18. Filliben, J. J.: The Probability Plot Correlation Coefficient Test for Normality, *Technometrics,* **17**: 111–117 (1975).
19. Fishman, G. S.: *Concepts and Methods in Discrete Event Digital Simulation,* Wiley, New York, 1973.
20. Fishman, G. S.: *Principles of Discrete Event Simulation,* Wiley, New York, 1978.
21. Forsythe, G. E.: von Neumann's Comparison Method for Random Sampling from the Normal and Other Distributions, *Math. Comput.,* **26**: 817–826 (1972).
22. Jöhnk, M. D.: Erzeugung von Betaverteilten und Gammaverteilten Zufallszahlen, *Metrika,* **8**: 5–15 (1964).
23. Johnson, M. E., and J. S. Ramberg: Transformations of the Multivariate Normal Distribution with Applications to Simulation, *Los Alamos Sci. Lab. Tech. Rep.* LA-UR-77-2595, Los Alamos, N.M., 1978.

24. Kinderman, A. J., and J. G. Ramage: Computer Generation of Normal Random Variables, *J. Am. Statist. Ass.*, **71:** 893–896 (1976).

25. Knuth, D. E.: *The Art of Computer Programming,* vol. 1, Addison-Wesley, Reading, Mass., 1975.

26. Kronmal, R. A., and A. V. Peterson, Jr.: On the Alias Method for Generating Random Variables from a Discrete Distribution, *Am. Statist.,* **33:** 214–218 (1979).

27. Lewis, P. A. W., and G. S. Shedler: Simulation of Nonhomogeneous Poisson Processes by Thinning, *Nav. Res. Logist. Q.,* **26:** 403–413 (1979).

28. Lilliefors, H. W.: On the Kolmogorov-Smirnov Test for Normality with Mean and Variance Unknown, *J. Am. Statist. Ass.,* **62:** 399–402 (1967).

29. MacLaren, M. D., G. Marsaglia, and T. A. Bray: A Fast Procedure for Generating Exponential Random Variables, *Commun. Ass. Comput. Mach.,* **7:** 298–300 (1964).

30. Marsaglia, G.: Generating Exponential Random Variables, *Ann. Math. Statist.,* **32:** 899–902 (1961).

31. Marsaglia, G., and T. A. Bray: A Convenient Method for Generating Normal Variables, *SIAM Rev.,* **6:** 260–264 (1964).

32. Marshall, A. W., and I. Olkin: A Multivariate Exponential Distribution, *J. Am. Statist. Ass.,* **62:** 30–44 (1967).

33. Mitchell, C. R., and A. S. Paulson: $M/M/1$ Queues with Interdependent Arrival and Service Processes, *Nav. Res. Logist. Q.,* **26:** 47–56 (1979).

34. Mitchell, C. R., A. S. Paulson, and C. A. Beswick: The Effect of Correlated Exponential Service Times on Single Server Tandem Queues, *Nav. Res. Logist. Q.,* **24:** 95–112 (1977).

35. Mood, A. M., F. A. Graybill, and D. C. Boes: *Introduction to the Theory of Statistics,* 3d ed., McGraw-Hill, New York, 1974.

36. Ramberg, J. S., and P. R. Tadikamalla: On the Generation of Subsets of Order Statistics, *J. Statist. Comput. Simul.,* **6:** 239–241 (1978).

37. Ronning, G.: A Simple Scheme for Generating Multivariate Gamma Distributions with Non-Negative Covariance Matrix, *Technometrics,* **19:** 179–183 (1977).

38. Scheuer, E. M., and D. S. Stoller: On the Generation of Normal Random Vectors, *Technometrics,* **4:** 278–281 (1962).

39. Schmeiser, B. W.: Generation of the Maximum (Minimum) Value in Digital Computer Simulation, *J. Statist. Comput. Simul.,* **8:** 103–115 (1978).

40. Schmeiser, B. W.: The Generation of Order Statistics in Digital Computer Simulation: A Survey, *Proc. 1978 Winter Simul. Conf., Miami, Fla., 1978,* pp. 137–140.

41. Schmeiser, B. W.: Generation of Variates from Distribution Tails, *Oper. Res.,* **28:** 1012–1017 (1980).

42. Schmeiser, B. W., and A. J. G. Babu: Beta Variate Generation via Exponential Majorizing Functions, *Oper. Res.,* **28:** 917–926 (1980).

43. Schmeiser, B. W., and R. Lal: Computer Generation of Bivariate Gamma Random Vectors, *Southern Methodist Univ. Dept. Oper. Res. Eng. Manage. Tech. Rep.* OR 79009, Dallas, Tex., 1979.

44. Schmeiser, B. W., and R. Lal: Squeeze Methods for Generating Gamma Variates, *J. Am. Statist. Ass.,* **75:** 679–682 (1980).

45. Schmeiser, B. W., and M. A. Shalaby: Rejection using Piece-wise Linear Majorizing Functions in Random Variate Generation, *Proc. Comput. Sci. Statist: 11th Ann. Symp. Interface,* Raleigh, N.C., 1978, pp. 230–233.

46. Schucany, W. R.: Order Statistics in Simulation, *J. Statist. Comput. Simul.,* **1:** 281–286 (1972).

47. Shapiro, S. S., and M. B. Wilk: An Analysis of Variance Test for Normality (Complete Samples), *Biometrika,* **52:** 591–611 (1965).

48. Tadikamalla, P. R.: Computer Generation of Gamma Random Variables–II, *Commun. Ass. Comput. Mach.,* **21:** 925–928 (1978).

49. von Neumann, J.: Various Techniques Used in Connection with Random Digits, *Nat. Bur. Std. Math. Ser.,* **12:** 36–38 (1951).

50. Walker, A. J.: An Efficient Method for Generating Discrete Random Variables with General Distributions, *ACM Trans. Math. Software,* **3:** 253–256 (1977).

EIGHT

OUTPUT DATA ANALYSIS FOR A SINGLE SYSTEM

8.1 INTRODUCTION

It has been our observation that in many simulation studies a large amount of time and money is spent on model development and programming but little effort is made to analyze the simulation output data in an appropriate manner. As a matter of fact, the most common mode of operation is to make a single simulation run of somewhat arbitrary length and then treat the resulting simulation estimates as being the "true" answers for the model. Since these estimates are random variables which may have large variances, they could, in a particular simulation run, differ greatly from the corresponding true answers. The net effect is, of course, that there may be a significant probability of making erroneous inferences about the system under study.

One reason for the historical lack of definitive output data analyses is that simulation output data are rarely, if ever, independent. Thus, classical statistical analyses based on IID observations are not directly applicable. At present there are still several output-analysis problems for which there is no completely accepted solution, and the solutions that do exist are often complicated to apply. Another impediment to getting accurate estimates of a model's true parameters or characteristics is the computer cost associated with collecting the necessary amount of simulation output data. Indeed, there are situations where an appropriate statistical procedure is available, but the cost of collecting the amount of data dictated by the procedure is prohibitive. We expect this latter difficulty to become less severe as the cost of computer time continues to drop.

Our goal in this chapter is to give a state-of-the-art treatment of statistical analyses for simulation output data and to present the material with a practical focus which should be accessible to a reader having a basic understanding of statistics. (Reviewing Chap. 4 might be advisable before reading this chapter.) The emphasis will be on statistical procedures which are relatively easy to understand, have been shown to perform well in practice, and have applicability to real-world problems. The remainder of the chapter is organized as follows. In Sec. 8.2 we define the two types of simulations with regard to analysis of the output, namely, terminating and steady-state simulations. Section 8.3 contrasts measures of performance for these two types of simulations, and Sec. 8.4 discusses the need to assess the accuracy of simulation output. In Secs. 8.5 and 8.6 we discuss how to construct a confidence interval for a measure of performance in the terminating and steady-state cases, respectively. In Sec. 8.7 we extend these analyses to multiple measures of performance, and the chapter is reviewed in Sec. 8.8.

On a first reading, we suggest restricting attention to Secs. 8.2 to 8.5 and 8.8.

8.2 TYPES OF SIMULATIONS WITH REGARD TO ANALYSIS OF THE OUTPUT

We begin by giving a precise definition of the two types of simulations with regard to analysis of the output data. A *terminating simulation* is one for which the desired measures of system performance are defined relative to the interval of simulated time $[0, T_E]$, where T_E is the instant in the simulation when a specified event E occurs. (Note that T_E may be a random variable.) The event E is specified before the simulation begins. Since measures of performance for terminating simulations explicitly depend on the state of the simulated system at time 0, care must be taken in choosing initial conditions. This point will be discussed further in the examples below and in Sec. 8.5.4.

Example 8.1 A retail establishment, e.g., a bank, closes each evening (physically terminating). If the establishment is open from 9 to 5, the objective of a simulation might be to estimate some measure of the quality of customer service over the period beginning at 9 and ending when the last customer who entered before the doors closed at 5 has been served. In this case $E = \{$at least 8 hours of simulated time have elapsed and the system is empty$\}$, and reasonable initial conditions for the simulation might be that no customers are present at time 0.

Example 8.2 Consider a telephone exchange which is always open (physically nonterminating). The objective of a simulation might be to determine the number of (permanent) telephone lines needed to service incoming calls adequately. Since the arrival rate of calls changes with the time of day, day of the week, etc., it is unlikely that a steady-state measure of performance (see Sec. 8.3), which is defined as a limit as time goes to infinity, will exist. A common objective in this case is to study the system during the period of peak loading, say, of length t hours, since the number of lines sufficient for this period will also do for the rest of the day. In this case, $E = \{t$ hours of simulated time have elapsed$\}$. However, care must be taken in choosing the number of waiting calls at time 0, since the actual system will probably be quite congested at the beginning of the period of peak loading. (See Sec. 8.5.4 for further discussion.)

Example 8.3 Consider a military confrontation between a defensive (fixed position) blue force and an offensive (attacking) red force. Relative to some initial force strengths, the objective of a simulation might be to estimate some function of the (final) force strengths when the red force moves to within a certain specified distance from the blue force. In this case, $E = \{$red force has moved to within a certain specified distance from the blue force$\}$. The choice of initial conditions, e.g., the number of troops and tanks for each force, for the simulation is generally not a problem here since they are specified by the military scenario under consideration.

Example 8.4 A company which sells a single product would like to decide how many items to have in inventory during a planning horizon of 120 months (see Sec. 1.5). Given some initial inventory level, the objective might be to determine how much to order each month so as to minimize the average cost per month of operating the inventory system. In this case $E = \{$120 months have been simulated$\}$, and the simulation is initialized with the current inventory level.

A *steady-state simulation* is one for which the measures of performance are defined as limits as the length of the simulation goes to infinity. Since there is no natural event E to terminate the simulation, the length of *one* simulation is made large enough to get "good" estimates of the quantities of interest. Alternatively, the length of the simulation could be determined by cost considerations; however, this may not produce acceptable results (see Sec. 8.6.1).

Example 8.5 A computer manufacturer is constructing a simulation model of a proposed computer system. Instead of using data from the arrival process of an existing computer system as input to the model, the manufacturer typically assumes that jobs arrive in accordance with a Poisson process (IID exponential interarrival times) with the rate equal to the predicted arrival rate of jobs during the period of peak loading. (This is done either because it is not clear that the arrival process of an existing system will be representative of that of the proposed system or for simplicity.) *The manufacturer is interested in estimating some characteristic of the response time of a job after the system has been running long enough for initial conditions, e.g., the number of jobs in the system at time 0, to cease to have any effect.*

Because the arrival rate of jobs will vary with the time of day, etc., steady-state measures for real-world computer systems will probably not exist. However, assuming that the arrival rate is constant over time in the model allows steady-state measures to exist. In performing a steady-state analysis of the proposed computer system, the model's developers are essentially trying to determine how the system will respond to a peak load of infinite duration.

Example 8.6 A chemical manufacturer constructs a simulation model of a proposed chemical process operation. In operation the process will be subject to randomly occurring breakdowns. The input rate of raw materials to the process and the controllable parameters, e.g., temperature and pressure, of the process are both assumed to be stationary with respect to time. *The company would like to estimate the production rate after the process has been running long enough for initial conditions no longer to have any effect.*

One might get the impression from the above discussion that for any system there is a unique type of simulation, i.e., terminating or steady state, which is appropriate. However, for some systems either type of simulation might be appropriate, *depending on what the analyst wants to learn about the system.* For example, consider a simulation model of a proposed assembly line which includes provision for the time for workers to learn their jobs. A steady-state simulation of this system might be designed to estimate the production rate after the assembly line has been in operation long enough for the workers to have learned their jobs. On the other hand, a terminating simulation of length 6 months, say, might be aimed at estimating the production rate during each of the first 6 months while the workers are still learning their jobs.

8.3 MEASURES OF SYSTEM PERFORMANCE

8.3.1 Contrast of Measures of Performance

In this section we contrast measures of performance for terminating and steady-state simulations by means of two examples for which the true measures of performance can be computed analytically. (This would not be possible, of course, for most complex real-world simulations.)

Example 8.7 Consider the output process $\{D_i, i \geq 1\}$ for the $M/M/1$ queue, where D_i is the delay in queue (exclusive of service time) of the ith customer. Recall that this is a single-server queueing system with IID exponential interarrival times with mean $1/\lambda$, IID exponential service times with mean $1/\omega$, and customers served in a FIFO manner. Assume that $\rho = \lambda/\omega < 1$. The objective of a terminating simulation of the $M/M/1$ queue might be to estimate the *expected average delay of the first m customers* (i.e., the terminating event is $E = \{m$ customers have completed their delays$\}$) given some initial condition—say that the number of customers in the system at time 0, $L(0)$, is zero. The desired quantity, which we denote by $d(m | L(0) = 0)$ (the vertical line is read "given that"), is then given by

$$d(m | L(0) = 0) = E\left[\frac{\sum_{i=1}^{m} D_i}{m} \,\middle|\, L(0) = 0 \right] \tag{8.1}$$

Although the expression on the right-hand side of (8.1) might seem imposing at a first glance, its interpretation is really quite simple. The random variable $X = \sum_{i=1}^{m} D_i/m$ is just the average delay of the first m customers, and we are interested in estimating $E(X)$ given that $L(0) = 0$. Since we may think of $E(X)$ as the average of the X's resulting from making a very large (infinite) number of independent simulation runs each of length m customers, one legitimate question is to ask how many independent runs of length m customers each are required to get a good estimate of $E(X)$. This issue is taken up in Sec. 8.5.

Note that measures of performance for terminating simulations explicitly depend on the state of the system at time 0. In particular, $d(m | L(0) = l_1) \neq d(m | L(0) = l_2)$ *for* $l_1 \neq l_2$.

The objective of a steady-state simulation of $\{D_i, i \geq 1\}$ for the $M/M/1$ queue would be to estimate the *steady-state expected average delay d,* given by

$$d = \lim_{m \to \infty} d(m | L(0) = l) \qquad \text{for any } l = 0, 1, \ldots \tag{8.2}$$

If $\rho < 1$, as we assume, then d exists; i.e., the limit exists and is finite. [If, however, $\rho > 1$, then customers are arriving faster, on the average, than they are served. As time gets large, the length of the queue will get longer and longer, and the right-hand side of (8.2) will diverge to plus infinity.]

Observe in (8.2) that d is independent of the state of the system at time 0, $L(0)$. In Fig. 8.1 we plot $d(m | L(0) = 0)$ (see Heathcote and Winer [18]) as a function of m. (The arrival rate $\lambda = 1$ and the service rate $\omega = \frac{10}{9}$, so $\rho = 0.9$.) The horizontal line that $d(m | L(0) = 0)$ asymptotically approaches is at height $d = 8.1$ (see Gross and Harris [17, p. 58]).

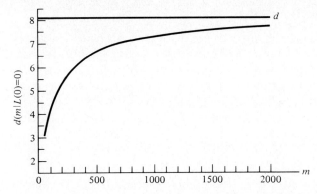

Figure 8.1 $d(m\,|\,L(0) = 0)$ as a function of m for the $M/M/1$ queue with $\rho = 0.9$.

Note $d(m\,|\,L(0) = 0)$ is small for small values of m because $L(0)$ was artificially chosen to be zero.

Example 8.8 As a second example consider the stochastic process $\{C_i, i \geq 1\}$ for the (s, S) inventory system with zero delivery lag and backlogging of Example 4.6, where C_i is the total cost in the ith month. A possible objective of a terminating simulation would be to estimate the *expected average cost for the first m months* given that the inventory level at the beginning of month 1, I_1, is S:

$$c(m\,|\,I_1 = S) = E\left[\frac{\sum_{i=1}^{m} C_i}{m}\,\middle|\,I_1 = S\right]$$

The objective of a steady-state simulation of $\{C_i, i \geq 1\}$ would be to estimate the *steady-state expected average cost*:

$$c = \lim_{m \to \infty} c(m\,|\,I_1 = l) \qquad \text{for any } l = 0, \pm 1, \pm 2, \ldots$$

(It can be shown that c exists.) We plot $c(m\,|\,I_1 = S)$ as a function of m and also $c = 112.108$ (see Wagner [38, p. A19]) in Fig. 8.2.

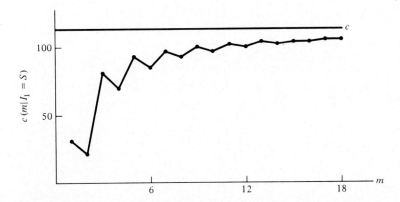

Figure 8.2 $c(m\,|\,I_1 = S)$ as a function of m for the (s, S) inventory system.

8.3.2 The Meaning of Steady State

In Example 8.7, d was defined as the limit (as the number of customers m goes to infinity) of the expected average delay of the first m customers. [That definition was convenient there because it allowed us to relate d to $d(m \mid L(0) = l)$.] The difficulty with this definition is that it implies that d is, in effect, the average delay over an infinite number of simulation runs, each of infinite duration. We therefore give a more pragmatic definition of d. If d, as defined by (8.2), exists and is finite, then d is also given by

$$ d = \lim_{m \to \infty} \frac{\sum_{i=1}^{m} D_i}{m} \qquad \text{w.p. 1} \qquad \text{for } L(0) = \text{any } l \qquad (8.3) $$

We now drop the adjective "expected" and call d the *steady-state average delay in queue*. What (8.3) says is that if one performs an infinite number of simulation runs, each resulting in a $\overline{D}(m) = \sum_{i=1}^{m} D_i / m$, and m is sufficiently large, then $\overline{D}(m)$ will be arbitrarily close to d for virtually (i.e., with probability 1) all simulation runs. We can therefore think of d as the average delay resulting from making *one* sufficiently long simulation run. In the remainder of this book, we shall define steady-state measures of performance similarly to the way d is defined in (8.3) (see Sec. 8.6).

> **Example 8.9** For the queueing system considered in Example 8.7, we plot in Fig. 8.3 $\overline{D}(m)$ as a function of m (computed from a single simulation run) and also d. Note that the convergence of $\overline{D}(m)$ to d as m goes to infinity is certainly not monotone as in Fig. 8.1, where $E[\overline{D}(m)]$ was plotted as a function of m. Observe, in addition, that $\overline{D}(m)$ (as a function of m) still exhibits some random fluctuation even for m as large as 5000.

Many books and papers on simulation make a statement like "It is desired to estimate some measure of performance for a system that is operating in steady state." Since we believe that this statement is not well understood, we now attempt to shed some light on the meaning of steady state. For the $M/M/1$ queue of Example 8.7 let

$$ F_{i,l}(x) = P\{D_i \leq x \mid L(0) = l\} $$

We call $F_{i,l}(x)$ the *transient distribution of delay at time i* given $L(0) = l$. (The word "transient" means that there is a different distribution for each time i.) Now it can be shown that for any $x \geq 0$,

$$ F(x) = \lim_{i \to \infty} F_{i,l}(x) \qquad \text{for } L(0) = \text{any } l \qquad (8.4) $$

exists, and we call $F(x)$ the *steady-state distribution of delay*. [The exact form of $F(x)$ is given by expression (4.13).] It follows from (8.4) that there exists a time index i' such that for all $i \geq i'$, $F_{i,l}(x) \approx F(x)$ for all $x \geq 0$. At the point in time when $F_{i,l}(x)$ is essentially no longer changing with i, we shall intuitively say that the process $\{D_i, i \geq 1\}$ is in "steady state." Thus, steady state does *not* mean that the

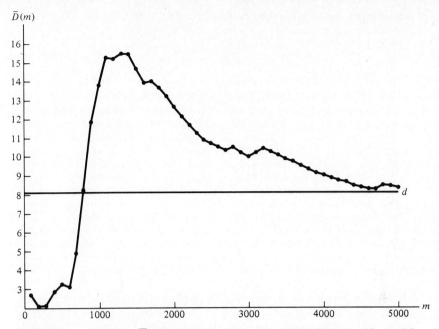

Figure 8.3 A realization of $\overline{D}(m)$ as a function of m for the $M/M/1$ queue with $\rho = 0.9$.

actual delays in a single realization (or run) of the simulation become constant after some point in time, but that the *distribution* of the delays becomes invariant.

Let D be the delay of a customer who arrives after the process $\{D_i, i \geq 1\}$ is in steady state. Then it can also be shown that $E(D) = d$. Although we have given three definitions of d, henceforth (as stated above) we shall use the one given by (8.3).

8.3.3 Measures of Performance Other than Averages

The usual criterion for comparing two or more systems is some sort of average system response. We now show by means of an example that this may result in misleading conclusions.

Example 8.10 Consider the bank of Example 8.1 with five tellers, customers arriving in accordance with a Poisson process at rate 1 per minute, and service times that are IID exponential random variables with mean 4 minutes. Thus, the utilization factor $\rho = \lambda/5\omega = 0.8$. We compare the policy of having one queue for each teller (and jockeying) with the policy of having one queue feed all tellers on the basis of *expected average delay in queue* and *expected time-average number of customers in queue*. These measures of performance are explicitly defined as follows (see Appendix 8B):

$$E\left(\frac{\sum_{i=1}^{N} D_i}{N}\right) \quad \text{and} \quad E\left[\frac{\int_{0}^{T} Q(t)\, dt}{T}\right]$$

where T = amount of time that the bank is operating ($T \geq 8$)
$\quad\quad N$ = number of customers served in the time interval $[0, T]$
$\quad\quad Q(t)$ = number of customers in queue at time t

Table 8.1 gives the results of making one simulation run of each policy. [These simulation runs were performed so that the time of arrival of the ith customer ($i = 1, 2, \ldots, N$) was identical for both policies and so that the service time of the ith customer to begin service ($i = 1, 2, \ldots, N$) was the same for both policies.] Thus, on the basis of "average system response," it would appear that the two policies are equivalent. However, this is clearly not the case. Since customers are not necessarily served in the order of their arrival with the multiqueue policy, we would expect this policy to result in greater variability of a customer's delay. Table 8.2 gives estimates, computed from the same two simulation runs used above, of the expected proportion of customers with a delay in the interval $[0, 5)$ (in minutes), the expected proportion of customers with a delay in $[5, 10)$, ..., the expected proportion of customers with a delay in $[40, 45)$ for both policies. (We did not estimate variances from these runs since, as pointed out in Chap. 4, variance estimates computed from correlated simulation output data are often highly biased.) Observe from Table 8.2 that a customer is more likely to have a large delay with the multiqueue policy than with the single-queue policy. (For larger values of ρ, the differences between the two policies would be even more significant.) This observation together with the greater equitability of the single-queue policy has probably led many organizations, e.g., banks and airlines, to adopt this policy.

We conclude from the above example that comparing alternative systems or policies strictly on the basis of average system behavior can sometimes result in misleading conclusions and, furthermore, that proportions can be a useful measure of system performance. Note also that proportions are really just a special case of averages. In particular, for the above example, the expected proportion of customers with a delay in the interval $[5(k - 1), 5k)$ ($k = 1, 2, \ldots, 9$) is given by

$$E\left[\frac{\sum_{i=1}^{N} I_i(5(k - 1), 5k)}{N} \right]$$

where

$$I_i(5(k - 1), 5k) = \begin{cases} 1 & \text{if } 5(k - 1) \leq D_i < 5k \\ 0 & \text{otherwise} \end{cases}$$

Although the indicator variables $I_i(5(k - 1), 5k)$ take on only the values 0 and 1, they *are* legitimate random variables and the specified proportion is just their average. Therefore, since proportions (as discussed here) are just averages, statistical procedures which can be used for estimating averages are also applicable to estimating proportions.

Table 8.1 Simulation results for the two bank policies: averages

	Estimates	
Measure of performance	Five queues	One queue
Expected operating time, hours	8.140	8.140
Expected average delay, minutes	5.567	5.567
Expected average number in queue	5.517	5.517

**Table 8.2 Simulation results for the
two bank policies: proportions**

Interval	Estimates of expected proportions	
	Five queues	One queue
[0, 5)	0.626	0.597
[5, 10)	0.182	0.188
[10, 15)	0.076	0.107
[15, 20)	0.047	0.095
[20, 25)	0.031	0.013
[25, 30)	0.020	0
[30, 35)	0.015	0
[35, 40)	0.003	0
[40, 45)	0	0

8.4 THE NEED FOR CONFIDENCE INTERVALS

Suppose we would like to estimate $d(25 \,|\, L(0) = 0) = 2.124$ for the $M/M/1$ queue with $\rho = 0.9$. The following are 10 independent realizations of the random variable $\sum_{i=1}^{25} D_i/25$ given $L(0) = 0$; that is, different random numbers were used for each realization:

$$1.051 \quad 6.438 \quad 2.646 \quad 0.805 \quad 1.505$$

$$0.546 \quad 2.281 \quad 2.822 \quad 0.414 \quad 1.307$$

Note that the estimators range from a minimum of 0.414 to a maximum of 6.438 and that most of the estimators are not very close to the true answer, 2.124. We conclude that one realization, or replication, is generally not sufficient to obtain an acceptable estimate of a measure of performance and that a method is needed for ascertaining how close an estimator is to the true measure. The usual approach to assessing the accuracy of an estimator is to construct a confidence interval for the true measure.

   Although the above discusssion was oriented toward terminating simulations, the same conclusion is valid for steady-state simulations, i.e., that one needs a way of assessing the accuracy of an estimator and that a confidence interval is the usual approach.

8.5 CONFIDENCE INTERVALS FOR TERMINATING SIMULATIONS

Suppose we make n independent replications of a terminating simulation, where the length of each replication is determined by the specified event E and each replication is begun with the same initial conditions (see Sec. 8.5.4). The independence of replications is accomplished by using different random numbers for each replication. (For a discussion of how this can easily be accomplished if the n replications are made in more than one submittal to the computer, see Chap. 6.) Assume for simplicity that there is a single performance measure of interest. (This assumption is dropped in Sec. 8.7.) If X_j is the estimator of the measure of performance from the jth replication, then the X_j's are IID random variables and classical statistical analysis can be used to construct a confidence interval for $\mu = E(X)$. For the $M/M/1$ queue of Example 8.7, X_j might be the average delay $\sum_{i=1}^{m} D_i/m$ from the jth replication. For the inventory system of Example 8.8, X_j might be the average cost $\sum_{i=1}^{m} C_i/m$ from the jth replication. Finally, for the bank of Example 8.10, X_j might be the time average $\int_0^T Q(t)\ dt/T$ or the proportion $\sum_{i=1}^{N} I_i(0, 5)/N$ from the jth replication.

8.5.1 Fixed-Sample-Size Procedure

The usual approach to constructing a confidence interval for μ is to make a fixed number of replications n ($n \geq 2$). If the estimators $X_1, X_2, \ldots, X_n$ are assumed to be normal random variables in addition to being IID, then a $100(1 - \alpha)$ percent ($0 < \alpha < 1$) confidence interval for μ is given by

$$\overline{X}(n) \pm t_{n-1,1-\alpha/2} \sqrt{\frac{s^2(n)}{n}} \tag{8.5}$$

Note that (8.5) is the same expression used in classical statistics to construct a confidence interval for the mean of a population (see Sec. 4.5).

> **Example 8.11** Suppose we want to construct a 90 percent confidence interval for $d(25 \mid L(0) = 0)$ in the case of the $M/M/1$ queue with $\rho = 0.9$. From the 10 replications presented in Sec. 8.4 we obtained
>
> $$\overline{X}(10) = 1.982 \qquad \text{and} \qquad s^2(10) = 3.172$$
>
> Then an approximate 90 percent confidence interval for $d(25 \mid L(0) = 0)$ is given by
>
> $$\overline{X}(10) \pm t_{9,0.95} \sqrt{\frac{s^2(10)}{10}} = 1.982 \pm 1.032$$
>
> Thus, subject to the correct interpretation to be given to confidence intervals (see Sec. 4.5), we can claim with approximately 90 percent confidence that $d(25 \mid L(0) = 0)$ is contained in the interval [0.950, 3.014].

The correctness of the confidence interval given by (8.5) (in terms of having coverage close to $1 - \alpha$) depends on the assumption that the X_j's are normal random variables; this is why we called the confidence interval in Example 8.11 an *approximate* 90 percent confidence interval. Since this assumption will rarely be strictly satisfied in practice, we now investigate empirically the robustness of the confidence interval to departures from normality. Our goal is to provide the simulation practitioner with some guidance as to how well the confidence interval will perform, in terms of coverage, in practice.

We first performed 500 independent simulation experiments for the $M/M/1$ queue with $\rho = 0.9$. For each experiment we considered $n = 5, 10, 20, 40$, and for each n we used (8.5) to construct an approximate 90 percent confidence interval for $d(25 \mid L(0) = 0) = 2.124$. Table 8.3 gives the proportion, $\hat{p}$, of the 500 confidence intervals which covered the true $d(25 \mid L(0) = 0)$, a 90 percent confidence interval for the true coverage p [the proportion of a very large number of confidence intervals which would cover $d(25 \mid L(0) = 0)$], and the average value of the confidence interval half-length [that is, $t_{n-1,1-\alpha/2} \sqrt{s^2(n)/n}$] divided by the point estimate $\overline{X}(n)$ over the 500 experiments. (This ratio is called the *relative precision* of the confidence interval; see Sec. 8.5.2 for further discussion.) The 90 percent confidence interval for the true coverage was computed from

$$\hat{p} \pm z_{0.95} \sqrt{\frac{\hat{p}(1-\hat{p})}{500}}$$

and is based on the fact that $(\hat{p} - p)/\sqrt{\hat{p}(1 - \hat{p})/500}$ is approximately distributed as a standard normal random variable (see Hogg and Craig [19, p. 187]).

From Table 8.3 it can be seen that 86.4 percent of the 500 confidence intervals based on $n = 10$ replications covered $d(25 \mid L(0) = 0)$ and we know with approximately 90 percent confidence that the true coverage for $n = 10$ is between 0.839 and 0.889. Considering that simulation models are always only an approximation to the corresponding real-world system, we believe that the estimated coverages presented in Table 8.3 are close enough to the desired 0.9 to be useful. Note also from the table that 4 times as many replications are required to decrease the relative precision by a factor of approximately 2. This is to be expected since there is a $\sqrt{n}$ in the denominator of the expression for the confidence-interval half-length in (8.5).

To show that the confidence interval given by (8.5) does *not* always produce coverages close to $1 - \alpha$, we considered a second example. A reliability model consisting of three components will function as long as component 1 works and either component 2 or 3 works. If G is the time to failure of the whole system and G_i is the time to failure of component i ($i = 1, 2, 3$), then $G = \min \{G_1, \max \{G_2, G_3\}\}$. We further assume that the G_i's are independent random variables and that each G_i has

Table 8.3 Fixed-sample-size results for $d(25 \mid L(0) = 0) = 2.124$ based on 500 experiments, $M/M/1$ queue with $\rho = 0.9$

n	Estimated coverage	Average of (confidence-interval half-length)/$\overline{X}(n)$
5	0.880 ± 0.024	0.672
10	0.864 ± 0.025	0.436
20	0.886 ± 0.023	0.301
40	0.914 ± 0.021	0.212

a Weibull distribution with shape parameter 0.5 and scale parameter 1 (see Chap. 5). This particular Weibull distribution is extremely nonnormal (skewed). Once again we performed 500 independent simulation experiments; for each experiment we considered $n = 5, 10, 20, 40$ and for each n we used (8.5) to construct a 90 percent confidence interval for $E(G|\text{all components new}) = 0.778$ (which was calculated by analytic reasoning). The results from these experiments are given in Table 8.4. Note that for small values of n there is definitely a significant degradation in coverage. Also, as n gets large, the coverage appears to be approaching 0.9, which is guaranteed by the central limit theorem.

We can see from the results in Tables 8.3 and 8.4 that the coverage actually obtained from the confidence interval given by (8.5) depends on the simulation model under consideration (actually on the distribution of the resulting X_j's) and also on the sample size n. It is therefore natural to ask why the confidence interval worked better for the $M/M/1$ queue than it did for the reliability model. Two possible reasons come to mind. First, an X_j for the queueing system is actually an average of 25 individual delays, while an X_j for the reliability model is computed from the three individual times to failure by a formula involving a minimum and a maximum. Furthermore, there are central limit theorems for certain types of correlated data which state that averages of these data become approximately normally distributed as the number of points in the average gets large. (See Sec. 8.6.1 for further discussion.) We would therefore expect that if X_j is the average of a large number of individual points, the degradation in coverage of the confidence interval might not be very severe. Our experience indicates that many real-world simulations produce X_j's of this type. A second reason is that the delays for the queueing system are themselves more normal-like than the times to failure for the reliability model. In fact, recall that the distribution of the times to failure was purposely chosen to be extremely nonnormal.

Results in the statistics literature (see, for example, Johnson [23]) indicate that the type of nonnormality which causes the greatest degradation in coverage is asymmetry of the distribution of an X_j, which is usually measured by a quantity called the *skewness* (see Kendall and Stuart [26] for the definition). Furthermore, empirical results in Law [31] suggest that there is a strong positive correlation between the skewness of a distribution and the amount of degradation in coverage. See [23] for a modification of the confidence interval given by (8.5) which may reduce the effect of skewness on coverage.

Table 8.4 Fixed-sample-size results for $E(G|\text{all components new}) = 0.778$ based on 500 experiments, reliability model

n	Estimated coverage	Average of (confidence-interval half-length)/$\overline{X}(n)$
5	0.708 $\pm$ 0.033	1.163
10	0.750 $\pm$ 0.032	0.820
20	0.800 $\pm$ 0.029	0.600
40	0.840 $\pm$ 0.027	0.444

8.5.2 Obtaining Confidence Intervals with a Specified Precision

One disadvantage of the fixed-sample-size approach to constructing a confidence interval is that the simulator has no control over the confidence-interval half-length; for fixed n, the half-length will depend on the population variance of the X_j's, $\sigma^2(X)$. In Example 8.11, the half-length of 1.032 (based on $n = 10$ replications) was probably too large to get an accurate idea of the true value of $d(25 \,|\, L(0) = 0)$. In this section we discuss procedures for determining the number of replications required to obtain a confidence interval with a specified precision.

We begin by defining two ways of measuring the precision of a confidence interval. We call the *actual* confidence-interval half-length the *absolute precision* of the confidence interval and we call the *ratio* of the confidence-interval half-length to the magnitude of the point estimator the *relative precision* of the confidence interval. [Although not strictly correct, one can think of the relative precision as the "proportion" of μ by which $\overline{X}(n)$ differs from μ]. Suppose that we have constructed a confidence interval for μ based on a fixed number of replications n but the confidence interval is too "large" to be of much practical value. If we assume that our estimate of the population variance, that is, $s^2(n)$, will not change (appreciably) as the number of replications increases, an *approximate* expression for the total number of replications, $n_a^*(\beta)$, required to reduce the absolute precision of the confidence interval to a desired value β ($\beta > 0$) is given by

$$n_a^*(\beta) = \min \left\{ i \geq n : t_{i-1,1-\alpha/2} \sqrt{s^2(n)/i} \leq \beta \right\} \tag{8.6}$$

We can determine $n_a^*(\beta)$ by iteratively increasing i by 1 until a value of i is obtained for which $t_{i-1,1-\alpha/2}\sqrt{s^2(n)/i} \leq \beta$. [Alternatively, $n_a^*(\beta)$ can be approximated as the smallest integer i satisfying $i \geq s^2(n)(z_{1-\alpha/2}/\beta)^2$.] Then, if we make $n_a^*(\beta) - n$ additional replications of the simulation and construct a confidence interval from all $n_a^*(\beta)$ replications, the resulting confidence interval should have an absolute precision of approximately β. Similarly, if we assume that our estimates of both the population mean and the population variance will not change (appreciably) as the number of replications increases, an *approximate* expression for the total number of replications, $n_r^*(\gamma)$, required to reduce the relative precision of the confidence interval to a desired value γ ($0 < \gamma < 1$) is given by

$$n_r^*(\gamma) = \min \left\{ i \geq n : \frac{t_{i-1,1-\alpha/2} \sqrt{s^2(n)/i}}{|\overline{X}(n)|} \leq \gamma \right\} \tag{8.7}$$

[Again, $n_r^*(\gamma)$ is approximately the smallest integer i satisfying $i \geq s^2(n)[z_{1-\alpha/2}/\gamma\overline{X}(n)]^2$.]

Example 8.12 For the 90 percent confidence interval constructed in Example 8.11, the absolute precision was 1.032, and the relative precision was $1.032/1.982 = 0.521$. If we want to estimate $d(25 \,|\, L(0) = 0)$ with an absolute precision of $\beta = 0.5$, the approximate total number of replications required is

$$n_a^*(0.5) = \min \left\{ i \geq 10 : t_{i-1,0.95} \sqrt{\frac{3.172}{i}} \leq 0.5 \right\} = 37$$

Thus, with approximately 37 total replications we can estimate $d(25|L(0) = 0)$ to within ± 0.5 with 90 percent confidence. If we want to estimate $d(25|L(0) = 0)$ with a relative precision of $\gamma = 0.15$, the approximate total number of replications required is

$$n_r^*(0.15) = \min \left\{ i \geq 10: \frac{t_{i-1,0.95} \sqrt{3.172/i}}{1.982} \leq 0.15 \right\} = 99$$

Thus, with approximately 99 total replications we can get an estimate of $d(25|L(0) = 0)$ which differs from $d(25|L(0) = 0)$ by no more than 15 percent of $d(25|L(0) = 0)$ with 90 percent confidence.

The difficulty with using (8.7) directly to obtain a confidence interval with a small relative precision γ is that if $s^2(n)$ is an overestimate of the population variance $\sigma^2(X)$, then the number of replications, $n_r^*(\gamma)$, used to construct the confidence interval may be significantly more than actually needed. (Compare the results from Example 8.13 below with those from Example 8.12.) Since the cost of making a replication of a real-world simulation may be great, the direct use of (8.7) may result in an unnecessarily large bill for computer time. We now present a *sequential* procedure (new replications are added one at a time) for constructing a confidence interval with a specified relative precision which takes only as many replications as are actually needed. The procedure assumes that $X_1, X_2, \ldots$ is a sequence of IID random variables which need not be normal.

The specific objective of the procedure is to construct a $100(1 - \alpha)$ percent confidence interval for μ such that the relative precision is less than or equal to γ, for $0 < \gamma < 1$. Choose an initial number of replications $n_0 \geq 2$ and let

$$\delta(n, \alpha) = t_{n-1,1-\alpha/2} \sqrt{\frac{s^2(n)}{n}}$$

be the half-length. [Note that $\delta(n, \alpha)$ is the same half-length used in the fixed-sample-size procedure.] Then the sequential procedure is as follows:

0. Make n_0 replications of the simulation and set $n = n_0$.
1. Compute $\overline{X}(n)$ and $\delta(n, \alpha)$ from $X_1, X_2, \ldots, X_n$.
2. If $\delta(n, \alpha)/|\overline{X}(n)| \leq \gamma$, use

$$I(\alpha, \gamma) = [\overline{X}(n) - \delta(n, \alpha), \overline{X}(n) + \delta(n, \alpha)] \tag{8.8}$$

as an approximate $100(1 - \alpha)$ percent confidence interval for μ and stop. Otherwise, replace n by $n + 1$, make an additional replication of the simulation, and go to step 1.

Note that the procedure computes a new estimate of $\sigma^2(X)$ after *each* replication is obtained, and that the total number of replications required by the procedure is a random variable.

Example 8.13 For the $M/M/1$ queue with $\rho = 0.9$, suppose that we want to construct a 90 percent confidence interval for $d(25|L(0) = 0)$ such that the relative precision is less than or equal to 0.15. Using $n_0 = 10$, we obtained the following results:

$$n = 68 \text{ (the total number of replications)}, \quad \overline{X}(68) = 1.872, \quad s^2(68) = 1.865,$$

and

$$I(0.10, 0.15) = [1.595, 2.148]$$

Note that the number of replications actually required, 68, was less than the 99 predicted in Example 8.12.

Although the sequential procedure described above is intuitively appealing, the question naturally arises as to how well it performs in terms of producing a confidence interval with coverage close to the desired $1 - \alpha$. In Law, Kelton, and Koenig [35], it is shown that if $\mu \neq 0$ [and $0 < \sigma^2(X) < \infty$], then the coverage of the confidence interval given by (8.8) will be arbitrarily close to $1 - \alpha$, provided the desired relative precision γ is sufficiently close to 0. Based on sampling from a large number of stochastic models and probability distributions (including the $M/M/1$ queue and the reliability model) for which the true value of μ is known, our recommendation is to use the sequential procedure with $n_0 \geq 10$ and $\gamma \leq 0.15$ (see [35]). It was found that if these recommendations are followed, the estimated coverage (based on 500 independent experiments for each model) for a desired 90 percent confidence interval was never less than 0.864.

Analogous to the sequential procedure described above, there is a sequential procedure due to Chow and Robbins [4] for constructing a $100(1 - \alpha)$ percent confidence interval for μ with a small absolute precision β. Furthermore, it can be shown that the coverage actually produced by the procedure will be arbitrary close to $1 - \alpha$ provided the desired absolute precision β is sufficiently close to 0. However, since the meaning of "*absolute precision β sufficiently small*" is extremely model-dependent, and since the coverage results in [31] indicate that the procedure is very sensitive to the choice of β, we do not recommend the use of the Chow and Robbins procedure in general.

8.5.3 Recommended Use of the Procedures

We now make our recommendations on the use of the fixed-sample-size and sequential procedures for terminating simulations. If one is performing an exploratory experiment where the precision of the confidence interval may not be overwhelmingly important, we recommend using the fixed-sample-size procedure. However, if the X_j's are highly nonnormal and the number of replications n is too small, the actual coverage of the constructed confidence interval may be somewhat lower than desired.

From an exploratory experiment consisting of n replications one can estimate the cost per replication and the population variance of the X_j's, and then estimate from (8.6) the approximate number of replications, $n_a^*(\beta)$, required to construct a confidence interval with a desired absolute precision β. Alternatively, one can estimate from (8.7) the approximate number of replications, $n_r^*(\gamma)$, required to construct a confidence interval with a desired relative precision γ. Sometimes the choice of β or γ might have to be tempered by the cost associated with the required number of replications. If it is finally decided to construct a confidence interval with a small relative precision γ, we recommend use of the sequential procedure with $\gamma \leq 0.15$ and $n_0 \geq 10$. If one wants a confidence interval with a relative precision γ greater than 0.15, we recommend several successive applications of the fixed-sample-size approach. In particular, one might estimate $n_r^*(\gamma)$, collect, say $[n_r^*(\gamma) - n]/2$ more replications, and then use (8.5) to construct a confidence interval based on the existing $[n + n_r^*(\gamma)]/2$ replications. If the relative precision of the resulting confidence interval is still greater than γ, then $n_r^*(\gamma)$ can be reestimated based on a new variance estimate, and some portion of the necessary additional replications may be collected, etc. To construct a confidence interval with a small absolute precision β, we once again recommend several successive applications of the fixed-sample-size approach. It should be mentioned that all the statistical analyses [except the calculation of $n_a^*(\beta)$] for terminating simulations thus far discussed in Sec. 8.5 can be performed automatically in SIMSCRIPT II.5 using a library routine called STAT.R (see Law [30]).

Depending on the complexity of the system of interest, the cost of making one replication of a simulation model may range from less than $1 per replication to an extreme of $500 or even more. Thus precise confidence intervals may simply not be affordable. Regardless of the cost per replication, we recommend always making at least three replications of the simulation to assess the variability of the X_j's. (With two replications it may be likely to get X_1 and X_2 very close together even though the X_j's are highly variable.) *If X_1, X_2, and X_3 are not very close together, additional replications must be made or any conclusions derived from the simulation study will probably be of doubtful validity.*

8.5.4 Approaches to Choosing Appropriate Initial Conditions

As stated in Sec. 8.2, the measures of performance for a terminating simulation depend explicitly on the state of the system at time 0; thus, care must be taken in choosing appropriate initial conditions. Let us illustrate this potential problem by means of an example. Suppose that we would like to estimate the expected average delay of all customers who arrive and complete their delays between 12 and 1 (the busiest period) in a bank. Since the bank will probably be quite congested at 12, starting the simulation at 12 with no customers present (the usual initial conditions for a queueing simulation) will cause our estimate of expected average delay to be biased low. We now discuss two heuristic approaches to this problem, the first of which appears to be used widely.

For the first approach let us assume that the bank opens at 9 with no customers present. Then we can start the simulation at 9 with no customers present and run it for 4 simulated hours. In estimating the desired expected average delay, we use only the delays of those customers who arrive and complete their delays between 12 and 1. The evolution of the simulation between 9 and 12 (the "warm-up period") determines the appropriate conditions for the simulation at 12. A disadvantage of this approach is that 3 hours of simulated time are wasted. As a result, one might compromise and start the simulation at some other time, say 11, with no customers present. However, there is no guarantee that the conditions in the simulation at 12 will be representative of the actual conditions in the bank at 12. This approach can be carried out in SIMLIB by reinitializing the statistical counters for subroutines SAMPST, TIMEST, and FILEST (see Prob. 2.5) at 12.

An alternative approach is to collect data on the number of customers present in the bank at 12 for several different days. Let $\hat{p}_i$ be the proportion of these days that i customers ($i = 0, 1, \ldots$) are present at 12. Then we simulate the bank from 12 to 1 with the number of customers present at 12 being randomly chosen from the distribution $\{\hat{p}_i\}$. (All customers who are being served at 12 might be assumed to be just beginning their services. Starting all services fresh at 12 results in an approximation to the actual situation in the bank, since the customers who are in the process of being served at 12 would have partially completed their services. However, the effect of this approximation should be negligible for a simulation of length 1 hour.)

If more than one simulation run from 12 to 1 is desired, then a different sample from $\{\hat{p}_i\}$ is drawn for each run. The X_j's which result from these runs are still identically distributed since the initial conditions for each run are chosen from the same distribution.

8.6 CONFIDENCE INTERVALS FOR STEADY-STATE SIMULATIONS

Let $Y_1, Y_2, \ldots$ be an output process resulting from a *single* simulation run. (For example, Y_i might be the delay of the ith customer, D_i, for a queueing system, or the total cost in the ith month, C_i, for an inventory system.) Then define the *steady-state average response* ν of $\{Y_i, i \geq 1\}$ (when it exists) by

$$\nu = \lim_{m \to \infty} \frac{\sum_{i=1}^{m} Y_i}{m} \qquad \text{w.p. } 1$$

[This definition is consistent with the definition of d given by (8.3).] We also assume that the limit ν is independent of the state of the simulation at time zero.

Two general approaches have been suggested in the simulation literature for constructing a confidence interval for ν:

1. *Fixed-sample-size procedures*. A simulation run of an *arbitrary* fixed length is performed, and then one of a number of available procedures is used to construct a confidence interval from the available data.
2. *Sequential procedures*. The length of a simulation is sequentially increased until an "acceptable" confidence interval can be constructed. There are several techniques for deciding when to stop the simulation run.

8.6.1 Fixed-Sample-Size Procedures

Five fixed-sample-size procedures have been suggested in the literature (see Law and Kelton [34] for a survey). Here we discuss the two of these five, namely, batch means and the regenerative method, which appear to have the greatest promise in terms of proved performance or applicability to real-world problems. Both procedures break the output data Y_1, Y_2, ... into (approximately) IID "observations" to which classical statistical analyses can be applied to construct a confidence interval for ν.

Batch means. Assume temporarily that $\{Y_i, i \geq 1\}$ is a covariance stationary process (see Sec. 4.3) with $E(Y_i) = \nu$ for all i. Suppose we make a simulation run of length m and then divide the resulting observations Y_1, Y_2, ... , Y_m into n batches of length l. (Assume that $m = nl$.) Thus, batch 1 consists of observations Y_1, ... , Y_l, batch 2 consists of observations Y_{l+1}, ... , Y_{2l}, etc. Let $\overline{Y}_j(l)$ ($j = 1, 2, ... , n$) be the sample (or batch) mean of the l observations in the jth batch and let $\overline{\overline{Y}}(n, l) = $

$$\sum_{j=1}^{n} \overline{Y}_j(l)/n = \sum_{i=1}^{m} Y_i/m$$ be the grand sample mean. We shall use $\overline{\overline{Y}}(n, l)$ as our

point estimator for ν. [The $\overline{Y}_j(l)$'s will eventually play the same role for batch means as the X_j's did for the fixed-sample-size confidence interval in Sec. 8.5.1.]

If we choose the batch size l large enough, it can be shown that the $\overline{Y}_j(l)$'s will be approximately uncorrelated (see Law and Carson [32]). Suppose we can choose l large enough also for the $\overline{Y}_j(l)$'s to be approximately normally distributed. This is not implausible since there are central limit theorems for certain types of correlated stochastic processes (see Anderson [2, p. 427]). Also, it can be shown that the sample mean of the first l delays, $\overline{D}(l)$, for the $M/M/1$ queue will be approximately normally distributed if l is large (see Law [28]). However, if the $\overline{Y}_j(l)$'s are both uncorrelated and normally distributed, it follows from Prob. 4.5 that the $\overline{Y}_j(l)$'s are independent and normally distributed. Denote these two properties by (P1).

Since Y_1, Y_2, ... is assumed to be covariance stationary with $E(Y_i) = \nu$, it easily follows that the $\overline{Y}_j(l)$'s have the same mean ν and the same variance [see Eq. (4.6)]. Denote these properties by (P2).

It follows from (P1) and (P2) that the $\overline{Y}_j(l)$'s are normal random variables with the same mean and variance. Since a normal random variable is completely determined by its mean and variance, it in turn follows that the $\overline{Y}_j(l)$'s are identically distributed with mean ν, which we denote by (P3). Therefore, if the batch size l is large enough, it follows from (P1) and (P3) that it is not unreasonable to treat the $\overline{Y}_j(l)$'s as if they were IID normal random variables with mean ν and to construct an approximate $100(1 - \alpha)$ percent confidence interval for ν from

$$\overline{\overline{Y}}(n, l) \pm t_{n-1,1-\alpha/2} \sqrt{\frac{s_{\overline{Y}_j(l)}^2(n)}{n}} \tag{8.9}$$

where $$s_{\overline{Y}_j(l)}^2(n) = \frac{\sum_{j=1}^{n} [\overline{Y}_j(l) - \overline{\overline{Y}}(n, l)]^2}{n - 1}$$

Expression (8.9) is analogous to the confidence interval given by (8.5) for terminating simulations.

There are three potential sources of error when one uses (8.9) to construct a confidence interval for v:

1. $Y_1, Y_2, \ldots$ will rarely, if ever, be covariance stationary in practice. However, as suggested in Appendix 4A, if v exists, in general $Y_{k+1}, Y_{k+2}, \ldots$ will be approximately covariance stationary if k is large enough.
2. If l is not large enough, the $\overline{Y}_j(l)$'s may not be approximately normally distributed.
3. If l is not large enough, the $\overline{Y}_j(l)$'s may be highly correlated and $s^2_{\overline{Y}_j(l)}(n)/n$ will be a severely biased estimator of $\sigma^2[\overline{Y}(n, l)]$; see Sec. 4.4. In particular, if the Y_i's are positively correlated (as is often the case in practice), the $\overline{Y}_j(l)$'s will be too, giving a variance estimate that is biased low and a confidence interval that is too small.

Empirical results presented in Law [29] indicate that, at least for simple systems like the $M/M/1$ queue, the correlation between the $\overline{Y}_j(l)$'s is the most serious source of error. These results also suggest that nonnormality of the $\overline{Y}_j(l)$'s will not be a problem if the number of batches n is large, say 40 or more. We present empirical results for batch means later in this section.

The method of batch means can also be used for continuous-time stochastic processes. Suppose that $\{Y(t), t \geq 0\}$ is a continuous-time output process and that we would like to construct a confidence interval for the steady-state time-average response

$$v = \lim_{t \to \infty} \frac{\int_0^t Y(u) \, du}{t} \qquad \text{w.p. 1}$$

From a simulation run of length t time units, divide the interval $[0, t]$ into n adjacent intervals of length Δt ($t = n \, \Delta t$), and then define the batch mean $\overline{Y}_j(\Delta t)$ ($j = 1, 2, \ldots, n$) by

$$\overline{Y}_j(\Delta t) = \frac{\int_{(j-1) \, \Delta t}^{j \, \Delta t} Y(u) \, du}{\Delta t}$$

The $\overline{Y}_j(\Delta t)$'s are then used in place of the $\overline{Y}_j(l)$'s in (8.9) to construct a confidence interval for v.

*Regenerative method. The regenerative method is an altogether different approach to simulation and thus leads to different approaches to constructing a confidence interval for v. The idea is to identify random times at which the process probabilistically "starts over," i.e., regenerates, and to use these regeneration points to obtain independent random variables to which classical statistical analysis can be applied to form point and interval estimates for v. This method was developed simultaneously by Crane and Iglehart [6–9] and by Fishman [12, 13]; we follow the presentation of the former authors.

Assume for the output process $\{Y_i, i \geq 1\}$ that there is a sequence of random indices $1 \leq B_1 < B_2 < \cdots$, called *regeneration points,* at which the process starts over probabilistically; i.e., the distribution of the process $\{Y_{B_j+i-1}, i = 1, 2, \ldots\}$ is the same for each $j = 1, 2, \ldots$, and the process from each B_j on is assumed to be independent of the process prior to B_j. The portion of the process between two successive B_j's is called a *regeneration cycle,* and it can be shown that successive cycles are IID replicas of each other. In particular, comparable random variables defined over the successive cycles are IID. Let $N_j = B_{j+1} - B_j$ for $j = 1, 2, \ldots$ and assume that $E(N_j) < \infty$. If $Z_j = \sum_{i=B_j}^{B_{j+1}-1} Y_i$, the random vectors $\mathbf{U}_j = (Z_j, N_j)^T$ ($\mathbf{A}^T$ is the transpose of the vector $\mathbf{A}$) are IID, and provided that $E(|Z_j|) < \infty$, the steady-state average response ν is given (see Prob. 8.9) by

$$\nu = \frac{E(Z)}{E(N)}$$

Example 8.14 Consider the output process of delays $\{D_i, i \geq 1\}$ for a single-server queue with IID interarrival times, IID service times, customers served in a FIFO manner, and $\rho < 1$. The indices of those customers who arrive to find the system completely empty are regeneration points (see Fig. 8.4). Let N_j be the total number of customers served in the jth cycle and let $Z_j = \sum_{i=B_j}^{B_{j+1}-1} D_i$ be the total delay of all customers served in the jth cycle. Then the steady-state average delay $d = \lim_{m\to\infty} \sum_{i=1}^{m} D_i/m$ (w.p. 1) is given by $d = E(Z)/E(N)$.

Note that the indices of customers who arrive to find l customers present ($l \geq 1$ and fixed) will not, in general, be regeneration points for the process $\{D_i, i \geq 1\}$. This is because the distribution of the remaining service time of the customer in service will be different for successive customers who arrive to find l customers present. However, if service times are exponential random variables, these indices *are* regeneration points because of the memoryless property of the exponential distribution (see Appendix 8A and also Probs. 8.8 and 8.10).

Example 8.15 For the time-shared computer model of Sec. 2.4, consider the output process of response times $\{R_i, i \geq 1\}$. The indices of those jobs which, upon completion of their response time, find all other terminals in the "think" state are regeneration points. (This would not be true if think times were not exponential random variables.) Let N_j be the number of jobs whose response times are completed in the jth cycle, and let $Z_j = \sum_{i=B_j}^{B_{j+1}-1} R_i$. Then the steady-state average response time $r = \lim_{m\to\infty} \sum_{i=1}^{m} R_i/m$ (w.p. 1) is given by $r = E(Z)/E(N)$.

Example 8.16 Up to now the regenerative method has been discussed for discrete-time processes; however, it is also relevant for continuous-time processes. Consider the number-in-queue process $\{Q(t), t \geq 0\}$ for the queueing system of Example 8.14. Those continuous time points at which a customer arrives to find the system completely empty are regeneration points for the process $\{Q(t), t \geq 0\}$. If H is the time between any two such successive points, the steady-state time-average number in queue $Q = \lim_{t\to\infty} \int_0^t Q(u)du/t$ (w.p. 1) is given by

$$Q = \frac{E\left[\int_0^H Q(u)\, du\right]}{E(H)}$$

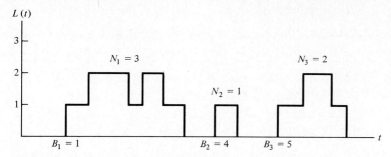

Figure 8.4 A realization of the number-in-system process $\{L(t), t \geq 0\}$ for a single-server queue.

We now discuss how to obtain a point estimator and a confidence interval for ν using the regenerative method. Suppose we simulate the process $\{Y_i, i \geq 1\}$ for exactly n' regeneration cycles, resulting in the following data:

$$Z_1, Z_2, \ldots, Z_{n'}$$

$$N_1, N_2, \ldots, N_{n'}$$

Each of these sequences consists of IID random variables; however, in general, Z_j and N_j are not independent. A point estimator for ν is then given by

$$\hat{\nu}(n') = \frac{\overline{Z}(n')}{\overline{N}(n')}$$

Although $\overline{Z}(n')$ and $\overline{N}(n')$ are unbiased estimators of $E(Z)$ and $E(N)$, respectively, $\hat{\nu}(n')$ is *not* an unbiased estimator of ν (see Appendix 8B). It is true, however, that $\hat{\nu}(n')$ is a strongly consistent estimator of ν, that is, $\hat{\nu}(n') \to \nu$ as $n' \to \infty$ (w.p. 1); see Prob. 8.9.

Let the covariance matrix of the vector $\mathbf{U}_j = (Z_j, N_j)^T$ be

$$\Sigma = \begin{bmatrix} \sigma_{11} & \sigma_{12} \\ \sigma_{12} & \sigma_{22} \end{bmatrix}$$

for example, $\sigma_{12} = E\{[Z_j - E(Z_j)][N_j - E(N_j)]\}$, and let $V_j = Z_j - \nu N_j$. Then the V_j's are IID random variables with mean 0 and variance $\sigma_V^2 = \sigma_{11} - 2\nu\sigma_{12} + \nu^2\sigma_{22}$ (see Prob. 4.11). Therefore, if $0 < \sigma_V^2 < \infty$, it follows from the classical central limit theorem (see Theorem 4.1 in Sec. 4.5) that

$$\frac{\overline{V}(n')}{\sqrt{\sigma_V^2/n'}} \xrightarrow{\mathcal{D}} N(0, 1) \qquad \text{as } n' \to \infty \tag{8.10}$$

where $\xrightarrow{\mathcal{D}}$ denotes convergence in distribution and $N(0, 1)$ denotes a standard normal random variable. Let

$$\hat{\Sigma}(n') = \begin{bmatrix} \hat{\sigma}_{11}(n') & \hat{\sigma}_{12}(n') \\ \hat{\sigma}_{12}(n') & \hat{\sigma}_{22}(n') \end{bmatrix} = \frac{\sum_{j=1}^{n'} [\mathbf{U}_j - \overline{\mathbf{U}}(n')][\mathbf{U}_j - \overline{\mathbf{U}}(n')]^T}{n' - 1}$$

be the estimated covariance matrix and let

$$\hat{\sigma}_V^2(n') = \hat{\sigma}_{11}(n') - 2\hat{v}(n')\hat{\sigma}_{12}(n') + [\hat{v}(n')]^2\hat{\sigma}_{22}(n')$$

be the estimate of σ_V^2 based on n' regeneration cycles. It can be shown that $\hat{\sigma}_V^2(n') \to \sigma_V^2$ as $n' \to \infty$ (w.p. 1). Consequently, we can replace σ_V^2 in (8.10) by $\hat{\sigma}_V^2(n')$ (see Chung [5, p. 93]), and dividing through the ratio by $\overline{N}(n')$ yields

$$\frac{\hat{v}(n') - v}{\sqrt{\hat{\sigma}_V^2(n')/n'[\overline{N}(n')]^2}} \xrightarrow{\mathcal{D}} N(0, 1) \qquad \text{as } n' \to \infty$$

Therefore, if the number of cycles n' is sufficiently large, an approximate (in terms of coverage) $100(1 - \alpha)$ percent confidence interval for v is given by

$$\hat{v}(n') \pm \frac{z_{1-\alpha/2}\sqrt{\hat{\sigma}_V^2(n')/n'}}{\overline{N}(n')} \tag{8.11}$$

We call this regenerative approach to constructing a confidence interval for v the *classical approach* (C). For an alternative regenerative approach to constructing a confidence interval for v, known as the *jackknife approach* (J), see Appendix 8B.

The difficulty with using the regenerative method in practice is that real-world simulations may not have regeneration points or (even if they do) the expected cycle length may be so large that only a very few cycles can be simulated [in which case the confidence interval given by (8.11) will not be valid]. For example, suppose one wants to estimate by simulation the steady-state average total delay in queue for a network consisting of k queueing systems in series. [A customer departing from queueing system i ($i = 1, 2, \ldots, k - 1$) proceeds to queueing system $i + 1$.] Then regeneration points for the process $\{D_i, i \geq 1\}$ (D_i is the total delay of the ith customer to arrive) are the indices of those customers who arrive at the first queueing system to find the entire network empty. If the queueing systems composing the network are highly utilized, regeneration points for the network will be few and far between.

Additional references on the regenerative method which may be of interest are Crane and Lemoine [10], Fishman [15], Iglehart [20, 21], Iglehart and Shedler [22], and Lavenberg and Sauer [27]. The first of these references is particularly recommended for a comprehensive introductory treatment.

Empirical comparison of the two procedures. Since the method of batch means and the regenerative method both depend on assumptions which may not be strictly satisfied, e.g., n' sufficiently large for the regenerative method, it is of interest to see how these procedures perform in practice. We first performed 200 independent simulation experiments for the $M/M/1$ queue with $\rho = 0.8$ ($\lambda = 1$ and $\omega = \frac{5}{4}$), and in each experiment our goal was to construct a 90 percent confidence interval for d = 3.2 (see [17, p. 58]) using both procedures. Not knowing how to choose definitively the total sample size m and the number of batches n for the method of batch means, we arbitrarily chose $m = 320, 640, 1280, 2560$ and $n = 5, 10, 20, 40$. Thus, for each experiment we constructed 16 different confidence intervals using batch means. For the regenerative method it can be shown that $E(N) = 1/(1 - \rho) = 5$

Table 8.5 Estimated coverages based on 200 experiments, $M/M/1$ queue with $\rho = 0.8$

	Batch means				Regenerative method approach	
$m(n')$	$n = 5$	$n = 10$	$n = 20$	$n = 40$	C	J
320(64)	0.740	0.630	0.495	0.375	0.570	0.685
640(128)	0.745	0.715	0.615	0.480	0.690	0.745
1280(256)	0.775	0.740	0.710	0.595	0.715	0.765
2560(512)	0.810	0.810	0.760	0.645	0.760	0.775

for the $M/M/1$ queue with $\rho = 0.8$. We therefore chose the number of regeneration cycles $n' = 64, 128, 256, 512$ so that, on the average, the two procedures used the same number of observations, that is, $m = n'E(N)$. Since both a classical and a jackknife confidence interval were constructed for each n', there were eight regenerative confidence intervals for each experiment. Table 8.5 gives the proportion of the 200 confidence intervals which covered d for each of the 24 cases discussed above. For example, in the case of $m = 320$ and $n = 5$ for batch means (i.e., each confidence interval was based on five batches of size 64), 74 percent of the 200 confidence intervals covered d, falling considerably short of the desired 90 percent. (Note that for a fixed m, the estimated coverage for batch means decreases as n increases. This is because as n increases, the batch means become more correlated, resulting in a more biased estimate of the variance of the sample mean.) For the regenerative method, the estimated coverages are even more disappointing than those for batch means, and the jackknife regenerative confidence interval seems preferable. For both batch means and the regenerative method, the estimated coverages improve as m(or n') gets larger. This is encouraging because it implies that both procedures might perform well if enough data were available (see Sec. 8.6.2).

We next performed 200 independent simulation experiments for the time-shared computer model with 35 terminals, which was discussed in Example 8.15 and Sec. 2.4. Our objective was to construct 90 percent confidence intervals for the steady-state average response time $r = 8.246$ (see Adiri and Avi-Itzhak [1]). We chose m and n as above and, since $E(N) \approx 32$ for the computer model, we took $n' = 10, 20, 40, 80$. Table 8.6 gives the proportion of the 200 confidence intervals which covered

Table 8.6 Estimated coverages based on 200 experiments, time-shared computer model

	Batch means				Regenerative method approach	
$m(n')$	$n = 5$	$n = 10$	$n = 20$	$n = 40$	C	J
320(10)	0.860	0.780	0.670	0.550	0.545	0.725
640(20)	0.890	0.855	0.790	0.685	0.730	0.830
1280(40)	0.910	0.885	0.880	0.795	0.830	0.865
2560(80)	0.905	0.875	0.895	0.855	0.870	0.915

r for each of the 24 cases. Even though the computer model is considerably more complex than the $M/M/1$ queue, it can be seen from Table 8.6 that batch means with $n = 5$ produces an estimated coverage very close to 0.90 for m as small as 640. Thus, the $M/M/1$ queue with $\rho = 0.8$ is much more difficult statistically, despite its highly simple structure. These two examples illustrate that one cannot infer anything about the statistical behavior of the output data by looking at how "complex" the model's structure might be. Note also the superiority of batch means over the regenerative method for small sample sizes.

Summary. From the empirical results presented in Tables 8.5 and 8.6 and also those given in [29] and [34], we came to the following conclusions with regard to the use of fixed-sample-size procedures:

1. If the total sample size m (or n') is chosen too small, the actual coverages of *all* existing fixed-sample-size procedures may be considerably lower than desired. This is really not surprising since a steady-state measure of performance is defined as a limit as the length of the simulation (total number of observations) goes to infinity.
2. The "appropriate" choice of m (or n') would appear to be extremely model-dependent and thus impossible to choose arbitrarily. For the method of batch means with $n = 5$, $m = 640$ gave good results for the computer model; however, even for m as large as 2560, we did not obtain good results for the $M/M/1$ queue.
3. If the total number of observations m (or n') which can be collected is restricted to be "small," batch means with $n = 5$ appears to work as well as any other procedure, and it is a simple method to apply.

*8.6.2 Sequential Procedures

We saw in Sec. 8.6.1 that fixed-sample-size procedures generally cannot be relied upon to produce confidence intervals with coverages close to the desired level. The results were encouraging, however, in that they indicated that these procedures would perform well if enough data were available. In this section we discuss sequential procedures for constructing a confidence interval for a steady-state average response ν which determine the amount of data required during the course of a simulation run.

In [33] Law and Kelton surveyed the published sequential procedures and found that only two of these procedures performed well when tested on a variety of stochastic models with a known value of ν. One procedure, developed by Fishman [14], is based on the regenerative method and thus, we feel, has limited applicability to many real-world problems at the present time. The other procedure (see Law and Carson [32]), which is based on the idea of batch means, we now describe.

For a simulation run resulting in the observations $Y_1, Y_2, \ldots, Y_m$, let the batch means $\overline{Y}_j(l)$ ($j = 1, 2, \ldots, n$) and the grand sample mean $\overline{\overline{Y}}(n, l)$ be defined as in Sec. 8.6.1. In addition, let $\rho_i(l) = \text{Cor}\,[\overline{Y}_j(l), \overline{Y}_{j+i}(l)]$ ($i = 1, 2, \ldots, n - j$) be the correlation between any two batch means, each based on l observations, separated by i batches, and let $b(n, l)$ be such that $E\{\hat{\sigma}^2[\overline{\overline{Y}}(n, l)]\} = b(n, l)\sigma^2[\overline{\overline{Y}}(n, l)]$, where $\hat{\sigma}^2[\overline{\overline{Y}}(n, l)] = s^2_{\overline{Y}_j(l)}(n)/n$. [We are assuming that $Y_1, Y_2, \ldots$ is covariance stationary, which makes the $\rho_i(l)$'s well defined. Note that $\rho_i(l)$ is sometimes called the *lag i correlation*.] In [32] it is shown that $\rho_i(l) \to 0$ ($i = 1, 2, \ldots, n - 1$) as the batch size $l \to \infty$, which in turn implies that $b(n, l) \to 1$ as $l \to \infty$ (see Prob. 8.6). Thus, if we could develop a method for choosing the batch size large enough for the batch means to be (essentially) uncorrelated, the estimate of $\sigma^2[\overline{\overline{Y}}(n, l)]$ would be (essentially) unbiased. Furthermore, as pointed out above, this appears to be the most important consideration in making the method of batch means produce acceptable coverages.

One approach which has been suggested in the literature for obtaining uncorrelated batch means is to fix the number of batches n and then increase the batch size l until the estimated value of $\rho_1(l)$ is small, say less than 0.05. The difficulty with this approach is that correlation estimators are generally biased and for small n have a large variance (see Sec. 4.4). For example, consider the process $\{D_i, i \geq 1\}$ for the (covariance stationary) $M/M/1$ queue with $\rho = 0.9$. Law and Carson made 100 independent simulation runs of this process, each of length 14,400 observations. Each run was divided into 30 batches of length 480, and $\rho_1(480)$ was estimated by the jackknifed estimator $\tilde{\rho}_1(30, 480)$, defined by (8.12) below. For 23 of the 100 runs, $\tilde{\rho}_1(30, 480)$ was less than 0.05 (22 were less than 0); however, it can be shown (see Daley [11]) that $\rho_1(480) = 0.284$ and furthermore that $b(30, 480) = 0.597$. Further empirical investigations showed that a sequential procedure based on directly estimating $\rho_1(l)$ from 30 (or any small number of) batch means would produce confidence intervals with coverages which may be considerably lower than desired. They also found that for some systems, n might have to be as large as 400 to get a precise estimate of $\rho_1(l)$. Unfortunately, obtaining 400 or more uncorrelated batch means is likely to require a prohibitive number of observations.

These considerations suggested using fn (f an integer ≥ 2) batches of length l to infer whether n batches of length fl are approximately uncorrelated. To investigate the relationships between $\rho_1(l)$ and $\rho_1(fl)$ which can occur in practice, Law and Carson studied the following processes for which $\rho_i(l)$ and $b(n, l)$ can be analytically computed:

1. $\{D_i, i \geq 1\}$ for the $M/M/1$ queue with $\rho = 0.5, 0.8$, and 0.9
2. $\{C_i, i \geq 1\}$ for the (s, S) inventory system described in Example 4.6
3. Thirty different AR(1), AR(2), and ARMA(1, 1) time-series models (see Box and Jenkins [3, p. 53]) with parameters chosen over the entire range of feasible values

From studying these 34 stochastic processes, they found essentially three types of behavior for $\rho_1(l)$ as a function of l, examples of which are shown in Figs. 8.5 to 8.7. For type 1 behavior the lag 1 correlation $\rho_1(l)$ strictly decreases to 0. For example, suppose $f = 10$ and $n = 40$. If, for some l, $\rho_1(l) < 0.4$, then $\rho_1(10l) < 0.05$ and $0.9 < b(40, 10l) < 1$. (This holds for all type 1 models they considered.) The $M/M/1$ queue exhibits type 1 behavior.

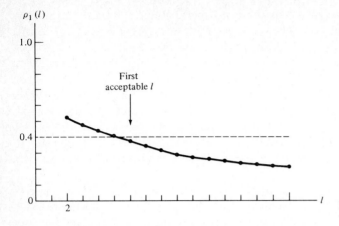

Figure 8.5 Type 1 behavior.

In type 2 behavior, $\rho_1(l)$ changes direction one or more times and then strictly decreases to zero. Consider again the example $f = 10$ and $n = 40$. If, for some l, $\rho_1(l) < 0.4$ and $\rho_1(l')$ is decreasing for $l' \geq l$, then $\rho_1(10l) < 0.05$ and $0.9 < b(40, 10l) < 1$. [This holds for all type 2 models considered with one exception, where $\rho_1(l) < 0.4$ and $\rho_1(l')$ decreasing for $l' \geq l$ implies $\rho_1(10l) = 0.059$ and $b(40, 10l) = 0.894$.] Some of the time-series models are of this type.

For type 3 behavior, $\rho_1(l) < 0$ and $b(40, 10l) > 1$, for all l. In this case the $\overline{Y}_j(10l)$'s may be correlated, but the coverage will be at least as great as that desired. The (s, S) inventory system exhibits type 3 behavior.

Law and Carson note that these three types of behavior are certainly not the only ones which can occur. In fact, for some of the time-series models they studied, $\rho_1(l)$ can be either positive or negative as l varies. However, if $0 < \rho_1(l) < 0.4$ for some l, then $\rho_1(10l) < 0.05$ (similar to type 1); and if $\rho_1(l) < 0$ for some l, then $b(40, 10l) > 1$ (similar to type 3).

The above discussion was predicated on knowing $\rho_1(l)$ which, in fact, must be

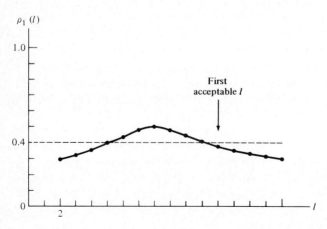

Figure 8.6 Type 2 behavior.

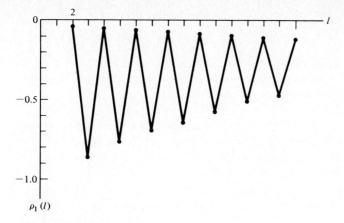

Figure 8.7 Type 3 behavior.

estimated. The usual estimator of $\rho_1(l)$ is given by

$$\hat{\rho}_1(n, l) = \frac{\sum\limits_{j=1}^{n-1} [\overline{Y}_j(l) - \overline{\overline{Y}}(n, l)][\overline{Y}_{j+1}(l) - \overline{\overline{Y}}(n, l)]}{\sum\limits_{j=1}^{n} [\overline{Y}_j(l) - \overline{\overline{Y}}(n, l)]^2}$$

However, if $\hat{\rho}_1^1(n/2, l)$ and $\hat{\rho}_1^2(n/2, l)$ are, respectively, the usual lag 1 estimators based on the first $n/2$ and the last $n/2$ batches (n is assumed to be even), we can also estimate $\rho_1(l)$ by the jackknifed estimator

$$\tilde{\rho}_1(n, l) = 2\hat{\rho}_1(n, l) - \frac{\hat{\rho}_1^1(n/2, l) + \hat{\rho}_1^2(n/2, l)}{2} \tag{8.12}$$

We shall use $\tilde{\rho}_1(n, l)$ rather than $\hat{\rho}_1(n, l)$ to estimate $\rho_1(l)$ since, in general, it will be less biased (see Miller [36]).

We now state the sequential procedure of Law and Carson, based on the above observations. Note that n was chosen to be 40 to obviate the effect of the nonnormality of the $\overline{Y}_j(l)$'s (see the discussion of batch means in Sec. 8.6.1) and f was chosen to be 10 so that $fn = 400$ batch means would be available to estimate lag 1 correlations.

   0. Fix $n = 40$, $f = 10$, $m_0 = 600$, $m_1 = 800$ (see note 1 below), the stopping value $u = 0.4$, the relative precision $\gamma > 0$; let $i = 1$; collect m_1 observations.

1a. Divide the m_i observations into fn batches of size $l = m_i/fn$. Compute $\tilde{\rho}_1(fn, l)$ from $\overline{Y}_j(l)$ ($j = 1, 2, \ldots, fn$). If $\tilde{\rho}_1(fn, l) \geq u$ (see note 2), go to step 2. If $\tilde{\rho}_1(fn, l) \leq 0$ (see note 3), go to step 1c. Otherwise, go to step 1b.

  b. Divide m_i into $fn/2$ batches of size $2l$. Compute $\tilde{\rho}_1(fn/2, 2l)$ from $\overline{Y}_j(2l)$ ($j = 1, 2, \ldots, fn/2$) (see note 4). If $\tilde{\rho}_1(fn/2, 2l) < \tilde{\rho}_1(fn, l)$ (see note 5), go to step 1c. Otherwise, go to step 2.

    c. Divide m_i into n batches of size fl. Compute $\overline{Y}(n,\ fl)$ and $\delta = t_{n-1,1-\alpha/2}\ \sqrt{\hat{\sigma}^2[\overline{\overline{Y}}(n,\ fl)]}$ from $\overline{Y}_j(fl)$ $(j = 1, 2, \ldots, n)$ (see note 4). If $\delta/|\overline{Y}(n, fl)| \leq \gamma$ (see note 6), use $\overline{Y}(n, fl) \pm \delta$ as an approximate $100(1 - \alpha)$ percent confidence interval for ν and stop. Otherwise, go to step 2.
2. Replace i by $i + 1$, set $m_i = 2m_{i-2}$ (see note 7), collect the additional $m_i - m_{i-1}$ observations required, and go to step 1a.

Note 1. The initial sample size $m_1 = 800$ was chosen since it is the smallest sample size which allows 400 batches of size 2, and $m_0 = 600$ was chosen to make $m_{2i} = (m_{2i-1} + m_{2i+1})/2$ for $i = 1, 2, \ldots$.

Note 2. This check was suggested by type 1 behavior.

Note 3. This check was suggested by type 3 behavior.

Note 4. An appropriate number of the $\overline{Y}_j(l)$'s can be averaged to compute the $\overline{Y}_j(2l)$'s or the $\overline{Y}_j(fl)$'s.

Note 5. This check was suggested by type 2 behavior. They tested to see whether $\rho_1(l')$ is decreasing for $l' \geq l$ by checking to see whether $\rho_1(2l) < \rho_1(l)$.

Note 6. This additional check allows a simulator to require that the relative precision of the confidence interval be less than or equal to a specified number γ.

Note 7. The successive sample sizes are 800, 1200, 1600, 2400, 3200, ... By doubling the sample size every other iteration, only 800 storage locations are required to store the batch means; the basic data $Y_1, Y_2, \ldots$ need not be stored.

    To see how well the sequential procedure performed in practice, Law and Carson made 100 independent simulation runs using the procedure for each of 13 stochastic models with a known value of ν (see [32] for details). For each run a 90 percent confidence interval was constructed, and it was determined whether the interval contained ν. They found that if $\gamma = 0.075$, the average coverage over the 13 models was 0.883 and for no model was the coverage excessively below 0.90. In particular, for the $M/M/1$ queue with $\rho = 0.8$, 87 percent of the 100 confidence intervals covered d, and the average sample size at termination was 75,648. For the time-shared computer model, 92 percent of the 100 confidence intervals covered r, and the average sample size was 17,696.

    If one wants to construct a confidence interval for a steady-state average response ν which is likely to have coverage close to the desired level, we recommend using the above sequential procedure with γ chosen to be less than or equal to 0.075. This parameter choice produced good results for all models tested but might require a "large" sample size for some models. On the other hand, no one has developed a procedure which will, in general, produce good results for a "small" fixed sample size. Although not specified in the algorithm above, it may be prudent to delete some number of observations, say k, before applying the sequential procedure. The data which are then used, $Y_{k+1}, Y_{k+2}, \ldots$, should more closely approximate covariance stationarity than the original data, $Y_1, Y_2, \ldots$ (see Appendix 4A). Unfortunately, there is no simple method for choosing k; see Sec. 8.6.3.

8.6.3 A Replication-Deletion Approach

The reader may have wondered why a simulator could not do a terminating simulation-type analysis of an output process Y_1, Y_2, ... to estimate the steady-state average response ν. To illustrate the danger of making independent replications (each starting from the same initial conditions) and of performing a terminating analysis of a system for which we *really* want to estimate a *steady-state* measure of performance, consider the $M/M/1$ queue with $\rho = 0.9$. Suppose we want to estimate the steady-state average delay $d = 8.1$ and make n independent replications each of length $m = 320$ customers and each with $L(0) = 0$. Since $E(X_j) = d(320|L(0) = 0) = 6.01$ (see Fig. 8.1), $E[\overline{X}(n)] = 6.01$ and $\overline{X}(n)$ is a biased estimator of d no matter how many replications are made. (Here X_j is the average delay of the 320 customers in the jth replication). Furthermore, as n gets large, the length of a confidence interval constructed from (8.5) or (8.8) will become smaller and smaller and the coverage of the confidence interval eventually approaches 0 (see [29]). We are actually constructing a confidence interval for $d(320|L(0) = 0)$, not d.

From Fig. 8.1 it becomes clear why the above terminating analysis does not perform well in the steady-state case. Because of a simulator's inability to start the simulation off at time 0 in a state which is representative of the steady-state behavior of the system (see Sec. 8.3.2), the output data at the beginning of the simulation are not "good" estimates of the steady-state average response ν. (This difficulty has been called the *start-up problem* or the *problem of the initial transient* in the simulation literature.) This suggests "warming up" the simulation (see Appendix 4A) for some amount of time, say k observations, before beginning data collection. The difficulty is in knowing how to choose k; a survey paper by Gafarian, Ancker, and Morisaku [16] indicates that no published procedure performs at all well in practice. We now briefly describe a procedure for this problem recently developed by Kelton [24] (see also Kelton and Law [25]).

Suppose we make n independent replications of the process Y_1, Y_2, ... each of length m resulting in the following observations:

$$Y_{11}, Y_{12}, \ldots, Y_{1m}$$

$$\cdot \cdot \cdot \cdot \cdot \cdot \cdot \cdot \cdot \cdot \cdot \cdot \cdot \cdot$$

$$Y_{n1}, Y_{n2}, \ldots, Y_{nm}$$

Thus, Y_{ji} is the ith observation from the jth replication. Delete the first k observations from each replication $(0 \leq k < m)$ and let

$$\overline{Y}_j(m, k) = \frac{\sum_{i=k+1}^{m} Y_{ji}}{m - k} \quad \text{and} \quad \overline{\overline{Y}}(n, m, k) = \frac{\sum_{j=1}^{n} \overline{Y}_j(m, k)}{n}$$

Using $n = 5$ replications and a time-series regression technique, Kelton developed an algorithm for choosing m and k such that $E[\overline{Y}_j(m, k)] \approx \nu$. Thus, if one uses

Table 8.7 Results for the replication-deletion procedure based on 100 experiments

Model	Measure of performance	Average m	Average k	Estimated bias in $\bar{\bar{Y}}(5, m, k)$, %
$M/M/1$ queue with $\rho = 0.8$	$d = 3.200$	1615	761	0.11
Time-shared computer model with 50 terminals	$r = 21.384$	1380	643	0.02

this procedure to determine m and k, the $\bar{Y}_j(m, k)$'s resulting from making additional replications of the process will be IID random variables which are approximately unbiased for ν.

Table 8.7 gives the results of applying this replication-deletion approach in 100 experiments with the $M/M/1$ queue with $\rho = 0.8$ and in 100 experiments with the time-shared computer model with 50 terminals. The table entry "estimated bias in $\bar{\bar{Y}}(5, m, k)$" is the average value of $100(|\bar{\bar{Y}}(5, m, k) - \nu|)/\nu$ over the 100 experiments. Note that the estimated bias is negligible in both cases.

A practical difficulty with applying the above procedure is that it may require restarting each of five replications which have been previously terminated; this is essentially a programming problem. A theoretical limitation of the procedure is that it basically makes the assumption that $E(Y_i)$ is a monotone function of i. Although many queueing and computer models share this monotonicity property (see [24]), this assumption does limit the overall applicability of the procedure.

8.7 MULTIPLE MEASURES OF PERFORMANCE

In Secs. 8.5 and 8.6 we presented procedures for constructing a confidence interval for a single measure of performance. However, for most real-world simulations several measures of performance are of interest. Suppose that I_l is a $100(1 - \alpha_l)$ percent confidence interval for the measure of performance μ_l ($l = 1, 2, \ldots, k$). (The μ_l's may all be measures of performance for a terminating simulation or may all be measures for a steady-state simulation.) Then the probability that all k confidence intervals *simultaneously* contain their respective true measures satisfies (see Prob. 8.7)

$$P\{\mu_l \in I_l \text{ for all } l = 1, 2, \ldots, k\} \geq 1 - \sum_{l=1}^{k} \alpha_l \qquad (8.13)$$

whether or not the I_l's are independent. This result, known as the *Bonferroni inequality* has serious implications for a simulation study. For example, suppose one constructs 90 percent confidence intervals, that is, $\alpha_l = 0.1$ for all l, for 10 different measures of performance. Then the probability that each of the 10 confidence intervals contains its true measure can only be claimed to be greater than or equal to *zero*. Thus one cannot have much overall confidence in any conclusions drawn from such a study. The difficulty we have just described is known in the statistics literature as the *multiple-comparisons problem.*

We now describe a practical solution to the above problem when the value of k is small. If one wants the overall confidence level associated with k confidence intervals to be at least $100(1 - \alpha)$ percent, choose the α_i's so that $\sum_{l=1}^{k} \alpha_l = \alpha$. (Note that the α_i's do *not* have to be equal. Thus, α_i's corresponding to more important measures could be chosen smaller.) Therefore, one could construct ten 99 percent confidence intervals and have the overall confidence level be *at least* 90 percent. The difficulty with this solution is that the confidence intervals will be larger than they were originally if a fixed-sample-size procedure is used, or more data will be required for a specified set of k relative precisions if a sequential procedure is used. For this reason, we recommend that k be no larger than about 10.

If one has a very large number of measures of performance, the only recourse available is to construct the usual 90 percent or 95 percent confidence intervals but to be aware that one or more of these confidence intervals probably do not contain their true measures.

Example 8.17 Consider the bank of Example 8.10 with five tellers and one queue. Table 8.8 gives the results of making 10 replications of the (terminating) simulation and using (8.5) to construct 96.667 percent confidence intervals for each of the measures of performance

$$ E\left[\int_0^T Q(t)\,dt/T \right], \quad E\left(\sum_{i=1}^{N} D_i/N \right), \text{ and } E\left[\sum_{i=1}^{N} I_i(0, 5)/N \right] $$

so that the overall confidence level is at least 90 percent.

Example 8.18 For the $M/M/1$ queue with $\rho = 0.8$ ($\lambda = 1$, $\omega = \frac{5}{4}$), suppose that it is desired to construct a confidence interval for the steady-state average delay $d = 3.2$ and also to construct a confidence interval for the steady-state proportion of customers who have a delay less than or equal to 8.318, so that the overall confidence level is at least 90 percent. The latter measure of perfor-

Table 8.8 Results of making 10 replications of the bank model with five tellers and one queue

Measure of performance	Point estimate	96.667% confidence interval	Relative precision
$E\left[\dfrac{\int_0^T Q(t)\,dt}{T} \right]$	1.973	[1.550, 2.395]	0.214
$E\left(\dfrac{\sum_{i=1}^{N} D_i}{N} \right)$	2.031	[1.590, 2.472]	0.217
$E\left[\dfrac{\sum_{i=1}^{N} I_i(0, 5)}{N} \right]$	0.853	[0.803, 0.902]	0.058

Table 8.9 Results of applying the steady-state sequential procedure to two output processes for the $M/M/1$ queue with $\rho = 0.8$

Measure of performance	Point estimate	95% confidence interval	Relative precision
$d = 3.2$	3.159	[2.924, 3.394]	0.074
$p(8.318) = 0.9$	0.907	[0.893, 0.921]	0.015

mance, which is known to have a true value of 0.9 (see [17, p. 57]), is defined by

$$p(8.318) = \lim_{m \to \infty} \frac{\sum_{i=1}^{m} I_i(0, 8.318)}{m} \quad \text{w.p. 1}$$

where

$$I_i(0, 8.318) = \begin{cases} 1 & \text{if } 0 \le D_i \le 8.318 \\ 0 & \text{otherwise} \end{cases}$$

Table 8.9 shows the results of applying the sequential procedure (of Sec. 8.6.2) to each of the processes $D_1, D_2, \ldots$ and $I_1(0, 8.318), I_2(0, 8.318), \ldots$, with $\alpha = 0.05$ and $\gamma = 0.075$ for each confidence interval. Thus, the simulation was run until the procedure's stopping criteria were satisfied for *each* output process. The sample size required to satisfy the stopping criteria for both processes was 102,400. (The procedure would have terminated for the indicator process itself at a sample size of 19,200.)

8.8 CONCLUDING THOUGHTS ON THE CHAPTER

Reading the simulation literature leads one to believe that only steady-state simulations are important; almost every paper and book written on the analysis of simulation output data deals with the steady-state case. This may be a carryover from mathematical queueing theory, where only a steady-state analysis is generally possible. However, we believe that terminating simulations are also important. We have discovered by talking to a large number of simulation practitioners that a significant proportion of simulations in the real world are actually of the terminating type. The following are some reasons why a steady-state analysis may not be appropriate:

1. The system under consideration is physically terminating. In this case, letting the length of a simulation be arbitrarily large may make no sense.
2. The input distributions for the system change over time. In this case, steady-state measures of performance will probably not exist.
3. One is often interested in studying the transient behavior (see Sec. 8.3.2) of a system even if steady-state measures of performance exist.

If one does a terminating-type analysis of a system, the most important thing to keep in mind is that the X_j resulting from replication j should be representative of what one actually wants to estimate (see Sec. 8.6.3). Terminating analyses have the advantage that each replication produces an IID "observation" and thus the procedures for constructing confidence intervals are relatively simple.

In the steady-state case, the procedures for constructing confidence intervals are considerably more complicated. If one makes one long simulation run to estimate a steady-state measure of performance, the start-up problem is less significant because the artificial initial conditions are experienced only once. If one wants to construct a confidence interval which is likely to have coverage close to the desired level, we believe that the sequential procedure described in Sec. 8.6.2 performs as well as any published procedure and has greater applicability to real-world problems.

There are some situations where it may not be clear whether to do a terminating or steady-state analysis. For example, consider a computer system where the arrival rate of jobs varies over the day but there is a peak period where the arrival rate is reasonably constant (see Example 8.5). Although this situation has usually been analyzed using a steady-state simulation (with the arrival rate of jobs equal to the peak rate), we believe that either type of analysis might be appropriate depending on the circumstances. One additional consideration to keep in mind is that if the peak period in the actual system is short or if the arrival rate before the peak period is considerably lower than the peak rate, a steady-state simulation may overestimate the level of congestion during the peak period in the system. This might result in purchasing a computer configuration that is more than actually needed.

APPENDIX 8A THE MEMORYLESS PROPERTY

A random variable X is said to have the *memoryless property* if

$$P\{X > t + s \mid X > t\} = P\{X > s\} \qquad \text{for all } t, s \geq 0$$

Thus, if X is the lifetime of some device, the "remaining life" is independent of how long it has already been in operation. It can easily be shown that the exponential random variable has the memoryless property (see Prob. 8.8) and furthermore that this is the only continuous random variable with this property (see Ross [37, p. 9]).

APPENDIX 8B RATIOS OF EXPECTATIONS AND JACKKNIFE ESTIMATORS

Much of this chapter has been concerned with estimating the expectation of a single random variable X, namely, $E(X)$. However, as the following examples show, there are many situations in simulation where it is of interest to estimate the ratio of two expectations, namely, $E(Y)/E(X)$:

1. For the regenerative method, we saw in Sec. 8.6.1 that steady-state measures can be expressed as the ratio of two expectations.

2. For the combat simulation of Example 8.3, it is sometimes of interest to estimate $E(R)/E(B)$, where R and B are the numbers of red losses and blue losses in a battle.

3. For the bank simulation of Example 8.10, let $P = \sum_{i=1}^{N} D_i$ be the total delay of all customers served in a day. Then it is of interest to estimate $E(P/N)$, which can be interpreted as the expectation of the average delay of a customer where the expectation is taken with respect to all possible days. However, it may also be of interest to estimate the long-run average delay of all customers, which can be shown to be equal to $E(P)/E(N)$.

Estimators of ratios of expectations, however, usually are biased. We now discuss a method of obtaining a less biased point estimator, as well as an alternative confidence interval.

Suppose that it is desired to estimate the ratio $\phi = E(Y)/E(X)$ from the data $Y_1, Y_2, \ldots, Y_n$ and $X_1, X_2, \ldots, X_n$, where the X_i's are IID random variables, the Y_i's are IID random variables, and $\text{Cov}(Y_i, X_j) = 0$ for $i \neq j$. The classical point estimator of ϕ is given by $\hat{\phi}_C(n) = \overline{Y}(n)/\overline{X}(n)$; see the discussion of the regenerative method in Sec. 8.6.1 for the classical confidence interval for ϕ. We now discuss the jackknife approach to point and interval estimation of ϕ (see [20] and [36]). First define

$$\theta_g = n\hat{\phi}_C(n) - (n-1)\frac{\sum\limits_{\substack{j=1 \\ j \neq g}}^{n} Y_j}{\sum\limits_{\substack{j=1 \\ j \neq g}}^{n} X_j} \qquad \text{for } g = 1, 2, \ldots, n$$

Then the jackknife point estimator for ϕ is given by $\hat{\phi}_J(n) = \sum\limits_{g=1}^{n} \theta_g/n$, which is, in general, less biased than $\hat{\phi}_C(n)$. Let

$$\hat{\sigma}_J^2(n) = \frac{\sum\limits_{g=1}^{n} [\theta_g - \hat{\phi}_J(n)]^2}{n-1}$$

Then it can be shown (see [36]) that

$$\frac{\hat{\phi}_J(n) - \phi}{\sqrt{\hat{\sigma}_J^2(n)/n}} \xrightarrow{D} N(0, 1) \qquad \text{as } n \to \infty$$

which gives the jackknife $100(1 - \alpha)$ percent confidence interval $\hat{\phi}_J(n) \pm z_{1-\alpha/2}\sqrt{\hat{\sigma}_J^2(n)/n}$ for ϕ. (See Sec. 8.6.1 for some empirical results on the relative performance of the classical and jackknife confidence intervals.)

PROBLEMS

8.1 For the multiteller bank with five tellers of Sec. 2.5, make $n = 5$ independent replications and use (8.5) to construct a 90 percent confidence interval for the expected average delay in queue of a customer. Approximately how many total replications would be required to obtain a confidence interval with an absolute precision of $\beta = 0.5$ minutes? To obtain a confidence interval with a relative precision of $\gamma = 0.25$?

8.2 For the bank of Prob. 8.1, use the sequential procedure of Sec. 8.5.2 to construct a 90 percent confidence interval for the expected average delay in queue of a customer, and make the relative precision of the confidence interval be less than or equal to $\gamma = 0.15$. Use $n_0 = 10$ initial replications.

8.3 For the time-shared computer model of Sec. 2.4 with 35 terminals, warm up the model for 50 response times (see Prob. 2.5) and then use batch means with $m = 640$ response times and $n = 5$ batches to construct confidence intervals for the steady-state average response time, r, and also for the steady-state proportion of response times which are less than or equal to 20 seconds, $p(20)$. Try to make the overall confidence level at least 90 percent (see Sec. 8.7).

*8.4 For the computer model of Prob. 8.3, use the sequential procedure of Sec. 8.6.2 to construct a 90 percent confidence interval for the steady-state average response time, r, whose relative precision is less than or equal to $\gamma = 0.05$.

8.5 If $Y_1, Y_2, \ldots$ is a covariance stationary process, show for the method of batch means that $C_j(l) = \text{Cov}\,[\overline{Y}_j(l), \overline{Y}_{j+i}(l)]$ is given by

$$C_i(l) = \sum_{k=-(l-1)}^{l-1} \frac{(1 - |k|/l)C_{il+k}}{l} \qquad \text{where } C_k = \text{Cov}\,(Y_i, Y_{i+k})$$

*8.6 If $Y_1, Y_2, \ldots$ is a covariance stationary process, show for the method of batch means that $\rho_i(l) \to 0$ (for $i = 1, 2, \ldots, n - 1$) as $l \to \infty$ implies that $E\{\hat{\sigma}^2[\overline{\overline{Y}}(n, l)]\} \to \sigma^2[\overline{\overline{Y}}(n, l)]$ as $l \to \infty$ (see Sec. 8.6.2). *Hint:* First show that

$$b(n, l) = \frac{\left\{ n \Big/ \left[1 + 2 \sum_{i=1}^{n-1} \left(1 - \frac{i}{n} \right) \rho_i(l) \right] \right\} - 1}{n - 1}$$

8.7 Let E_l be an event which occurs with probability $1 - \alpha_l$ for $l = 1, 2, \ldots, k$. Then prove that

$$P\left\{ \bigcap_{l=1}^{k} E_l \right\} \geq 1 - \sum_{l=1}^{k} \alpha_l$$

where $\bigcap_{l=1}^{k} E_l$ is the intersection of the events $E_1, E_2, \ldots, E_k$. Do not assume the E_l's are independent. [This result is called the Bonferroni inequality; see Eq. (8.13).] *Hint:* The proof is by mathematical induction. That is, first show that $P\{E_1 \cap E_2\} \geq 1 - \alpha_1 - \alpha_2$. Then show that if $P\left\{ \bigcap_{l=1}^{k-1} E_l \right\} \geq 1 - \sum_{l=1}^{k-1} \alpha_l$ is true, then the desired result is also true.

8.8 Show that the exponential random variable has the memoryless property (see Appendix 8A).

*8.9 For the regenerative method, show that $\nu = E(Z)/E(N)$. [*Hint:* Observe that

$$\frac{\sum_{j=1}^{n'} Z_j}{\sum_{j=1}^{n'} N_j} = \frac{\sum_{i=1}^{M(n')} Y_i}{M(n')}$$

where n' is the number of regeneration cycles and $M(n')$ is the total number of observations (a random variable) in the n' cycles. Let $n' \to \infty$ and apply the strong law of large numbers (see Sec. 4.6) to the left-hand side of the above equation.] Also conclude that $\hat{\nu}(n') = \overline{Z}(n')/\overline{N}(n') \to \nu$ as $n' \to \infty$ (w.p. 1), so that $\hat{\nu}(n')$ is a strongly consistent estimator of ν. (See Secs. 8.6.1 and 4.6.)

*8.10 For the queueing system considered in Example 8.14, are the indices of those customers who depart and leave exactly l customers behind ($l \geq 0$ and fixed) regeneration points for the process $\{D_i, i \geq 1\}$? If not, under what circumstances would they be?

*8.11 For the inventory example of Sec. 1.5, identify a sequence of regeneration points for the process $\{C_i, i \geq 1\}$. Repeat assuming that the interdemand times are not exponential random variables.

*8.12 For the job-shop model of Sec. 2.6, identify a sequence of regeneration points for the process $\{D_i, i \geq 1\}$, where D_i is the total delay in queue of the ith job to complete its delay.

*8.13 Run a simulation model of the $M/M/1$ queue with $\rho = 0.8$ ($\lambda = 1$ and $\omega = 5/4$) for $n' = 100$ regeneration cycles (as defined in Example 8.14) and construct point and interval estimates for the steady-state average delay, d, and the steady-state proportion of customers with a delay less than or equal to 8.318, $p(8.318)$ (see Sec. 8.7). Try to make the overall confidence level at least 90 percent.

REFERENCES

1. Adiri, I., and B. Avi-Itzhak: A Time-Sharing Queue with a Finite Number of Customers, *J. Ass. Comput. Mach.,* **16:** 315–323 (1969).
2. Anderson, T. W.: *The Statistical Analysis of Time Series,* Wiley, New York, 1971.
3. Box, G. E. P., and G. M. Jenkins: *Time Series Analysis: Forecasting and Control,* revised ed., Holden-Day, San Francisco, 1976.
4. Chow, Y. S., and H. Robbins: On the Asymptotic Theory of Fixed-Width Sequential Confidence Intervals for the Mean, *Ann. Math. Statist.,* **36:** 457–462 (1965).
5. Chung, K. L.: *A Course in Probability Theory,* 2d ed., Academic, New York, 1974.
6. Crane, M. A., and D. L. Iglehart: Simulating Stable Stochastic Systems, I: General Multiserver Queues, *J. Ass. Comput. Mach.,* **21:** 103–113 (1974).
7. Crane, M. A., and D. L. Iglehart: Simulating Stable Stochastic Systems, II: Markov Chains, *J. Ass. Comput. Mach.,* **21:** 114–123 (1974).
8. Crane, M. A., and D. L. Iglehart: Simulating Stable Stochastic Systems, III: Regenerative Processes and Discrete-Event Simulations, *Oper. Res.,* **23:** 33–45 (1975).
9. Crane, M. A., and D. L. Iglehart: Simulating Stable Stochastic Systems, IV: Approximation Techniques, *Manage. Sci.,* **21:** 1215–1224 (1975).
10. Crane, M. A., and A. J. Lemoine: *An Introduction to the Regenerative Method for Simulation Analysis,* Lecture Notes in Control and Information Sciences, vol. 4, Springer-Verlag, New York, 1977.
11. Daley, D. J.: The Serial Correlation Coefficients of Waiting Times in a Stationary Single Server Queue, *J. Aust. Math. Soc.,* **8:** 683–699 (1968).
12. Fishman, G. S.: Statistical Analysis for Queueing Simulations, *Manage. Sci.,* **20:** 363–369 (1973).
13. Fishman, G. S.: Estimation in Multiserver Queueing Simulations, *Oper. Res.,* **22:** 72–78 (1974).
14. Fishman, G. S.: Achieving Specific Accuracy in Simulation Output Analysis, *Commun. Ass. Comput. Mach.,* **20:** 310–315 (1977).
15. Fishman, G. S.: *Principles of Discrete Event Simulation,* Wiley, New York, 1978.
16. Gafarian, A. V., C. J. Ancker, Jr., and T. Morisaku: Evaluation of Commonly Used Rules for Detecting "Steady State" in Computer Simulation, *Nav. Res. Logist. Q.,* **25:** 511–529 (1978).
17. Gross, D., and C. M. Harris: *Fundamentals of Queueing Theory,* Wiley, New York, 1974.
18. Heathcote, C. R., and P. Winer: An Approximation for the Moments of Waiting Times, *Oper. Res.,* **17:** 175–186 (1969).
19. Hogg, R. V., and A. T. Craig: *Introduction to Mathematical Statistics,* 3d ed., Macmillan, New York, 1970.

20. Iglehart, D. L.: Simulating Stable Stochastic Systems, V: Comparison of Ratio Estimators, *Nav. Res. Logist. Q.*, **22:** 553–565 (1975).
21. Iglehart, D. L.: Simulating Stable Stochastic Systems, VI: Quantile Estimation, *J. Ass. Comput. Mach.*, **23:** 347–360 (1976).
22. Iglehart, D. L., and G. S. Shedler: *Regenerative Simulation of Response Times in Networks of Queues,* Lecture Notes in Control and Information Sciences, vol. 26, Springer-Verlag, New York, 1980.
23. Johnson, N. J.: Modified *t* Tests and Confidence Intervals for Asymmetrical Populations, *J. Am. Statist. Ass.*, **73:** 536–544 (1978).
24. Kelton, W. D.: The Startup Problem in Discrete-Event Simulation, *Univ. Wis. Dept. Ind. Eng. Tech. Rep.* 80-1, Madison, 1980.
25. Kelton, W. D., and A. M. Law: A New Approach for Dealing with the Startup Problem in Discrete Event Simulation, *Univ. Wis. Dept. Ind. Eng. Tech. Rep.* 80-2, Madison, 1980.
26. Kendall, M. G., and A. Stuart: *The Advanced Theory of Statistics,* 3d ed., vol. 1, Hafner, New York, 1969.
27. Lavenberg, S. S., and C. H. Sauer: Sequential Stopping Rules for the Regenerative Method of Simulation, *IBM J. Res. Dev.*, **21:** 545–558 (1977).
28. Law, A. M.: Efficient Estimators for Simulated Queueing Systems, *Univ. Calif. Oper. Res. Cent.* ORC 74-7, Berkeley, 1974.
29. Law, A. M.: Confidence Intervals in Discrete Event Simulation: A Comparison of Replication and Batch Means, *Nav. Res. Logist. Q.*, **24:** 667–678 (1977).
30. Law, A. M.: Statistical Analysis of Simulation Output Data with SIMSCRIPT II.5, CACI, Inc., Los Angeles, 1979.
31. Law, A. M.: Statistical Analysis of the Output Data from Terminating Simulations, *Nav. Res. Logist. Q.*, **27:** 131–143 (1980).
32. Law, A. M., and J. S. Carson: A Sequential Procedure for Determining the Length of a Steady-State Simulation, *Oper. Res.*, **27:** 1011–1025 (1979).
33. Law, A. M., and W. D. Kelton: Confidence Intervals for Steady-State Simulations, II: A Survey of Sequential Procedures. *Univ. Wis. Dept. Ind. Eng. Tech. Rep.* 78–6, Madison, 1978. Also to appear in *Manage. Sci.*, **28:** (1982).
34. Law, A. M., and W. D. Kelton: Confidence Intervals for Steady-State Simulations, I: A Survey of Fixed Sample Size Procedures, *Univ. Wis. Dept. Ind. Eng. Tech. Rep.* 78-5, Madison, 1979.
35. Law, A. M., W. D. Kelton, and L. W. Koenig: Relative Width Sequential Confidence Intervals for the Mean, *Commun. Statist.*, **B10:** 29–39 (1981).
36. Miller, R. G.: The Jackknife– A Review, *Biometrika*, **61:** 1–15 (1974).
37. Ross, S. M.: *Applied Probability Models with Optimization Applications,* Holden-Day, San Francisco, 1970.
38. Wagner, H. M: *Principles of Operations Research,* Prentice-Hall, Englewood Cliffs, N.J., 1969.

STATISTICAL TECHNIQUES FOR COMPARING ALTERNATIVE SYSTEMS

9.1 INTRODUCTION

In Chap. 8 we have just seen the importance of applying appropriate statistical analyses to the output from a simulation model of a *single* system. In this chaper we address the question of how the simulator should analyze the output from several *different* simulation models, which might represent alternative system designs or operating policies. This is a very important subject since the real usefulness of the simulation technique is, by its very nature, in studying such alternatives before their actual implementation. As the following example illustrates, appropriate statistical methods are essential if we are to avoid making serious errors leading to fallacious conclusions and, ultimately, poor decisions. We hope that this example will demonstrate the danger inherent in making decisions based on the output from a *single* run (or replication) of each alternative system.

Example 9.1 A bank planning to install an automated teller station must choose between buying one Zippytel machine or two Klunkytel machines. Although one Zippy costs twice as much to purchase, install, and operate as one Klunky, the Zippy works twice as fast. Since the total cost to the bank is thus the same regardless of its decision, the managers would like to install the system that will provide its customers with the best service. From available data, it is estimated that during a certain rush period, customers arrive one at a time according to a Poisson process with rate 1 per minute. Further, if the Zippy is purchased, it is felt that it can provide service to these customers (in a FIFO manner) so that the service times are IID exponential random variables (independent of the arrival process) with mean 0.9 minute. Alternatively, if two Klunkies are installed, each will yield service times that are IID exponential random variables with mean 1.8 minutes; if two Klunkies are installed, a single FIFO line will be formed rather than two separate lines. (Thus, we are comparing an $M/M/1$ queue with an $M/M/2$ queue, each with utilization factor $\rho = 0.9$; see

Fig. 9.1.) The performance measure of interest is the expected average delay in queue of the first 100 customers, assuming that the first customer arrives to find the system(s) empty and idle; we denote these (true) quantities by $d_Z(100)$ and $d_K(100)$ for the Zippytel and Klunkytel installations, respectively. (The bank decided to ignore the actual service times of the customers in its performance measure, since it was felt that waiting in line is the most irritating experience and that customers are reasonably pacified as long as they are being served.) The bank's systems analyst decided to make one simulation run of length 100 customers for each of the two alternative systems (using independent random-number streams for each system) and to use the average of the 100 delays in each case to decide whether $d_Z(100)$ or $d_K(100)$ is smaller, and thus make a recommendation.

How likely is it that the analyst will make the right recommendation? To find out, we performed 100 independent experiments of the entire scheme and noted how many times the analyst would have recommended the best system, which is actually the two-Klunky installation since $d_K(100) < d_Z(100)$ [$d_Z(100) = 4.134$, and $d_K(100) = 3.711 \pm 0.060$ with 99.9 percent confidence, where the latter quantity was estimated by simulation]. That is, we performed 100 independent pairs of independent simulations of the two systems and averaged the delays in each simulation to obtain $\hat{d}_Z(100)$ and $\hat{d}_K(100)$, say, and then recommended the Zippy or Klunky system according as $\hat{d}_Z(100)$ or $\hat{d}_K(100)$ was smaller; some of the results are in Table 9.1. In only 56 of our 100 experiments was $\hat{d}_K(100) < \hat{d}_Z(100)$, so that our estimate of the probability that the analyst would have made the *wrong* recommendation is nearly 45 percent.

We have an uneasy feeling that many simulation studies are carried out in a manner similar to that described in Example 9.1.

Note that in Example 9.1, we dealt with terminating simulations (see Sec. 8.2). As we shall see in this chaper, a basic requirement for using any statistical method for comparing alternative systems is the ability to collect IID observations with an expectation equal to the desired measure of performance. For terminating simulations, this is easily accomplished by simply making independent replications; e.g., a basic unit of observation in Example 9.1 should be the average of the 100 delays in a single entire replication of the system being simulated.

If we want to compare alternative systems on the basis of their steady-state behavior, however, the situation is not so simple since we cannot readily obtain IID observations having an expectation equal to the desired steady-state average

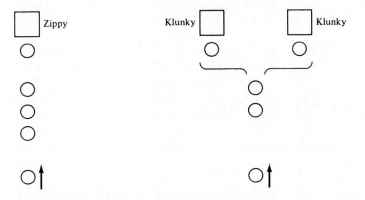

Figure 9.1 One Zippy or two Klunkies?

Table 9.1 Testing the analyst's decision rule

Experiment	$\hat{d}_Z(100)$	$\hat{d}_K(100)$	Recommendation
1	3.848	1.787	Klunky (right)
2	3.218	5.667	Zippy (wrong)
. . . .	. . . .	. . . .	. . . .
100	4.549	3.755	Klunky (right)

response. Although the entire question of how one should perform such steady-state comparisons is still open, we can suggest several possible approaches. Perhaps the most direct route would be the use of the replication-deletion idea of Sec. 8.6.3 on a system-by-system basis to mitigate the start-up bias separately for each system and then proceed by making independent replications, as in the terminating case; this idea has been successfully implemented for the selection problem of Sec. 9.3. Another route might involve the batch-means approach of Secs. 8.6.1 and 8.6.2, where we would use the batch means as the basic IID unbiased observations. Since the critical factor in the successful use of a batch-means approach is eliminating the correlation between the actual batch means, we could use the procedure of Law and Carson (see Sec. 8.6.2) to determine a batch size l large enough to do this. Although this idea has not been explicitly tested, we can get an idea of how well it might perform from the results in [10]. By way of example, for the $M/M/1$ queue with ρ = 0.5 (taking u = 0.4 and γ = 0.075; see Sec. 8.6.2), the average batch size $\bar{l}$ was 487, and for batches of this size the correlation between adjacent batch means, $\rho_1(487)$, is approximately 0.006. [For the $M/M/1$ queue with ρ = 0.8, the corresponding values are $\bar{l}$ = 1891 and $\rho_1(1891)$ ≈ 0.014.] Thus, it appears that their procedure does well in establishing a batch size l yielding batch means that are nearly uncorrelated. The procedure also results in 40 batches of this size, so that if more "observations" are needed for the final analysis, the simulation could be continued for as many additional batches as are needed. The determination of the appropriate l should be done, of course, on a system-by-system basis. (See Dudewicz and Zaino [5] for an approach which could be useful if there is still correlation between the batch means.) Finally, Iglehart [8] has considered the selection problem of Sec. 9.3 in concert with the regenerative method.

Our purpose in this chapter is to present several different types of comparison and selection problems which we feel could be useful in simulation, together with appropriate statistical procedures for their solution, and numerical examples. The model we shall use for the examples is the (terminating) inventory system of Sec. 1.5. We assume for this chapter that the various alternative systems are simply *given*. In many situations (such as our inventory model) care should be taken in choosing *which* particular system variants to simulate; see Chap. 12 for discussion of how to choose appropriate alternative systems for comparison. For discussion of other kinds of comparison and selection problems, see Gibbons, Olkin, and Sobel [6], Gupta and Panchapakesan [7], and Miller [11].

In Sec. 9.2 we treat the special but important case of comparing two systems by constructing a confidence interval for the difference between their measures of performance. Then in Sec. 9.3 we discuss the problem of choosing the "best" system from among k ($k \geq 2$) alternatives; Secs. 9.4 and 9.5 deal with choosing certain "good" subsets from these k alternatives. Section 9.6 is concerned with justification of the selection procedures of Secs. 9.3 to 9.5 and is intended for the advanced reader.

9.2 CONFIDENCE INTERVALS FOR THE DIFFERENCE BETWEEN MEASURES OF PERFORMANCE OF TWO SYSTEMS

Here we consider the special case of comparing two systems on the basis of some mean (or expected) response (or measure of performance). Our approach is to construct a confidence interval for the *difference* in the two expectations, rather than performing a hypothesis test to see whether the observed difference can be distinguished from zero. Whereas a test results only in a "reject" or "fail to reject" conclusion, a confidence interval gives us this information (according as the confidence interval misses or contains zero, respectively) as well as a measure of the *degree* to which the system responses are likely to differ, if at all. Also, we take a parametric, i.e., normal-theory, approach here, even though nonparametric analogues could alternatively be employed (see, for example, Conover [1]). We have chosen the parametric approach for its simplicity and familiarity but also because we feel that in the present context parametric procedures should be quite robust, since troublesome skewness (see Sec. 8.5.1) in the underlying distributions of the output random variables should be largely ameliorated upon subtraction.

For $i = 1, 2$, let $X_{i1}, X_{i2}, \ldots, X_{in_i}$ be a sample of n_i IID observations from system i, and let $\mu_i = E(X_{ij})$ be the mean response of interest; we want to construct a confidence interval for $\zeta = \mu_1 - \mu_2$. Whether or not X_{1j} and X_{2j} are independent depends on how the simulations are executed and on which of the following two confidence-interval approaches is used.

If $n_1 = n_2$ ($= n$, say) (or we are willing to throw away some observations from the system on which we actually have more observations), we can *pair* X_{1j} with X_{2j} to define $Z_j = X_{1j} - X_{2j}$ for $j = 1, 2, \ldots, n$. Then the Z_j's are IID random variables and $E(Z_j) = \zeta$, the quantity for which we want to construct a confidence interval. Thus, we can let

$$\overline{Z}(n) = \frac{\sum_{j=1}^{n} Z_j}{n} \quad \text{and} \quad \hat{\sigma}^2[\overline{Z}(n)] = \frac{\sum_{j=1}^{n} [Z_j - \overline{Z}(n)]^2}{n(n-1)}$$

and form the (approximate) $100(1 - \alpha)$ percent confidence interval

$$\overline{Z}(n) \pm t_{n-1, 1-\alpha/2} \sqrt{\hat{\sigma}^2[\overline{Z}(n)]} \tag{9.1}$$

If the Z_j's are normally distributed, this confidence interval is exact; i.e., it covers ζ with probability $1 - \alpha$; otherwise, we rely on the central limit theorem (Sec. 4.5), which implies that this coverage probability is *near* $1 - \alpha$ for large n. An important point here is that we did *not* have to assume that X_{1j} and X_{2j} are independent; nor did we have to assume that Var (X_{1j}) and Var (X_{2j}) are equal. Allowing positive correlation between X_{1j} and X_{2j} can be of great importance since this leads to a reduction in Var (Z_j) and thus to a smaller confidence interval. Section 11.2 discusses a method (common random numbers) that can often induce this positive correlation between the observations on the different systems. The confidence interval in (9.1) will be called the *paired-t confidence interval,* and in its derivation we essentially reduced the two-system problem to one involving a single sample, namely, the Z_j's. In this sense, the paired-t approach is the same as the method discussed in Sec. 8.5.1 for analysis of a single system. (Thus, the sequential confidence-interval procedures of Sec. 8.5.2 could be applied here.) It is important to note that the X_{ij}'s are random variables defined over an entire *replication*; for example, X_{1j} might be the average of the 100 delays on the jth replication of the Zippytel system of Example 9.1; it is *not* the delay of some individual customer.

> **Example 9.2** For the inventory model of Sec. 1.5, suppose we want to compare two different (s, S) policies in terms of their effect on the expected average total cost per month for the first 120 months of operation, where we assume that the initial inventory level is 60. For the first policy $(s, S) = (20, 40)$, and the second policy sets $(s, S) = (20, 80)$. Here, X_{ij} is the average total cost per month of policy i on the jth independent replication. We made the runs for policy 1 and policy 2 independently of each other and made $n = n_1 = n_2 = 10$ independent replications of the model under each policy; Table 9.2 contains the results. Using the paired-t approach, we obtained $\overline{Z}(10) = 3.418$ and $\hat{\sigma}^2[\overline{Z}(10)] = 2.891$, leading to the (approximate) 90 percent confidence interval [0.302, 6.534] for $\zeta = \mu_1 - \mu_2$. Thus, with approximately 90 percent confidence, we can say that μ_1 differs from μ_2, and it furthermore appears that policy 2 is superior, since it leads to a lower average operating cost (between 0.302 and 6.534 lower, which would *not* have been evident from a hypothesis test).

A second approach to forming a confidence interval for ζ does not pair up the observations from the two systems but *does* require that the X_{1j}'s be independent of the X_{2j}'s. However, n_1 and n_2 now can be different. In order to apply the classical two-sample-t approach to this case, we *must* have Var $(X_{1j}) =$ Var (X_{2j}); if these variances are not equal, the two-sample-t confidence interval can exhibit serious coverage degradation. (If, however, $n_1 = n_2$, the two-sample-t approach is fairly safe even if the variances differ; see Scheffé [13] for further discussion.) Since equality of variances is probably not a safe assumption in simulation, we would recommend against using the two-sample-t methods. Instead, we shall give an old but reliable approximate solution, due to Welch [14], to this problem of comparison of two sys-

Table 9.2 Comparing two inventory policies

j	X_{1j}	X_{2j}	j	X_{1j}	X_{2j}
1	129.351	127.397	6	118.385	118.042
2	127.113	122.524	7	130.170	123.672
3	124.031	123.080	8	129.771	121.593
4	122.131	119.197	9	125.517	127.382
5	120.438	124.460	10	133.754	119.135

tems with unequal and unknown variances, called the *Behrens-Fisher problem* when the X_{ij}'s are normally distributed (see also [13]). As usual, let

$$\overline{X}_i(n_i) = \frac{\sum\limits_{j=1}^{n_i} X_{ij}}{n_i}$$

and

$$s_i^2(n_i) = \frac{\sum\limits_{j=1}^{n_i} [X_{ij} - \overline{X}_i(n_i)]^2}{n_i - 1}$$

for $i = 1, 2$. Then compute the *estimated* degrees of freedom

$$\hat{f} = \frac{[s_1^2(n_1)/n_1 + s_2^2(n_2)/n_2]^2}{[s_1^2(n_1)/n_1]^2/(n_1 - 1) + [s_2^2(n_2)/n_2]^2/(n_2 - 1)}$$

and form the confidence interval

$$[\overline{X}_1(n_1) - \overline{X}_2(n_2)] \pm t_{\hat{f},1-\alpha/2} \left[\frac{s_1^2(n_1)}{n_1} + \frac{s_2^2(n_2)}{n_2} \right]^{1/2} \tag{9.2}$$

as an approximate $100(1 - \alpha)$ percent confidence interval for ζ. Since $\hat{f}$ will not, in general, be an integer, interpolation in the t tables will probably be necessary. The confidence interval given by (9.2), which we call the *Welch confidence interval,* can also be used for validating a simulation model of an existing system (see Sec. 10.6.2). If "system 1" is the real-world system on which we have physically collected data and "system 2" is the corresponding simulation model from which we have simulation output data, it is likely that n_1 will be far less than n_2. Finally, if we are comparing two simulated systems and want a "small" confidence interval, a sequential procedure due to Robbins, Simons, and Starr [12] can be employed, which is efficient in the sense of minimizing the final value of $n_1 + n_2$, and is asymptotically correct in the sense that the confidence interval will have approximately the correct coverage probability as the prespecified confidence-interval width becomes small.

Example 9.3 Since the runs for the two different inventory policies of Example 9.2 were done independently, we can apply the Welch approach to forming an approximate 90 percent confidence interval for ζ; we use the same X_{ij} data as given in Table 9.2. We get $\overline{X}_1(10) = 126.066$, $\overline{X}_2(10) = 122.648$, $s_1^2(10) = 23.574$, $s_2^2(10) = 10.675$, and $\hat{f} = 15.764$. Interpolating in the t tables leads to $t_{\hat{f},0.95} = 1.748$. Thus, the Welch confidence interval is $[0.183, 6.653]$.

Since the inventory system data of Table 9.2 were collected so that $n_1 = n_2$ and the X_{1j}'s were independent of the X_{2j}'s, we could apply either the paired-t or Welch approach to construct a confidence interval for ζ. It happened that the confidence interval for the paired-t approach was slightly smaller in this case, but in general we will not know which confidence interval will be smaller. The choice of either the paired-t or the Welch approach will usually be made according to the situation. If common random numbers (see Sec. 11.2) are used for simulating the two systems, we must have $n_1 = n_2$ and use the paired-t approach; the use of common numbers can often lead to a considerable reduction in Var (Z_j) and thus to a much smaller confidence interval. On the other hand, if $n_1 \neq n_2$ (and we want to use all the available data), the Welch approach should be used; this requires independence of the X_{1j}'s from the X_{2j}'s and so in particular would preclude the use of common random numbers.

9.3 SELECTING THE BEST OF k SYSTEMS

In this and the next two sections we consider certain selection problems when we have $k \geq 2$ alternative systems. The problem of this section concerns selecting *one* of the k systems as being the "best" in a certain sense, and knowing that we are making the correct selection with a specified probability; the next two sections discuss selection of certain "good" subsets from among the k alternatives. We refer the reader to Sec. 9.6 for a discussion of the validity of all three selection procedures.

As in Sec. 9.2, let X_{ij} be the random variable of interest from the jth independent replication of the ith system, and let $\mu_i = E(X_{ij})$. For all these selection problems, $X_{i1}, X_{i2}, \ldots$ are assumed to be IID random variables, and the runs for different systems must be made independently of each other. Now, however, i can range from 1 through k. (For example, X_{ij} might be the average total cost per month for the jth replication of policy i for the inventory model of Examples 9.2 and 9.3.) Let μ_{i_l} be the lth smallest of the μ_i's, so that $\mu_{i_1} \leq \mu_{i_2} \leq \cdots \leq \mu_{i_k}$. Our goal in this section is to select a system with the *smallest* expected response, μ_{i_1}. (If we want the largest mean μ_{i_k}, the signs of the X_{ij}'s and μ_i's can simply be reversed.) Let CS denote this event of "correct selection."

The inherent randomness of the observed X_{ij}'s implies that we can never be *absolutely* sure that we shall make the CS, but we would like to be able to prespecify the *probability* of CS. Further, if μ_{i_1} and μ_{i_2} are actually very close together, we might not care if we erroneously choose system i_2 (the one with mean μ_{i_2}), so that we want a method that avoids making a large number of replications to resolve this unimportant difference. The exact problem formulation, then, is that we want $P\{CS\} \geq P^*$ provided that $\mu_{i_2} - \mu_{i_1} \geq d^*$, where the minimal CS probability $P^* > 1/k$ and the "indifference" amount $d^* > 0$ are both specified by the analyst. It is natural to ask what happens if $\mu_{i_2} - \mu_{i_1} < d^*$. The procedure stated below has the nice property that, with a probability of at least P^*, the true mean of the *selected* system will be no larger than $\mu_{i_1} + d^*$. Thus, we are in any case protected against selecting a system with mean that is more than d^* worse than that of the best system.

The statistical procedure for solving this problem, as developed by Dudewicz and Dalal [4], involves "two-stage" sampling from each of the k systems. In the first stage we make a fixed number of replications of each system, then use the resulting variance estimates to determine how many additional replications from each system are necessary in a second stage of sampling in order to reach a decision. (Work is currently being done by Dudewicz and Hsu on sequential analogues for these two-stage procedures.) It must be assumed that the X_{ij}'s are normally distributed, but (importantly) we need *not* assume that the values of $\sigma_i^2 = \text{Var}(X_{ij})$ are known; nor do we have to assume that the σ_i^2's are the same for different i's. (Assuming known or equal variances is very unrealistic in simulation.) The procedure's performance should be robust to departures from the normality assumption, especially if the X_{ij}'s are sample means. (We have verified this robustness when X_{ij} is the sample mean of a fixed number of delays in queue for an $M/M/1$ queueing system.) In the first-stage sampling, we make n_0 ($n_0 \geq 2$) replications of each of the k systems and define the first-stage sample means and variances

$$\overline{X}_i^{(1)}(n_0) = \frac{\sum_{j=1}^{n_0} X_{ij}}{n_0}$$

and
$$s_i^2(n_0) = \frac{\sum_{j=1}^{n_0} [X_{ij} - \overline{X}_i^{(1)}(n_0)]^2}{n_0 - 1}$$

for $i = 1, 2, \ldots, k$. Then we compute the total sample size N_i needed for system i as

$$N_i = \max \left\{ n_0 + 1, \left\lceil \frac{h_1^2 s_i^2(n_0)}{(d^*)^2} \right\rceil \right\} \tag{9.3}$$

where $\lceil z \rceil$ is the smallest integer that is greater than or equal to the real number z and h_1 (which depends on k, P^*, and n_0) is a constant that can be obtained from Table 9.7 in Appendix 9A. Next, we make $N_i - n_0$ *more* replications of system i ($i = 1, 2, \ldots, k$) and obtain the second-stage sample means

$$\overline{X}_i^{(2)}(N_i - n_0) = \frac{\sum_{j=n_0+1}^{N_i} X_{ij}}{N_i - n_0}$$

Then define the weights

$$W_{i1} = \frac{n_0}{N_i} \left(1 + \left\{ 1 - \frac{N_i}{n_0} \left[1 - \frac{(N_i - n_0)(d^*)^2}{h_1^2 s_i^2(n_0)} \right] \right\}^{1/2} \right)$$

and $W_{i2} = 1 - W_{i1}$, for $i = 1, 2, \ldots, k$. Finally, define the weighted sample means

$$\tilde{X}_i(N_i) = W_{i1} \overline{X}_i^{(1)}(n_0) + W_{i2} \overline{X}_i^{(2)}(N_i - n_0)$$

and select the system with the smallest $\tilde{X}_i(N_i)$. (See Sec. 9.6 for an explanation of the seemingly bizarre definition of W_{i1}.)

The choice of P^* and d^* depend on the analyst's goals and the particular systems under study; their specification might be tempered by the computing cost of obtaining a large N_i associated with a large P^* or small d^*. (Note that P^* and d^* could be chosen *after* the first-stage sampling.) However, choosing n_0 is more troublesome, and we can at present only recommend, on the basis of our experiments and

Table 9.3 The five alternative (s, S) inventory policies

Policy (i)	s	S
1	20	40
2	20	80
3	40	60
4	40	100
5	60	100

various statements in the literature, that n_0 be at least 15. If n_0 is too small, we might get a poor estimate $s_i^2(n_0)$ of σ_i^2; in particular, it could be likely that $s_i^2(n_0)$ is much greater than σ_i^2, leading to an unnecessarily large value of N_i. On the other hand, if n_0 is too large, we could "overshoot" the necessary number of replications for some of the systems, which is wasteful. Table 9.7 gives values of h_1 for $P^* = 0.90$ and 0.95, $n_0 = 20$ and 40, and for $k = 2, 3, \ldots, 10$. (The inclusion of $n_0 = 40$ was motivated by possible use of the Law and Carson batch-means procedure for steady-state selection problems, since we would automatically start out with 40 nearly uncorrelated batch means as our X_{ij}'s; see Sec. 9.1.) If values of h_1 are needed for other P^*, n_0, or k values, we refer the reader to Dudewicz and Dalal [4] or Koenig and Law [9].

Example 9.4 For the inventory model of Sec. 1.5 (and Examples 9.2 and 9.3) suppose that we want to compare the $k = 5$ different (s, S) policies, as given in Table 9.3, on the basis of their corresponding expected average total cost per month for the first 120 months of operation, which we denote by μ_i for the ith policy. Our goal is to select a system with the smallest μ_i and to be $100P^*$ percent = 90 percent sure that we have made the correct selection provided that $\mu_{i_2} - \mu_{i_1} \geq d^* = 1$. We made $n_0 = 20$ initial independent replications of each system, so that from Table 9.7, $h_1 = 2.747$. The results of the first-stage sampling are given in the $\overline{X}_i^{(1)}(20)$ and $s_i^2(20)$ columns of Table 9.4. From the $s_i^2(20)$'s, h_1, and d^*, we next computed the total sample size value N_i for each system, as shown in Table 9.4. Then we made $N_i - 20$ additional replications for each policy, i.e., 90 more replications for policy 1, 41 more for policy 2, etc., and computed the second-stage sample means $\overline{X}_i^{(2)}(N_i - 20)$, as shown. Finally, we calculated the weights W_{i1} and W_{i2} for each system and the weighted sample means $\tilde{X}_i(N_i)$. Since $\tilde{X}_2(N_2)$ is the smallest weighted sample mean, we select policy 2 ($s = 20$ and $S = 80$) as being the lowest-cost configuration. Note from the $s_i^2(20)$ and N_i columns of Table 9.4 that the procedure calls for higher values of the final N_i if the variance estimate $s_i^2(20)$ is high; this is simply reflecting the fact that we need more data on the more variable systems.

It might be that making between 47 and 110 replications of each of five systems is unreason-

Table 9.4 Selecting the best of the five inventory policies

i	$\overline{X}_i^{(1)}(20)$	$s_i^2(20)$	N_i	$\overline{X}_i^{(2)}(N_i - 20)$	W_{i1}	W_{i2}	$\tilde{X}_i(N_i)$
1	126.484	14.521	110	124.453	0.206	0.794	124.871
2	121.915	7.961	61	121.633	0.386	0.614	121.742
3	127.160	9.451	72	126.105	0.321	0.679	126.444
4	130.710	8.246	63	132.031	0.369	0.631	131.543
5	144.072	6.197	47	144.833	0.460	0.540	144.483

ably expensive. If we had looked at the values of $\overline{X}_i^{(1)}(20)$ after the first-stage sampling, setting $d^* = 2$ instead of 1 would probably be sufficiently accurate, since 2 is less than 2 percent of our initial estimates of the μ_i's. With $d^* = 2$, we would have obtained $N_1 = 28$ and $N_i = 21$ for $i = 2, 3, 4, 5$, resulting in much less computing in the second-stage sampling.

9.4 SELECTING A SUBSET OF SIZE m CONTAINING THE BEST OF k SYSTEMS

Now we consider a different kind of selection problem, that of selecting a subset of exactly m of the k systems (m is prespecified) so that (with probability at least P^*) the selected subset will contain a system with the smallest mean response, μ_{i_1}. This could be a useful goal in the initial stages of a simulation study where there may be a large number (k) of alternative systems and we would like to perform an initial screening to eliminate those which appear to be clearly inferior. Thus, we could avoid expending a large amount of computer time getting accurate estimates of the behavior of these inferior systems.

We define X_{ij}, μ_i, μ_{i_l}, and σ_i^2 as in Sec. 9.3. Again, all X_{ij}'s are independent and normal, and for fixed i, X_{i1}, X_{i2}, ... are IID; the σ_i^2's are unknown and need not be equal. Here, correct selection (CS) is defined to mean that the subset of size m which is selected contains a system with mean μ_{i_1} and we want $P\{CS\} \geq P^*$ provided that $\mu_{i_2} - \mu_{i_1} \geq d^*$; here we must have $1 \leq m \leq k - 1$, $P^* > m/k$, and $d^* > 0$. (If $\mu_{i_2} - \mu_{i_1} < d^*$, then with a probability of at least P^*, the subset selected will contain a system with expected response that is no larger than $\mu_{i_1} + d^*$.)

The procedure is very similar to that of Sec. 9.3 and has recently been derived by Koenig and Law [9]. We take a first-stage sample of n_0 ($n_0 \geq 2$) replications from each system and define $\overline{X}_i^{(1)}(n_0)$ and $s_i^2(n_0)$ for $i = 1, 2, \ldots, k$ exactly as in Sec. 9.3. Next compute the total number of replications, N_i, needed for the ith system exactly as in (9.3), except that h_1 should be replaced by h_2 (which depends on m as well as on k, P^*, and n_0), as found in Table 9.8. (For values of h_2 which might be needed for other P^*, n_0, k, or m values, see [9].) Then make $N_i - n_0$ more replications, form the second-stage sample means $\overline{X}_i^{(2)}(N_i - n_0)$, weights W_{i1} and W_{i2}, and weighted sample means $\tilde{X}_i(N_i)$, exactly as in Sec. 9.3. Finally, define the selected subset to consist of the m systems corresponding to the m smallest values of the $\tilde{X}_i(N_i)$'s. The comments concerning the choice of P^*, d^*, and n_0 made in Sec. 9.3 also apply here.

Example 9.5 Consider again our five inventory systems of Example 9.4, as defined in Table 9.3. Now, however, suppose we want to select a subset of size $m = 3$ from among the $k = 5$ systems and be assured with a confidence level of at least $P^* = 0.90$ that the selected subset contains the best (least-cost) system provided that $\mu_{i_2} - \mu_{i_1} \geq d^* = 1$. Again we made $n_0 = 20$ initial replications of each system, and the complete results for the subset selection procedure are given in Table 9.5. (From Table 9.8, $h_2 = 1.243$.) The subset selected consists of policies 1, 2, and 3.

Comparing the value of h_2 ($= 1.243$) used here with that of h_1 ($= 2.747$) used in Example 9.4, we see from the form of (9.3) that the more modest goal of selecting

Table 9.5 Selecting a subset of size 3 containing the best of the five inventory policies

i	$\overline{X}_i^{(1)}(20)$	$s_i^2(20)$	N_i	$\overline{X}_i^{(2)}(N_i - 20)$	W_{i1}	W_{i2}	$\tilde{X}_i(N_i)$
1	124.707	17.156	27	125.637	0.799	0.201	124.894
2	121.197	12.637	21	125.685	1.011	−0.011	121.149
3	125.572	9.066	21	123.508	1.103	−0.103	125.784
4	132.390	6.219	21	133.368	1.184	−0.184	132.210
5	144.266	4.228	21	143.674	1.269	−0.269	144.426

a subset of size 3 *containing* the best system requires considerably fewer replications on the average than the more ambitious goal of selecting *the* best system. (In fact, the selection problem of Sec. 9.3 is really just a special case of the present subset-selection problem, with $m = 1$.) This effect exemplifies what we meant at the beginning of this section by referring to this subset-selection problem as an inexpensive initial "screening."

9.5 SELECTING THE m BEST OF k SYSTEMS

As a final type of selection problem, consider the goal of selecting a subset of specified size m ($1 \leq m \leq k - 1$) so that with a probability of at least P^* the selected subset consists exactly of systems corresponding to the m smallest expected responses, $\mu_{i_1}, \mu_{i_2}, \ldots, \mu_{i_m}$. It is important to note that we are *not* saying that the m selected systems are ranked or ordered in any way among themselves but only that the unordered *set* of m selected systems is the same as the unordered *set* of the m best systems. This particular selection goal might be useful if it is desired to identify several good options, since the best system might prove unacceptable for other reasons, e.g., political or environmental considerations. The solution procedure was mentioned in Dudewicz and Dalal [4] and developed by Koenig and Law [9].

The setup (independence, normality, unknown and unequal variances, etc.) is exactly as in Sec. 9.4 except that the indifference-zone configuration and constraint on P^* must be changed. We want $P\{CS\} \geq P^*$ provided that $\mu_{i_{m+1}} - \mu_{i_m} \geq d^*$; CS, of course, is redefined to mean that the selected set is equal to a set containing the m best systems. (If the condition $\mu_{i_{m+1}} - \mu_{i_m} \geq d^*$ fails here, then with a prob-

Table 9.6 Selecting the three best of the five inventory policies

i	$\overline{X}_i^{(1)}(20)$	$s_i^2(20)$	N_i	$\overline{X}_i^{(2)}(N_i - 20)$	W_{i1}	W_{i2}	$\tilde{X}_i(N_i)$
1	123.666	11.500	105	124.858	0.214	0.786	124.603
2	120.624	8.804	81	121.749	0.293	0.707	121.420
3	125.240	7.160	66	125.134	0.356	0.644	125.172
4	132.050	6.178	57	131.262	0.408	0.592	131.583
5	144.815	3.266	30	144.235	0.713	0.287	144.649

ability of at least P^*, the expected responses of the m selected systems will not exceed $\mu_{i_m} + d^*$.) Also for this problem, we must have $P^* > m!(k - m)!/k!$. The solution procedure (including the final subset selection) here is furthermore exactly the same as that for the problem in Sec. 9.4 except that the constant h_2 used there must be replaced by h_3, which can be found in Table 9.9. (See [9] for an algorithm to compute h_3 for other values of P^*, n_0, k, and m.) Note that the problem of Sec. 9.3 is also a special case of this problem, for $m = 1$.

Example 9.6 Once again, we use the five inventory systems of Example 9.4, as specified in Table 9.3, to illustrate this third selection problem. Our goal is to select the $m = 3$ best systems from the $k = 5$ systems, and we want $P\{CS\} \geq P^* = 0.90$ provided that $\mu_{i_4} - \mu_{i_3} \geq d^* = 1$. Making $n_0 = 20$ initial replications and carrying out the procedure, we obtained the results in Table 9.6. (For these parameters, we got $h_3 = 3.016$ from Table 9.9.) The selected subset consists of policies 1, 2, and 3, which we claim are the three best systems but not in any particular order.

The value of h_3 in Example 9.6 is quite a bit larger than the values of h_1 and h_2 used in Examples 9.4 and 9.5, resulting in this selection problem's calling for larger average values of N_i than those of the problems in Secs. 9.3 and 9.4. (For our particular realizations, however, the N_i's of Table 9.6 are mostly *lower* than those of Table 9.4, since the variance estimates in Table 9.6 *happened* to be mostly lower than those in Table 9.4.) Intuitively, this is reasonable since the selection problem of this section allows us to make a considerably stronger final statement than we could for either of the previous two selection problems, so that we should expect to have to supply more supporting evidence.

*9.6 VALIDITY OF THE SELECTION PROCEDURES

The purpose of this section is to give a brief indication of how the procedures of Secs. 9.3 to 9.5 are justified and how the values for h_1, h_2, and h_3 in Appendix 9A were computed. For a more complete discussion, we refer the interested reader to Dudewicz and Dalal [4], Dudewicz and Bishop [3], Desu and Sobel [2], and Koenig and Law [9].

All three procedures are based on the fact that for $i = 1, 2, \ldots, k$,

$$T_i = \frac{\tilde{X}_i(N_i) - \mu_i}{d^*/h}$$

has a t distribution with $n_0 - 1$ df, where h is either h_1, h_2, or h_3 depending on which selection procedure is used; the T_i's are also independent. The rather curious form of the expressions for the weights W_{i1} and W_{i2} was chosen specifically to make $\tilde{X}_i(N_i)$ such that T_i *would* have this t distribution. [Other ways of defining W_{i1} and $\tilde{X}_i(N_i)$ also result in the T_i's having this t distribution; see [4].]

For the selection problem of Sec. 9.3 assume that $\mu_{i_2} - \mu_{i_1} \geq d^*$. Then correct selection occurs if and only if $\tilde{X}_{i_1}(N_{i_1})$ is the smallest of the $\tilde{X}_i(N_i)$'s. (i_1 is the index of a system with smallest expected response, μ_{i_1}.) Thus if we let f and F denote the density and distribution function, respectively, of the t distribution with $n_0 - 1$ df, we can write

$$
\begin{aligned}
P\{CS\} &= P\{\tilde{X}_{i_1}(N_{i_1}) < \tilde{X}_{i_l}(N_{i_l}) \text{ for } l = 2, 3, \dots, k\} \\
&= P\left\{ \frac{\tilde{X}_{i_1}(N_{i_1}) - \mu_{i_1}}{d^*/h_1} \le \frac{\tilde{X}_{i_l}(N_{i_l}) - \mu_{i_l}}{d^*/h_1} \right. \\
&\qquad \left. + \frac{\mu_{i_l} - \mu_{i_1}}{d^*/h_1} \text{ for } l = 2, 3, \dots, k \right\} \\
&= P\left\{ T_{i_l} \ge T_{i_1} - \frac{\mu_{i_l} - \mu_{i_1}}{d^*/h_1} \text{ for } l = 2, 3, \dots, k \right\} \\
&= \int_{-\infty}^{\infty} \prod_{l=2}^{k} F\left(\frac{\mu_{i_l} - \mu_{i_1}}{d^*/h_1} - t \right) f(t) \, dt
\end{aligned}
\tag{9.4}
$$

[The last equation in (9.4) follows by conditioning on $T_{i_1} = t$ and by the independence of the T_i's.] Now since we assumed that $\mu_{i_2} - \mu_{i_1} \ge d^*$ and the μ_{i_l}'s are increasing with l, we know that $\mu_{i_l} - \mu_{i_1} \ge d^*$ for $l = 2, 3, \dots, k$. Thus, since F is monotone increasing, (9.4) yields (after a change of variable in the integral)

$$
P\{CS\} \ge \int_{-\infty}^{\infty} [F(t + h_1)]^{k-1} f(t) \, dt
\tag{9.5}
$$

and equality holds in (9.5) exactly when $\mu_{i_1} + d^* = \mu_{i_2} = \cdots = \mu_{i_k}$, an arrangement of the μ_i's called the *least favorable configuration* (LFC). Table 9.7 was thus obtained by setting the integral on the right-hand side of (9.5) to P^* and solving (numerically) for h_1.

Demonstrating the validity of the subset selection procedures of Secs. 9.4 and 9.5 is more complicated but follows a similar line of reasoning. For the procedure in Sec. 9.4, we can show (see [9]) ultimately that

$$
P\{CS\} \ge (k - m) \binom{k - 1}{k - m} \int_{-\infty}^{\infty} F(t + h_2)[F(t)]^{m-1}[F(-t)]^{k-m-1} f(t) \, dt
$$

and we equate the right-hand side to P^* to solve for h_2, as given in Table 9.8. The LFC for this problem (in which case $P\{CS\} = P^*$) is the same as that for the problem in Sec. 9.3.

Finally, for the problem of Sec. 9.5 it can be shown (see [9]) that

$$
P\{CS\} \ge m \int_{-\infty}^{\infty} [F(t + h_3)]^{k-m}[F(-t)]^{m-1} f(t) \, dt
$$

and we again set the right-hand side to P^* and solve for the values of h_3 in Table 9.9. For this problem, however, the LFC occurs when $\mu_{i_1} + d^* = \cdots = \mu_{i_m} + d^* = \mu_{i_{m+1}} = \cdots = \mu_{i_k}$, when we again get $P\{CS\} = P^*$.

APPENDIX 9A CONSTANTS FOR THE SELECTION PROCEDURES

Table 9.7 Values of h_1 for the procedure of Sec. 9.3

P^*	n_0	$k = 2$	$k = 3$	$k = 4$	$k = 5$	$k = 6$	$k = 7$	$k = 8$	$k = 9$	$k = 10$
0.90	20	1.896	2.342	2.583	2.747	2.870	2.969	3.051	3.121	3.182
0.90	40	1.852	2.283	2.514	2.669	2.785	2.878	2.954	3.019	3.076
0.95	20	2.453	2.872	3.101	3.258	3.377	3.472	3.551	3.619	3.679
0.95	40	2.386	2.786	3.003	3.150	3.260	3.349	3.422	3.484	3.539

Table 9.8 Values of h_2 for the procedure of Sec. 9.4

For $m = 1$, use Table 9.7

m	$k = 3$	$k = 4$	$k = 5$	$k = 6$	$k = 7$	$k = 8$	$k = 9$	$k = 10$
				$P^* = 0.90$, $n_0 = 20$				
2	1.137	1.601	1.860	2.039	2.174	2.282	2.373	2.450
3		0.782	1.243	1.507	1.690	1.830	1.943	2.038
4			0.556	1.012	1.276	1.461	1.603	1.718
5				0.392	0.843	1.105	1.291	1.434
6					0.265	0.711	0.971	1.156
7						0.162	0.603	0.861
8							0.075	0.512
9								†
				$P^* = 0.90$, $n_0 = 40$				
2	1.114	1.570	1.825	1.999	2.131	2.237	2.324	2.399
3		0.763	1.219	1.479	1.660	1.798	1.909	2.002
4			0.541	0.991	1.251	1.434	1.575	1.688
5				0.381	0.824	1.083	1.266	1.408
6					0.257	0.693	0.950	1.133
7						0.156	0.587	0.841
8							0.072	0.497
9								†
				$P^* = 0.95$, $n_0 = 20$				
2	1.631	2.071	2.321	2.494	2.625	2.731	2.819	2.894
3		1.256	1.697	1.952	2.131	2.267	2.378	2.470
4			1.021	1.458	1.714	1.894	2.033	2.146
5				0.852	1.284	1.539	1.720	1.860
6					0.721	1.149	1.402	1.583
7						0.615	1.038	1.290
8							0.526	0.945
9								0.449

Table 9.8 (*Continued*)

m	k = 3	k = 4	k = 5	k = 6	k = 7	k = 8	k = 9	k = 10
				$P^* = 0.95$, $n_0 = 40$				
2	1.591	2.023	2.267	2.435	2.563	2.665	2.750	2.823
3		1.222	1.656	1.907	2.082	2.217	2.325	2.415
4			0.990	1.420	1.672	1.850	1.987	2.098
5				0.824	1.248	1.499	1.678	1.816
6					0.695	1.114	1.363	1.541
7						0.591	1.004	1.252
8							0.505	0.913
9								0.430

†Recall that for this selection problem we must have $P^* > m/k$. (If $P^* = 0.90$, $m = 9$, and $k = 10$, we can obtain $P\{CS\} = P^*$ by selecting nine systems at random, without any data collection at all.)

Table 9.9 Values of h_3 for the procedure of Sec. 9.5

For $m = 1$, use Table 9.7

m	k = 3	k = 4	k = 5	k = 6	k = 7	k = 8	k = 9	k = 10
				$P^* = 0.90$, $n_0 = 20$				
2	2.342	2.779	3.016	3.177	3.299	3.396	3.477	3.546
3		2.583	3.016	3.251	3.411	3.532	3.629	3.709
4			2.747	3.177	3.411	3.571	3.691	3.787
5				2.870	3.299	3.532	3.691	3.811
6					2.969	3.396	3.629	3.787
7						3.051	3.477	3.709
8							3.121	3.546
9								3.182
				$P^* = 0.90$, $n_0 = 40$				
2	2.283	2.703	2.928	3.081	3.195	3.285	3.360	3.424
3		2.514	2.928	3.151	3.302	3.415	3.505	3.579
4			2.669	3.081	3.302	3.451	3.564	3.653
5				2.785	3.195	3.415	3.564	3.675
6					2.878	3.285	3.505	3.653
7						2.954	3.360	3.579
8							3.019	3.424
9								3.076
				$P^* = 0.95$, $n_0 = 20$				
2	2.872	3.282	3.507	3.662	3.779	3.873	3.952	4.019
3		3.101	3.507	3.731	3.885	4.001	4.094	4.172
4			3.258	3.662	3.885	4.037	4.153	4.246
5				3.377	3.779	4.001	4.153	4.269
6					3.472	3.873	4.094	4.246
7						3.551	3.952	4.172
8							3.619	4.019
9								3.679
				$P^* = 0.95$, $n_0 = 40$				
2	2.786	3.175	3.386	3.530	3.639	3.725	3.797	3.858
3		3.003	3.386	3.595	3.738	3.845	3.931	4.002
4			3.150	3.530	3.738	3.879	3.986	4.071
5				3.260	3.639	3.845	3.986	4.092
6					3.349	3.725	3.931	4.071
7						3.422	3.797	4.002
8							3.484	3.858
9								3.539

PROBLEMS

9.1 Consider the two systems of Example 9.1, with the same initial conditions and performance measures given there; let $\zeta = d_Z(100) - d_K(100)$.

    (*a*) Make $n_1 = n_2 = 5$ independent replications of each system and construct an approximate 90 percent confidence interval for ζ. (Perform the simulations for the different systems independently of each other.) Use the paired-*t* approach.

    (*b*) Make $n_1 = 5$ replications of the Zippytel system and $n_2 = 10$ replications of the Klunkytel system, and construct an approximate 90 percent confidence interval for ζ. (Again make the runs of the two systems independently.)

    (*c*) Use the selection procedure of Sec. 9.3 to select the best of the $k = 2$ systems. Let $n_0 = 20$, $P^* = 0.90$, and $d^* = 0.4$.

9.2 For the time-shared computer model of Sec. 2.4, suppose that the company is considering a change in the service quantum length q in an effort to reduce the *steady-state* average response time of a job; the values for q under consideration are 0.05, 0.10, 0.20, and 0.40. Assume that there are $n = 35$ terminals and that the other parameters and initial conditions are the same as those in Sec. 2.4. To obtain IID observations with expectation essentially equal to the steady-state average response time of a job, it is felt that warming up the models for 50 response times is adequate, after which the next 640 response times are averaged to obtain a basic X_{ij} observation; independent replications of these 690 response times are then made, as needed. Use an appropriate selection procedure from Sec. 9.3 to 9.5 with $n_0 = 20$, $P^* = 0.90$, and $d^* = 0.7$ to solve each of the following problems.

    (*a*) Select the best of the four values for q.

    (*b*) Select two values of q, one of which is the best.

    (*c*) Select the best two values of q (without ordering the two selected).

9.3 For the job-shop model of Sec. 2.6, we can now carry out a better analysis of the question of deciding which machine group should be given an additional machine. [Reread Sec. 2.6.3 and note from Fig. 2.36 that (on the basis of a single replication of the existing system) machine groups 2, 4, and 1 appear to be the three most congested systems.] Use the procedure of Sec. 9.3 to recommend whether a machine should be added to group 2, 4, or 1, assuming that these are the only three possibilities; let $n_0 = 20$, $P^* = 0.90$, and $d^* = 1$. Use the overall *steady-state* average job total delay as the measure of performance; to obtain the X_{ij} observations, warm up the model for 10 eight-hour days and use the data from the next 90 days, as in Prob. 2.5. (*Beware!* This could be a case where considerations on the cost of simulating might temper the choice of d^*; perhaps you should pause after the first-stage sampling and reflect on the values of N_i mandated by the choice of d^*.) Compare your conclusions with those at the end of Sec. 2.6.3. From the moral of Example 9.1, how might this entire study be improved? *Hint:* The conclusion that machine groups 2, 4, and 1 *are* the bottlenecks was based on the results of a *single* replication, as reported in Fig. 2.36.

9.4 Consider the original time-shared computer model of Sec. 2.4 and the alternative processing policy described in Prob. 2.3, both with $n = 35$ terminals. Use the selection procedure of Sec. 9.3 with $n_0 = 20$ to recommend which processing policy results in the lowest steady-state average response time of a job. To obtain the X_{ij}'s here, warm up the model for 50 response times, then use the average of the next 640 response times, and replicate as needed. Choose your own P^* and d^*, perhaps based on the results of the initial 20 replications, cost considerations, or your own feeling about what constitutes an "important" difference in average response time.

9.5 For the manufacturing shop of Prob. 1.5, use the selection procedure of Sec. 9.4 to choose three out of the five values of s (s is the number of repairmen), one of which results in the smallest expected average cost per hour. Use $n_0 = 20$, $P^* = 0.90$, and $d^* = 5$.

REFERENCES

1. Conover, W. J.: *Practical Nonparametric Statistics*, Wiley, New York, 1971.
2. Desu, M., and M. Sobel: A Fixed Subset-Size Approach to a Selection Problem, *Biometrika*, **55**: 401–410 (1968).

3. Dudewicz, E. J., and T. A. Bishop: The Heteroscedastic Method, *Ohio State Univ. Dept. Statist. Tech. Rep.* 153, Columbus, 1977.
4. Dudewicz, E. J., and S. R. Dalal: Allocation of Measurements in Ranking and Selection with Unequal Variances, *Sankhya,* **B37:** 28–78 (1975).
5. Dudewicz, E. J., and N. A. Zaino, Jr.: Allowance for Correlation in Setting Simulation Run-Length via Ranking-and-Selection Procedures, *TIMS Stud. Manage. Sci.,* **7:** 51–61 (1977).
6. Gibbons, J. D., I. Olkin, and M. Sobel: *Selecting and Ordering Populations: A New Statistical Methodology,* Wiley, New York, 1977.
7. Gupta, S. S., and S. Panchapakesan: *Multiple Decision Procedures: Theory and Methodology of Selecting and Ranking Populations,* Wiley, New York, 1979.
8. Iglehart, D. L.: Simulating Stable Stochastic Systems, VII: Selecting the Best System, *TIMS Stud. Manage. Sci.,* **7:** 37–50 (1977).
9. Koenig, L. W., and A. M. Law: A Procedure for Selecting a Subset of Size m Containing the l Best of k Independent Normal Populations with Unknown and Unequal Variances, *Univ. Wis. Dept. Ind. Eng. Tech. Rep.* 80-3, Madison, 1980.
10. Law, A. M., and J. S. Carson: A Sequential Procedure for Determining the Length of a Steady-State Simulation, *Oper. Res.,* **27:** 1011–1025 (1979).
11. Miller, R. G., Jr.: Developments in Multiple Comparisons, 1966–1976, *J. Am. Statist. Ass.,* **72:** 779–788 (1977).
12. Robbins, H., G. Simons, and N. Starr: A Sequential Analogue of the Behrens-Fisher Problem, *Ann. Math. Statist.,* **38:** 1384–1391 (1967).
13. Scheffé, H.: Practical Solutions of the Behrens-Fisher Problem, *J. Am. Statist. Ass.,* **65:** 1501–1508 (1970).
14. Welch, B. L.: The Significance of the Difference Between Two Means when the Population Variances are Unequal, *Biometrika,* **25:** 350–362 (1938).

TEN

VALIDATION OF SIMULATION MODELS

10.1 INTRODUCTION

One of the most important problems facing a real-world simulator is that of trying to determine whether a simulation model is an accurate representation of the actual system being studied, but a review of the validation literature indicates that relatively little has been written on this subject. Furthermore, what has been written is often philosophical in nature rather than in the form of practical recommendations. (Important works on validation include [7], [13], [14], [15], and [17].) Somewhat surprised by this state of affairs, we decided to engage in a two-phase study to develop definitive qualitative and statistical procedures which actually can be used by simulators in their validation efforts. We first present in Secs. 10.2 to 10.5 an overview of the entire field of validation and survey techniques that can be used for verifying and validating a simulation model. (See below for the distinction between these terms.) Information for this survey came not only from existing papers and books on validation, but also from conversations with notable members of the academic and industrial communities who have had first-hand experience with validation. We hoped to uncover some validation techniques which have not been previously documented. The second phase of our study, which is still in progress, seeks to develop statistical procedures which can be used for comparing the output data from a simulation model and a corresponding real-world system (if the system exists). Our results to date for this phase are given in Sec. 10.6.

Since there appears to be some confusion in the simulation literature over the meaning of verification, validation, and output analysis, we begin by giving simple definitions of these terms. (Fishman and Kiviat [5] appear to be the first ones to have given definitions similar to these.) *Verification* is determining whether a simulation model performs as intended, i.e., debugging the computer program. Although verification is simple in concept, debugging a large-scale simulation model can be quite an arduous task. *Validation* is determining whether a simulation model (as opposed to the computer program) is an accurate representation of the real-world system under study. This is to be contrasted with *output analysis* (the subject of Chap. 8) which is concerned with determining a simulation *model's* (not necessarily the system's) true parameters or characteristics.

10.2 VERIFICATION OF SIMULATION MODELS

In this section we discuss five techniques which can be used for debugging the computer program of a simulation model. Some of these techniques may be used for debugging any computer program, while others we believe to be unique to simulation modeling.

Technique 1. In developing a simulation model, write and debug the computer program in modules or subprograms. By way of example, for a 10,000-statement simulation model it would be poor programming practice to write the entire program before attempting any debugging. When this large, untested program is finally run, it almost certainly will not execute, and determining the location in the program of the errors will be extremely difficult. Instead, the simulation model's main program and a few of the key subprograms should be written and debugged first, perhaps representing the other required subprograms as "dummies" or "stubs." Then, additional subprograms or levels of detail are successively added and debugged until a model is developed which satisfactorily represents the system under study. In general, it is always better to start with a simple model which is gradually made as complex as needed, than to develop "immediately" a complex model which may turn out to be more detailed than necessary and excessively expensive to run (see Sec. 10.4.2 for further discussion).

> **Example 10.1** For the multiteller bank with jockeying considered in Sec. 2.5, a good programming approach would be to write and debug first the computer program without letting customers jockey from queue to queue.

Technique 2. It is advisable when developing large simulation models to have more than one person read the computer program since the person who writes a particular subprogram may get into a mental rut and thus not be a good evaluator of its correctness. In some organizations, this idea is implemented formally and is called a *structured walk-through.* For example, all members of the modeling team, e.g., systems analysts, programmers, etc., are assembled in a room and each has a copy of a particular set of subprograms to be debugged. Then the subprograms' developer goes through the computer code but does not proceed from one statement to another until everyone is convinced that a statement is correct.

Technique 3. One of the most powerful techniques that can be used to debug a discrete-event simulation model is a *trace*. In a trace, the state of the simulated system, i.e., the contents of the event list, the state variables, certain statistical counters, etc., is printed out just after each event occurs in order to see whether the program is operating as intended. In performing a trace it is desirable to evaluate each possible program path and also the program's ability to deal with "extreme" conditions. Sometimes in order to effect such a thorough evaluation it may be necessary to prepare special (perhaps deterministic) input data for the model. It should be mentioned that all three of the major simulation languages in the United States (GASP, GPSS, and SIMSCRIPT) explicitly provide the capability to perform traces.

Example 10.2 Table 10.1 shows a trace for the intuitive explanation of the single-server queue considered in Sec. 1.4.2. The first row of the table is a snapshot of the system just after initialization at TIME $= 0$, the second row is a snapshot of the system just after the first event (an arrival) has occurred, etc.

Technique 4. In order to determine whether a simulation model is operating as intended, the model should, when possible, be run under simplifying assumptions for which the model's true characteristics are known or can easily be computed.

Example 10.3 For the job-shop model presented in Sec. 2.6 it is not possible to compute the desired system characteristics analytically. Therefore, one must resort to simulation. In order to debug the simulation model, one could first run the general model of Sec. 2.6.2 with one machine group, one machine in that group, and only type 1 jobs (which have an arrival rate of $0.3/0.25 = 1.2$ jobs per hour). The resulting model is known as the $M/E_2/1$ queue and has known steady-state characteristics (see Gross and Harris [8, p. 226]). Table 10.2 gives the theoretical values of the steady-state average number in queue, average utilization, and average delay in queue and also estimates of these quantities from a simulation run of length 2000 eight-hour days. Since the estimates are very close to the true values, this gives us some degree of confidence in the correctness of the computer program.

A more definitive test of the correctness of the computer program can be achieved by running the general model of Sec. 2.6.2 with the original number of machine groups (5), the original number of machines in each group (3, 2, 4, 3, 1), only type 1 jobs, and with exponential service times (with the same mean as the corresponding 2-Erlang service time) at each machine group. The resulting model is, in effect, four multiserver queues in series, with the first queue an $M/M/3$, the second an $M/M/2$, etc. [The interdeparture times from an $M/M/s$ queue (s is the number of servers) which has been in operation for a long time are IID exponential random variables; see [8, p. 198].] Furthermore, steady-state characteristics are known for the $M/M/s$ queue (see [8, p. 95]). Table 10.3 gives, for each machine group, the theoretical values of the steady-state average number in queue, average utilization, and average delay in queue and also estimates of these quantities from a simulation run of length 2000 eight-hour days. Once again the simulation estimates are quite close to the theoretical values, which gives us increased confidence in the computer program's correctness.

Technique 5. With some types of simulation models, it may be helpful to display the simulation output on a graphics terminal as the simulation actually progresses.

Example 10.4 A simulation model of a network of automobile traffic intersections was developed, supposedly debugged, and used for some time to study such issues as the effect of various light-sequencing policies. However, when the simulated flow of traffic was displayed on a graphics ter-

Table 10.1 Trace for the single-server queue considered in Sec. 1.4.2

Event	Time	Times of arrival	Status	Number in queue	Event list		Number of customers delayed	Total delay	Area under number in queue function
					Arrive	Depart			
INIT	0		0	0	55	10^{30}	0	0	0
ARRIVE	55		1	0	87	98	1	0	0
ARRIVE	87	87	1	1	111	98	1	0	0
DEPART	98		1	0	111	134	2	11	11
ARRIVE	111	111	1	1	151	134	2	11	11
DEPART	134		1	0	151	168	3	34	34
ARRIVE	151	151	1	1	163	168	3	34	34
ARRIVE	163	151, 163	1	2	192	168	3	34	46

Table 10.2 Theoretical values (T) and simulation estimates (S) (both to three decimal places) for a simplified job-shop model ($M/E_2/1$ queue)

Average number in queue		Average utilization		Average delay in queue	
T	S	T	S	T	S
0.676	0.685	0.600	0.604	0.563	0.565

minal, it was found that simulated cars were actually colliding in the intersections; subsequent inspection of the computer program revealed several undetected errors.

10.3 GENERAL PERSPECTIVES ON VALIDATION

We now describe six general perspectives on validation. They should not be thought of as definitive recommendations on how to validate a simulation model but as somewhat philosophical considerations to be kept in mind when contemplating how to validate a model of a real-world system.

1. Experimentation with a simulation model is a surrogate for actually experimenting with an existing or proposed system. Thus, a reasonable goal in validation is to ensure that a model is developed which can actually be used by a decision maker to make the same decision that would be made if it *were* feasible and cost-effective to experiment with the system itself. Although this statement is hard to disagree with in theory, knowing how to effect it in practice is a different story. We hope to shed some light on this matter in the next section, where we discuss a three-step approach to validation.

2. A simulation model of a complex, real-world system is always only an *approximation* to the actual system, regardless of how much effort is put into developing the model. Thus, one should not speak of the absolute validity or invalidity of a model, but rather of the degree to which the model agrees with the system. The more

Table 10.3 Theoretical values (T) and simulation estimates (S) (both to three decimal places) for a simplified job-shop model (four multiserver queues in series)

Machine group	Average number in queue		Average utilization		Average delay in queue	
	T	S	T	S	T	S
3	0.001	0.001	0.150	0.149	0.001	0.001
1	0.012	0.012	0.240	0.238	0.010	0.010
2	0.359	0.350	0.510	0.508	0.299	0.292
5	0.900	0.902	0.600	0.601	0.750	0.752

time (and hence money) that is spent on validation, the closer the agreement of the model with the system should be. However, the most "valid" model will not necessarily be the most cost-effective. One should always keep in mind the overall objective of the simulation study, which is often to save money by determining an efficient system design.

3. A simulation model should always be developed for a particular purpose. Indeed, a model valid for one purpose may not be valid for another. (Since simulation models often evolve over time and are used for different purposes, every simulation study should include thorough documentation not only of the computer program but also of the assumptions underlying the model itself.) For example, consider a company which builds a simulation model of its computer system. Since simulation models are generally better at comparing alternatives than at determining absolute answers, a model of the computer system which is sufficiently valid to compare, in a relative sense, three proposed job-scheduling policies may not be valid enough to determine quite as precisely the average response time of the computer for a particular scheduling policy when the arrival rate of jobs is hypothesized to increase by 50 percent.

4. A simulation model should be validated relative to a specified set of criteria, namely, the criteria that will actually be used for decision making.

5. Validation is not something to be attempted after the simulation model has already been developed and only if there is time and money still remaining. Instead, model development and validation should be done hand in hand throughout the course of the simulation study. (Our experience indicates that this recommendation is often not followed.)

6. The use of formal statistical procedures is only part of the validation process; at present most of the "validation" done in practice seems to be of the subjective variety as discussed in Sec. 10.4.1. One reason for this is that most classical statistical techniques cannot be directly applied in the context of simulation-model validation. (See Sec. 10.4.3 for further discussion.)

10.4 A THREE-STEP APPROACH TO VALIDATION

Probably the most important paper in the validation literature is that of Naylor and Finger [13], where a three-step approach is given for "validating" a simulation model. Here, we augment their approach by giving specific recommendations and examples of how to carry out each of the three steps.

10.4.1 Develop a Model with High Face Validity

The primary objective during the first step of validation is to develop a model with high *face validity*, i.e., a model which, on the surface, seems reasonable to people who are knowledgeable about the system under study. In order to develop such a model, the simulation modelers should make use of all existing information, including the following.

Conversations with "experts." A simulation model is not an abstraction developed by a modeler working in isolation; instead the modeler should work closely with people who are intimately familiar with the system.

Existing theory. For example, if one is modeling a service system such as a bank and the arrival rate of customers is constant over some period of time, theory tells us that the interarrival times of customers are quite likely to be IID exponential random variables; in other words, customers arrive in accordance with a Poisson process (see Sec. 5.7).

Observations of the system. If one is modeling a multiteller bank with jockeying (see Sec. 2.5), then interarrival times are collected and used to fit a theoretical inter-arrival-time distribution, service times are collected and used to fit a theoretical ser-vice-time distribution, and the bank is observed in order to construct a model of how people jockey from one line to another. [In collecting data on the system under study, however, care must be taken to ensure that the data are representative of what one actually wants to model. For example, the data collected during a military field test (see Sec. 10.4.3) may not be representative of actual combat conditions due to dif-ferences in troop behavior and lack of battlefield smoke (see also Prob. 10.1). Schellenberger [14] discusses this and other aspects of data validity.]

General knowledge. In building a model, one should seek out and use relevant results from similar models, to avoid "reinventing the wheel" with each new study.

Intuition. It will often be necessary to use one's intuition to hypothesize how certain components of a complex system operate. It is hoped that these hypotheses can be substantiated during the later steps of the validation process.

It is also very important for the modelers to interact with the decision makers (or managers) throughout the course of the simulation study. When a study is first conceptualized, a decision maker may not understand the system well enough to know the ultimate objectives of the study precisely. Thus, as the study proceeds and a better understanding of the system is obtained, this information should be conveyed to the decision maker by the modeler, who in turn may revise his objectives for the study. Not only will this approach increase the actual validity of the model, but, in addition, the "perceived validity" to the decision maker of the model will be increased. Decision makers are much more likely to accept as valid and to use models in whose development they were actively involved.

10.4.2 Test the Assumptions of the Model Empirically

The goal of the second step of validation is to test quantitatively the assumptions made during the initial stages of model development. We now give some examples of techniques which can be used for this purpose, all of which are of general appli-cability. If a theoretical probability distribution has been fitted to some observed data and used as input to the simulation model, the adequacy of the fit can be assessed by the use of the chi-square or Kolmogorov-Smirnov goodness-of-fit tests, discussed in Sec. 5.5.

As stated in Sec. 10.4.1, it is important to use representative data in building a model; however, it is equally important to exercise care when structuring these data. For example, if two or more sets of observed data have been merged and used for some purpose in a model, whether this pooling is correct can be determined by use of the Mann-Whitney or Kruskal-Wallis tests of homogeneity of populations (see Breiman [3, chap. 9]). (In a simulation study of a post office we performed, it was found that the service-time distributions of different postal clerks were not the same, since one clerk engaged in a conversation with each customer. Thus, it was not appropriate to fit one distribution to a pooled set of observed service-time data.)

One of the most useful tools during the second step of validation is *sensitivity analysis*. For example, this technique can be used to determine how much the model output will vary with a small change in an input parameter. If the output is particularly sensitive to some parameter, a better estimate of it should be obtained (see Sec. 5.4 for further discussion). Another important use of sensitivity analysis is to determine the level of detail at which a particular subsystem is to be modeled. Sometimes a simulation model is developed which is so detailed that one can afford to run it for only a few replications and thus a thorough analysis of the system under study is impossible. In this case, the modelers might determine what subsystem's model is contributing most to the excessive running time and try to develop a simpler (and less expensive) model of this subsystem. Both representations of the entire system are then run, and the output data are compared for significant differences. If the simpler model produces "similar" results, it probably can safely be used for a detailed study of the system. This use of sensitivity analysis was employed in the freeway simulation model discussed in Gafarian and Walsh [6] (and conveyed to us in a personal communication with the first author).

10.4.3 Determine How Representative the Simulation Output Data Are

Probably the most definitive test of the validity of a simulation model is to establish that the model output data closely resemble the output data that would be expected from the actual system. If a system similar to the one being studied now exists, a simulation model of the existing system is developed and its output data are compared with data from the actual existing system. (These system data might be available from historical records or might have to be collected explicitly for validation purposes. Furthermore, the time required to construct a model of the existing system will probably not be wasted, since such a model will be needed to compare definitively the present system with proposed system designs.) If the two sets of output data compare favorably, the model of the existing system is modified so that it represents the proposed system. Although we cannot be sure that the model of the proposed system is "valid," we should have more confidence than if the comparison had not been made.

The above idea will be used to validate a simulation model of a welfare office's operations being developed by The Department of Health and Human Services for the purpose of evaluating the effect of various proposed administrative policies, using such performance measures as applicant delay and accuracy of welfare payments. Here the "existing system" will be a welfare office in Massachusetts run under current administrative policy.

A number of statistical tests have been suggested in the validation literature for comparing the output data from a simulation model with those from the corresponding real-world system (see, for example, Shannon [15, p. 208]). However, the comparison is not so simple as it might appear, since the output processes of almost all real-world systems and simulations are nonstationary (the distributions of the successive observations change over time) and autocorrelated (the observations in the process are correlated with each other). Thus, classical statistical tests based on IID observations are not *directly* applicable. Furthermore, we question whether hypothesis tests, compared with constructing confidence intervals for differences, are even the appropriate statistical approach. Since the model is only an approximation to the actual system, a null hypothesis that the system and model are the "same" is clearly false. We believe that it is more useful to ask whether or not the differences between the system and the model are significant enough to affect any conclusions derived from the model. For a discussion of statistical procedures which can be used for comparing system and model output data, see Sec. 10.6 and also Law [11].

In addition to statistical procedures, one can use a *Turing test* to compare the output data from the model to those of the system. People knowledgeable about the system are asked to examine one or more sets of system data and one or more sets of model data without knowing which sets are which. If these "experts" can differentiate between the system and model data, their explanation of how they were able to do it is used to improve the model. Even if a similar existing system exists but definitive output data are not readily available, the same experts can be asked to evaluate how reasonable the simulation output data are, and this information might be used to improve the model. This idea was put to good use by the developers of the ISEM simulation model of the Air Force Manpower and Personnel System. (This model was designed to provide Air Force policy analysts with a system-wide view of the effects of various proposed personnel policies.) The model was run under the Air Force's baseline personnel policy, and the results were shown to Air Force analysts and decision makers, who subsequently identified some discrepancies between model and perceived system behavior. This information was used to improve the model, and after several additional evaluations and improvements, a model was obtained which appeared to approximate current Air Force policy closely.

If the decisions to be made with a simulation model are of particularly great importance, field tests are sometimes used (primarily by the military) to obtain system output data for validation purposes. For example, suppose some military organization is thinking of purchasing a weapons system for which it is infeasible or too expensive to perform a complete set of evaluational tests. As an alternative, a simulation model of the system is developed, and then a prototype of the actual system is field-tested on a military reservation for one or more specified scenarios. If the model and system output data compare closely for each of the specified scenarios, the "validated" simulation model is used to evaluate the system for scenarios for which system field tests are not possible. For further discussion of field tests, see [15, p. 231].

Up to now we have discussed validating a simulation model relative to past or present system output data; however, a perhaps more definitive test of a model is to establish its ability to predict future system behavior. Since models often evolve over time and are used for more than one application, there is often an opportunity for such prospective validation. For example, if a model is used to decide which version of a proposed system to build, then after the system has been built and sufficient time has elapsed for output data to be collected, these data can be compared with the predictions of the model. If there is reasonable agreement, we have increased confidence in the "validity" of the model. On the other hand, discrepancies between the two data sets should be used to update the model. Regardless of the accuracy of a model's past predictions, a model should be carefully scrutinized before each new application, since a change in purpose or the passage of time may have invalidated some aspect of the existing model.

10.5 ADDITIONAL CONSIDERATIONS IN VALIDATION

In Sec. 10.4.3 we discussed comparing the output data from a simulation model with those from a corresponding existing system. However, if the system input and output data are complete enough and in the proper form, it may be possible to perform the suggested comparison in a statistically more efficient manner. Since this idea is best illustrated by means of an example, consider the multiteller bank discussed under "Observations of the system" in Sec. 10.4.1. Suppose that it is desired to validate a simulation model of the bank relative to the criterion of average delay of a customer between 12 and 1 P.M. (the busiest period in the bank). Suppose further that in collecting data from the bank it is possible to observe the number of customers in the bank at 12 and (more importantly) the interarrival time, the service time, and the delay in queue corresponding to each customer who arrives (and completes his delay) between 12 and 1. Then, rather than running the model by generating the required interarrival and service times from the fitted theoretical distributions, it is preferable to drive the model with the actual observed interarrival and service times (i.e., no random variables are generated) and to initialize the model at 12 with the number of customers actually observed in the bank. (For this simple example we are, in effect, validating our model of jockeying, while for a more complex model, we would be validating everything in the model but the fitted theoretical distributions.) By comparing the bank and the model under a similar statistical environment, we reduce the variance of the difference between the average delay in the bank and the average delay in the model, resulting in a more precise assessment of the actual difference between the model and the bank.

The idea of comparing a model and the corresponding system under the same statistical conditions is similar to the use of the variance-reduction technique known as common random numbers in simulation (see Sec. 11.2) and the use of "blocking" in statistical experimental design (see Chap. 12). It should be mentioned, however, that we do not recommend using historical system input data to drive a model for the purpose of making production runs.

Sometimes one uses historical input data to build a model and then compares the model output data with the corresponding historical output data. If the agreement is not good, the parameters or the structure of the model are manipulated and the resulting output data are again compared with the historical output data. This procedure, which we call *calibration* of a model, is continued until the two data sets agree closely. However, we must ask whether this procedure produces a valid model for the system, in general, or whether the model is only representative of the particular set of input data. To answer this question (in effect, to validate the model), one can use a completely independent set of historical input and output data. The calibrated model might be driven by the second set of input data (in a manner similar to that described above) and the resulting model output data compared with the second set of historical output data. This idea of using one set of data for calibration and another independent set for validation seems to be fairly common in economics and the biological sciences. In particular, it was used by the Crown Zellerbach Corporation in developing a simulation model of tree growth. Here the historical data were available from the U.S. Forest Service.

10.6 STATISTICAL PROCEDURES FOR COMPARING REAL-WORLD OBSERVATIONS AND SIMULATION OUTPUT DATA

Suppose that $R_1, R_2, \ldots, R_k$ are observations from a real-world system and that $M_1, M_2, \ldots, M_l$ are output data from a corresponding simulation model. We would like to compare the two data sets, in some sense, to determine whether the model is an accurate representation of the real-world system. The first approach which comes to mind is to use one of the classical statistical tests (t, Mann-Whitney, two-sample chi-square, two-sample Kolmogorov-Smirnov, etc.) to determine whether the underlying distributions of the two data sets can be safely regarded as being the same. (For a good discussion of these tests, which assume IID data, see [3].) However, as pointed out above, the output processes of almost all real-world systems and simulations are nonstationary and autocorrelated, and thus none of these tests is *directly* applicable. In Secs. 10.6.1 to 10.6.3 we discuss, respectively, inspection, confidence-interval, and time-series approaches to this comparison problem.

10.6.1 An Inspection Approach

The approach which seems to be used by most simulation practitioners (who attempt the third step of the suggested validation approach) is to compute one or more statistics from the real-world observations and corresponding statistics from the output data from the model, and then compare the resulting model statistics with those from the system without the use of a formal statistical procedure. (For an example of the use of the inspection approach in the context of computer performance evaluation, see Anderson and Sargent [1].) Examples of statistics which might be used for this purpose are the sample mean, the sample variance (see Sec. 4.4 for a discussion of the danger in using the sample variance), the sample correlation function, and "histograms." (The word histogram is put in quotation marks since histograms are usually derived from IID data.) The difficulty with this inspection approach, which is graphically illustrated below in Example 10.5, is that each statistic is essentially a sample of size 1 from some underlying population, making this idea particularly vulnerable to the inherent randomness of the observations from both the real system and the simulation model.

Example 10.5 In order to illustrate the danger in using inspection, suppose that the real-world system of interest is the $M/M/1$ queue with $\rho = 0.6$ and that the corresponding simulation model is the $M/M/1$ queue with $\rho = 0.5$. Suppose that the output process of interest is $\{D_i, i \geq 1\}$ (D_i is the delay in queue of the ith customer) and let

$$X = \frac{\sum_{i=1}^{200} D_i}{200} \quad \text{for the system}$$

and

$$Y = \frac{\sum_{i=1}^{200} D_i}{200} \quad \text{for the model}$$

(Thus, the sample size for the system, k, and the sample size for the model, l, are both equal to 200.) We shall attempt to determine how good a representation the model is for the system by comparing an estimate of $\mu_Y = E(Y) = 0.490$ [the expected average delay of the first 200 customers for the model; see Heathcote and Winer [9] for a discussion of how to compute $E(Y)$] with an estimate of $\mu_X = E(X) = 0.872$. Table 10.4 gives the results of three independent simulation experiments, each corresponding to a possible application of the inspection approach. For each experiment, $\hat{\mu}_X$ and $\hat{\mu}_Y$ represent the sample mean of the 200 delays for the system and model, respectively, and $\hat{\mu}_X - \hat{\mu}_Y$ is an estimate of $\mu_X - \mu_Y = 0.382$, which is what we are really trying to estimate. Note that $\hat{\mu}_X - \hat{\mu}_Y$ varies greatly from experiment to experiment. Also observe for experiment 2 that $\hat{\mu}_X - \hat{\mu}_Y = -0.016$, which would tend to lead one to think that the model is a good representation for the system. However, we believe that the model is really a poor representation of the system for purposes of estimation of the expected average delay in the real-world system, since μ_Y is nearly 44 percent smaller than μ_X.

In summary, we believe that the inspection approach may provide valuable insight into the adequacy of a simulation model for some simulation studies (partic-

Table 10.4 Results for three experiments with the inspection approach

Experiment	$\hat{\mu}_X$	$\hat{\mu}_Y$	$\hat{\mu}_X - \hat{\mu}_Y$
1	0.902	0.702	0.200
2	0.696	0.712	−0.016
3	1.075	0.353	0.722

ularly if the idea suggested at the beginning of Sec. 10.5 can be used). As a matter of fact, for some studies it may be the only approach which is feasible due to severe limitations on the amount of data available on the operation of the real system. However, as the above example shows, extreme care must be used in interpreting the results of this approach.

10.6.2 A Confidence-Interval Approach

We now describe a more reliable approach for comparing a model with a system for the situation where it is possible to collect a potentially large amount of data from both the model and the system. This might be the case, for example, when the system is an existing computer facility from which a large amount of data can be readily obtained.

In the spirit of terminating simulations (see Chaps. 8 and 9), suppose we collect m independent sets of data from the system and n independent sets of data from the model. Let X_j be the average of the observations in the jth set of system data, and let Y_j be the average of the observations in the jth set of model data. The X_j's are IID random variables (assuming that the m sets of system data are homogeneous) with mean $\mu_X = E(X_j)$ and the Y_j's are IID random variables (assuming that the n data sets for the model were produced by independent replications) with mean $\mu_Y = E(Y_j)$. We shall attempt to compare the model with the system by constructing a confidence interval for $\zeta = \mu_X - \mu_Y$. We believe that constructing a confidence interval for ζ is preferable to testing the null hypothesis $H_0: \mu_X = \mu_Y$ for the following reasons:

1. Since the model is only an approximation to the system, H_0 will clearly be false in almost all cases.
2. A confidence interval provides more information than the corresponding hypothesis test. If the hypothesis test indicates that $\mu_X \neq \mu_Y$, then the confidence interval will provide this information and also give an indication of the magnitude by which μ_X differs from μ_Y.

Constructing a confidence interval for ζ is a special case of the problem of comparing two systems by means of a confidence interval discussed in Sec. 9.2. Thus, we may construct a confidence interval for ζ by using either the paired-t approach or the Welch approach. (In the notation of Sec. 9.2, $n_1 = m$, $n_2 = n$, $X_{1j} = X_j$, and $X_{2j} = Y_j$.) The paired-t approach requires $m = n$ but allows X_j to be correlated with Y_j, which would be the case if the idea suggested at the beginning of Sec. 10.5 is used. The Welch approach can be used for any values of $m \geq 2$ and $n \geq 2$ but requires that the X_j's be independent of the Y_j's.

Suppose that we have constructed a $100(1 - \alpha)$ percent confidence interval for ζ by using either the paired-t or Welch approaches, and let $l(\alpha)$ and $u(\alpha)$ be the corresponding lower and upper confidence interval endpoints, respectively. If $0 \notin [l(\alpha), u(\alpha)]$, then the observed difference between μ_X and μ_Y, $\overline{X}(m) - \overline{Y}(n)$, is said to be *statistically significant*. This is equivalent to rejecting the null hypothesis

H_0: $\mu_X = \mu_Y$ in favor of the two-sided alternative hypothesis H_1: $\mu_X \neq \mu_Y$. If $0 \in [l(\alpha), u(\alpha)]$, any observed difference between μ_X and μ_Y is not statistically significant and might be caused by sampling fluctuation. Even if the observed difference between μ_X and μ_Y is statistically significant, this need not mean that the model is, for practical purposes, not a "valid" representation of the system. For example, if $\zeta = 1$ but $\mu_X = 1000$ and $\mu_Y = 999$, then the difference which exists between the model and the system is probably of no practical consequence. We shall say that the difference between a model and a system is *practically significant* if the "magnitude" of the difference is large enough to invalidate any inferences about the system which would be derived from the model. Clearly, the decision as to whether the difference between a model and a system is practically significant is a subjective one, which depends on such factors as the purpose of the model and the utility function of the person who is going to use the model.

If the length of the confidence interval for ζ is not small enough to decide practical significance, it will be necessary to obtain additional X_j's and/or Y_j's. It should be noted, however, that for the Welch approach it is not possible to make the confidence interval arbitrarily small by adding only X_j's or only Y_j's. Thus, if the number of sets of system data, m, cannot be increased, it may not be possible to determine practical significance by making more and more replications of the model.

Example 10.6 Suppose that X_j and Y_j are defined similarly to X and Y in Example 10.5, and suppose that we would like to construct a 90 percent confidence interval for $\zeta = \mu_X - \mu_Y$ using the paired-t approach to determine whether the model (the $M/M/1$ queue with $\rho = 0.5$) is an accurate representation of the system (the $M/M/1$ queue with $\rho = 0.6$). Letting $Z_j = X_j - Y_j$ and $m = n = 10$, we obtained

$$\overline{Z}(10) = \overline{X}(10) - \overline{Y}(10) = 0.797 - 0.441 = 0.356 \text{ (point estimator for } \zeta)$$

$$\hat{\sigma}^2[\overline{Z}(10)] = \frac{\sum_{j=1}^{10} [Z_j - \overline{Z}(10)]^2}{(10)(9)} = 0.0156$$

and the 90 percent confidence interval for ζ is

$$\overline{Z}(10) \pm t_{9,0.95} \sqrt{\hat{\sigma}^2[\overline{Z}(10)]} = 0.356 \pm 0.229$$

Therefore, with 90 percent confidence we claim that ζ is in the interval [0.127, 0.585]. (Recall from Example 10.5 that ζ is, in fact, 0.382.) Since the confidence interval does not contain 0, the observed difference between μ_X and μ_Y is statistically significant. One approach for deciding whether this difference is practically significant might be to compare 0.127 (the lower confidence interval endpoint for $\zeta = \mu_X - \mu_Y$) with $\overline{X}(10) = 0.797$ (the point estimator for μ_X), which results in the ratio $0.127/0.797 = 0.159$. Thus, loosely speaking, the model is at least 16 percent different from the system relative to the measure "expected average delay of the first 200 customers." It remains to decide the practical consequence of such a difference.

Two difficulties with the above replication approach are that it requires a large amount of data (each set of output data produces only one "observation") and it provides no information about the autocorrelation structures of the two output processes.

10.6.3 Time-Series Approaches

In this section we briefly discuss two time-series approaches for comparing model output data with system output data. (A *time series* is a finite realization of a stochastic process. For example, the delays D_1, D_2, ... ,D_{200} from a queueing model or system form a time series.) These approaches require only one set of each type of output data and also yield information on the autocorrelation structures of the two output processes. Thus, the two difficulties of the replication approach mentioned above are not present here. There are, however, other difficulties.

The *spectral-analysis* approach (see Fishman and Kiviat [4], Law [11], and Naylor [12, p. 247]) proceeds by computing the sample spectrum, i.e., the Fourier cosine transformation of the estimated autocovariance function, of each output process and then using existing theory to construct a confidence interval for the difference of the logarithms of the spectra. This confidence interval can be potentially used to assess the degree of similarity of the two autocorrelation functions. Two drawbacks of spectral analysis are that it requires an output process to be covariance stationary (an assumption often not satisfied in practice) and that a very high level of mathematical sophistication is required in order to apply it. The method can also be quite expensive to apply in terms of computer time or storage.

Spectral analysis is a nonparametric approach in that it makes no assumption about the distributions of the observations in a time series. Hsu and Hunter [10] suggest an alternative approach which consists of fitting a parametric time-series model (see Box and Jenkins [2]) to each set of output data and then applying a hypothesis test to see whether the two models are the same.

PROBLEMS

10.1 As stated in Sec. 10.4.1, care must be taken that data collected on a system are representative of what one actually wants to model. Discuss this potential problem with regard to a study which will involve observing the efficiency of workers on an assembly line for the purpose of building a simulation model. (The phenomenon you have identified is called the *Hawthorne effect*.)

10.2 Discuss why validating a model of a computer system might be easier than validating a military combat model. Assume that the computer system of interest is similar to an existing computer system.

10.3 If one constructs a confidence interval for $\zeta = \mu_X - \mu_Y$ using the confidence-interval approach of Sec. 10.6.2, which of the following outcomes are possible?

	Statistically significant	Practically significant
(a)	Yes	Yes
(b)	Yes	No
(c)	Yes	?
(d)	No	Yes
(e)	No	No
(f)	No	?

10.4 Use the Welch approach with $m = 5$ and $n = 10$ to construct a 90 percent confidence interval for $\zeta = \mu_X - \mu_Y$ given the following data:

$$X_j\text{'s: } 0.920, 0.908, 0.567, 0.863, 0.902$$

$$Y_j\text{'s: } 0.278, 0.316, 0.476, 0.486, 0.702, 0.513, 0.385, 0.279, 0.446, 0.573$$

Is the confidence interval statistically significant? Use your own criterion to decide whether or not the confidence interval is practically significant.

REFERENCES

1. Anderson, H. A., Jr., and R. G. Sargent: Investigation into Scheduling for an Interactive Computing System, *IBM J. Res. Dev.*, **18:** 125–137 (1974).
2. Box, G. E. P., and G. M. Jenkins: *Time Series Analysis: Forecasting and Control,* revised ed., Holden-Day, San Francisco, 1976.
3. Breiman, L.: *Statistics: With a View Toward Applications,* Houghton Mifflin, Boston, 1973.
4. Fishman, G. S., and P. J. Kiviat: The Analysis of Simulation-Generated Time Series, *Manage. Sci.,* **13:** 525–557 (1967).
5. Fishman, G. S., and P. J. Kiviat: The Statistics of Discrete-Event Simulation, *Simulation,* **10:** 185–195 (1968).
6. Gafarian, A. V., and J. E. Walsh: Methods for Statistical Validation of a Simulation Model for Freeway Traffic Near an On-Ramp, *Transp. Res.,* **4:** 379–384 (1970).
7. Gass, S. I.: Evaluation of Complex Models, *Comput. Oper. Res.,* **4:** 25–37 (1977).
8. Gross, D., and C. M. Harris: *Fundamentals of Queueing Theory,* Wiley, New York, 1974.
9. Heathcote, C. R., and P. Winer: An Approximation to the Moments of Waiting Times, *Oper. Res.,* **17:** 175–186 (1969).
10. Hsu, D. A., and J. S. Hunter: Analysis of Simulation-Generated Responses Using Autoregressive Models, *Manage. Sci.,* **24:** 181–190 (1977).
11. Law, A. M.: Validation of Simulation Models, II: Comparison of Real-World and Simulation Output Data, *Univ. Wis. Dept. Ind. Eng. Tech. Rep.* 78-15, Madison, 1981.
12. Naylor, T. H.: *Computer Simulation Experiments with Models of Economic Systems,* Wiley, New York, 1971.
13. Naylor, T. H., and J. M. Finger: Verification of Computer Simulation Models, *Manage. Sci.,* **14:** 92–101 (1967).
14. Schellenberger, R. E.: Criteria for Assessing Model Validity for Managerial Purposes, *Decis. Sci.,* **5:** 644–653 (1974).
15. Shannon, R. E.: *Systems Simulation: The Art and Science,* Prentice-Hall, Englewood Cliffs, N.J., 1975.
16. U.S. General Accounting Office: Guidelines for Model Evaluation, *Rep.* PAD-79-17, Washington, 1979.
17. Van Horn, R. L: Validation of Simulation Results, *Manage. Sci.,* **17:** 247–258 (1971).

ELEVEN

VARIANCE-REDUCTION TECHNIQUES

11.1 INTRODUCTION

One of the points we have tried to emphasize throughout this book is that simulations driven by random inputs will produce random output. Thus, proper statistical techniques applied to simulation output data are imperative if the results are to be properly analyzed, interpreted, and used (see Chaps. 8, 9, and 12). Since many large-scale simulations require great amounts of computer time and storage, proper statistical analyses (which may require multiple replications of the model, for example) can become extremely costly. Sometimes the cost of making even a modest statistical analysis of the output can be so high that the precision of the results, perhaps measured by confidence-interval width, will be unacceptably poor. The simulator should therefore try to use any means possible to increase the efficiency of the simulation.

Of course, "efficiency" mandates careful programming to expedite execution and minimize storage requirements. In this chapter, however, we focus on *statistical* efficiency, as measured by the *variances* of the output random variables from a simulation. If we can somehow reduce the variance of an output random variable of interest (such as average delay in queue, or average cost per month in an inventory system) without disturbing its expected value, we can obtain greater precision, e.g., smaller confidence intervals, for the same amount of simulating or, alternatively, achieve a prespecified precision with less simulating. Sometimes such a *variance-reduction technique* (VRT), properly applied, can make the difference between an impossibly expensive simulation project and a frugal, useful one.

As we shall see, the method of applying VRTs usually depends on the particular model (or models) of interest. Therefore, a thorough understanding of the workings of the model(s) is required for proper use of VRTs. Furthermore, it is generally impossible to know beforehand how great a variance reduction might be realized, or (worse) whether or not the variance will be reduced at all in comparison with straightforward simulation. However, preliminary pilot runs could be made (if affordable) to compare the results of applying a VRT with the results of straightforward simulation. A third point is that some VRTs themselves will increase computing cost, and this decrease in computational efficiency must be traded off against the potential gain in statistical efficiency. Almost all VRTs require *some* extra effort on the part of the analyst (if only to understand the technique) and this, as always, must be considered.

Many VRTs were developed originally in the early days of computers, to be applied in Monte Carlo simulations or distribution sampling (see Sec. 1.7.3, as well as Hammersley and Handscomb [12]). Thus, many of the original VRTs cannot easily be applied to simulations of complex dynamic systems. We have chosen to discuss five general types of VRTs in the remainder of this chapter, which we feel have the most promise of successful application to a wide variety of simulations. (We refer the reader to Kleijnen [18] for detailed discussions of other VRTs, such as stratified sampling and importance sampling.)

On a first reading, we suggest that attention be focused on Sec. 11.2 and possibly Sec. 11.3. These two VRTs are probably the most useful, general, and easily understood.

11.2 COMMON RANDOM NUMBERS

The first VRT we consider, *common random numbers* (CRN), applies when we are comparing two or more alternative system designs (see Chap. 9) and is probably the most useful and popular VRT. The basic idea is that we should compare the alternative systems "under similar experimental conditions" so that we can be more confident that any observed differences in performance are due to the differences in the system designs rather than to fluctuations of the "experimental conditions." In simulation, the experimental conditions are the generated random variables that are used to drive the models through simulated time. In queueing simulations, for example, these would include interarrival times and service requirements of the customers; in inventory simulations we might want to include interdemand times and demand sizes. The name of this technique stems from the possibility in some situations of using the *same* stream of basic $U(0, 1)$ random variables to drive each of the alternative models through time; as we shall see later in this section, however, there are programming techniques which are often needed to facilitate the implementation of CRN. In the terminology of classical experimental design, CRN is a form of *blocking,* i.e., "comparing like with like"; CRN has also been called *correlated sampling* in some simulation contexts.

To see the rationale for CRN more clearly, consider the case of *two* alternative systems, as in Sec. 9.2, where X_{1j} and X_{2j} are the observations from the first and second systems, respectively, on the jth independent replication, and we want to estimate $\zeta = E(X_{1j}) - E(X_{2j})$. If we make n replications of each system and let $Z_j = X_{1j} - X_{2j}$ for $j = 1, 2, \ldots, n$, then $E(Z_j) = \zeta$ and so $\overline{Z}(n) = \sum_{j=1}^{n} Z_j/n$ is an unbiased estimator of ζ. Since the Z_j's are IID random variables,

$$\text{Var}\,[\overline{Z}(n)] = \frac{\text{Var}\,(Z_j)}{n} = \frac{\text{Var}\,(X_{1j}) + \text{Var}\,(X_{2j}) - 2\,\text{Cov}\,(X_{1j}, X_{2j})}{n}$$

[see Eq. (4.4) and Prob. 4.11]. If the simulations of the two different systems are done independently, i.e., with separate random-number streams, X_{1j} and X_{2j} are independent, so that $\text{Cov}\,(X_{1j}, X_{2j}) = 0$. On the other hand, if we could somehow carry out the simulations of system 1 and system 2 so that X_{1j} and X_{2j} are *positively* correlated, then $\text{Cov}\,(X_{1j}, X_{2j}) > 0$, so that the variance of our estimator $\overline{Z}(n)$ is reduced. CRN is a technique by which we try to induce this positive correlation.

Unfortunately, there is no general proof that CRN "works"; nor can we know beforehand how great a reduction in variance we might experience. (Heidelberger and Iglehart [15] have recently shown that CRN guarantees a variance reduction for certain types of regenerative simulations.) The efficacy of the CRN technique depends wholly on the particular models being compared, and its use must be based on the analyst's belief that the different models will respond "similarly" to large or small values of the random variables driving the models. (For example, we would expect that smaller interarrival times at any of several designs of a queueing facility would result in larger delays and queue lengths for each system.) If affordable, one could make a preliminary check on the efficacy of CRN for a given set of alternative systems by estimating the variances under CRN *and* under independent sampling in a small pilot study. More directly, the covariances or correlations between the output random variables of the alternative systems could be estimated to provide a numerical check on the assumption that the desired positive correlation *is* being induced. (Keep in mind, however, that both these suggestions provide only *estimates* which are still random variables.) Of course, any extra programming that might be necessary to implement CRN would have to be done for such pilot studies, whether CRN is ultimately adopted or not.

While there are some examples of CRN's backfiring, i.e., causing $\text{Cov}\,(X_{1j}, X_{2j}) < 0$ and thus leading to an *increase* in variance, as demonstrated recently by Wright and Ramsay [34] for an inventory simulation, we feel that CRN is generally a valuable tool which should be given careful consideration by an analyst faced with the task of comparing two or more alternative systems. Another possible drawback to CRN is that formal statistical analyses when we have *more* than two systems can be complicated by the induced correlation (adaptations for standard analysis of variance tests in the presence of this correlation are discussed by Heikes, Montgomery, and Rardin [16] and by Kleijnen [19]).

To implement CRN, we must match up, or *synchronize*, the random numbers across the different systems so that a random number used for a particular purpose in one system is used for the *same* purpose in all other systems. The difficulty of maintaining this synchronization is completely dependent on the model structure and parameters and on the methods used to generate the random variables needed in the simulations. Several programming "tricks" can be considered to maintain synchronization in a given simulation: (1) If it is possible to have several different random-number generators operating simultaneously (as is the case in some specialized simulation languages), we can "devote" a generator to generating the random numbers for a particular type of random variable; e.g., in a queueing simulation one generator could be devoted to generating $U(0, 1)$ random variables to generate the interarrival-time random variables, and a different generator could be devoted to service times. (2) We might find it advantageous to "waste" some random numbers at certain points in the simulation of some models; Prob. 11.1 gives an example of a model where this technique is useful. (3) Another trick is to generate the required random variables ahead of time and store them (perhaps in secondary or auxiliary storage) for use as needed in simulating *each* of the alternative systems. (4) In some queueing simulations another technique for maintaining synchronization is to generate the service requirement(s) of a customer at the time of arrival instead of when the customer actually enters service. Example 11.2 below illustrates this idea for implementing CRN for the alternative job-shop models of Sec. 2.6.3. (5) The general inverse-transform method for generating random variables (see Sec. 7.2.1) can facilitate maintenance of synchronization since we always need *exactly one* $U(0, 1)$ random variable to produce each value of the desired random variable, as contrasted with, for example, the acceptance-rejection method of Sec. 7.2.4 where a *random* number of $U(0, 1)$ random variables is needed to produce a single value of the desired random variable.

Even armed with these programming tricks (as well as other techniques which could be devised for a particular situation), it may simply be impossible to attain full synchronization across all models under study. Also, the extra programming effort, computation time, or storage costs needed for full synchronization might not be worth the realized variance reduction. Thus, we might consider synchronizing *some* of the input random variables and generate others independently across the various systems. (For example, it might be convenient to synchronize interarrival times but not service times in a complex network of queues.) In the final analysis, the use of CRN and the degree to which we synchronize the input random variables are quite model-dependent. Thus, we close this section with three examples of the use of CRN in particular situations.

Example 11.1 Recall the two competing designs for the automated teller station of Example 9.1; the first system is an $M/M/1$ queue, and the second is an $M/M/2$ queue, both with traffic intensity $\rho = 0.9$, and the performance measure is the expected average delay in queue of the first 100 customers given that the first customer finds the system empty and idle. Thus, X_{ij} is the average delay of the first 100 customers in the $M/M/i$ queue on the jth replication, for $i = 1, 2$. In Example 9.1, we generated X_{1j} and X_{2j} independently for the 100 independent replications, but we could have used CRN. For example, if $A_l(i)$ is the time between the arrivals of customers $l-1$ and l (see Chap. 1) for system i on a particular replication, we could generate $A_l(1)$ for $l = 1, 2, \ldots$, and set $A_l(2) = A_l(1)$ for each l. Furthermore, if $S_l(i)$ is the service time of customer l in system i, we could generate $S_l(1)$ for $l = 1, 2, \ldots$, and set $S_l(2) = 2S_l(1)$ for each l. (Recall that the mean service time in the $M/M/2$ queue must be twice that of the $M/M/1$ queue if the value of ρ is to remain the same.) To estimate the effect of various degrees of synchronization in

Table 11.1 CRN for the $M/M/1$ queue versus the $M/M/2$ queue

	I	A	S	A&S
$\hat{\sigma}^2$	25.491	11.647	10.473	0.103
$\hat{p}$	0.44	0.37	0.40	0.05

CRN, we made four sequences of 100 pairs of simulations each. In the first sequence, denoted I, all runs were independent, i.e., the interarrival and service times of the two models were generated independently. In the second sequence (A) the interarrival times for the two models were the same, but service times were independent. For the third sequence (S) the interarrivals were independent, but the service times were matched up by setting $S_i(2) = 2S_i(1)$. Finally, the fourth sequence (A&S) matched up both interarrival and service times. From these 100 pairs of simulations we estimated Var (Z_j) by the usual unbiased variance estimator $\hat{\sigma}^2 = \sum_{j=1}^{100} [Z_j - \overline{Z}(100)]^2/99$, and computed the proportion $\hat{p}$ of the 100 pairs for which the "wrong" decision would be made, i.e., when $X_{1j} < X_{2j}$; the results are given in Table 11.1. The variance reduction attained by full synchronization (A&S) compared with independent sampling (I) is quite striking here, being a reduction of more than 99 percent; the probability of making the wrong decision based on a single replication pair is reduced from 44 to 5 percent. Lesser variance reductions are observed for the two types of partial synchronization, but $\hat{p}$ was not greatly reduced. The results in Table 11.1 indicate that from a given number of replications of each of the two systems, a confidence interval for ζ formed by the paired-t approach of Sec. 9.2 would be about 16 times smaller under completely synchronized CRN than under independent sampling. Alternatively, if we want a given precision in our estimate $\overline{Z}(n)$ for ζ (perhaps measured in terms of confidence-interval width), independent sampling would require about 247 times as many replications of each system than under completely synchronized CRN. (In carrying out the simulations for this example we actually generated all necessary random variables ahead of time and stored them. CRN could have been implemented, however, without this extra storage by generating a customer's service requirement upon his arrival to the system or by devoting a separate random-number generator to interarrival-time and service-time generation if a simulation language is used that has this feature. If separate generators are used, a particular generator must use the same seed for the jth replication of each system.)

Example 11.2 Consider the job-shop model of Sec. 2.6, and recall specifically the discussion at the end of Sec. 2.6.3. As in the last three rows of Table 2.4, let systems 1, 2, and 3 be, respectively, the job shop obtained by adding a machine to machine group 2, 4, and 1, and let μ_i be the *steady-state* overall average job total delay in system i for $i = 1$, 2, and 3. Suppose that we want to estimate $\zeta_{12} = \mu_1 - \mu_2$, $\zeta_{13} = \mu_1 - \mu_3$, and $\zeta_{23} = \mu_2 - \mu_3$ by making simulations of length 100 eight-hour days of each of the three systems but using the first 10 of these 100 days as a warm-up period and collecting data on only the last 90 days (see Prob. 2.5); let X_{ij} be the overall average job total delay over these 90 days for system i as observed on the jth replication and let $Z_{12j} = X_{1j} - X_{2j}$, $Z_{13j} = X_{1j} - X_{3j}$, and $Z_{23j} = X_{2j} - X_{3j}$. [Note that $E(Z_{i_1i_2j}) \approx \zeta_{i_1i_2}$, provided that the 10-day warm-up period is sufficient.] One way to carry out the simulations would be simply to make the runs of the different systems independent of each other (denoted I in Table 11.2 below). Alternatively, we could use CRN across the three systems on each replication, as follows. For each system, use the same interarrival times for the jobs and make the sequence of job types the same. Furthermore, when a job arrives at the shop and its type is determined, immediately generate its service times that will be needed later as it moves along its route through the shop. Thus, when a job arrives, its service requirements are generated and stored as extra attributes of this job. When a job enters service at a particular machine group, its service time is no longer generated at that point but is taken from the appropriate location in the array MASTER. (Therefore, event routines ARRIVE and DEPART of Sec. 2.6.2 must be changed.) Let $\hat{\sigma}_{i_1i_2}^2$ be the usual unbiased estimate

Table 11.2 CRN for three job-shop configurations

	I	CRN
$\hat{\sigma}_{12}^2$	10.399	2.351
$\hat{\sigma}_{13}^2$	23.078	0.873
$\hat{\sigma}_{23}^2$	6.272	1.459

of Var $(Z_{i(i2j)})$, which we computed from 10 independent replications using both independent sampling and CRN, as given in Table 11.2. Here, CRN leads to variance reductions ranging from 77 to 96 percent, depending on which two policies are being compared.

Example 11.3 In this example, complete synchronization between the systems is not possible, but CRN can still be used by matching up *some* of the random variables. The general model is the inventory system of Sec. 1.5 (with an initial inventory level of 60 and a run length of 120 months), and the two particular alternative systems are those in Example 9.2, that is, $(s, S) = (20, 40)$ for the first system and $(s, S) = (20, 80)$ for the second. For both systems we can schedule demands of the same size which occur at the same time; i.e., we use common interdemand times and common demand sizes. However, due to the different values of s and S, ordering will generally take place at different times for the two models, and so the number of orders placed will also be different under the two policies. Thus, it is not clear how we could sensibly match up the delivery-lag random variables, and we therefore generated them independently for the two models. As in Example 9.2, we made 10 independent pairs of simulations, but here using the same interdemand times and demand sizes for both models within each pair. Using the paired-t approach to confidence-interval formation exactly as in Example 9.2, we obtained $\overline{Z}(10) = 4.332$, $\hat{\sigma}^2[\overline{Z}(10)] = 0.125$, and an approximate 90 percent confidence interval of [3.684, 4.979]. Comparing these results with those of Example 9.2 (which were obtained by independent sampling), we get a variance reduction of approximately 96 percent, and the width of the final confidence interval is reduced by 79 percent. Thus, CRN gave us a considerable gain in precision even though we could only maintain partial synchronization.

Finally, we refer the reader to Schruben and Margolin [31] and Schruben [30] for a general treatment of random-number assignment in simulations of alternative systems as it relates to the overall experimental design.

11.3 ANTITHETIC VARIATES

Antithetic variates (AV) is a VRT which is applicable to the simulation of a *single* system, as are the rest of the VRTs discussed in this chapter. As in CRN, we try to induce correlation between separate runs, but we now seek *negative* correlation. The central idea (which dates back at least to 1956 with the paper of Hammersley and Morton [13] in the context of Monte Carlo simulation) is to make *pairs* of runs of the system such that a small observation on the first run tends to be offset by a large observation on the second run, or vice versa. (Thus, the two observations are negatively correlated.) Then if we use the *average* of the two observations in the pair as a basic data point for analysis, this average should tend to be closer to the expectation of an observation which we want to estimate. In other words, we reduce the variance of the average of the two observations in the pair compared with the variance of this average if the two runs in the pair had been made independently of each other. Roughly speaking, AV tries to induce this negative correlation by using complementary random numbers to drive the two runs in a pair; i.e., if U_k is a U(0, 1) random variable used *for a particular purpose* in the first run, we use $1 - U_k$ *for this same purpose* in the second run. [Recall that if $U \sim$ U(0, 1), then $1 - U \sim$ U(0, 1) as well.]

As with CRN, we can give an explicit mathematical rationale for AV. Suppose that we make n *pairs* of runs of the system resulting in observations $(X_1^{(1)}, X_1^{(2)}), \ldots, (X_n^{(1)}, X_n^{(2)})$ such that each pair is independent of every other pair; i.e., for $j_1 \neq j_2$, $X_{j_1}^{(l_1)}$ and $X_{j_2}^{(l_2)}$ are independent. (Note that the total number of simulation runs is $2n$.) For $j = 1, 2, \ldots, n$, let $X_j = (X_j^{(1)} + X_j^{(2)})/2$, and let $\overline{X}(n) = \sum_{j=1}^{n} X_j/n$ be the point estimator of $\mu = E(X_j^{(l)}) = E(X_j) = E[\overline{X}(n)]$. Then since the X_j's are IID random variables,

$$\text{Var}\left[\overline{X}(n)\right] = \frac{\text{Var}\left(X_j\right)}{n} = \frac{\text{Var}\left(X_j^{(1)}\right) + \text{Var}\left(X_j^{(2)}\right) + 2 \text{Cov}\left(X_j^{(1)}, X_j^{(2)}\right)}{4n}$$

If the two runs within a pair were made independently, then $\text{Cov}\,(X_j^{(1)}, X_j^{(2)}) = 0$. On the other hand, if we can indeed induce negative correlation between $X_j^{(1)}$ and $X_j^{(2)}$, then $\text{Cov}\,(X_j^{(1)}, X_j^{(2)}) < 0$, which reduces $\text{Var}\,[\overline{X}(n)]$, as desired. AV attempts to induce this desired negative correlation.

No general guarantee of the success of AV can be given; its feasibility and efficacy are perhaps even more model-dependent than for CRN. (In a few specific cases AV has been analytically shown to lead to variance reductions, although the magnitude of the reduction is usually not known; see Andréasson [1], George [11], Hammersley and Handscomb [12], Mitchell [27], and Wilson [33].) Furthermore, we cannot know beforehand how great a variance reduction might be achieved; a small pilot study like that described for CRN might be useful to get an idea whether or not AV is a good idea in a specific case. The basic requirement which the model must satisfy if AV is to be successful is that a large value of U_k used for a particular purpose in the model must have an effect on the final response opposite that realized if this U_k had happened to be small. Then, if U_k *is* large, $1 - U_k$ *will* be small, inducing the opposite effect in $X_j^{(2)}$ compared with the effect of the large U_k on $X_j^{(1)}$. Since we want this antithetic behavior of the U_k's to propagate initially to the random variables actually used to drive the model (such as interarrival and service times, and inventory interdemand times and demand sizes), the inverse-transform method (Sec. 7.2.1) is recommended for generating these random variables; if U_k is large, $Y^{(1)} = F^{-1}(U_k)$ will be large and $Y^{(2)} = F^{-1}(1 - U_k)$ will be small, since the inverse distribution function F^{-1} is monotone increasing. (Franta [7] gives examples of the failure of AV if other methods, such as acceptance-rejection, are used to generate random variables.) Furthermore, the final response should be, in some sense, monotone with respect to the input random variables; i.e., if Y is an input random variable (such as an interarrival time) and X is the response (such as an average delay in queue), then large and small values of Y should tend to make X large and small, respectively (or vice versa). If this monotonicity does not hold, AV might backfire, since *either* large *or* small Y could produce a large value of X, creating *positive* correlation. We can only urge the analyst to provide some kind of evidence that AV *will* work in a given case, either by arguing from "physical" properties of the model's structure or by initial experimentation.

Before giving examples of AV, we should make an important point which seems to have been omitted in many discussions of the technique. As we have implicitly emphasized in this section, if we use U_k for a particular purpose in the first run of a pair to obtain the final observation $X_j^{(1)}$, then $1 - U_k$ must be used for the *same* purpose in the antithetic simulation producing $X_j^{(2)}$. In other words, the use of the random numbers in the two runs producing the pair $(X_j^{(1)}, X_j^{(2)})$ must be *synchronized*. This presents many of the same potential difficulties inherent in synchronization in the use of CRN, and many of the same programming tricks (using separate random-number generators, judicious wasting of random numbers, storing the random variables, generating service requirements upon a customer's arrival in queueing systems) can be used for AV synchronization as well.

Finally, we can sometimes use partial AV (generating some random variables antithetically and others independently) if complete AV is too difficult to program or does not make sense physically (see Example 11.5).

Example 11.4 Consider the $M/M/1$ queue with $\rho = 0.9$, as in Example 11.1, where the first customer arrives at an empty and idle system, and we want to estimate the expected average delay in queue of the first 100 customers. (Thus, an "observation" $X_j^{(l)}$ is the average of the delays of the first 100 customers in a simulation run.) From the model's structure it is reasonably safe to assume that large interarrival times would tend to make $X_j^{(l)}$ smaller (and vice versa) and large service times would generally result in a larger $X_j^{(l)}$. Further, if we use the method of Sec. 7.3.2 to generate the exponential interarrival-time and service-time random variables, we would expect AV to induce the desired negative correlation between $X_j^{(l)}$ and $X_j^{(2)}$. We made $n = 100$ independent pairs of runs using both independent sampling within a pair [so Cov $(X_j^{(1)}, X_j^{(2)}) = 0$] and using AV [synchronization was maintained by generating the necessary U(0, 1) random variables ahead of time and storing them, although other methods could have been used]. Under independent sampling, our estimate of Var (X_j) was 6.355, while AV led to a variance estimate of 2.731; thus AV reduced the estimated variance by about 57 percent. Note that the extra cost of AV over independent sampling is negligible here, since AV requires almost no extra programming and only the subtraction of the U(0, 1) random variables from 1; both methods required 200 separate simulation runs. (Another type of "antithetic" sampling that can be used for simple queueing simulations is to generate the interarrival times in the second run of a pair using the U_k's that were used to generate the service times in the first run, and vice versa. Implementing this idea, due to Page [28], for the present $M/M/1$ model led to an estimated variance reduction of 65 percent compared with independent sampling. This general method of interchanging the use of random numbers might be useful in inducing negative correlation for other types of models as well.)

To illustrate the importance of proper synchronization in the antithetic use of U(0, 1) random variables, we made another set of $n = 100$ pairs of runs of this model, *without* taking care to maintain synchronization. That is, we made the second run of each pair by starting at the same point in the random-number sequence that was used for the first run but simply replaced the variable U in the subroutine EXPON (see Sec. 1.4.3) by 1. $-$ U immediately before taking the logarithm. Upon examination of the actual working of the program, we see that this scheme will guarantee *only* that synchronization is maintained in generating the time to the arrival of the first customer, the time between the first and second arrivals, and the service time of the first customer. After that point, the random-number streams will generally get mixed up; e.g., a particular U_k

might have been used in the first run to generate a service-time random variable, but (due to lack of synchronization) it is quite possible that $1 - U_k$ would be used to generate an interarrival time in the second run. This defeats the purpose of AV and in this case markedly decreases the realized variance reduction. Our estimate of Var (X_j) in this case is 4.478, which is only about a 30 percent variance reduction (with respect to the independent-sampling approach), compared with the 57 percent reduction obtained by properly synchronized AV.

We hope that this example will help dispel the notion that AV can be implemented by simply "replacing U by $1 - U$ everywhere in the program" and impress upon the reader the importance of synchronization in the use of the random numbers. In fact, it seems possible that for some models, ignoring synchronization in applying AV could result in no variance reduction at all or (worse) in actually *increasing* the variance.

> **Example 11.5** Although somewhat more work is required to see a physical rationale for the success of AV (see Prob. 11.2), it can also be applied to the inventory model of Sec. 1.5. Take the case $(s, S) = (20, 40)$, and assume the same parameters and output variables as in Example 11.3. Also as done in Example 11.3, we shall apply AV only to the interdemand times and to the demand sizes and generate the delivery lags independently between the two runs of a pair. Again we made $n = 100$ independent pairs of runs, first making $X_j^{(1)}$ and $X_j^{(2)}$ independent, and obtained 8.554 as an estimate of Var (X_j), whereas the variance estimate under AV was 3.260, a reduction of some 62 percent. Thus we see that AV was successful here even though we only applied it to some of the types of input random variables (interdemand times and demand sizes), and generated another type (delivery lags) independently.

We close this section with a word of caution on a seemingly good idea, that of using *both* AV *and* CRN when several alternative systems are to be compared. At first it would appear that we could obtain greater variance reduction by using AV for each system separately and CRN over the several systems. However, upon closer examination we can see that if both AV and CRN "work," i.e., induce correlations of the desired sign, certain "cross covariances" (specifically, the covariance between the first run of an antithetic pair of runs of system 1 and the second run of an antithetic pair of runs of system 2, and vice versa) enter the relevant variance expression with the *wrong* sign, which might *increase* the variance. (For details, see Kleijnen [18, pp. 207–238].) Thus, it is by no means clear that combining AV with CRN for comparing alternative systems is a good idea. More recently, Schruben and Margolin [31] have re-examined this issue in a more general experimental design context.

11.4 CONTROL VARIATES

Like CRN and AV, the method of *control variates* (CV) attempts to take advantage of correlation between certain random variables to obtain a variance reduction. Depending on the specific type of CV technique used, this correlation might arise naturally in the course of a simulation run, or be induced by using CRN in an auxillary simulation.

Let X be an output random variable and suppose we want to estimate $\mu =$

$E(X)$. (X might be the average of the delays of customers in a simulation run, for example.) Suppose that Y is another random variable which is believed to be correlated with X (either positively or negatively) and has *known* expectation $\nu = E(Y)$. Then the random variable $X_C = X - a(Y - \nu)$ is also an unbiased estimator of μ, for any real number a. Furthermore,

$$\text{Var } (X_C) = \text{Var } (X) + a^2 \text{ Var } (Y) - 2a \text{ Cov } (X, Y) \qquad (11.1)$$

so that X_C has a smaller variance than X if and only if

$$2a \text{ Cov } (X, Y) > a^2 \text{ Var } (Y)$$

The random variable Y is called a *control variate* for X since it partially "controls" X in the sense that it is correlated with X and has known expectation. The definition of X_C can be generalized if there are m control variates $Y_1, Y_2, \ldots, Y_m$ with respective known means $\nu_1, \nu_2, \ldots, \nu_m$, to

$$X_C = X - \sum_{l=1}^{m} a_l(Y_l - \nu_l)$$

where the a_l's are any real numbers. (The Y_l's may or may not be independent of each other.) In this general case,

$$\text{Var } (X_C) = \text{Var } (X) + \sum_{l=1}^{m} a_l^2 \text{ Var } (Y_l) - 2 \sum_{l=1}^{m} a_l \text{ Cov } (X, Y_l)$$

$$+ 2 \sum_{l_1=2}^{m} \sum_{l_2=1}^{l_1-1} a_{l_1} a_{l_2} \text{ Cov } (Y_{l_1}, Y_{l_2})$$

from which we can easily see when a variance reduction will occur.

It is evident from the above discussion that the two critical problems in applying the CV technique are those of finding good control variates, and of specifying the weights $a_1, a_2, \ldots, a_m$; we address these problems next.

Good control variates should be strongly correlated with X, either positively or negatively. Then if the observed value of Y_l is larger than the known constant ν_l, we have the information that the observed value of X is quite likely to be either above the unknown μ [if Cov $(X, Y_l) > 0$] or below μ [if Cov $(X, Y_l) < 0$], and the CV technique makes use of this information to obtain a variance reduction. Choosing Y_l's with this desirable strong correlation could be done based on an analysis of a model's structure or could rely on initial experimentation.

We can identify three general methods that have been used to obtain control variates, although other methods may be useful for a given model. First, the input random variables (such as interarrival times, service times, demand sizes, etc.), or simple functions of them, are possibilities, since their expectations will be known and analysis of the model's use of them could identify at least the sign of the correlation with the output random variable. For example, in the queueing problem of Example 11.4, the output from a single replication is $X = $ the average delay of the first 100 customers, and possible control variates are $Y_1 = $ the average of the interarrival times and Y_2 = the average of the service times; we would expect that Cov $(X, Y_1) < 0$ and Cov $(X, Y_2) > 0$. These kinds of control variates have been called *internal* or *concomitant* since they must be (essentially) generated anyway during the simulation to get an observed value of X and therefore add essentially nothing to the cost of the simulation. Detailed accounts of various kinds of internal CV applications can be found in Iglehart and Lewis [17], Lavenberg, Moeller, and Sauer [20], and Lavenberg, Moeller, and Welch [21, 22].

A second method of obtaining control variates, which we might call *external* control variates, is to simulate simultaneously a "similar" but analytically tractable system, *using* CRN, and use the corresponding output Y from the simulation of this second model as a control variate. By "analytically tractable" we mean specifically that $E(Y)$ can be computed exactly, and we hope that the "similarity" of the simpler model to the original one will induce positive correlation between Y and the random variable X observed from the original system (see Sec. 11.2 on CRN). Unlike internal CV, this approach is *not* costless since it involves a second simulation to get the control variate. Thus Cov (X, Y) will have to be larger than for internal CV to make external CV worthwhile. Examples of external CV can be found in Burt, Gaver, and Perlas [3], Gaver and Shedler [9], Gaver and Thompson [10], and in Prob. 11.10.

The third general method for obtaining control variates arises when we have several unbiased estimators of μ, say $X^{(1)}, X^{(2)}, \ldots, X^{(m)}$, where the $X^{(l)}$'s may or may not be independent. This might arise, for example, when we can use the method of indirect estimators as described in the following section. If $b_1, b_2, \ldots, b_m$ are any real numbers which sum to 1, then $X_C = \sum_{l=1}^{m} b_l X^{(l)}$ is also an unbiased estimator

of μ. However, since $b_1 = 1 - \sum_{l=2}^{m} b_l$, we can express X_C as

$$X_C = \left(1 - \sum_{l=2}^{m} b_l \right) X^{(1)} + \sum_{l=2}^{m} b_l X^{(l)} = X^{(1)} - \sum_{l=2}^{m} b_l (X^{(1)} - X^{(l)})$$

so that we can view $Y_l = X^{(1)} - X^{(l)}$ for $l = 2, 3, \ldots, m$ as $m - 1$ control variates for the estimator $X^{(1)}$.

We now turn to the question of how the weights a_l should be specified. For simplicity, we assume that $m = 1$; that is, that there is only one control variate Y, and $X_C = X - a(Y - \nu)$. The methods for $m > 1$ are quite similar in essence but somewhat more involved in implementation, and we recommend Lavenberg and Welch [24] for a good exposition of the general case. In many treatments of CV, only the special cases $a = 1$ [if it is believed that Cov $(X, Y) > 0$] or $a = -1$ [if Cov $(X, Y) < 0$] are considered, but this requires that $|\text{Cov} (X, Y)| > \text{Var} (Y)/2$ for a variance reduction. Thus, simply setting $a = \pm 1$ places the entire burden for success upon the choice of Y; by allowing other values for a we can do better. From (11.1) the *optimal* value of a, that is, the one which minimizes Var (X_C), is

$$a^* = \frac{\text{Cov} (X, Y)}{\text{Var} (Y)} \tag{11.2}$$

(see Prob. 11.8), and for $a = a^*$ we get

$$\text{Var}(X_C) = \text{Var}(X) - \frac{[\text{Cov}(X, Y)]^2}{\text{Var}(Y)} = (1 - \rho_{XY}^2)\,\text{Var}(X)$$

where ρ_{XY} is the correlation between X and Y. Thus we *always* get a variance reduction with the optimal value of a provided that X and Y are *at all* correlated, and the reduction is greater if this correlation is stronger. Unfortunately, however, we generally cannot calculate $\text{Cov}(X, Y)$ and $\text{Var}(Y)$, so that a^* will not be known. Accordingly, several methods have been proposed for estimating a^* from the simulations. We next describe one of the simpler of these methods, which also culminates in a confidence interval for μ (see [22, 24]). [As stated, the method applies to terminating simulations where the basic approach is that of independent replications (see Sec. 8.2), although it might also be applicable to steady-state simulations by replacing the replication observations by batch means.]

The method essentially replaces $\text{Cov}(X, Y)$ and $\text{Var}(Y)$ in (11.2) by their sample equivalents. Suppose we make n independent replications to obtain the n IID observations $X_1, X_2, \ldots, X_n$ on X and the n IID observations $Y_1, Y_2, \ldots, Y_n$ on the control variate Y. Let

$$\bar{X}(n) = \frac{\sum_{j=1}^{n} X_j}{n}, \qquad \bar{Y}(n) = \frac{\sum_{j=1}^{n} Y_j}{n}, \qquad \hat{C}_{XY}(n) = \frac{\sum_{j=1}^{n} [X_j - \bar{X}(n)][Y_j - \bar{Y}(n)]}{n - 1},$$

and

$$\hat{\sigma}_Y^2(n) = \frac{\sum_{j=1}^{n} [Y_j - \bar{Y}(n)]^2}{n - 1}$$

[see Eq. (4.8)]. Then the estimator for a^* is

$$\hat{a}^*(n) = \frac{\hat{C}_{XY}(n)}{\hat{\sigma}_Y^2(n)}$$

and the final point estimator for μ is

$$\bar{X}_C(n) = \bar{X}(n) - \hat{a}^*(n)[\bar{Y}(n) - \nu]$$

Immediately we must note that $\bar{X}_C(n)$ need *not* be unbiased for μ, since $\hat{a}^*(n)$ and $\bar{Y}(n)$ are generally not independent. (Alternative estimators of a^* based on jackknifing, which reduce the bias of the final point estimator, are discussed by Kleijnen [18] and in [22].) The severity of this bias, as well as the variance reduction which might be obtained from this scheme, are investigated in [22]. For $m > 1$ (multiple control variates) the optimal values of $a_1, a_2, \ldots, a_m$ can similarly be estimated as the least-squares estimators of the coefficients in a certain linear-regression model; indeed, the CV technique is sometimes called *regression sampling*.

Example 11.6 As mentioned earlier in this section, averages of interarrival or service times can serve as internal control variates in simple queueing models, such as the $M/M/1$ queue with $\rho = 0.9$. Again, we wish to estimate $\mu = $ the expected average delay in queue of the first 100 customers, where the initial conditions are empty and idle. We made $n = 10$ independent replications, and observed X_j = the average of the 100 delays and Y_j = the average of all generated interarrival times, on the jth replication. Applying the above procedure to estimate a^*, we obtained $\overline{X}(10) = 4.497$, $\overline{Y}(10) = 0.998$, $\hat{C}_{XY}(10) = -0.264$ (confirming our feeling that the average delay should be negatively correlated with the average interarrival time), $\hat{\sigma}_Y^2(10) = 0.015$, so that $\hat{a}^*(10) = -17.600$ and $\overline{X}_C(10) = 4.462$, since the expected interarrival time is 1. To see whether Var $[\overline{X}_C(10)]$ is smaller than Var $[\overline{X}(10)]$, we replicated this set of 10 simulations 100 times to estimate these variances, as well as the expected value of $\overline{X}_C(10)$. [$\overline{X}(10)$ is unbiased for μ, which is actually 4.134.] Our estimate of Var $[\overline{X}(10)]$ was 0.873, whereas we estimated Var $[\overline{X}_C(10)]$ to be 0.583, a reduction of 33 percent. However, from these same runs we estimated $E[\overline{X}_C(10)]$ to be 3.941 ± 0.150 (with 95 percent confidence), indicating that by estimating a^* by $\hat{a}^*(10)$ we have introduced some bias into the estimator $\overline{X}_C(10)$. (See [22] for an assessment of the impact of this biasing effect on confidence-interval coverage; it did not appear to be troublesome in the experiments reported there.)

Other internal control variates could have been used in Example 11.6; see Prob. 11.9.

11.5 INDIRECT ESTIMATION

This VRT has been developed for $GI/G/s$ queueing simulations and for some tandem queues (queues in series) when the quantities to be estimated are steady-state measures of performance, such as d, w, Q, and L (see Appendix 1B.). Proofs that variance reductions are obtained have been given for these systems (see Law [25, 26], Carson [4], and Carson and Law [5]), but the idea might be applicable to other models as well; again, initial experimentation could reveal whether worthwhile variance reductions are being experienced. The basic tool is use of the theoretical relations between d, w, Q, and L given in Appendix 1B.

Let D_i and W_i be, respectively, the delay in queue and the total wait in system of the ith customer arriving at a $GI/G/s$ queue. Thus, if S_i is the service time of the ith customer, $W_i = D_i + S_i$. Also, let $Q(t)$ and $L(t)$ be, respectively, the number of customers in queue and in system at time t. From a simulation run in which n customers complete their service and which lasts for T units of simulated time, the *direct estimators* of d, w, Q, and L, respectively, are

$$\hat{d}(n) = \frac{\sum_{i=1}^{n} D_i}{n}, \qquad \hat{w}(n) = \frac{\sum_{i=1}^{n} W_i}{n}, \qquad \hat{Q}(n) = \frac{\int_0^T Q(t)\,dt}{T},$$

and
$$\hat{L}(n) = \frac{\int_0^T L(t)\,dt}{T}$$

Now $\hat{w}(n) = \hat{d}(n) + \overline{S}(n)$, where $\overline{S}(n) = \sum_{i=1}^{n} S_i/n$, and $E[\overline{S}(n)] = E(S)$, the expected service time, which would be known in a simulation. Thus, an alternative estimator of w might be

$$\tilde{w}(n) = \hat{d}(n) + E(S)$$

i.e., we replace the estimate $\overline{S}(n)$ by its *known* expectation $E(S)$. $\tilde{w}(n)$ is called an *indirect estimator* of w, and it seems reasonable to suspect that $\tilde{w}(n)$ might be less variable than $\hat{w}(n)$, since the random term $\overline{S}(n)$ in $\hat{w}(n)$ is replaced by the fixed number $E(S)$ to obtain $\tilde{w}(n)$. For any $GI/G/s$ queue and for any n, this is indeed the case, as shown in [25]. [The proof is not as simple as it might seem, since $\overline{S}(n)$ and $\hat{d}(n)$ are not independent.] Thus, the indirect estimator $\tilde{w}(n)$ is better than the more obvious direct estimator.

The variance reduction of the previous paragraph is suggested by the equation $w = d + E(S)$. Other equations that suggest indirect estimators of Q and L are

$$Q = \lambda d \tag{11.3}$$

and

$$L = \lambda w \tag{11.4}$$

where λ is the arrival rate (see Appendix 1B), which would again be known in a simulation. An indirect estimator of Q, as suggested by (11.3), is

$$\tilde{Q}(n) = \lambda \hat{d}(n)$$

and it is shown in [4, 5] that *asymptotically* (as the length of the simulation, and thus n and T, becomes large) $\tilde{Q}(n)$ has a smaller variance than the direct estimator $\hat{Q}(n)$. Similarly, using (11.4) and the superior indirect estimator $\tilde{w}(n)$ of w, we can show that the indirect estimator

$$\tilde{L}(n) = \lambda \tilde{w}(n) = \lambda[\hat{d}(n) + E(S)]$$

asymptotically has a smaller variance than $\hat{L}(n)$. Thus, we see that it is better to estimate w, Q, and L by deterministic functions of $\hat{d}(n)$ than to estimate them directly. (This is why we have emphasized estimation of the delay in queue in our examples.) An additional advantage of indirect estimation is that only the delays D_1, D_2, ... and not W_i, $Q(t)$, or $L(t)$ need to be collected in the simulation, even if we really want to estimate w, Q, or L.

Example 11.7 The exact asymptotic variance reductions obtained by estimating Q (for example) indirectly with $\tilde{Q}(n)$ rather than directly with $\hat{Q}(n)$ can be calculated for $M/G/1$ queues (see [25]). Table 11.3 gives these reductions (in percent) for exponential, 4-Erlang, and hyperexponential (see [25]) service times and for $\rho = 0.5, 0.7,$ and 0.9.

One possible weakness of the above indirect estimation technique is that as ρ approaches 1, the variance reductions evidently diminish toward 0. (This was shown in [25] for the $M/G/1$ queue.) A more general use of indirect estimators developed in [4], which is related to techniques devised by Heidelberger [14], does better for ρ near 1 and generally achieves greater variance reductions. Again taking the example of estimating Q, we note that we have two estimators, namely $\hat{Q}$ and $\tilde{Q}$ (we drop n from the notation for convenience). This leads to the possibility of forming an

Table 11.3 Exact asymptotic variance reductions for indirect estimation of Q, $M/G/1$ **queue**

Service-time distribution	Reduction, %		
	$\rho = 0.5$	$\rho = 0.7$	$\rho = 0.9$
Exponential	15	11	4
4-Erlang	22	17	7
Hyperexponential	4	3	2

estimator using *both* $\hat{Q}$ and $\tilde{Q}$, defined as

$$Q(a_1, a_2) = a_1 \hat{Q} + a_2 \tilde{Q}$$

where $a_1 + a_2 = 1$. (a_1 and a_2 need *not* satisfy any other constraints, such as non-negativity.) Then a_1 and a_2 could be chosen to minimize Var $[Q(a_1, a_2)]$ subject to the constraint that $a_1 + a_2 = 1$. Note that $Q(1, 0) = \hat{Q}$ and $Q(0, 1) = \tilde{Q}$, so that this *linear-combination technique* includes both direct and indirect estimation as special cases. Thus, for the optimal (a_1, a_2), Var $[Q(a_1, a_2)]$ will be at least as small as the variance of $\hat{Q}$ or of $\tilde{Q}$. As with the method of control variates, the difficulty is in estimating the optimal (a_1, a_2). Carson [4] gives an asymptotically valid way to do this, based on the regenerative method, and also considers the general case of more than two alternative estimators; his theoretical and empirical studies indicate that variance reductions of at least 40 percent, in comparison with direct estimators, were often achieved.

11.6 CONDITIONAL EXPECTATIONS

The final VRT we consider, that of *conditioning,* is aimed at exploiting some special property of a model's structure so that we can sometimes replace an estimate of a quantity by its true, theoretical value. In removing this source of random fluctuation, we hope that the variance of the final output random variable will be reduced, although there can be no absolute guarantee of a variance reduction; again, pilot studies comparing the conditioning technique with a straightforward sampling approach could indicate whether (and to what extent) the estimated variance is being reduced. Since this VRT is highly model-dependent, we cannot give any general discussion of how it can be accomplished or how effective it may be. The general conditioning technique as we shall discuss it is in the same spirit as the "conditional Monte Carlo technique" used in Monte Carlo simulation (see Hammersley and Handscomb [12]).

Suppose that Z is an output random variable of interest (such as a delay in queue of a customer) and we seek to estimate $\mu = E(Z)$. Suppose that there is some other random variable Y such that we can calculate (exactly) the *conditional* expectation $E(Z|Y = y)$ for any real number y. [Note that $E(Z|Y = y)$ is a function of the real number y, whereas $E(Z|Y)$ is a random variable.] Then $\mu = E(Z) = E[E(Z|Y)]$, so that the random variable $E(Z|Y)$ is unbiased for μ. Further,

$$\text{Var } [E(Z|Y)] = \text{Var } (Z) - E[\text{Var } (Z|Y)] \le \text{Var } (Z) \qquad (11.5)$$

(see Ross [29, p. 108]), indicating that observing $E(Z|Y)$ (as computed analytically from the random variable Y) instead of direct observation of Z will result in a smaller variance. The trick, of course, is specifying a Y so that $E(Z|Y)$ *can* be computed (one would hope efficiently) and so that $E[\text{Var } (Z|Y)]$ is large. The situation is further complicated by the fact that (11.5) will not generally be applicable to the *final* output random variables (such as an average of customers' delays) due to autocorrelation in the simulation output, so that a variance reduction is not guaranteed.

Since this VRT is so heavily model-dependent, we illustrate it by describing successful implementations which have been reported in the literature. The following example, taken from Lavenberg and Welch [23], illustrates the use of conditioning to obtain variance reductions in estimates of several expected delays in a queueing network.

Example 11.8 We consider a model of a time-shared computer system which has both similarities to, and differences with, the model of Sec. 2.4. There is a single central processing unit (CPU) and 15 terminals, as well as a disk drive and a tape drive, as shown in Fig. 11.1. Each terminal is occupied by a user who "thinks" for an amount of time which is an exponential random variable with mean 100 seconds and then sends a job to the computer, where it joins a FIFO queue at the CPU (unless the CPU is idle, in which case the job immediately begins service). Each job entering the CPU occupies it for an amount of time which is an exponential random variable S_C with mean 1 second. Upon leaving the CPU, a job is either finished (with probability 0.20, independent of the system state) and returns to its terminal to begin another think time, or requires data from the disk drive (with probability 0.72), or needs some data stored on tape (with probability 0.08). If a job leaving the CPU is sent to the disk drive, it may have to join a FIFO queue there until the disk drive is free; the service time at the disk drive is an exponential random variable S_D with mean 1.39 seconds. Upon finishing disk service the job queues up again at the CPU. A job leaving the CPU bound for the tape drive has an experience similar to a disk job, except that the service time

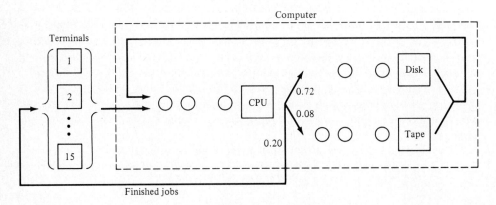

Figure 11.1 Another time-shared computer model.

at the tape drive is an exponential random variable S_T with mean 12.5 seconds. All service times and think times are independent, and all jobs are initially in the think state at their terminals. The goal is to estimate d_C, d_D, and d_T, which are the steady-state average delays in queue at, respectively, the CPU, disk drive, and tape drive. Straightforward simulation could be used to obtain estimates of d_C, d_D, and d_T by simply taking the average of the delays actually experienced by jobs in the queues for the CPU, disk drive, and tape drive, respectively. Thus, the number of jobs used in the estimate of d_T, for example, is the number of jobs which were actually sent to the tape drive from the CPU, which is only about 8 percent of the number of jobs that leave the CPU.

We can obtain a different estimate of d_T by observing the total number N_T of jobs (in queue and in service) at the tape drive at the instant that *each* job leaves the CPU, no matter where this job will eventually go. Then *given* that this job just leaving the CPU will go to the tape drive, its expected delay in queue at the tape drive is $E(S_T)N_T = 12.5N_T$ seconds. (Since the job in service, if any, has an exponential service time, its remaining service time has this same exponential distribution; see Appendix 8A. Conditioning is still possible for nonexponential service times but requires more information; see [23].) In this way we get information on d_T for *every* job that leaves the CPU, not just the 8 percent that actually go to the tape drive, so that averaging the values of $12.5N_T$ over all jobs leaving the CPU includes many more terms. Further, we use the true value of $E(S_T)$ rather than values of the random variable S_T that would be generated in the straightforward simulation.

A better estimate of d_D can be obtained exactly as in the previous paragraph, and simultaneously. (That is, *each* job exiting from the CPU is used to estimate *both* d_T *and* d_D by observing both N_T and N_D = the total number of jobs at the disk drive at the instant that a job leaves the CPU.) This will also increase the number of observations but not as dramatically as for the estimate of d_T; we still can expect to do better, however, by using $1.39N_D$ instead of the sum of N_D IID observations of S_D. Finally, by conditioning on N_C = the total number of jobs at the CPU when a job leaves either its terminal, the disk drive, or the tape drive, we can average the values of $1N_C$ to try to get a better estimate of d_C; we do not obtain any more terms in the average but still can exploit knowledge of the expected CPU service time.

Lavenberg and Welch made 100 independent simulation runs (each lasting until 400 jobs had been processed and returned to their terminals) and estimated each of d_C, d_D, and d_T by both straightforward sampling and the conditional methods outlined above; they obtained estimated variance reductions of 19, 28, and 56 percent respectively. (The extra computing time needed for the conditional methods was negligible.) As expected, the greatest variance reduction was for the estimate of d_T, since the tape drive was used in the straightforward simulation very infrequently. (Lavenberg and Welch also simulated seven other versions of this system and estimated second moments as well; estimated variance reductions were always experienced and ranged between 9 and 86 percent depending on the particular model and the quantity being estimated.)

As the preceding example shows, the use of conditioning as a VRT requires careful analysis of the probabilistic aspects of a model's structure. Also, the VRT's success was evidently due in part to increasing the number of observations on a "rare" event (a job's requiring service at the tape drive) artificially, as well as to replacing observed values on the service-time random variables by their known expectations. These two factors are also important in the success of using conditional expectations in the following example, due to Carter and Ignall [6].

Example 11.9 A simulation model was developed to compare alternative policies for dispatching fire trucks to fires in the Bronx. Certain fires are classified as "serious," since there is considerable danger that lives will be lost and property damage will be high unless the fire department is able to respond quickly with enough fire trucks. The goal of the simulation was to estimate the expected response time to a serious fire under a given dispatching policy.

Historical data indicated that about 1 out of every 30 fires is serious. Thus, the model would have to progress through about 30 simulated fires to get a single observation on the response time to a serious fire, which could lead to very long and expensive runs to generate enough serious fires to get a good estimate of the desired expected response time. However, the model's specific structure was such that, given the state of the system (the location of all fire trucks) at any instant, the *true* expected response time to a serious fire could be calculated, should one occur at that instant. Furthermore, the probabilistic assumptions (in particular, serious fires were assumed to occur in accordance with a Poisson process) enabled the simulators to condition on the event of a serious fire's occurring at *every* instant when the system state was observed regardless of whether or not a serious fire actually *did* occur, without introducing bias. Thus, the simulation was simply interrupted periodically to observe the system state, and the expected response time to a serious fire, given the current state, was calculated and recorded, and the simulation was resumed. The final estimator was the average of these conditional expected response times and included many more terms than the number of serious fires actually simulated.

Carter and Ignall found that the conditional-expectation approach reduced the estimated variance of their estimator by about 95 percent in comparison with the straightforward estimator. Computationally, however, the conditional expectation approach was more expensive, so that for the same computing cost the variance reduction was about 92 percent.

There are several other examples of using the conditioning approach as a VRT which might be helpful. Carter and Ignall [6] also consider an inventory model, where the event on which conditioning occurs is a shortage, which occurred infrequently but had a large impact on system performance when it did occur. Burt and Garman [2] considered simulation of stochastic PERT networks and conditioned on certain task times which were common to more than one path through the network; in their use of conditioning, the concept of a rare event is not present. Further VRTs based on conditioning in stochastic network simulations are discussed by Garman [8] and by Sigal, Pritsker, and Solberg [32].

PROBLEMS

11.1 Consider the queueing model depicted in Fig. 11.2. Customers arrive according to a Poisson process with rate 1 per minute and must all be served by the first server, where service times are IID exponential random variables with mean 0.7 minute; the queueing discipline is FIFO. When a customer finishes service at the first server, he leaves the system with probability p, independent of the state of the system, and requires a second stage of service with probability $1 - p$. The service times at the second server are IID exponential random variables with mean 0.9 minute, and the second-stage queue is also FIFO. All service times and interarrival times are independent of each other, and the initial conditions are empty and idle. The measure of performance is the expected average total delay in queue of the first 100 customers. (If a customer visits the second server, his total delay is the sum of his delays in the two queues; if a customer leaves the system after being served by the first server, his total delay is just his delay in the first queue.)

(*a*) Consider comparison of two such systems, where p is either 0.3 or 0.8. Make 10 replications of each system using both independent sampling and CRN, and compare the estimated variances of the resulting estimate of the difference between the measures of performance. Take care to maintain proper synchronization when using CRN.

(*b*) For $p = 0.3$, make five pairs of runs using both independent sampling and AV within a pair, and compare the estimated variances of the estimated measure of performance. Again, pay attention to synchronization.

11.2 Recall the inventory model of Sec. 1.5, as used in Example 11.5 to illustrate the use of AV. There

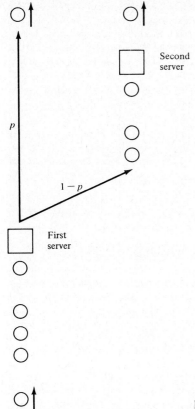

Figure 11.2 The queueing model of Prob. 11.1.

are three types of input random variables (interdemand times, demand sizes, and delivery lags), and three types of costs (ordering, holding, and shortage). Analyze this model, as programmed in Sec. 1.5.2, to provide a rationale for the use of AV. Specifically, see what the effect of a small (or large) U(0, 1) random variable would be on each of the three types of costs if it is used to generate each of the three types of input random variables. For example, suppose that a small U is used to generate an interdemand time. Would this tend to make the ordering cost generally large or small?

11.3 Recall the bank model of Sec. 2.5, and suppose that the bank's management would like an estimate of the effect of adding a sixth teller *and* of adding a seventh teller (in comparison with the current configuration of five tellers) which is more reliable than the results in Fig. 2.25. Use CRN to do this, and make enough replications of the three systems to obtain what you feel are accurate estimates of the differences in the expectations of the average delays in queue. *Hint:* Consider generating the customer service time when the customer arrives (rather than enters service).

11.4 For the harbor model of Prob. 2.4, discuss the following issues:

(*a*) Consider using AV for the model as stated originally. Specifically, which input random variables should be generated antithetically, and how could proper synchronization be maintained?

(*b*) Suppose that thought is being given to replacing the two existing cranes with two faster cranes, which would have the result that the time for one crane to unload a ship would be uniformly distributed between 0.2 and 1.0 day; everything else remains the same. Discuss the proper application and implementation of CRN to compare the original system with the proposed new one.

11.5 Discuss the use of CRN to compare job-processing policies (*a*) and (*b*) for the computer model of Prob. 2.6.

11.6 For the two priority policies in the computer model of Prob. 2.8, use CRN to sharpen the comparison between the expected average delay in queue under each policy.

11.7 Consider two $M/G/1$ queues with exponential service times in the first queue and gamma service times in the second queue. Discuss problems of synchronization of the basic U(0, 1) random variables in implementing CRN to compare these two queues on the basis, say, of the expected average delay of the first 100 customers given empty and idle initial conditions. Sections 7.2.1 and 7.3.4 may be of use.

11.8 Derive the expression in (11.2) for a^*, the optimal weight when using a single control variate. Show directly that Var (X_C) is made at least as small by choosing $a = a^*$ rather than $a = 0$, $a = 1$, or $a = -1$.

***11.9** In Example 11.6, we used the average of the interarrival times as a control variate. Repeat the study of that example, i.e., use $n = 10$ replications and estimate the optimal weight and repeat this set of 10 replications 100 times, for each of the following two internal control variates in place of the average interarrival time:

    (*a*) The average of the service times

    (*b*) The difference between the average service time and average interarrival time

    Which of the three control variates results in the largest variance reduction? Using the fact that the true μ is 4.134, comment on the bias in $\overline{X}_C(10)$ for each type of control variate.

***11.10** Suppose we want to estimate the expected average delay in queue of the first 100 customers in a FIFO $M/G/1$ queue where the initial conditions are empty and idle, the mean interarrival time is 1 minute, and service times have a Weibull distribution with shape parameter $\alpha = 2$ and scale parameter $\beta = 1.8/\sqrt{\pi}$ minutes. Thus, the mean service time is $\beta\Gamma[(1/\alpha) + 1] = (1.8/\sqrt{\pi})(\sqrt{\pi}/2) = 0.9$ minute, and the utilization factor is $\rho = 0.9$. (Recall that Weibull random variables can easily be generated by the inverse-transform method, as discussed in Sec. 7.3.5.) As an external control variate, we could use CRN to simulate the $M/M/1$ queue for 100 customers with the same mean interarrival and service times, which is precisely the model of Example 11.6, and use the fact that the *known* expected average delay in queue for this $M/M/1$ queue is 4.134. Use the estimation technique given in Sec. 11.4 to estimate the optimal weight a^* from $n = 10$ replications, and repeat the whole process 100 times to see the extent of the variance reduction in comparison with straightforward simulation of this $M/G/1$ queue. Is the variance reduction worthwhile, or should the computing time that is needed to simulate the $M/M/1$ queue be devoted to making additional direct replications of the $M/G/1$ queue?

***11.11** Discuss proper use of AV for the time-shared computer model of Sec. 2.4. For alternative designs of this model (such as buying a faster CPU or changing the service quantum), how could CRN be appropriately applied for making comparative simulations?

REFERENCES

1. Andréasson, I. J.: Antithetic Methods in Queueing Simulations, *R. Inst. Technol. Dept. Comput. Sci. Tech. Rep.* NA 72.58, Stockholm, 1972.
2. Burt, J. M., Jr., and M. B. Garman: Conditional Monte Carlo: A Simulation Technique for Stochastic Network Analysis, *Manage. Sci.,* **18:** 207–217 (1971).
3. Burt, J. M., Jr., D. P. Gaver, and M. Perlas: Simple Stochastic Networks: Some Problems and Procedures, *Nav. Res. Logist. Q.,* **17:** 439–459 (1970).
4. Carson, J. S.: Variance Reduction Techniques for Simulated Queueing Processes, *Univ. Wis. Dept. Ind. Eng. Tech. Rep.* 78-8, Madison, 1978.
5. Carson, J. S., and A. M. Law: Conservation Equations and Variance Reduction in Queueing Simulations, *Oper. Res.,* **28:** 535–546 (1980).
6. Carter, G., and E. J. Ignall: Virtual Measures: A Variance Reduction Technique for Simulation, *Manage. Sci.,* **21:** 607–616 (1975).
7. Franta, W. R.: A Note on Random Variate Generators and Antithetic Sampling, *INFOR,* **13:** 112–117 (1975).

8. Garman, M. B.: More on Conditioned Sampling in the Simulation of Stochastic Networks, *Manage. Sci.,* **19:** 90–95 (1972).

9. Gaver, D. P., and G. S. Shedler: Control Variable Methods in the Simulation of a Model of a Multiprogrammed Computer System, *Nav. Res. Logist. Q.,* **18:** 435–450 (1971).

10. Gaver, D. P., and G. L. Thompson: *Programming and Probability Models,* Wadsworth, Monterey, Calif., 1973.

11. George, L. L.: Variance Reduction for a Replacement Process, *Simulation,* **29:** 65–74 (1977).

12. Hammersley, J. M., and D. C. Handscomb: *Monte Carlo Methods,* Methuen, London, 1964.

13. Hammersley, J. M., and K. W. Morton: A New Monte Carlo Technique: Antithetic Variates, *Proc. Camb. Phil. Soc.,* **52:** 449–475 (1956).

14. Heidelberger, P.: Variance Reduction Techniques for the Simulation of Markov Processes, I: Multiple Estimates, *Stanford Univ. Dept. Oper. Res. Tech. Rep.* 42, Stanford, Calif., 1977.

15. Heidelberger, P., and D. L. Iglehart: Comparing Stochastic Systems Using Regenerative Simulation with Common Random Numbers, *Adv. Appl. Prob.,* **11:** 804–819 (1979).

16. Heikes, R. G., D. C. Montgomery, and R. L. Rardin: Using Common Random Numbers in Simulation Experiments—An Approach to Statistical Analysis, *Simulation,* **25:** 81–85 (1976).

17. Iglehart, D. L., and P. A. W. Lewis: Regenerative Simulation with Internal Controls, *J. Ass. Comput. Mach.,* **26:** 271–282 (1979).

18. Kleijnen, J. P. C.: *Statistical Techniques in Simulation,* pt. I, Dekker, New York, 1974.

19. Kleijnen, J. P. C.: Analysis of Simulation with Common Random Numbers: A Note on Heikes et al. (1976), Version 2, *Katholieke Hogeschool Fac. Econ. Wet. Tech. Rep.* 79.095, Tilburg, Netherlands, 1979.

20. Lavenberg, S. S., T. L. Moeller, and C. H. Sauer: Concomitant Control Variables Applied to the Regenerative Simulation of Queueing Systems, *Oper. Res.,* **27:** 134–160 (1979).

21. Lavenberg, S. S., T. L. Moeller, and P. D. Welch: Control Variables Applied to the Simulation of Queueing Models of Computer Systems, *IBM Res. Rep.* RC 6630, Yorktown Heights, N.Y., 1977.

22. Lavenberg, S. S., T. L. Moeller, and P. D. Welch: Statistical Results on Multiple Control Variables with Application to Variance Reduction in Queueing Network Simulation, *IBM Res. Rep.* RC 7423, Yorktown Heights, N.Y., 1978.

23. Lavenberg, S. S., and P. D. Welch: Using Conditional Expectation to Reduce Variance in Discrete Event Simulation, *Proc. 1979 Winter Simul. Conf., San Diego, Calif., 1979,* pp. 291–294.

24. Lavenberg, S. S., and P. D. Welch: A Perspective on the Use of Control Variables to Increase the Efficiency of Monte Carlo Simulations, *IBM Res. Rep.* RC 8161, Yorktown Heights, N.Y., 1980.

25. Law, A. M.: Efficient Estimators for Simulated Queueing Systems, *Univ. Calif. Oper. Res. Cent.* ORC 74-7, Berkeley, 1974.

26. Law, A. M.: Efficient Estimators for Simulated Queueing Systems, *Manage. Sci.,* **22:** 30–41 (1975).

27. Mitchell, B.: Variance Reduction by Antithetic Variates in $GI/G/1$ Queueing Simulations, *Oper. Res.,* **21:** 988–997 (1973).

28. Page, E. S.: On Monte Carlo Methods in Congestion Problems: II. Simulation of Queueing Systems, *Oper. Res.,* **13:** 300–305 (1965).

29. Ross, S. M.: *Introduction to Probability Models,* 2d ed. Academic, New York, 1980.

30. Schruben, L. W.: Designing Correlation Induction Strategies for Simulation Experiments, chap. 16 in N. R. Adam and A. Dogramaci (eds.), *Current Issues in Computer Simulation,* Academic, New York, 1979.

31. Schruben, L. W., and B. H. Margolin: Pseudorandom Number Assignment in Statistically Designed Simulation and Distribution Sampling Experiments, *J. Am. Statist. Ass.,* **73:** 504–520 (1978).

32. Sigal, C. E., A. A. B. Pritsker, and J. J. Solberg: The Use of Cutsets in Monte Carlo Analysis of Stochastic Networks, *Math. Comput. Simul.,* **21:** 376–384 (1979).

33. Wilson, J. R.: Proof of the Antithetic-Variates Theorem for Unbounded Functions, *Math. Proc. Camb. Phil. Soc.,* **86:** 477–479 (1979).

34. Wright, R. D., and T. E. Ramsay, Jr.: On the Effectiveness of Common Random Numbers, *Manage. Sci.,* **25:** 649–656 (1979).

TWELVE

EXPERIMENTAL DESIGN AND OPTIMIZATION

12.1 INTRODUCTION

This chapter provides an introduction to the use of statistical experimental design and optimization techniques when the "experiment" is the execution of a computer simulation model. As in Chap. 9, we shall be discussing simulation of alternative system designs and examining and comparing the results from these simulations. In Chap. 9, however, we assumed that the various alternative systems were simply *given*, having been externally specified as *the* alternatives (perhaps based on physical constraints or political considerations). This chapter, on the other hand, deals with a situation in which there is less structure in the goal of the simulation study; we might want to learn about how the various parameters and particular structural assumptions affect a measure of performance for a model, or which set of model specifications appears to lead to optimal performance. For these broader (and more ambitious) objectives, we generally shall not be able to carry out formal statistical analyses like those of Chap. 9 or make such formal probabilistic statements at the end of our analyses.

In the terminology of experimental design, the (input) parameters and particular structural assumptions composing a model are called *factors,* and the (output) measure of performance is called the *response*. Factors can be either quantitative or qualitative. *Quantitative factors* are those which naturally assume numerical values, e.g., the number of tellers in a bank or the maximum delivery lag in an inventory system. *Qualitative factors* typically represent structural assumptions in a model which do not have a natural numerical meaning, such as the queue discipline, e.g., FIFO or LIFO, or the disposition of demands in excess of on-hand inventory, e.g., sales lost or put on back order. In simulation experiments we can also classify factors as being controllable or uncontrollable. *Controllable factors* represent policy options available to the managers of the real-world system being modeled, e.g., the number of tellers and the queue discipline. *Uncontrollable factors,* while still being inputs to the model and thus generally having an effect on the response, cannot be manipulated in the real-world system at will by management; arrival rates or mean demand sizes are examples of uncontrollable factors. Usually we shall focus on controllable factors in simulation experiments, since they are most relevant to decisions which must be made about implementation of a real-world system. However, Biles [2] has pointed out that uncontrollable factors might also be of interest in simulation experiments; e.g., we might want to assess how an abrupt increase in the arrival rate of customers would affect the expected average delay in queue. In a given model, the decision as to which parameters and structural assumptions are considered fixed aspects of the model and which are the experimental factors depends on the goals of the study, rather than on the inherent form of the model.

In the simulation context, *experimental design* provides a way of deciding beforehand which particular system variants to simulate so that the desired information can be obtained at minimal cost, i.e., with the least amount of simulating. Carefully thought-out, or "designed," experiments are thus much more efficient than a "hit-or-miss" sequence of runs in which we simply "try" a number of alternative systems unsystematically to see what happens. The designs we discuss in Secs. 12.2 and 12.3 are particularly useful in the early stages of experimentation when we are pretty much in the dark about which factors are important and how they might affect the response. As we learn more about the behavior of a model (in particular, which factors really matter and how they appear to be affecting the response), we may want to move on and become more precise in our goals; specifically, one often seeks to find the *optimal* combination of factor specifications (where the response is either maximized or minimized). A whole variety of techniques known as *response-surface methodologies* can then be used to make progress toward finding this optimum; we briefly discuss this topic in Sec. 12.4.

This chapter is by no means intended to be a complete treatment of experimental design and optimization; whole books are devoted to this subject. We only hope to make the reader aware of the existence of these kinds of techniques and strongly recommend that readers consult some of the many excellent books on the general topic of experimental design or response-surface methodology before proceeding with an involved and expensive simulation study. These books include, for example, Box, Hunter, and Hunter [5], Cochran and Cox [6], Davies [7], Hicks [8], John [11], Montgomery [14], and Myers [17].

Although one can think of simulation "experiments" as just a certain kind of experimentation in general, there are some peculiarities about simulation which distinguish it from the usual "physical" industrial, laboratory, or agricultural experiments traditionally used as examples in the experimental-design literature. In simulation, we have much more control over the experimental conditions than is usually possible in physical experiments. Thus, we can actually control "uncontrollable" factors such as the arrival rate of customers; by contrast, if we were to conduct an actual physical experiment in a bank, the arrival rate would truly be beyond our control.

This allows the inclusion of these "uncontrollable" factors as experimental factors in simulation. More fundamentally (and more importantly), simulation allows us to control the basic randomness in the experiment due to the deterministic nature of random-number generators (see Chap. 6). In particular, we can use variance-reduction techniques (see Chap. 11) in simulating the various system designs called for by the overall experimental design; the technique of using common random numbers (see Sec. 11.2) across the different system designs is especially appealing and really amounts to blocking, in the terminology of (physical) experimental design. Finally, most physical experimentation calls for "randomization" of "treatments" and "run orders" to protect against systematic variation contributed by uncontrollable experimental conditions, such as a steady rise in ambient laboratory temperature during the course of a sequence of biological experiments not thermally isolated. Randomization in simulation experimentation is not necessary, assuming that the random-number generator is operating properly (see Chap. 6). References which treat experimental design and optimization particularly in the simulation context include Biles [2], Biles and Swain [3, 4], Hunter and Naylor [9], Ignall [10], Kleijnen [12, 13], Montgomery [15], Montgomery and Bettencourt [16], and Smith [18–20].

Section 12.2 presents the ideas behind what is probably the simplest kind of experimental design; for the reader who only wants to learn what experimental design is about, reading this section would probably suffice. Section 12.3 then discusses a similar kind of design which is useful in the very beginning of a study to "screen out" factors which appear to be unimportant. Finally, Sec. 12.4 introduces some basic ideas of response-surface methodology.

12.2 2^k FACTORIAL DESIGNS

If a model only has one factor, the experimental design is relatively simple; we just run the simulation at various values, or *levels,* of the factor, perhaps forming a confidence interval for the true response at each of the levels of the factor. For quantitative factors, a graph of the response as a function of the level of the factor is often useful. Thus, we assume in the remainder of this chapter that we have at least two factors.

Suppose that we have identified k ($k \geq 2$) factors which could influence our model's response, and we want to get an initial estimate of how each factor affects the response as well as whether the factors *interact* with each other, i.e., whether the effect of a factor depends on the level of other factors. One way to measure the effect of a particular factor would be to fix the levels of the *other* $k - 1$ factors at some set of values and make simulation runs for each of several levels of the factor of interest to see how the response reacts to changes in this single factor. The whole process is then repeated to examine each of the other factors, one at a time. Such a strategy turns out to be quite inefficient in terms of the number of simulation runs needed (see [5, pp. 312–313]) and furthermore does not allow us to measure any interactions. (Indeed, it assumes that there are no interactions between the factors.)

A much more economical strategy (with which we can also measure interac-

Table 12.1 Design matrix for a 2^3 factorial design

Factor combination	Factor 1	Factor 2	Factor 3	Response
1	−	−	−	R_1
2	+	−	−	R_2
3	−	+	−	R_3
4	+	+	−	R_4
5	−	−	+	R_5
6	+	−	+	R_6
7	−	+	+	R_7
8	+	+	+	R_8

tions), called a *2^k factorial design,* requires us to choose just *two* levels for each factor and then calls for simulation runs at each of the 2^k possible combinations of factor levels. Usually we associate a minus sign with one level of a factor and a plus sign with the other level; which sign is associated with which level is quite arbitrary, although for quantitative factors it is less confusing if we associate the minus sign with the lower numerical value. No general prescription can be given for how one should specify the levels. We hope that the analyst will have some intuitive feel for the model that will allow specification of reasonable values for the quantitative factors and realistic options for the qualitative factors. The form of the experiment can be compactly represented in tabular form, as exemplified in Table 12.1 for $k = 3$. The variables R_i for $i = 1, 2, \ldots , 8$ are the values of the response when running the simulation with the ith combination of factor levels. For example, R_6 is the response resulting from running the simulation with factor 1 at its + level, factor 2 at its − level, and factor 3 at its + level. We shall see later that writing down this array of + and − signs, called the *design matrix,* facilitates calculation of the factor effects and interactions.

The *main effect* of factor j is the average *change* in the response due to moving factor j from its − level to its + level while holding all the other factors fixed. For the 2^3 factorial design of Table 12.1, the main effect of factor 1 is thus

$$e_1 = \frac{(R_2 - R_1) + (R_4 - R_3) + (R_6 - R_5) + (R_8 - R_7)}{4}$$

Note that in combinations 1 and 2, factors 2 and 3 remain fixed, as they do in combinations 3 and 4, 5 and 6, and 7 and 8. The main effect of factor 2 is

$$e_2 = \frac{(R_3 - R_1) + (R_4 - R_2) + (R_7 - R_5) + (R_8 - R_6)}{4}$$

and that of factor 3 is

$$e_3 = \frac{(R_5 - R_1) + (R_6 - R_2) + (R_7 - R_3) + (R_8 - R_4)}{4}$$

Examination of Table 12.1 and the above expressions for the e_j's leads to an alternative way of defining main effects, as well as a simpler way of computing them. Namely, e_j is the *difference* between the average response when factor j is at its $+$ level and the average response when factor j is at its $-$ level. Thus, to compute e_j we simply apply the signs in the "Factor j" column to the corresponding R_i's, add them up, and divide by 2^{k-1}. For example, in the 2^3 factorial design of Table 12.1,

$$e_2 = \frac{-R_1 - R_2 + R_3 + R_4 - R_5 - R_6 + R_7 + R_8}{4}$$

which is equivalent to the earlier expression for e_2.

The main effects measure the *average* change in the response due to a change in an individual factor. It could be, however, that the effect of factor j_1 depends on the level of some other factor, j_2, in which case factors j_1 and j_2 are said to *interact*. We measure the degree of this interaction by the (two-factor) *interaction effect*, $e_{j_1 j_2}$, between factors j_1 and j_2; it is defined to be *half* the difference between the average effect of factor j_1 when factor j_2 is at its $+$ level (and all factors other than j_1 and j_2 are held constant) and the average effect of j_1 when j_2 is at its $-$ level. ($e_{j_1 j_2}$ is also called the $j_1 \times j_2$ *interaction*.) For example, in the design of Table 12.1 we have

$$e_{12} = \frac{1}{2}\left[\frac{(R_4 - R_3) + (R_8 - R_7)}{2} - \frac{(R_2 - R_1) + (R_6 - R_5)}{2}\right]$$

$$e_{13} = \frac{1}{2}\left[\frac{(R_6 - R_5) + (R_8 - R_7)}{2} - \frac{(R_2 - R_1) + (R_4 - R_3)}{2}\right]$$

and $$e_{23} = \frac{1}{2}\left[\frac{(R_7 - R_5) + (R_8 - R_6)}{2} - \frac{(R_3 - R_1) + (R_4 - R_2)}{2}\right]$$

As with main effects, there is a much simpler way to compute interaction effects, based on examination of the design matrix. If we rearrange the above expression for e_{13}, for example, so that the R_i's appear in increasing order of the i's, we get

$$e_{13} = \frac{R_1 - R_2 + R_3 - R_4 - R_5 + R_6 - R_7 + R_8}{4}$$

Now if we create a new column, labeled "1 $\times$ 3," of 8 signs by "multiplying" the ith sign in the "Factor 1" column by the ith sign in the "Factor 3" column (the product of like signs is a $+$, and the product of opposite signs is a $-$), we get a column of signs which gives us precisely the signs of the R_i's used to form e_{13}. (As with main effects, the divisor is 2^{k-1}.) We leave it to the reader to compute e_{12} and e_{23} in this way. Thus, the interaction effect between factors 1 and 3 can be thought of as the difference between the average response when factors 1 and 3 are at the same (both $+$ or both $-$) level and the average response when factors 1 and 3 are at opposite levels. Finally, we note that two-factor interaction effects are completely symmetric; that is, $e_{12} = e_{21}$, $e_{23} = e_{32}$, etc.

Although their interpretations become more difficult, we can define (and compute) three- and higher-factor interaction effects, all the way up to a k-factor interaction. For example, in the 2^3 factorial design of Table 12.1, the three-factor interaction between factors 1, 2, and 3 is half the difference between the average two-factor interaction effect between factors 1 and 2 when factor 3 is at its + level and the average two-factor interaction effect between factors 1 and 2 when factor 3 is at its − level. That is,

$$
\begin{aligned}
e_{123} &= \frac{1}{2}\left[\frac{(R_8 - R_7) - (R_6 - R_5)}{2} - \frac{(R_4 - R_3) - (R_2 - R_1)}{2}\right] \\
&= \frac{-R_1 + R_2 + R_3 - R_4 + R_5 - R_6 - R_7 + R_8}{4}
\end{aligned}
$$

The second expression for e_{123} is obtained by multiplying the ith signs from the columns for factors 1, 2, and 3 in Table 12.1 and applying them to R_i; the denominator is once again 2^{k-1}. Three- and higher-factor interaction effects are also symmetric; for example, $e_{123} = e_{132} = e_{213}$, etc.

In the following example, we perform a 2^2 factorial experiment with the inventory model which was introduced in Sec. 1.5 and used in the examples throughout Chap. 9. The important question of how to assess the statistical significance of effects is also discussed in this example.

Example 12.1 We use the inventory model of Sec. 1.5 and identify two experimental factors, s and S. The "low" and "high" levels we chose for s and S are given in the "coding chart" in Table 12.2; recall that we must have $s < S$ for this model. The design matrix and corresponding response variables are given in Table 12.3. (The signs for the $s \times S$ interaction effect are also included.) Each R_i is the average total cost per month from a single 120-month replication; we used independent random-number streams for each R_i, but common random-number streams could have been used (see Example 11.3 and Prob. 12.1). The main effects are

$$
e_s = \frac{-118.280 + 141.060 - 136.807 + 152.789}{2} = 19.381
$$

and

$$
e_S = \frac{-118.280 - 141.060 + 136.807 + 152.789}{2} = 15.128
$$

and the interaction effect between s and S is

$$
e_{sS} = \frac{118.280 - 141.060 - 136.807 + 152.789}{2} = -3.399
$$

Thus, the average effect of raising s from 20 to 60 was to raise the monthly cost by 19.381, and raising S from 70 to 120 increased the monthly cost by an average of 15.128. Therefore, it appears that the smaller values of both s and S would be preferable, since lower monthly costs are desired. Since the $s \times S$ interaction effect is negative, there is indication that lower costs are observed by setting *both* s and S at either their − or + levels rather than one at the − level and one at the + level. The magnitude (absolute value) of the interaction effect is much smaller than the magnitudes of the main effects, which often happens in factorial experiments.

Table 12.2 Coding for s and S in the inventory model

	−	+
s	20	60
S	70	120

Table 12.3 Design matrix and empirical results for the 2^2 factorial design on s and S for the inventory model

Factor combination	s	S	$s \times S$	Response
1	−	−	+	118.280
2	+	−	−	141.060
3	−	+	−	136.807
4	+	+	+	152.789

Since the R_i's are random variables, the effects are also random. To ascertain whether the effects are "real," as opposed to being explainable by random fluctuation, we need to estimate their variances. Several methods could be used (see, for example, [5, pp. 319–322]); a very simple approach is to replicate independently the *whole design* n times and obtain n independent values of e_s, e_S, and e_{sS}. We took $n = 10$ and obtained an average value of $\bar{e}_s(10) = 21.539$ for e_s; the variance estimate of $\bar{e}_s(10)$ was 0.879. Thus, an approximate 90 percent confidence interval (based on the t distribution with 9 df) for the *expected* main effect of s is 21.539 ± 1.719, and the main effect of s indeed appears to be real. Similarly, approximate 90 percent confidence intervals for $E(e_S)$ and $E(e_{sS})$ were 10.459 ± 2.002 and -2.971 ± 0.794, respectively. Therefore, from 10 replications of the whole design, all effects appear to be real and the main effects are much stronger than the interaction effect.

Calculation of main effects and interactions of 2^k factorial experiments is actually equivalent to estimating the parameters in a particular statistical *regression model* of how the response depends on the factors. For Example 12.1 this regression model is

$$R(s, S) = a + bx_s + cx_S + dx_s x_S + \epsilon$$

where $R(s, S) =$ response as a function of s and S
$x_s = (s - 40)/20$ (to transform s to the values -1 and $+1$)
$x_S = (S - 95)/25$

and ϵ is a random variable with mean zero. Given this regression model, we could estimate a, b, c, and d by ordinary least-squares regression and use the fitted model to *forecast* the value of $E[R(s, S)]$ at combinations of s and S where no simulation has been done. Moreover, the main effect e_s is exactly twice $\hat{b}$, the least-squares estimator of b. Similarly, $e_S = 2\hat{c}$, $e_{sS} = 2\hat{d}$, and $\hat{a} = \sum_{i=1}^{4} R_i/4$. However, direct computation of e_s, e_S, and e_{sS} (as in Example 12.1) is much easier than performing a regression. The theoretical validity of factorial experiments is based on the validity of the corresponding regression model; see [5, pp. 329–336] for ways of checking the validity of a regression model.

12.3 2^{k-p} FRACTIONAL FACTORIAL DESIGNS

For a model with k factors, the designs of the previous section require at least one simulation run at each of the 2^k possible combinations of factors. It is not at all difficult to imagine a simulation model with as many as $k = 11$ factors, for which a full 2^k factorial design would require at least 2048 simulation runs; if we wanted to estimate the variances of the effects by the method in Example 12.1 with, say, $n = 5$ replications at each design point, we would need 10,240 total replications. If a single replication of the model took, say, 1 minute of CPU time (which is a modest amount of time for many complex real-world simulations), we would need over a full week of round-the-clock computing to complete the experiment.

Fractional factorial designs provide a way to get estimates of (for example) the main effects or low-order interactions of interest at a fraction of the experimental effort required by a full 2^k factorial design. These kinds of designs are especially useful as a first step in experimentation when many factors are present and we want to screen out those factors which appear to be relatively unimportant without having to perform an excessive amount of simulation, thus saving the bulk of the computing budget for a more intensive study of the important factors. Basically, a 2^{k-p} fractional factorial design is constructed by choosing a certain subset (of size 2^{k-p}) of the 2^k possible factor combinations and then running the simulation only for these chosen combinations. Thus only $1/2^p$ of the 2^k factor combinations are actually run. The important question of *which* 2^{k-p} combinations to choose is a whole subject unto itself, discussed at length in most books on experimental design (see, for example, [5, chaps. 12 and 13]). This choice should obviously be made carefully and might depend on which main effects and interactions are of greatest interest. As we shall see after the following example, the price paid for only having to do a fraction of the work is that we can no longer obtain estimates of *all* the expected main and interaction effects.

Example 12.2 Consider a generalization of the inventory model of Example 12.1 in which there are two new factors, in addition to s and S. The first new factor is the inventory-evaluation interval m, which is the number of months between successive evaluations of the inventory level to determine whether an order will be placed. In the original model $m = 1$, but consideration is being given to changing m to 3. The second new factor arose since the supplier has introduced an "express" delivery option. Originally, if Z items were ordered, the ordering cost was $32 + 3Z$ and the delivery lag was a $U(0.5, 1.0)$ random variable. With express delivery, the supplier will make delivery in half the time; i.e., the delivery lag is a $U(0.25, 0.50)$ random variable, but will charge an amount $48 + 4Z$ instead. The delivery priority P is thus either "normal" or "express" and is a qualitative factor for the experiment. In this generalized model, then, we have $k = 4$ factors, which we code as $-$ or $+$ according to Table 12.4.

    A full 2^4 factorial design would require simulation of each of 16 possible factor combinations. However, if our goal is simply to obtain acceptable estimates of the expected *main* effects, we can

Table 12.4 Coding for s, S, m, and P in the generalized inventory model

	$-$	$+$
s	20	60
S	70	120
m	1	3
P	Normal	Express

Table 12.5 Design matrix and empirical results for a 2^{4-1} fractional factorial design on s, S, m, and P for the generalized inventory model

Factor combination	s	S	m	P	Response
1	−	−	−	−	118.686
2	+	−	−	+	196.119
3	−	+	−	+	166.674
4	+	+	−	−	149.542
5	−	−	+	+	148.045
6	+	−	+	−	135.754
7	−	+	+	−	153.202
8	+	+	+	+	181.885

get away with only considering *half* these 16 combinations. What we lose is the ability to compute any interactions, as we shall see immediately following this example. Thus, we consulted Box, Hunter, and Hunter [5, p. 410] to decide which eight factor combinations to consider and constructed the 2^{4-1} fractional factorial design given in Table 12.5. We then performed the corresponding simulation runs. The effects are calculated exactly as for the full 2^k designs; e.g., the main effect of s is obtained by applying the eight signs in the "s" column to the corresponding responses, adding them up, and dividing by $2^{k-p-1} = 4$ (half the total number of runs). Thus, $e_s = 19.173$, $e_S = 13.175$, $e_m = -3.034$, and $e_P = 33.885$. To estimate the variances of the main effects, we replicated the design independently $n = 10$ times and constructed approximate 90 percent confidence intervals for the expected main effects, exactly as in Example 12.1. These confidence intervals were 15.478 ± 1.831 for $E(e_s)$, 14.431 ± 2.017 for $E(e_S)$, -1.217 ± 1.449 for $E(e_m)$, and 34.915 ± 1.775 for $E(e_P)$. Thus, the main effects of s and S still appear to be significantly positive, as in Example 12.1, but seem to have somewhat different magnitudes than before. As for m, its main effect on cost is very small and statistically insignificant; it thus appears that m really does not matter (at least over the range in which we specified its levels), so that we would not need to include it as a factor in future experimentation. The other new option, express delivery, appears to raise operating costs markedly; therefore, we conclude that the faster delivery times of the express delivery option do not justify the extra cost.

Conspicuously absent from Example 12.2 were any calculations involving interactions; this is where we have to pay the piper. For example, try computing the $s \times S$ interaction and then calculate the $m \times P$ interaction. Since these two expressions are exactly the same, we cannot compute these two interactions separately; they are said to be *confounded* with each other. Similarly, an attempt to compute the $s \times S \times m$ interaction leads precisely to the main effect of P, so that e_{sSm} and e_P are also confounded. Fractional factorial designs purposely confound groups of effects in this way and in return call for only $1/2^p$ of the 2^k combinations. It is possible to choose which effects are confounded with which other effects in order to obtain the desired information. For example, the design of Example 12.2 was constructed so that main effects are not confounded with each other or with two-factor interaction effects; however, the main effects *are* confounded with three-factor interaction effects, and the two-factor interaction effects are confounded with each other. Thus, if we are willing to assume that the three-factor interaction effects are insignificant in comparison with the main effects (as often turns out to be the case), this design allows us to obtain relatively "clear" main effects. (See [5, p. 410] for a useful table on constructing these kinds of designs, which are called *resolution IV* fractional factorials.) On the other hand, if there is particular interest in a certain two-factor interaction effect, for example, one could construct a fractional factorial design to estimate it free of confounding with main effects or other two-factor interactions. Again, we refer the reader to the experimental design literature.

The construction of fractional factorials is a very useful and powerful technique. Returning to our 11-factor example in the first paragraph of this section, we could construct a 2^{11-6} resolution IV fractional factorial design which would allow us to obtain main effects confounded only with three- and higher-factor interactions. Since this design would require only 32 (rather than 2048) runs per replication, we could replicate it $n = 5$ times in 2 hours and 40 minutes of CPU time. This is still not exactly inexpensive, but it beats a week.

*12.4 RESPONSE-SURFACE METHODOLOGY

As experimentation with a simulation model progresses, we might become interested in obtaining information that is more precise than what can be obtained from full or fractional factorial designs. An important example of a general program of experimentation is one in which we would first use full or fractional factorial designs to identify which factors are important and then examine these factors more intensively to find a combination of levels for which the response is maximized (or minimized). A number of experimental designs and procedures known as response-surface methodologies (RSMs) can be of use in dealing with this optimization problem when all factors are quantitative.

A *response surface* is simply the expected response of a system viewed as a function of the factors. The term "surface" is used since the expected response function for the case of $k = 2$ factors *is* a surface of some sort in three-dimensional space. For example, the dashed lines in Fig. 12.1 are the contours, i.e., curves of constant response, of an estimate (from 10 independent replications) of a portion of the surface (average monthly cost) for the inventory model of Example 12.1, as a function of s and S. [It appears that the optimal (s, S) combination is somewhere near (25, 65).] To obtain these contours, however, we had to make 4650 replications of the model (we let $S = 5, 10, 15, \ldots, 150$, and $s = 0, 5, 10, \ldots, S - 5$ for each value of S), which is not the kind of analysis that is generally possible for large-scale simulations. RSMs try to gain this same kind of information about the optimum without having to perform such an exhaustive search of the space of factor combinations. There are many different kinds of RSMs, and the following example is meant to illustrate only the general idea; see, for example, [5, chap. 15] or Myers [17] for more detailed accounts.

Example 12.3 For the original two-factor (s and S) inventory model, a RSM could begin with the 2^2 factorial design of Example 12.1. Factor combinations 1, 2, 3, and 4 from Table 12.3 are marked as the corners of the rectangle in Fig. 12.1, and the average responses (over the 10 independent

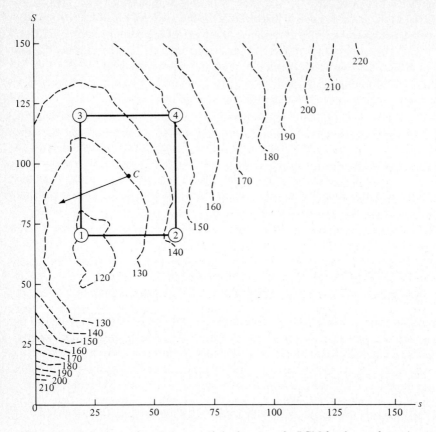

Figure 12.1 Response-surface contours and the first step of a RSM for the two-factor inventory model.

replications) at these points were 119.684, 144.194, 133.114, and 151.682, respectively. As an approximation to the response surface in the region covered by this design, we could use ordinary least-squares regression to fit the linear (or planar) regression model

$$E[R(s, S)] = \beta_0 + \beta_1 s + \beta_2 S$$

to the response at the four design points. Carrying out the computations, we obtain the least-squares coefficients $\hat{\beta}_0 = 95.757$, $\hat{\beta}_1 = 0.538$, and $\hat{\beta}_2 = 0.209$. Since we are interested in searching for a lower response (cost) in this case, we examine the fitted linear regression model $\hat{\beta}_0 + \hat{\beta}_1 s + \hat{\beta}_2 S$ to ascertain which direction in (s, S) space we should move to decrease the response most rapidly; this is called the *direction of steepest descent*. From calculus, we know that the *negative* of the vector of partial derivatives of a function points in the direction of steepest descent, so that for our fitted linear-regression model we should move through the (s, S) plane in a line parallel to the vector $-(\hat{\beta}_1, \hat{\beta}_2) = (-0.538, -0.209)$. Usually RSMs move from the center of a design, so that our direction of search is shown by the arrow in Fig. 12.1 which starts at the point labeled "*C*." If we continued our search, we would perform additional simulations for (s, S) combinations along this line (or near it, since s and S must be integers) and continue moving away from point *C* for as long as we keep observing steadily decreasing responses. If the response began to rise, we would back up to the previous lowest response and use it as the center point for a new 2^2 factorial design to which we fit a new regression model and obtain a new direction of steepest descent. Eventually, the fitted linear regression model will result in a nearly flat plane ($\hat{\beta}_1$ and $\hat{\beta}_2$

are both near zero), which indicates that we are near the "bottom of the bowl." At this point, we could perform a design more elaborate than a rectangular 2^2 factorial which would allow us to fit a quadratic (or second-order) regression model

$$E[R(s, S)] = \beta_0 + \beta_1 s + \beta_2 S + \beta_{12} sS + \beta_{11} s^2 + \beta_{22} S^2$$

The fitted quadratic regression model is then minimized by standard mathematical techniques.

We wish to emphasize that the preceding example gives a very simplified view of RSM. In practice, designs other than 2^k factorials (such as fractional factorials or more intricate composite or circular designs with center points) can be used to fit the regression models; these regression models themselves can also be more sophisticated, such as quadratic functions throughout. In addition, tests for lack of fit of the regression model are useful for identifying its adequacy and for indicating when a possible optimum is being approached.

The problem of optimization in simulation is an extremely difficult one, since it combines the problems of deterministic mathematical programming (see, for example, Avriel [1]) and of statistical estimation; i.e., deterministic optimization is in general a hard problem itself, and we are further hindered since the inherent randomness of the simulation output makes it impossible for us even to evaluate exactly the objective function (response surface) to be optimized. Thus, there can be no guarantee that the result of a RSM procedure will always identify a truly optimal system design. Furthermore, RSMs typically call for a large number of simulation runs, which may be simply unaffordable. It is our feeling that the analyst should therefore be circumspect in applying RSMs in simulation studies and interpreting the results, rather than simply applying a "black box" RSM algorithm and accepting its prescription without question.

PROBLEMS

12.1 The simulations carried out for the 2^2 factorial design on s and S in Example 12.1 were all done independently. Repeat Example 12.1 using common random numbers to simulate the four combinations of factors in Table 12.3 by the method discussed in Example 11.3 (matching up interdemand times and demand sizes but generating the delivery lags independently). Make $n = 10$ independent replications, construct 90 percent confidence intervals for the expected main and interaction effects, and compare the half-lengths of these confidence intervals with those in Example 12.1.

12.2 For the generalized four-factor inventory model of Example 12.2, carry out a full 2^4 factorial experiment with the same factor-level coding given in Table 12.4. (Use either completely independent sampling or common interdemand times and demand sizes as in Prob. 12.1.) Replicate the design independently $n = 10$ times and compute all the main effects, as well as two-, three-, and four-factor interaction effects, together with 90 percent confidence intervals on their expectations. Compare your results with those obtained from the fractional factorial design of Example 12.2. In particular, do the main effects seem to be the same? Was the assumption made in Example 12.2 that three- and four-factor interactions are "small" (in comparison with the main effects) a valid one? In your opinion, was anything lost by doing only the half fraction (rather than your full 16-run experiment) in Example 12.2?

12.3 Recall the model of the manufacturing shop in Prob. 1.5, with five machines, which are subject to breakdowns, and s repairmen. Suppose that the shop has not yet been built and that in addition to deciding how many repairmen to hire, management has two other decisions to make. (1) There is a

Table 12.6 Coding for the generalized machine-breakdown model

	$-$	$+$
s	2	4
Machine type	Standard	Deluxe
Repairman type	Standard	Expert

higher-quality deluxe machine on the market which is more reliable, in that it will run for an amount of time which is an exponential random variable with a mean of 16 hours (rather than the 8 hours for the standard machine). However, the higher price of these deluxe machines means that it costs the shop $100 (rather than $50) for each hour that each deluxe machine is broken down. (Since deluxe machines work no faster, the shop would still need five of them. Assume also that the shop cannot purchase some of each kind of machine; i.e., the machines must be either all standard or all deluxe.) (2) Instead of hiring the standard repairmen, the managers have the option of hiring a team of better-trained expert repairmen, who would have to be paid $15 an hour (rather than the $10 an hour for the standard repairmen) but can repair a broken machine (regardless of whether it is standard or deluxe) in an exponential amount of time with a mean of 1.5 hours (rather than 2 hours). (The repairmen hired must be either all standard or all expert.) Use the coding in Table 12.6 to perform a full 2^3 factorial experiment, replicated $n = 5$ times, and compute 90 percent confidence intervals for all expected main and interaction effects. (Each simulation run is for 800 hours and begins with all five machines in working order. Make all runs independently.) What are your recommendations?

12.4 For the time-shared computer model of Sec. 2.4, suppose that consideration is being given to adjusting the service quantum length q (as in Prob. 9.2) as well as to adopting the alternative processing policy discussed in Probs. 2.3 and 9.4. Perform a 2^2 factorial experiment with these two factors ($q = 0.05$ or 0.40, and the processing policy either as described originally in Sec. 2.4 or as in Prob. 2.3), running the model for 500 job completions (without warming it up), 35 terminals, and all terminals initially in the think state; make all runs independently. Replicate the design as you see fit to obtain useful estimates of the expected main and interaction effects.

*12.5 Consult the references on RSM and conduct a more thorough optimization study of the two-factor inventory model of Example 12.3. Compare your recommended optimal (s, S) pair with the dashed contour lines in Fig. 12.1.

REFERENCES

1. Avriel, M.: *Nonlinear Programming: Analysis and Methods*, Prentice-Hall, Englewood Cliffs, N.J., 1976.
2. Biles, W. E.: Experimental Design in Computer Simulation, *Proc. 1979 Winter Simul. Conf., San Diego, Calif., 1979*, pp. 3–9.
3. Biles, W. E., and J. J. Swain: Mathematical Programming and the Optimization of Computer Simulations, *Math. Program. Stud.*, **11**: 189–207 (1979).
4. Biles, W. E., and J. J. Swain: *Optimization and Industrial Experimentation*, Wiley, New York, 1980.
5. Box, G. E. P., W. G. Hunter, and J. S. Hunter: *Statistics for Experimenters: An Introduction to Design, Data Analysis, and Model Building*, Wiley, New York, 1978.
6. Cochran, W. G., and G. M. Cox: *Experimental Designs*, 2d ed., Wiley, New York, 1957.
7. Davies, O. L.: *The Design and Analysis of Industrial Experiments*, Hafner, New York, 1956.
8. Hicks, C. R.: *Fundamental Concepts in the Design of Experiments*, 2d ed., Holt, New York, 1973.
9. Hunter, J. S., and T. H. Naylor: Experimental Designs for Computer Simulation Experiments, *Manage. Sci.*, **16**: 422–434 (1970).

10. Ignall, E. J.: On Experimental Designs for Computer Simulation Experiments, *Manage. Sci.,* **18:** 384–388 (1972).
11. John, P. M. W.: *Statistical Design and Analysis of Experiments,* Macmillan, New York, 1971.
12. Kleijnen, J. P. C.: *Statistical Techniques in Simulation,* pt. II, Dekker, New York, 1975.
13. Kleijnen, J. P. C.: Design and Analysis of Simulations: Practical Statistical Techniques, *Simulation,* **28:** 81–90 (1977).
14. Montgomery, D. C.: *Design and Analysis of Experiments,* Wiley, New York, 1976.
15. Montgomery, D. C.: Methods for Factor Screening in Computer Simulation Experiments, Georgia Institute of Technology School of Industrial and Systems Engineering, Atlanta, 1979.
16. Montgomery, D. C., and V. M. Bettencourt, Jr.: Multiple Response Surface Methods in Computer Simulation, *Simulation,* **29:** 113–121 (1977).
17. Myers, R. H.: *Response Surface Methodology,* Allyn and Bacon, Boston, 1971.
18. Smith, D. E.: An Empirical Investigation of Optimum-Seeking in the Computer Simulation Situation, *Oper. Res.,* **21:** 475–497 (1973).
19. Smith, D. E.: Requirements of an "Optimizer" for Computer Simulations, *Nav. Res. Logist. Q.,* **20:** 161–179 (1973).
20. Smith, D. E.: Automatic Optimum-Seeking Program for Digital Simulation, *Simulation,* **27:** 27–31 (1976).

APPENDIX

Table T.1 Critical points $t_{\nu,\gamma}$ for the t distribution with ν df, and z_γ for the standard normal distribution

($\gamma = P\{T_\nu \leq t_{\nu,\gamma}\}$, where T_ν is a random variable having the t distribution with ν df; the last row, where $\nu = \infty$, gives the normal critical points satisfying $\gamma = P(Z \leq z_\gamma)$, where Z is a standard normal random variable)

ν	0.6000	0.7000	0.8000	0.9000	0.9333	0.9500	0.9600	0.9667	0.9750	0.9800	0.9833	0.9875	0.9900	0.9917	0.9938	0.9950
1	0.325	0.727	1.376	3.078	4.702	6.314	7.916	9.524	12.706	15.895	19.043	25.452	31.821	38.342	51.334	63.657
2	0.289	0.617	1.061	1.886	2.456	2.920	3.320	3.679	4.303	4.849	5.334	6.205	6.965	7.665	8.897	9.925
3	0.277	0.584	0.978	1.638	2.045	2.353	2.605	2.823	3.182	3.482	3.738	4.177	4.541	4.864	5.408	5.841
4	0.271	0.569	0.941	1.533	1.879	2.132	2.333	2.502	2.776	2.999	3.184	3.495	3.747	3.966	4.325	4.604
5	0.267	0.559	0.920	1.476	1.790	2.015	2.191	2.337	2.571	2.757	2.910	3.163	3.365	3.538	3.818	4.032
6	0.265	0.553	0.906	1.440	1.735	1.943	2.104	2.237	2.447	2.612	2.748	2.969	3.143	3.291	3.528	3.707
7	0.263	0.549	0.896	1.415	1.698	1.895	2.046	2.170	2.365	2.517	2.640	2.841	2.998	3.130	3.341	3.499
8	0.262	0.546	0.889	1.397	1.670	1.860	2.004	2.122	2.306	2.449	2.565	2.752	2.896	3.018	3.211	3.355
9	0.261	0.543	0.883	1.383	1.650	1.833	1.973	2.086	2.262	2.398	2.508	2.685	2.821	2.936	3.116	3.250
10	0.260	0.542	0.879	1.372	1.634	1.812	1.948	2.058	2.228	2.359	2.465	2.634	2.764	2.872	3.043	3.169
11	0.260	0.540	0.876	1.363	1.621	1.796	1.928	2.036	2.201	2.328	2.430	2.593	2.718	2.822	2.985	3.106
12	0.259	0.539	0.873	1.356	1.610	1.782	1.912	2.017	2.179	2.303	2.402	2.560	2.681	2.782	2.939	3.055
13	0.259	0.538	0.870	1.350	1.601	1.771	1.899	2.002	2.160	2.282	2.379	2.533	2.650	2.748	2.900	3.012
14	0.258	0.537	0.868	1.345	1.593	1.761	1.887	1.989	2.145	2.264	2.359	2.510	2.624	2.720	2.868	2.977
15	0.258	0.536	0.866	1.341	1.587	1.753	1.878	1.978	2.131	2.249	2.342	2.490	2.602	2.696	2.841	2.947
16	0.258	0.535	0.865	1.337	1.581	1.746	1.869	1.968	2.120	2.235	2.327	2.473	2.583	2.675	2.817	2.921
17	0.257	0.534	0.863	1.333	1.576	1.740	1.862	1.960	2.110	2.224	2.315	2.458	2.567	2.657	2.796	2.898
18	0.257	0.534	0.862	1.330	1.572	1.734	1.855	1.953	2.101	2.214	2.303	2.445	2.552	2.641	2.778	2.878
19	0.257	0.533	0.861	1.328	1.568	1.729	1.850	1.946	2.093	2.205	2.293	2.433	2.539	2.627	2.762	2.861
20	0.257	0.533	0.860	1.325	1.564	1.725	1.844	1.940	2.086	2.197	2.285	2.423	2.528	2.614	2.748	2.845
21	0.257	0.532	0.859	1.323	1.561	1.721	1.840	1.935	2.080	2.189	2.277	2.414	2.518	2.603	2.735	2.831
22	0.256	0.532	0.858	1.321	1.558	1.717	1.835	1.930	2.074	2.183	2.269	2.405	2.508	2.593	2.724	2.819
23	0.256	0.532	0.858	1.319	1.556	1.714	1.832	1.926	2.069	2.177	2.263	2.398	2.500	2.584	2.713	2.807
24	0.256	0.531	0.857	1.318	1.553	1.711	1.828	1.922	2.064	2.172	2.257	2.391	2.492	2.575	2.704	2.797
25	0.256	0.531	0.856	1.316	1.551	1.708	1.825	1.918	2.060	2.167	2.251	2.385	2.485	2.568	2.695	2.787
26	0.256	0.531	0.856	1.315	1.549	1.706	1.822	1.915	2.056	2.162	2.246	2.379	2.479	2.561	2.687	2.779
27	0.256	0.531	0.855	1.314	1.547	1.703	1.819	1.912	2.052	2.158	2.242	2.373	2.473	2.554	2.680	2.771
28	0.256	0.530	0.855	1.313	1.546	1.701	1.817	1.909	2.048	2.154	2.237	2.368	2.467	2.548	2.673	2.763

29	0.256	0.530	0.854	1.311	1.544	1.699	1.814	1.906	2.045	2.150	2.233	2.364	2.462	2.543	2.667	2.756
30	0.256	0.530	0.854	1.310	1.543	1.697	1.812	1.904	2.042	2.147	2.230	2.360	2.457	2.537	2.661	2.750
40	0.255	0.529	0.851	1.303	1.532	1.684	1.796	1.886	2.021	2.123	2.203	2.329	2.423	2.501	2.619	2.704
50	0.255	0.528	0.849	1.299	1.526	1.676	1.787	1.875	2.009	2.109	2.188	2.311	2.403	2.479	2.594	2.678
75	0.254	0.527	0.846	1.293	1.517	1.665	1.775	1.861	1.992	2.090	2.167	2.287	2.377	2.450	2.562	2.643
100	0.254	0.526	0.845	1.290	1.513	1.660	1.769	1.855	1.984	2.081	2.157	2.276	2.364	2.436	2.547	2.626
∞	0.253	0.524	0.842	1.282	1.501	1.645	1.751	1.834	1.960	2.054	2.127	2.241	2.326	2.395	2.501	2.576

Table T.2 Critical points $\chi^2_{\nu,\gamma}$ for the chi-square distribution with ν df

($\gamma = P\{Y_{\nu} \leq \chi^2_{\nu,\gamma}\}$, where Y_{ν} has a chi-square distribution with ν df; for large ν, use the approximation for $\chi^2_{\nu,\gamma}$ in Sec. 6.4.1)

ν	γ 0.250	0.500	0.750	0.900	0.950	0.975	0.990
1	0.102	0.455	1.323	2.706	3.841	5.024	6.635
2	0.575	1.386	2.773	4.605	5.991	7.378	9.210
3	1.213	2.366	4.108	6.251	7.815	9.348	11.345
4	1.923	3.357	5.385	7.779	9.488	11.143	13.277
5	2.675	4.351	6.626	9.236	11.070	12.833	15.086
6	3.455	5.348	7.841	10.645	12.592	14.449	16.812
7	4.255	6.346	9.037	12.017	14.067	16.013	18.475
8	5.071	7.344	10.219	13.362	15.507	17.535	20.090
9	5.899	8.343	11.389	14.684	16.919	19.023	21.666
10	6.737	9.342	12.549	15.987	18.307	20.483	23.209
11	7.584	10.341	13.701	17.275	19.675	21.920	24.725
12	8.438	11.340	14.845	18.549	21.026	23.337	26.217
13	9.299	12.340	15.984	19.812	22.362	24.736	27.688
14	10.165	13.339	17.117	21.064	23.685	26.119	29.141
15	11.037	14.339	18.245	22.307	24.996	27.488	30.578
16	11.912	15.338	19.369	23.542	26.296	28.845	32.000
17	12.792	16.338	20.489	24.769	27.587	30.191	33.409
18	13.675	17.338	21.605	25.989	28.869	31.526	34.805
19	14.562	18.338	22.718	27.204	30.144	32.852	36.191
20	15.452	19.337	23.828	28.412	31.410	34.170	37.566
21	16.344	20.337	24.935	29.615	32.671	35.479	38.932
22	17.240	21.337	26.039	30.813	33.924	36.781	40.289
23	18.137	22.337	27.141	32.007	35.172	38.076	41.638
24	19.037	23.337	28.241	33.196	36.415	39.364	42.980
25	19.939	24.337	29.339	34.382	37.652	40.646	44.314
26	20.843	25.336	30.435	35.563	38.885	41.923	45.642
27	21.749	26.336	31.528	36.741	40.113	43.195	46.963
28	22.657	27.336	32.620	37.916	41.337	44.461	48.278
29	23.567	28.336	33.711	39.087	42.557	45.722	49.588
30	24.478	29.336	34.800	40.256	43.773	46.979	50.892
40	33.660	39.335	45.616	51.805	55.758	59.342	63.691
50	42.942	49.335	56.334	63.167	67.505	71.420	76.154
75	66.417	74.334	82.858	91.061	96.217	100.839	106.393
100	90.133	99.334	109.141	118.498	124.342	129.561	135.807